POLITICAL MAP OF THE WORLD

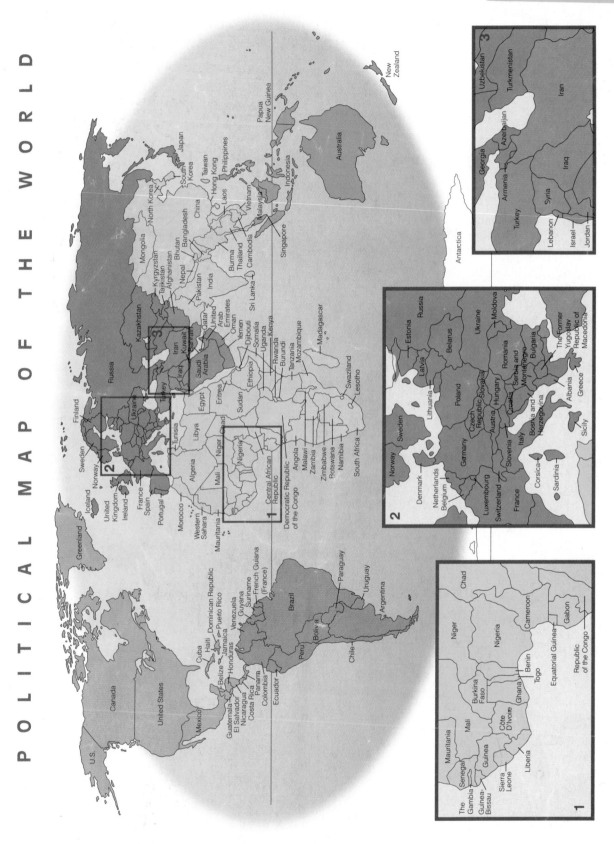

Sociology

Your Compass for a New World,
The Brief Edition

ENHANCED
SECOND EDITION

Robert J. Brym
University of Toronto

John Lie
University of California at Berkeley

★ WADSWORTH
CENGAGE Learning™

Australia • Brazil • Japan • Korea • Mexico • Singapore • Spain • United Kingdom • United States

**Sociology: Your Compass for a New World,
The Brief Edition, Enhanced Second Edition**
Robert J. Brym and John Lie

Senior Acquisitions Editor: Chris Caldeira

Associate Development Editor:
Dan Moneypenny

Assistant Editor: Melanie Cregger

Editorial Assistant: Rachael Krapf

Media Editor: Lauren Keyes

Marketing Manager: Andrew Keay

Marketing Assistant: Jillian Myers

Marketing Communications Manager:
Laura Localio

Content Project Manager: Cheri Palmer

Creative Director: Rob Hugel

Art Director: Caryl Gorska

Print Buyer: Paula Vang

Rights Acquisitions Account Manager, Text:
Roberta Broyer

Rights Acquisitions Account Manager, Image:
Mandy Groszko

Production Service: Graphic World Inc.

Text Designer: Norman Baugher

Photo Researcher: Kathleen Olson

Illustrator: Graphic World Illustration Studio

Cover Designer: RHDG

Cover Image: Photograph/RHDG

Compositor: Graphic World Inc.

For product information and technology assistance, contact us at
Cengage Learning Customer & Sales Support, 1-800-354-9706.

For permission to use material from this text or product,
submit all requests online at **cengage.com/permissions.**
Further permissions questions can be emailed to
permissionrequest@cengage.com.

Library of Congress Control Number: 2009925540

Student Edition:

ISBN-13: 978-0-495-59893-0

ISBN-10: 0-495-59893-3

Wadsworth
10 Davis Drive
Belmont, CA 94002-3098
USA

Cengage Learning is a leading provider of customized learning solutions with office locations around the globe, including Singapore, the United Kingdom, Australia, Mexico, Brazil, and Japan. Locate your local office at **www.cengage.com/global.**

Cengage Learning products are represented in Canada by Nelson Education, Ltd.

To learn more about Wadsworth, visit **www.cengage.com/wadsworth.**

Purchase any of our products at your local college store or at our preferred online store **www.ichapters.com.**

Printed in the United States of America
1 2 3 4 5 6 7 13 12 11 10 09

Dedication

Many authors seem to be afflicted with stoic family members who gladly allow them to spend endless hours buried in their work. I suffer no such misfortune. The members of my family have demanded that I focus on what really matters in life. I think that focus has made this a better book. I am deeply grateful to Rhonda Lenton, Shira Brym, Talia-Lenton-Brym, and Ariella Lenton-Brym. I dedicate this book to them with thanks and love.

ROBERT J. BRYM

For Charis Thompson, Thomas Cussins, Jessica Cussins, and Charlotte Lie, with thanks and love.

JOHN LIE

Robert J. **B**rym (pronounced "brim") studied sociology in Canada and Israel and received his Ph.D from the University of Toronto, where he is now on faculty and where he especially enjoys teaching introductory sociology. He is the winner of the 2007 Northrop Frye Award for excellence in fusing research with teaching.

In 2008, he was elected a Fellow of the Royal Society of Canada. Bob's work has been translated into half a dozen languages, and he has lectured at universities in Brazil, Israel, Russia, and the United States. His research focuses on the social bases of politics. His major books include *Intellectuals and Politics* (London and Boston: Allen & Unwin, 1980); *From Culture to Power* (Toronto: Oxford University Press, 1989); *The Jews of Moscow, Kiev, and Minsk* (New York: New York University Press, 1994); and *Sociology as a Life or Death Issue* (Belmont, CA: Wadsworth Cengage Learning, 2009). He is now writing a book on suicide bombers in Israel and Palestine.

John **L**ie (pronounced "Lee") was born in South Korea, grew up in Japan and Hawaii, and attended Harvard University, where he received his A.B., A.M., and Ph.D. Currently he is Class of 1959 Professor and Dean of International and Area Studies at the University of California, Berkeley.

Lie's dissertation probed the political origins of market society and proposed the concept of mode of exchange. He then embarked on the "sociological imagination trilogy" that analyzed contemporary East Asia and the United States through the thread of his biography: *Han Unbound: The Political Economy of South Korea* (Stanford University Press, 1998); *Multiethnic Japan* (Harvard University Press, 2001); and *Blue Dreams: Korean Americans and the Los Angeles Riots* (co-authored, Harvard University Press, 1995). His most recent book is *Modern Peoplehood* (Harvard University Press, 2004), which is a comparative, historical, and theoretical analysis of race, ethnicity, nation, racism, and identity. He is currently working on two books, both tentatively to be published by the University of California Press: *Violence* and *The Consolation of Social Theory.*

Before joining the Berkeley faculty, he held appointments at the University of Oregon, University of Illinois at Urbana–Champaign, and the University of Michigan. He has also held visiting professorships at Yonsei University (South Korea), Keio University (Japan), University of Waikato (New Zealand), and Harvard University.

Lie has taught introductory sociology courses ranging in size from 3 to 700 students in several different countries. He hopes that this book will contribute to the development of the reader's sociological imagination.

Brief Contents

P A R T   V
Social Change

Contents

P A R T   I I
Basic Social Processes

P A R T   I I I
Inequality

Chapter 7
Social Stratification: United States and Global Perspectives 170

P A R T   I V
Institutions

Chapter 11
Families 292

P A R T   V
Social Change

Chapter 15
Collective Action and Social Movements 426

Boxes

Sociology at the Movies

Social Policy: What Do You Think?

Mass Media and Society

You and the Social World

Maps

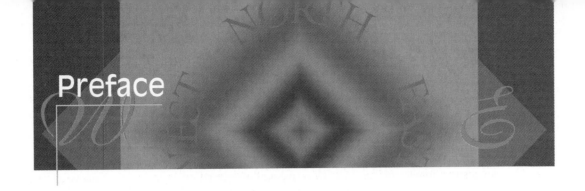

Preface

Why a Compass for a New World?

Soon after European explorers arrived in North and South America, they started calling the twin continents the "New World." Everything was different here. A native population perhaps a hundredth as large as Europe's occupied a territory more than four times larger. The New World was unimaginably rich in resources. European rulers saw that by controlling it they could increase their power and importance. Christians recognized new possibilities for spreading their religion. Explorers discerned fresh opportunities for rewarding adventures. A wave of excitement swelled as word spread of the New World's vast potential and challenges.

Today, it is easy for us to appreciate that wave of excitement. For we, too, have reached the frontiers of a New World. And we are also full of anticipation. Our New World is one of virtually instant long-distance communication, global economies and cultures, weakening nation-states, and technological advances that often make the daily news seem like reports from a distant planet. In a fundamental way, the world is not the same place it was just 50 years ago. Orbiting telescopes that peer to the fringes of the universe, human genetic code laid bare like a road map, fiber-optic cable that carries a trillion bits of information per second, and spacecraft that transport robots to Mars help to make this a New World.

Five hundred years ago, the early European explorers of North and South America set themselves the preliminary task of mapping the contours of the New World. We set ourselves a similar task here. Their frontiers were physical. Ours are social. Their maps were geographical. Ours are sociological. But in terms of functionality, our maps are much like theirs. All maps allow us to find our place in the world and see ourselves in the context of larger forces. *Sociological* maps, as C. Wright Mills wrote, allow us to "grasp the interplay of [people] and society, of biography and history" (Mills, 1959: 4). This book, then, shows you how to draw sociological maps so that you can see your place in the world, figure out how to navigate through it, and perhaps discover how to improve it. It is your sociological compass.

We are not as naive as the early European explorers were. Where they saw only hope and bright horizons, minimizing the significance of the violence required to conquer the people of the New World, our anticipation is mixed with dread. Scientific breakthroughs are announced almost daily, but the global environment has never been in worse shape, and AIDS is now the leading cause of death in Africa. Marriages and nations unexpectedly break up and then reconstitute themselves in new and unanticipated forms. We celebrate the advances made by women and racial minorities only to find that some people oppose their progress, sometimes violently. Waves of people suddenly migrate between continents, establishing cooperation, but also conflict, between previously separated groups. New technologies make work more interesting and creative for some, offering unprecedented opportunities to get rich and become famous. They also make jobs more onerous and routine for others. The standard of living goes up for many people but stagnates for many more.

Is it any wonder that amid all this contradictory news, good and bad, uncertainty about the future prevails? We wrote this book to show undergraduate college students that sociology can help them make sense of their lives, however uncertain they may appear to be. Moreover, we show that sociology can be a liberating practical activity, not just an abstract intellectual exercise. By revealing the opportunities and constraints you face, sociology can help to teach you who you are and what you can become in this particular social and historical context. We cannot know what the future will bring, but we can at least know the choices we confront and the likely consequences of our actions. From this point of view, sociology can help us create the best possible future. That has always been sociology's principal justification, and so it should be today.

Distinctive Features

We have tried to keep sociology's main purpose and relevance front and center in this book. As a result, *Sociology: Your Compass for a New World,* Enhanced Second Brief Edition, differs from comparable introductory sociology textbooks in five ways:

1. **Drawing connections between one's self and the social world.** To varying degrees, all introductory sociology textbooks try to show students how their personal experiences are connected to the larger social world. However, we employ two devices to make these connections clearer than in other textbooks. First, we illustrate key sociological ideas by using examples from popular culture that resonate deeply with student interests and experiences. For example, we conclude our discussion of culture in Chapter 2 by showing how radical subcultures often become commercialized, focusing on the development of rap and heavy metal music. In Chapter 10 we examine the causes and consequences of glamorizing thin bodies in advertising. We analyze the Super Bowl to highlight key features of Durkheim's theory of religion in Chapter 12. We think these and many other examples speak directly to today's students about important sociological ideas in terms they understand, thus making the connection between self and society clear.

   Second, we developed several unique pedagogical features to draw the connection between students' experiences and the larger social world. **You and the Social World** is a feature that repeatedly challenges students to consider how and why their own lives conform to, or deviate from, various patterns of social relations and actions. We also enter into a social policy debate in each chapter with a feature entitled **Social Policy: What Do You Think?** Here we set out public policy alternatives on a range of pressing social issues and teach students that sociology can be a matter of the most urgent practical importance. Students also learn that they can have a say in the development of public policy. **Mass Media and Society** is a feature unique to this book. It examines the World Wide Web, television, and other means of modern mass communication to illustrate such concepts as globalization, social networks, minority representation, body image, political protest, and the establishment of community. **Sociology at the Movies** takes a universal and popular element of contemporary culture and renders it sociologically relevant. We provide brief reviews of movies, most of them recent releases, and highlight the sociological issues they raise and the sociological insights they contain. Each of the boxed features ends with Critical Thinking Questions that can be used to stimulate classroom discussion or for assignments, many of them research based.

2. **What to think versus how to think.** All textbooks teach students both *what* to think about a subject and *how* to think about it from a particular disciplinary perspective. In our judgment, however, introductory sociology textbooks usually place too much stress on the "what" and not enough on the "how." The result: They sometimes read more like encyclopedias than enticements to look at the world in a new way. We have tipped the balance in the other direction. To be sure, *Sociology: Your Compass for a New World,* Enhanced Second Brief Edition, contains definitions and literature reviews. Each chapter features standard pedagogical aids such as a list of **Chapter Objectives,** a **Summary,** companion **Web Resources,** and a set of **Questions to Consider.** Key terms are defined both in the margins of the text and in a cumulative **Glossary** at the end of the book. However, we devote more space than other authors to showing how sociologists think. We often relate an anecdote to highlight an issue's importance, present contending interpretations of the issue, and then adduce data to judge the merits of the various interpretations. We do not just refer to tables and graphs, we analyze them. When evidence warrants, we reject theories and endorse others. Thus, many sections of the book read more like a simplified journal article than an encyclopedia. If all this sounds just like what sociologists do professionally, then we have achieved our aim: to present a less antiseptic, more realistic, and therefore intrinsically exciting account of how sociologists practice their craft. Said differently, one of the strengths of this book is that it does not present sociology as a set of immutable truths carved in stone tablets. Instead, it shows how sociologists actually go about the business of solving sociological puzzles.

3. **Objectivity versus subjectivity.** Sociologists since Max Weber have understood that sociologists—indeed, all scientists—are members of society whose thinking and research are influenced by the social and historical context in which they work. Yet most introductory sociology textbooks present a stylized and not very sociological view of the research process. Textbooks tend to emphasize sociology's objectivity and the hypothetico-deductive method of reasoning, for the most part ignoring the more subjective factors that go into the research mix (Lynch and Bogen, 1997). We think this emphasis is a pedagogical error. In our own teaching, we have found that drawing the connection between objectivity and subjectivity in sociological research makes the discipline more appealing to students. It shows how research issues are connected to the lives of real flesh-and-blood women and men and how sociology is related to students' existential concerns. Therefore, in most chapters of *Sociology: Your Compass for a New World,* Enhanced Second Brief Edition, we feature a **Personal Anecdote** that explains how certain sociological issues first arose in our own minds. We often adopt a narrative style because stories let students understand ideas on an emotional as well as an intellectual level; and when we form an emotional attachment to ideas, they stay with us more effectively than if our attachment is solely intellectual. We place the ideas of important sociological figures in social and historical context. We show how sociological methodologies serve as a reality check, but we also make it clear that socially personal concerns often lead sociologists to decide which aspects of reality are worth checking on in the first place. We believe that *Sociology: Your Compass for a New World,* Enhanced Second Brief Edition, is unique in presenting a realistic and balanced account of the role of objectivity and subjectivity in the research process.

4. **Diversity and a global perspective.** It is gratifying to see how much less parochial American introductory sociology textbooks are today than they were just 20 years ago. Contemporary textbooks highlight gender and race issues. They broaden the student's understanding of the world by comparing the United States with other societies. They

show how global processes affect local issues and how local issues affect global processes. *Sociology: Your Compass for a New World,* Enhanced Second Brief Edition, is no different in this regard. We have made diversity and globalization prominent themes of this book. We make frequent and effective use of crossnational comparisons between the United States and countries as diverse as India and Sweden. We incorporate original maps that illustrate the distribution of sociological variables globally and regionally and the relationship among variables across time and space. We remain sensitive to gender and race issues throughout. This has been easy for us because we are members of racial and ethnic minority groups. We are multilingual. We have lived in other countries for extended periods. And we have published widely on five countries other than the United States. Robert Brym specializes in the study of Russia, Canada, and Israel and Palestine, while John Lie's research focuses on South Korea and Japan. As you will see in the following pages, our backgrounds have enabled us to bring greater depth to issues of diversity and globalization than other textbooks.

5. **Currency.** Every book bears the imprint of its time. It is significant, therefore, that the first editions of the leading American introductory sociology textbooks were published in the late 1980s. At that time just over 10 percent of Americans owned PCs. The World Wide Web did not exist. Genetic engineering was in its infancy. The USSR was a major world power. Nobody could imagine teenage boys committing mass murder at school with semi-automatic weapons. *Sociology: Your Compass for a New World,* Enhanced Second Brief Edition, is one of the first American introductory sociology textbooks of the 21st century, and it is the most up-to-date. This is reflected in the currency of our illustrations and references. For instance, Web resources form an integral part of this book; more than one-sixth of our citations are to materials on the Web.

It made sense in the 1980s to simplify the sociological universe for introductory students by claiming that three main theoretical perspectives—functionalism, symbolic interactionism, and conflict theory—pervade all areas of the discipline. However, that approach is no longer adequate. Functionalism is less influential than it once was. Feminism is an important theoretical perspective in its own right. Conflict theory and symbolic interactionism have become internally differentiated. For example, there is no longer a single conflict theory of politics but several important variants. Highly influential new theoretical perspectives, such as postmodernism and social constructionism, have emerged, and not all of them fit neatly into the old categories. *Sociology: Your Compass for a New World,* Enhanced Second Brief Edition, highlights the contributions of traditional theoretical approaches, but it also notes recent theoretical innovations that are given insufficient attention in other major textbooks.

New in the Enhanced Second Brief Edition

We were gratified and moved by the overwhelmingly positive response to previous editions of this book. At the same time, we benefited from the constructive criticisms generously offered by dozens of our readers and reviewers. *Sociology: Your Compass for a New World,* Enhanced Second Brief Edition, is a response to many of their suggestions. We have thoroughly updated the Enhanced Second Brief Edition as follows:

● written six new reviews of popular movies for the **Sociology at the Movies** feature, including *Borat, Wedding Crashers, Shake Hands with the Devil, The Great Debaters, The Corporation,* and *Sicko;*

- inserted new census and research data throughout the text, including more than 40 updated figures and tables;
- extensively revised the discussion of norms and values in Chapter 2;
- extensively revised the discussion of status in Chapter 4;
- added substantial new material on globalization in Chapter 8;
- added a new **You and the Social World** feature on the 2008 U.S. presidential election in Chapter 13;
- added new material on the 2008–2009 global financial crisis in Chapter 13; and
- added substantial new material on global warming in Chapter 16.

We are delighted with the final product and very much hope our readers will be too.

Supplements

Sociology: Your Compass for a New World, Enhanced Second Brief Edition, is accompanied by a wide array of supplements prepared to create the best learning environment inside as well as outside the classroom for both the instructor and the student. All the continuing supplements for *Sociology: Your Compass for a New World,* Enhanced Second Brief Edition, have been thoroughly revised and updated, and several are new to this edition. We invite you to take full advantage of the teaching and learning tools available to you.

For the Instructor

Instructor's Resource Manual. This supplement offers the instructor brief chapter outlines, chapter summaries, chapter-specific summaries, key terms, student learning objectives, extensively detailed chapter lecture outlines, essay/discussion questions, lecture suggestions, student activities, chapter review questions, InfoTrac® College Edition discussion exercises, Internet exercises, video suggestions, suggested resources for instructors, and creative lecture and teaching suggestions. Also included is a list of additional print, video, and online resources, and concise user guides for CengageNOW™, InfoTrac College Edition, and WebTutor™.

Test Bank. This test bank consists of 75–100 multiple-choice questions and 15–20 true/false questions for each chapter of the text, all with answer explanations and page references to the text. Each multiple-choice item has the question type (factual, applied, or conceptual) indicated. Also included are 10–20 short-answer and 5–10 essay questions for each chapter. All questions are labeled as new, modified, or pickup and have corresponding learning objectives to help instructors streamline their lectures and tests.

ExamView Computerized Testing for Macintosh and Windows. Create, deliver, and customize printed and online tests and study guides in minutes with this easy-to-use assessment and tutorial system. ExamView includes a Quick Test Wizard and an Online Test Wizard to guide instructors step by step through the process of creating tests. The test appears on screen exactly as it will print or display online. Using ExamView's complete word processing capabilities, instructors can enter an unlimited number of new questions or edit questions included with ExamView.

Extension: Wadsworth's Sociology Reader Database. Create your own customized reader for your Sociology class drawing from dozens of classic and contemporary articles found on the exclusive Cengage Learning TextChoice database. Using the TextChoice website (http://www.TextChoice.com) you can preview articles, select your content, and add your own original material. TextChoice will then produce your materials as a printed supplementary reader for your class.

Spicing Up Sociology. Written by Marisol Clark-Ibanez and Richelle Swan of California State University, San Marcos, *Spicing Up Sociology* is designed to address the growing interest in using film in the classroom. The authors start the book with the rationale for using film in the classroom, methods for incorporating film into the classroom, and learning outcomes. They choose a feature film for every chapter in *Sociology: Your Compass for a New World,* Enhanced Second Brief Edition, and some of the films in this book's "Sociology at the Movies" features are included. The authors give a synopsis of the film and a description of what concept in that chapter it gets across. Accompanying each feature film is an activity for students to complete.

Classroom Presentation Tools for the Instructor

JoinIn™ on TurningPoint®. Transform your lecture into an interactive student experience with *JoinIn.* Combined with your choice of keypad systems, *JoinIn* turns your PowerPoint® application into audience response software. With a click on a handheld device, students can respond to multiple-choice questions, short polls, interactive exercises, and peer review questions. You can also take attendance, check student comprehension of concepts, collect student demographics to better assess student needs, and even administer quizzes. In addition, there are interactive text-specific slide sets that you can modify and merge with any of your own PowerPoint lecture slides.

Multimedia Manager Instructor Resource CD: A Microsoft® PowerPoint® Link Tool. With this one-stop digital library and presentation tool, instructors can assemble, edit, and present custom lectures with ease. The Multimedia Manager contains figures, tables, graphs, and maps from this text, pre-assembled Microsoft PowerPoint lecture slides, video clips from Dallas TeleLearning, ShowCase presentational software, tips for teaching, the instructor's manual, and more.

Videos. Adopters of *Sociology: Your Compass for a New World,* Enhanced Second Brief Edition have several different video options available with the text. Please consult with your Cengage Learning sales representative to determine whether you are a qualified adopter for a particular video.

Wadsworth's Lecture Launchers for Introductory Sociology. An exclusive offering jointly created by Wadsworth, Cengage Learning and Dallas Telelearning, this video contains a collection of video highlights taken from the *Exploring Society: An Introduction to Sociology Telecourse* (formerly *The Sociological Imagination*). Each 3- to 6-minute video segment has been specially chosen to enhance and enliven class lectures and discussions of 20 key topics covered in the Introduction to Sociology course. Accompanying the video is a brief written description of each clip, along with suggested discussion questions to help effectively incorporate the material into the classroom. Available on VHS or DVD.

Sociology: Core Concepts Video. Another exclusive offering jointly created by Wadsworth, Cengage Learning and Dallas TeleLearning, this video contains a collection of video highlights taken from the *Exploring Society: An Introduction to Sociology Telecourse* (formerly *The Sociological Imagination*). Each 15- to 20-minute video segment will enhance student learning of the essential concepts in the introductory course and can be used to initiate class lectures, discussion, and review. The video covers topics such as the sociological imagination, stratification, race and ethnic relations, social change, and more. Available on VHS or DVD.

ABC Videos. Launch your lectures with exciting video clips from the award-winning news coverage of ABC. Addressing topics covered in a typical course, these videos are divided into short segments—perfect for introducing key concepts in contexts relevant to students' lives.

Wadsworth Sociology Video Library. Bring sociological concepts to life with videos from Wadsworth's Sociology Video Library, which includes thought-provoking offerings from Films for Humanities, as well as other excellent educational video sources. This extensive collection illustrates important sociological concepts covered in many sociology courses.

Supplements for the Student

CengageNow™. Students can sign in, save time, and get the grade they want with CengageNOW, our online study system that includes an integrated eBook and a personalized study plan. Access to CengageNOW also includes access to InfoTrac College Edition, which puts a complete online university library at students' fingertips 24/7.

Study Guide with Practice Tests. This student study tool contains learning objectives, a list of key terms with page references to the text, detailed chapter outlines, study activities, learning objectives, InfoTrac College Edition discussion exercises, Internet exercises, and practice tests consisting of 25–30 multiple-choice questions, 10–15 true-false questions, 5–10 short-answer questions, 5 essay questions. All multiple-choice, true-false, short-answer, and essay questions include answer explanations and page references to the text.

InfoTrac® College Edition with InfoMarks™. Available as a free option with newly purchased texts, InfoTrac College Edition gives instructors and students four months of free access to an extensive online database of reliable, full-length articles (not just abstracts) from thousands of scholarly and popular publications going back as much as 22 years. Among the journals available 24/7 are *American Journal of Sociology, Social Forces, Social Research,* and *Sociology.* InfoTrac College Edition now also comes with InfoMarks™, a tool that allows you to save your search parameters, as well as save links to specific articles. (Available to North American college and university students only; journals are subject to change.)

WebTutor™ for WebCT® and Blackboard®. WebTutor combines easy-to-use course management tools with rich, text-specific content. Ready to use as soon as you log on—or, customize WebTutor with web links, images, and other resources.

Turnitin™ Online Originality Checker. This online "originality checker" is a simple solution for professors who want to put a strong deterrent against plagiarism into place and make sure their students are employing proper research techniques. Students upload their papers to their professor's personalized website and within seconds, the paper is checked against three databases—a constantly updated archive of over 4.5 billion web pages; a collection of millions of published works, including a number of Cengage Learning texts; and the millions of student papers already submitted to Turnitin. For each paper submitted, the professor receives a customized report that documents any text matches found in Turnitin's databases. At a glance, the professor can see if the student has used proper research and citation skills, or if he or she has simply copied the material from a source and pasted it into the paper without giving credit where credit was due. Our exclusive deal with iParadigms, the producers of Turnitin, gives instructors the ability to package Turnitin™ with the *Sociology: Your Compass for a New World* Cengage Learning textbook. Please consult with your Cengage Learning sales representative to find out more!

Companion Website for *Sociology: Your Compass for a New World,* **Enhanced Second Brief Edition** (www.cengage.com/sociology). The book's companion site includes chapter-specific resources for instructors and students. For instructors, the site offers a password-protected instructor's manual, Microsoft PowerPoint presentation slides, and more. For students, there is a multitude of text-specific study aids, including the following:

- Tutorial practice quizzes that can be scored and e-mailed to the instructor
- Web Links
- InfoTrac College Edition exercises
- Flash cards
- MicroCase Online data exercises
- Crossword puzzles
- Virtual Explorations
- And much more!

Acknowledgments

Anyone who has gone sailing knows that when you embark on a long voyage you need more than a compass. Among other things, you need a helm operator blessed with a strong sense of direction and intimate knowledge of likely dangers. You need crew members who know all the ropes and can use them to keep things intact and in their proper place. And you need sturdy hands to raise and lower the sails. On the voyage to complete this book, our crew demonstrated all these skills. Our acquisitions editor, Chris Caldeira, saw this book's promise from the outset, understood clearly the direction we had to take to develop its potential, and on several occasions steered us clear of threatening shoals. We still marvel at how Cheri Palmer, our production project manager, and Dan Fitzgerald, production editor, were able to keep the many parts of this project in their proper order and prevent the whole thing from flying apart at the seams. But it was Dan Moneypenny, our developmental editor, who made this book sail. He knew just when to trim the jib and when to hoist the mainsail. We are deeply grateful to him and to all the members of our crew for a successful voyage.

This book would have been of far inferior quality if the following people had not generously shared their knowledge with us and offered painstaking criticisms for the Enhanced Second Brief Edition:

Yasemin Besen-Cassino, Montclair State University
Paul E. Calarco, Jr., State University of New York at Albany
Karyn Daniels, Long Beach City College
Jennifer L. Holz, University of Akron–Wayne College
Sue Wika, Minnesota State Community and Technical College
Yih-Jin Young, Nassau Community College

We are also grateful to the following colleagues who reviewed the manuscript for the first and second editions and provided a wealth of helpful suggestions: David Allen, Temple University; Kay Andrews, Chattanooga State Technical Community College; Aurora Bautista, Bunker Hill Community College; Shelly Brown, University of North Carolina, Greensboro; John F. Brusati, Virginia Western Community College; William Carter, Middle Tennessee State University; Andrew Cho, Tacoma Community College;

Margaret Choka, Pellissippi State Technical Community College; William M. Cross, Illinois College; Jessica Dumas, Maple Woods Community College; Gianna Durso-Finley, Mercer County Community College; Charles R. Gray, Old Dominion University; Mara Kent-Skruch, Anne Arundel Community College; William Lockhart, McLennan Community College; Muketiwa W. Madzura, Normandale Community College; Ron Matson, Wichita State University; Deborah McCarthy, College of Charleston; John S. Rice, University of North Carolina at Wilmington; Donald D. Ricker, Mott Community College; Terina M. Roberson, Central Piedmont Community College; William E. Snizek, Virginia Tech; Tom Waller, Tallahassee Community College; M. Nicole Warehime, University of Oklahoma; James Wright, Chattanooga State Technical Community College.

CHAPTER 1

A Sociological Compass

Zigy Kaluzny/Getty Images

In this chapter, you will learn that:

- The causes of human behavior lie mostly in the patterns of social relations that surround and permeate us.

- Sociology is the systematic study of human behavior in social context.

- Sociologists are often motivated to do research by the desire to improve people's lives. At the same time, sociologists adopt scientific methods to test their ideas.

- The main methods of collecting sociological data include systematic observations of natural social settings, experiments, surveys, and analyses of existing documents and official statistics. Each research method has characteristic strengths and weaknesses.

- The founders of sociology diagnosed the massive social transformations of their day and suggested ways of overcoming the social problems created by the Industrial Revolution. Today's Postindustrial Revolution and the process of globalization similarly challenge us.

- At the personal level, sociology can help clarify the opportunities and constraints you face. It suggests what you can become in today's social and historical context.

Introduction

Robert Brym's Indirect Road to Sociology

Personal Anecdote

"When I started college at the age of 18," says Robert Brym, "I was bewildered by the wide variety of courses I could choose from. Having now taught sociology for more than 30 years and met thousands of undergraduates, I am quite sure most students today feel as I did then.

"One source of confusion for me was uncertainty about why I was in college in the first place. Like you, I knew higher education could improve one's chance of finding good work. But, like most students, I also had a sense that higher education is supposed to provide something more than just the training necessary to embark on a career that is interesting and pays well. Several high school teachers and guidance counselors had told me that college was also supposed to 'broaden my horizons' and teach me to 'think critically.' I wasn't sure what they meant, but they made it sound interesting enough to encourage me to know more. Thus, I decided in my first year to take mainly 'practical' courses that might prepare me for a law degree (economics, political science, and psychology). I also enrolled in a couple of other courses to indulge my 'intellectual' side (philosophy, drama). One thing I knew for sure: I didn't want to study sociology.

CENGAGENOW™

This icon signals when CengageNOW has important resources available for you to use in conjunction with the text. See the foldout at the front of this text for information on how to access CengageNOW.

"Sociology, I came to believe, was thin soup with uncertain ingredients. When I asked a few sophomores and juniors in my dorm what sociology is, I received different answers. They variously defined sociology as the science of social inequality, the study of how to create the ideal society, the analysis of how and why people assume different roles in their lives, and the method of figuring out why people don't always do what they are supposed to do. I found all this confusing and decided to forgo sociology for what seemed to be tastier courses."

A Change of Mind

"Despite the opinion I'd formed, I found myself taking no fewer than four sociology courses a year after starting college. That revolution in my life was partly due to the influence of an extraordinary professor I happened to meet just before I began my sophomore year. He set me thinking in an altogether new way about what I could and should do with my life. He exploded some of my deepest beliefs. He started me thinking sociologically.

"Specifically, he first encouraged me to think about the dilemma of all thinking people. Life is finite. If we want to make the most of it, we must figure out how best to live. That is no easy task. It requires study, reflection, and the selection of values and goals. Ideally, he said, higher education is supposed to supply students with just that opportunity. Finally, I was beginning to understand what I could expect from college apart from job training.

"The professor also convinced me that sociology in particular could open up a new and superior way of comprehending my world. Specifically, he said, it could clarify my place in society, how I might best maneuver through it, and perhaps even how I might contribute to improving it, however modestly. Before beginning my study of sociology, I had always taken for granted that things happen in the world—and to me—because physical and emotional forces cause them. Famine, I thought, is caused by drought, war by territorial greed, economic success by hard work, marriage by love, suicide by bottomless depression, rape by depraved lust. But now this professor repeatedly threw evidence in my face that contradicted my easy formulas. If drought causes famine, why have so many famines occurred in perfectly normal weather conditions or involved some groups hoarding or destroying food so others would starve? If hard work causes prosperity, why are so many hard workers poor? If love causes marriage, why does violence against women and children occur in so many families? And so the questions multiplied.

"As if it were not enough that the professor's sociological evidence upset many of my assumptions about the way the world worked, he also challenged me to understand sociology's unique way of explaining social life. He defined **sociology** as the systematic study of human behavior in social context. He explained that social causes are distinct from physical and emotional causes. Understanding social causes can help clarify otherwise inexplicable features of famine, marriage, and so forth. In public grade school and high school, my teachers taught me that people are free to do what they want with their lives. However, my new professor taught me that the organization of the social world opens some opportunities and closes others, thus constraining our freedom and helping to make us what we are. By examining the operation of these powerful social forces, he said, sociology can help us to know ourselves, our capabilities and limitations. I was hooked. And so, of course, I hope you will be too."

Sociology: The systematic study of human behavior in social context.

The Sociological Perspective

Before showing how sociology can help you understand and improve *your* world, we briefly examine the problem of suicide. This will help illustrate how the sociological perspective can clarify and sometimes overturn commonsense beliefs. By analyzing suicide sociologically, you can put to a tough test our claim that sociology takes a unique, surprising, and enlightening perspective on social events. After all, suicide appears to be the supremely antisocial and nonsocial act. It is condemned by nearly everyone in society. It is typically committed in private, far from the public's intrusive glare. It is rare. There are about 11 suicides for every 100,000 Americans annually (Centers for Disease Control and Prevention, 2002: 425). When we think about why people commit such acts, we are likely to focus on their individual states of mind rather than on the state of society. In other words, what usually interests us are the aspects of specific individuals' lives that caused them to become depressed or angry enough to commit suicide. We usually do not think about the patterns of social relations that might encourage such actions in general.

"Pacific." Alex Colville. 1967.

If sociology can reveal the hidden social causes of such an apparently antisocial and nonsocial phenomenon, there must be something to it!

CENGAGENOW™

Learn more about the **sociological perspective** by going through the Sociological Perspective Learning Module.

The Sociological Explanation of Suicide

At the end of the 19th century, French sociologist Émile Durkheim, one of the pioneers of the discipline, demonstrated that suicide is more than just an individual act of desperation resulting from a psychological disorder, as people commonly believed at the time (Durkheim, 1951 [1897]). Suicide rates, he showed, are strongly influenced by social forces.

Durkheim made his case by first examining the relationship between rates of suicide and rates of psychological disorder for different groups. The idea that a psychological disorder causes suicide would be supported, he reasoned, only if suicide rates were high where rates of psychological disorder were high and were low where rates of psychological disorder were low. Yet his analysis of European government statistics and hospital records revealed nothing of the kind. He discovered that slightly more women than men were in insane asylums, yet four men committed suicide for every woman who did so. Jews had the highest rate of psychological disorder among the major religious groups in France. They also had the lowest suicide rate. Psychological disorder occurred most frequently when a person reached maturity. Suicide rates, though, increased steadily with advancing age.

So, rates of suicide and psychological disorder did not rise and fall together. What, then, accounts for variations in suicide rates? Durkheim argued that suicide rates vary because of differences in the degree of **social solidarity** in different groups. According to Durkheim, the greater the degree to which a group's members share beliefs and values, and the more frequently and intensely they interact, the more social solidarity exists in the group. In turn, the higher the level of social solidarity, the more firmly anchored individuals are to the social world and the less likely they are to commit suicide

Social solidarity: (1) The degree to which group members share beliefs and values and (2) the intensity and frequency of their interaction.

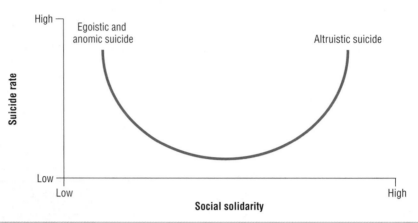

▶FIGURE 1.1
Durkheim's Theory of Suicide
Durkheim argued that as the level of social solidarity increases, the suicide rate declines. Then, beyond a certain point, it starts to rise. Hence the U-shaped curve in this graph. Durkheim called suicides that occur in high-solidarity settings *altruistic.* "Altruism" means devotion to the interests of others. **Altruistic suicide** occurs when norms tightly govern behavior, so individual actions are often in the group interest. For example, when soldiers knowingly give up their lives to protect members of their unit, they commit altruistic suicide out of a deep sense of comradeship. In contrast, suicide that occurs in low-solidarity settings is *egoistic* or *anomic,* said Durkheim. **Egoistic suicide** results from a lack of integration of the individual into society because of weak social ties to others. For example, the rate of egoistic suicide is likely to be high among people who lack friends and are unmarried. Anomie means "without order." **Anomic suicide** occurs when norms governing behavior are vaguely defined. For example, when people live in a society lacking a widely shared code of morality, the rate of anomic suicide is likely to be high.

CENGAGENOW™

Learn more about **Suicide** by going through the Suicide Death Rate per 100,000 Map Exercise.

Altruistic suicide: Durkheim's term for suicide that occurs in high-solidarity settings, where norms tightly govern behavior. *Altruism* means devotion to the interests of others. Altruistic suicide is suicide in the group interest.

Egoistic suicide: Durkheim's term for a type of suicide that occurs in low-solidarity settings. It results from a lack of integration of the individual into society because of weak social ties to others.

Anomic suicide: Durkheim's term for a type of suicide that occurs in low-solidarity settings, where norms governing behavior are vaguely defined. *Anomie* (from which the adjective is derived) means "without order."

if adversity strikes. In other words, Durkheim expected groups with a high degree of solidarity to have lower suicide rates than groups with a low degree of solidarity—at least to a point (▶Figure 1.1).

To support his argument, Durkheim showed that married adults were half as likely as unmarried adults to commit suicide because marriage typically created social ties and a moral cement that bound the individuals to society. Similarly, women were less likely to commit suicide than men. Why? Women were generally more involved in the intimate social relations of family life. Jews, Durkheim wrote, were less likely to commit suicide than Christians. The reason? Centuries of persecution had turned them into a group that was more defensive and tightly knit. Elderly people were more prone than young and middle-aged people to take their own lives when faced with misfortune because they were most likely to live alone, to have lost a spouse, and to lack a job and a wide network of friends.

Durkheim's theory is not just a historical curiosity. It also sheds light on suicide here and now. As the cluster of bars at the far left of ▶Figure 1.2 shows, the suicide rate in the United States today varies with age, just as it did more than a century ago in France. Elderly people are most likely to commit suicide because they are the least firmly rooted in society. Moreover, among elderly individuals, suicide is most common among the divorced and widowed (National Center for Injury Prevention and Control, 2000). Figure 1.2 also shows that suicide rates in the United States differ between men and women. As in France in the late 1800s, men typically are less involved than women in child care and other duties involving family life and are about four times more likely than women to commit suicide.

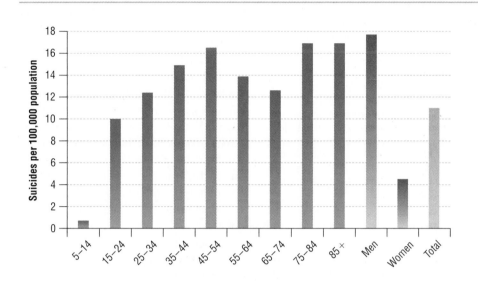

▶FIGURE 1.2
Suicide Rate by Age Cohort and Sex, United States, 2005 (per 100,000 people)

Source: American Association of Suicidology (2008).

Research also shows that parts of the United States with high rates of church membership have low suicide rates, whereas areas with high divorce rates have high suicide rates (Breault, 1986). This finding, too, is consistent with Durkheim's theory that "suicide varies with the degree of integration of the social groups of which the individual forms a part" (Durkheim, 1951 [1897]: 209).

The Sociological Imagination

You have known for a long time that you live in a society. Yet until now, you may not have fully appreciated that society also lives in you. Patterns of social relations such as the level of social solidarity affect your innermost thoughts and feelings, influence your actions, and thus help shape who you are. Sociologists call stable patterns of social relations **social structures.**

Nearly half a century ago, the great American sociologist C. Wright Mills (1916–62) called the ability to see the connection between personal troubles and social structures the **sociological imagination.** One of the sociologist's main tasks is to identify and explain the connection between people's personal troubles and the social structures in which they are embedded. An important step in broadening one's sociological awareness involves recognizing that three levels of social structure surround and permeate us. Think of these structures as concentric circles radiating out from you.

Microstructures are patterns of intimate social relations. They are formed during face-to-face interaction. Families, friendship circles, and work associations are all examples of microstructures. **Macrostructures** are patterns of social relations that lie outside and above your circle of intimates and acquaintances. One important macrostructure is **patriarchy,** the traditional system of economic and political inequality between women and men in most societies. Other macrostructures include religious institutions and social classes. The third level of society that surrounds and permeates us is composed of **global structures.** International organizations, patterns of worldwide travel and communication, and the economic relations between and among countries are examples of global structures. Global structures are increasingly important, because inexpensive travel and

Social structures: Stable patterns of social relations.

Sociological imagination: The quality of mind that enables one to see the connection between personal troubles and social structures.

Microstructures: Patterns of social relations formed during face-to-face interaction. Families, friendship circles, and work associations are all examples of microstructures.

Macrostructures: Overarching patterns of social relations that lie outside and above one's circle of intimates and acquaintances. Macrostructures include classes and power systems such as patriarchy.

Patriarchy: The traditional system of economic and political inequality between women and men.

Global structures: Patterns of social relations that lie outside and above the national level. They include international organizations, patterns of worldwide travel and communication, and the economic relations between and among countries.

Brown Brothers, Sterling PA

C. Wright Mills (1916–62) argued that the sociological imagination is a unique way of thinking. It allows people to see how their actions and potential are affected by the social and historical context in which they live. Mills employed the sociological imagination effectively in his most important works. For example, *The Power Elite* (1956) is a study of the several hundred men who occupied the "command posts" of major U.S. institutions. It suggests that economic, political, and military power is highly concentrated in U.S. society, which is therefore less of a democracy than we are often led to believe. The implication of Mills's study is that to make our society more democratic, power must be more evenly distributed among the citizenry.

communication allow all parts of the world to become interconnected culturally, economically, and politically.[1]

Personal problems are connected to social structures at the micro, macro, and global levels. Whether the personal problem involves finding a job, keeping a marriage intact, or acting justly to end world poverty, considering the influence of social structures on us broadens our understanding of the problems we face and suggests appropriate courses of action (Box 1.1).

The sociological imagination is a recent addition to the human repertoire. It is only about as old as the United States. Although in ancient and medieval times some philosophers wrote about society, their thinking was not sociological. They believed that God and nature controlled society. These philosophers spent much of their time sketching blueprints for the ideal society and urging people to follow those blueprints. They relied on speculation rather than evidence to reach conclusions about how society worked.

Origins of the Sociological Imagination

The sociological imagination was born when three modern revolutions pushed people to think about society in an entirely new way.

The Scientific Revolution

The **Scientific Revolution** began about 1550. It encouraged the view that sound conclusions about the workings of society must be based on solid evidence, not just speculation.

People often link the Scientific Revolution to specific ideas, such as Newton's laws of motion and Copernicus's theory that the Earth revolves around the Sun. However, science is less a collection of ideas than a method of inquiry. For instance, in 1609 Galileo pointed his newly invented telescope at the heavens, made some careful observations, and showed that his observations fit Copernicus's theory. This is the core of the scientific method: using evidence to make a case for a particular point of view. By the mid-1600s, some philosophers were calling for a science of society. When sociology emerged as a distinct discipline in the 19th century, commitment to the scientific method was one firm pillar of the sociological imagination.

The Democratic Revolution

The **Democratic Revolution** began about 1750. It suggested that people are responsible for organizing society and that human intervention can therefore solve social problems. Before the Democratic Revolution, most people thought otherwise. They believed that God ordained the social order. The American Revolution (1775–83) and the French Revolution (1789–99) helped undermine that idea. These democratic political upheavals showed that society could experience massive change in a short period. They proved that people could replace unsatisfactory rulers. They suggested

Scientific Revolution: Began in Europe about 1550. It encouraged the view that sound conclusions about the workings of society must be based on solid evidence, not just speculation.

Democratic Revolution: Began about 1750, during which the citizens of the United States, France, and other countries broadened their participation in government. This revolution suggested that people organize society and that human intervention can therefore resolve social problems.

---

[1]Some sociologists also distinguish "mesostructures," which are social relations that link microstructures and macrostructures.

BOX 1.1
SOCIOLOGY AT THE MOVIES

Minority Report
(2002)

The year is 2054 and the place is Washington, D.C. John Anderton (played by Tom Cruise) is a police officer who uses the latest technologies to apprehend murderers *before* they commit their crimes. This remarkable feat is possible because scientists have nearly perfected the use of "Pre-Cogs"—or so, at least, it seems. The Pre-Cog system consists of three psychics whose brains are wired together and who are kept sedated so they can develop a collective vision about impending murders. Together with powerful computers, the Pre-Cogs are apparently helping to create a crime-free society.

All is well until one of the psychic's visions shows Anderton himself murdering a stranger in less than 36 hours. Suddenly, Anderton is on the run from his own men. Desperate to figure out whether the Pre-Cog system is somehow mistaken, he breaks into the system, unwires one of the psychics, and discovers that they do not always agree about what the future will bring. Sometimes there is a "minority report." Sometimes the minority report is correct. Sometimes people are arrested even though they never would have broken the law. The authorities have concealed this system flaw and allowed the arrest of potentially innocent people in their zeal to create a crime-free society.

And so Anderton comes to realize that not everything is predetermined—that, in his words, "It's not the future if you stop

John Anderton (Tom Cruise) in *Minority Report*.

it." And stop it he does. Herein lies an important sociological lesson. Many people believe two contradictory ideas with equal conviction: first, that they are perfectly free to do whatever they want; second, that the "system" (or "society") is so big and powerful they are unable to do anything to change it. Neither idea is accurate. As we emphasize throughout this book, various aspects of society exert powerful influences on our behavior; we are not perfectly free. Nonetheless, it is possible to change many aspects of society; we are not wholly determined either. As you will learn, changing various aspects of society is possible under certain specifiable circumstances, with the aid of specialized knowledge and often through great individual and collective effort. As John Anderton says, "It's not the future if you stop it."

Understanding the social constraints and possibilities for freedom that envelop us requires an active sociological imagination. The sociological imagination urges us to connect our biography with history and social structure—to make sense of our lives against a larger historical and social background and to act in light of our understanding. Although movies are just entertainment to many people, they often achieve by different means what the sociological imagination aims for. Therefore, in each chapter of this book, we review a movie to shed light on topics of sociological importance.

Critical Thinking

- Have you ever tried to put events in your own life in the context of history and social structure? Did the exercise help you make sense of your life? Did it in any way lead to a life more worth living?

- Is the sociological imagination a worthy goal?

that *people* control society. The implications for social thought were profound, for if it was possible to change society through human intervention, a science of society could play a big role. The new science could help people find ways of overcoming social problems, improving the welfare of citizens, and effectively reaching given goals. Much of the justification for sociology as a science arose out of the democratic revolutions that shook Europe and North America.

Eugène Delacroix. Liberty Leading the People, July 28, 1830. The democratic forces unleashed by the French Revolution suggested that people are responsible for organizing society and that human intervention can therefore solve social problems. Democracy was thus a foundation stone of sociology.

Industrial Revolution: The rapid economic transformation that began in Britain in the 1780s. It involved the large-scale application of science and technology to industrial processes, the creation of factories, and the formation of a working class. It created a host of new and serious social problems that attracted the attention of many social thinkers.

The Industrial Revolution

The **Industrial Revolution** began about 1780. It created a host of new and serious social problems that attracted the attention of social thinkers. As a result of the growth of industry, masses of people moved from countryside to city, worked agonizingly long hours in crowded and dangerous mines and factories, lost faith in their religions, confronted faceless bureaucracies, and reacted to the filth and poverty of their existence by means of strikes, crime, revolutions, and wars. Scholars had never seen a sociological laboratory like this. The Scientific Revolution suggested that a science of society was possible. The Democratic Revolution suggested that people could intervene to improve society. The Industrial Revolution now presented social thinkers with a host of pressing social problems crying out for solution. They responded by giving birth to the sociological imagination.

Auguste Comte and the Tension between Science and Values

French social thinker Auguste Comte (1798–1857) coined the term sociology in 1838 (Comte, 1975). Comte tried to place the study of society on scientific foundations. He said he wanted to understand the social world as it was, not as he or anyone else imagined it should be. Yet there was a tension in his work. For although Comte was eager to adopt the scientific method in the study of society, he was a conservative thinker, motivated by strong opposition to rapid change in French society. That is evident in his writings. When he moved from his small, conservative hometown to Paris, Comte witnessed the democratic forces unleashed by the French Revolution, the early industrialization of society, and the rapid growth of cities. What he saw shocked and saddened him. Rapid social change was destroying much of what he valued, especially respect for traditional authority. He therefore urged slow change and the preservation of all that was traditional in social life. Thus, scientific methods of research and a vision of the ideal society were evident in sociology at its origins.

To varying degrees, we see the same tension in the work of the three giants in the early history of sociology: Karl Marx (1818–83), Émile Durkheim (1858–1917), and Max Weber (pronounced VAY-ber; 1864–1920). The lives of these three men spanned just over a century. They witnessed various phases of Europe's wrenching transition to industrial capitalism. They wanted to explain the great transformation of Europe and suggest ways of improving people's lives. Like Comte, they were committed to the scientific method of research. However, the ideas they developed are not just diagnostic tools from which we can still learn, but, like many sociological ideas, prescriptions for combating social ills.

Durkheim, Marx, and Weber stood close to the origins of the major theoretical traditions in sociology: functionalism, conflict theory, and symbolic interactionism. A fourth theoretical tradition, feminism, has arisen in recent decades to correct some deficiencies in the three long-established traditions. It will become clear as you read this book that many more theories exist in addition to these four. However, because these four traditions have been especially influential in the development of sociology, we present a thumbnail sketch of each at the beginning.

Sociological Theory and Theorists

Functionalism

Durkheim

Durkheim's theory of suicide is an early example of what sociologists now call functionalism. **Functionalist theories** incorporate four features:

1. Functionalist theories stress that human behavior is governed by stable patterns of social relations, or social structures. For example, Durkheim emphasized how patterns of social solidarity influence suicide rates. The social structures typically analyzed by functionalists are macrostructures.

2. Functionalist theories show how social structures maintain or undermine social stability. This is why functionalists are sometimes called *structural functionalists;* they analyze how the parts of society (structures) fit together and how each part contributes to the stability of the whole (its function). Thus, Durkheim argued that high social solidarity contributes to the maintenance of social order. However, the growth of industries and cities in 19th-century Europe lowered the level of social solidarity and contributed to social instability. One aspect of instability, wrote Durkheim, is a higher suicide rate. Another is frequent strikes by workers.

3. Functionalist theories emphasize that social structures are based mainly on shared values. Thus, when Durkheim wrote about social solidarity, he sometimes meant the frequency and intensity of social interaction, but more often he thought of social solidarity as a kind of moral cement that binds people together.

4. Functionalism suggests that reestablishing equilibrium can best solve most social problems. Durkheim said that social stability could be restored in late 19th-century Europe by creating new associations of employers and workers that would lower workers' expectations about what they should hope for in life. If more people could agree on wanting less, Durkheim wrote, social solidarity would rise and there would be fewer strikes and lower suicide rates. Functionalism, then, was a conservative response to widespread social unrest in late 19th-century France. A more liberal or radical response would have been to argue that if people were expressing discontent because they were getting less out of life than they expected, discontent could be lowered by finding ways for them to get more out of life.

Parsons and Merton

Although functionalist thinking influenced American sociology at the end of the 19th century, it was only during the Great Depression of 1929–39 that it took deep root (Russett, 1966). With about 30 percent of the labor force unemployed and labor unrest reaching unprecedented levels by 1934, sociologists with a conservative frame of mind were attracted to a theory that focused on how social equilibrium could be restored. Functionalist theory remained popular in the United States for approximately 30 years. It experienced a minor revival in the early 1990s but never regained the dominance it enjoyed from the 1930s to the early 1960s.

Sociologist Talcott Parsons (1902–79) was a leading American proponent of functionalism. He is best known for identifying how various institutions must work to ensure the smooth operation of society as a whole. He argued that society is well integrated and in equilibrium when the family successfully raises new generations, the military successfully defends society against external threats, schools are able to teach students the skills

Émile Durkheim (1858–1917) was the first professor of sociology in France and is often considered to be the first modern sociologist. In *The Rules of the Sociological Method* (1895) and *Suicide* (1897), he argued that human behavior is shaped by "social facts," or the social context in which people are embedded. In Durkheim's view, social facts define the constraints and opportunities within which people must act. Durkheim was also keenly interested in the conditions that promote social order in "primitive" and modern societies, and he explored this problem in depth in such works as *The Division of Labor in Society* (1893) and *The Elementary Forms of the Religious Life* (1912).

Functionalist theory: Stresses that human behavior is governed by relatively stable social structures. It underlines how social structures maintain or undermine social stability. It emphasizes that social structures are based mainly on shared values or preferences, and it suggests that reestablishing equilibrium can best solve most social problems.

Robert Merton (1910–2003) made functionalism a more flexible theory from the late 1930s to the 1950s. *In Social Theory and Social Structure* (1949), he proposed that social structures are not always functional. They may be dysfunctional for some people. Moreover, not all functions are manifest; some are latent. Merton also made major contributions to the sociology of science, notably in *On the Shoulders of Giants* (1956), a study of creativity, tradition, plagiarism, the transmission of knowledge, and the concept of progress.

and values they need to function as productive adults, and religions create a shared moral code among people (Parsons, 1951).

Parsons was criticized for exaggerating the degree to which members of society share common values and social institutions contribute to social harmony. This criticism led Robert Merton (1910–2003), the other leading functionalist in the United States, to propose that social structures may have different consequences for different groups. Merton noted that some of those consequences may be disruptive or **dysfunctional** (Merton, 1968 [1949]). Moreover, said Merton, while some functions are **manifest** (intended and easily observed), others are **latent** (unintended and less obvious). For instance, a manifest function of schools is to transmit skills from one generation to the next. A latent function of schools is to encourage the development of a separate youth culture that often conflicts with parents' values (Coleman, 1961; Hersch, 1998).

Conflict Theory

The second major theoretical tradition in sociology emphasizes the centrality of conflict in social life. Conflict theory incorporates the following four features:

1. **Conflict theory** generally focuses on large, macro-level structures, such as "class relations" or patterns of domination, submission, and struggle between people of high and low standing.

2. Conflict theory shows how major patterns of inequality in society produce social stability in some circumstances and social change in others.

3. Conflict theory stresses how members of privileged groups try to maintain their advantages while subordinate groups struggle to increase theirs. From this point of view, social conditions at a given time are the expression of an ongoing power struggle between privileged and subordinate groups.

4. Conflict theory typically leads to the suggestion that lessening privilege will lower the level of conflict and increase total human welfare.

Marx

Conflict theory originated in the work of German social thinker Karl Marx. A generation before Durkheim, Marx observed the destitution and discontent produced by the Industrial Revolution and proposed a sweeping argument about the way societies develop (Marx, 1904 [1859]; Marx and Engels, 1972 [1848]). Marx's theory radically differed from Durkheim's. **Class conflict,** the struggle between classes to resist and overcome the opposition of other classes, lies at the center of his ideas.

Marx argued that owners of industry are eager to improve the way work is organized and to adopt new tools, machines, and production methods. These innovations allow them to produce more efficiently, earn higher profits, and drive inefficient competitors out of business. However, the drive for profits also causes capitalists to concentrate workers in larger and larger establishments, keep wages as low as possible, and invest as little as possible in improving working conditions. It thus comes about, wrote Marx, that a large and growing class of poor workers opposes a small and shrinking class of wealthy owners.

Dysfunctions: Effects of social structures that create social instability.

Manifest functions: Visible and intended effects of social structures.

Latent functions: Invisible and unintended effects of social structures.

Conflict theory: Generally focuses on large, macro-level structures, such as the relations between or among classes. It shows how major patterns of inequality in society produce social stability in some circumstances and social change in others. It stresses how members of privileged groups try to maintain their advantages, while subordinate groups struggle to increase theirs. It typically leads to the suggestion that eliminating privilege will lower the level of conflict and increase the sum total of human welfare.

Class conflict: The struggle between classes to resist and overcome the opposition of other classes.

Marx believed that workers would ultimately become aware of belonging to the same exploited class. He called this awareness **class consciousness.** He believed that working-class consciousness would encourage the growth of trade unions and labor parties. According to Marx, these organizations would eventually seek to put an end to private ownership of property, replacing it with a communist society, defined as a system in which there is no private property and everyone shares property and wealth according to their needs.

Weber

Although some of Marx's ideas have been usefully adapted to the study of contemporary society, his predictions about the inevitable collapse of capitalism have been questioned. Max Weber, a German sociologist who wrote his major works four decades after Marx did, was among the first to find flaws in Marx's argument (Weber, 1946). Weber noted the rapid growth of the service sector of the economy, with its many nonmanual workers and professionals. He argued that many members of these occupational groups stabilize society because they enjoy higher status and income than manual workers employed in the manufacturing sector. In addition, Weber showed that class conflict is not the only driving force of history. In his view, politics and religion are also important sources of historical change. Other social thinkers pointed out that Marx did not understand how investing in technology would make it possible for workers to toil fewer hours under less oppressive conditions. Nor did he foresee that higher wages, better working conditions, and welfare-state benefits would pacify manual workers. Thus, we see that many of the particulars of Marx's theory were called into question by Weber and other sociologists.

Du Bois

Nonetheless, Marx's general insights about the fundamental importance of conflict in social life were influential, and still are today. For example, William Edward Burghardt Du Bois (1868–1963) was an early advocate of conflict theory in the United States. For a man writing at the end of the 19th century, Du Bois had a remarkably liberal and even radical frame of mind. The first African American to receive a Ph.D. from Harvard, Du Bois went to Berlin to hear Max Weber lecture and conducted pioneering studies of race in the United States. He was also a founder of the National Association for the Advancement of Colored People (NAACP) and of the country's second Department of Sociology, at Atlanta University, in 1897.[2]

Du Bois's best-known work is *The Philadelphia Negro,* a book based on the first major sociological research project conducted in the United States. Du Bois showed that poverty and other social problems faced by African Americans were not due to some "natural" inferiority (which was widely believed at the time) but to white prejudice (Du Bois, 1967 [1899]). He believed that the elimination of white prejudice would reduce racial conflict and create more equality between blacks and whites. Du Bois was also critical of economically successful African Americans. He faulted them for failing to help less fortunate blacks and segregating themselves from the African American community to win acceptance among whites. Du Bois was disappointed with the slow improvement in race relations in the United States. He eventually became a Marxist, and near the end of his life he moved to Ghana, where he died.

Karl Marx (1818–83) was a revolutionary thinker whose ideas affected not just the growth of sociology but the course of world history. He held that major socio-historical changes are the result of conflict between society's main social classes. In his major work, *Capital* (1867–94), Marx argued that capitalism would produce such misery and collective strength among workers that they would eventually take state power and create a classless society in which production would be based on human need rather than profit.

The Art Archive/Corbis

---

[2]The country's first Department of Sociology was formed at the University of Kansas in 1892. The country's third and, for decades, most influential Department of Sociology was formed at the University of Chicago in 1899.

Class consciousness: Awareness of being a member of a class.

Brown Brothers, Sterling PA

Max Weber (1864–1920), Germany's greatest sociologist, profoundly influenced the development of the discipline worldwide. Engaged in a lifelong "debate with Marx's ghost," Weber held that economic circumstances alone do not explain the rise of capitalism. As he showed in *The Protestant Ethic and the Spirit of Capitalism* (1904–05), independent developments in the religious realm had unintended, beneficial consequences for capitalist development in some parts of Europe. He also argued that capitalism would not necessarily give way to socialism. Instead, he regarded the growth of bureaucracy and the overall "rationalization" of life as the defining characteristics of the modern age. These themes were developed in *Economy and Society* (1922).

Bettmann/CORBIS

W. E. B. Du Bois (1868–1963), Harvard's first African American Ph.D., was a pioneer in the study of race in the United States and a founder of the NAACP. His book *The Philadelphia Negro* (1899) is a classic that went against the grain of much contemporary social thought. In his view, social inequality and discrimination—between blacks and whites, and between successful and less successful blacks—were the main sources of problems faced by African Americans. He argued that only a decline in inequality and prejudice would solve the problems of the African American community.

C. Wright Mills

Du Bois was a pioneer in American conflict theory, particularly as it applied to race and ethnic relations. Conflict theory had some advocates in the United States after Du Bois. Most noteworthy is C. Wright Mills, who laid the foundations for modern conflict theory in the United States in the 1950s. Mills conducted pioneering research on American politics and class structure. One of his most important books is *The Power Elite*, a study of the several hundred men who occupy the "command posts" of the American economy, military, and government. He argued that power is highly concentrated in American society, which is therefore less of a democracy than we are often led to believe (Mills, 1956).

Exceptions like Mills notwithstanding, conflict theory did not really take hold in the United States until the 1960s, a decade that was rocked by growing labor unrest, antiwar protests, the rise of the Black Power movement, and the first stirrings of feminism. Strikes, demonstrations, and riots were frequent occurrences in the 1960s and early 1970s, and therefore many sociologists of that era thought that conflict between and among classes, nations, races, and generations was the very essence of society. Many of today's leading sociologists attended graduate school in the 1960s and 1970s and were strongly influenced by the spirit of the times. As you will see throughout this book, they have made important contributions to conflict theory during their professional careers.

Symbolic Interactionism

Weber and the Protestant Ethic

We noted earlier that Weber criticized Marx's interpretation of the development of capitalism. Among other things, Weber argued that early capitalist development was not caused by favorable economic circumstances alone. In addition, he said, certain *religious* beliefs facilitated robust capitalist growth. In particular, 16th- and 17th-century Protestants believed that their religious doubts could be reduced and a state of grace assured if they worked diligently and lived modestly. Weber called this belief the **Protestant ethic.** He believed it had an unintended effect: people who adhered to the Protestant ethic saved and invested more money than did others. Thus, capitalism developed most robustly where the Protestant ethic took hold. He concluded that capitalism did not develop as a result of the operation of economic forces alone, as Marx argued. Instead, it depended partly on the religious meaning that individuals attached to their work (Weber, 1958 [1904–05]). In much of his research, Weber emphasized the importance of empathically understanding people's motives and the meanings they attach to things to gain a clear sense of the significance of their actions. He called this aspect of his approach to sociological research the method of *Verstehen* ("understanding" in German).

Protestant ethic: The 16th- and 17th-century Protestant belief that religious doubts could be reduced and a state of grace assured if people worked diligently and lived ascetically. According to Weber, the Protestant ethic had the unintended effect of increasing savings and investment and thus stimulating capitalist growth.

The idea that subjective meanings and motives must be analyzed in any complete sociological analysis was only one of Weber's contributions to early sociological theory. Weber was also an important conflict theorist, as you will learn in later chapters of this book. It is enough to note here that his emphasis on subjective meanings found rich soil in the United States in the late 19th and early 20th centuries because his ideas resonated deeply with the individualism of American culture. A century ago, people widely believed that individual talent and initiative could allow one to achieve just about anything in this land of opportunity. Much of early American sociology therefore focused on the individual or, more precisely, on the connection between the individual and the larger society.

George Herbert Mead

The connection between the individual and the larger society was certainly a focus of sociologists at the University of Chicago, which established the most influential Department of Sociology in the country before World War II. For example, George Herbert Mead (1863–1931) was the driving force behind the study of how the individual's sense of self is formed in the course of interaction with other people. We discuss his contribution in Chapter 3, "Socialization." Here, we note only that the work of Mead and his colleagues gave birth to symbolic interactionism, a distinctively American theoretical tradition that continues to be a major force in sociology today.

Functionalist and conflict theories assume that people's group memberships—whether they are rich or poor, male or female, black or white—help shape their behavior. This can sometimes make people seem like balls on a pool table that get knocked around and cannot choose their own destinations. We know from our everyday experience, however, that people are not like that. You often make choices, sometimes difficult ones. You sometimes change your mind. Moreover, two people with similar group memberships may react differently to similar social circumstances because they interpret those circumstances differently.

The Symbolic Interactionism of Erving Goffman

Recognizing these issues, some sociologists focus on the subjective side of social life. They work in the symbolic interactionist tradition, a school of thought that was given its name by sociologist Herbert Blumer (1900–86), who was Mead's student at the University of Chicago. **Symbolic interactionism** incorporates these four features:

1. It focuses on interpersonal communication in micro-level social settings, distinguishing it from both functionalist and conflict theories.

2. Symbolic interactionism emphasizes that social life is possible only because people attach meanings to things. It follows that an adequate explanation of social behavior requires understanding the subjective meanings that people associate with their social circumstances.

3. Symbolic interactionism stresses that people help create their social circumstances and do not merely react to them. For example, Canadian-born sociologist Erving Goffman (1922–82), one of the most influential symbolic interactionists, analyzed the many ways in which people present themselves to others in everyday life so as to appear in the best possible light. Goffman compared social interaction to a carefully staged play, complete with stage, backstage, defined roles, and props. In this play, a person's age, gender, race, and other characteristics may help shape his or her actions, but there is much room for individual creativity as well (Goffman, 1959 [1956]).

The Granger Collection, New York

George Herbert Mead (1863–1931) was the driving force behind the study of how individual identity is formed in the course of interaction with other people. The work of Mead and his colleagues gave birth to symbolic interactionism, a distinctively American theoretical tradition that continues to be a major force in sociology today.

Symbolic interactionist theory: Focuses on interpersonal communication in micro-level social settings. It emphasizes that an adequate explanation of social behavior requires understanding the subjective meanings people attach to their social circumstances. It stresses that people help create their social circumstances and do not merely react to them. By underscoring the subjective meanings people create in small social settings, it validates unpopular and nonofficial viewpoints. This increases our understanding and tolerance of people who may be different from us.

Harriet Martineau (1802–76) was the first woman sociologist. Unlike most women of her time and place, she was able to live the life of a scholar because she came from a wealthy family and never married or had children. She translated Comte into English and conducted studies on research methods, slavery, factory laws, and gender inequality. As a leading advocate of voting rights, higher education for women, and gender equality in the family, Martineau was one of the first feminists.

4. By focusing on the subjective meanings people create in small social settings, symbolic interactionists sometimes validate unpopular and nonofficial viewpoints. This increases our understanding and tolerance of people who may be different from us.

Social Constructionism

One variant of symbolic interactionism that has become especially popular in recent years is **social constructionism.** Social constructionists argue that when people interact, they typically assume things are naturally or innately what they seem to be. However, apparently natural or innate features of life are often sustained by *social* processes that vary historically and culturally. For example, many people assume that differences in the way women and men behave are the result of their different biological makeup. In contrast, social constructionists show that many of the presumably natural differences between women and men depend on the way in which power is distributed between them and the degree to which certain ideas about women and men are widely shared (see Chapter 10, "Sexuality and Gender"; Berger and Luckmann, 1966). People usually do such a good job of building natural-seeming social realities in their everyday interactions that they do not notice the materials used in the construction process. Social constructionists identify those materials and analyze how they are pieced together.

Feminist Theory

Few women figured prominently in the early history of sociology. The strict demands placed on them by the 19th-century family and the lack of opportunity in the larger society prevented most of them from earning a higher education and making major contributions to the discipline. Women who made their mark on sociology in its early years tended to have unusual biographies. Some of these exceptional people introduced gender issues that were largely ignored by Marx, Durkheim, Weber, Mead, and other early sociologists. Appreciation for the sociological contribution of these pioneering women has grown in recent years because concern regarding gender issues has come to form a substantial part of the modern sociological enterprise.

Harriet Martineau

Harriet Martineau (1802–76) is often called the first woman sociologist. Born in England to a prosperous family, she never married. She supported herself comfortably from her journalistic writings. Martineau translated Comte into English and wrote one of the first books on research methods. She undertook critical studies of slavery, factory laws, and gender inequality. She was a leading advocate of voting rights and higher education for women and of gender equality in the family. As such, Martineau was one of the first feminists (Martineau, 1985).

Jane Addams

In the United States in the early 20th century, a few women from wealthy families attended university, received training as sociologists, and wanted to become professors of sociology, but they were denied faculty appointments. Typically, they turned to social activism and social work instead. A case in point is Jane Addams (1860–1935). Addams was cofounder of Hull House, a shelter for the destitute in Chicago's slums, and she spent a lifetime fighting for social reform. She also provided a research platform for sociologists from the University of Chicago, who often visited Hull House to interview its clients. In recognition of her efforts, Addams in 1931 received the ultimate academic award—the Nobel Prize.

Social constructionists: Sociologists who argue that apparently natural or innate features of life are often sustained by *social* processes that vary historically and culturally.

Modern Feminism

Despite its early stirrings, feminist thinking had little impact on sociology until the mid-1960s, when the rise of the modern women's movement drew attention to the many remaining inequalities between women and men. Because of feminist theory's major influence on sociology, it may fairly be regarded as sociology's fourth major theoretical tradition. Modern feminism has several variants (see Chapter 10, "Sexuality and Gender"). However, the various strands of **feminist theory** share the following four features:

1. Feminist theory focuses on various aspects of patriarchy, the system of male domination in society. Patriarchy, feminists contend, is as important as class inequality, if not more so, in determining a person's opportunities in life.

2. Feminist theory holds that male domination and female subordination are determined not by biological necessity but by structures of power and social convention. From this point of view, women are subordinate to men only because men enjoy more legal, economic, political, and cultural rights.

3. Feminist theory examines the operation of patriarchy in both micro- and macro-level settings.

4. Feminist theory contends that existing patterns of gender inequality can and should be changed for the benefit of all members of society. The main sources of gender inequality include differences in the way boys and girls are reared; barriers to equal opportunity in education, paid work, and politics; and the unequal division of domestic responsibilities between women and men.

The theoretical traditions just outlined are summarized in ▶Concept Summary 1.1 and ▶Figure 1.3. As you will see in the following pages, sociologists in the United States and elsewhere have applied these traditions to all of the discipline's branches and have elaborated and refined each of them. Some sociologists work exclusively within one tradition. Others conduct research that borrows from more than one tradition. But all sociologists are deeply indebted to the founders of the discipline.

Note, however, that theorizing without research is like painting a portrait without paint. You might have a spectacular idea for the portrait, but you can never be sure it's going to work out until you get your hands dirty and commit the idea to canvas. Similarly,

▶Concept Summary 1.1
Four Theoretical Traditions in Society

Theoretical Tradition	Main Levels of Analysis	Main Focus	Main Question
Functionalist	Macro	Values	How do the institutions of society contribute to social stability and instability?
Conflict	Macro	Inequality	How do privileged groups seek to maintain their advantages and subordinate groups seek to increase theirs, often causing social change in the process?
Symbolic interactionist	Micro	Meaning	How do individuals communicate to make their social settings meaningful?
Feminist	Macro and micro	Patriarchy	Which social structures and interaction processes maintain male dominance and female subordination?

Feminist theory: Claims that patriarchy is at least as important as class inequality in determining a person's opportunities in life. It holds that male domination and female subordination are determined not by biological necessity but by structures of power and social convention. It examines the operation of patriarchy in both micro- and macro-level settings and contends that existing patterns of gender inequality can and should be changed for the benefit of all members of society.

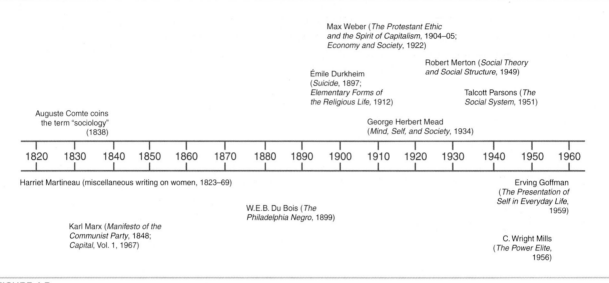

▶FIGURE 1.3
A Sociological Timeline of Some Major Figures in the Development of Sociological Theory, 1820–1960

sociologists conduct research to see how well their theories "fit" the real world. We devote the second half of this chapter to outlining the research process, given its importance to the sociological enterprise as a whole.

Conducting Research

Social conditions often color theoretical speculation. Think of the influence of the Great Depression on the functionalists and the influence of the radical 1960s on the conflict theorists. The personal values of individual theorists also come into play when they formulate theories. Remember how the biases of theorists since Comte have helped shape theories. Should we conclude that theories are merely speculative and totally subjective? Not at all. Sociologists have a powerful means of controlling bias and assessing the validity of theories: conducting **research.**

Before we do research, we rarely see things as they are. We see them as *we* are. Then, in the research process, a sort of waltz begins. Subjectivity leads, objectivity follows. When the dance is finished, we see things more accurately. As many advances in sociological thinking show, subjective experiences often enhance objective sociological knowledge, leading to the discovery of new problems and new solutions to old problems. Acknowledging that our experiences inspire us to ask particular questions about the social world is not the same as saying that those questions, or the answers we eventually uncover, are biased. Bias arises only when we remain unaware of our subjectivity. It is the purpose of research to help us become aware of our biases and to test theories against systematic observations of the social world that other researchers can repeat to check on us. On the basis of research, we reject some theories, modify others, and are forced to invent new ones. Having outlined the main theoretical approaches in sociology, it is now time to discuss the research process in detail.

Research: The process of systematically observing reality to assess the validity of a theory.

Carol Wainio. *We Can Be Certain.* 1982. Research involves taking the plunge from speculation to testing ideas against evidence.

Courtesy of Carol Wainio, London, Ontario, Canada

The Research Cycle

Ideally, sociological research is a cyclical process that involves six steps (▶Figure 1.4). The sociologist's first step is *formulating a research question.* A research question must be stated so that it can be answered by systematically collecting and analyzing sociological data.

Sociological research cannot determine whether God exists or what the best political system is. Answers to such questions require faith more than evidence. However, sociological research can determine why some people are more religious than others and which political system creates more opportunities for higher education. Answers to such questions require evidence more than faith.

The second step involves *reviewing the existing research literature.* Researchers must elaborate their research questions in the clear light of what other sociologists have already debated and discovered. Why? Because reading the relevant sociological literature stimulates researchers' sociological imaginations, allows them to refine their initial questions, and prevents duplication of effort.

Selecting a research method is the third step in the research cycle. As we will see in detail later in this chapter, each data collection method has strengths and weaknesses. Each method is therefore best suited to studying a different kind of problem. When choosing a method, one must keep these strengths and weaknesses in mind.

The fourth stage of the research cycle involves *collecting data* by observing subjects, interviewing them, reading documents produced by or about them, and so forth. Many researchers think this is the most exciting stage of the research cycle because it brings them face to face with the puzzling sociological reality that so fascinates them.

Other researchers find the fifth step of the research cycle, *analyzing the data,* the most challenging. During data analysis you can learn things that nobody knew before. At this stage, data confirm some of your expectations and confound others, requiring you to think creatively about familiar issues, reconsider the relevant theoretical and research literature, and abandon pet ideas.

Research is not useful for the sociological community, the subjects of the research, or the wider society if researchers do not complete the sixth step—*publishing the results* in a report, a scientific journal, or a book. Publication serves another important function, too. It allows other sociologists to scrutinize and criticize the research. On that

CENGAGENOW™

Learn more about **Observation** by going through the Role of The Observer Animation.

CENGAGENOW™

Learn about **Qualitative Research** by going through the Qualitative Field Research Learning Module.

▶FIGURE 1.4
The Research Cycle

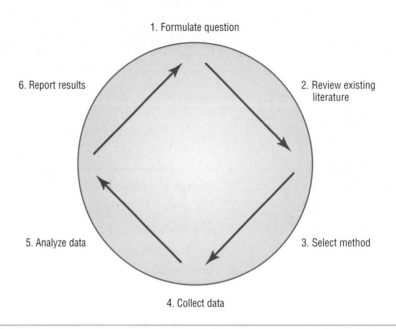

1. Formulate question

6. Report results

2. Review existing
   literature

5. Analyze data

3. Select method

4. Collect data

basis, errors can be corrected and new and more sophisticated research questions can be formulated for the next round of research. Science is a social activity governed by rules defined and enforced by the scientific community.

Ethics in Sociological Research

Researchers must be mindful of the need to respect their subjects' rights throughout the research cycle. This means, first, that researchers must do their subjects no harm. This is the right to *safety*. Second, research subjects must have the right to decide whether their attitudes and behaviors may be revealed to the public and, if so, in what way. This is the right to *privacy*. Third, researchers cannot use data in a way that allows them to be traced to a particular subject. This is the subject's right to *confidentiality*. Fourth, subjects must be told how the information they supply will be used. They must also be allowed to judge the degree of personal risk involved in answering questions so that they can decide whether they may be studied and, if so, in what way. This is the right to *informed consent*.

Ethical issues arise not only in the treatment of subjects but also in the treatment of research results. For example, plagiarism is a concern in academic life, especially among students, who write research papers and submit them to professors for evaluation. A 2003 study found that 38 percent of American college students admitted to committing "cut and paste" plagiarism when writing essays, up from just 10 percent in 2000 (Edmundson, 2003). Ready-made essays are also widely available for purchase.

Increased plagiarism is a consequence of the spread of the World Wide Web and the growing view that everything on it is public and therefore does not have to be cited. That view is wrong. The Code of Ethics of the American Sociological Association states that we must "explicitly identify, credit, and reference the author" when we make any use of another person's written work, "whether it is published, unpublished, or electronically available" (American Sociological Association, 1999: 16). Making such ethical standards better known can help remedy the problem of plagiarism. So can better policing. Powerful web-based applications are now available that help college instructors determine whether essays are plagiarized in whole or in part (visit http://www.turnitin.com). Perhaps the most effective remedy, however, is for instructors to ensure that what they teach really matters to their students. If they do, students won't be as inclined to plagiarize because they will regard essay writing as a process of personal discovery. You can't cut and paste or buy enlightenment (Edmundson, 2003).

Bearing in mind our thumbnail sketch of the research cycle, we devote the rest of this chapter to exploring its fourth and fifth stages—gathering and analyzing evidence. We will now describe each of sociology's major research methods: field research, experiments, surveys, and the analysis of existing documents and official statistics. We turn first to field research.

The Main Methods of Sociological Research

Experiments

In the mid-1960s, the first generation of North American children exposed to high levels of TV violence virtually from birth reached their mid-teens. At the same time, the rate of violent crime began to increase. Some commentators said that TV violence made violence in the real world seem normal and acceptable. As a result, they concluded, North American teenagers in the 1960s and subsequent decades were more likely than pre-1960s teens to commit violent acts. The increasing prevalence of violence in movies, video games, and popular music seemed to add weight to their conclusion.

Social scientists soon started investigating the connection between media and real-world violence using experimental methods. An **experiment** is a carefully controlled artificial situation that allows researchers to isolate presumed causes and measure their effects precisely (Campbell and Stanley, 1963).

Experiments use a procedure called **randomization** to create two similar groups. Randomization involves assigning individuals to two groups by chance processes. For example, researchers may ask 50 children to draw a number from 1 to 50 from a covered box. The researchers assign children who draw odd numbers to one group and those who draw even numbers to the other group. By assigning subjects to the two groups using a chance process, researchers ensure that each group has about the same proportion of boys and girls, members of different races, children highly motivated to participate in the study, and so forth, if the experiment is performed many times.

After subjects have been randomly assigned to the two groups, the researchers may put the groups in separate rooms and give them toys to play with. They observe the children through one-way mirrors, rating each child in terms of the aggressiveness of his or her play. This is the child's initial score on the "dependent variable," aggressive behavior. The **dependent variable** is the effect in any cause-and-effect relationship.

Then the researchers introduce the hypothesized cause to one group—now called the **experimental group.** They may show children in the experimental group an hour-long TV program in which many violent acts take place. They do not show the program to children in the other group, now called the **control group.** In this case, the violent TV show is the "independent variable." The **independent variable** is the presumed cause in any cause-and-effect relationship.

CENGAGENOW™

Learn more about **Experiments** by going through the Independent and Dependent Variables Animation.

CENGAGENOW™

Learn more about **Variables** by going through the Understanding Variables Learning Module.

Experiment: A carefully controlled artificial situation that allows researchers to isolate hypothesized causes and measure their effects precisely.

Randomization: In an experiment, involves assigning individuals to experimental and control groups by chance processes.

Dependent variable: The presumed effect in a cause-and-effect relationship.

Experimental group: The group in an experiment that is exposed to the independent variable.

Control group: The group in an experiment that is not exposed to the independent variable.

Independent variable: The presumed cause in a cause-and-effect relationship.

When children fight at home, an adult is often present to intervene. By repeatedly separating children and discouraging their aggressive behavior, the adult can teach them that fighting is unacceptable. In contrast, experiments on the effect of TV on aggressive behavior lack validity, in part because they may facilitate violence.

CENGAGENOW™

Learn more about **Measurement** by going through the Levels of Measurement Learning Module.

Immediately after the children see the TV show, the researchers again observe the children in both groups at play. Each child's play is given a second aggressiveness score. By comparing the aggressiveness scores of the two groups before and after only one of the groups has been exposed to the presumed cause, an experiment can determine whether the presumed cause (watching violent TV) has the predicted effect (increasing violent behavior).

Many experiments show that exposure to media violence has a short-term effect on violent behavior in young children, especially boys. However, the results of experiments are mixed when it comes to assessing longer-term effects, especially on older children and teenagers (Anderson and Bushman, 2002; Browne and Hamilton-Giachritsis, 2005; Freedman, 2002).

Experiments allow researchers to isolate the single cause of theoretical interest and measure its effect with high **reliability,** that is, consistently from one experiment to the next. Yet many sociologists argue that experiments are highly artificial situations. They believe that removing people from their natural social settings lowers the **validity** of experimental results, that is, the degree to which they measure what they are actually supposed to measure.

To understand why experiments on the effects of media violence may lack validity, consider that, in the real world, violent behavior usually means attempting to harm another person physically. Shouting or kicking a toy is not the same thing. In fact, such acts may enable children to relieve frustrations in a fantasy world, lowering their chance of acting violently in the real world. Moreover, in a laboratory situation, aggressive behavior may be encouraged because it is legitimized. Simply showing a violent TV program may suggest to subjects how the experimenter expects them to behave. Nor is aggressive behavior punished or controlled in the laboratory setting as it is in the real world. If a boy watching a violent TV show stands up and delivers a karate kick to his brother, a parent or other caregiver is likely to take action to prevent a recurrence. This usually teaches the boy not to engage in aggressive behavior. In the lab, the lack of disciplinary control may facilitate unrealistically high levels of aggression (Felson, 1996).

Reliability: The degree to which a measurement procedure yields consistent results.

Validity: The degree to which a measure actually measures what it is intended to measure.

Surveys

Surveys are the most widely used sociological research method, and they have also been used to measure the effects of media violence on behavior. Overall, the results of surveys show a weaker relationship between exposure to violent mass media and violent behavior than do experiments, and some surveys show no relationship at all between these two variables (Anderson and Bushman, 2002; Huesmann et al., 2003; Johnson et al., 2002; see ▶Table 1.1).

In a **survey,** people are asked questions about their knowledge, attitudes or behavior. All survey researchers aim to study part of a group—a **sample**—to learn about the whole group of interest—the **population.** To safely generalize about the population on the basis of findings from a sample, researchers must be sure that the characteristics of the people in the sample match those of the population. To draw a sample from which one can safely generalize, researchers must choose respondents at random, and an individual's chance of being chosen must be known and greater than zero. A sample with these characteristics is known as a **probability sample.**

To draw a probability sample you first need a **sampling frame,** a list of all the people in the population of interest. You also need a randomizing method, a way of ensuring that every person in the sampling frame has a known and nonzero chance of being selected. A frequently used sampling frame is the telephone directory, which is now available for the entire country on CD-ROM. Researchers program computers to dial residential phone numbers at random, thus allowing them to create samples based on all households with phones—roughly 99 percent of United States households.

CENGAGENOW™

Learn more about **Sampling** by going through the Types of Sample Designs Learning Module.

CENGAGENOW™

Learn more about **Questionnaire Construction** by going through the Questionnaire Construction Coached Problem.

▶Table 1.1

Watching TV and Approval of Violence (in percent)

TV Viewing	0–2 hrs/day	3+ hrs/day	Total
Punching approval			
Yes	69	65	67
No	31	35	33
Total	100	100	100
n	5,188	5,022	10,210

This table comes from one of the most respected surveys in the United States, the General Social Survey, conducted most years since 1972. The survey regularly asks **respondents** (people who answer the survey questions) how many hours of TV they watch every day. Until 1994, it also asked respondents if they ever approve of a man punching an adult male. This table shows the results for these two questions, combining responses from 1972 to 1994.

An **association** between two variables exists if the value of one variable changes with the value of the other. For example, if the percentage of people who approve of a man punching an adult male is *higher* among those who watch 3 or more hours of TV a day, a *positive* association exists between the two variables. If the percentage of people who approve of a man punching an adult male is *lower* among those who watch 3 or more hours of TV a day, a *negative* association exists between the two variables. The greater the percentage difference between frequent and infrequent TV viewers, the stronger the association. This table shows that 69 percent of respondents who watched TV 0–2 hours a day approved punching compared with 65 percent of respondents who watched TV 3 or more hours. Is this a positive or a negative association?

To interpret tables, you must pay careful attention to what adds up to 100 percent. The table says that 69 percent *of people who watched TV 0–2 hours a day* approved of a man punching an adult male. It does *not* say that 69 percent of all people who approved of a man punching an adult male watched TV 0–2 hours a day. We know this because each category of the "TV viewing" variable equals 100 percent.

To test your understanding, calculate the number of respondents represented by the table's 69%, 65%, 31%, and 35%. Answers are given below.

```
Answers:
69% = (69/100) × 5,188 = 3,580 respondents
65% = (65/100) × 5,022 = 3,264 respondents
31% = (31/100) × 5,188 = 1,608 respondents
35% = (35/100) × 5,022 = 1,758 respondents
```

Source: National Opinion Research Center (2006).

Survey: Asks people questions about their knowledge, attitudes, or behavior, either in a face-to-face interview, telephone interview, or paper-and-pencil format.

Sample: Part of the population of research interest that is selected for analysis.

Population: The entire group about which the researcher wishes to generalize.

Probability sample: Sample in which units have a known and nonzero chance of being selected.

Sampling frame: A list of all the people (or other social units, such as organizations) in the population of interest to a researcher.

Respondents: People who answer survey questions.

Association: Exists between two variables if the value of one variable changes with the value of the other.

Jeff Greenberg/PhotoEdit

Researchers collect information using surveys by asking people in a representative sample a set of identical questions. People interviewed on a downtown street corner do not constitute a representative sample of American adults. That is because the sample does not include people who live outside the urban core, it underestimates the number of elderly and disabled people, it does not take into account regional diversity, and so on.

When sociologists conduct a survey, they may mail a form to respondents containing questions. Respondents then mail the completed questionnaire back to the researcher. Alternatively, sociologists may conduct face-to-face interviews in which questions are presented to the respondent by the interviewer during a meeting. Sociologists may also conduct surveys by means of telephone interviews.

Questionnaires may contain two types of questions. A **closed-ended question** provides the respondent with a list of permitted answers. Each answer is given a numerical code so the data can later be easily input into a computer for statistical analysis. Often, the numerical results of surveys are arranged in tables like Table 1.1. An **open-ended question** allows respondents to answer in their own words. Open-ended questions are particularly useful when researchers don't have enough knowledge to create a meaningful and complete list of possible answers.

To ensure that survey questions elicit valid responses, researchers must guard against four dangers:

1. The exclusion of part of the population from the sampling frame;
2. The refusal of some people to participate in the survey;
3. The unwillingness of some respondents to answer questions frankly;
4. The asking of confusing, leading or inflammatory questions or questions that refer to several, unimportant, or noncurrent events.

Much of the art and science of survey research involves overcoming these threats to validity (Converse and Presser, 1986; Ornstein, 1998). Recall that surveys tend to show a weaker relationship than do experiments between exposure to violent mass media and violent behavior. That may be because survey researchers have developed more valid measures of violent behavior.

Field Research

The method that comes closest to people's natural social settings is **field research.** Field research involves systematically observing people wherever they meet, from the ethnic slum to the alternative hard rock scene to the public school classroom (Schippers, 2002; Whyte, 1981 [1943]).

When they go into the field, researchers come prepared with strategies to ensure that their observations are accurate. One such strategy is **detached observation,** which involves classifying and counting the behavior of interest according to a predetermined scheme. Although useful for some purposes, two main problems confound direct observation. First, the presence of the researcher may cause **reactivity;** the observed people may conceal certain things or act artificially to impress the researcher (Webb et al., 1966). Second, the meaning of the observed behavior may remain obscure to the researcher. A wink may be an involuntary muscle contraction, an indication of a secret being kept, a sexual come-on, etc. We can't know what a wink means just by observing it.

To avoid reactivity and understand the meaning of behavior, we must be able to see it in its social context and from the point of view of the people we are observing. To do that,

Closed-ended question: In a survey, a type of question that provides the respondent with a list of permitted answers. Each answer is given a numerical code so that the data can later be easily input into a computer for statistical analysis.

Open-ended question: In a survey, a type of question that allows respondents to answer in their own words.

Field research: Research based on the observation of people in their natural settings.

Detached observation: A type of field research that involves classifying and counting the behavior of interest according to a predetermined scheme.

Reactivity: The tendency of people who are observed by a researcher to react to the presence of the researcher by concealing certain things or acting artificially to impress the researcher.

researchers must immerse themselves in their subjects' world by learning their language and their culture in depth. When sociologists observe a social setting systematically *and* take part in the activities of the people they are studying, they are engaging in **participant observation** research (Lofland and Lofland, 1995 [1971]).

Participant observation research helps us better understand how media violence may influence youth violence. For example, sociologists have spent time in schools where shooting rampages have taken place. They have developed a deep appreciation of the social and cultural context of school shootings by living in the neighborhoods where they occur, interviewing students, teachers, neighborhood residents, and shooters' family members, and studying police and psychological reports, the shooters' own writings, and other relevant materials (Harding, Fox, and Mehta, 2002; Sullivan, 2002). They have tentatively concluded that only a small number of young people—those who are weakly connected to family, school, community, and peers—seem to be susceptible to translating media violence into violent behavior. Lack of social support allows their personal problems to become greatly magnified, and if guns are readily available they are prone to using violent media messages as models for their own behavior. In contrast, for the overwhelming majority of young people, violence in the mass media is just a source of entertainment and a fantasy outlet for emotional issues, not a template for action (Anderson, 2003).

Like other research methods, participant observation has strengths and weaknesses. On the plus side, it allows researchers to develop a deep and sympathetic understanding of the way people see the world. It is especially useful in the "exploratory" stage of research, when investigators have only a vague sense of what they are looking for and little sense of what they will discover. On the minus side, because participant observation research usually involves just one researcher in one social setting, it is difficult to know if other researchers would measure things in the same way (this is the problem of reliability) and it is difficult to know how broadly findings may be generalized to other settings.

Analysis of Existing Documents and Official Statistics

The fourth important sociological research method involves the **analysis of existing documents and official statistics.** What do existing documents and official statistics have in common? They are created by people other than the researcher for purposes other than sociological research.

The three types of existing documents that sociologists have mined most deeply are diaries, newspapers, and published historical works. Census data, police crime reports, and records of key life events are perhaps the most frequently used sources of official statistics. The modern census tallies the number of American residents and classifies them by place of residence, race, ethnic origin, occupation, age, and hundreds of other variables. The FBI publishes an annual Uniform Crime Report giving the number of crimes in the United States and classifying them by location and type of crime, the age and sex of offenders and victims, and other variables. The Centers for Disease Control and Prevention regularly publish "vital statistics" reports on births, deaths, marriages, and divorces by sex, race, age, and so forth.

Census and crime data put into perspective the limited effect of media violence on violent behavior. For example, researchers have discovered big differences in violent behavior when they compare the United States and Canada. The homicide rate (the number of murders per 100,000 people) has historically been about four times higher in the United States. Yet TV programming, movies, and video games are nearly identical in the two countries, so exposure to media violence can't account for the difference. Researchers instead attribute the difference in homicide rates to the higher level of economic and so-

Participant observation: A type of field research that involves carefully observing people's face-to-face interactions and participating in their lives over a long period, thus achieving a deep and sympathetic understanding of what motivates them to act in the way they do.

Analysis of existing documents and official statistics: A nonreactive research method that involves the analysis of diaries, newspapers, published historical works, and statistics produced by government agencies, all of which are created by people other than the researcher for purposes other than sociological research.

cial inequality and the wider availability of handguns in the United States (Government of Canada, 2002; Lenton, 1989; National Rifle Association, 2005).

Existing documents and official statistics have several advantages over other types of data. They can save the researcher time and money because they are usually available at no cost in libraries or on the World Wide Web. Official statistics usually cover entire populations and are collected using rigorous and uniform methods, thus yielding highly reliable data. Existing documents and official statistics are especially useful for historical analysis. Finally, since the analysis of existing documents and official statistics does not require live subjects, reactivity is not a problem. The researcher's presence does not influence the subjects' behavior.

Existing documents and official statistics also share one big disadvantage. They are not created with the researcher's needs in mind. In a sense, the researcher starts at stage 4 of the research cycle (data collection; see Figure 1.4) and then works within the limitations imposed by available data, including biases that reflect the interests of the individuals and organizations that created them.

The Points of the Compass

By now, you should have a pretty good idea of the basic methodological issues that confront any sociological research project. You should also know the strengths and weaknesses of some of the most widely used data collection techniques (see ▶Concept Summary 1.2). In the remainder of this chapter, we outline what you can expect to learn from this book.

The founders of sociology developed their ideas to help solve the great sociological puzzle of their time—the causes and consequences of the Industrial Revolution. This raises two interesting questions: What are the great sociological puzzles of *our* time? How are today's sociologists responding to the challenges presented by the social settings in which *we* live? We devote the rest of this book to answering these questions in depth.

It would be wrong to suggest that the research of tens of thousands of sociologists around the world is animated by just a few key issues. Viewed up close, sociology today is a heterogeneous enterprise enlivened by hundreds of theoretical debates, some focused on small issues relevant to particular fields and geographical areas, others focused on big issues that seek to characterize the entire historical era for humanity as

▶Concept Summary 1.2
Strengths and Weaknesses of Four Research Methods

Method	Strengths	Weaknesses
Experiment	High reliability; excellent for establishing cause-and-effect relationships	Low validity for many sociological problems because of the unnaturalness of the experimental setting
Survey	Good reliability; useful for establishing cause-and-effect relationships	Validity problems exist unless researchers make strong efforts to deal with them
Participant observation	Allows researchers to develop a deep and sympathetic understanding of the way people see the world; especially useful in exploratory research	Low reliability and generalizability
Analysis of existing documents and official statistics	Often inexpensive and easy to obtain; provides good coverage; useful for historical analysis; nonreactive	Often contains biases reflecting the interests of their creators and not the interests of the researcher

a whole. Among the big issues, two stand out. Perhaps the greatest sociological puzzles of our time are the causes and consequences of the Postindustrial Revolution and globalization.

The **Postindustrial Revolution** is the technology-driven shift from employment in factories to employment in offices, and the consequences of that shift for nearly all human activities (Bell, 1973; Toffler, 1990). For example, as a result of the Postindustrial Revolution, nonmanual occupations now outnumber manual occupations, and women have been drawn into the system of higher education and the paid labor force in large numbers. This shift has transformed the way we work and study, our standard of living, the way we form families, and much else. **Globalization** is the process by which formerly separate economies, states, and cultures are becoming tied together and people are becoming increasingly aware of their growing interdependence (Giddens, 1990: 64; Guillén, 2001). Especially in recent decades, rapid increases in the volume of international trade, travel, and communication have broken down the isolation and independence of most countries and people. Also contributing to globalization is the growth of many institutions that bind corporations, companies, and cultures together. These processes have caused people to depend more than ever on people in other countries for products, services, ideas, and even a sense of identity.

Sociologists agree that globalization and postindustrialism promise many exciting opportunities to enhance the quality of life and increase human freedom. However, they also see many social-structural barriers to the realization of that promise. We can summarize both the promise and the barriers by drawing a compass—a sociological compass (▶Figure 1.5). Each axis of the compass contrasts a promise with the barriers to its realization. The vertical axis contrasts the promise of equality of opportunity with the barrier of inequality of opportunity. The horizontal axis contrasts the promise of individual freedom with the barrier of constraint on that freedom. Let us consider these axes in more detail because much of our discussion in the following chapters turns on them.

Postindustrial Revolution: The technology-driven shift from manufacturing to service industries and the consequences of that shift for virtually all human activities.

Globalization: The process by which formerly separate economies, states, and cultures are being tied together and people are becoming increasingly aware of their growing interdependence.

▶FIGURE 1.5
A Sociological Compass

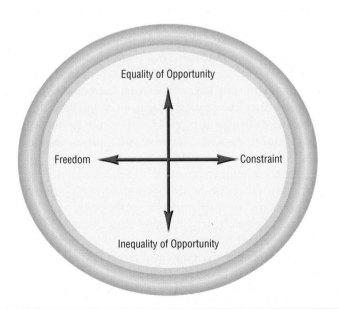

Equality versus Inequality of Opportunity

Optimists forecast that postindustrialism will provide more opportunities for people to find creative, interesting, challenging, and rewarding work. In addition, the postindustrial era will generate more equality of opportunity, that is, better chances for *all* people to get an education, influence government policy, and find good jobs.

You will find evidence to support these claims in the following pages. For example, we show that the average standard of living and the number of good jobs are increasing in postindustrial societies such as the United States. Women are making rapid strides in the economy, the education system, and other institutions. Postindustrial societies like the United States are characterized by a decline in discrimination against members of ethnic and racial minorities, while democracy is spreading throughout the world. The desperately poor form a declining percentage of the world's population.

Yet, as you read this book, it will also become clear that all of these seemingly happy stories have a dark underside. For example, it turns out that the number of routine jobs with low pay and few benefits is growing faster than the number of creative, high-paying jobs. Inequality between the wealthiest and poorest Americans has grown in recent decades. An enormous opportunity gulf still separates women from men. Racism and discrimination are still a part of our world. Our health-care system is in crisis just as our population is aging rapidly and most in need of health care. Scientific discoveries do not always involve unambiguous progress. Many of the world's new democracies are only superficially democratic, while Americans and citizens of other postindustrial societies are increasingly cynical about the ability of their political systems to respond to their needs. They are looking for alternative forms of political expression. The absolute number of desperately poor people in the world continues to grow, as does the gap between rich and poor nations. Many people attribute the world's most serious problems to globalization. They have formed organizations and movements—some of them violent—to oppose it. In short, equality of opportunity is an undeniably attractive ideal, but it is unclear whether it is the inevitable outcome of a globalized, postindustrial society.

Individual Freedom versus Individual Constraint

We may say the same about the ideal of freedom. In an earlier era, most people retained their religious, ethnic, racial, and sexual identities for a lifetime, even if they were not particularly comfortable with them. They often remained in social relationships that made them unhappy. One of the major themes of this book is that many people are now freer to construct their identities and form social relationships in ways that suit them. To a greater degree than ever before, it is possible to *choose* who you want to be, with whom you want to associate, and how you want to associate with them. The postindustrial and global era frees people from traditional constraints by encouraging virtually instant global communication, international migration, greater acceptance of sexual diversity and a variety of family forms, the growth of ethnically and racially diverse cities, and so forth. For instance, in the past people often stayed in marriages even if they were dissatisfied with them. Families often involved a father working in the paid labor force and a mother keeping house and raising children without pay. Today, people are freer to end unhappy marriages and create family structures that are more suited to their individual needs.

Again, however, we must face the less rosy aspects of postindustrialism and globalization. In many of the following chapters, we point out how increased freedom is experienced only within certain limits and how social diversity is limited by a strong push to conformity in some spheres of life. For example, we can choose a far wider variety of consumer products than ever before, but consumerism itself increasingly seems a compulsory way of life. Moreover, it is a way of life that threatens the natural environment. Large, impersonal bureaucracies and standardized products and services dehumanize both staff and customers. The tastes and the profit motive of vast media conglomerates, most of them U.S. owned, govern most of our diverse cultural consumption and arguably threaten the survival of distinctive national cultures. Powerful interests are trying to shore up the traditional nuclear family even though it does not suit some people. As these examples show, the push for uniformity counters the trend toward growing social diversity.

Postindustrialism and globalization may make us freer in some ways, but they also place new constraints on us.

Where Do You Fit In?

Our overview of themes in this book drives home the fact that we live in an era "suspended between extraordinary opportunity . . . and global catastrophe" (Giddens, 1987: 166). A whole range of environmental issues; profound inequalities in the wealth of nations and of classes; religious, racial, and ethnic violence; and unsolved problems in the relations between women and men continue to stare us in the face and profoundly affect the quality of our everyday lives.

Giving in to despair and apathy is one possible response to these complex issues, but it is not a response that humans often favor. If it were our nature to give up hope, we would still be sitting around half-naked in the mud outside a cave. People are more inclined to look for ways of improving their lives, and this period of human history is full of opportunities to do so. We have, for example, advanced to the point at which for the first time we have the means to feed and educate everyone in the world. Similarly, it now seems possible to erode some of the inequalities that have always been the major source of human conflict.

Sociology offers useful advice on how to achieve these goals—for sociology is more than just an intellectual exercise; it is also an applied science with practical, everyday uses. Sociologists teach at all levels, from high school to graduate school. They conduct research for local, state, and federal governments; colleges; corporations; the criminal justice system; public opinion firms; management consulting firms; trade unions; social service agencies; international nongovernmental organizations; and private research and testing firms. They are often involved in the formulation of **public policy,** the creation of laws and regulations by organizations and governments (Box 1.2). This is because sociologists are trained not just to see what is, but to see what is possible.

So please consider this book an invitation to explore your society's, and your own, possibilities. We don't provide easy answers. However, we are sure that if you try to grapple with the questions we raise, you will find that sociology can help you figure out where you fit into society and how you can make society fit you.

Public policy: Involves the creation of laws and regulations by organizations and governments.

BOX 1.2
SOCIAL POLICY: WHAT DO YOU THINK?

In 2002 the Sloan School of Management at the Massachusetts Institute of Technology conducted a survey of 600 graduates as part of its 50th anniversary observance. Sixty percent of survey respondents said that honesty, integrity, and ethics were the main factors making a good corporate leader. Most alumni believed that living a moral professional life was more important than pulling in large paychecks and generous perks. "Demonstrate daily that your word is your bond and always try to give something back to your community and those less fortunate than yourself," said Michael Campbell, a 1976 Sloan graduate and the current president of Nova Technology Corporation in Portsmouth, New Hampshire (Goll, 2002).

Unfortunately, the behavior of American executives sometimes fails to reflect Mr. Campbell's high ethical standards. In 2002, for example, investigators uncovered the biggest corporate scandals ever to rock America. Things got so bad that Andy Grove, a founder of Intel, said he was "embarrassed and ashamed" to be a corporate executive in America today (quoted in Hochberg, 2002), and the Wall Street investment firm of Charles Schwab ran a highly defensive television ad claiming to be "almost the opposite of a Wall Street firm." What brought about such astonishing statements was that corporate giants, including Enron, WorldCom, Tyco, Global Crossings, and Adelphia Communications, were shown to have engaged in accounting

Are Corporate Scandals a Problem of Individual Ethics or Social Policy?

fraud to make their earnings appear higher than they actually were. This practice kept their stock prices artificially high—until investigators made public what was going on, at which time their stock prices took a nosedive. Ordinary stockholders lost hundreds of billions of dollars. Many company employees lost their pensions (because they had been encouraged or compelled to place their retirement funds in company stock) and their jobs (because their companies soon filed for bankruptcy). In contrast, accounting fraud greatly benefited senior executives. They had received stock options as part of their compensation package. If you own stock options, you can buy company stock whenever you want at a fixed low price, even if the market price for the stock is much higher. Senior executives typically exercised their stock options *before* the stocks crashed, netting them billions of dollars in profit.

Ethics courses have been taught at nearly all of the country's business schools for years, but as the acting dean of the Haas School of Business (University of California-Berkeley) re-

cently noted, these courses can't "turn sinners into saints. . . . If a company does a lot of crazy stuff but its share price continues to rise, a lot of people will look the other way and not really care whether senior management is behaving ethically or not" (quoted in Goll, 2002).

Because individual ethics often seem weak in the face of greed, some observers have suggested that new public policies, that is, laws and regulations passed by organizations and governments, are required to regulate executive compensation. For example, some people think that the practice of granting stock options to senior executives should be outlawed, stiff jail terms imposed on anyone who engages in accounting fraud, and strong legal protection offered to anyone who blows the whistle on executive wrongdoing.

Sociology helps us see what may appear to be personal issues in the larger context of public policy. Even our tendency to act ethically or unethically is shaped in part by public policy—or the lack of it. Therefore, we review a public policy debate in each chapter of this book. It is good exercise for the sociological imagination, and it will help you gain more control over the forces that shape your life.

Critical Thinking

- Can we rely on individual morality or ethics to show senior executives how to behave responsibly, that is, in the long-term interest of their companies and society as a whole?

CHAPTER SUMMARY

1. **What does the sociological study of suicide tell us about society and about sociology?**

   Durkheim noted that suicide is apparently a nonsocial and antisocial action that people often but unsuccessfully try to explain psychologically. In contrast, he showed that suicide rates are influenced by the level of social solidarity of the groups to which people belong.

This argument suggests that a distinctively *social* realm influences all human behavior.

2. **What is the sociological perspective?**

   The sociological perspective analyzes the connection between personal troubles and three levels of social structure: microstructures, macrostructures, and global structures.

3. **What are the major theoretical traditions in sociology?**

   Sociology has four major theoretical traditions. *Functionalism* analyzes how social order is supported by macrostructures. The *conflict approach* analyzes how social inequality is maintained and challenged. *Symbolic interactionism* analyzes how meaning is created when people communicate in micro-level settings. *Feminism* focuses on the social sources of patriarchy in both macro- and micro-level settings.

4. **What were the main influences on the rise of sociology?**

   The rise of sociology was stimulated by the Scientific, Democratic, and Industrial Revolutions. The Scientific Revolution encouraged the view that sound conclusions about the workings of society must be based on solid evidence, not just speculation. The Democratic Revolution suggested that people are responsible for organizing society and that human intervention can therefore solve social problems. The Industrial Revolution created a host of new and serious social problems that attracted the attention of many social thinkers.

5. **Does sociological research have a subjective side?**

   It does. The subjective side of the research enterprise is no less important than the objective side. Creativity and the motivation to study new problems from new perspectives arise from individual passions and interests.

6. **What methodological issues must be addressed in any research project?**

   To maximize the scientific value of a research project, one must address issues of reliability (consistency in measurement) and validity (precision in measurement).

7. **What is participant observation?**

   Participant observation is one of the main sociological methods. It involves carefully observing people's face-to-face interactions and actually participating in their lives over a long period. Participant observation is particularly useful for enabling researchers to understand how their subjects understand the world and for conducting exploratory research. Issues of reliability and generalizability make participant observation less useful for other research purposes.

8. **What is an experiment?**

   An experiment is a carefully controlled artificial situation that allows researchers to isolate hypothesized causes and measure their effects by randomizing the allocation of subjects to experimental and control groups and exposing only the experimental group to an independent variable. Experiments get high marks for reliability and analysis of causality, but validity issues make them less than ideal for many research purposes.

9. **What is a survey?**

   In a survey, people are asked questions about their knowledge, attitudes, or behavior, in either a face-to-face interview, a telephone interview, or a paper-and-pencil format. Surveys rank high on reliability and validity as long as researchers phrase questions carefully and take measures to ensure high response rates.

10. **What are the advantages and disadvantages of using official documents and official statistics as sources of sociological data?**

    Existing documents and official statistics are inexpensive and convenient sources of high-quality data. However, they must be used cautiously because they often reflect the biases of the individuals and organizations that created them rather than the interests of the researcher.

11. **What are the main influences on and concerns of sociology today?**

    The Postindustrial Revolution is the technology-driven shift from manufacturing to service industries. Globalization is the process by which formerly separate economies, states, and cultures are becoming tied together and people are becoming increasingly aware of their growing interdependence. The causes and consequences of postindustrialism and globalization form the great sociological puzzles of our time. The tensions between equality and inequality of opportunity, and between freedom and constraint, are among the chief interests of sociology today.

Questions to Consider

1. In this chapter, you learned how variation in the level of social solidarity affects the suicide rate. How do you think variation in social solidarity might affect other areas of social life, such as criminal behavior and political protest?

2. Is a science of society possible? If you agree that such a science is possible, what are its advantages over common sense? What are its limitations?

3. What is the connection between objectivity and subjectivity in sociological research?

4. What criteria do sociologists apply to select one method of data collection over another?

5. What are the methodological strengths and weaknesses of various methods of data collection?

6. Do you think the promise of freedom and equality will be realized in the 21st century? Why or why not?

Web Resources

CENGAGENOW™

Maximize your study time by using CengageNOW's diagnostic study plan to help you review this chapter. The Study Plan will

- help you identify areas on which you should concentrate;
- provide interactive exercises to help you master the chapter concepts; and
- provide a post-test to confirm you are ready to move on to the next chapter.

The Companion Website for *Sociology: Your Compass for a New World, The Brief Edition,* Enhanced Second Edition

www.cengage.com/sociology/brym

Supplement your review of this chapter by going to the companion website to take one of the tutorial quizzes, use flash cards to master key terms, and check out the many other study aids you'll find there. You'll also find special features such as GSS Data and Census 2000 information that will put data and resources at your fingertips to help you with that special project or help you do some research on your own.

Kevin Frayer/CP PHOTO

In this chapter, you will learn that:

- Culture is the sum of shared ideas, practices, and material objects that people create to adapt to, and thrive in, their environments.

- Humans have thrived in their environments because of their unique ability to think abstractly, cooperate with one another, and make tools.

- In some respects, the development of culture makes people freer. For example, culture has become more diversified and consensus has declined in many areas of life, allowing people more choice in how they live.

- In other respects, the development of culture puts limits on who we can become. For example, the culture of buying consumer goods has become a virtually compulsory national pastime. Increasingly, therefore, people define themselves by the goods they purchase.

Culture as Problem Solving

If you follow professional baseball, you probably know that star shortstop Nomar Garciaparra can take 10 seconds to repeatedly pull up his batting gloves and kick the dirt with the toes of his cleats before he swings the bat. He believes this routine brings him luck. Garciaparra has other superstitious practices as well. For example, he never changes his cap. And although his name is really Anthony, he adopted "Nomar," his father's name spelled backward, for good luck. Garciaparra's nervous prebatting dance and his other superstitious practices make some people chuckle. But they put Garciaparra at ease. They certainly didn't hurt his league-leading .372 batting average in 2000. As Garciaparra says: "I have some superstitions, definitely, and they're always going to be there. I think a lot of people have them in baseball. . . . [It] definitely helps because it gets you in the mindset" ("Garciaparra Explains His Superstitions," 2000).

When some people say "culture," they are referring to opera, ballet, art, and fine literature. For sociologists, however, this definition is too narrow. Sociologists define **culture** broadly as all the ideas, practices, and material objects that people create to deal with real-life problems. For example, when Nomar Garciaparra developed the practice of pulling at his gloves, he was creating culture in the sociological sense. His habit helped him deal with the real-life problem of high anxiety. Sociologists call opera, ballet, art, and similar activities **high culture.** They distinguish high culture from **popular culture** or **mass cul-**

Culture: The sum of practices, languages, symbols, beliefs, values, ideologies, and material objects that people create to deal with real-life problems. Cultures enable people to adapt to and thrive in their environments.

High culture: Culture consumed mainly by upper classes.

Popular culture (or mass culture): Culture consumed by all classes.

Mass culture: *(See popular culture).*

CENGAGENOW™

This icon signals when CengageNOW has important resources available for you to use in conjunction with the text. See the foldout at the front of this text for information on how to access CengageNOW.

33

Nomar Garciaparra creates a little culture as he prepares to hit one out of Fenway Park.

Andrew Woolley

ture. Whereas popular or mass culture is consumed by all classes, high culture tends to be consumed mainly by upper classes.

Similarly, tools help people solve the problem of how to plant crops and build houses. Religion helps people come to terms with death and gives meaning to life. Tools and religion are also elements of culture because they, too, help people solve real-life problems. Note, however, that religion, technology, and many other elements of culture differ from the superstitions of Garciaparra in an important way. Superstitions may be unique to the individuals who create them. Religion and technology are widely shared. They are even passed on from one generation to the next. How does cultural sharing take place? By means of communication and learning. Thus, shared culture is socially transmitted. It requires a society to persist. (In turn, a **society** is a number of people who interact, usually in a defined territory, and share a culture.) We conclude that culture is composed of the *socially transmitted ideas,* practices, and material objects that enable people to adapt to, and thrive in, their environments.

The Origins and Components of Culture

You can appreciate the importance of culture for human survival by considering the predicament of early humans about 100,000 years ago. They lived in harsh natural environments. They had poor physical endowments, being slower runners and weaker fighters than many other animals. Yet they survived despite these disadvantages. More than that: They prospered and came to dominate nature. That was possible largely because they were the smartest creatures around. Their sophisticated brains enabled them to create cultural survival kits of enormous complexity and flexibility. These cultural survival kits contained three main tools. Each tool was a uniquely human talent, and each gave rise to a different element of culture.

Society: People who interact, usually in a defined territory, and share a culture.

Mark Richards/PhotoEdit

By acquiring specialized skills, people are able to accomplish things that no person could possibly do on his or her own.

Symbols

The first tool in the human cultural survival kit is **abstraction,** the ability to create general ideas or ways of thinking. **Symbols,** for example, are ideas. They are things that carry particular meanings. Languages and mathematical notations are sets of symbols. They allow us to classify experiences and generalize from them. For example, we recognize that we can sit on many objects but that only some of them have four legs, a back, and space for one person. We distinguish the latter from other objects by giving them a name: chairs. By the time most babies reach the end of their first year, they have heard the word "chair" repeatedly and understand that it refers to a certain class of objects.

Norms and Values

Cooperation is the second main tool in the human cultural survival kit. It is the capacity to create a complex social life by establishing **norms,** or generally accepted ways of doing things, and **values,** or ideas about what is right and wrong, good and bad, beautiful and ugly. For example, family members cooperate to raise children, and in the process, they develop and apply norms and values about which child-rearing practices are appropriate and desirable. Note, however, that different times and places give rise to different norms and values. In our society today, parents might ground children for swearing, but in Puritan times, parents would typically "beat the devil out of them." As this example suggests, by analyzing how people cooperate and produce norms and values, we can learn much about what distinguishes one culture from another.

Material and Nonmaterial Cultures

Production is the third main tool in the human cultural survival kit. It involves making and using tools and techniques that improve our ability to take what we want from nature. Such tools and techniques are known as **material culture** because they are tangible, whereas the symbols, norms, values, and other elements of **nonmaterial culture** are in-

CENGAGENOW

Learn more about **Norms** by going through the Norms Video Exercise.

Abstraction: The human capacity to create general ideas or ways of thinking that are not linked to particular instances.

Symbol: Ideas that carry a particular meaning, including the components of language, mathematical notations, and signs.

Cooperation: The human capacity to create a complex social life.

Norms: Generally accepted ways of doing things.

Values: Ideas about what is right and wrong, good and bad, beautiful and ugly.

Production: The human capacity to make and use tools that improve our ability to take what we want from nature.

Material culture: Culture composed of the tools and objects that enable people to get tasks accomplished.

Nonmaterial culture: Culture composed of symbols, norms, and other nontangible elements of culture.

tangible. All animals take from nature to subsist, and an ape may sometimes use a rock to break another object. But only humans are sufficiently intelligent and dexterous to make tools and use them to produce everything from food to computers. Understood in this sense, production is a uniquely human activity.

▶Concept Summary 2.1 illustrates each of the basic human capacities and their cultural offshoots in the field of medicine. As in medicine, so in all fields of human activity: abstraction, cooperation, and production give rise to specific kinds of ideas, norms, and elements of material culture.

Three Types of Norms: Folkways, Mores, and Taboos

If a man walks down a busy street wearing nothing on the top half of his body, he is violating a **folkway.** If he walks down the street wearing nothing on the bottom half of his body, he is violating a **more** (the Latin word for "custom," pronounced MORE-ay). Folkways are norms that specify social *preferences.* Mores are norms that specify social *requirements.* People are usually punished when they violate norms, but the punishment is usually minor if the norm is a folkway. Some onlookers will raise their eyebrows at the shirtless man. Others will shake their head in disapproval. In contrast, the punishment for walking down the street without pants is bound to be moderately harsh. Someone is bound to call the police, probably sooner than later (Sumner (1940 [1907]). The strongest and most central norms, however, are **taboos.** When someone violates a taboo, it causes revulsion in the community, and punishment is severe. Incest is one of the most widespread taboos.

Social scientists generally agree that folkways, mores, and most taboos change over time and vary from one society to the next. However, they traditionally single out the incest taboo as an exception. They hold that sexual relations between close relatives have been strictly forbidden throughout the history of all societies, because the prohibition is grounded in biological necessity. In this view, people have always observed that sexual relations between close relatives result in a relatively high incidence of congenital birth defects. As a result, people have always made sexual relations between close relatives taboo.

However, recent research suggests that the traditional view may be inaccurate (Leavitt, 2007). For example, incestuous mating was widespread among Egyptians in Roman times, and close inbreeding was common in the small and isolated communities of Samaritans in Israel and Jordan in the 1980s. Yet in both cases, congenital birth defects appear not to have been especially widespread, and in both cases, sexual relations between close relatives were acceptable. Such findings cast doubt on the view that incest is always problematic for biological reasons and that it is always a taboo practice. Different social and geographical conditions (still unknown) may determine the incidence of congenital birth defects that result from incest and close inbreeding, and whether, in rare instances, incest is culturally approved.

Folkways: A relatively unimportant norm that many people prefer to uphold. The violation of a folkway evokes mild punishment.

More: A core norm that most people believe must be upheld. The violation of a more evokes moderately harsh punishment.

Taboos: The strongest and most central norms. When someone violates a taboo, it causes revulsion in the community, and punishment is severe.

▶**Concept Summary 2.1**
The Building Blocks of Culture

The human capacity for . . .	Abstraction	Cooperation	Production
Gives rise to these elements of culture . . .	Ideas	Norms and values	Material culture
In medicine, for example . . .	*Theories* are developed about how a certain drug might cure a disease.	*Experiments* are conducted to test whether the drug works as expected.	*Treatments* are developed on the basis of the experimental results.

Language and the Sapir-Whorf Thesis

Many sociologists say that language is the most important part of culture. A **language** is a system of symbols strung together to communicate thought. Equipped with language, we can share understandings, pass experience and knowledge from one generation to the next, and make plans for the future. In short, language allows culture to develop. Consequently, sociologists commonly think of language as a cultural invention that distinguishes humans from other animals.

In the 1930s, linguists Edward Sapir and Benjamin Lee Whorf proposed an influential argument about the connection between experience, thought, and language. It came to be known as the **Sapir-Whorf thesis.** The Sapir-Whorf thesis holds that we experience certain things in our environment and form concepts about those things (path 1 to 2 in ▶Figure 2.1). We then develop language to express our concepts (path 2 to 3). Finally, language itself influences how we see the world (path 3 to 1).

Whorf saw speech patterns as "interpretations of experience" (Whorf, 1956: 137), and this view seems uncontroversial. The Garo of Burma, a rice-growing people, distinguish many types of rice. Nomadic Arabs have more than 20 different words for *camel* (Sternberg, 1998 [1995]: 305). Verbal distinctions among types of rice and camels are necessary for different groups of people because these objects are important in their environment. As a matter of necessity, they distinguish among many different types of what we may regard as "the same" object. Similarly, terms that apparently refer to the same things or people may change to reflect a changing reality. For example, a committee used to be headed by a "chairman." Then, when women started entering the paid labor force in large numbers in the 1960s and some of them became committee heads, the term changed to "chairperson" or simply "chair." In such cases, we see clearly how the environment or experience influences language.

The controversial part of the Sapir-Whorf thesis is path 3 to 1. In what sense does language *in and of itself* influence the way we experience the world? In the first wave of studies based on the Sapir-Whorf thesis, researchers focused on whether speakers of different languages perceive color in different ways. By the 1970s, researchers concluded that they do not. People who speak different languages may have a different number of basic color terms, but everyone with normal vision is able to see the full visible spectrum. The Russian language has two words for *blue*, whereas the English language has only one. This does not mean that English speakers are handicapped in their ability to distinguish shades of blue.

In the 1980s and 1990s, researchers found that language itself can affect perception. For example, the German word for *key* is masculine, whereas the Spanish word for *key* is feminine. When German and Spanish speakers are asked to describe keys, German speakers tend to use words like *hard, heavy,* and *jagged,* whereas Spanish speakers use words such as *lovely, shiny,* and *shaped.* Apparently, the gender of the noun in and of itself influences how people see the thing to which the noun refers (Minkel, 2002). Still, the degree to which language itself influences thought is a matter of controversy. Some men use terms like *fox, babe, bitch, ho,* and *doll* to refer to women. These terms are deeply offensive to many people. They certainly reflect underlying inequalities between women and men. Some people assert that these terms *in and of themselves* influence people to think of

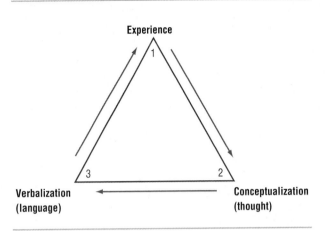

▶FIGURE 2.1
The Sapir-Whorf Thesis

According to the Sapir-Whorf thesis, we form concepts about things that we experience (path 1 to 2) and develop language to express our concepts (path 2 to 3). Controversially, however, the Sapir-Worf thesis holds that language itself then influences how we see the world (path 3 to 1).

Language: A system of symbols strung together to communicate thought.

Sapir-Whorf thesis: Holds that we experience certain things in our environment and form concepts about those things. We then develop language to express our concepts. Finally, language itself influences how we see the world.

BOX 2.1
SOCIOLOGY AT THE MOVIES

Borat: Cultural Learnings of America for Make Benefit Glorious Nation of Kazakhstan (2006)

Borat is a journalist from Kazakhstan who visits the United States so that he can learn about American culture and return home with useful lessons. The movie's humor turns on the apparent differences between Borat's culture and that of his audience and the people he meets. His values, beliefs, and norms seem deeply offensive to the Americans he encounters. Since Borat is capable of seeing the world only from his own cultural viewpoint, the movie at one level is a story of ethnocentrism gone mad.

The joke is apparent from the get-go. Many DVDs let you choose to hear the dialogue in English, French, or Spanish. The *Borat* DVD appears to give you the additional options of hearing the dialogue in Russian or Hebrew. However, when you select "Hebrew," you hear a series of anti-Semitic slurs.

We soon discover that Kazakhs are not just anti-Semites. They are racists, homophobes, and sexists too. At the film's Toronto Film Festival debut, Borat (played by Sacha Baron Cohen) sat with a horse in a cart pulled by four women dressed as peasants. As Borat explained in an interview, in Kazakhstan, the highest being is God. Next comes man, followed by the horse, the snake, "the little crawly thing," and, finally, woman.

Borat directs many of our biggest laughs against Americans. At one point he secures the agreement of a rodeo organizer in Salem, Virginia, to let him sing the national anthem before the show begins. Borat first makes a little speech: "My name Borat, I come from Kazakhstan. Can I say first, we support your war of terror. May we show our support to our boys in Iraq. May US and A kill every single terrorist! May George Bush drink the blood of every single man, woman and child of Iraq! May you destroy their country so that for the next 1,000 years not even a single lizard will survive in their desert!" After thus demonstrating the inhumanity of his audience, Borat sings the Kazakh national anthem in English to the tune of the United States national anthem:

> Kazakhstan is the greatest country in the world.
> All other countries are run by little girls.
> Kazakhstan is number one exporter of potassium.
> Other Central Asian countries have inferior potassium.
> Kazakhstan is the greatest country in the world.
> All other countries is the home of the gays.

To the suggestion that another country exceeds the United States in glory, the audience responds with jeers and boos that grow so loud, one fears for Borat's life. In this and other scenes, the movie forces us to conclude that American culture is as biased in its own way as Kazakh culture allegedly is.

Borat deeply offended many people, none more than the Kazakhs. When the president of Kazakhstan visited President George W. Bush at the White House in 2006, he discussed the bad image that the movie was giving his country. A spokesperson from the Kazakh Foreign Ministry

women simply as sexual objects, but social scientists have yet to demonstrate the degree to which they do so.

Culture as Freedom and Constraint

Culture and Ethnocentrism: A Functionalist Analysis of Culture

Despite its central importance in human life, culture is often invisible. That is, people tend to take their own culture for granted. It usually seems so sensible and natural that they rarely think about it. In contrast, people are often startled when confronted by cul-

threatened to sue Sacha Baron Cohen, referring to his actions as "a concoction of bad taste and ill manners which is completely incompatible with the ethics and civilized behaviour of Kazakhstan's people" (quoted in "Bush to hold talks…," 2006). The Kazakh ambassador to the UK wrote a letter to the editor of *The Guardian,* a leading British newspaper, explaining that Kazakhstan is an increasingly modern, prosperous, and secular country that is ethnically diverse and tolerant of ethnic minorities. "Once you know something of the true Kazakhstan," wrote the ambassador, [Borat's] antics will leave a nasty aftertaste. Indeed, you may not laugh at all" (Idrissov, 2006).

Is *Borat* just one long prejudiced rant against Jews, Americans, Kazakhs, blacks, gays, women, and so on? Some people think so. But that opinion is not credible for two reasons. First, it is inconsistent with who Sacha Baron Cohen is. He is a well-educated liberal who completed a degree in history at Cambridge and wrote his thesis on the civil rights movement in the United States. And he is a Jew who strongly identifies with his ethnic heritage. (One of the movie's biggest and largely unappreciated

Borat holds a news conference defending his film against its critics.

jokes is that Borat speaks mostly Hebrew to his sidekick, Azamat Bagatov [Ken Davitian].)

Borat certainly is one long and very funny rant, but the real objects of its satire are the world's racists, sexists, anti-Semites, and homophobes, regardless of their race, creed, or national origin. The deeper mes-

sage of Borat is anything but ethnocentric: respect for human dignity is a value that rises above all cultures, and people who think otherwise deserve to be laughed at.

Critical Thinking

● Does *Borat* help you see the prejudices of other people more clearly?

● Does *Borat* help you see your own prejudices more clearly?

● Borat talks and acts like a bigot from the opening title to the closing credits. Do you think that the expression of bigotry is inherently offensive and should always be avoided? Or do you believe that the satirical expression of bigotry can usefully reveal hidden prejudices?

tures other than their own. The ideas, norms, values, and techniques of other cultures frequently seem odd, irrational, and even inferior.

Judging another culture exclusively by the standards of one's own is known as **ethnocentrism** (Box 2.1). Ethnocentrism impairs sociological analysis. This can be illustrated by Marvin Harris's (1974) functionalist analysis of a practice that seems bizarre to many Westerners: cow worship among Hindu peasants in India.

Hindu peasants refuse to slaughter cattle and eat beef because, for them, the cow is a religious symbol of life. Pinup calendars throughout rural India portray beautiful women with the bodies of fat, white cows, milk jetting out of each teat. Cows are permitted to wander the streets, defecate on the sidewalks, and stop to chew their cud in busy intersections or on railroad tracks, forcing traffic to a complete halt. In Madras, police stations maintain fields where stray cows that have fallen ill can graze and be nursed back to health.

Ethnocentrism: The tendency to judge other cultures exclusively by the standards of one's own.

The government even runs old-age homes for cows, where dry and decrepit cattle are kept free of charge. All this special care seems mysterious to most Westerners, for it takes place amid poverty and hunger that could presumably be alleviated if only the peasants would slaughter their "useless" cattle for food instead of squandering scarce resources to feed and protect these animals.

According to Harris, however, ethnocentrism misleads many Western observers (Harris, 1974: 3–32). Cow worship, it turns out, is an economically rational practice in rural India. For one thing, Indian peasants can't afford tractors, so cows are needed to give birth to oxen, which are in high demand for plowing. For another, the cows produce hundreds of millions of pounds of recoverable manure, about half of which is used as fertilizer and half as a cooking fuel. With oil, coal, and wood in short supply, and with the peasants unable to afford chemical fertilizers, cow dung is, well, a godsend. What is more, cows in India don't cost much to maintain because they eat mostly food that is not fit for human consumption. And they represent an important source of protein as well as a livelihood for members of low-ranking castes, who have the right to dispose of the bodies of dead cattle. These "untouchables" eat beef and form the workforce of India's large leather craft industry. The protection of cows by means of cow worship is thus a perfectly sensible and highly efficient economic practice. It seems irrational only when judged by Western standards.

Harris's analysis of cow worship in rural India is interesting for two reasons. First, it illustrates how functionalist theory can illuminate otherwise mysterious social practices. Harris uncovers a range of latent functions performed by cow worship, thus showing how a particular social practice has unintended and nonobvious consequences that make social order possible. Second, we can draw an important lesson about ethnocentrism from Harris's analysis. If you refrain from judging other societies by the standards of your own, you will have taken an important first step toward developing a sociological understanding of culture.

Culture as Freedom

Culture has two faces. First, culture provides us with an opportunity to exercise our *freedom*. We create elements of culture in our everyday life to solve practical problems and express our needs, hopes, joys, and fears.

However, creating culture is just like any other act of construction in that we need raw materials to get the job done. The raw materials for the culture we create consist of cultural elements that either existed before we were born or were created by other people since our birth. We may put these elements together in ways that produce something genuinely new. But there is no other well to drink from, so existing culture puts limits on what we can think and do. In that sense, culture *constrains* us. This is culture's second face. In the rest of this chapter, we take a close look at both faces of culture.

Cultural Production and Symbolic Interactionism

Until the 1960s, most sociologists argued that culture is a "reflection" of society. Using the language introduced in Chapter 1, we can say that they regarded culture as a dependent variable. Harris's analysis of rural Indians certainly fits that mold. In Harris's view, the social necessity of protecting cows caused the cultural belief that cows are holy.

In recent decades, the symbolic interactionist tradition we discussed in Chapter 1 has influenced many sociologists of culture. Symbolic interactionists are inclined to regard culture as an *independent* variable. In their view, people do not accept culture passively; we are not empty vessels into which society pours a defined assortment of beliefs, symbols, and values. Instead, we actively produce and interpret culture, creatively fashioning it and attaching meaning to it in accordance with our diverse needs.

The idea that people actively produce and interpret culture implies that, to a degree, we are at liberty to choose how culture influences us. Let us linger a moment on the question of why we enjoy that freedom today more than ever before.

Cultural Diversity

Part of the reason we are increasingly able to choose how culture influences us is that a greater diversity of culture is available from which to choose. Like most societies in the world, American society is undergoing rapid cultural diversification. That is evident in all aspects of life, from the growing popularity of Latino music to the ever-broadening international assortment of foods consumed by most Americans. Marriage between people of different races is increasingly common. While only 1 percent of African Americans married nonblacks in 1970, the figure had increased to 7 percent by 2000. Some 5.5 percent of all marriages were interracial in 2005 (Rosenfeld, 2008). We also witness cultural diversity in Hollywood stars' names. While Jewish and other ethnic names were often Anglicized in the past—Bernard Schwartz became Tony Curtis, Anna Italiano became Anne Bancroft, and Ramon Estevez became Martin Sheen—by the 1990s there was a greater openness to "ethnic" names for stars, such as Renée Zellweger, Jennifer Lopez, Benicio Del Toro, and Emilio Estevez (Martin Sheen's son). In fact, some accentuated their difference; gangster rappers took on names like 50 Cent and DMX rather than gentle-sounding Curtis Jackson and Earl Simmons.

Many Westerners find the Indian practice of cow worship bizarre. However, cow worship performs a number of useful economic functions and is in that sense entirely rational. By viewing cow worship exclusively as an outsider (or, for that matter, exclusively as an insider), we fail to see its rational core.

World Religions Photo Library/Alamy

Multiculturalism

At the political level, cultural diversity has become a source of conflict. The conflict is most evident in the debates that have surfaced in recent years concerning curricula in the American educational system.

Until recent decades, the American educational system stressed the common elements of American culture, history, and society. Students learned the story of how European settlers overcame great odds, prospered, and forged a united nation from diverse ethnic and racial elements. School curricula typically neglected the contributions of nonwhites and non-Europeans to America's historical, literary, artistic, and scientific development. Moreover, students learned little about the less savory aspects of American history, many of which involved the use of force to create a racial hierarchy that persists to this day, albeit in modified form (see Chapter 9, "Race and Ethnicity").

History books did not deny that African Americans were enslaved and that force was used to wrest territory from Native Americans and Mexicans. They did, however, make it

© 1992 Joel Gordon

The United States continues to diversify culturally.

Multiculturalism: The view that
the curricula of America's public
schools and colleges should
reflect the country's ethnic and
racial diversity and recognize
the equality of all cultures.

Cultural relativism: The belief
that all cultures have equal
value.

seem as if these unfortunate events were part of the American past, with few implications for the present. The history of the United States was presented as a history of progress involving the *elimination* of racial privilege.

In contrast, for the past several decades, advocates of **multiculturalism** have argued that school and college curricula should present a more balanced picture of American history, culture, and society—one that better reflects the country's ethnic and racial diversity in the past and its growing ethnic and racial diversity today (Nash, Crabtree, and Dunn, 1997). A multicultural approach to education highlights the achievements of nonwhites and non-Europeans in American society. It gives more recognition to the way European settlers came to dominate nonwhite and non-European communities. It stresses how racial domination resulted in persistent social inequalities, and it encourages Spanish-language, elementary-level instruction in the states of California, Texas, New Mexico, Arizona, and Florida, where a substantial minority of people speak Spanish at home. (About one in seven Americans older than age 5 speaks a language other than English at home. Of these people, more than half speak Spanish. Most Spanish speakers live in the states just listed.)

Most critics of multiculturalism do not argue against teaching cultural diversity. What they fear is that multiculturalism is being taken too far (Glazer, 1997; Schlesinger, 1991). They believe that multiculturalism has three negative consequences:

1. Multiculturalism distracts students from essential subjects. Critics believe that multicultural education hurts minority students by forcing them to spend too much time on noncore subjects. To get ahead in the world, they say, one needs to be skilled in English and math. By taking time away from these subjects, multicultural education impedes the success of minority-group members in the work world. (Multiculturalists counter that minority students develop pride and self-esteem from a curriculum that stresses cultural diversity. They argue that pride and self-esteem help minority students get ahead in the work world.)

2. Multiculturalism encourages conflict. Critics also believe that multicultural education causes political disunity and results in more interethnic and interracial conflict. Therefore, they want schools and colleges to stress the common elements of the national experience and highlight Europe's contribution to American culture. (Multiculturalists reply that political unity and interethnic and interracial harmony maintain inequality in American society. Conflict, they say, although unfortunate, is often necessary to achieve equality between majority and minority groups.)

3. Multiculturalism encourages **cultural relativism.** Cultural relativism is the opposite of ethnocentrism. It is the belief that all cultures and all cultural practices have equal value. The trouble with this view is that some cultures oppose the most deeply held values of most Americans. Other cultures promote practices that most Americans consider inhumane. Should we respect racist and antidemocratic cultures, such as the apartheid regime that existed in South Africa from 1948 until 1992? How about

BOX 2.2
SOCIAL POLICY: WHAT DO YOU THINK?

Female Genital Mutilation: Cultural Relativism or Ethnocentrism?

The World Health Organization (WHO) defines female genital mutilation as "all procedures involving partial or total removal of the external female genitalia or other injury to the female genital organs whether for cultural or other nontherapeutic reasons" (World Health Organization, 2001). Elderly women who lack medical training usually perform these procedures.

Female genital mutilation results in pain, humiliation, psychological trauma, and loss of sexual pleasure. In the short term it is associated with infection, shock, injury to neighboring organs, and severe bleeding. Long-term effects include infertility, chronic infections in the urinary tract and reproductive system, and increased susceptibility to hepatitis B and HIV/AIDS.

Although frequently associated with Islam, female genital mutilation is rare in many predominantly Muslim countries. It is a social custom, not a religious practice. It is nearly universal in parts of Africa. About 2 million girls, mainly between the ages of 4 and 14, are at risk of undergoing it every year (Ahmad, 2000; World Health Organization, 2001).

In some cultures, people think female genital mutilation enhances female fertility. Furthermore, they commonly assume that women are naturally "unclean" and "masculine" inasmuch as they possess a vestige of the male sex organ, the clitoris. From this point of view, women who have not experienced genital mutilation are more likely to demonstrate "masculine" levels of sexual interest and activity. They are less likely to remain virgins before marriage and faithful within marriage. Accordingly, some people think female genital mutilation lessens or eradicates sexual arousal in women.

One reaction to female genital mutilation is a "human rights perspective." In this view, the practice is simply one manifestation of gender-based oppression and the violence that women experience in societies worldwide. Adopting this perspective, the United Nations has defined female genital mutilation as a form of violence against women. This perspective is also reflected in a growing number of international, regional, and national agreements that commit governments to preventing female genital mutilation, assisting women at risk of undergoing it, and punishing people who commit it. In the United States, the penalty for conducting female genital mutilation is up to 5 years in prison. The law stresses that "belief . . . that the operation is required as a matter of custom or ritual" is irrelevant in determining its illegality (U.S. Code, 1998).

Proponents of a second perspective on female genital mutilation are cultural relativists. They regard the human rights perspective as ethnocentric. The cultural relativists view interventions that interfere with the practice as little more than neo-imperialist attacks on African cultures. From their point of view, all talk of "universal human rights" denies cultural sovereignty to less powerful peoples. Moreover, opposition to female genital mutilation undermines tolerance and multiculturalism while reinforcing racist attitudes. Accordingly, cultural relativists argue that we should affirm the right of other cultures to practice female genital mutilation even if we regard it as destructive, senseless, oppressive, and abhorrent. We should respect the fact that other cultures regard female genital mutilation as meaningful and as serving useful functions.

Critical Thinking

- Which of these perspectives do you find more compelling?
- Do you believe that certain principles of human decency transcend the particulars of any specific culture? If so, what are those principles?
- If you do not believe in the existence of any universal principles of human decency, then does anything go?
- Would you agree that, say, genocide is acceptable if most people in a society favor it? Or are there limits to your cultural relativism?
- In a world where supposedly universal principles often clash with the principles of particular cultures, where do you draw the line?

the Australian aboriginal practice of driving spears through the limbs of criminals (Garkawe, 1995)? Or female circumcision, which is still widely practiced in Somalia, Sudan, and Egypt? (Box 2.2). Critics argue that by promoting cultural relativism, multiculturalism encourages respect for practices that are abhorrent to most Americans. (Multiculturalists reply that cultural relativism need not be taken to an extreme. *Moderate* cultural relativism encourages tolerance and should be promoted.)

The Rights Revolution: A Conflict Analysis of Culture

What are the social roots of cultural diversity and multiculturalism? Conflict theory suggests where to look for an answer. Recall from Chapter 1 the central argument of conflict theory: Social life is an ongoing struggle between more and less advantaged groups. Privileged groups try to maintain their advantages while subordinate groups struggle to increase theirs. And sure enough, if we probe beneath cultural diversification and multiculturalism, we find what has been called the **rights revolution,** the process by which socially excluded groups have struggled to win equal rights under the law and in practice.

After the outburst of nationalism, racism, and genocidal behavior among the combatants in World War II, the United Nations proclaimed the Universal Declaration of Human Rights in 1948. It recognized the "inherent dignity" and "equal and inalienable rights of all members of the human family" and held that "every organ of society" should "strive by teaching and education to promote respect for these rights and freedoms and by progressive measures, national and international, to secure their universal and effective recognition and observance" (United Nations, 1998c). Fanned by such sentiment, the rights revolution was in full swing by the 1960s. Today, women's rights, minority rights, gay and lesbian rights, the rights of people with special needs, constitutional rights, and language rights are all part of our political discourse. Because of the rights revolution, democracy has been widened and deepened (see Chapter 13, "Politics, Work, and the Economy"). The rights revolution is by no means finished. Many categories of people are still discriminated against socially, politically, and economically. However, in much of the world, all categories of people now participate more fully than ever before in the life of their societies (Ignatieff, 2000).

The rights revolution raises some difficult issues. For example, some members of groups that have suffered extraordinarily high levels of discrimination historically, such as Native Americans and African Americans, have demanded reparations in the form of money, symbolic gestures, land, and political autonomy (see Chapter 9, "Race and Ethnicity"). Much controversy surrounds the extent to which today's citizens are obligated to compensate past injustices.

Such problems notwithstanding, the rights revolution is here to stay and it affects our culture profoundly. Specifically, the rights revolution fragments American culture by (1) legitimizing the grievances of groups that were formerly excluded from full social participation and (2) renewing their pride in their identity and heritage. Our history books, our literature, our music, our use of languages, and our very sense of what it means to be American have diversified culturally. White, male, heterosexual property owners of northern European origin are still disproportionately influential in the United States, but our culture is no longer dominated by them in the way that it was just four decades ago.

From Diversity to Globalization

Rights revolution: The process by which socially excluded groups have struggled to win equal rights under the law and in practice since the 1960s.

Rites of passage: Cultural ceremonies that mark the transition from one stage of life to another (e.g., from childhood to adulthood) or from life to death (e.g., funerals).

The cultural diversification we witness today is not evident in preliterate or tribal societies. In such societies, cultural beliefs and practices are virtually the same for all group members. For example, many tribal societies organize **rites of passage.** These cultural ceremonies mark the transition from one stage of life to another (e.g., from childhood to adulthood) or from life to death (e.g., funerals). They involve elaborate procedures such as body painting and carefully orchestrated chants and movements. They are conducted in public, and no variation from prescribed practice is allowed. Culture is homogeneous (Durkheim, 1976 [1915]).

In contrast, preindustrial western Europe and North America were rocked by artistic, religious, scientific, and political forces that fragmented culture. The Renaissance, the Protestant Reformation, the Scientific Revolution, the French and American Revolutions—between the 14th and 18th centuries, all of these movements involved people questioning old ways of seeing and doing things. Science placed skepticism about established authority at the very heart of its method. Political revolution proved there was nothing ordained about who should rule and how they should do so. Religious dissent ensured that the Catholic Church would no longer be the supreme interpreter of God's will in the eyes of all Christians. Authority and truth became divided as never before.

In the 1980s, big American food companies started expanding into non-Western countries to find new markets, but they recognized that globalization would have to involve adapting to local tastes and traditions. For example, rather than selling corn flakes in India, Kellogg's has been promoting basmati flakes (made from basmati rice) since 1992.

Cultural fragmentation picked up steam during industrialization as the variety of occupational roles grew and new political and intellectual movements crystallized. The pace of cultural fragmentation is quickening again today in the postindustrial era as a result of globalization. **Globalization** is the process by which formerly separate economies, states, and cultures are becoming tied together and people are becoming increasingly aware of their growing interdependence.

One of the most important roots of globalization is the expansion of international trade and investment. Even a business as "American" as McDonald's now earns 60 percent of its profits outside the United States, and its international operations are growing much faster than its U.S. outlets (Commins, 1997). At the same time, members of different ethnic and racial groups are migrating and coming into sustained contact with one another. The number of influential "transnational" organizations, such as the International Monetary Fund, the World Bank, the European Union, Greenpeace, and Amnesty International, is multiplying. Relatively inexpensive international travel and communication make contacts between people from diverse cultures routine. The mass media make Vin Diesel and *The Apprentice* nearly as well known in Warsaw as in Wichita. MTV brings rock music to the world via MTV Canada, MTV Latino, MTV Brazil, MTV Europe, MTV Asia, MTV Japan, MTV Mandarin, and MTV India (Hanke, 1998). In short, globalization destroys political, economic, and cultural isolation, bringing people together in what Canadian media analyst Marshall McLuhan (1964) first called a "global village" (Box 2.3). As a result of globalization, people are less obliged to accept the culture into which they were born and are freer to combine elements of culture from a wide variety of historical periods and geographical settings. Globalization is a schoolboy in New Delhi, India, listening to Avril Lavigne on his MP3 player as he rushes to slip into his Levis, wolf down a bowl of Kellogg's Basmati Flakes, and say good-bye to his parents in Hindi because he is late for his English-language school.

Aspects of Postmodernism

Some sociologists think that so much cultural fragmentation and reconfiguration has taken place in the last few decades that a new term is needed to characterize the culture of our times: **postmodernism.** Scholars often characterize the last half of the 19th century

Globalization: The process by which formerly separate economies, states, and cultures are being tied together and people are becoming increasingly aware of their growing interdependence.

Postmodernism: A style of thought characterized by an eclectic mixing of cultural elements and the erosion of authority and of consensus around some core values.

BOX 2.3
MASS MEDIA AND SOCIETY

English, Globalization, and the Internet

A good indicator of the influence and extent of globalization is the spread of English. In 1600, English was the mother tongue of between 4 and 7 million people. Not even all people in England spoke it. Today, more than 1.5 billion people speak English worldwide, more than half as a second language (McCrum, Cran, and MacNeil, 1992; Peritz, 2006) (▶Figure 2.2). English is the most widespread language on Earth. Most of the world's technical and scientific periodicals are written in English. English is the official language of the Olympics, of the Miss Universe contest, of navigation in the air and on the seas, and of the World Council of Churches.

English is dominant because Britain and the United States have been the world's most powerful and influential countries—economically, militarily, and culturally—for more than 200 years. (Someone once defined "language" as a dialect backed up by an army.) In recent decades, the global spread of capitalism, the popularity of Hollywood movies and American TV shows, and widespread access to instant communication via telephone and the Internet have increased the reach of the English language. There are now more speakers of excellent English in India than in Britain, and when a construction company jointly owned by German, French, and Italian interests undertakes a building project in Spain, the language of business is English (▶Figure 2.3).

Due to the rise of English (as well as the influence of French, Spanish, and the languages of a few other colonizing nations), several thousand languages around the world are in the process of being eliminated. These endangered languages are spoken by the tribes of Papua, New Guinea; the Native peoples of the Americas; the national and tribal minorities of Asia, Africa, and Oceania; and marginalized European peoples such as the Irish and the Basques. The Linguistic Society of America estimates that the 5,000 to 6,000 languages spoken in the world today will be reduced to 1,000 to 3,000 in a century. Much of the culture of a people—its prayers, humor, conversational styles, technical vocabulary, myths, and so on—is expressed through language. Therefore, the loss of language amounts to the disappearance of tradition and perhaps even identity. These are often replaced by the traditions and identity of the colonial

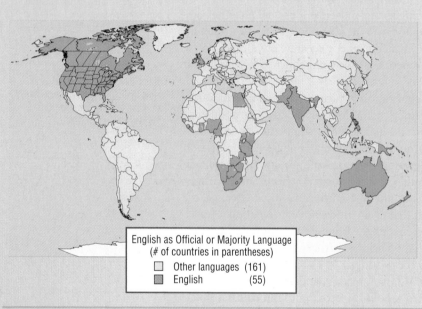

▶FIGURE 2.2
English as Official or Majority Language

Sources: United Nations Educational, Scientific, and Cultural Organization (2001); Central Intelligence Agency (2002).

and the first half of the 20th century as the era of modernity. During that 100-year period, belief in the inevitability of progress, respect for authority, and consensus around core values characterized much of Western culture. In contrast, postmodern culture involves an eclectic mixing of elements from different times and places, the erosion of authority, and the decline of consensus of some core values. Let us consider each of these aspects of postmodernism in turn.

power, with television playing an important role in the transformation (Woodbury, 2003).

Still, major languages other than English are holding their own and even pushing back the English onslaught in some areas, such as the Internet. Consider the pie charts in Figure 2.3, which show how language use on the Internet changed from June 2001 to June 2008. In this 7-year period, English usage dropped nearly 15 percent, while Chinese usage jumped 12 percent. This suggests that globalization does not necessarily involve the homogenization of culture—an important theme that we will take up again in Chapter 8 ("Globalization, Inequality, and Development").

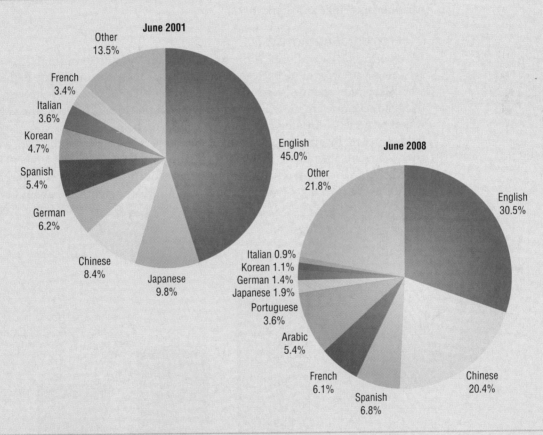

▶FIGURE 2.3
Internet Usage by Language Group, June 2001 and June 2008

Source: Global Reach (2001, 2004); Internet World Statistics (2008).

Blending Cultures

An eclectic mixing of cultural elements from different times and places is the first aspect of postmodernism. In the postmodern era, it is easier to create individualized belief systems and practices by blending facets of different cultures and historical periods. Consider religion. In the United States today, people enjoy many more ways to worship than they used to. *The Encyclopedia of American Religions* lists more than

2,100 religious groups; and one can easily construct a personalized religion involving, say, belief in the divinity of Jesus *and* yoga (Melton, 1996 [1978]). In the words of one journalist, "In an age when we trust ourselves to assemble our own investment portfolios and cancer therapies, why not our religious beliefs?" (Creedon, 1998).

Nor are religious beliefs and practices drawn from conventional sources alone. Even fundamentalist Christians who believe that the Bible is the literal word of God often supplement Judeo-Christian beliefs and practices with less conventional ideas about astrology, psychic powers, and communication with the dead (▶Figure 2.4). Individuals thus draw on religious practices as if they are selecting a variety of foods in a buffet. Meanwhile, churches, synagogues, and other religious institutions have diversified their "menus" to appeal to the spiritual, leisure, and social needs of religious consumers and retain their loyalties in the competitive market for congregants and parishioners (Finke and Stark, 1992).

Erosion of Authority

The erosion of authority is the second aspect of postmodernism. Half a century ago, Americans were more likely than they are today to defer to authority in the family, schools, politics, and medicine. As the social bases of authority and truth have multiplied, however, we are more likely to challenge authority. Authorities who were once widely respected, including parents, physicians, and politicians, have come to be held in lower regard by many people. In the 1950s, Robert Young played the firm, wise, and always-present father in the TV hit *Father Knows Best.* Fifty years later, Homer Simpson plays a fool in *The Simpsons.* In the 1950s, three-fourths of Americans expressed confidence in the federal government's ability to do what is right "just about always" or

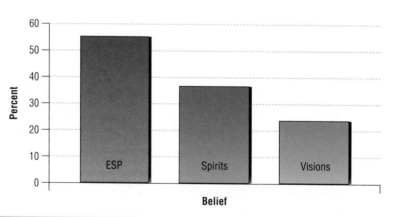

▶FIGURE 2.4

Unconventional Beliefs Among Christian Fundamentalists, United States (in percent; n = 312)

"How often have you had any of the following experiences: Felt in touch with someone when they were far away from you ('ESP')? Felt as though you were really in touch with someone who had died ('spirits')? Seen events that happened at a great distance as they were happening ('visions')?" Responses are shown for respondents who said they are Protestant or Catholic and who believe the Bible is the literal word of God.

Note: Data are for 1989.

Source: National Opinion Research Center, 2006. General Social Survey, 1972–2002. Machine-readable file. Copyright © 2006 NORC. Used with permission.

A hallmark of postmodernism is the combining of cultural elements from different times and places. Architect I. M. Pei unleashed a storm of protest when his 72-foot glass pyramid became an entrance to the Louvre in Paris. This pyramid created a postmodern nightmare in the eyes of some critics.

Owen Franken/CORBIS

"most of the time." Fifty years later, the confidence level stood at just one-third of the American people. The rise of Homer Simpson and the decline of confidence in government both reflect the society-wide erosion of traditional authority (Nevitte, 1996).

Instability of Core American Values

The decline of consensus around core values is the third aspect of postmodernism. More than half a century ago, sociologist Robin M. Williams, Jr., identified a dozen core American values (Williams, 1951). Americans, he wrote, value:

- achievement and success
- individualism
- activity and work
- efficiency and practicality
- science and technology
- progress
- material comfort
- humanitarianism
- freedom
- democracy
- equality
- groups to which they belong above other groups

Many Americans still believe in these values, and some of them have even become stronger, as we will see later. However, other values are less likely to remain stable over time, and consensus has broken down on some of them.

Value instability is evident in voting patterns, for example. In the middle of the 20th century, the great majority of adults remained loyal to one political party from one election to the next. By the third quarter of the 20th century, however, specific issues and personalities began to eclipse party loyalty as the driving forces of American politics (Nie, Verba, and Petrocik, 1979 [1976]). Today, people are more likely to vote for different parties in succeeding elections than they were in 1950, though party identification and loyalty remain significant (Green, Schickler, and Palmquist, 2002). Similarly, although Americans are among the most optimistic people in the world regarding the effects of science on humanity, they have become more pessimistic in the last two decades, as have the citizens of other rich countries.

Postmodernism has many parents, teachers, politicians, religious leaders, and university professors worried. Given the eclectic mixing of cultural elements from different times and places, the erosion of authority, and the decline of consensus around some core values, how can we make binding decisions? How can we govern? How can we teach children and adolescents the difference between right and wrong? How can we transmit accepted literary tastes and artistic standards from one generation to the next? These kinds of issues plague people in positions of authority today.

Although their concerns are legitimate, many authorities seem not to have considered the other side of the coin. The postmodern condition empowers ordinary people and makes them more responsible for their own fate. It frees people to adopt religious, ethnic, and other identities with which they are comfortable, as opposed to identities imposed on them by others. It makes them more tolerant of difference, which is no small matter in a world torn by group conflict. Finally, the postmodern attitude encourages healthy skepticism about rosy and naive scientific and political promises.

Culture as Constraint

We noted previously that culture has two faces. One we labeled freedom, the other constraint. Diversity, globalization, the rights revolution, and postmodernism are all aspects of the new freedoms that culture allows us today. We now examine several aspects of culture that act as constraining forces on our lives.

Values

American Values and the Problem of Cultural Lag

Earlier we listed a dozen core American values identified by Robin M. Williams, Jr., in the 1950s (p. 49). We noted the erosion of consensus on some of those values in recent decades. Now, however, we must add that some of the values Williams identified seem not to have eroded at all. Instead, they have become more important in the lives of many Americans. Those persistent values act as enduring cultural constraints on our lives.

Consider, for example, that the United States is one of just a few countries that do not allow homosexuals to serve openly in the military. If you are gay or lesbian and are found out, you can expect to be discharged. True, given the shortage of personnel in the armed forces, the military increasingly ignores the rule. Discharges on grounds of homosexuality numbered about 1,200 in 2001, but only about 600 in 2007 (60 Minutes, 2007). Still, the rule is on the books and is often applied, placing the United States in the same category as China, Cuba, Egypt, Saudi Arabia, Syria, and Yemen, which have similar policies. In

British naval personnel march in the Gay Pride parade in London, July 5, 2008.

contrast, most countries do not care whether homosexuals serve openly in the military, believing that mutual tolerance and respect for difference increase troop morale. For example, Australia and Canada have allowed homosexuals to serve openly in the military since 1992, and in the UK since 2000. In the UK and Canada, homosexuals in the military are even free to march in uniform on Gay Pride Day.

Sociologically speaking, the position of the United States on gays and lesbians in the military is unexpected. Nearly half a century ago, sociologist Seymour Martin Lipset (1963) emphasized that the United States was born in open rebellion against the British motherland. Its Western frontier was lawless. Vast opportunities for striking it rich bred a spirit of individualism. Thus, the United States developed anti-authoritarian values emphasizing equality and freedom. Yet opposition to homosexuals in the military limits freedom, reinforces inequality, and seeks to impose unquestioning respect for authority. Surveys show that countries similar to the United States economically and politically became more freedom-loving, tolerant, and critical of authority in the 1980s and 1990s—in short, more American. Meanwhile, the United States moved in the opposite direction (Adams, 1997; Inglehart and Baker, 2000). In a sense, we became less American. Our culture became more *constraining* than did the cultures of other, similar countries.

Said differently, over the past few decades the United States has developed a case of what sociologists call **cultural lag.** Cultural lag exists when change in material culture outpaces change in values and other aspects of symbolic culture (Ogburn, 1966 [1922]). Economically and technologically, the rich English-speaking democracies grew robustly, and in three cases (Australia, Canada, and the UK) their cultures became less traditional. In the United States, however, cultural modernization lagged, largely because of a strong religious revival that emphasized traditional values (Inglehart and Baker, 2000). In recent

Cultural lag: The tendency of symbolic culture to change more slowly than material culture.

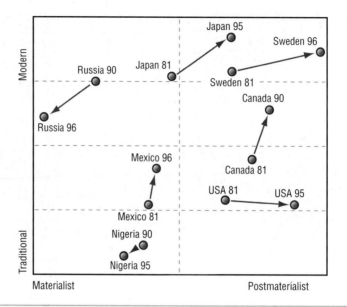

▶FIGURE 2.5
Value Change in Seven Countries

The World Values Survey allows us to see how people's values have changed over time in many countries. This graph shows that, unlike other rich countries, the United States became more traditional (that is religious, patriotic, respectful of authority, and so on) between 1981 and 1995. However, like other rich countries, the United States also became more "postmaterialist," meaning that Americans gave higher priority to self-expression and quality of life in 1995 than they did in 1981. Does a tension exist between the simultaneous movement toward greater traditionalism and greater postmaterialism in American society? If so, how is that tension expressed socially and politically?

Source: Ronald Inglehart and Wayne Baker (2000), "Modernization, Cultural Change and the Persistence of Traditional Values," *American Sociological Review* 65: 19–51. Copyright © 2000 American Sociological Association. Reprinted with permission of the publisher and author.

decades, a substantial number of Americans have joined religious organizations. They started attending religious services more frequently, taking their scriptures literally, and supporting conservative social issues, including opposition to homosexuality (Chapter 12, "Religion and Education"). This situation caused a gap to grow between American values and the country's modern economic, technological, and political systems. Because of this cultural lag, our culture now constrains us more than the cultures of Australia and the other rich English-speaking democracies constrain their citizens (▶Figure 2.5).

The Regulation of Time

One of the American values identified by Robin M. Williams, Jr., in the 1950s that has grown stronger in the past few decades is our value of efficiency. This is evident, for example, in the way we allow the clock to regiment our daily lives.

People did not always let the clock determine the pace of daily life. When the first mechanical clocks were installed in public squares in Germany nearly 700 years ago to signal the beginning of the workday, the timing of meals, and quitting time, workers resisted. They were accustomed to enjoying many holidays and a flexible and vague work schedule regulated only approximately by the seasons and the rising and setting of the sun. The strict regime imposed by the work clocks made their lives harder. They staged uprisings to silence the clocks—but to no avail. City officials sided with employers and imposed fines for ignoring the work clocks. Harsher penalties, including death, were imposed on anyone trying to use the clocks' bells to signal a revolt (Thompson, 1967).

Today, nearly 700 years later, many people seem like slaves of the work clock. This is especially true of urban North American couples who are employed full time in the paid labor force and have preteen children. For them, life often seems an endless round of waking up at 6:30 a.m.; getting everyone washed and dressed; preparing the kids' lunches; getting them out the door in time for the school bus or the car pool; driving to work through rush-hour traffic; facing the speedup at work resulting from the recent downsizing; driving back home through rush-hour traffic; preparing dinner; taking the kids to their soccer game; returning home to clean up the dishes and help with homework; getting the kids washed, their teeth brushed, and then into bed; and (if they have not brought some office work home) grabbing an hour of TV before collapsing, exhausted, for approximately 6½ hours' sleep before

▲
Have we come to depend too heavily on the work clock?

the story repeats itself. At the end of the 1990s, married couples with children younger than 6 years worked for pay 16 hours a week longer than they did in the late 1960s (U.S. Department of Labor, 1999c: 100). Managers were more likely than any other category of workers to be working for pay 49 hours a week or more. Next came sales personnel who earn commissions, transportation workers (especially truck drivers), and professionals (Rones, Ilg, and Gardner, 1997: 9). Life is less hectic for residents of small towns, unmarried people, couples without small children, retirees, and the unemployed. But the lives of many people are so packed with activities that they must carefully regulate time and parcel out each moment precisely so that they may tick off item after item from an evergrowing list of tasks that need to be completed on schedule (Schor, 1992). After 700 years of conditioning, it is unusual for people to rebel against the clock anymore. We now wear a watch on our wrist without giving it a second thought, as it were. This signifies that we have accepted and internalized the regime of the work clock. Allowing clocks to precisely regulate our activities seems the most natural thing in the world, although there is nothing natural about it.

The precise regulation of time is a rational means of ensuring efficiency. Minding the clock maximizes how much work you get done in a day. The regulation of time makes it possible for trains to run on schedule, university classes to begin punctually, and business meetings to start on time. But even if we allow that minding the clock is rational as a means of achieving efficiency, is it rational as an end in itself? For many people, it is not. They complain that the precise regulation of time has gotten out of hand. Life has simply become too hectic for many people to enjoy. How rational is it that a restaurant in Japan has installed a punch-clock for its customers? The restaurant offers all you can eat for 35 yen per minute. As a result, "the diners rush in, punch the clock, load their trays from the buffet table, and concentrate intensely on efficient chewing and swallowing, trying not to waste time talking to their companions before rushing back to punch out" (Gleick, 2000 [1999]: 244). Meanwhile, in New York and Los Angeles some upscale restaurants have gotten in on the act. An increasingly large number of business clients are so pressed for time, they pack in two half-hour lunches with successive guests. The restaurants oblige, making the resetting of tables "resemble the pit-stop activity at the Indianapolis 500" (Gleick, 2000 [1999]: 155). Arguably, as these examples illustrate, a *rational means* (the use of the work clock) has been applied to a *given goal* (maximizing work) but has led to an *irrational end* (a too-hectic life).

Rationalization

This, in a nutshell, is Max Weber's thesis about what he called the rationalization process: **Rationalization,** in Weber's usage, means (1) the application of the most efficient means to achieve given goals and (2) the unintended, negative consequences of doing so.

Weber claimed that rationalization of means has crept into all spheres of life, leading to unintended consequences that dehumanize and constrain us (▶Figure 2.6). As our analysis of the way we use time shows, rationalization enables us to do just about everything more efficiently, but at a steep cost. In Weber's view, rationalization is one of the most constraining aspects of contemporary culture; rationalization makes life in the modern world akin to living inside an "iron cage," wrote Weber.

Consumerism

A second constraining aspect of culture is consumerism. **Consumerism** is the tendency to define ourselves in terms of the goods and services we purchase. As artist Barbara Krueger put it: "I shop, therefore I am." It is the contemporary form of valuing "material progress that makes life easier," which Robin M.Williams, Jr., identified as a core American value in the 1950s.

The rationalization process, when applied to the production of goods and services, enables us to produce more efficiently, to have more of just about everything than our parents did. But it is consumerism, the tendency to define ourselves in terms of the goods we purchase, that ensures all the goods we produce will be bought. Of course, we have lots of choices. We can select from dozens of styles of running shoes, cars, toothpaste, and all the rest. We can also choose to buy items that help define us as members of a particular **subculture,** adherents of a set of distinctive values, norms, and practices within a larger culture (Box 2.4).

But, individual taste aside, we all have one thing in common: we tend to be good consumers. We are motivated by advertising, which is based on the accurate insight that people will tend to be considered cultural outcasts if they fail to conform to stylish trends.

CENGAGENOW™

Learn more about **Consumerism** by going through the Number of Shopping Centers in the U.S. Map Exercise.

Rationalization: The application of the most efficient means to achieve given goals and the unintended, negative consequences of doing so.

Consumerism: The tendency to define oneself in terms of the goods one purchases.

Subculture: A set of distinctive values, norms, and practices within a larger culture.

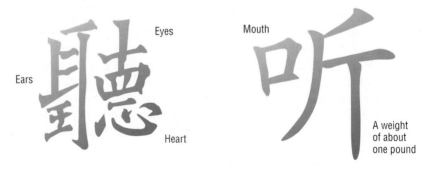

Ears   Eyes   Mouth   Heart   A weight of about one pound

▶FIGURE 2.6
The Rationalization of Chinese Script

Reprinted here are the Chinese characters for "listening" (*t'ing*) in traditional Chinese script (left) and simplified, modern script (right). Each character is composed of several word-symbols. In classical script, listening is depicted as a process involving the eyes, the ears, and the heart. It implies that listening demands the utmost empathy and involves the whole person. In contrast, modern script depicts listening as something that involves merely one person speaking and the other "weighing" speech. Modern Chinese script has been rationalized. Has empathy been lost in the process?

BOX 2.4
YOU AND THE SOCIAL WORLD

Ads 'Я Us

Because advertising stimulates sales, businesses tend to spend more on advertising over time. Because advertising is widespread, most people unquestioningly accept it as part of their lives. In fact, many people have *become* ads. When your father was a child and quickly threw on a shirt, allowing the label to hang out, your grandmother might have told him to "tuck in that label." Today, many people proudly display consumer labels as marks of status and identity. Advertisers teach us to associate the words "Gucci" and "Nike" with different kinds of people, and when people display these labels on their clothes, they are telling us something about

the kind of people they are. Advertising becomes us.

Record all labels displayed on the clothes worn by your three closest college friends over a week. During the same week, record all labels displayed on the clothes worn by three classmates who seem like they could never be your friends. Finally, record all labels displayed on the clothes you wear over the week.

WRITING ASSIGNMENT

In about 500 words, write an essay addressing the following questions:

Do your labels resemble those of your friends or nonfriends? What do the labels worn by your friends and nonfriends tell you about who your friends and nonfriends are? On the basis of your observations, do you think it is reasonable to conclude that clothing labels are cultural artifacts that increase the solidarity of social groups and segregate them from other groups? (Note: If you, your friends, or your nonfriends don't display clothing labels, what does this tell you?)

By creating those trends, advertisers push us to buy, even if doing so requires that we work more and incur large debts (Schor, 1999). That is why the "shop-till-you-drop" lifestyle of many North Americans prompted French sociologist Jean Baudrillard to remark pointedly that even what is best in America is compulsory (Baudrillard, 1988 [1986]). And it is why we say that consumerism, like rationalization, acts as a powerful constraint on our lives.

From Counterculture to Subculture

In concluding our discussion of culture as a constraining force, we note that consumerism is remarkably effective at taming countercultures. **Countercultures** are subversive subcultures. They oppose dominant values and seek to replace them. The hippies of the 1960s formed a counterculture and so do environmentalists today. Countercultures rarely pose a serious threat to social stability. Most often, the system of social control, of rewards and punishments, keeps countercultures at bay. In our society, consumerism acts as a social control mechanism that normally prevents countercultures from disrupting the social order. It does that by transforming deviations from mainstream culture into means of making money and by enticing rebels to become entrepreneurs (Frank and Weiland, 1997). Two examples from popular music help illustrate the point:

- Ozzy Osbourne was an important figure in the counterculture that grew up around heavy metal music beginning in the late 1960s. He and his band, Black Sabbath, inspired Metallica, Marilyn Manson, and others to play loud music, reject conventional morality, embrace death and violence, and spark youthful rebellion and parental panic. In the early 1980s, Tipper Gore, wife of future presidential candidate Al Gore, formed the Parental Music Resource Committee to fight against violence and sex in the lyrics of popular music. Osbourne was one of the com-

Countercultures: Subversive subcultures. They oppose dominant values and seek to replace them.

The Osbournes

mittee's principal targets. The "Prince of Darkness," as he was often called, was about as rebellious a figure as one could imagine in 1982. Flash forward 20 years. In 2002, Osbourne, now 55, was the star of a popular MTV show. MTV placed a dozen cameras throughout his Beverly Hills mansion, and every Tuesday night viewers got to see everything going on in the Osbourne household for half an hour. According to *USA Today,* Osbourne is "a lot like anyone's adorable dad. Shuffles a bit. Forgets things. Worries about the garbage. Snores on the couch while the TV blares. Walks the dog" (Gundersen, Keveney, and Oldenburg, 2002: 1A). Rosie O'Donnell said to Ozzy's wife, Sharon, "What I love most about [your show] is not only the relationship you have with Ozzy—and you obviously adore each other—but the honesty with which you relate to your children. The love is so evident between all of you. It's heartwarming" (Gundersen, Keveney, and Oldenburg, 2002: 2A). Sharon and Ozzy were invited to dinner at the White House in 2002. *The Osbournes,* it seems, was a comfort to many people. It proved that heavy metal's frightening rejection of mainstream culture in the 1970s and 1980s was just a passing phase and that the nuclear family remained intact. Ozzy Osbourne was thus transformed from the embodiment of rebellion against society to a family man, a small industry, and a conservative media icon.

● The development of hip-hop also illustrates the commercialization and taming of rebellion (Brym, 2009b). Originating in the poverty and despair of inner-city American ghettos in the 1970s, hip-hop gave rise to a highly politicized counterculture. Early hip-hop artists glorified the mean streets of the inner city and held the police, the mass media, and other pillars of white society in contempt, blaming them for arbitrary arrests, the political suppression of black activists, and the spreading of lies about African Americans. However, by the time Public Enemy became a hit in the late 1980s, MTV had aired its first regular program devoted to the genre, and much of hip-hop's audience was composed of white, middle-class youth. Hip-hop artists were quick to see the potential of commercialization. Soon Wu-Tang Clan had its own line of clothes, and Versace was marketing clothing influenced by ghetto styles. Puff Daddy reminded his audience in his 1999 CD *Forever*: "N_____ get money, that's simply the plan." According to *Forbes* magazine, he became one of the country's forty richest men under 40. By 2005, he had his own line of popular clothing, Sean John, and renamed himself Diddy. No less than heavy metal and punk, hip-hop's radicalism gave way to the lures of commerce.

The fate of heavy metal and hip-hop is testimony to the capacity of consumerism to change countercultures into mere subcultures, thus constraining dissent and rebellion.

The Points of the Compass

In this chapter, we have focused on the freedom-versus-constraint points of the sociological compass that we introduced in Chapter 1 (see Figure 1.5). Here is what we have learned:

Today's culture grants people more freedom to explore and fulfill their individual and collective aspirations than at any time in human history. Although much distance remains to be covered, previously marginalized groups such as women, gays and lesbians, and members of racial minorities are closer than ever to equality with majority groups. They have the rights revolution to thank for that. At the same time, multiculturalism, globalization, and postmodernism give people more freedom than they enjoyed in the past to choose their religion, ethnicity, nationality, and sexuality—in short, their very identity.

We would develop a distorted picture of social reality, however, if we ignored the opposite point of the compass. Today's culture also constrains us, putting limits on what we can become. The constraints first became evident when we examined the drift toward traditional religious and moral values in the United States in recent decades. As we saw, strengthening traditionalism sets limits on our individualism and freedom of self-expression. Growing rationalization and the spread of consumerism also limit what we can become. Rationalization limits us by focusing our attention on how we can do things more efficiently while diverting our attention from the ultimate consequences of our actions, even if those consequences are undesirable for most people. Consumerism acts as a constraint too, pushing us to want and buy more things while simultaneously acting as a form of social control and driving us into unmanageable debt. Some freedoms, it emerges, are also straightjackets.

Diddy

Kurt Krieger/Corbis

CHAPTER SUMMARY

1. What are the main components of culture, and what is culture's main function?

Culture is composed of various types of ideas (e.g., symbols, language, values, beliefs), norms of behavior, and human-made material objects. The ability to create symbols, cooperate, and make tools has enabled humans to thrive in their environments.

2. What does it mean to say that culture has "two faces"?

First, culture provides us with increasing opportunities to exercise our freedom in some respects. The rights revolution, multiculturalism, globalization, and postmodernism all reflect this tendency. Second, culture constrains us in other respects, putting limits on what we can become. The shift of values towards traditionalism, the growth of rationalization, and the spread of consumerism all reflect this tendency.

3. What is the multiculturalism debate?

Advocates of multiculturalism want school and college curricula to reflect the country's growing ethnic and racial diversity. They also want school and college curricula to stress that all cultures have equal value. They believe that multicultural education will promote self-esteem and economic success among members of racial minorities. Critics fear that multiculturalism results in declining educational standards. They believe that multicultural education causes political disunity and interethnic and interracial conflict, promoting an extreme form of cultural relativism.

4. What is the rights revolution?

The rights revolution is the process by which socially excluded groups have struggled to win equal rights under the law and in practice. In full swing by the 1960s, the rights revolution involves the promotion of women's rights, minority rights, gay and lesbian rights, the rights of people with special needs, constitutional rights, and language rights. The rights revolution fragments American culture by legitimizing the grievances of groups that were formerly excluded from full social participation and renewing their pride in their identity and heritage.

5. What causes the globalization of culture?

The globalization of culture results from the growth of international trade and investment, ethnic and racial migration, influential transnational organizations, and inexpensive travel and communication.

6. What is postmodernism?

Postmodernism involves an eclectic mixing of elements from different times and places, the decline of authority, and the erosion of consensus around core values.

7. What is rationalization?

Rationalization involves the application of the most efficient means to achieve given goals and the unintended, negative consequences of doing so. Rationalization is evident in the increasingly regulated use of time and in many other areas of social life.

8. What is consumerism?

Consumerism is the tendency to define ourselves in terms of the goods we purchase. Excessive consumption limits who we can become and constrains our capacity to dissent from mainstream culture.

Questions to Consider

1. To what extent do we shape our culture and to what extent does it shape us?

2. Select a subcultural practice that seems odd, inexplicable, or irrational to you. By interviewing members of the subcultural group and reading about them, explain how the subcultural practice that you chose to research makes sense to members of the subcultural group.

3. Do you think the freedoms afforded by postmodern culture outweigh the constraints it places on us? Why or why not?

Web Resources

CENGAGENOW™

Maximize your study time by using CengageNOW's diagnostic study plan to help you review this chapter. The Study Plan will

- help you identify areas on which you should concentrate;
- provide interactive exercises to help you master the chapter concepts; and
- provide a post-test to confirm you are ready to move on to the next chapter.

The Companion Website for *Sociology: Your Compass for a New World, The Brief Edition,* Enhanced Second Edition

www.cengage.com/sociology/brym

Supplement your review of this chapter by going to the companion website to take one of the tutorial quizzes, use flash cards to master key terms, and check out the many other study aids you'll find there. You'll also find special features such as GSS Data and Census 2000 information that will put data and resources at your fingertips to help you with that special project or help you do some research on your own.

Jim West/The Image Works

In this chapter, you will learn that:

- The view that social interaction unleashes human abilities is supported by studies showing that children raised in isolation do not develop normal language and other social skills.

- While the socializing influence of the family decreased in the 20th century, the influence of schools, peer groups, and the mass media increased.

- People's identities change faster, more often, and more completely than they did just a couple of decades ago; the self has become more plastic.

- The main socializing institutions often teach children and adolescents contradictory lessons, making socialization a more confusing and stressful process than it used to be.

- Declining parental supervision and guidance, increasing assumption of adult responsibilities by youth, and declining participation in extracurricular activities are transforming the character of childhood and adolescence today.

Social Isolation and Socialization

One day in 1800, a 10- or 11-year-old boy walked out of the woods in southern France. He was filthy, naked, and unable to speak and had not been toilet trained. After the police took him to a local orphanage, he repeatedly tried to escape and refused to wear clothes. No parent ever claimed him. He became known as "the wild boy of Aveyron." A thorough medical examination found no major physical or mental abnormalities. Why, then, did the boy seem more animal than human? Because, until he walked out of the woods, he apparently had been raised in isolation from other human beings (Shattuck, 1980).

Similar horrifying reports lead to the same conclusion. Occasionally a child is found locked in an attic or a cellar, where he or she saw another person for only short periods each day to receive food. Like the wild boy of Aveyron, such children rarely develop normally. Typically, they remain disinterested in games. They cannot form intimate social relationships with other people. They develop only the most basic language skills.

Some of these children may suffer from congenitally subnormal intelligence. The amount and type of social contact they had before they were discovered is unknown. Some may have been abused. Therefore, their condition may not be a result of social isolation alone. However, these examples do at least suggest that the ability to learn culture and become human is only a potential. To be actualized, **socialization** must unleash

CENGAGENOW™

This icon signals when CengageNOW has important resources available for you to use in conjunction with the text. See the foldout at the front of this text for information on how to access CengageNOW.

Socialization: The process by which people learn their culture. They do so by entering and disengaging from a succession of roles and becoming aware of themselves as they interact with others.

Nina Leen/Time Life Pictures/Getty Images

In the 1960s, researchers Harry and Margaret Harlow placed baby rhesus monkeys in various conditions of isolation to witness and study the animals' reactions. They discovered that baby monkeys raised with an artificial mother made of wire mesh, a wooden head, and the nipple of a feeding tube for a breast were later unable to interact normally with other monkeys. However, when the artificial mother was covered with a soft terry cloth, the infant monkeys clung to it in comfort and later revealed less emotional distress. Infant monkeys preferred the cloth mother even when it gave less milk than the wire mother. The Harlows concluded that emotional development requires affectionate cradling.

this human potential. Socialization is the process by which people learn their culture. They do so by (1) entering into and disengaging from a succession of roles and (2) becoming aware of themselves as they interact with others. A **role** is the behavior expected of a person occupying a particular position in society.

Convincing evidence of the importance of socialization in unleashing human potential comes from a study conducted by René Spitz (1945, 1962). Spitz compared children who were being raised in an orphanage with children who were being raised in a nursing home attached to a prison for women. Both institutions were hygienic and provided good food and medical care. However, the children's mothers cared for them in the nursing home, whereas just six nurses cared for the 45 children in the orphanage. The orphans therefore had much less contact with other people. Moreover, from their cribs, the nursing home infants could taste a slice of society. They saw other babies playing and receiving care. They saw mothers, doctors, and nurses talking, cleaning, serving food, and giving medical treatment. In contrast, the nurses in the orphanage would hang sheets from the cribs to prevent the infants from seeing the activities of the institution. Depriving the infants of social stimuli for most of the day apparently made them less demanding.

Social deprivation had other effects too. Because of the different patterns of child care just described, by the age of 9 to 12 months the orphans were more susceptible to infections and had a higher death rate than the children in the nursing home. By the time they were 2 to 3 years old, all the children from the nursing home were walking and talking, compared with fewer than 8 percent of the orphans. Normal children begin to play with their own genitals by the end of their first year. Spitz found that the orphans began this sort of play only in their fourth year. He took this behavior as a sign that they might have an impaired sexual life when they reached maturity. This outcome had occurred in rhesus monkeys raised in isolation. Spitz's natural experiment thus amounts to quite compelling evidence for the importance of childhood socialization in making us fully human. Without childhood socialization, most of our human potential remains undeveloped.

The Crystallization of Self-Identity

The formation of a sense of self continues in adolescence. Adolescence is a particularly turbulent period of rapid self-development. Consequently, many people can remember experiences from their youth that helped crystallize their self-identity. Do you? Robert Brym clearly recalls one such defining moment.

Personal Anecdote

"I can date precisely the pivot of my adolescence," says Robert. "I was in grade 10. It was December 16. At 4 p.m. I was a nobody and knew it. Half an hour later, I was walking home from school, delighting in the slight sting of snowflakes melting on my upturned face, knowing I had been swept up in a sea change.

"About 200 students sat impatiently in the auditorium that last day of school before the winter vacation. We were waiting for Mr. Garrod, the English teacher who headed the school's drama program, to announce the cast of *West Side Story*. I was hoping for a small speaking part and was not surprised when Mr. Garrod failed

Role: The behavior (or set of behaviors) expected of a person occupying a particular position in society.

to read my name as a chorus member. However, as the list of remaining characters grew shorter, I became despondent. Soon only the leads remained. I knew an unknown kid in grade 10 couldn't possibly be asked to play Tony, the male lead. Leads were almost always reserved for more experienced, grade-12 students.

"Then the thunderclap. 'Tony,' said Mr. Garrod, 'will be played by Robert Brym.' "'Who's Robert Brym?' whispered a girl seated two rows ahead of me. Her friend merely shrugged in reply. If she had asked *me* that question, I might have responded similarly. Like nearly all 15-year-olds, I was deeply involved in the process of figuring out exactly who I was. I had little idea of what I was good at. I was insecure about my social status. I wasn't sure what I believed in. In short, I was a typical teenager. I had only a vaguely defined sense of self.

"A sociologist once wrote that 'the central growth process in adolescence is to define the self through the clarification of experience and to establish self-esteem' (Friedenberg, 1959: 190). From this point of view, playing Tony in *West Side Story* turned out to be the first section of a bridge that led me from adolescence to adulthood. Playing Tony raised my social status in the eyes of my classmates, made me more self-confident, taught me I could be good at something, helped me to begin discovering parts of myself I hadn't known before, and showed me that I could act rather than merely be acted upon. In short, it was through my involvement in the play (and, subsequently, in many other plays throughout high school) that I began to develop a clear sense of who I am."

The crystallization of self-identity during adolescence is just one episode in a lifelong process of socialization. To paint a picture of the socialization process in its entirety, we must first review the main theories of how one's sense of self develops during early childhood. We then discuss the operation and relative influence of society's main socializing institutions, or "agents of socialization": families, schools, peer groups, and the mass media. In these settings, we learn, among other things, how to control our impulses, think of ourselves as members of different groups, value certain ideals, and perform various roles. You will see that these institutions do not always work hand in hand to produce happy, well-adjusted adults. They often give mixed messages and are commonly at odds with each other. They teach children and adolescents different and even contradictory lessons. You will also see that although recent developments give us more freedom to decide who we are, they can make socialization more disorienting than ever. Finally, in the concluding section of this chapter, we examine how decreasing supervision and guidance by adult family members, increasing assumption of adult responsibilities by youth, and declining participation in extracurricular activities are changing the nature of childhood and adolescence today. Some analysts even say that childhood and adolescence are vanishing before our eyes. Thus, the main theme of this chapter is that the development of one's self-identity is often a difficult and stressful process—and it is becoming more so.

It is during childhood that the contours of one's self are first formed. We therefore begin by discussing the most important social-scientific theories of how the self originates in the first years of life.

Theories of Childhood Socialization

Socialization begins soon after birth. Infants cry out, driven by elemental needs, and are gratified with food, comfort, and affection. Because their needs are usually satisfied immediately, at first they do not seem able to distinguish themselves from their main care-

Sigmund Freud (1856–1939) was the founder of psychoanalysis.

givers, usually their mothers. However, social interaction soon enables infants to begin developing a self-image or sense of **self**—a set of ideas and attitudes about who they are as independent beings.

Freud

Sigmund Freud proposed the first social-scientific interpretation of the process by which the self emerges (Freud, 1962 [1930], 1973 [1915–17]). Freud referred to the part of the self that demands immediate gratification as the **id.** According to Freud, a self image begins to emerge as soon as the id's demands are denied. For example, at a certain point, parents usually decide not to feed and comfort a baby every time it wakes up in the middle of the night. The parents' refusal at first incites howls of protest. Eventually, however, the baby learns certain practical lessons from the experience: to eat more before going to bed, to sleep for longer periods, and to go back to sleep if it wakes up. Equally important, the baby begins to sense that its needs differ from those of its parents, it has an existence independent of others, and it must somehow balance its needs with the realities of life.

Because of many such lessons in self-control, including toilet training, the child eventually develops a sense of what constitutes appropriate behavior and a moral sense of right and wrong. Soon a personal conscience, or to use Freud's term, a **superego,** crystallizes. The superego is a repository of cultural standards. In addition, the child develops a third component of the self, the **ego.** According to Freud, the ego is a psychological mechanism that, in well-adjusted individuals, balances the conflicting needs of the pleasure-seeking id and the restraining superego.

In Freud's view, the emergence of the superego is a painful and frustrating process. In fact, said Freud, to get on with our daily lives we have to repress memories of denying the id immediate gratification. Repression involves storing traumatic memories in a part of the self that we are not normally aware of: the **unconscious.** Repressed memories influence emotions and actions even after they are stored away. Particularly painful instances of childhood repression may cause various types of psychological problems later in life that require therapy to correct. However, some repression is the cost of civilization. As Freud said, we cannot live in an orderly society unless we deny the id (Freud, 1962 [1930]).

Criticisms of Freud's Analysis

Researchers have called into question many of the specifics of Freud's argument. Three criticisms stand out:

1. *The connections between early childhood development and adult personality are more complex than Freud assumed.* Freud wrote that when the ego fails to balance the needs of the id and the superego, individuals develop personality disorders. Typically, he said, this occurs if a young child is raised in an overly repressive atmosphere. To avoid later psychiatric problems, Freud and his followers recommended that young children should be raised in a relaxed and permissive environment. Such an environment is characterized by prolonged breast-feeding, nursing on demand, gradual weaning, lenient and late bladder and bowel training, frequent mothering, freedom from restraint and punishment, and so forth. However, sociological research reveals no connection between these aspects of early childhood training and the development of well-adjusted adults (Sewell, 1958).

2. *Many sociologists criticize Freud for gender bias in his analysis of male and female sexuality.* Freud argued that psychologically normal women are immature and dependent on men because they envy the male sexual organ. Women who are mature and in-

Self: Consists of one's ideas and attitudes about who one is.

Id: According to Freud, the part of the self that demands immediate gratification.

Superego: According to Freud, the part of the self that acts as a repository of cultural standards.

Ego: According to Freud, a psychological mechanism that balances the conflicting needs of the pleasure-seeking id and the restraining superego.

Unconscious: According to Freud, the part of the self that contains repressed memories that we are not normally aware of.

dependent he classified as abnormal. We discuss this fallacy in detail in Chapter 10, "Sexuality and Gender."

3. *Sociologists often criticize Freud for neglecting socialization after childhood.* Freud believed that the human personality is fixed by about the age of 5. However, sociologists have shown that socialization continues throughout the life course. We devote much of this chapter to exploring socialization after early childhood.

Despite these shortcomings, the sociological implications of Freud's theory are profound. His main sociological contribution was his insistence that the self emerges during early social interaction and that early childhood experience exerts a lasting impact on personality development. As we will now see, American sociologists and social psychologists took these ideas in a still more sociological direction.

Cooley's Symbolic Interactionism

More than a century ago, the American sociologist Charles Horton Cooley introduced the idea of the **looking-glass self,** making him a founding father of the symbolic interactionist tradition and an early contributor to the sociological study of socialization. Cooley observed that when we interact with others, they gesture and react to us. This allows us to imagine how we appear to them. We then judge how others evaluate us. Finally, from these judgments we develop a self-concept or a set of feelings and ideas about who we are. In other words, our feelings about who we are depend largely on how we see ourselves evaluated by others. Just as we see our physical body reflected in a mirror, so we see our social selves reflected in people's gestures and reactions to us (Cooley, 1902). When teachers evaluate students negatively, for example, students may develop a negative self-concept that causes them to do poorly in school. Poor performance may have as much to do with teachers' negative evaluations as with students' innate abilities (Hamachek, 1995; see Chapter 12, "Religion and Education"). Here, succinctly put, we have the hallmarks of what came to be known as symbolic interactionism—the idea that in the course of face-to-face communication, people engage in a creative process of attaching meaning to things.

Mead

George Herbert Mead (1934) took up and developed Cooley's idea of the looking-glass self. Like Freud, Mead noted that a subjective and impulsive aspect of the self is present from birth. Mead called it simply the **I.** Again like Freud, Mead argued that a repository of culturally approved standards emerges as part of the self during social interaction. Mead called this objective, social component of the self the **me.** However, whereas Freud focused on the denial of the id's impulses as the mechanism that generates the self's objective side, Mead drew attention to the unique human capacity to "take the role of the other" as the source of the "me."

Mead understood that human communication involves seeing yourself from other people's points of view. How, for example, do you interpret your mother's smile? Does it mean "I love you," "I find you humorous," or something else entirely? According to Mead, you can find the answer by using your imagination to take your mother's point of view for a moment and see yourself as she sees you. In other words, you must see yourself objectively as a "me" to understand your mother's communicative act. All human communication depends on being able to take the role of the other, wrote Mead. The self thus emerges from people using symbols such as words and gestures to com-

Looking-glass self: Cooley's description of the way our feelings about who we are depend largely on how we see ourselves evaluated by others.

I: According to Mead, the subjective and impulsive aspect of the self that is present from birth.

Me: According to Mead, the objective component of the self that emerges as people communicate symbolically and learn to take the role of the other.

By emphasizing that moral development is socially differentiated and does not follow universal rules, researcher Carol Gilligan made a major sociological contribution to our understanding of childhood development.

municate. It follows that the "me" is not present from birth. It emerges only gradually during social interaction.

Mead's Four Stages of Development: Role Taking

Unlike Freud, Mead did not view the emergence of the self as a trauma. On the contrary, he thought it was fun. Mead saw the self as developing in four stages of role taking. At first, children learn to use language and other symbols by *imitating* important people in their lives, such as their mother and father. Mead called such people **significant others.** Second, children pretend to *be* other people. That is, they use their imaginations to role-play in games such as "house," "school," and "doctor." Third, about the time they reach the age of 7, children learn to play complex games that require them to simultaneously take the role of *several* other people. In baseball, for example, the infielders have to be aware of the expectations of everyone in the infield. A shortstop may catch a line drive. If she wants to make a double play, she must almost instantly be aware that a runner is trying to reach second base and that the person playing second base expects her to throw there. If she hesitates, she probably cannot execute the double play. Once a child can think in this complex way, she can begin the fourth stage in the development of the self, which involves taking the role of what Mead called the **generalized other.** Years of experience may teach an individual that other people, employing the cultural standards of their society, usually regard her as funny or temperamental or intelligent. A person's image of these cultural standards and how they are applied to her is what Mead meant by the generalized other.

Since Mead, some psychologists interested in the problem of childhood socialization have analyzed how the style, complexity, and abstractness of thinking (or "cognitive skills") develop in distinct stages from infancy to the late teenage years (Piaget and Inhelder, 1969). Other psychologists have analyzed how the ability to think in abstract moral terms develops in stages (Kohlberg, 1981). From a sociological point of view, however, it is important to recognize that the development of cognitive and moral skills is more than just the unfolding of a person's innate characteristics. It is also shaped by the structure of one's society and one's position in it.

Gilligan and Gender Differences

One of the best-known examples of how social position affects socialization comes from the research of Carol Gilligan. Gilligan demonstrated that sociological factors help explain differences in the sense of self that boys and girls usually develop. Parents and teachers tend to pass on different cultural standards to boys and girls. Such adult authorities usually define the ideal woman as eager to please and therefore nonassertive. Most girls learn this lesson as they mature. The fact that girls usually encounter more male and fewer female teachers and other authority figures as they grow up reinforces the lesson. Consequently, much research shows that girls tend to develop lower self-esteem than boys, although it seems doubtful that teenage girls in general experience the decline in self-esteem that Gilligan detected in her early work (Brown and Gilligan, 1992; Kling et al., 1999).

Civilizational Differences

In a like manner, sociological factors help explain the development of different ways of thinking or cognitive styles of different civilizations (Cole, 1995; Vygotsky, 1987). Consider, for example, the contrast between ancient China and ancient Greece. In part because of complex irrigation needs, the rice agriculture of ancient southern China required substantial cooperation among neighbors. It had to be centrally organized in

Significant others: People who play important roles in the early socialization experiences of children.

Generalized other: According to Mead, a person's image of cultural standards and how they apply to him or her.

an elaborate hierarchy within a large state. Harmony and social order were therefore central to ancient Chinese life. Ancient Chinese thinking, in turn, tended to stress the importance of mutual social obligation and consensus rather than debate. Ancient Chinese philosophies focused on the way in which whole systems, not analytical categories, cause processes and events.

In contrast, the hills and seashores of ancient Greece were suited to small-scale herding and fishing rather than large-scale, centrally organized agriculture. Ancient Greece was less socially complex than ancient China. It was more politically decentralized, and it gave its citizens more personal freedom. As a result, philosophies tended to be analytical, which means, among other things, that processes and events were viewed as the result of discrete categories rather than whole systems. Markedly different civilizations grew up on these different cognitive foundations; ways of thinking depended less on people's innate characteristics than on the structure of society (Nisbett, Peng, Choi, and Norenzayan, 2001).

We thus see that society plays a major role in shaping the way we think and the way we think of ourselves. It does so through various "agents of socialization," including families, schools, peer groups, and, in modern times, the mass media. Let us now consider in detail how these institutions socialize us.

Agents of Socialization

Families

The family is the most important agent of **primary socialization,** the process of mastering the basic skills required to function in society during childhood. Marriage is less popular than it once was (Box 3.1), but the family is still well suited to providing the kind of careful, intimate attention required for primary socialization. The family is a small group. Its members are in frequent face-to-face contact. Most parents love their children and are therefore highly motivated to care for them. These characteristics make most families ideal for teaching small children everything from language to their place in the world.

The socialization function of the family was more pronounced a century ago, partly because adult family members were more readily available for child care than they are today. As industry grew across the United States, families left farming for city work in factories and offices. Especially after the 1950s, many women had to work outside the home for a wage to maintain an adequate standard of living for their families. Fathers, for the most part, did not compensate by spending more time with their children. In fact, because divorce rates have increased and many fathers have less contact with their children after divorce, children probably see less of their fathers on average now than they did a century ago. In some countries, such as Sweden and France, the creation of state-funded child-care facilities compensated for these developments by helping teach, supervise, and discipline children (see Chapter 11, "Families"). In the United States, however, child care—and therefore childhood socialization—became a big social problem, leading in some cases to child neglect and abuse.

Schools

For children older than 5, the child-care problem was resolved partly by the growth of the public school system, which was increasingly responsible for **secondary socialization,** or socialization outside the family after childhood. In addition, American industry needed

Primary socialization: The process of acquiring the basic skills needed to function in society during childhood. Primary socialization usually takes place in a family.

Secondary socialization: Socialization outside the family after childhood.

BOX 3.1
SOCIOLOGY AT THE MOVIES

Wedding Crashers (2005)

John Beckwith (Owen Wilson) and Jeremy Gray (Vince Vaughn) are 30-something partners in a divorce mediation firm. Neither is married because of their belief that, as Jeremy says during one particularly heated mediation, "the real enemy here is the institution of marriage. It's not realistic. It's crazy."

So what do these handsome, single, professional men do for excitement come spring? They crash weddings, party till dawn, and bed the unsuspecting beauties who fall for their fast talk and scripted charm.

Their activities raise an important sociological issue. How did it come about that people old enough to be considered adults just a couple of generations ago now seem stuck between adolescence and adulthood? They aren't married. Some of them live with their parents. They may still be in school. And some of them lack steady, well-paying, full-time jobs. They represent a growing category of young adults who are often a big worry to their elders.

The number of Americans in their 20s and early 30s living with their parents has increased rapidly in recent decades. One reason for this phenomenon is economic. In the first few decades after World War II, housing and education costs were low, and the number of years one had to spend in school to get a steady, well-paying job was

John Beckwith (Owen Wilson) and Jeremy Gray (Vince Vaughn) stuck between adolescence and adulthood in *Wedding Crashers*.

© New Line/courtesy Everett Collection

modest. Today, housing and education costs are high, and young people must typically spend more years in school before starting their careers (Furstenberg et al., 2004). As a result, many young people continue to live in their parents' home into their 20s and 30s as a matter of economic necessity.

For upper-middle-class families, a change in child-rearing practices also seems to account in part for the reluctance of some young adults to grow up. Many well-educated and well-to-do parents seem to be raising children who are simply too

dependent. They are reluctant to insist that their children get part-time jobs when they are in their mid-teens, and they neglect to teach them the importance of saving money by always giving them as much money as they want. They provide too much assistance with schoolwork (either by themselves or by hiring tutors), and they organize too many extracurricular activities for their children, thus not giving them enough space to figure out their interests for themselves.

In *Wedding Crashers*, John and Jeremy finally seem able to break the mould when Jeremy marries Gloria Cleary (Isla Fisher) and John commits to her sister, Claire (Rachel McAdams). But as the happy foursome drive away, they get the bright idea of posing as a folk-singing quartet from Utah and crashing a wedding for the great Japanese food that is bound to be served. It seems that their parents' worries are far from over.

Critical Thinking

- Some people call today's young adults "slackers." They justify their opinion by pointing to the willingness of many young adults to live with their parents. Do you think their opinion is justified? Why or why not?

CENGAGENOW

Learn more about **Agents of Socialization** by going through the Agents of Socialization Learning Module.

better trained and educated employees. Therefore, by 1918, every state required children to attend school until the age of 16 or the completion of grade 8. By the beginning of the 21st century, more than four-fifths of Americans older than 25 had graduated from high school and about one-fourth had graduated from college. By these standards, Americans are the most highly educated people in the world.

Although schools help prepare students for the job market, they do not necessarily give them an accurate picture of what the job market requires. In 1992, for example, a nationwide survey highlighted the mismatch between the ambitions of American high school students and the projected needs of the American economy in 2005 (Schneider and Stevenson, 1999: 77–8). The number of high school students wanting to become lawyers and judges was five times the projected number needed. The number who wanted to become writers, artists, entertainers, and athletes was 14 times higher than expected openings in 2005. At the other extreme, there were projected to be five times more administrative and clerical jobs in 2005 than students interested in such work in 1992. Seven times more service jobs were projected to be available than teenagers who wanted them. American high school students, it seems safe to say, often have unrealistically high expectations about the kinds of jobs they are likely to get when they finish their formal education (▶Figure 3.1).

Class, Race, and Conflict Theory

Instructing students in academic and vocational subjects is just one part of the school's job. In addition, a **hidden curriculum** teaches students what will be expected of them in the larger society after they graduate. The hidden curriculum teaches them how to be conventionally "good citizens." Most parents approve of this instruction. According to a survey conducted in the United States and the highly industrialized countries of Europe, the capacity of schools to socialize students is more important to the public than the teaching of all academic subjects except mathematics (Galper, 1998).

What is the content of the hidden curriculum? In the family, children tend to be evaluated on the basis of personal and emotional criteria. As students, however, they are led to believe that they are evaluated solely on the basis of their performance on impersonal, standardized tests. They are told that similar criteria will be used to evaluate them in the world of work. The lesson is only partly true. As you will see in Chapter 7 ("Social

Hidden curriculum: Instruction in what will be expected of students as conventionally good citizens once they leave school.

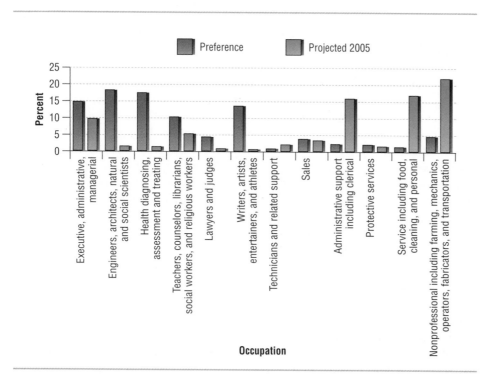

▶FIGURE 3.1
Adolescent Job Preferences and Projected Jobs in Paid Labor Force, United States, 2005 (in percent)

Source: *The Ambitious Generation* by B. Schneider and D. Stevenson, copyright 1999 Yale University Press. Reprinted by permission.

Stratification: United States and Global Perspectives"), Chapter 9 ("Race and Ethnicity"), Chapter 10 ("Sexuality and Gender"), and Chapter 12 ("Religion and Education"), not just performance but also class, gender, and racial criteria help determine success in school and in the work world. But the accuracy of the lesson is not the issue here. The important point is that the hidden curriculum has done its job if it convinces students that they are judged on the basis of performance alone. A successful hidden curriculum also teaches students punctuality, respect for authority, the importance of competition in leading to excellent performance, and other conformist behaviors and beliefs that are expected of good citizens, conventionally defined.

The idea of the hidden curriculum was first proposed by conflict theorists, who, you will recall, see an ongoing struggle between privileged and disadvantaged groups whenever they probe beneath the surface of social life (Willis, 1984 [1977]). From the point of view of conflict theory, some poor and racial-minority students accept the hidden curriculum, thereby learning to act like conventionally good citizens. Other such students reject the hidden curriculum, consequently doing poorly in school and eventually entering the work world near the bottom of the socioeconomic hierarchy. In either case, the hidden curriculum helps sustain the overall structure of society, with its privileges and disadvantages.

The Self-Fulfilling Prophecy

Why do some poor and racial-minority students reject the hidden curriculum? Because their experience and the experience of their friends, peers, and family members may make them skeptical about the ability of school to open job opportunities for them. As a result, they rebel against the authority of the school. Expected to be polite and studious, they openly violate rules and neglect their work.

Believing that education does not lead to economic success can become a **self-fulfilling prophecy,** which is an expectation that helps cause the situation it predicts. William Isaac Thomas and Dorothy Swaine Thomas had a similar idea in stating what became known as the **Thomas theorem:** "Situations we define as real become real in their consequences" (Thomas, 1966 [1931]: 301). For example, believing that school won't help you get ahead may cause you to perform poorly in school, and you are more likely to end up near the bottom of the class structure if you perform poorly in school.

Teachers, for their part, can also develop expectations that turn into self-fulfilling prophecies. In one famous study, two researchers informed the teachers in a primary school that they were going to administer a special test to the pupils to predict intellectual "blooming." In fact, the test was just a standard IQ test. After the test, they told teachers which students they could expect to become high achievers and which they could expect to become low achievers. In fact, the researchers assigned pupils to the two groups at random. At the end of the year, the researchers repeated the IQ test. They found that the students singled out as high achievers scored significantly higher than those singled out as low achievers. Because the only difference between the two groups of students was that teachers expected one group to perform well and the other to perform poorly, the researchers concluded that teachers' expectations alone influenced students' performance (Rosenthal and Jacobson, 1968). The clear implication of this research is that if a teacher believes that poor or minority-group children are likely to perform poorly in school, chances are they will. That is because students who are members of groups that are widely expected to perform poorly *internalize* social expectations; they feel anxiety about their performance, and the anxiety lowers their performance level (Steele, 1995).

Self-fulfilling prophecy: An expectation that helps bring about the result that it predicts.

Thomas theorem: States that "situations we define as real become real in their consequences."

Peer Groups

A second socialization agent whose importance increased in the 20th century is the **peer group.** Peer groups consist of individuals who are not necessarily friends but are about the same age and of similar status. (**Status** refers to a recognized social position that an individual can occupy.) Peer groups help children and adolescents separate themselves from their families and develop independent sources of identity. They are especially influential in lifestyle issues such as appearance, social activities, and dating. In fact, from middle childhood through adolescence, the peer group is often the dominant socializing agent.

As you probably learned from your own experience, conflict often exists between the values promoted by the family and those promoted by the adolescent peer group. Adolescent peer groups are controlled by youth. Through these groups, young people begin to develop their own identities by rejecting some parental values, experimenting with new elements of culture, and engaging in various forms of rebellious behavior, which include consuming alcohol and drugs and smoking cigarettes (▶Table 3.1). In contrast, parents control families. They represent the values of childhood. Under these circumstances, such issues as tobacco, drug, and alcohol use; hair and dress styles; political views; music; and curfew times are likely to become points of conflict between the generations.

We should not, however, overstate the significance of adolescent-parent conflict. For one thing, the conflict is usually temporary. Once adolescents mature, the family exerts a more enduring influence on many important issues. Research shows that families have more influence than do peer groups over the educational aspirations and the political, social, and religious preferences of adolescents and college students (Davies and Kandel, 1981; Milem, 1998; Sherkat, 1998).

A second reason why we should not exaggerate the extent of adolescent-parent discord is that peer groups are not just sources of conflict. They also help *integrate* young people into the larger society. A study of preadolescent children in a small city in the Northwest illustrates this point. Over 8 years, sociologists Patricia and Peter Adler conducted in-depth interviews with school children between the ages of 8 and 11. They lived in a well-to-do community composed of about 80,000 whites and 10,000 Hispanics and other minority-group members (Adler and Adler, 1998). In each school they visited, they found a system

Peer group: A group composed of people who are about the same age and of similar status. The peer group acts as an agent of socialization.

Status: A recognized social position that an individual can occupy.

▶TABLE 3.1

Yearly Alcohol-Related Problems in American Colleges

Problem	Number of College Students between the Ages of 18 and 24 Who Experience the Problem Each Year
Students who die from alcohol-related unintentional injuries, including motor vehicle crashes	1,700
Students assaulted by another student who has been drinking	696,000+
Students who are victims of alcohol-related sexual assault or date rape	97,000
Students who have sex but are too intoxicated to know if they consented	100,000+
Students who develop an alcohol-related health problem	150,000
Students who drive under the influence of alcohol	2,100,000

Source: "A Snapshot..." (2007).

of cliques arranged in a strict hierarchy, much like the arrangement of classes and racial groups in adult society. In schools with a substantial number of Hispanics and nonwhites, cliques were divided by race.

Nonwhite and Hispanic cliques were usually less popular than white cliques. In all schools, the most popular boys were highly successful in competitive and aggressive achievement-oriented activities, especially athletics. The most popular girls came from well-to-do and permissive families. One of the main bases of their popularity was that they had the means and the opportunity to participate in the most interesting social activities, ranging from skiing to late-night parties. Physical attractiveness was also an important basis of girls' popularity. Thus, elementary school peer groups prepared these youngsters for the class and racial inequalities of the adult world and the gender-specific criteria that would often be used to evaluate them as adults, such as competitiveness in the case of boys and attractiveness in the case of girls. (For more on gender socialization, see the discussion of the mass media following in this chapter and in Chapter 10, "Sexuality and Gender.") What we learn from this research is that the function of peer groups is not just to help adolescents form an independent identity by separating them from their families. In addition, peer groups teach young people how to adapt to the ways of the larger society.

The Mass Media

Like the school and the peer group, the mass media also became an increasingly important socializing agent in the 20th century. The mass media include TV, radio, movies, videos, CDs, audiotapes, the Internet, newspapers, magazines, and books.

The fastest-growing mass medium is the Internet (▶Figure 3.2). However, TV viewing still consumes more of the average American's time than any other mass medium. More than 98 percent of American households own a TV. On average, each TV is turned on for 7 hours a day. The University of Maryland's Americans' Use of Time Project collected national survey data showing that watching TV was the most time-consuming waking activity for women between the ages of 18 and 24 and the second

▶FIGURE 3.2
Number of Internet Users, 1996–2005

Source: "Face of the Web . . ." (2000); "Internet Growth" (2000); "Internet Usage Statistics . . ." (2005, 2008).

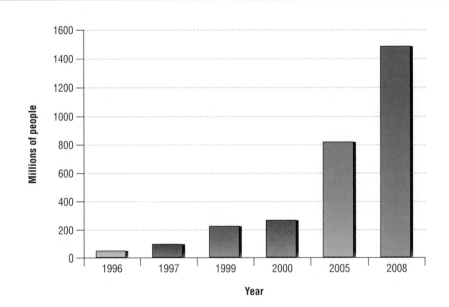

most time-consuming waking activity for men in the same age-group (▶Figure 3.3). Survey research shows that American adults watched more TV in the 1970s than in the 1960s, more in the 1980s than in the 1970s, and more in the early 1990s than in the 1980s. Since the mid-1990s, however, Internet use has been eating into TV viewing hours, especially among more highly educated Americans. Heavy watchers of TV are concentrated among socially disadvantaged groups, and that trend is intensifying over time (Hao, 1994; Robinson and Bianchi, 1997) (▶Table 3.2).

Self-Socialization

Children and adolescents use the mass media for entertainment and stimulation. The mass media also help young people cope with anger, anxiety, and unhappiness. Finally, the cultural materials provided by the mass media help young people construct their identities—for example, by emulating the appearance and behavior of appealing movie stars, rock idols, and sports heroes. In performing these functions, the mass media offer youth much choice. Many Americans have access to scores of radio stations and TV channels, hundreds of magazines, thousands of CD titles, hundreds of

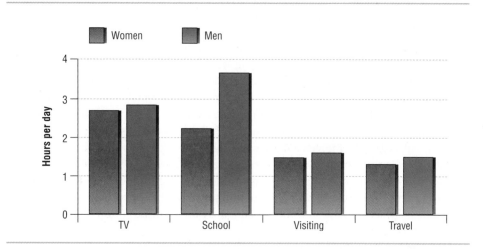

▶FIGURE 3.3
Top Four Waking Activities of American Women and Men, Ages 18–24 (hours per day)

Source: "The Children's Hours" by John P. Robinson and Suzanne Bianchi, *American Demographics*, Vol. 20, No. 4, December 1997.

▶TABLE 3.2
Hours of TV Viewing per Week by Highest Year of School Completed, United States, 2006, in percent (n = 1,984)

Hours per Day Watching TV	HIGHEST YEAR OF SCHOOL COMPLETED				
	0–11	12	13–14	15–16	17–20
0	3.1	1.8	4.0	6.1	5.7
1	15.4	16.0	21.6	25.0	31.9
2	23.7	27.5	28.5	30.6	36.9
3	15.1	20.4	16.9	18.0	11.4
4	13.5	13.7	10.8	9.8	7.6
5	7.1	8.5	9.7	4.2	2.7
6+	22.2	12.1	8.5	6.3	3.8
Total	100.0	100.0	100.0	100.0	100.0
n	325	495	473	428	263

Source: National Opinion Research Center (2008a).

thousands of books, and millions of websites. Most of us can gain access to hip-hop, heavy metal, or Haydn with equal ease. Thus, whereas adolescents have little choice over how they are socialized by their family and their school, the very proliferation of the mass media gives them more say over which media messages will influence them. To a degree, the mass media allow adolescents to engage in what sociologist Jeffrey Jensen Arnett (1995) calls **self-socialization,** or choosing socialization influences from the wide variety of mass media offerings.

Gender Roles, the Mass Media, and the Feminist Approach to Socialization

Although people are to some extent free to choose socialization influences from the mass media, they choose some influences more than others. Specifically, they tend to choose influences that are more pervasive, fit existing cultural standards, and are made especially appealing by those who control the mass media. We can illustrate this point by considering how feminist sociologists analyze gender roles. **Gender roles** are widely shared expectations about how males and females are supposed to act. They are of special interest to feminist sociologists, who claim that people are not born knowing how to express masculinity and femininity in conventional ways. Instead, say feminist sociologists, people *learn* gender roles, in part through the mass media.

The learning of gender roles through the mass media begins when small children see that only a kiss from Prince Charming will save Snow White from eternal sleep. Here is an early lesson about who can expect to be passive and who potent. The lesson continues in magazines, romance novels, television, advertisements, music, and the Internet. A central theme in popular romance novels, for example, is the transformation of women's bodies into objects for men's pleasure. In the typical popular romance, men are expected to be the sexual aggressors. They are typically more experienced and promiscuous than women. Women are expected to desire love before intimacy. They are assumed to be sexually passive, giving only subtle cues to indicate their interest in male overtures. Supposedly lacking the urgent sex drive that preoccupies men, women are often held accountable for moral standards and contraception (Grescoe, 1996; Jensen, 1984) (Box 3.2).

Boys and girls do not passively accept such messages about appropriate gender roles. They often interpret them in unique ways and sometimes resist them. For the most part, however, they try to develop skills that will help them perform gender roles in a conventional way (Eagley and Wood, 1999: 412–13). Of course, conventions change. What children learn about femininity and masculinity today is less sexist than what they learned just a generation or two ago. Comparing *Cinderella* and *Snow White* with *Mulan,* for example, we immediately see that children who watch Disney movies today are sometimes presented with more assertive and heroic female role models than the passive heroines of the 1930s and 1940s. Yet we must not exaggerate the amount of change in gender socialization. *Cinderella* and *Snow White* are still popular movies. Moreover, for every *Mulan* there is a *Little Mermaid,* a movie that simply modernizes old themes about female passivity and male conquest.

As the learning of gender roles through the mass media suggests, not all media influences are created equal. We may be free to choose which media messages influence us. However, most people are inclined to choose the messages that are most widespread, most closely aligned with existing cultural standards, and made most enticing by the mass media. As feminist sociologists remind us, in the case of gender roles these messages support conventional expectations about how males and females are supposed to act.

CENGAGENOW™

Learn more about **Gender Roles** by going through the Gender Roles and Videos Animation.

Self-socialization: Involves choosing socialization influences from the wide variety of mass media offerings.

Gender roles: The set of behaviors associated with widely shared expectations about how males and females are supposed to act.

BOX 3.2
MASS MEDIA AND SOCIETY

Learning Gender Roles through Popular Romance Novels

"Frantically she got up, her eyes flooding with tears, knocking over her chair in her desperate attempt to avoid crying in front of Alex and completely humiliating herself. But as she tried to run to the sanctuary of the bathroom the length of her bathrobe hampered her, and she had only taken a few steps before Alex caught up with her, bodily grabbed hold of her and swung her around to face him, his own face taut with emotion . . .

'Men aren't worth loving . . .'

'No?' Alex asked her huskily.

'No,' Beth repeated firmly, but somehow or other her denial had lost a good deal of its potency. Was that perhaps because of the way Alex was cupping her face, his mouth gently caressing hers, his lips teasing the stubbornly tight line of hers, coaxing it to soften and part . . . ?

As Alex continued to kiss her, the most dizzying sweet sensation filled Beth. She had the most overpowering urge to cling blissfully to Alex and melt into his arms like an old-fashioned Victorian maiden. Behind her closed eyelids she could have sworn there danced sunlit images of tulle and confetti scented with the lilies of a bridal bouquet, and the sound of a triumphant 'Wedding March' swelled and boomed and gold sunbeams formed a circle around her.

Dreamily Beth sighed, and then smiled beneath Alex's kiss, her own lips parting in happy acquiescence to the explorative thrust of his tongue."

———————

Source: Jordan (1999: 97-8).

Critical Thinking

● What are the characteristics of the male and female gender roles presented in this passage from a popular romance novel?

● What role if any do such novels play in reinforcing traditional gender roles?

A Harlequin Romance

Resocialization and Total Institutions

In concluding our discussion of socialization agents, we must underline the importance of **resocialization** in contributing to the lifelong process of social learning. Resocialization takes place when powerful socializing agents deliberately cause rapid change in people's values, roles, and self-conceptions, sometimes against their will.

You can see resocialization at work in the ceremonies that are staged when someone joins a fraternity, a sorority, the U.S. Marines, or a religious order. Such a ceremony, or **initiation rite,** signifies the transition of the individual from one group to another and ensures his or her loyalty to the new group. Initiation rites require new recruits to abandon old self-perceptions and assume new identities. When initiation rites take place during resocialization, they typically involve a three-stage ceremony: (1) separation from one's old status and identity (ritual rejection); (2) degradation, disorientation, and stress (ritual death); and (3) acceptance of the new group culture and status (ritual rebirth).

Much resocialization takes place in what sociologist Erving Goffman (1961) called **total institutions.** Total institutions are settings where people are isolated from the larger society and under the strict control and constant supervision of a specialized staff. Asylums

Resocialization: Occurs when powerful socializing agents deliberately cause rapid change in one's values, roles, and self-conception, sometimes against one's will.

Initiation rite: A ritual that signifies the transition of the individual from one group to another and ensures his or her loyalty to the new group.

Total institutions: Settings where people are isolated from the larger society and under the strict control and constant supervision of a specialized staff.

Jonathan Blair/CORBIS

Not all initiation rites or "rites of passage" involve resocialization. Some rites of passage are a normal part of primary and secondary socialization and merely signify the transition from one status to another. Here, an Italian family celebrates the first communion of a young boy.

CENGAGENOW™

Learn more about **Resocialization** by going through the Resocialization Animation.

and prisons are examples of total institutions. Because of the "pressure cooker" atmosphere in such institutions, resocialization in total institutions is often rapid and thorough, even in the absence of initiation rites.

A famous failed experiment illustrates the immense resocializing capacity of total institutions (Haney, Banks, and Zimbardo, 1973; Zimbardo, 1972). In the early 1970s, researchers at Stanford University created their own mock prison. They paid two dozen male volunteers to act as guards and inmates. The volunteers were mature, emotionally stable, intelligent college students from middle-class homes. By the flip of a coin, half the volunteers were designated prisoners, the other half guards. At the mock prison, each prisoner was stripped, deloused, put into prison-issue clothes, given a number, and placed in a cell with two other inmates. The guards made up their own rules for maintaining law and order.

To understand better what it means to be a prisoner or a prison guard, the researchers wanted to observe and record social interaction in the mock prison for 2 weeks. However, they were forced to end the experiment abruptly after only 6 days because what they witnessed frightened them. In less than a week, the prisoners and prison guards could no longer tell the difference between the roles they were playing and their "real" selves. Much of the socialization that these young men had undergone over a period of about 20 years was quickly suspended.

About a third of the guards began to treat the prisoners like despicable animals, taking pleasure in cruelty. Even the guards who were regarded by the prisoners as tough but fair stopped short of interfering in the tyrannical and arbitrary use of power by the most sadistic guards. All of the prisoners became servile and dehumanized, thinking only about survival, escape, and their growing hatred of the guards. If they were thinking as college students, they could have walked out of the experiment at any time. Some of the prisoners did in fact beg for parole. However, by the fifth day of the experiment they were so programmed to think of themselves as prisoners that they returned docilely to their cells when their request for parole was denied.

The Stanford experiment suggests that your sense of self and the roles you play are not as fixed as you may think. Radically alter your social setting, and like the college students in the experiment, your self-conception and patterned behavior are likely to change too. Such change is most evident among people undergoing resocialization in total institutions. However, the sociological eye is able to observe the flexibility of the self in all social settings, including those that routinely greet the individual in adult life.

Socialization across the Life Course

Adult Socialization and the Flexible Self

The development of the self is a lifelong process (Mortimer and Simmons, 1978). When young adults enter a profession or get married, they must learn new occupational and family roles. Retirement and old age present an entirely new set of challenges. Giving up a job, seeing children leave home and start their own families, and losing a spouse and close friends—all these changes later in life require people to think of themselves in new ways and to redefine who they are. Many new roles are predictable. To help us learn them we often engage in **anticipatory socialization,** which involves beginning to take on the norms and behaviors of the roles to which we aspire. (Think of 15-year-old fans of the

Anticipatory socialization: Involves beginning to take on the norms and behaviors of a role to which one aspires but does not yet occupy.

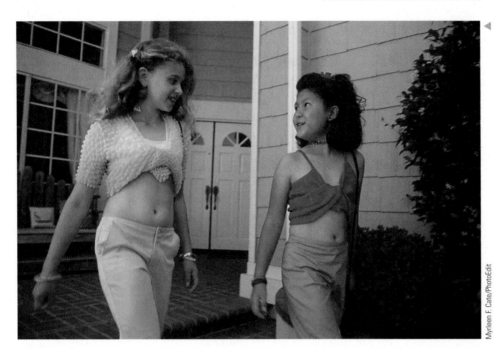

Myrleen F. Cate/PhotoEdit

Much socialization takes place informally, with the participants unaware that they are being socialized. These girls are learning gender roles as they go to the mall dressed like Britney Spears.

TV show *Friends* learning from the show what it might mean to be a young adult.) Other new roles are unpredictable. You might unexpectedly fall in love and marry someone from a different ethnic, racial, or religious group. You might experience a sudden and difficult transition from peace to war. If so, you will have to learn new roles and adopt new cultural values or at least modify old ones. Even in adulthood, then, the self remains flexible.

Today, people's identities change faster, more often, and more completely than they did just a couple of decades ago. One factor contributing to the growing flexibility of the self is globalization. People are now less obliged to accept the culture into which they are born. Because of globalization, they are freer to combine elements of culture from a wide variety of historical periods and geographical settings.

A second factor increasing our freedom to design our selves is our growing ability to fashion new bodies from old. People have always defined themselves partly in terms of their bodies; your self-conception is influenced by whether you're a man or a woman, tall or short, healthy or ill, conventionally attractive or plain. But our bodies used to be fixed by nature. People could do nothing to change the fact that they were born with certain features and grew older at a certain rate.

Now, however, you can change your body, and therefore your self-conception, radically and virtually at will—if, that is, you can afford it. Some examples of such changes include the following:

- Bodybuilding, aerobic exercise, and weight reduction regimens are more popular than ever.
- Sex-change operations, although infrequent, are no longer a rarity.
- Plastic surgery allows people to buy new breasts, noses, lips, eyelids, and hair—and to remove unwanted fat, skin, and hair from various parts of their bodies. In 2007, more than 5.5 million Americans had cosmetic surgery—and that excludes "minimally

CENGAGENOW

Learn more about **Roles** by going through the Roles and Status Learning Module.

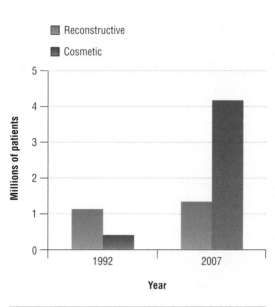

▶FIGURE 3.4
Plastic Surgery, United States, 1992–2007

Source: American Society of Plastic Surgeons (2008).

invasive" procedures such as collagen and Botox (▶Figure 3.4). Although the vast majority of people who undergo cosmetic surgery are women, the number of men opting for cosmetic surgery has doubled in the past two decades.

● The use of collagen, Botox, and other nonsurgical procedures to remove facial wrinkles is increasingly common. In fact, a growing number of plastic surgeons organize Botox parties— sort of like Tupperware parties but with needles. At a typical Botox party, a plastic surgeon invites about 10 clients to an evening of champagne, chocolate truffles, brie, and botulinum toxin type A. When injected in the face, at a cost of about $300 per injection, the toxin relaxes muscles and erases signs of aging for a few months.

● Organ transplants are routine. At any given time about 50,000 Americans are waiting for a replacement organ. Brisk, illegal international trade in human hearts, lungs, kidneys, livers, and eyes enables well-to-do people to enhance and extend their lives (Rothman, 1998).

● In 2002 Kevin Warwick, a professor of cybernetics in the United Kingdom, became the first cyborg (part man, part computer) when he had a computer chip implanted in his wrist and connected to about 100 neurons. A wire now runs under the skin up his arm to a point just below his elbow, where a junction box allows data from his neurons to be transmitted wirelessly to a computer. He plans on implanting a similar device in his wife. Through an Internet connection, they will each be able to feel what the other feels in his or her arm. Warwick predicts that before 2020 more sophisticated implants will allow a primitive form of telepathy (Akin, 2002).

As these examples illustrate, many new opportunities for changing one's self-conception have been introduced in recent decades.

Identity and the Internet

Further complicating the process of identity formation today is the growth of the Internet and its audiovisual component, the World Wide Web. In the 1980s and early 1990s most observers believed that social interaction by means of computer would involve only the exchange of information among individuals. It turns out they were wrong. Computer-assisted social interaction can profoundly affect how people think of themselves (Brym and Lenton, 2001; Haythornwaite and Wellman, 2002;).

Internet users interact socially by exchanging text, images, and sound via e-mail, messaging services such as MSN Messenger, Facebook, Internet phone, videoconferencing, computer-assisted work groups, and online dating services. In the process, they form **virtual communities.** Virtual communities are associations of people, scattered across the country or the planet, who communicate via computer and modem about subjects of common interest. For example, research shows that undergraduates use Facebook to get information and emotional support. In the process, they tend to solidify existing offline relationships and, thus, help to strengthen their community. The top three perceived audiences for undergraduate Facebook users are "my old high school friends," "people in my

Virtual community: An association of people, scattered across the country, continent, or planet, who communicate via computer and modem about a subject of common interest.

classes," and "other friends." "Total strangers" are the fourth-ranked audience, followed by "someone I met at a party" and "family." Even when students meet total strangers online, they tend to be strangers within a known and trusted institution, notably their college (Ellison, Steinfeld, and Lampe, 2007).

Some virtual communities are short-lived and loosely structured in the sense that they have few formal rules and people quickly drift in and out of them. Chat groups are typical of this genre. Other virtual communities are more enduring and structured. For example, discussion groups cater to people's interest in specialized subjects such as Latino culture, BMWs, dating, or white-water canoeing. Still other virtual communities are highly structured, with many formal rules and relatively stable membership. For example, MUDs (multiple user dimensions), such as Second Life, are computer programs that allow people to role-play and engage in a sort of collective fantasy. These programs define the aims and rules of the virtual community and the objects and spaces it contains. Users around the world log on to the MUD from their computers and define their character—their identity—any way they wish. They interact with other users by exchanging text messages or by having their "avatars" (graphical representations) act and speak for them.

Because virtual communities allow interaction using concealed identities, people are free to assume new identities and are encouraged to discover parts of themselves they were formerly unaware of. In virtual communities, shy people can become bold, normally assertive people can become voyeurs, old people can become young, straight people can become gay, and women can become men (Turkle, 1995). Experience on the Internet thus reinforces our main point. In recent decades, the self has become increasingly flexible, and people are freer than ever to shape their selves as they choose.

However, this freedom comes at a cost, particularly for young people. In concluding this chapter, we consider some of the socialization challenges American youth faces today. To set the stage for this discussion, we first examine the emergence of childhood and adolescence as categories of social thought and experience some 400 years ago.

Dilemmas of Childhood and Adolescent Socialization

In preindustrial societies, children were thought of as small adults. From a young age, they were expected to conform as much as possible to the norms of the adult world, largely because they were put to work as soon as they could contribute to the welfare of their families. Often, this meant doing chores by the age of 5 and working full time by the age of 10 or 12. Marriage, and thus the achievement of full adulthood, was common by the age of 15 or 16.

Children in Europe and North America fit this pattern until the late 1600s, when the idea of childhood emerged as a distinct stage of life. At that time, the feeling grew among well-to-do Europeans and North Americans that boys should be allowed to play games and receive an education that would allow them to develop the emotional, physical, and intellectual skills they would need as adults. Girls continued to be treated as "little women" (the title of Louisa May Alcott's 1869 novel) until the 19th century. Most working-class boys didn't enjoy much of a childhood until the 20th century. Only in the last century did the idea of childhood as a distinct and prolonged stage of life become universal in the West (Ariès, 1962).

The Emergence of Childhood and Adolescence

The idea of childhood emerged when and where it did because of social necessity and social possibility. Prolonged childhood was *necessary* in societies that required better-educated adults to do increasingly complex work because it gave young people a chance to prepare for adult life. Prolonged childhood was *possible* in societies where improved hygiene and nutrition allowed most people to live more than 35 years, the average life span in Europe in the early 1600s. In other words, before the late 1600s, most people did not live long enough to permit the luxury of childhood. Moreover, there was no social need for a period of extended training and development before the comparatively simple demands of adulthood were thrust upon young people.

In general, wealthier and more complex societies whose populations enjoy a long average life expectancy stretch out the preadult period of life. For example, in Europe in 1600 most people reached mature adulthood by the age of about 16. In contrast, in the United States today, most people are considered to reach mature adulthood only around the age of 30, by which time they have completed their formal education, married, and "settled down." Once teenagers were relieved of adult responsibilities, a new term had to be coined to describe the teenage years: *adolescence.* Subsequently, the term *young adulthood* entered popular usage as an increasingly large number of people in their late teens and 20s delayed marriage to attend college.

Although these new terms describing the stages of life were firmly entrenched in North America by the middle of the 20th century, some of the categories of the population they were meant to describe soon began to change dramatically. Somewhat excitedly, a number of analysts began to write about the "disappearance" of childhood and adolescence altogether (Friedenberg, 1959; Postman, 1982). Although undoubtedly overstating their case, these social scientists identified some of the social forces responsible for the changing character of childhood and adolescence in recent decades. We examine these social forces in the concluding section of this chapter.

Problems of Childhood and Adolescent Socialization Today

Declining adult supervision and guidance, increasing mass media and peer group influence, and the increasing assumption of substantial adult responsibilities to the neglect of extracurricular activities have done much to change the socialization patterns of American youth over the past 40 years or so (Box 3.3). Let us consider each of these developments in turn.

Declining Adult Supervision and Guidance

In a 6-year, in-depth study of American adolescence, Patricia Hersch wrote that "in all societies since the beginning of time, adolescents have learned to become adults by observing, imitating and interacting with grown-ups around them" (Hersch, 1998: 20). However, in the contemporary United States, notes Hersch, adults are increasingly absent from the lives of adolescents. Why? According to Hersch, "American society has left its children behind as the cost of progress in the workplace" (Hersch, 1998: 19). What she means is that more American adults are working longer hours than ever before. Consequently, they have less time to spend with their children than they used to. Young people are increasingly left alone to socialize themselves and build their own community.

This community sometimes revolves around high-risk behavior. To be sure, more is involved in high-risk behavior than socialization patterns (Box 3.4). However, it is not coincidental that the peak hours for juvenile crime are between 3 p.m. and 6 p.m. on weekdays—that is, after school and before most parents return home from work (Hersch, 1998: 362). Also of significance in this connection is that girls are less likely to engage in juvenile crime than boys, partly because parents tend to supervise and socialize their sons

Your Adolescent Socialization

Ask yourself and a parent the following questions: When you were between the ages of 10 and 17, how often were you at home or with friends but without adult supervision? How often did you have to prepare your own meals or take care of a younger sibling while your parent or parents were at work? How many hours a week did you spend cleaning house? How many hours a week did you have to work at a part-time job to earn spending money and save for college? How many hours a week did you spend on extracurricular activities associated with

your school? How many hours a week did you watch TV and spend on other mass media use? If you compare your experiences with those of your parents, chances are, many more of your waking hours outside of school were spent without adult supervision and assuming substantial adult responsibilities such as those just listed. Compared with

your parents, you are unlikely to have spent much time on extracurricular activities associated with your school but quite a lot of time viewing TV and using other mass media. What consequences have these different patterns of socialization had for your life and that of your parent?

WRITING ASSIGNMENT

In about 500 words, write a comparison of your parents' and your own socialization experiences during adolescence.

---

and daughters differently (Hagan, Simpson, and Gillis, 1987). These research findings suggest that many of the teenage behaviors commonly regarded as problematic result from declining adult guidance and supervision.

Increasing Media Influence

Declining adult supervision and guidance also leaves American youth more susceptible to the influence of the mass media and peer groups. As one parent put it, "When they hit the teen years, it is as if they can't be children anymore. The outside world has invaded the school environment" (quoted in Hersch, 1998: 111). In an earlier era, family, school, church, and community usually taught young people more or less consistent beliefs and values. Now, however, the mass media and peer groups often pull young people in different directions from the school and the family, leaving them uncertain about what constitutes appropriate behavior and making the job of growing up more stressful than it used to be (Arnett, 1995).

Declining Extracurricular Activities and Increasing Adult Responsibilities

As the chapter's opening anecdote about Robert Brym's involvement in high school drama illustrates, extracurricular activities are important for adolescent personality development. By training and playing hard on a football team, mastering electric guitar, or acting in plays, you can learn something about your physical, emotional, and social capabilities and limitations; about what you are made of; and about what you can and can't do. Adolescents require these types of activities for healthy self-development.

However, if you're like most young Americans today, you spent fewer hours per week on extracurricular activities associated with school than your parents did when they went to school. Educators estimate that only about one-fourth of today's high school students take part in extracurricular activities such as sports, drama, and music (Hersch, 1998). Many of them are simply too busy with household chores, child-care responsibilities, and part-time jobs to enjoy the benefits of school activities outside the classroom. The need

BOX 3.4
SOCIAL POLICY: WHAT DO YOU THINK?

Socialization versus Gun Control

On April 20, 1999, Columbine High School in Littleton, Colorado, was the scene of a mass killing by two students. The shooters murdered 13 of their fellow students and then turned their guns on themselves.

After the massacre at Columbine High School, newspapers, magazines, Internet chat rooms, and radio and TV talk shows were abuzz with the problem of teenage violence. "What is to be done?" people asked. One solution that seems obvious to many people is to limit the availability of firearms. All postindustrial societies except the United States restrict gun ownership. Other countries have problems with teenage violence, but because guns are not readily available, teenage violence more rarely leads to mass killings in, say, Canada, Australia, Britain, or Japan. According to a Canadian government report, the rate of homicide using firearms per 100,000 people is 2.2 in Canada, 1.8 in Australia, 1.2 in Japan, 1.3 in Britain, and 9.3 in the United States (Department of Justice, Canada, 1995).

In the United States, however, most political discussions about teenage violence focus on socialization, not on gun control. Soon after the Columbine tragedy, for example, the House of Representatives passed a "juvenile crime bill." It cast blame on the entertainment industry, especially Hollywood movies, and the decline of

Citizens of most developed countries must purchase a license before they can possess firearms and buy ammunition. Licensing allows officials to require that applicants pass a safety course and a background check. This practice lowers the risk that firearms will be used for illegal purposes.

"family values." Henry Hyde, an Illinois Republican, complained, "People were misled and disinclined to oppose the powerful entertainment industry" (quoted in Lazare, 1999: 57). Tom DeLay, a Republican congressman from Texas, worried: "We place our children in daycare centers where they learn their socialization skills . . . under the law of the jungle . . ." (quoted in Lazare, 1999: 58). In other words, according to these politicians, teenage massacres result from poor childhood socialization: the corrupting influence of Hollywood movies and declining family values.

Some politicians, including Hyde and DeLay, want to reintroduce Christianity into public schools to help overcome this presumed decay. In support of this idea, DeLay reported an e-mail message he received, which read: "'Dear God, why didn't you stop the shootings at Columbine?' And God writes, 'Dear student, I would have, but I wasn't allowed in school'" (quoted in Lazare, 1999: 57–8). One consequence of the Columbine massacre was not a gun control bill, but a bill to display the Ten Commandments in public schools.

Critical Thinking

- Is the problem of students shooting each other a problem of socialization, lack of gun control, another factor, or a combination of factors?

---

for part-time or even full-time work increases when adolescents enter college, often with negative consequences for their grades (▶Figure 3.5).

"The Vanishing Adolescent"

Some analysts wonder whether the assumption of so many adult responsibilities, the lack of extracurricular activities, declining adult supervision and guidance, and increasing mass media and peer group influence are causing childhood and adolescence to disappear. As early as 1959, one sociologist spoke of "the vanishing adolescent" in American society (Friedenberg, 1959). More recently, another commentator remarked: "I think that we who were small in the early sixties were perhaps the last generation of Americans who actually had a childhood, in the . . . sense of . . . a space distinct in roles and customs from the

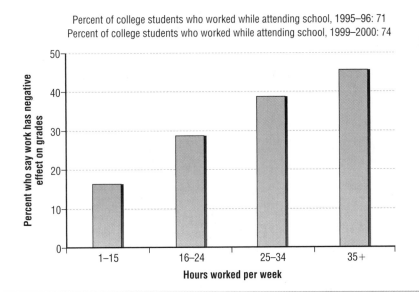

Percent of college students who worked while attending school, 1995–96: 71
Percent of college students who worked while attending school, 1999–2000: 74

▶FIGURE 3.5
Negative Effect of Employment on Grades among Full-Time College Students Who Work, United States

Source: Marklein (2002).

world of adults, oriented around children's own needs and culture rather than around the needs and culture of adults" (Wolf, 1997: 13). Childhood and adolescence became universal categories of social thought and experience in the 20th century. Under the impact of the social forces discussed previously, the experience and meaning of childhood and adolescence now seem to be changing radically.

The Points of the Compass

In this chapter, we have again drawn attention to the freedom-versus-constraint points of the sociological compass, but this time we have done so at two levels of analysis.

First, we focused on the *individual.* Beginning in the early twentieth century, social scientists established the existence of a tension between an impulsive, freedom-seeking part of the self (Freud's id and Mead's I) and a constraining part that helps to impose the norms of society on the individual (Freud's superego and Mead's me). From the point of view of Freud, Mead, and other leading students of socialization, people cannot develop normally unless they interact socially. That is because only social interaction allows the socializing and constraining part of the self to temper the impulsive, freedom-seeking part. Our identity emerges out of this interaction. Tension between the desire to satisfy our impulses and the imposition of social constraint forges our sense of who we are and how we should act in the world.

We also analyzed the interplay between freedom and constraint at the level of *social institutions.* The family, the peer group, the school, and the mass media are powerful socializing agents. Within their constraints, people learn and relearn society's values, beliefs, and norms. For three reasons, however, institutions allow people varying degrees of freedom to choose socializing influences. First, the influence of the most powerful socializing agent, the family, has weakened in the past century or so. Second, institutions do not act as a monolithic and coordinated socializing force. Instead, they promote patterns of socialization that are often at odds with each other. Third, technological innovation and globalization have created new opportunities for socialization. Institutional weakening and competition, and the proliferation of socialization opportunities, increase people's freedom to select the socializing influences that best suit them.

In the next two chapters, we elaborate the idea that freedom and constraint are two points of the sociological compass at various levels of analysis.

C H A P T E R   S U M M A R Y

1. Why is social interaction necessary?

Studies show that children raised in isolation do not develop normally. This finding corroborates the view that social interaction unleashes human potential.

2. What are the major theories of childhood socialization?

Freud called the part of the self that demands immediate gratification the *id*. He argued that a self-image begins to emerge when the id's demands are denied. Because of many lessons in self-control, a child eventually develops a sense of what constitutes appropriate behavior, a moral sense of right and wrong, and a personal conscience, or superego. The *superego* is a repository of cultural standards. A third component of the self, the *ego*, develops to balance the demands of the id and the superego.

Like Freud, Mead noted that an impulsive aspect of the self is present from birth. He called it the *I*. Developing Cooley's idea of the "looking-glass self," Mead also argued that a repository of culturally approved standards emerges as part of the self during social interaction. Mead called it the *me*. However, Mead drew attention to the unique human capacity to take the role of the other as the source of the *me*. People develop, he wrote, by first imitating and pretending to be their significant others, then learning to play complex games that require understanding several roles simultaneously, and finally developing a sense of cultural standards and how they apply.

Since the early 20th century, psychologists have contributed to our understanding of cognitive and moral socialization, but sociologists have done more to underline the social conditions that account for variations in cognitive and moral development. Specifically, their work suggests that gender and economic and political structures shape socialization patterns.

3. How has the influence of various social agents changed over the past century?

Over the past century, the increasing socializing influence of schools, peer groups, and the mass media has

been matched by the decreasing socializing influence of the family.

4. In what sense is the self more flexible than it used to be?

People's self-conceptions are subject to more flux now than they were even a few decades ago. Cultural globalization, medical advances, and computer-assisted communication are among the factors that have made the self more plastic.

5. What social forces have caused change in the character and experience of childhood and adolescence?

Childhood as a distinct stage of life emerged for well-to-do boys in the late 1600s, when life expectancy started to increase and boys had to be trained for more complex work tasks. Girls were treated as "little women" until the 19th century, and most working-class boys first experienced childhood as a distinct stage of the life course only in the 20th century. Once teenagers were relieved of adult responsibilities, the term *adolescence* was coined to describe the teenage years. Subsequently, the term *young adulthood* entered popular usage as an increasingly large number of people in their late teens and 20s delayed marriage to attend college.

Today, decreasing parental supervision and guidance, the increasing assumption of substantial adult responsibilities by children and adolescents, declining participation in extracurricular activities, and increased mass media and peer group influence are causing changes in the character and experience of childhood and adolescence. According to some analysts, childhood and adolescence as they were known in the first half of the 20th century are disappearing.

Questions to Consider

1. Do you think of yourself in a fundamentally different way from the way your parents (or other close relatives or friends at least 20 years older than you) thought of themselves when they were your age? Interview your parents,

relatives, or friends to find out. Pay particular attention to the way in which the forces of globalization may have altered self-conceptions over time.

2. Watch an hour of prime-time TV. How are gender, racial, ethnic, class, age, and disability roles portrayed? Are stereotypes used to characterize different types of people? What impact might such portrayals have on children watching TV?

3. Have you ever participated in an initiation rite in college, the military, or a religious organization? If so, describe the ritual rejection, ritual death, and ritual rebirth that made up the rite. Do you think that the rite increased your identification with the group you were joining? Did it increase the sense of solidarity—the *we* feeling—of group members?

4. List the contradictory lessons that different agents of socialization taught you as an adolescent. How have you resolved those contradictory lessons? If you have not, how do you intend to do so?

Web Resources

CENGAGENOW™

Maximize your study time by using CengageNOW's diagnostic study plan to help you review this chapter. The Study Plan will

- help you identify areas on which you should concentrate;
- provide interactive exercises to help you master the chapter concepts; and
- provide a post-test to confirm you are ready to move on to the next chapter.

The Companion Website for *Sociology: Your Compass for a New World, The Brief Edition*, Enhanced Second Edition

www.cengage.com/sociology/brym

Supplement your review of this chapter by going to the companion website to take one of the tutorial quizzes, use flash cards to master key terms, and check out the many other study aids you'll find there. You'll also find special features such as GSS Data and Census 2000 information that will put data and resources at your fingertips to help you with that special project or help you do some research on your own.

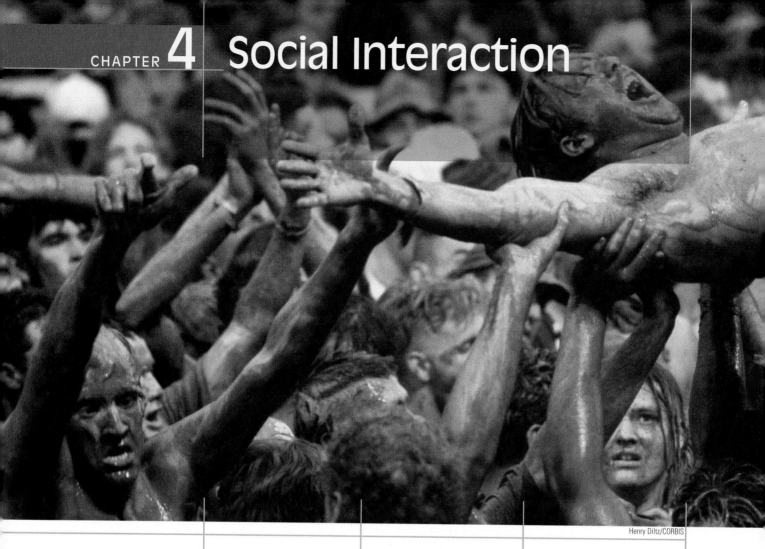

Henry Diltz/CORBIS

In this chapter, you will learn that:

- Social interaction involves people communicating face-to-face, acting and reacting in relation to one another. The character of every social interaction depends on people's distinct positions in the interaction (statuses), their standards of conduct (norms), and their sets of expected behaviors (roles).

- Humor, fear, anger, grief, disgust, love, jealousy, and other emotions color social interactions.

However, emotions are not as natural, spontaneous, authentic, and uncontrollable as we commonly believe. Various aspects of social structure influence the texture of our emotional life.

- Nonverbal means of communication, including facial expressions, gestures, body language, and "status cues," are as important as language in social interaction.

- Sociological theories focus on six aspects of social interaction: (1) the way people exchange valued resources; (2) the way people maximize gains and minimize losses; (3) the way people interpret, negotiate, and modify norms, roles, and statuses; (4) the way people manage the impressions they give to others; (5) the way preexisting norms influence social interaction; and (6) the way status hierarchies influence social interaction.

What Is Social Interaction?

In the early decades of the 20th century, the service personnel on ocean liners and trains were mostly men. When commercial airlines first started operating in Germany in the first decade of the 20th century and the United States in the 1920s, hiring cabin boys and stewards therefore seemed the natural thing to do.

Things began to change a little in the 1930s, and even more by the early 1950s. The government tightly regulated the airline industry at the time. It decided where and when planes could fly and how much they could charge. On transatlantic flights, the government even decided the allowable amount of passenger legroom and the number and types of courses that constituted a meal. This regulation made all the airlines pretty much identical. How then could one airline stand out from the others and thereby win more business? The airlines came up with a creative answer. In the 1950s, they started hiring large numbers of women as stewardesses (known today by the gender-neutral term *flight attendants*). The airlines outdid one another in training and marketing stewardesses as glamorous sex objects, using them to lure the still largely male clientele to fly with them rather than with their competitors.

The plan required the establishment of a new form of **social interaction,** the creation of a novel way for people to communicate face-to-face (or, today, via computer), acting and reacting in relation to one another. As is generally the case, this social interaction was structured around specific statuses, roles, and norms.

CENGAGENOW™

Learn more about **Social Interaction** by going through the Social Interaction: The Ropes Course, Video Exercise.

Social interaction: Involves people communicating face-to-face or via computer, acting and reacting in relation to other people. It is structured around norms, roles, and statuses.

CENGAGENOW™

This icon signals when CengageNOW has important resources available for you to use in conjunction with the text. See the foldout at the front of this text for information on how to access CengageNOW.

The Structure of Social Interaction

Status

A **status** is a recognized social position that an individual can occupy. Flight attendants and passengers occupy distinct statuses. Each person occupies many statuses. Thus, an individual may be a flight attendant, a wife, and a mother at the same time. Sociologists call the entire ensemble of statuses occupied by an individual a **status set.** If a status is involuntary, it is an **ascribed status.** If it is voluntary, it is an **achieved status.** "Daughter" is an ascribed status, "flight attendant" an achieved status. Some statuses matter more than others for a person's identity. One's **master status** is the status that is most influential in shaping one's life at a given time.

Roles

Social interaction also requires **roles,** or sets of expected behaviors. Whereas people *occupy* statuses, they *perform* roles. For example, people who occupy the status of flight attendant have to play several roles—in-flight server, in-flight safety expert, and so on. Expectations define the role. The entire cluster of roles attached to a single status is called a **role set** (▶Figure 4.1).

Norms

Finally, social interaction requires **norms,** or generally accepted ways of doing things. Norms may be prescriptive or proscriptive. *Prescriptive* norms suggest what a person is expected to do while performing a particular role. *Proscriptive* norms suggest what a person is expected *not* to do while performing a particular role. Norms often change over time. At one point in time, some norms are universal, whereas others differ from situation to situation and from role to role.

Status: A recognized social position that an individual can occupy.

Status set: The entire ensemble of statuses occupied by an individual.

Ascribed status: An involuntary status.

Achieved status: A voluntary status.

Master status: The status that is most influential in shaping one's life at a given time and hence one's overriding public identity.

Role: A set of expected behaviors.

Role set: A cluster of roles attached to a single status.

Norms: Generally accepted ways of doing things.

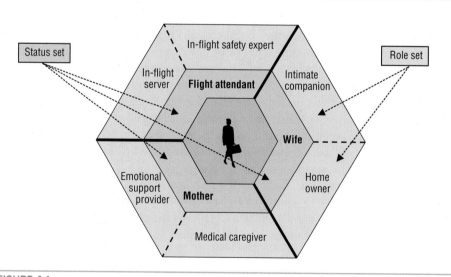

▶FIGURE 4.1

Role Set and Status Set

A person occupies several recognized positions or statuses at the same time—for example, mother, wife, and flight attendant. All of these statuses together form a status set. Each status is composed of several sets of expected behaviors or roles; for example, a wife is expected to act as an intimate companion to her husband and to assume certain legal responsibilities as co-owner of a house. In this figure, dashed lines separate roles and dark solid lines separate statuses.

Case Study: Stewardesses and Their Clientele

Let's now consider how these three elements of social interaction shaped the evolution of the stewardess's job.

The Changing Role of Stewardess

In 1930, Boeing Air Transport hired the world's first stewardess (United Airlines, 2003). In 1965, a revolution in the role of stewardess began with the first of a series of radical uniform changes. An advertising executive persuaded now-defunct Braniff International Airways to hire a leading fashion designer to redesign its stewardesses' uniforms. The resulting op-art pastels and hemlines 6 inches above the knee were a sensation. Everyone wanted to fly Braniff. Its stock rose from $24 to $120 per share. Soon all the airlines were in on the act. Advertising reflected the new expectations surrounding the stewardess's role. "Does your wife know you're flying with us?" one Braniff ad teased. A National Airlines ad used this blunt come-on: "I'm Linda. Fly me." Pan Am's radio commercials asked: "How do you like your stewardesses?" Continental, which painted its planes with splashes of gold and whose stewardesses wore golden uniforms, advertised itself as "The Proud Bird with the Golden Tail" and later emphasized, "We really move our tail for you." Movies and books solidified the stewardess's new role as sex object. The 1965 movie *Boeing, Boeing* featured Tony Curtis juggling three stewardess girlfriends on different flight schedules. *Coffee, Tea or Me,* a novel published in 1967, advertised itself as an exposé of the stewardess's life behind the scenes, "the uninhibited memoirs of two airline stewardesses," according to the book jacket. It was translated into 12 languages and sold 3 million copies (Handy, 2002). The 2002 hit movie *Catch Me If You Can,* starring Leonardo DiCaprio and Tom Hanks, gives us a glimpse of the airline industry's attitudes toward the role of stewardess in the 1960s.[1]

The Enforcement of Norms

The airlines specified and enforced many norms pertaining to the stewardess's role. The expectations of passengers helped reinforce those norms. For example, until 1968 stewardesses had to be single. Until 1970 they could not be pregnant. They had to be attractive, have a good smile, and achieve certain standards on IQ and other psychological tests. In 1954, American Airlines imposed a mandatory retirement age of 32 that became the industry standard. Stewardesses had to have a certain "look"—slim, wholesome, and not too buxom. They were assigned an ideal weight based on their height and figure. Preflight weigh-ins ensured they didn't deviate from the ideal. All stewardesses had to wear girdles, and supervisors did a routine "girdle check" by flicking an index finger against a buttock. Weight and height standards were not abolished until 1982 (Lehoczky, 2003). Then there was the question of "personality." Stewardesses were expected to be charming and solicitous at all times. They also had to at least appear "available" to the mainly male clientele.

A Braniff International Airways ad featuring stewardesses in designer uniforms considered racy at the time.

Bettmann/CORBIS

---

[1]Incidentally, Frank Abagnale, Jr., the impostor and forger played by DiCaprio, eventually became a sociology professor at Brigham Young University.

Dany Saval, Tony Curtis, and Thelma Ritter (left to right) in *Boeing, Boeing* (1965).

Role Conflict and Role Strain

Role conflict occurs when two or more statuses held at the same time place contradictory role demands on a person. Today's female flight attendants experience role conflict to the degree that working in the airline industry requires frequent absences from home, whereas being a mother and a wife require spending considerable time at home. In contrast, in the 1950s and 1960s role conflict was minimal. Back then, sick children and demanding husbands could hardly interfere with the performance of the stewardess role because the airlines didn't allow stewardesses to become mothers or wives. On the other hand, the demands and expectations placed on the stewardess in the 1960s maximized role strain. **Role strain** occurs when incompatible role demands are placed on a person in a single status. For instance, constantly having to be suggestive while also politely warding off unwanted, impolite, and even crude overtures made the stewardess role a lot more stressful than it appeared in the ads (▶Figure 4.2).

Change in Status

From the 1950s to the late 1970s or early 1980s, the role of stewardess was certainly glamorous. People often stared enviously at stewardesses marching proudly through an airport terminal on their way to a presumably exotic location, sporting the latest fashions

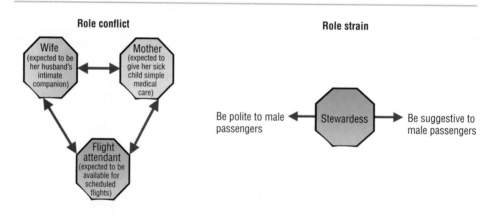

Role conflict taks place when different role demands are placed on a person by two or more statuses held at the same time. How might a flight attendant experience role conflict due to the contradictory demands of the statuses diagrammed above?

Role strain occurs when incompatible role demands are placed on a person in a single status. Why was the status of stewardess in the 1960s and 1970s high in role strain?

▶FIGURE 4.2
Role Conflict and Role Strain

and hairstyles. On the other hand, the pay was anything but glamorous. Stewardesses typically had to live four or five to an apartment and, as one stewardess said, "If you wanted to eat, you had to find a boyfriend real quick" (quoted in Handy, 2002: 220). Moreover, working conditions were far from ideal. One stewardess described her job to *Newsweek* in 1968 as "food under your fingernails, sore feet, complaints and insults" (quoted in Handy, 2002: 220).

In the past couple of decades, the status of the stewardess (i.e., the position of the stewardess in relation to others) has changed. In the era of shoe searches, deep discount no-frills service, and packaged peanut snacks, little of the glamour remains. However, in the 1960s and 1970s what is now called the Association of Flight Attendants won changes in rules regarding marriage, pregnancy, retirement, and the hiring of men. Stewardesses, once considered sex objects, became flight attendants, and what often used to be a 2-year stint leading to marriage became a career.

What Shapes Social Interaction?

Norms, roles, and statuses are the building blocks of all face-to-face communication. Whenever people communicate face-to-face, these building blocks structure their interaction. This assertion flies in the face of common sense. We typically think of our interactions as outcomes of our emotional states. We interact differently with people depending on whether they love us, make us angry, or make us laugh. We usually think our emotions are evoked involuntarily and result in uncontrollable action. So, can we truthfully say that norms, roles, and statuses shape our interactions? We answer this question in the affirmative in the next section. As you will see, our emotions are not as unique, involuntary, and uncontrollable as we are often led to believe. Underlying the turbulence of emotional life is a measure of order and predictability governed by sociological principles.

Just as building blocks need cement to hold them together, so norms, roles, and statuses require a sort of "social cement" to prevent them from falling apart and to turn them into a durable social structure. What is the nature of the cement that holds the building blocks of social life together? Asked differently, exactly how is social interaction maintained? This is the most fundamental sociological question one can ask, for it is really a question about how social structures, and society as a whole, are possible. There are three main ways of maintaining social interaction and thereby cementing social structures and society as a whole: by means of domination, competition, and cooperation. In this chapter's second section, we investigate each of these modes of interaction in detail. First, however, we turn to the problem of emotions, beginning with laughter and humor.

The Sociology of Emotions

Laughter and Humor

Robert Provine (2000) and his research assistants eavesdropped on 1,200 conversations of people laughing in public places such as shopping malls. When they heard someone laughing, they recorded who laughed (the speaker, the listener, or both) and the gender of the speaker and the listener. To simplify things, they eavesdropped only on two-person groups, or *dyads*.

Provine found that in general, speakers laugh more often than listeners do. Moreover, interesting patterns emerged when Provine considered the gender of the speaker and the listener. Women, it turns out, laugh more than men in everyday conversations. The biggest discrepancy in laughing occurs when the speaker is a woman and the listener is a man. In such cases, women laugh more than twice as often as men. However, even when a man speaks and a woman listens, the woman is more likely to laugh than the man. In contrast, men get more laughs from their audiences than women do. Not surprisingly, only a small percentage of standup comics in the United States are women.

Some people might think that Provine's findings confirm the stereotype of the giggling female. Others might think his data support the view that when dealing with men, women have more to laugh at. A sociologist, however, would notice that the gender distribution of laughter fits a more general pattern. In social situations where people of different statuses interact, laughter is unevenly distributed across the status hierarchy. People with higher status get more laughs. People with lower status laugh more. That is perhaps why class clowns are nearly always boys. It is also why a classic sociological study of laughter among staff members in a psychiatric hospital discovered "downward humor" (Coser, 1960). At a series of staff meetings, psychiatrists averaged 7.5 witticisms, medical students doing their residency averaged 5.5, and paramedics averaged a mere 0.7. Moreover, the psychiatrists most often made the residents the target of their humor, whereas the residents and the paramedics targeted the patients or themselves. Laughter in everyday life, it turns out, is not as spontaneous as we may think. It is often a signal of dominance or subservience; social structure influences what we find funny.

Humor and Social Status

Much social interaction takes place among status equals—among members of the same national or racial group, for example. If status equals enjoy a privileged position in the larger society, they often direct their humor at perceived social inferiors. White Americans of northern European origin make jokes about "Polacks" and blacks. The English laugh about the Irish and, more recently, the Welsh. The French howl at the Belgians. The Canadians tell "Newfie" jokes (about Newfoundlanders). And the Russians make jokes about the impoverished and oppressed Chukchi people of northern Siberia ("When a Chukchi man comes back from hunting he first wants his supper on the table. Then he wants to make love to his wife. Then he wants to take off his skis"). Similarly, when people point out that the only good thing about having Alzheimer's disease is that you can hide your own Easter eggs, they are making a joke about a socially marginal and powerless group. It has the effect of excluding outsiders, making the teller of the joke feel superior, and reinforcing group norms and the status hierarchy itself.

Chris Rock onstage.

Sipkin Corey/Corbis Sygma

"Ain't nothing more horrifying than a bunch of poor white people," Chris Rock once quipped. "They blame n_____ for everything. . . . 'Space shuttle blew up! Them damn n_____, that's what it was!'" Chris Rock is, of course, an African American, a member of a group that, on the whole, is disadvantaged in American society. Disadvantaged people often laugh at the privileged majority, but not always. Nation of Islam leader Louis Farrakhan organized the Million Man March in Washington, D.C., in 1996 as a celebration of black solidarity and pride. One of the speakers at the march was Marion Barry, the black mayor of Washington, D.C., who had been arrested on cocaine charges 6 years earlier. Here is what Chris Rock had to say about the incident in front of a black Washington audience: "Marion Barry at the Million Man March.

You know what that means? That means even at our finest hour, we had a crackhead onstage!" (Farley, 1998). When members of disadvantaged groups are not laughing at the privileged majority, they are typically laughing at themselves.

Humor and the Structure of Society

People sometimes direct humor against government. Some scholars argue that the more repressive a government and the less free its mass media, the more widespread antigovernment jokes are (Davies, 1998). Sometimes, humor merely has a political edge, "political" here being understood broadly as having to do with the distribution of power and privilege in society. And sometimes, humor seems to have no political content at all; one would be hard pressed to discern the political significance of a chicken crossing a road to get to the other side. Yet in a sense all jokes, even those about chickens crossing the road, are "little revolutions," as George Orwell once remarked, for all jokes invert or pervert reality. They suddenly and momentarily let us see beyond the serious, taken-for-granted world. Analyzed sociologically, jokes even enable us to see the structure of society that lies just beneath our laughter (Zijderveld, 1983).

Emotion Management

Some scholars think that emotions are like the common cold. In both cases, an external disturbance causes a reaction that we experience involuntarily. The external disturbance may involve exposure to a grizzly bear attack that causes us to experience fear or exposure to a virus that causes us to catch cold. In either case, we can't control our body's patterned response. Emotions, like colds, just happen to us (Thoits, 1989: 319).

The trouble with this argument is that we can and often do *control* our emotions. Emotions don't just happen to us. We manage them. If a grizzly bear attacks you in the woods, you can run as fast as your legs will carry you or you can calm yourself, lie down, play dead, and silently pray for the best. You are more likely to survive the grizzly bear attack if you control your emotions and follow the second strategy.[2] You will also temper your fear with a new emotion: hope (▶Figure 4.3).

When we manage our emotions, we usually follow certain cultural "scripts," like the culturally transmitted knowledge that lying down and playing dead gives you a better chance of surviving a grizzly bear attack. That is, we usually know the culturally designated emotional response to a particular external stimulus and we try to respond appro-

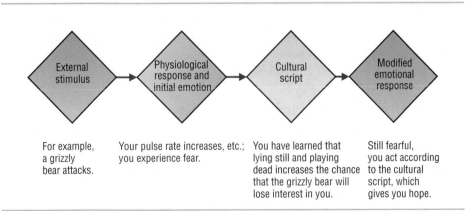

▶FIGURE 4.3
How We Get Emotional

External stimulus	→	Physiological response and initial emotion	→	Cultural script	→	Modified emotional response
For example, a grizzly bear attacks.		Your pulse rate increases, etc.; you experience fear.		You have learned that lying still and playing dead increases the chance that the grizzly bear will lose interest in you.		Still fearful, you act according to the cultural script, which gives you hope.

---

[2]Standard advice for polar and black bear attacks is to yell and fight back.

priately. If we don't succeed in achieving the culturally appropriate emotional response, we are likely to feel guilt, disappointment, or (as in the case of the grizzly bear attack) something much worse.

Sociologist Arlie Russell Hochschild is a leading figure in the study of **emotion management.** In fact, she coined the term. She argues that emotion management involves people obeying "feeling rules" and responding appropriately to the situations in which they find themselves (Hochschild, 1979, 1983). So, for example, people talk about the "right" to feel angry and they acknowledge that they "should" have mourned a relative's death more deeply. We have conventional expectations not only about what we should feel but also about how much we should feel, how long we should feel it, and with whom we should share our feelings. For example, we are expected to mourn the end of a love relationship. Shedding tears would be regarded as completely natural today among Americans, though if you should shoot yourself—as was the fad among some European Romantics in the early 19th century—then you would be regarded as deranged. If you should go on a date minutes after you break up with your longtime girlfriend or boyfriend, then most people would regard you as callous. Norms and rules thus govern our emotional life.

Emotion Labor

Hochschild distinguishes emotion management (which everyone does in their everyday life) from **emotion labor** (which many people do as part of their job and for which they are paid). We've all seen teachers deal with students who routinely hand in assignments late, pass notes, chatter during class, talk back, and act as class clowns. Those teachers do emotion labor. Similarly, sales clerks, nurses, and flight attendants must be experts in emotion labor. They spend a considerable part of their workday dealing with other people's misbehavior, anger, rudeness, and unreasonable demands. They spend another part of their workday in what is essentially promotional and public relations work on behalf of the organizations that employ them. ("We hope you enjoyed your flight on Americans Airlines and that we can serve you again the next time your travel.") In all these tasks, they carefully manage their own emotions while trying to render their clientele happy and orderly. Hochschild estimates that in the United States, nearly half the jobs women do and one-fifth of the jobs men do involve substantial amounts of emotion labor.

Moreover, as the focus of the economy shifts from the production of goods to the production of services, the market for emotion labor grows. More and more people are selected, trained, and paid for their skill in emotion labor. Hence, employers look for people not just with high IQs but also with "emotional intelligence." Emotion labor becomes a commodity that employers buy in much the same way a furniture manufacturer buys fabric to upholster chairs. The emotional life of workers—or at least the way they openly express their feelings—is increasingly governed by the organizations for which they work and is therefore less and less spontaneous and authentic.

Emotions in Historical Perspective

We can glean additional evidence of the impact of society on our emotional life from historical studies. It turns out that feeling rules take different forms under different social conditions, which vary historically. Three examples from the social history of emotions help illustrate the point:

● *Grief.* Among other factors, the *crude death rate* (the annual number of deaths per 1,000 people in a population) helps determine our experience of grief (Lofland, 1985). In Europe as late as 1600, life expectancy was only 35 years. Many infants

Emotion management: Involves people obeying "feeling rules" and responding appropriately to the situations in which they find themselves.

Emotion labor: Emotion management that many people do as part of their job and for which they are paid.

died at birth or in their first year of life. Infectious diseases decimated entire populations. The medical profession was in its infancy. The risk of losing family members, especially babies, was thus much greater than today. As a result, people invested less emotionally in their children than we typically do. As health conditions improved and the infant mortality rate fell over the years, emotional investment in children increased. It intensified especially in the 19th century, when women started having fewer babies on average as a result of industrialization (see Chapter 16, "Population, Urbanization, and the Environment"). As emotional investment in children increased, grief response to child deaths intensified and lasted longer. To put it crudely, in Europe and North America in 1600 it was "normal" to lose a few children in birth. Today, in contrast, every child's death is a major tragedy.

Manners in Europe during the Middle Ages were utterly disgusting by our standards today.

- *Anger.* Industrialization and the growth of competitive markets in 19th-century North America and Europe turned the family into an emotional haven from a world increasingly perceived as heartless (see Chapter 11, "Families"). In keeping with the enhanced emotional function of the family, anger control, particularly by women, became increasingly important for the establishment of a harmonious household. The early 20th century witnessed mounting labor unrest and the growth of the service sector. Avoiding anger thus became an important labor relations goal. This trend influenced family life too. Childrearing advice manuals increasingly stressed the importance of teaching children how to control their anger (Stearns and Stearns, 1985, 1986).

- *Disgust.* Manners in Europe in the Middle Ages were disgusting by our standards. Even the most refined aristocrats spat in public and belched shamelessly during banquets (with the king in attendance, no less). Members of high society didn't flinch at scratching themselves and passing gas at the dinner table, where they ate with their hands and speared food with knives. What was acceptable then causes revulsion now because feeling rules have changed. Specifically, manners began to change with the emergence of the modern political state, especially after 1700. The modern political state raised armies and collected taxes, imposed languages, and required loyalty. All this coordination of effort necessitated more self-control on the part of the citizenry. Changes in standards of public conduct—signaled by the introduction of the fork, the nightdress, the handkerchief, the spittoon, and the chamber pot—accompanied the rise of the modern state. Good manners also served to define who had power and who lacked it. For example, there is nothing inherently well mannered about a father sitting at the head of the table carving the turkey and children waiting to speak until they are spoken to. These rules about the difference between good manners and improper or disgusting behavior were created to signify the distribution of power in the family by age and gender (Elias, 1994 [1939]; Scott, 1998).

We thus see that although emotions form an important part of all social interactions, they are not universal, nor are they constant. They have histories and deep sociological underpinnings in statuses, roles, and norms. In turn, big social structures and social changes—industrialization, the rise of the state, improvements in health conditions, and so forth—shape statuses, roles, and norms. Bearing these lessons in mind, we may now turn to the second main task of this chapter, analyzing the "social cement" that binds together the building blocks of social life and turns them into durable social structures.

Modes of Social Interaction

Interaction as Competition and Exchange

Have you ever been in a conversation where you can't get a word in edgewise? If you are like most people, this situation is bound to happen from time to time. The longer a one-sided conversation persists, the more neglected you feel. You may make increasingly less subtle attempts to turn the conversation your way. But if you fail, you may decide to end the interaction altogether. If this experience repeats itself—if the person you're talking to consistently monopolizes conversations—you're likely to want to avoid getting into conversations with him or her in the future. Maintaining interaction (and maintaining a relationship) requires that the need for attention by both parties is met.

Most people don't consistently try to monopolize conversations. If they did, there wouldn't be much talk in the world. In fact, turn-taking is one of the basic norms that govern conversations; people literally take turns talking to make conversation possible. Nonetheless, a remarkably large part of all conversations involves a subtle competition for attention. Consider the following snippet of dinner conversation:

> John: "I'm feeling really starved."
> Mary: "Oh, I just ate."
> John: "Well, I'm feeling really starved."
> Mary: "When was the last time you ate?"

Sociologist Charles Derber recorded this conversation (Derber, 1979: 24). John starts by saying how hungry he is. The attention is on him. Mary replies that she's not hungry, and the attention shifts to her. John insists he's hungry, shifting attention back to him. Mary finally allows the conversation to focus on John by asking him when he last ate. John thus "wins" the competition for attention (Box 4.1).

Derber recorded 1,500 conversations in family homes, workplaces, restaurants, classrooms, dormitories, and therapy groups. He concluded that Americans usually try to turn conversations toward themselves. They usually do so in ways that go unnoticed. Nonetheless, says Derber, the typical conversation is a covert competition for attention. Derber is careful to point out that conversations are not winner-take-all competitions. Unless both people in a two-person conversation receive some attention, the interaction is likely to cease. Therefore, conversation typically involves the exchange of attention.

Exchange and Rational Choice Theories

The idea that social interaction involves trade in attention and other valued resources is the central insight of **exchange theory** (Blau, 1964; Homans, 1961). Exchange theorists believe, as did the Beatles, that "in the end, the love you take is equal to the love you make." But not just love: social exchange theorists argue that *all* social relationships involve a literal give and take. From this point of view, when people interact, they exchange valued resources (including attention, pleasure, approval, prestige, information, and money) or punishments. With payoffs, relationships endure and can give rise to various organizational forms. Without payoffs, relationships end. Paradoxically, relationships can also endure because *punishments* are exchanged. The classic case involves "tit-for-tat" violence,

Exchange theory: Holds that social interaction involves trade in valued resources.

BOX 4.1
YOU AND THE SOCIAL WORLD

Competing for Attention

You can observe the competition for attention yourself. Record a couple of minutes of conversation in your dorm, home, or workplace. Then play it back.

WRITING ASSIGNMENT

Write a 500-word essay evaluating each statement in the conversation. Does the statement try to change who is the subject of the conversation? Or does it say something about the *other* conversationalist(s) or ask them about what *they* said? How does not responding, or merely saying "uh-huh" in response, operate to shift attention? Are other conversational techniques especially effective in shifting attention? Who "wins" the conversation? What is the winner's gender, race, and class position? Is the winner popular or unpopular? Do you think a connection exists between the person's status in the group and his or her ability to win? What other factors might account for winning?

---

where one party to a conflict engages in violence, another party retaliates, the first party seeks revenge, and so on.

A variant of this approach is **rational choice theory** (Coleman, 1990; Hechter, 1987). Rational choice theory focuses less on the resources being exchanged than the way interacting people weigh the benefits and costs of interaction. According to rational choice theory, interacting people always try to maximize benefits and minimize costs. Businesspeople want to keep their expenses to a minimum so that they can keep their profits as high as possible. Similarly, everyone wants to gain the most from their interactions—socially, emotionally, and economically—while paying the least.

Undoubtedly, one can explain many types of social interaction in terms of exchange and rational choice theories. However, some types of interaction cannot be explained in these terms. For example, people get little or nothing of value out of some relationships, yet they persist. Slaves remain slaves not because they are well paid or because they enjoy the work but because they are forced to do it. Some people remain in abusive relationships because their abusive partner keeps them socially isolated and psychologically dependent. They lack the emotional or material resources needed to get out of the abusive relationship.

At the other extreme, people often act in ways they consider fair or just, even if this does not maximize their personal gain (Frank, 1988; Gamson, Fireman, and Rytina, 1982). Some people even engage in altruistic or heroic acts from which they gain nothing. Heroes respond to cries for help based on emotion (which, physiologists tell us, takes 1/125th of a second to register in the brain), not rational calculation (which takes seconds or even minutes). When people behave fairly or altruistically, they are interacting with others based on *norms* they have learned—norms that say they should act justly and help people in need, even if substantial costs are attached. Such norms are for the most part ignored by exchange and rational choice theorists. Exchange and rational choice theorists think that you do for others what they do for you because if you don't, then others will stop doing things for you (Homans, 1950). But social life is richer than this narrow view suggests. Interaction is not all selfishness. One researcher found that freshman sociology and economics majors were equally "selfish," but by the time they graduated, the economics majors were much more likely than the sociology majors to consider "selfish" actions natural and normal (Frank, 1988). Clearly, what we learn has an impact on our norms and expectations regarding social interaction.

Moreover, we cannot *assume* what people want, because norms (as well as roles and statuses) are not presented to us fully formed, nor do we accept them me-

Rational choice theory: Focuses on the way interacting people weigh the benefits and costs of interaction. According to rational choice theory, interacting people always try to maximize benefits and minimize costs.

chanically. Instead, we constantly negotiate and modify norms—as well as roles and statuses—as we interact with others. We will now explore this theme by considering the ingenious ways in which people manage the impressions they give to others during social interaction.

Interaction as Symbolic

The best way of impressing [advisers] with your competence is asking questions you know the answer to. Because if they ever put it back on you, "Well, what do you think?" then you can tell them what you think and you'd give a very intelligent answer because you knew it. You didn't ask it to find out information. You ask it to impress people.

—A THIRD-YEAR MEDICAL STUDENT

CENGAGENOW™

Learn more about **Impression Management** by going through the Impression Management Animation.

Impression management has been important in U.S. politics for a long time. President George W. Bush wanted to project himself as a man of the people—a Texan interested in sports and ranching—rather than a member of the East Coast elite. President Franklin D. Roosevelt, who suffered from polio, wanted to project a sense of strength, so his staff went to great lengths never to show him in a wheelchair.

Soon after they enter medical school, students become adept at managing the impression they make on other people. As Jack Haas and William Shaffir (1987) show in their study of professional socialization, medical students adopt a new, medical vocabulary and wear a white lab coat to set themselves apart from patients. They try to model their behavior after the doctors who have authority over them. They may ask questions they know the answer to so that they can impress their teachers. When dealing with patients, they may hide their ignorance under medical jargon to maintain their authority. By engaging in these and related practices, medical students reduce the distance between their premedical-school selves and the role of doctor. By the time they finish medical school, they have reduced the distance so much that they no longer see any difference between the two. They come to take for granted a fact they once had to socially construct—the fact that they are doctors (Haas and Shaffir, 1987: 53–83).

Haas and Shaffir's study is an application of symbolic interactionism, a theoretical approach introduced in Chapter 1. Symbolic interactionists regard people as active, creative, and self-reflective. Whereas exchange theorists *assume* what people want, symbolic interactionists argue that people create meanings and desires in the course of social interaction (Blumer, 1969; Berger and Luckmann, 1966; Strauss, 1993).

PAUL BUCK/AFP/Getty Images

Ewing Galloway/Index Stock Imagery/Photolibrary

Dramaturgical Analysis: Role-Playing

Although there are several distinct approaches to symbolic interactionism (Denzin, 1992), probably the most widely applied approach is **dramaturgical analysis.** As first developed by sociologist Erving Goffman (1959 [1956]), dramaturgical analysis takes literally Shakespeare's line from *As You Like It:* "All the world's a stage and all the men and women merely players."

From Goffman's point of view, we are constantly engaged in role-playing. This fact is most evident when we are "front stage" in public settings. Just as being front stage in a drama requires the use of props, set gestures, and memorized lines, so does acting in public space. A server in a restaurant, for example, must dress in a uniform, smile, and recite fixed lines ("How are you? My name is Sam and I'm your server today. May I get you a drink before you order your meal?"). When the server goes "backstage," he or she can relax from the front-stage performance and discuss it with fellow actors ("Those kids at table six are driving me nuts!"). Thus, we often distinguish between our public roles and our "true" selves. Note, however, that even backstage we engage in role-playing and impression management. It's just that we are less likely to be aware of it. For instance, in the kitchen, a server may try to present herself in the best possible light to impress another server so that she can eventually ask him out for a date. Thus, the implication of dramaturgical analysis is that there is no single self, just the ensemble of roles we play in various social contexts (Box 4.2). Servers in restaurants play many roles off the job. They play on basketball teams, sing in church choirs, and hang out with friends at shopping malls. Each role is governed by norms about what kinds of clothes to wear, what kind of conversation to engage in, and so on. We play on many front stages in everyday life.

We do not always do so enthusiastically. If a role is stressful, we may engage in role distancing. **Role distancing** involves giving the impression that we are just "going through the motions" but actually lack serious commitment to a role. Thus, when people think a role they are playing is embarrassing or beneath them, they typically want to give their peers the impression that the role is not their "true" self. My parents force me to sing in the church choir; I'm working at McDonald's just to earn a few extra dollars, but I'll be going back to college next semester; this old car I'm driving is just a loaner. When we distance ourselves from a role, we invent those kinds of rationalizations.

Ethnomethodology

By emphasizing how we construct social reality in the course of interaction, symbolic interactionists downplay the importance of norms and understandings that *precede* any given interaction. **Ethnomethodology** tries to correct that shortcoming. Ethnomethodology is the study of the methods ordinary people use, often unconsciously, to make sense of what others do and say. Ethnomethodologists stress that everyday interactions could not take place without preexisting shared norms and understandings.

To illustrate the importance of preexisting shared norms and understandings, Harold Garfinkel conducted a series of experiments. In one such experiment he asked one of his students to interpret a casual greeting in an unexpected way (Garfinkel, 1967: 44):

Acquaintance: [waving cheerily] How are you?

Student: How am I in regard to what? My health, my finances, my schoolwork, my peace of mind, my . . . ?

Acquaintance: [red in the face and suddenly out of control] Look! I was just trying to be polite. Frankly, I don't give a damn how you are.

As this example shows, social interaction requires tacit agreement between the actors about what is normal and expected. Without shared norms and understandings, no sus-

Dramaturgical analysis: An approach that views social interaction as a sort of play in which people present themselves so that they appear in the best possible light.

Role distancing: Involves giving the impression that we are just going through the motions and that we lack serious commitment to a role.

Ethnomethodology: The study of how people make sense of what others do and say by adhering to preexisting norms.

BOX 4.2
SOCIOLOGY AT THE MOVIES

Miss Congeniality (2000)

Sandra Bullock in *Miss Congeniality* (2000)

RON BATZDORFF/CASTLE ROCK/FORTIS/THE KOBAL COLLECTION

Scene: A New Jersey schoolyard in 1982. An 8-year-old schoolyard bully is picking a fight with another, smaller boy. Unexpectedly, a girl comes to the rescue, telling the bully to back off. The following dialogue ensues:

Bully: "If you weren't a girl, I'd beat your face off."
Girl: "If *you* weren't a girl I'd beat *your* face off."
Bully: "You calling me a girl?"
Girl: "You called *me* one."

Whereupon the bully takes a swing at the girl, which she neatly evades, and she proceeds to deck him. She then approaches the other boy, and says sweetly: "Forget those guys. They're just jealous. You're funny. You're smart. Girls like that."
Other boy: "Well I don't like you. Now everyone thinks I need a girl to fight for me. You're a dork brain." Girl punches other boy in nose. End of scene.

Almost predictably, the girl grows up to become a tough-talking and tomboyish undercover agent (played by Sandra Bullock) without a boyfriend. The plot thickens when Bullock is forced to take an undercover assignment as a contestant in a beauty pageant. Someone is plotting a terrorist act during the pageant and she has to find out who it is. First, however, she has to undergo a role change, something far deeper than a mere makeover. A beauty consultant (played by Michael Caine) teaches her how to walk like a stereotypical woman, wear makeup, and dress to kill. In her interaction with the other contestants, she begins to learn how to behave in a conventionally feminine way. She even becomes a finalist in the beauty pageant. In the end, she gets the bad guy, captures the heart of the handsome FBI agent (played by Benjamin Bratt), and wins the pageant's "Miss Congeniality" award. Her true self emerges, and everyone goes home happy.

This movie's theme is at least as old as Cinderella. In Hollywood, as in fairy tales, the emergence of one's "true self" is often the resolution of the conflict that animates the story. Yet life rarely comes in such neat packages. The sociological study of social interaction shows how we balance different selves in center stage and backstage performances, play many roles simultaneously, get pulled in different directions by role strain and role conflict, and distance ourselves from some of our roles. To make matters even more complex and dynamic, sociology underlines how we continuously enter new stages, roles, conflicts, strains, and distancing maneuvers as we mature. This social complexity makes our "true self" not a thing we discover once and for all time but a work in progress. The resolution of every conflict that animates our lives is temporary. *Miss Congeniality* is an entertaining escape from reality's messiness, but a poor guide to life as we actually live it. For that we need sociology.

Critical Thinking

- Do you have a "true self"? Or are you just a bundle of roles that you perform?

- When do we act and when do we stop acting?

---

tained interaction can occur. People are likely to get upset and end an interaction when one violates the assumptions underlying the stability and meaning of daily life.

Assuming the existence of shared norms and understandings, let us now inquire briefly into the way people communicate in face-to-face interaction. The issue may seem trivial. However, as you will soon see, having a conversation is actually a wonder of intricate complexity. Even today's most advanced supercomputer cannot conduct a natural-sounding conversation with a person (Kurzweil, 1999: 61, 91).

Verbal and Nonverbal Communication

Fifty years ago an article appeared in the British newspaper *News Chronicle,* trumpeting the invention of an electronic translating device at the University of London. According to the article, "As fast as [a user] could type the words in, say, French, the equivalent in Hungarian or Russian would issue forth on the tape" (quoted in Silberman, 2000: 225). The report was an exaggeration, to put it mildly. It soon became a standing joke that if you asked a computer to translate "The spirit is willing, but the flesh is weak" into Russian, the output would read, "The vodka is good, but the steak is lousy." Today we are closer to high-quality machine translation than we were in the 1950s. However, a practical universal translator exists only on *Star Trek.*

The Social Context of Language

The main problem with computerized translation systems is that computers find it difficult to make sense of the *social and cultural context* in which language is used. The same words may mean different things in different settings, so computers, lacking contextual cues, routinely botch translations. For this reason, metaphors are notoriously problematic for computers. The following machine translation, which contains both literal and metaphorical text, illustrates this point:

English original:

Babel Fish is a computerized translation system (at http://babelfish.yahoo.com/) that is available on the World Wide Web. You can type a passage in a window and receive a nearly instant translation in one of four languages. Simple, literal language is translated fairly accurately. But when understanding requires an appreciation of social context, as most of our everyday speech does, the computer can quickly get you into a pickle. What a drag!

Machine translation from English to Spanish:

El pescado de Babel es un sistema automatizado de la traducción que está disponible en el World Wide Web (en http://babelfish.yahoo.com/). Usted puede pulsar un paso en un Window y recibir una traducción casi inmediata en varias idiomas. El lenguaje simple, literal se traduce bastante exactamente. Pero cuando la comprensión requiere un aprecio del contexto social, como la mayoría de nuestro discurso diario, el ordenador puede conseguirle rápidamente en una salmuera. Una qué fricción!

Machine translation from Spanish back to English:

The fish of Babel is an automated system of the translation that is available in the World Wide Web (in http://babelfish.yahoo.com/). You can press a passage in a Window and receive an almost immediate translation in several languages. The simple, literal language is translated rather exactly. But when it does, the understanding requires an esteem of the social context, like most of our daily speech, the computer can obtain to him in a brine quickly. One what friction!

Despite the complexity involved in accurate translation, human beings are much better at it than computers. Why is this so? A hint comes from computers themselves. Machine translation works best when applications are restricted to a single social context—say, weather forecasting or oil exploration. In such cases, specialized vocabularies and meanings specific to the context of interest can be built into the program. Ambiguity is thus reduced and computers can "understand" the meaning of words well enough to translate them with reasonable accuracy. Similarly, humans must be able to reduce ambiguity and make sense of words to become good translators. They do so by learning the nuances of meaning in different cultural and social contexts over an extended period of time.

Mastery of one's own language happens the same way. People are able to understand one another not just because they are able to learn words—computers can do that well enough—but because they can learn the social and cultural contexts that give words meaning. They are greatly assisted in that task by *nonverbal* cues.

Facial Expressions, Gestures, and Body Language

Cosmopolitan magazine once featured an article advising female readers on "how to reduce otherwise evolved men to drooling, panting fools." Basing his analysis on the work of several psychologists, the author of the article first urges readers to "[d]elete the old-school seductress image (smoky eyes, red lips, brazen stare) from your consciousness." Then, he writes, you must "[u]pload a new inner temptress who's equal parts good girl and wild child." The article recommends invading a man's personal space and entering his "intimate zone" by finding an excuse to touch him. Picking a piece of lint off his jacket ought to do the trick. Then you can tell him how much you like his cologne (Willardt, 2000). If things progress, another article in the same issue of *Cosmopolitan* explains how you can read his body language to tell whether he's lying (Dutton, 2000).

Whatever we may think of the soundness of *Cosmopolitan*'s advice or the images of women and men it tries to reinforce, this example drives home the point that social interaction typically involves a complex mix of verbal and nonverbal messages. The face alone is capable of more than 1,000 distinct expressions, reflecting the whole range of human emotion. Arm movements, hand gestures, posture, and other aspects of body language send many more messages to one's audience (Wood, 1999 [1996]).

Despite the wide variety of facial expressions in the human repertoire, most researchers believed until recently that the facial expressions of six emotions are similar across cultures. These six emotions are happiness, sadness, anger, disgust, fear, and surprise (Ekman, 1978). Especially since the mid-1990s, however, some researchers have questioned whether a universally recognized set of facial expressions reflects basic human emotions. Among other things, critics have argued that "facial expressions are not the readout of emotions but displays that serve social motives and are mostly determined by the presence of an audience" (Fernandez-Dols, Sanchez, Carrera, and Ruiz-Belda, 1997: 163). From this point of view, a smile will reflect pleasure if it serves a person's interest to present a smiling face to his or her audience. On the other hand, a person may be motivated to conceal anxiety by smiling or to conceal pleasure by suppressing a smile. At times, different cultural expectations can lead to colossal misunderstanding. Until recently, it was considered rude among educated Japanese to say "no." Disagreement was instead conveyed by discreetly changing the subject and smiling politely. Consequently, it was common for visiting Americans to think that their Japanese hosts were saying "yes" because of the politeness, the smile, and the absence of a "no" when in fact they were saying "no."

No gestures or body postures mean the same thing in all societies and all cultures. In our society, people point with an outstretched hand and an extended finger. However, people raised in other cultures tip their head or use their chin or eyes to point out something. We nod our heads "yes" and shake "no," but others nod "no" and shake "yes."

Finally, we must note that in all societies people communicate by manipulating the space that separates them from others (Hall, 1959, 1966). This point is well illustrated in our *Cosmopolitan* example. Sociologists commonly distinguish four zones that surround us. The size of these zones varies from one society to the next. In North America, an inti-

Robert J. Brym

◁ Among other things, body language communicates the degree to which people conform to gender roles, or widely shared expectations about how males and females are supposed to act. In these photos, which postures suggest power and aggressiveness? Which suggest pleasant compliance? Which are "appropriate" to the sex of the person?

mate zone extends about 18 inches from the body. It is restricted to people with whom we want sustained, intimate physical contact. A personal zone extends from about 18 inches to 4 feet away. It is reserved for friends and acquaintances. We tolerate only a little physical intimacy from such people. The social zone is situated in the area roughly 4 to 12 feet away from us. Apart from a handshake, no physical contact is permitted from people we restrict to that zone. The public zone starts around 12 feet from our bodies. It is used to distinguish a performer or a speaker from an audience.

Status Cues

Aside from facial expressions, gestures, and body language, nonverbal communication takes place by means of **status cues,** or visual indicators of other people's social position. Goffman (1959 [1956]) observed that when individuals come into contact, they typically try to acquire information that will help them define the situation and make interaction easier. That goal is accomplished in part by attending to status cues.

Elijah Anderson (1990) developed this idea by studying the way African Americans and European Americans interact on the street in two adjacent urban neighborhoods. Members of both groups visually inspect strangers before concluding that they are not dangerous. They make assumptions about others on the basis of skin color, age, gender, companions, clothing, jewelry, and the objects they carry with them. They evaluate the movements of strangers, the time of day, and other factors to establish how dangerous they might be. In general, children pass inspection easily. White women and white men are treated with greater caution, but not as much caution as African American women and

Status cues: Visual indicators of a person's social position.

Which stereotypes about Japanese people are reinforced by this American World War II poster?

Appeared in *Leatherneck*, March, 1945/Pantheon Books/Random House, Inc.

African American men. Urban dwellers are most suspicious of African American male teenagers. People are most likely to interact verbally with individuals who are perceived as the safest.

Although status cues may be useful in helping people define the situation and thus greasing the wheels of social interaction, they also pose a social danger, for status cues can quickly degenerate into **stereotypes,** or rigid views of how members of various groups act, regardless of whether individual group members really behave that way. Stereotypes create social barriers that impair interaction or prevent it altogether. For instance, police officers in some states routinely stop young African American male drivers without cause to check for proper licensing, possession of illegal goods, and other similar violations. In this case, a social cue has become a stereotype that guides police policy. Young African American males, the great majority of whom never commit an illegal act, view this police practice as harassment. Racial stereotyping therefore helps perpetuate the sometimes poor relations between the African American community and law enforcement officials.

As these examples show, face-to-face interaction may at first glance appear to be straightforward and unproblematic. Most of the time it is. However, underlying the taken-for-granted surface of human communication is a wide range of cultural assumptions, unconscious understandings, and nonverbal cues that make interaction possible.

Power and Conflict Theories of Social Interaction

In our discussion of the social cement that binds statuses, roles, and norms together, we have made four main points (▶Concept Summary 4.1):

1. One of the most important forces that cements social interaction is the competitive exchange of valued resources. People communicate to the degree they get something valuable out of the interaction. Simultaneously, however, they must engage in a careful balancing act. If they compete too avidly and prevent others from getting much

Stereotypes: Rigid views of how members of various groups act, regardless of whether individual group members really behave that way.

▶CONCEPT SUMMARY 4.1

Theories of Social Interaction

Theory	Focus	Principal Theorist(s)
Exchange theory	Exchange of valued resources	Homans, Blau
Rational choice theory	Maximization of gains and minimization of losses	Coleman, Hechter
Symbolic interactionism	Interpretation, negotiation, and modification of norms, roles, and statuses	Blumer, Denzin
Dramaturgical analysis	Impression management	Goffman
Ethnomethodology	Influence of preexisting norms	Garfinkel
Conflict theory	Influence of status hierarchies	Bourdieu, Collins

out of the social interaction, communication will break down. This is exchange and rational choice theory in a nutshell.

2. Nobody hands values, norms, roles, and statuses to us fully formed, nor do we accept them mechanically. We mold them to suit us as we interact with others. For example, we constantly engage in impression management so that others will see the roles we perform in the best possible light. This is a major argument of symbolic interactionism and its most popular variant, dramaturgical analysis.

3. Norms do not emerge entirely spontaneously during social interaction, either. In general form, they exist before any given interaction takes place. Indeed, sustained interaction would be impossible without preexisting shared understandings. This is the core argument of ethnomethodology.

4. Nonverbal mechanisms of communication greatly facilitate social interaction. These mechanisms include facial expressions, hand gestures, body language, and status cues.

We now want to highlight a final point that has been lurking in the background of our discussion. **Conflict theories of social interaction** emphasize that when people interact, their statuses are often arranged in a hierarchy. People on top enjoy more **power** than those on the bottom—that is, they are "in a position to carry out [their] own will despite resistance" (Weber, 1947: 152). This disparity in power is well illustrated by the mass media, where the conversation is overwhelmingly one-sided; in most cases, the media speak and we listen (Box 4.3). More generally, in face-to-face communication the degree of inequality strongly affects the character of social interaction between the interacting parties (Bourdieu, 1977 [1972]; Collins, 1982).

We can see how the distribution of power affects interaction by examining male–female interaction. Women are typically socialized to assume subordinate positions, whereas men are typically socialized to assume superordinate positions. This distribution of power is evident in the way men usually learn to be aggressive and competitive, and women learn to be cooperative and supportive (see Chapter 3, "Socialization," and Chapter 10, "Sexuality and Gender"). Because of this learning, men often dominate conversations. Thus, conversation analyses conducted by Deborah Tannen show that men are more likely than women to engage in long monologues and interrupt when others are talking (Tannen, 1994a, 1994b; Box 4.4). They are also less likely to ask for help or directions because doing so would imply a reduction in their authority. Many male–female conflicts result from these differences. A stereotypical case is the lost male driver and the helpful female passenger. The female passenger, seeing that the male driver is lost, suggests

Conflict theories of social interaction: Theories which emphasize that when people interact, their statuses are often arranged in a hierarchy. Those on top enjoy more power than those on the bottom. The degree of inequality strongly affects the character of social interaction between the interacting parties.

Power: The probability that one actor in a social relationship will be in a position to carry out his or her own will despite resistance.

BOX 4.3
MASS MEDIA AND SOCIETY

The Problem of Domination

The mass media include print, radio, television, and other communication technologies. Often, *mass media* and *mass communication* are used interchangeably to refer to the transmission of information from one person or group to another. The word *mass* implies that the media reach many people. The word *media* signifies that communication does not take place directly through face-to-face interaction. Instead, technology intervenes or mediates in transmitting messages from senders to receivers.

Communication via the mass media is usually one way, or at least one sided. There are few senders (or producers) and many receivers (or audience members). Ordinary people may appear on the *Oprah Winfrey Show* or *Late Night with David Letterman,* compete in *American Idol* or *The Apprentice,* or even delight in a slice of fame on *Survivor* or *Big Brother.* However, producers choose the guests and create the content for these programs.

Usually, then, members of the audience cannot exert much influence on the mass media. They can choose only to tune in or tune out. And even tuning out is difficult because it excludes one from the styles, news, gossip, and entertainment most people depend on to grease the wheels of social interaction. Few people want to be cultural misfits.

This does not mean that people are always passive consumers of the mass media. For one thing, we may filter, interpret, and resist what we see and hear if it contradicts our experience and beliefs. For another, at least one mass medium, the Internet, allows consumers to become producers with relative ease. Many millions of Internet users participate in discussion groups, chat groups, and role-playing communities; create their own websites; and develop and use free music-sharing programs such as Napster and Kazaa. True, the original Napster was shut down, and a group of recording companies tried to close Kazaa by taking it to an American court for copyright infringement late in 2002. However, the companies discovered that the distributor of Kazaa software is incorporated in the tiny South Pacific island of Vanuatu. Kazaa is managed from Australia, its servers are in Denmark, its source code is stored in Estonia, its developers live in the Netherlands, and it has 60 million users in 150 countries. It is therefore highly doubtful that a decision on behalf of the recording companies could be enforced ("Digital Dilemmas," 2003). It seems that as soon as one illegal music-sharing service is shut down, another pops up. Nonetheless, the Internet is an exception to the general rule. In the interaction between audiences and all other media sources, the media sources dominate.

Critical Thinking

- To what degree do you think the mass media shape your life?
- To what degree do you think you shape the mass media?
- Is your relationship (and the relationship of your peers) to the mass media acceptable or would you like to see it change in some way? If so, how? How might change be accomplished?

Domination: A mode of interaction in which nearly all power is concentrated in the hands of people with similar status. Fear is the dominant emotion in systems of interaction based on domination.

Cooperation: A mode of social interaction in which power is more or less equally distributed between people of different status. The dominant emotion in cooperative interaction is trust.

Competition: A mode of interaction in which power is unequally distributed but the degree of inequality is less than in systems of domination. Envy is an important emotion in competitive interactions.

that they stop and ask for directions. The male driver doesn't want to ask for directions because he thinks that would make him look incompetent. If both parties remain firm in their positions, an argument is bound to result.

Types of Interaction

Domination represents one extreme type of interaction. In social interaction based on domination, nearly all power is concentrated in the hands of people of similar status, whereas people of a different status enjoy almost no power. In extreme cases of domination, subordinates live in a state of near-constant fear. The opposite is interaction based on **cooperation.** Here, power is more or less equally distributed between people of different statuses. Cooperative interaction is based on feelings of trust. Between the two extremes of interaction based on domination and interaction based on cooperation is interaction based on **competition.** In this mode of interaction, power is unequally distributed, but the degree of inequality is less than in systems of domination. Most of the social interactions analyzed by exchange and rational choice theorists are of this type. Envy is an important emotion in most competitive interactions (▶Concept Summary 4.2).

BOX 4.4
SOCIAL POLICY: WHAT DO YOU THINK?

Allocating Time Fairly in Class Discussions

When John Lie was Chair of the Department of Sociology at the University of Illinois (Urbana-Champaign), he often heard student complaints. Sometimes they were reasonable. Sometimes they were not. A particularly puzzling complaint came from a self-proclaimed feminist taking a women's studies class. She said: "The professor lets the male students talk in class. They don't seem to have done much of the reading, but the professor insists on letting them say something even when they don't really have anything to say." John later talked to the professor, who claimed she was only trying to let different opinions come out in class.

Policy debates often deal with important issues at the state, national, and international levels. However, they may revolve around everyday social interaction. For instance, as Deborah Tannen's work suggests, gender differences in conversational styles have a big impact on gender inequality. Thus, many professors use class participation to evaluate students. Your grade may depend in part on how often you speak up and whether you have something interesting to say. But Tannen's study suggests that men tend to speak up more

often and more forcefully than women. Men are more likely to dominate classroom discussions. Therefore, does the evaluation of class participation in assigning grades unfairly penalize female students? If so, what policies can you recommend that might overcome the problem?

One possibility is to eliminate class participation as a criterion for student evaluation. Most professors would object to this approach on the grounds that good discussions can demonstrate students' familiarity with course material, sharpen one's ability to reason logically, and enrich everyone's educational experience. A college lacking energetic discussion and debate wouldn't be much of an educational institution.

A second option is to systematically encourage women to participate in classroom discussion. A third option is to allot

equal time for women and men or to allot each student equal time. Criticisms of such an approach come readily to mind. Shouldn't time be allocated only to people who have done the reading and have something interesting to say? The woman who complained to John Lie made that same point. Encouraging everyone to speak or forcing each student to speak for a certain number of minutes, even if they don't have something interesting to contribute, would probably be boring or frustrating for better-prepared students.

As you can see, the question of how time should be allocated in class discussions has no obvious solution. In general, the realm of interpersonal interaction and conversation is an extremely difficult area in which to impose rules and policies.

Critical Thinking

- What should your professor do to ensure that class discussion time is allocated fairly?

- Should people regulate social interaction and conversation? If so, how?

The Points of the Compass

Society fits together like a set of nested Russian dolls, with face-to-face interaction constituting the smallest doll in the set (▶Figure 4.4). Norms, roles, and statuses are the building blocks of social life. They form the *micro-structures* within which face-to-face interac-

▶CONCEPT SUMMARY 4.2
Main Modes of Interaction

	MODE OF INTERACTION		
	Domination	**Competition**	**Cooperation**
Level of inequality	High	Medium	Low
Characteristic emotion	Fear	Envy	Trust
Example	Plantation	Corporation	Marriage

tion takes place. Sustained micro-level interaction is shaped by higher-level structures (sometimes called *mesostructures;* see Chapter 5, "Networks, Groups, and Organizations") (Maines, 1982). Still larger *macrostructures,* including classes, states, and systems of patriarchy, constrain the functioning of networks, groups, and organizations. Finally, international trade, global communication, state relations, and organizations that span many countries form the overarching *global structures* that limit the freedom of the smaller

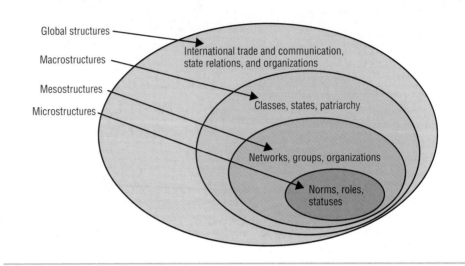

▶FIGURE 4.4
Big Structures, Small Processes

Global structures → International trade and communication, state relations, and organizations

Macrostructures → Classes, states, patriarchy

Mesostructures → Networks, groups, organizations

Microstructures → Norms, roles, statuses

structures operating within them (on macrostructures and global structures, see Part III, "Social Inequality" and Part IV, "Institutions"). Social structures thus constrain our actions at various levels of analysis.

The process of people interpreting, negotiating, and modifying their immediate social settings, which we have analyzed in this chapter, gives social structures their dynamism and their life. Society involves people exercising creativity and freedom within limits shaped by social structures; but human creativity and freedom modify those social structures, and therefore, eventually, the constraints that shape human thought and action. Social life is shaped by both points on the sociological compass, freedom and constraint.

CHAPTER SUMMARY

1. What is social interaction?

Social interaction involves verbal and nonverbal communication between people acting and reacting to one another. It is ordered by norms, roles, and statuses.

2. Don't emotions govern all social interaction? Aren't emotions natural, spontaneous, and largely uncontrollable?

Emotions do form an important part of all social interactions. However, they are less spontaneous and uncontrollable than we commonly believe. For example, your status in an interaction and in the larger society affects how much you laugh and what you laugh at. Similarly, people manage their emotions in personal life and at work according to "feeling rules" that reflect historically changing cultural standards and the demands of organizations.

3. In what sense is social interaction based on competition?

When we interact socially we exchange valued resources—everything from attention and pleasure to prestige and money. However, because people typically try to maximize their rewards and minimize their losses, social interaction may be seen as a competition for scarce resources.

4. Is competition the only basis of social interaction?

No, it is not. People may interact cooperatively and altruistically because they have been socialized to do so. They may also maintain interaction based on domination.

5. How do symbolic interactionists analyze social interaction?

Symbolic interactionists focus on how people create meaning in the course of social interaction and on how they negotiate and modify roles, statuses, and norms. Symbolic interactionism has several variants. For example, dramaturgical analysis is based on the idea that people play roles in their daily lives in much the same way as actors on stage. When we are center stage, we act publicly, sometimes from ready-made scripts. Backstage, we relax from our public performances and allow what we regard as our "true" selves to emerge (even though we engage in role performances backstage, too). We may distance ourselves from our roles when they embarrass us, but role-playing nonetheless pervades social interaction. Together with various norms of interaction, role-playing enables society to function. Ethnomethodology is another symbolic interactionist approach to social interaction. It analyzes the methods people use to make sense of what others do and say. It insists on the importance of preexisting shared norms and understandings in making everyday interaction possible.

6. **Is all social interaction based on language?**

No, it is not. Nonverbal communication, including socially defined facial expressions, gestures, body language, and status cues, are as important as verbal communication in conveying meaning.

Questions to Consider

1. Draw up a list of your current and former girlfriends or boyfriends. Indicate the race, religion, age, and height of each person on the list. How similar or different are you from the people with whom you have chosen to be intimate? What does this list tell you about the social distribution of intimacy? Is love blind? What criteria other than race, religion, age, and height might affect the social distribution of intimacy?

2. Is it accurate to say that people always act selfishly to maximize their rewards and minimize their losses? Why or why not?

3. In what sense (if any) is it reasonable to claim that all of social life consists of role-playing and that we have no "true self," just an ensemble of roles?

Web Resources

CENGAGENOW™

Maximize your study time by using CengageNOW's diagnostic study plan to help you review this chapter. The Study Plan will

- help you identify areas on which you should concentrate;
- provide interactive exercises to help you master the chapter concepts; and
- provide a post-test to confirm you are ready to move on to the next chapter.

The Companion Website for *Sociology: Your Compass for a New World, The Brief Edition*, Enhanced Second Edition

www.cengage.com/sociology/brym

Supplement your review of this chapter by going to the companion website to take one of the tutorial quizzes, use flash cards to master key terms, and check out the many other study aids you'll find there. You'll also find special features such as GSS Data and Census 2000 information that will put data and resources at your fingertips to help you with that special project or help you do some research on your own.

Networks, Groups, and Organizations

In this chapter, you will learn that:

- We commonly explain the way people act in terms of their interests and emotions. However, sometimes people act against their interests and suppress their emotions because various social collectivities (i.e., groups, networks, and bureaucracies) exert a powerful influence on them.

- The patterns of social ties through which emotional and material resources flow form social networks. Among other things, information, communicable diseases, and social support typically spread through social networks.

- People who are bound together by interaction and a common identity form social groups. Groups impose conformity on members and draw boundary lines between those who belong and those who do not.

- Bureaucracies are large, impersonal organizations that operate with varying degrees of efficiency.

- Efficient bureaucracies keep hierarchy to a minimum, distribute decision making to all levels of the bureaucracy, and keep lines of communication open between different units of the bureaucracy.

- Although our freedom is constrained by various social collectivities, we can also use them to increase our freedom. Networks, groups, and organizations can be mobilized for good or evil.

Beyond Individual Motives

The Holocaust

Personal Anecdote

In 1941, the large stone and glass train station was one of the proudest structures in Smolensk, a provincial capital of about 100,000 people on Russia's western border. Always bustling, it was especially busy on the morning of June 28. For besides the usual passengers and well-wishers, hundreds of Soviet Red Army soldiers were nervously talking, smoking, writing hurried letters to their loved ones, and sleeping fitfully on the station floor waiting for their train. Nazi troops had invaded the nearby city of Minsk in Belarus a couple of days before. The Soviet soldiers were being positioned to defend Russia against the inevitable German onslaught.

Robert Brym's father, then in his 20s, had been standing in line for nearly 2 hours to buy food when he noticed flares arching over the station. Within seconds, Stuka bombers, the pride of the German air force, swept down, releasing their bombs just before pulling out of their dive. Inside the station, shards of glass, blocks of stone, and mounds of earth fell indiscriminately on sleeping soldiers and nursing mothers alike. Everyone panicked. People trampled over one another to get out. In minutes, the train station was rubble.

Nearly 2 years earlier, Robert's father had managed to escape Poland when the Nazis invaded his hometown near Warsaw. Now he was on the run again. By the time the Nazis occupied Smolensk a few weeks after their dive-bombers destroyed

---

CENGAGENOW™

This icon signals when CengageNOW has important resources available for you to use in conjunction with the text. See the foldout at the front of this text for information on how to access CengageNOW.

its train station, Robert's father was deep in the Russian interior serving in a workers' battalion attached to the Soviet Red Army.

"My father was one of 300,000 Polish Jews who fled eastward into Russia before the Nazi genocide machine could reach them," says Robert. "The remaining 3 million Polish Jews were killed in various ways. Some died in battle. Many more, like my father's mother and younger siblings, were rounded up like diseased cattle and shot. However, most of Poland's Jews wound up in the concentration camps. Those deemed unfit were shipped to the gas chambers. Those declared able to work were turned into slaves until they could work no more. Then they, too, met their fate. A mere 9 percent of Poland's 3.3 million Jews survived World War II. The Nazi regime was responsible for the death of 6 million Jews in Europe.

"One question that always perplexed my father about the war was this: How was it possible for many thousands of ordinary Germans—products of what he regarded as the most advanced civilization on earth—to systematically murder millions of defenseless and innocent Jews, Roma ('Gypsies'), homosexuals, and mentally disabled people in the death camps?" To answer this question adequately, we must borrow ideas from the sociological study of networks, groups, and bureaucracies.

How Social Groups Shape Our Actions

How could ordinary German citizens commit the crime of the century? The conventional, nonsociological answer is that many Nazis were evil, sadistic, or deluded enough to think that Jews and other undesirables threatened the existence of the German people. Therefore, in the Nazi mind, the innocents had to be killed. This answer is given in the 1993 movie *Schindler's List* and in many other accounts. Yet it is far from the whole story. Sociologists emphasize three other factors.

The movie, *Schindler's List,* turns the history of Nazism into a morality play, a struggle between good and evil forces. It does not probe into the sociological roots of good and evil.

Everett Collection

Norms of Solidarity

Norms of solidarity demand conformity. When we form relationships with friends, lovers, spouses, teammates, and comrades-in-arms, we develop shared ideas, or "norms of solidarity," about how we should behave toward them to sustain the relationships. Because these relationships are emotionally important to us, we sometimes pay more attention to norms of solidarity than to the morality of our actions. For example, a study of the Nazis who roamed the Polish countryside to shoot and kill Jews and other "enemies" of Nazi Germany found that the soldiers often did not hate the people they systematically slaughtered, nor did they have many qualms about their actions (Browning, 1992). They simply developed deep loyalty to each other. They felt they had to get their assigned job done or face letting down their comrades. Thus, they committed atrocities partly because they just wanted to maintain group morale, solidarity, and loyalty. They committed evil deeds not because they were extraordinarily bad but because they were quite ordinary—ordinary in the sense that they acted to sustain their friendship ties and to serve their group, just like most people.

The case of the Nazi regime may seem extreme, but other instances of going along with criminal behavior uncover a similar dynamic at work. Why do people rarely report crimes committed by corporations? Employees may worry about getting reprimanded or fired if they become "whistleblowers," but they also worry about letting down their coworkers. Why do gang members engage in criminal acts? They may seek financial gain, but they also regard crime as a way of maintaining a close social bond with their fellow gang members (Box 5.1).

A study of the small number of Polish Christians who helped save Jews during World War II helps clarify why some people violate group norms (Tec, 1986). The heroism of these Polish Christians was not correlated with their educational attainment, political orientation, religious background, or even attitudes toward Jews. In fact, some Polish Christians who helped save Jews were quite anti-Semitic. Instead, these Christian heroes were for one reason or another estranged or cut off from mainstream norms. Because they were poorly socialized into the norms of their society, they were freer not to conform and instead act in ways they believed were right. We could tell a roughly similar story about corporate whistleblowers or people who turn in their fellow gang members. They are disloyal from an insider's point of view but heroic from an outsider's point of view, often because they have been poorly socialized into the group's norms.

Corporate whistleblowers were widely celebrated in 2002 as news of corporate and bureaucratic scandals proliferated in the mass media.

Obedience to Structures of Authority

Structures of authority tend to render people obedient. Most people find it difficult to disobey authorities because they fear ridicule, ostracism, and punishment. This was strikingly demonstrated in an experiment conducted by social psychologist Stanley Milgram (1974). Milgram informed his experimental subjects that they were taking part in a study on punishment and learning. He brought each subject to a room where a man was strapped to a chair. An electrode was attached to the man's wrist. The experimental subject sat in front of a console. It contained 30 switches with labels ranging from "15 volts" to "450 volts" in 15-volt increments. Labels ranging from "slight shock" to "danger: severe shock" were pasted below the switches. The experimental subjects were told to administer a 15-volt shock for the man's first wrong answer and then increase the voltage each time he made an error. The man strapped in the chair was in fact an actor. He did not actually receive a shock. As the experimental subject increased the current, however, the actor began to writhe, shouting for mercy and

BOX 5.1
SOCIAL POLICY: WHAT DO YOU THINK?

Group Loyalty or Betrayal?

Group cohesion led Nazi soldiers to commit genocide. Group loyalty led many ordinary German citizens to support them. Although the Nazis are an extreme case, ordinary people often face a stark choice between group loyalty and group betrayal.

Glen Ridge, New Jersey, is an affluent white suburb. It was also the site of a terrible rape case in 1989. A group of 13 teenage boys lured a sweet-natured young woman with an IQ of 49 and the mental age of a second-grader into a basement. There, 4 of them raped her while 3 others looked on; 6 left when they realized what was going to happen. The rapists used a baseball bat and a broomstick. The boys were the most popular students in the local high school. They had everything going for them. Nor was the young woman a stranger to them. Some of them had known her since she was 5 years old, when they convinced her to lick the point of a ballpoint pen that had been coated in dog feces.

What possessed these boys to gangrape a helpless young woman? How can we explain the subsequent actions of many of the leading citizens of Glen Ridge? It was weeks before anyone reported the rape to the police and years before the boys went to trial. At the trial, many members of the community rallied behind the boys, blaming and ostracizing the rape victim. The courts eventually handed out only light sentences. Why did members of the community refuse to believe the clear-cut evidence? What made them defend the rapists? Why did the boys get off so easily?

Bernard Lefkowitz (1997b) interviewed 250 key players and observers in the Glen Ridge rape case. Ultimately, he indicted the *community* for the rape. He concluded that "[the rapists] adhered to a code of behavior that mimicked, distorted, and exaggerated the values of the adult world around them," while "the citizens supported the boys because they didn't want to taint the town they treasured" (Lefkowitz, 1997b: 493). What were some of the community values the elders upheld and the boys aped?

- *The subordination of women.* All of the boys had grown up in families where men were the dominant personalities. Only one of them had a sister. Not a single woman occupied a position of authority in Glen Ridge High School. The boys classified their female classmates either as "little mothers" who fawned over them or "bad girls" who were simply sexual objects.

- *Lack of compassion for the weak.* According to the minister of Glen Ridge Congregational Church, "Achievement was honored and respected almost to the point of pathology, whether it was the achievements of high school athletes or the achievements of corporate world conquerors." Adds Lefkowitz: "Compassion for the weak wasn't part of the curriculum" (Lefkowitz, 1997b: 130).

- *Tolerance of male misconduct.* The boys routinely engaged in delinquent acts, including one spectacular trashing of a house. However, their parents always paid damages, covered up the misdeeds, and rationalized them with phrases like "boys will be boys." Especially because they were town football heroes, many people felt they could do no wrong.

- *Intense group loyalty.* "The guys prized their intimacy with each other far above what could be achieved with a girl," writes Lefkowitz (1997b: 146). The boys formed a tight clique, and team sports reinforced group solidarity. Under such circumstances, the probability of someone "ratting" on his friends was very low. In the end, of course, there was a "rat." His name was Charles Figueroa. He did not participate in the rape, but he was an athlete, part of the jock clique, and therefore aware of what had happened. Significantly, he was one of the few black boys in the school, tolerated because of his athletic ability but never trusted because of his race and often called a n_____ by his teammates behind his back. This young man's family was highly intelligent and morally sensitive. He was the only one to have the courage to betray the group (Lefkowitz, 1997a, 1997b).

Lefkowitz raises the important question of where we ought to draw the line between group loyalty and group betrayal. You may have to choose between group loyalty and betrayal on more than one occasion, so thinking about these criteria—and clearly understanding the values for which your group stands—will help you make a more informed choice.

Critical Thinking

- Considering your own group loyalties, are there times when you regret not having spoken up?

- Are there times when you regret not having been more loyal? What is the difference between these two types of situations?

- Can you specify criteria for deciding when loyalty is required and when betrayal is the right thing to do?

begging to be released. If the experimental subjects grew reluctant to administer more current, Milgram assured them the man strapped in the chair would be fine and insisted that the success of the experiment depended on the subject's obedience. The subjects were, however, free to abort the experiment at any time.

Remarkably, 71 percent of experimental subjects were prepared to administer shocks of 285 volts or more, even though the switches at that level were labeled "intense shock," "extreme intensity shock," and "danger: severe shock" and despite the fact that the actor appeared to be in great distress at this level of current (▶Figure 5.1).

Milgram's experiment teaches us that as soon as we are introduced to a structure of authority, we are inclined to obey those in power. This is the case even if the authority structure is new and highly artificial, even if we are free to walk away from it with no penalty, and even if we think that by remaining in its grip we are inflicting terrible pain on another human being. In this context, the actions and inactions of German citizens in World War II become more understandable if not more forgivable.

Bureaucratic Organization

Bureaucracies are highly effective structures of authority. The Nazi genocide machine was also so effective because it was bureaucratically organized. As Max Weber (1978 [1968]) defined the term, a **bureaucracy** is a large, impersonal organization composed of many clearly defined positions arranged in a hierarchy. A bureaucracy has a permanent, salaried staff of qualified experts and written goals, rules, and procedures. Staff members always try to find ways of running their organization more efficiently. *Efficiency* means achieving the bureaucracy's goals at the least cost. The goal of the Nazi genocide machine was to kill Jews and other undesirables. To achieve that goal with maximum efficiency, the job was broken into many small tasks. Most officials performed only one function, such as checking train schedules, organizing entertainment for camp guards, maintaining supplies of Zyklon B gas, and removing ashes from the crematoria. The full horror

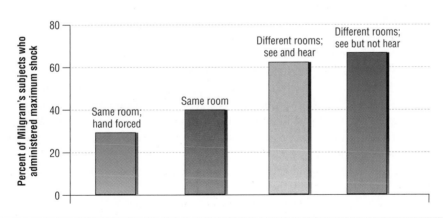

▶FIGURE 5.1

Obedience to Authority Increases with Separation from the Negative Effects of One's Actions

Milgram's experiment supports the view that separating people from the negative effects of their actions increases the likelihood of compliance.

Source: Bar graph based on information in Chapter 4, "Closeness of the Victim," in *Obedience to Authority,* by Stanley Milgram. Copyright © 1974 by Stanley Milgram.

Bureaucracy: A large, impersonal organization composed of many clearly defined positions arranged in a hierarchy. A bureaucracy has a permanent, salaried staff of qualified experts and written goals, rules, and procedures. Staff members always try to find ways of running the bureaucracy more efficiently.

of what was happening eluded many officials or at least could be conveniently ignored as they concentrated on their jobs, most of them far removed from the gas chambers and death camps in occupied Poland. Many factors account for variation in Jewish victimization rates across Europe during World War II. One factor was bureaucratic organization. Not coincidentally, the proportion of Jews killed was highest not in the Nazi-controlled countries where the hatred of Jews was most intense (e.g., Romania), but in countries where the Nazi bureaucracy was best organized (e.g., Holland) (Bauman, 1991 [1989]; Sofsky, 1997 [1993]).

In short, the sociological reply to the question posed by Robert's father is that it was not just blind hatred but the nature of groups and bureaucracies that made it possible for the Nazis to kill innocent people so ruthlessly.

We commonly think that *individual* motives prompt our actions. And for good reason: As we saw in Chapter 4 ("Social Interaction"), we often make rational calculations to maximize gains and minimize losses. In addition, our deeply held emotions partly govern our behavior. However, this chapter asks you to make a conceptual leap beyond the individual motives that prompt us to act in certain ways. We ask you to consider the way three kinds of social *collectivities* shape our actions: networks, groups, and bureaucratic organizations. The limitations of an analysis based exclusively on individual motives should be clear from our discussion of the social roots of evil. The advantages of considering how social collectivities affect us will become clear below. We begin by considering the nature and effects of social networks.

Social Networks: It's a Small World

Let's say someone asked you to have a letter delivered to a complete stranger on the other side of the country, but only by using acquaintances to pass the letter along. You could give the letter to an acquaintance, who could give the letter to one of his or her acquaintances, and so forth. On average, it would take no more than about six acquaintances to get the letter to the stranger. This fact suggests that in a fundamental sociological sense, we live in a small world: Few social ties separate us from everyone else.

Our world is small because we are enmeshed in overlapping sets of social relations, or "social networks." Although any particular individual may know a small number of people, his or her family members, friends, coworkers, and others know many more people who extend far beyond that individual's "personal network." So, for example, the authors of this textbook are likely to be complete strangers to you. Yet your professor may know one of us or at least know someone who knows one of us. Probably no more than two links separate us from you. Put differently, although our personal networks are small, they lead quickly to much larger networks. We live in a small world because our social networks connect us to the larger world.

Sociologists define a **social network** as a bounded set of units (individuals, organizations, countries, etc.) linked by the exchange of material or emotional resources, everything from money to friendship. The patterns of exchange determine the boundaries of the network. Network members exchange resources more frequently with each other than with nonmembers. Individuals in a network think of themselves as network members. Social networks may be formal (i.e., defined in writing) or informal (i.e., defined only in practice). The people you know personally form the boundaries of your personal network. However, each of your network members is linked to other people. This is what connects you to people you have never met, creating a "small world" that extends far beyond your personal network (Box 5.2).

Social network: A bounded set of individuals who are linked by the exchange of material or emotional resources. The patterns of exchange determine the boundaries of the network. Members exchange resources more frequently with each other than with nonmembers. They also think of themselves as network members. Social networks may be formal (defined in writing), but they are more often informal (defined only in practice).

Six Degrees of Kevin Bacon

The *Internet Movie Database* (2003) contains information on the half million actors who have ever performed in a commercially released movie. While this number is large, you might be surprised to learn that, socially, they form a small world. We can demonstrate this fact by first selecting an actor who is not an especially big star—someone like Kevin Bacon. We can then use the *Internet Movie Database* to find out which other actors have ever been in a movie with him (University of Virginia, 2003). Acting in a movie with *another* actor constitutes a link. Actors two links away from Bacon have never been in a movie with him but have been in a movie with another actor who has been in a movie with him. Remarkably, more than 85 percent of the half million actors in the database have one, two, or three links to Bacon. We conclude that although film acting stretches back more than a century and has involved people in many countries, the half million people who have ever acted in films form a pretty small world.

What is true for the world of film actors turns out to be true for the rest of us, too. Jeffrey Travers and Stanley Milgram (1969) conducted a famous study in which they asked 300 randomly selected people to mail a document to a complete stranger. However, the people could not mail the document directly to him. They had to mail it to a person they knew on a first-name basis who, in turn, could send it only to a person *he* or *she* knew on a first-name basis, and so forth. Travers and Milgram defined this passing of a letter from one person to another as a link, or a "degree of separation." Remarkably, it took only six links on average for the document to reach the stranger. The idea soon became widespread that there are no more than six degrees of separation between any two people in the United States. An attempt to apply the idea to the entire world via the Internet is under way at Columbia University's Department of Sociology.

Kevin Bacon

Reuters/CORBIS

Critical Thinking

- Think about your tastes in fashion and music. Are they yours and yours alone? Do you accept them mechanically and directly from the mass media? Or does the mass media provide a "menu" of fashions and tastes that are then filtered by the personal network to which you belong and then selectively adopted by you in accordance with your interests and desires?

- How important is your personal network (relative to the mass media and your personal interests and desires) in the process through which you construct your taste in clothing and music?

The Value of Network Analysis

The study of social networks is not restricted to ties among individuals (Wasserman and Faust, 1994; Wellman and Berkowitz, 1997[1988]). The units of analysis (or "nodes") in a network can be individuals, groups, organizations, and even countries. Thus, social network analysts have examined everything from intimate relationships between lovers to diplomatic relations among nations. For example, in Chapter 8 ("Globalization, Inequality, and Development") we show how patterns in the flow of international trade divide the world into three major trading blocs, dominated respectively by the United States, Germany, and Japan. In Chapter 13 ("Politics, Work, and the Economy"), we show how American corporate networks create alliances that are useful for exchanging information and influencing government. In both cases, our analysis of social networks teaches us something new and unexpected about the social bases of economic and political affairs.

Unlike organizations, most networks lack names and offices. There is a Boy Scouts of America but no American Trading Bloc. In a sense, networks lie beneath the more visible collectivities of social life. However, that makes them no less real or important. Some analysts claim that we can gain only a partial sense of why certain things happen in the social world by focusing on highly visible collectivities. From their point of view, the whole story requires probing below the surface and examining the network level. The study of social networks clarifies a wide range of social phenomena, including how people find jobs; how information, innovations, and communicable diseases spread; and how some people exert influence over others. To illustrate further the value of network analysis, we now focus on each of these issues in turn.

Finding a Job

Many people learn about important events, ideas, and opportunities from their social networks. Friends and acquaintances often introduce you to everything from an interesting college course or a great restaurant to a satisfying occupation or a future spouse. Of course, social networks aren't the only source of information, but they are highly significant.

Consider how people find jobs. Do you look in the Help Wanted section of your local newspaper, scan the Internet, or walk around certain areas of town looking for "Employee Wanted" signs? Although these strategies are common, people often learn about employment opportunities from other people.

What kind of people? According to Mark Granovetter (1973), you may have strong or weak ties to another person. You have strong ties to people who are close to

Parents can help their graduating children find jobs by getting them "plugged into" the right social networks. Here, in the 1968 movie *The Graduate*, a friend of the family advises Dustin Hoffman that the future lies in the plastics industry.

Everett Collection

you, such as family members and friends. You have weak ties to mere acquaintances, such as people you meet at parties and friends of friends. In his research, Granovetter found that weak ties are more important than strong ties in finding a job, which is contrary to common sense. One might reasonably assume that a mere acquaintance wouldn't do much to help you find a job, whereas a close friend or relative would make a lot more effort in this regard. However, by focusing on the flow of information in personal networks, Granovetter found something different.

Mere acquaintances are more likely to provide useful information about employment opportunities than friends or family members because people who are close to you typically share overlapping networks. Therefore, the information they can provide about job opportunities is often redundant. In contrast, mere acquaintances are likely to be connected to *diverse* networks. They can therefore provide information about many different job openings and make introductions to many different potential employers. Moreover, because people typically have more weak ties than strong ties, the sum of weak ties holds more information about job opportunities than the sum of strong ties. These features of personal networks allowed Granovetter to conclude that the "strength of weak ties" lies in their diversity and abundance.

Urban Networks

We rely on social networks for a lot more than job information. Consider everyday life in the big city. We often think of big cities as cold and alienating places where few people know one another. In this view, urban acquaintanceships tend to be few and functionally specific; we know someone fleetingly as a bank teller or a server in a restaurant but not as a whole person. Even dating can involve a series of brief encounters. In contrast, people often think of small towns as friendly, comfortable places where everyone knows everyone else (and everyone else's business). Indeed, some of the founders of sociology emphasized just this distinction. Notably, German sociologist Ferdinand Tönnies (1988 [1887]) contrasted *community* with *society*. According to Tönnies, a community is marked by intimate and emotionally intense social ties, whereas a society is marked by impersonal relationships held together largely by self-interest. A big city is a prime example of a society in Tönnies's judgment.

Tönnies's view prevailed until network analysts started studying big city life in the 1970s. Where Tönnies saw only sparse, functionally specific ties, network analysts found elaborate social networks, some functionally specific and some not. For example, Barry Wellman and his colleagues studied personal networks in Toronto, Canada (Wellman, Carrington, and Hall, 1997 [1988]). They found that each Torontonian had an average of about 400 social ties, including immediate and extended kin, neighbors, friends, and coworkers. These ties provided everything from emotional aid (e.g., visits after a personal tragedy) and financial support (e.g., small loans) to minor services (e.g., fixing a car) and information of the kind Granovetter studied.

Strong ties that last a long time are typically restricted to immediate family members, a few close relatives and friends, and a close coworker or two. Beyond that, however, people rely on a wide array of ties for different purposes at different times. Downtown residents sitting on their front stoops on a summer evening, sipping soda and chatting with neighbors as the kids play stickball or road hockey may be less common than they were 50 years ago. However, the automobile, public transportation, the telephone, and the Internet help people stay in close touch with a wide range of contacts for a variety of purposes (Haythornwaite and Wellman, 2002). Far from living in an impersonal and alienating world, the lives of today's city dwellers are network rich.

BOX 5.3
YOU AND THE SOCIAL WORLD

Social Networks and Illness

Social networks exert a powerful influence on health. People who are well integrated into cohesive social networks of family, extended kin, and friends are less likely to suffer heart attacks, complications during pregnancy, and so forth. Surprisingly, although more social contacts may expose you to more germs, research shows that you are *less* likely to come down with an infectious disease the more social contacts you have (Jones, Gallagher, and McFalls, 1995: 109–11).

If you are skeptical about this claim, you can try this exercise to see how social networks affect your health and that of your classmates. Ask everyone in your sociology class to answer two questions: (1) How many times have you caught cold or had the flu during the past 3 months? (2) How many relatives and family members did you see face-to-face at least three times in the last 3 months? After you have collected the answers to these questions, tally the responses. (If your class is large, you will want to do this exercise with a group of your classmates.) Create a four-cell table such as Table 1.1 on p. 21 showing how, if at all, the frequency of face-to-face contact with relatives and family members influences the likelihood of catching cold or the flu. Our prediction is that the greater the contact, the less the chance of catching cold or the flu. (If you want to explore this matter further, you can also ask: (3) How many relatives and family members did you contact by phone and the Internet at least three times in the last 3 months? You may find that the frequency of non–face-to-face contacts also influences the chance of catching cold or the flu.)

WRITING ASSIGNMENT

In 250–500 words, explain whether your results support or refute our hypothesis or whether they are inconclusive. Outline how researchers might pursue this line of inquiry to determine whether your results are credible or idiosyncratic.

CENGAGENOW™

Learn more about **HIV/AIDS** by going through the # of AIDS Cases Map Exercise.

From HIV/AIDS to the Common Cold

Another example of the usefulness of focusing on concrete social ties rather than abstract attributes comes from the study of how communicable diseases spread. Human immunodeficiency virus/acquired immune deficiency syndrome (HIV/AIDS) was widely considered a "gay disease" in the 1980s. HIV/AIDS spread rapidly in the gay community during that decade. However, network analysis helped to show that the characterization of HIV/AIDS as a "gay disease" was an oversimplification (Watts, 2003). The disease did not spread uniformly throughout the community. Rather, it spread along the friendship and acquaintanceship networks of people first exposed to it. Meanwhile, in India and parts of Africa, HIV/AIDS did not initially spread among gay men at all. Instead, it spread through a network of long-distance truck drivers and the prostitutes who catered to them. Again, concrete social networks—not abstract categories such as gay men or truck drivers—track the spread of the disease (Box 5.3)

CENGAGENOW™

Learn more about **Dyads and Triads** by going through the Group Size Effects Animation.

Dyad: A social relationship between two nodes, or social units (people, firms, organizations, countries).

Triad: A social relationship among three nodes, or social units (people, firms, organizations, countries).

The Building Blocks of Social Networks: The Dyad and the Triad

Researchers often use mathematical models and computer programs to analyze social networks. However, no matter how sophisticated the mathematics or the software, network analysts begin from an understanding of the basic building blocks of social networks.

The most elementary network form is the **dyad,** a social relationship between two nodes or social units (people, firms, organizations, countries). A **triad** is a social relationship among three nodes. The difference between a dyad and a triad may seem small. However, the social dynamics of these two elementary network forms are fundamentally different, as sociologist Georg Simmel showed early in the 20th century (Simmel, 1950; ▶Figure 5.2).

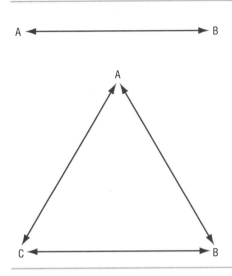

Characteristics of the dyad:
1. Both partners are intensely absorbed in the relationship.
2. The dyad needs both partners to live but only one to die.
3. No "free riders" are possible.
4. Neither partner can deny responsibility by shifting it to a larger collectivity.

Characteristics of the triad:
1. Intensity and intimacy are reduced.
2. The triad restricts individuality by allowing a partner to be constrained for the collective good. A partner may be outvoted by a majority, for example.
3. Coalitions are possible.
4. Third-party mediation of conflict between two partners is possible.
5. Third-party exploitation of rivalry between two partners is possible.
6. A third-party divide-and-conquer strategy is possible.
7. "Free riders" are possible.
8. It is possible to shift responsibility to the larger collectivity.

Dyads

In a dyadic relationship such as a marriage, both partners tend to be intensely and intimately involved. Moreover, the dyad needs both partners if it is to survive. A marriage, for example, can endure only if both partners are intensely involved. If one partner ceases active participation, the marriage is over in practice if not in law. This need for intense involvement on the part of both partners is also why a dyad can have no "free riders," or partners who benefit from the relationship without contributing to it. Finally, in a dyadic relationship, the partners must assume full responsibility for all that transpires. Neither partner can shift responsibility to some larger collectivity, because no larger collectivity exists beyond the relationship between the two partners.

Triads

When a third person (or other social unit) enters the picture, a triad is created. A triad allows a social relationship to continue even if one person (or other social unit) departs. In a triad, relationships tend to be less intimate and intense than in a dyad. Equally significantly, the triad restricts individuality by allowing one partner to be constrained for the collective good. This situation occurs when a majority outvotes one partner. The existence of a triad also allows coalitions or factions to form. Furthermore, it allows one partner to mediate conflict between the other two, exploit rivalry between the other two, or encourage rivalry between the other two to achieve dominance. Thus, the introduction of a third partner makes possible a whole new set of social dynamics that are structurally impossible in a dyadic relationship.

Groups

Although intensity and intimacy characterize dyadic relationships, outside forces often destroy them. For instance, the star-crossed lovers in *Romeo and Juliet* are torn between their love for one another and their loyalty to the feuding Montague and Capulet families. In the end, Romeo and Juliet lie dead, victims of the feud.

Love thwarted by conflicting group loyalty is the stuff of many tragic plays, novels, and movies. Most audiences have no problem grasping the fact that group loyalty is often more powerful than romantic love. However, why group loyalty holds such power over

The family is the most important primary group.

us is unclear. The sociological study of groups provides some useful answers.

Social groups are composed of one or more networks of people who identify with one another, routinely interact, and adhere to defined norms, roles, and statuses. We usually distinguish social groups from **social categories,** people who share similar status but do not routinely interact or identify with one another. Coffee drinkers form a social category. They do not normally share norms, routinely interact, and identify with each other. In contrast, members of a group such as a family, sports team, or college are aware of shared membership. They think of themselves as members of a collectivity and routinely interact.

Primary and Secondary Groups

Many kinds of social groups exist. However, sociologists make a basic distinction between primary and secondary groups. In **primary groups,** norms, roles, and statuses are agreed upon but are not put in writing. Social interaction creates strong emotional ties. It extends over a long period and involves a wide range of activities. It results in group members knowing one another well. The family is the most important primary group.

Secondary groups are larger and more impersonal than primary groups. Compared with primary groups, social interaction in secondary groups creates weaker emotional ties. It extends over a shorter period and involves a narrow range of activities. It results in most group members having at most a passing acquaintance with one another. Your sociology class is an example of a secondary group. Bearing these distinctions in mind, we can begin to explore the power of groups to ensure conformity.

Group Conformity

Television's first reality TV show was *Candid Camera.* In an early episode, an unsuspecting man waits for an elevator. When the elevator door opens, he finds four people, all confederates of the show, facing the elevator's back wall. Seeing the four people with their backs to him, the man at first hesitates. He then tentatively enters the elevator. However, rather than turning around so he faces the door, he remains facing the back wall, just like the others. The scene is repeated several times. Men and women, black and white, all behave the same. Confronting unanimously bizarre behavior, they all choose conformity over common sense.

Conformity is an integral part of group life, and primary groups generate more pressure to conform than secondary groups. Strong social ties create emotional intimacy. They also ensure that primary group members share similar attitudes, beliefs, and information. Beyond the family, friendship groups (or cliques) and gangs demonstrate these features. Group members tend to dress and act alike, speak the same lingo, share the same likes and dislikes, and demand loyalty, especially in the face of external threat. Conformity ensures group cohesion.

Asch's Experiment

A famous experiment conducted by social psychologist Solomon Asch half a century ago demonstrates how group pressure creates conformity (Asch, 1955). Asch assembled seven men. One of them was the experimental subject. The other six were Asch's confederates. Asch showed the seven men a card with a line drawn on it. He then showed them a second card with three lines of varying length drawn on it (▶Figure 5.3). One by one, he asked the confederates to judge which line on card 2 was the same length as the line on card 1. The answer was obvious. One line on card 2 was much shorter than the line on card 1. One line was much longer. One was exactly the same length. Yet, as instructed by Asch, all six confederates said that either the shorter or the longer line was the same length as the line on card 1. When it came time for the experimental subject to make his judgment, he typically overruled his own perception and agreed with the majority. Only 25 percent of Asch's experimental subjects consistently gave the right answer. Asch thus demonstrated how easily group pressure can overturn individual conviction and result in conformity.

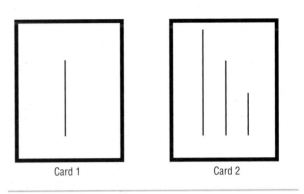

Card 1   Card 2

▶FIGURE 5.3
The Asch Experiment

Factors Affecting Conformity

Asch's work and subsequent research show that several factors affect the likelihood of conformity (Sternberg, 1998 [1995]: 499–500). First, the likelihood of conformity increases as *group size* increases to three or four members. For groups larger than four, the likelihood of conformity generally does not increase. Second, as *group cohesiveness* increases, so does the likelihood of conformity. Where greater intimacy and sharing of values occur, group members are less likely to express dissent. Third, *social status* affects the likelihood of conformity. People with low status in a group (e.g., because of their gender or race) are less likely to dissent than people with high status. Fourth, culture matters. People in individualistic societies like the United States tend to conform less than people in collectivist societies like China. Fifth, the *appearance of unanimity* affects the likelihood of conformity. Even one dissenting voice greatly increases the chance that others will dissent.

Groupthink

The power of groups to ensure conformity is often a valuable asset. Sports teams could not excel without the willingness of players to undergo personal sacrifice for the good of the group, nor could armies function. In fact, as sociologists have demonstrated and as high-ranking military officers have observed, group cohesion—not patriotism or bravery—is the main factor motivating soldiers to engage in combat (Stouffer et al., 1949; Marshall, 1947: 160–1). As one soldier says in the 2001 movie *Black Hawk Down:* "When I go home people will ask me: 'Hey, Hoot, why do you do it, man? Why? Are you some kinda war junkie?' I won't say a goddamn word. Why? They won't understand. They won't understand why we do it. They won't understand it's about the men next to you. And that's it. That's all it is."

However, being a "good team player" can have a downside, because the consensus of a group can sometimes be misguided or dangerous. Dissent might save the group from making mistakes (Box 5.4), but the pressure to conform despite individual misgivings—sometimes called **groupthink** (Janis, 1972)—can lead to disaster.

Great managers are able to encourage frank and open discussion, assess ideas based on their merit, develop a strategy that incorporates the best ideas voiced, and *then* create consensus on how to implement the ideas. Inadequate managers feel they know it all. They rationalize their plan of action, squelch dissent, and fail to examine alternatives.

Social group: A group that is composed of one or more networks of people who identify with one another and adhere to defined norms, roles, and statuses.

Social category: A category that is composed of people who share similar status but do not identify with one another.

Primary groups: Groups in which norms, roles, and statuses are agreed upon but are not put in writing. Social interaction leads to strong emotional ties. It extends over a long period and involves a wide range of activities. It results in group members knowing one another well.

Secondary groups: Groups that are larger and more impersonal than primary groups. Compared with primary groups, social interaction in secondary groups creates weaker emotional ties. It extends over a shorter period, and it involves a narrow range of activities. It results in most group members having at most a passing acquaintance with one another.

Groupthink: Group pressure to conform despite individual misgivings.

They create a group culture that inhibits people from expressing their misgivings and use the fact that people do not want to appear disloyal to impose consensus on the group. They all pretend to see the "emperor's clothes"—until an outsider points out that the emperor is in fact naked. High-stress situations—a war room, an operating theater—often do not allow a democratic managerial style. Therefore, it is precisely in high-stress situations that the dangers of groupthink are greatest.

Examples of Groupthink

Arguably, groupthink was operating when President Roosevelt and his advisers refused to believe the Japanese would bomb Pearl Harbor, President Kennedy decided to embark on his ill-fated invasion of Cuba, President Johnson escalated the bombing of North Vietnam, and President Nixon decided to cover up the Watergate break-in. Groupthink was also at work in high-level meetings preceding the space shuttle Columbia disaster in 2003. Transcripts of those meetings at the National Aeronautics and Space Administration (NASA) show that the official who ran shuttle management meetings, a nonengineer, believed from the outset that foam insulation debris could not damage the spacecraft. She dismissed the issue and cut off discussion when an engineer expressed his concerns. The others present quickly fell into line with the nonengineer running the meeting (Wald and Schwartz, 2003). A few days later, damage caused by foam insulation debris caused Columbia to break apart on reentry into the Earth's atmosphere.

Other famous examples of how the lack of a single dissenting voice can result in tragedy come from two homicide cases that grabbed the world's attention. In 1964 in Queens, New York, 28-year-old Kitty Genovese parked her car after returning home from work. When she got out, a man grabbed and stabbed her. She screamed for help. For 35 minutes, at least 38 middle-class, law-abiding neighbors watched from darkened windows as the man repeatedly attacked Genovese and stabbed her 17 times. Finally, one neighbor called the police, but only after he had called a friend and asked what to do. Some of the neighbors later pleaded ignorance. Others said they thought it was just a lovers' quarrel or "some kids having fun." Still others admitted they didn't want to get involved (Gado, 2003).

A similar thing happened in 1993 near Liverpool, England. Two 10-year-old boys abducted 2-year-old James Bulger from a shopping mall. They took him on a long, aimless walk, torturing him along the way—dropping him on his head and kicking him in the ribs. Motorists and pedestrians saw the toddler crying, noticed his wounds, and even witnessed some of the violence. "A persuading kick" was the way one motorist later described the blow to the ribs (Scott, 2003). Nobody called the police. These cases illustrate "bystander apathy." As the number of bystanders increases, the likelihood of any one bystander helping decreases, because the greater the number of bystanders, the less responsibility any one individual feels. This behavior shows that people usually take their cues for action from others and again demonstrates the power of groups over individuals. If no one else in a large collectivity responds, most people figure nothing is wrong. This is in part what made the Holocaust possible.

Inclusion and Exclusion: In-Groups and Out-Groups

If a group exists, it follows that some people must not belong to it. Accordingly, sociologists distinguish in-group members (those who belong) from out-group members (those who do not). Members of an **in-group** typically draw a boundary separating themselves from members of the **out-group,** and they try to keep out-group members

In-group: Composed of people who belong to a group.

Out-group: Composed of people who are excluded from the in-group.

from crossing the line. Anyone who has gone to high school knows all about in-groups and out-groups. They have seen first-hand how race, class, athletic ability, academic talent, and physical attractiveness act as boundaries separating groups. Sadly, only in the movies can someone in a high school out-group get a chance to return to school as a young adult and use her savvy to become a member of the in-group (see the 1999 movie *Never Been Kissed*, starring Drew Barrymore).

Group Boundaries: Competition and Self-Esteem

Why do group boundaries crystallize? One theory is that group boundaries emerge when people compete for scarce resources. For example, old immigrants may greet new immigrants with hostility if the latter are seen as competitors for scarce jobs (Levine and Campbell, 1972). Another theory is that group boundaries emerge when people are motivated to protect their self-esteem. From this point of view, drawing group boundaries allows people to increase their self-esteem by believing that out-groups have low status (Tajfel, 1981).

Natural or artificial boundaries—rivers, mountains, highways, railway tracks—typically separate groups or communities.

Both theories are supported by a classic experiment on prejudice, the Robber's Cave Study (Sherif et al., 1988 [1961]). Researchers brought two groups of 11-year-old boys to a summer camp at Robber's Cave State Park in Oklahoma in 1954. The boys were strangers to one another, and for about a week the two groups were kept apart. They swam, camped, and hiked. Each group chose a name for itself, and the boys printed their group's name on their caps and T-shirts. Then the two groups met. A series of athletic competitions was set up between them. Soon, each group became highly antagonistic toward the other. Each group came to hold the other in low esteem. The boys ransacked cabins, started food fights, and stole various items from members of the other group. Thus, under competitive conditions, the boys quickly drew sharp group boundaries.

The investigators next stopped the athletic competitions and created several apparent emergencies whose solution required cooperation between the two groups. One such emergency involved a leak in the pipe supplying water to the camp. The researchers assigned the boys to teams composed of members of *both* groups. Their job was to inspect the pipe and fix the leak. After engaging in several such cooperative ventures, the boys started playing together without fighting. Once cooperation replaced competition and the groups ceased to hold each other in low esteem, group boundaries melted away as quickly as they had formed. Significantly, the two groups were of equal status—the boys were all white, middle-class, and 11 years old—and their contact involved face-to-face interaction in a setting where norms established by the investigators promoted a reduction of group prejudice. Social scientists today recognize that all these conditions must be in place before the boundaries between an in-group and an out-group fade away (Sternberg, 1998 [1995]: 512).

Dominant Groups

The boundaries separating groups often seem unchangeable and even natural. In general, however, dominant groups construct group boundaries in particular circumstances to further their goals (Barth, 1969; Tajfel, 1981). Consider Germans and Jews. By the early 20th century, Jews were well integrated into German society. They were economically successful, culturally innovative, and politically influential, and many of them considered themselves more German than Jewish. In 1933, the year Hitler seized power, 44 percent of marriages involving at least one German Jew were to a non-Jew. In addition, some German Jews converted before marrying non-Jewish Germans (Gordon, 1984). Yet, although the boundary separating Germans from Jews was quite weak, the Nazis chose to redraw and reinforce it. Defining a Jew as anyone who had at least one Jewish grandparent, they passed a whole series of anti-Jewish laws and, in the end, systematically slaughtered the Jews of Europe. The division between Germans and Jews was not "natural." It came into existence because of its perceived usefulness to a dominant group.

Groups and Social Imagination

So far, we have focused almost exclusively on face-to-face interaction in groups. However, people also interact with other group members in their imagination. Take reference groups, for example. A **reference group** is composed of people against whom an individual evaluates his or her situation or conduct. Put differently, members of a reference group function as "role models." A classic study of reference groups is Theodore Newcomb's (1943) research on students at Bennington College in Vermont, an institution well known for its liberalism. Although nearly all the students came from politically conservative families, they tended to become more liberal with every passing year. Twenty years later, they remained liberals. Newcomb argued that their liberalism grew because over time they came to identify less with their conservative parents (members of their primary group) and more with their liberal professors (their reference group).

The Influence of Reference Groups

Interestingly, reference groups may influence us even though they represent a largely imaginary ideal. Thus, the advertising industry promotes certain body ideals that many people try to emulate, although we know that hardly anyone looks like a runway model or a Barbie doll (see Chapter 10, "Sexuality and Gender," and Chapter 14, "Health, Medicine, Disability, and Aging").

Imagined Communities

We have to exercise our imaginations vigorously to participate in the group life of a large, complex society like ours because much social life involves belonging to secondary groups without knowing or interacting with most group members. For an individual to interact with any more than a small fraction of the more than 300 million people living in this country is impossible. Nonetheless, most Americans feel a strong emotional bond to their fellow citizens. Similarly, think about the employees and students at your school. They know they belong to the same secondary group, and many of them are probably fiercely loyal to it. Yet, how many people at your school have you met? You have probably met no more than a small fraction of the total. One way to make sense of the paradox of intimacy despite distance is to think of your school or the United States as an "imagined community." It is imagined because you cannot possibly meet most members of the group and can only speculate about what they must be like. It is nonetheless a community because people believe strongly in its existence and importance (Anderson, 1991).

Many secondary groups are **formal organizations,** or secondary groups designed to achieve explicit objectives. In complex societies like ours, the most common and influential formal organizations are bureaucracies. We now turn to an examination of these often frustrating but necessary organizational forms.

Reference group: A group composed of people against whom an individual evaluates his or her situation or conduct.

Formal organizations: Secondary groups designed to achieve specific and explicit objectives.

Bureaucracy

Bureaucratic Inefficiency

At the beginning of this chapter, we noted that Weber regarded bureaucracies as the most efficient type of secondary group. This runs against the grain of common knowledge. In everyday speech, when someone says "bureaucracy," people commonly think of bored clerks sitting in small cubicles spinning out endless trails of "red tape" that create needless waste and frustrate the goals of clients. The idea that bureaucracies are efficient may seem very odd.

Real events often reinforce the common view. Consider, for instance, the case of the Challenger space shuttle, which exploded shortly after takeoff on January 28, 1986, killing all seven crew members. The weather was cold, and the flexible O-rings that were supposed to seal the sections of the booster rockets had become rigid and allowed burning gas to leak. The burning gas triggered the explosion. Some engineers at NASA and at the company that manufactured the O-rings knew they wouldn't function properly in cold weather. However, this information did not reach NASA's top bureaucrats:

> [The] rigid hierarchy that had arisen at NASA . . . made communication between departments formal and not particularly effective. [In the huge bureaucracy,] most communication was done through memos and reports. Everything was meticulously documented, but critical details tended to get lost in the paperwork blizzard. The result was that the upper-level managers were kept informed about possible problems with the O-rings . . . but they never truly understood the seriousness of the issue (Pool, 1997: 257).

As this incident shows, bureaucratic inefficiencies can sometimes have tragic consequences. Indeed, some of the lessons of the 1986 disaster appear to have gone unheeded. In the case of the 2003 Columbia shuttle disaster mentioned earlier, NASA administrator Sean O'Keefe was roundly criticized for bureaucratic mismanagement. The critics demanded to know why O'Keefe hadn't received internal NASA e-mails that expressed safety concerns about damage caused by debris during the takeoff. As U.S. Representative Anthony Weiner told O'Keefe: "I read this stuff before you did. That's crazy" (quoted in Stenger, 2003).

How can we square the reality of bureaucratic inefficiencies—even tragedies—with Weber's view that bureaucracies are the most efficient type of secondary group? The answer is twofold. First, we must recognize that when Weber wrote about the efficiency of bureaucracy, he was comparing it with older organizational forms. These had operated on the basis of either traditional practice ("We do it this way because we've always done it this way") or the charisma of their leaders ("We do it this way because our chief inspires us to do it this way"). Compared with such "traditional" and "charismatic" organizations, bureaucracies are generally more efficient. Second,

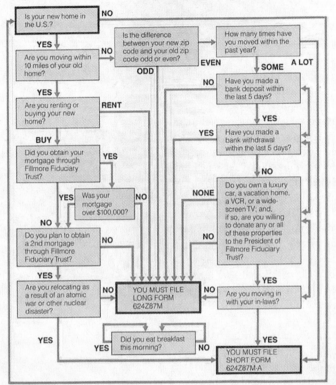

Red Tape. The 1980s Infocom game "Bureaucracy" satirized the conventional view of bureaucratic red tape.

Infocom, 2000/Activision

BOX 5.4
SOCIOLOGY AT THE MOVIES

Shake Hands with the Devil (2004)

Over a period of 100 days in 1994, the Hutus of Rwanda massacred 800,000 Tutsis—more than a tenth of Rwanda's population—with guns, machetes, hammers, and spears. Bodies were scattered everywhere, and the streets literally flowed with blood. The French trained and armed the Hutus in full knowledge of what would transpire. The Belgians knew too, and their 2,000 troops could have done much to prevent it, but they withdrew their "peacekeepers" just before the massacre began. Canadian General Roméo Dallaire, who led a contingent of United Nations (UN) troops in Rwanda, reported to his bosses at the UN that he knew where the Hutu arms caches were located and requested permission to destroy them. Permission was denied. Most North Americans were busy watching the O. J. Simpson trial on TV and barely noticed the genocide.

Dallaire and his 450 soldiers from Canada, Ghana, Tunisia, and Bangladesh nonetheless risked their lives to save an estimated 30,000 Rwandans in one of the 20th century's great heroic acts. Like the Swedish World War II hero Raoul Wallenberg in Hungary and Japanese consular official Chiune Sugihara in Lithuania, both of whom risked their lives to save thousands of Jews from the Nazis, Dallaire courageously swam against the stream of world apathy. *Shake Hands with the Devil,* which won the 2007 Emmy for best docu-

General Roméo Dallaire in *Shake Hands with the Devil.*

Ryan Remiorz/CP PHOTO

mentary, details Dallaire's actions, the heavy toll they took on his mental health, and his recovery from the trauma of 1994.

Although we know much about the origins of the 1994 Rwandan genocide, we know little about the conditions that create heroes. We do know that heroes are typically raised in an atmosphere of high moral principle and ethical standards of conduct. We know that they often demonstrate an independence of character and a willingness to defy authority and convention in the years preceding their heroic acts. Thus, while heroism sometimes requires a split-second decision, it is usually preceded by years of socialization that predispose the future hero to act compassionately, even if doing so involves refusing to follow the herd (Franco and Zimbardo, 2006–2007). As such, we have much to learn from the example of people like General Roméo Dallaire. (For more on obedience to unreasonable demands, see "The Points of the Compass" on page 134.)

Critical Thinking

- Describe any aspects of your upbringing that taught you to act heroically if called upon to do so.

- Do you think that young people today need more and better instruction in how to act heroically? If so, who should be responsible for such instruction—schools, political parties, religious organizations, or parents? Why?

- Is heroism incompatible with conformism? If so, how? If not, why not?

we must recognize that Weber thought bureaucracies could operate efficiently only in the ideal case. He wrote extensively about some of bureaucracy's less admirable aspects in the real world. In other words, he understood that reality is often messier than the ideal case. So should we. In reality, bureaucracies vary in efficiency. Therefore, rather than proclaiming bureaucracy efficient or inefficient, we should find out what makes bureaucracies work well or poorly. We can then apply this knowledge to improving the operation of bureaucracies.

Dehumanization, Ritualism, Oligarchy, and Inertia

Traditionally, sociologists have lodged four main criticisms against bureaucracies. First is the problem of **dehumanization.** Instead of treating clients and personnel as people with unique needs, bureaucracies sometimes treat clients as standard cases and personnel as cogs in a giant machine. This treatment frustrates clients and lowers worker morale. Second is the problem of **bureaucratic ritualism** (Merton, 1968 [1949]). Bureaucrats sometimes become so preoccupied with rules and regulations that they make it difficult for the organization to fulfill its goals. Third is the problem of **oligarchy,** or "rule of the few" (Michels, 1949 [1911]). Some sociologists have argued that in all bureaucracies, power tends to become increasingly concentrated in the hands of a few people at the top of the organizational pyramid. This tendency is particularly problematic in political organizations because it hinders democracy and renders leaders unaccountable to the public. Fourth is the problem of **bureaucratic inertia.** Bureaucracies are sometimes so large and rigid that they lose touch with reality and continue their policies even when their clients' needs change. Like the *Titanic,* they are so big that they find it difficult to shift course and steer clear of dangerous obstacles. Two main factors underlie bureaucratic inefficiency: size and social structure.

Size

Consider size first. Something can be said for the view that bigger is almost inevitably more problematic. Some of the problems caused by size are evident even when you remember some of the differences between dyads and triads. When only two people are involved in a relationship, they may form a strong social bond. If they do, communication is direct and sometimes unproblematic. Once a third person is introduced, however, a secret may be kept, a coalition of two against one may crystallize, and jealousy may result. Thus, triads are usually more conflict ridden than dyads.

Problems can multiply in groups of more than three people. For example, as ▶Figure 5.4 shows, only one dyadic relationship can exist between two people, whereas three

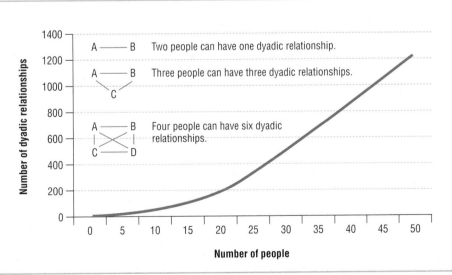

▶FIGURE 5.4

Number of Possible Dyadic Relationships by Number of People in Group

Note: The number of dyadic relationships $= n^2 - n/2$, where n is the number of people.

Dehumanization: Occurs when bureaucracies treat clients as standard cases and personnel as cogs in a giant machine. This treatment frustrates clients and lowers worker morale.

Bureaucratic ritualism: A situation that involves bureaucrats becoming so preoccupied with rules and regulations that they make it difficult for the organization to fulfill its goals.

Oligarchy: Means "rule by the few." Bureaucracies have a supposed tendency for power to become increasingly concentrated in the hands of a few people at the top of the organizational pyramid.

Bureaucratic inertia: The tendency of large, rigid bureaucracies to continue their policies even when their clients' needs change.

dyadic relationships can exist among three people, and six dyadic relationships can exist among four people. The number of potential dyadic relationships increases exponentially with the number of people. Hence, 300 dyadic relationships are possible among 25 people and 1,225 dyadic relationships are possible among 50 people. The possibility of clique formation, rivalries, conflict, and miscommunication rises as quickly with the number of possible dyadic social relationships in an organization.

Social Structure

The second factor underlying bureaucratic inefficiency is social structure. ▶Figure 5.5 shows a typical bureaucratic structure. Note that it is a hierarchy. The bureaucracy has a head. Below the head are three divisions. Below the divisions are six departments. As you move up the hierarchy, the power of the staff increases. Note also the lines of communication that join the various bureaucratic units. Departments report only to their divisions. Divisions report only to the head.

Usually, the more levels in a bureaucratic structure, the more difficult communication becomes. That is because people have to communicate indirectly, through department and division heads, rather than directly with each other. Information may be lost, blocked, reinterpreted, or distorted as it moves up the hierarchy, or an excess of information may cause top levels to become engulfed in a "paperwork blizzard" that prevents them from clearly seeing the needs of the organization and its clients. Bureaucratic heads may have only a vague and imprecise idea of what is happening "on the ground" (Wilensky, 1967).

Consider also what happens when the lines of communication directly joining departments or divisions are weak or nonexistent. As the lines joining units in Figure 5.5 suggest, department A1 may have information that could help department B1 do its job better, but A1 may have to communicate that information indirectly through the division level. At the division level, the information may be lost, blocked, reinterpreted, or distorted. Thus, just as people who have authority may lack information, people who have information may lack the authority to act on it directly (Crozier, 1964 [1963]).

Later we consider some ways of overcoming bureaucratic inefficiency. As you will see, these typically involve establishing patterns of social relations that flatten the bureaucratic hierarchy and cut across the sort of bureaucratic rigidities illustrated in Figure 5.5. As a useful prelude to this discussion, we first note some shortcomings of Weber's analysis of bureaucracy. Weber tended to ignore both bureaucracy's "informal" side and the role of leadership in influencing bureaucratic performance. Yet, as you will learn, it is precisely by paying attention to such issues that we can make bureaucracies more efficient.

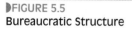
▶FIGURE 5.5
Bureaucratic Structure

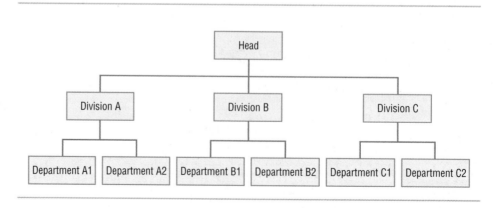

Bureaucracy's Informal Side

Social Relations within Bureaucracies

Weber was concerned mainly with the formal structure, or chain of command, in a bureaucracy. He paid little attention to the social networks that underlie the chain of command.

Evidence for the existence of social networks and their importance in the operation of bureaucracies goes back to the 1930s. Officials at the Hawthorne plant of the Western Electric Company near Chicago wanted to see how various aspects of the work environment affected productivity. They sent social scientists in to investigate. Among other things, researchers found that workers in one section of the plant had established a norm for daily output. Workers who failed to meet the norm were helped by coworkers until their output increased. Workers who exceeded the norm were reproached by coworkers until their productivity fell. Company officials and researchers previously regarded employees merely as individuals who worked as hard or as little as they could in response to wage levels and work conditions. However, the Hawthorne study showed that employees are members of social networks that regulate output (Roethlisberger and Dickson, 1939).

Informal interaction is common even in highly bureaucratic organizations. A water cooler, for example, can be a place for exchanging information and gossip, and even a place for decision making.

Rob Lewine/Corbis

In the 1970s, Rosabeth Moss Kanter conducted another landmark study of informal social relations in bureaucracies (Kanter, 1977). Kanter studied a corporation in which most women were sales agents. They were locked out of managerial positions. However, she did not find that the corporation discriminated against women as a matter of policy. She did find a male-only social network whose members shared gossip, went drinking, and told sexist jokes. The cost of being excluded from the network was high: To get good raises and promotions, one had to be accepted as "one of the boys" and be sponsored by a male executive, which was impossible for women. Thus, despite a company policy that did not discriminate against women, an informal network of social relations ensured that the company discriminated against women in practice.

Despite their overt commitment to impersonality and written rules, bureaucracies rely profoundly on informal interaction to get the job done (Barnard, 1938; Blau, 1963 [1955]). This is true even at the highest levels. For example, executives usually make important decisions in face-to-face meetings, not in writing or via phone. That is because people feel more comfortable in intimate settings, where they can get to know "the whole person." Meeting face-to-face, people can use their verbal and nonverbal interaction skills to gauge other people's trustworthiness. Socializing—talking over dinner, for example—is an important part of any business because the establishment of trust lies at the heart of all social interactions that require cooperation (Gambetta, 1988).

Leadership Styles

Apart from overlooking the role of informal relations in the operation of bureaucracies, Weber also paid insufficient attention to the issue of leadership. Weber thought that the formal structure of a bureaucracy largely determines how it operates. However, sociologists now realize that leadership style also has a major bearing on bureaucratic performance (Barnard, 1938; Ridgeway, 1983).

Research shows that the least effective leader is the one who allows subordinates to work things out largely on their own, with little direction from above. This is known as *laissez-faire* **leadership,** from the French expression "let them do." True, *laissez-faire* leadership can be effective under some circumstances. It works best when group members are highly experienced, trained, motivated, and educated and when trust and confidence in group members are high. In such conditions, a strong leader is not really needed for the group to accomplish its goals.

At the other extreme from *laissez-faire* leadership is **authoritarian leadership.** Authoritarian leaders demand strict compliance from subordinates. They are most effective in a crisis such as a war or the emergency room of a hospital. They may earn grudging respect from subordinates for achieving the group's goals in the face of difficult circumstances, but they rarely win popularity contests.

Democratic leadership offers more guidance than the *laissez-faire* variety but less control than the authoritarian type. Democratic leaders try to include all group members in the decision-making process, taking the best ideas from the group and molding them into a strategy that all can identify with. Except in crisis situations, democratic leadership is usually the most effective leadership style.

In sum, contemporary researchers have modified Weber's characterization of bureaucracy in two main ways. First, they have stressed the importance of informal social networks in shaping bureaucratic operations. Second, they have shown that democratic leaders are most effective in noncrisis situations because they tend to distribute decision-making authority and rewards widely. As you will now see, these are important principles for making bureaucracies more efficient.

Overcoming Bureaucratic Inefficiency

In the business world, large bureaucratic organizations sometimes find themselves unable to compete against smaller, innovative firms, particularly in industries that are changing quickly (Burns and Stalker, 1961). This situation occurs partly because innovative firms tend to have flatter and more democratic organizational structures, such as the network illustrated in ▶Figure 5.6. Compare the flat network structure in Figure 5.6 with the traditional bureaucratic structure in Figure 5.5. Note that the network structure has fewer levels than the traditional bureaucratic structure. Moreover, in the network structure, lines of communication link all units. In the traditional bureaucratic structure, information flows only upward.

Much evidence suggests that flatter bureaucracies with decentralized decision making and multiple lines of communication produce more satisfied workers, happier clients, and bigger profits (Kanter, 1989). Some of this evidence comes from Sweden and Japan. Beginning in the early 1970s, corporations such as Volvo and Toyota were at the forefront of bureaucratic innovation in those countries. They began eliminating middle-management positions. They allowed worker participation in a variety of tasks related to their main functions. They delegated authority to autonomous teams of a dozen or so workers that were allowed to make many decisions themselves. They formed "quality circles" of workers to monitor and correct defects in products and services. As a result, product quality, worker morale, and profitability improved. Today, these ideas have spread well beyond the Swedish and Japanese automobile industries and are evident in such American corporate giants as General Motors, Ford, Boeing, and Caterpillar.

In the 1980s and 1990s, companies outside the manufacturing sector introduced similar bureaucratic reforms, again with positive effects. Consider the case of Bob R., who works as a field technician for Bell South. His company created small teams of field

Laissez-faire **leadership:** A leadership style that allows subordinates to work things out largely on their own, with almost no direction from above. It is the least effective type of leadership.

Authoritarian leadership: A leadership style that demands strict compliance from subordinates. Authoritarian leaders are most effective in a crisis such as a war or in the emergency room of a hospital.

Democratic leadership: A leadership style that offers more guidance than the *laissez-faire* variety but less control than the authoritarian type. Democratic leaders try to include all group members in the decision-making process, taking the best ideas from the group and molding them into a strategy with which all can identify. Outside of crisis situations, democratic leadership is usually the most effective leadership style.

technicians that are each responsible for keeping a group of customers happy. The technicians set their own work schedule. They figure out when they need to do preventive maintenance, when they need to conduct repairs, and when it is time to try to sell customers new services. Bob describes his job after the changes were implemented:

> "I've been at the company for twenty-three years, and I always thought we were overmanaged, over-controlled, and oversupervised. They treated us like children. We're having a very good time under the new system. They've given us the freedom to work on our own. This is the most intelligent thing this company has done in years. It's fun" (quoted in Hammer, 1999: 87).

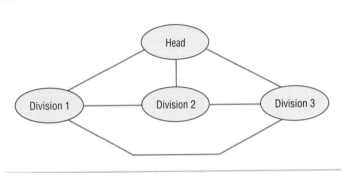

▶FIGURE 5.6
Network Structure

Managers and workers in many industries have offered similar testimonies to the benefits of more democratic, network-like structures.

Organizational Environments

If flatter organizations are more efficient, why aren't all bureaucracies flatter? Mainly, say sociologists, because of the environments in which they operate. An **organizational environment** is composed of a host of economic, political, and cultural factors that lie outside an organization and affect the way it works (Aldrich, 1979; Meyer and Scott, 1983). Some organizational environments are conducive to the formation of flatter, network-like bureaucracies. Others are not. We can illustrate the effects of organizational environments by discussing two cases that have attracted much attention in recent years: the organizational environments in the United States and Japan.

The Japanese Organizational Environment

In the 1970s, American business bureaucracies tended to be more hierarchical than their Japanese counterparts. This was one reason why worker dissatisfaction was high and labor productivity was low in the United States. In Japan, where corporate decision making was more decentralized, worker morale and productivity were high (Dore, 1983). Several aspects of the organizational environment help to explain Japanese–American differences in the 1970s. Specifically:

1. *Japanese workers were in a position to demand and achieve more decision-making authority than U.S. workers.* After World War II, the proportion of Japanese workers in unions increased, whereas the proportion of American workers in unions declined (see Chapter 15, "Collective Action and Social Movements"). Unions gave Japanese workers more clout than their American counterparts enjoyed.

2. *International competition encouraged bureaucratic efficiency in Japan.* Many big Japanese corporations matured in the highly competitive post–World War II international environment. Many big American corporations had originated earlier, in an international environment with few competitors. Thus, Japanese corporations had a bigger incentive to develop more efficient organizational structures (Harrison, 1994).

3. *The availability of external suppliers allowed Japanese firms to remain lean.* Many large American companies matured when external sources of supply were scarce.

Organizational environment: A host of economic, political, cultural, and other factors that lie outside an organization and affect the way it works.

For example, when IBM (International Business Machines Corporation) entered the computer market in the 1950s, it had to produce all components internally because nobody else was making them. This situation led IBM to develop a large, hierarchical bureaucracy. In contrast, Japanese computer manufacturers could rely on many external suppliers in the 1970s. Therefore, they could develop flatter organizational structures (Podolny and Page, 1998).

The U.S. Organizational Environment Today

Today, Japanese–American differences have substantially decreased because most big businesses in America have introduced Japanese-style bureaucratic reforms (Tsutsui, 1998). For instance, Silicon Valley, the center of the American computer industry today, is full of companies that fit the "Japanese" organizational pattern. These companies originated in the 1980s and 1990s, when external suppliers were abundant and international competitiveness was intense. In addition, American companies started to copy Japanese business structures because they saw them as successful (DiMaggio and Powell, 1983). We thus see how changes in the organizational environment help account for convergence between Japanese and American bureaucratic forms.

The experience of the United States over the past few decades holds out hope for increasing bureaucratic efficiency and the continued growth of employee autonomy and creativity at work. It does not mean, however, that bureaucracies in Japan and the United States will be alike in all respects in 20 or 50 or 100 years. The organizational environment is unpredictable, and sociologists are just beginning to understand its operation. It is therefore anyone's guess how far convergence will continue.

 ## The Points of the Compass

CENGAGENOW

Learn more about **Groups** by going through the Group Dynamics Learning Module.

Throughout this chapter, we have emphasized the capacity of networks, groups, and bureaucracies to constrain human behavior. As we have seen, such social collectivities can even encourage dangerously high levels of conformity, compel people to act against their better judgment, and dominate people in a vise of organizational rigidities.

We stressed the constraining aspect of social collectivities because we wanted to counter the commonsense view that motives alone determine the way people act. In conclusion, however, we should remember that people are often free to exercise two options other than bowing to the will of their social collectivities: "exit" and "voice" (Hirschman, 1970). In some circumstances, they can leave the social collectivities to which they belong (exit). In other circumstances, they can struggle against the constraints their social collectivities seek to impose on them (voice). After all, it is always possible to say no, even to the worst tyrant. Less dramatically but no less importantly, knowledge, including sociological knowledge, can increase the ability of people to resist the constraints imposed on them. Recall the Milgram experiment we discussed at the beginning of this chapter, in which subjects administered what they thought were painful shocks to people just because the experimenters told them to. When the experiment was replicated years later, many of the subjects refused to go along with the demands of the experimenters. Some invoked the example of the Nazis to justify their refusal to comply. Others mentioned Milgram's original experiment. Their knowledge, some of it perhaps gained in sociology courses, enabled them to resist unreasonable demands (Gamson, Fireman, and Rytina, 1982).

Paradoxically, to succeed in challenging social collectivities, people must sometimes form a new social collectivity themselves. Half a century ago, Seymour Martin Lipset, Martin A. Trow, and James S. Coleman (1956) conducted a classic sociological study that made just this point. They investigated the remarkable case of the International Typographical Union—remarkable because in the 1950s it was the outstanding exception to the tendency of trade union bureaucracies to turn into oligarchies, or organizations run by the few. The International Typographical Union remained democratic because the nature of printing as an occupation and an industry made the resources for democratic politics more widely available than is typical in trade unions. Strong local unions that valued their autonomy had founded the international union. The local and regional markets typical of the printing industry at the time strengthened their autonomy. At the same time, strong factions in the union prevented any one faction from becoming dominant. Finally, robust social networks on the shop floor enabled ordinary printers to fight for their rights and resist the slide into oligarchy and dull obedience. This case illustrates that people can exercise their freedom to form social collectivities that counteract other social collectivities. Embedded in social relations, we can use them for good or evil.

CHAPTER SUMMARY

1. **Do people act the way they do only because of their interests and emotions?**

   People's motives are important determinants of their actions, but social collectivities also influence the way we behave. Because of the power of social collectivities, people sometimes act against their interests, values, and emotions.

2. **Is it a small world?**

   It *is* a small world. Most people interact repeatedly with a small circle of family members, friends, coworkers, and others with whom they have strong ties. However, our personal networks overlap with other social networks, which is why only a few links separate us from complete strangers.

3. **What is network analysis?**

   Network analysis is the study of the concrete social relations linking people. By focusing on concrete ties, network analysts often come up with surprising results. For example, network analysis has demonstrated the strength of weak ties in job searches, explained patterns in the flow of information and communicable disease, and demonstrated that a rich web of social affiliations underlies urban life.

4. **What are groups?**

   Groups are clusters of people who identify with each other. Primary groups involve intense, intimate, enduring relations; secondary groups involve less personal and intense ties; and reference groups are groups against which people measure their situation or conduct. Groups impose conformity on members and seek to exclude nonmembers.

5. **Is bureaucracy just "red tape"? Is it possible to overcome bureaucratic inefficiency?**

   Although bureaucracies often suffer from various forms of inefficiency, they are generally efficient compared with other organizational forms. Bureaucratic inefficiency increases with size and degree of hierarchy. By flattening bureaucratic structures, decentralizing decision-making authority, and opening lines of communication between bureaucratic units, efficiency can often be improved.

6. **How accurate is Weber's analysis of bureaucracy?**

   Social networks underlie the chain of command in all bureaucracies and affect their operation. Weber ignored this aspect of bureaucracy. He also downplayed the importance of leadership in the functioning of bureaucracy. However, research shows that democratic leadership improves the efficiency of bureaucratic operations in noncrisis situations, authoritarian leadership works best in crises, and *laissez-faire* leadership is the least effective form of leadership in most situations.

7. **What impact does the organizational environment have on bureaucracy?**

   The organizational environment influences the degree to which bureaucratic efficiency can be achieved. For example, bureaucracies are less hierarchical where workers are more powerful, competition with other bureaucracies is high, and external sources of supply are available.

8. What does the sociological analysis of networks, groups, and bureaucracies tell us about the possibility of human freedom?

Networks, groups, and bureaucracies influence and constrain everyone. However, people also use these social collectivities to increase their freedom from other social collectivities. In this sense, social collectivities are a source of both constraint and freedom.

Questions to Consider

1. Would you have acted any differently from ordinary Germans if you were living in Nazi Germany? Why or why not? What if you were a member of a Nazi police battalion? Would you have been a traitor to your group? Why or why not?

2. Read the profiles of the 16 finalists on the first season of *The Apprentice* at http://www.nbc.com/nbc/The_Apprentice/contestants/index.shtml and develop an explanation for why Bill won the competition. Rely on insights learned from this chapter. For example, analyze the strengths and weaknesses of the contestants' leadership styles, problems with conformity and groupthink, and issues concerning group structure.

3. If you were starting your own business, how would you organize it? Why? Base your answers on theories and research discussed in this chapter.

Web Resources

CENGAGENOW™

Maximize your study time by using CengageNOW's diagnostic study plan to help you review this chapter. The Study Plan will

- help you identify areas on which you should concentrate;
- provide interactive exercises to help you master the chapter concepts; and
- provide a post-test to confirm you are ready to move on to the next chapter.

The Companion Website for *Sociology: Your Compass for a New World, The Brief Edition*, Enhanced Second Edition

www.cengage.com/sociology/brym

Supplement your review of this chapter by going to the companion website to take one of the tutorial quizzes, use flash cards to master key terms, and check out the many other study aids you'll find there. You'll also find special features such as GSS Data and Census 2000 information that will put data and resources at your fingertips to help you with that special project or help you do some research on your own.

CHAPTER 6

Deviance, Crime, and Social Control

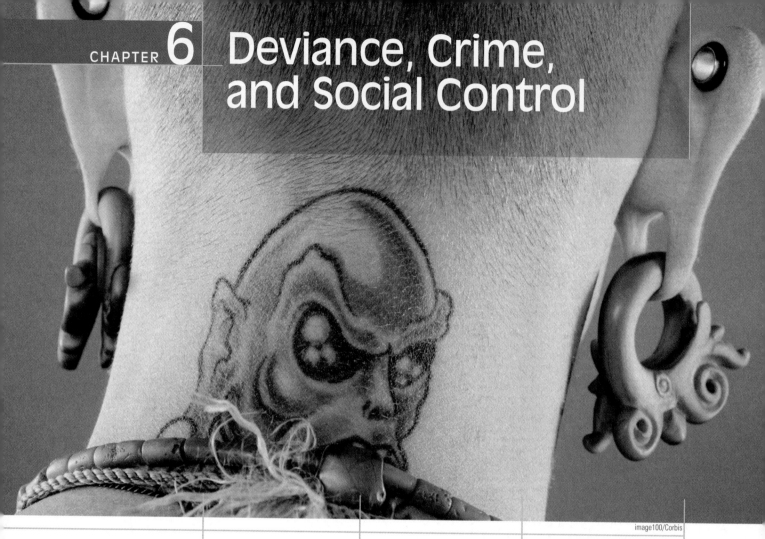

image100/Corbis

In this chapter, you will learn that:

- Deviance and crime vary among cultures, across history, and from one social context to another.

- Rather than being inherent in the characteristics of individuals or actions, deviance and crime are socially defined and constructed. The distribution of power is especially important in the social construction of deviance and crime.

- Many theories exist regarding deviance and crime. Each theory illuminates a different aspect of the process by which people break rules and are defined as deviants and criminals.

- As with deviance and crime, conceptions of appropriate punishment vary culturally and historically.

- Many forms of deviance that used to be considered voluntary forms of evil are now regarded as involuntary types of sickness that need to be treated by medical and psychiatric professionals.

- Imprisonment is one of the main forms of punishment in industrial societies; in the United States the prison system has grown quickly in the past 30 years, and punishment has become harsher.

- Fear of crime is increasing, but it is based less on rising crime rates than on manipulation by commercial and political groups that benefit from it.

- There are cost-effective and workable alternatives to the regime of punishment currently in place in the United States.

The Social Definition and Social Construction of Deviance

If you happen to come across members of the Tukano tribe in northern Brazil, don't be surprised if they greet you with a cheery "Have you bathed today?" You would probably find the question insulting, but think how you would feel if you were greeted by the Yanomamö people in Brazil's central highlands. A French anthropologist reports that when he first encountered the Yanomamö they rubbed mucus and tobacco juice into their palms, then inspected him by running their filthy hands over his body (Chagnon, 1992). He must have been relieved to return to urban Brazil and be greeted with a simple kiss on the cheek.

Rules for greeting people vary widely from one country to the next and among different cultural groups within one country. That is why a Boston marketing company recently found it useful to create an animated website showing business travelers how to greet their hosts in the fifteen countries where the firm does business ("The Business of Touch," 2006). After all, violating local norms can cause great offense and result in the loss of a contract, a fact that one visitor to South Korea found out too late. He beckoned his host with an index finger, after which the host grew quiet. He discovered after he lost the deal that Koreans beckon only cats and dogs with an index finger. If you want to beckon someone politely in South Korea, you should do so with all four fingers facing down, much like Americans wave good-bye.

CENGAGENOW

This icon signals when CengageNOW has important resources available for you to use in conjunction with the text. See the foldout at the front of this text for information on how to access CengageNOW.

Police arrest Martin Luther King, Jr., on September 4, 1958, in Montgomery, Alabama.

Bettmann/CORBIS

CENGAGENOW™

Learn more about **the Difference between Deviance and Crime** by going through the Difference between Deviance and Crime Animation.

Deviance: Occurs when someone departs from a norm and evokes a reaction from others.

Crime: Deviance that is against the law.

Law: A norm stipulated and enforced by government bodies.

Sanctions: Actions indicating disapproval of deviance.

Informal punishment: Involves a mild sanction that is imposed during face-to-face interaction, not by the judicial system.

Stigmatized: A marker that distinguishes some people from others and allows them to be negatively evaluated and treated.

Formal punishment: Punishment that takes place when the judicial system penalizes someone for breaking a law.

Because norms vary widely, deviance is relative. What some people consider normal, others consider deviant, and vice versa. No act is deviant in and of itself. People commit deviant acts only when they break a norm and cause others to react negatively. From a sociological point of view, *everyone* is a deviant in one social context or another.

The Difference between Deviance and Crime

Deviance involves breaking a norm and evoking a negative reaction from others. Societies establish some norms as laws. **Crime** is deviance that breaks a **law,** which is a norm stipulated and enforced by government bodies.

Just as deviance is relative, so is crime. Thus, in 1872, Susan B. Anthony—whose image graced the original dollar coin—was arrested and fined because she "knowingly, wrongfully and unlawfully voted for a representative to the Congress of the United States." That's right. She was arrested and fined because she voted. At trial, Justice Ward Hunt advised the jury, "There is no question for the jury, and the jury should be directed to find a verdict of guilty" (quoted in Flexner, 1975: 170). Or consider that in the late 1950s and early 1960s, Martin Luther King, Jr., whose birthday we now celebrate as a federal holiday, was repeatedly arrested for marching in the streets of Birmingham, Alabama, and other Southern cities for African Americans' civil rights, including their right to vote. Susan B. Anthony and Martin Luther King, Jr., were considered criminal in their lifetimes. In the 1870s, American law restricted voting to men. Anthony disagreed with the law and in acting on her deviant belief, she committed a crime. Similarly, in the 1950s most people in the American South believed in white superiority. They expressed that belief in many ways, including so-called Jim Crow laws that prevented many African Americans from voting. Martin Luther King, Jr., and other Civil Rights movement participants challenged existing laws and were therefore arrested.

Most of you would consider the sexist and racist society of the past, rather than Anthony and King, deviant or criminal. That is because norms and laws have changed dramatically. The 19th Amendment guaranteed woman suffrage in 1920. The Voting Rights Act of 1965 guaranteed voting rights for African Americans. Today, anyone arguing that women or African Americans should not be allowed to vote is considered deviant. Preventing them from voting is a crime. Crime is a special type of deviance because laws define certain deviant acts as criminal, but crime is just as relative as deviance. What is considered criminal in some times and places is considered perfectly normal in other times and places (see Box 6.3, pages 164–165).

Sanctions

Many otherwise deviant acts go unnoticed or are considered too trivial to warrant negative **sanctions,** or actions indicating disapproval of deviance. People who are observed committing more serious acts of deviance are typically punished, either informally or formally. **Informal punishment** is mild. It may involve raised eyebrows, a harsh stare, an ironic smile, gossip, ostracism, "shaming," or stigmatization (Braithwaite, 1989). When people are **stigmatized,** they are negatively evaluated because of a marker that distinguishes them from others (Goffman, 1963b). For example, until recently people with physical or mental disabilities were often treated with scorn or as a source of amusement. Pope Leo X (1475–1521) is said to have retained several mentally retarded dwarfs as a form of entertainment. **Formal punishment** results from people breaking laws. For example, criminals may be formally punished by having to serve time in prison or perform community service.

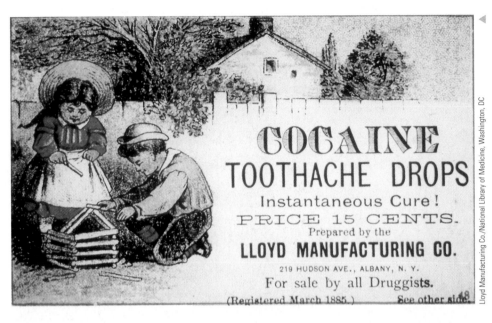

Lloyd Manufacturing Co./National Library of Medicine, Washington, DC

◀ Until the early part of the 20th century, people considered cocaine a medicine.

Types of Deviance and Crime

Sociologist John Hagan (1994) usefully classifies various types of deviance and crime along three dimensions. The first dimension is the *severity of the social response*. At one extreme, homicide and other very serious forms of deviance result in the most severe negative reactions, such as life imprisonment or capital punishment. At the other end of the spectrum, slight deviations from a norm, such as wearing a nose ring, will cause some people to do little more than express mild disapproval.

The second dimension of deviance and crime is the *perceived harmfulness* of the deviant or criminal act. Some deviant acts, such as rape, are generally seen as very harmful, whereas others, such as tattooing, are commonly regarded as being of little consequence. Note that actual harmfulness is not the only issue here. *Perceived* harmfulness is. Coca-Cola got its name because, in the early part of the 20th century, it contained a derivative of cocaine. Now cocaine is an illegal drug because people's perceptions of its harmfulness changed.

The third characteristic of deviance is the *degree of public agreement* about whether an act should be considered deviant. For example, people disagree about whether smoking marijuana should be considered a crime, especially because it may have therapeutic value in treating pain associated with cancer. In contrast, virtually everyone agrees that murder is seriously deviant. Note, however, that even the social definition of murder varies over time and across cultures and societies. Whether we classify the death of a miner as an accident or manslaughter depends on the kind of worker-safety legislation in existence. Some societies have more stringent worker-safety rules than others, and deaths considered accidental in some societies are classified as criminal offenses in others. So we see that even when it comes to consensus crimes, social definitions are variable.

Hagan's analysis allows us to classify four types of deviance and crime:

1. **Social diversions** are minor acts of deviance such as participating in fads and fashions. People usually perceive such acts as harmless. At most they evoke a mild societal reaction such as amusement or disdain, because many people are apathetic or unclear about whether social diversions are in fact deviant.

Social diversion: A minor act of deviance that is generally perceived as relatively harmless and that evokes, at most, a mild societal reaction such as amusement or disdain.

Is transvestism a social diversion, a social deviation, a conflict crime, or a consensus crime? Why?

Weegee (Arthur Fellig)/International Center of Photography/Getty Images

2. **Social deviations** are more serious acts. Large proportions of people agree that these acts are deviant and somewhat harmful, and they usually are subject to institutional sanction.

3. **Conflict crimes** are deviant acts that the state defines as illegal, but the definition is controversial in the wider society.

4. Finally, **consensus crimes** are widely recognized to be bad in themselves. There is little controversy over their seriousness. The great majority of people agree that such crimes should be met with severe punishment.

Power and the Social Construction of Deviance

To truly understand deviance and crime, you have to study how people socially construct norms and laws. The school of sociological thought known as *social constructionism* emphasizes that various social problems, including deviance and crime, are not inherent in certain actions themselves. Instead, some people are in a position to create norms and pass laws that stigmatize other people. Therefore, one must study how norms and laws are created (or "constructed") to understand why particular actions get defined as deviant or criminal in the first place. Relatively powerful groups are generally able to create norms and laws that suit their interests. Relatively powerless groups are usually unable to do so. The powerless, however, often struggle against stigmatization. If their power increases, they may succeed in their struggle. We now illustrate the importance of power in the social construction of deviance and crime by analyzing crimes against women and white-collar crime.

Social deviations: Noncriminal departures from norms that are nonetheless subject to official control. Some members of the public regard them as somewhat harmful, whereas other members of the public don't.

Conflict crimes: Illegal acts that many people consider harmful to society and that other people think are not very harmful. Such crimes are punishable by the state.

Consensus crimes: Illegal acts that nearly all people agree are bad and harm society greatly. The state inflicts severe punishment for consensus crimes.

Crimes against Women

Until recently, many types of crimes against women—including rape—were largely ignored in the United States and most other parts of the world. Admittedly, so-called aggravated rape involving strangers was sometimes severely punished. But so-called simple rape, which involved a friend or an acquaintance, was rarely prosecuted. Marital rape was viewed as a contradiction in terms, as if it were logically impossible for a married woman to be raped by her spouse. In her research, Susan Estrich (1987) found that rape law was not taught at American law schools in the 1970s. Law professors, judges, police officers, rapists, and even victims did not think that simple rape was "real rape." Similarly, judges, lawyers, and social scientists rarely discussed physical violence against women and sexual harassment until the 1970s. Governments did not collect data on the topic, and few social scientists showed any interest in what has now become a large and important area of study.

Today, the situation has improved. To be sure, rape is still associated with a low rate of prosecution (Scully, 1990). Rapists often hold women in contempt and do not regard rape as a real crime. Yet efforts by Estrich and others to have all forced sex defined as rape have raised people's awareness of date, acquaintance, and marital rape. Rape is prosecuted more often now than it used to be. The same is true for violence against women and sexual harassment.

Why the change? In part because women's position in the economy, the family, and other social institutions has improved over the past half century. Women now have more autonomy in the family, earn more, and enjoy more political influence. They also created a movement for women's rights that heightened concern about crimes disproportionately affecting them. For instance, until recently male sexual harassment of female workers was considered normal. Following Catharine MacKinnon's pathbreaking work on the subject, however, feminists succeeded in having the social definition of sexual harassment transformed (MacKinnon, 1979). Sexual harassment is now considered a social deviation and, in some circumstances, a crime. Increased public awareness of the extent of sexual harassment has probably made it less common. We thus see how social definitions of crimes against women have changed with a shift in the distribution of power.[1]

The 1873 Comstock Law was meant to stop trade in "obscene literature" (including information on sexually transmitted diseases) and "immoral articles" (including birth control devices). This 1915 cartoon satirizes the law. The caption reads: "Your honor, this woman gave birth to a naked child!"

White-Collar Crime

White-collar crime refers to illegal acts "committed by a person of respectability and high social status in the course of his [or her] occupation" (Sutherland, 1949: 9). Such crimes include embezzlement, false advertising, tax evasion, insider stock trading, fraud, unfair labor practices, copyright infringement, and conspiracy to fix prices and restrain trade. Sociologists often contrast white-collar crimes with **street crimes.** The latter include arson, burglary, robbery, assault, and other illegal acts. Street crime is committed disproportionately by people from lower classes, whereas white-collar crime is committed disproportionately by people from middle and upper classes.

White-collar crime is underreported. A recent Federal Bureau of Investigation (FBI) study notes that local law enforcement agencies are responsible for reporting white-collar

White-collar crime: An illegal act committed by a respectable, high-status person in the course of work.

Street crimes: Crimes that include arson, burglary, assault, and other illegal acts disproportionately committed by people from lower classes.

---

[1]Significantly, black rapists of white women receive much more severe punishments than white rapists of white women (LaFree, 1980). This pattern suggests that race is still an important power factor in the treatment of crime, a subject we have much to say about in the following.

crime but only on a voluntary basis (Barnett, n.d.). Because they receive no funding for compiling the data, few law enforcement agencies do. The FBI rarely bothers to analyze the data and publish results. Thus, for 1997–99, the most recent period for which data seem to be available, local agencies covering a mere 12 percent of the U.S. population reported white-collar crime data.

Despite underreporting, many sociologists think that white-collar crime is costlier to society than street crime. Consider that armed robbers netted perhaps $400 million in the 1980s, but the savings and loan scandal, in which bankers mismanaged funds and committed fraud, cost the American public $500 to $600 *billion* during that decade (Brouwer, 1998). Nonetheless, white-collar criminals, including corporations, are prosecuted relatively infrequently, and they are convicted even less often. This is true even in extreme cases, when white-collar crimes result in environmental degradation or death due, for example, to the illegal relaxation of safety standards. The police and the FBI routinely pursue burglars, but few of the corporate leaders whose mismanagement helped fuel the world financial crisis of 2008–2009 were even charged with a misdemeanor.

White-collar crime results in few prosecutions and still fewer convictions for two main reasons. First, much white-collar crime takes place in private and is therefore difficult to detect. For example, corporations may illegally decide to fix prices and divide markets, but executives make these decisions in boardrooms and private clubs that are not generally subject to police surveillance. Second, corporations can afford legal experts, public relations firms, and advertising agencies that advise their clients on how to bend laws, build up their corporate image in the public mind, and influence lawmakers to pass laws "without teeth" (Sherrill, 1997; Sutherland, 1949).

Governments also commit serious crimes. However, punishing political leaders is difficult (Chambliss, 1989). Authoritarian governments often call their critics terrorists and even torture people who are fighting for democracy, but such governments rarely have to account for their deeds (Herman and O'Sullivan, 1989). Some analysts argue that even the U.S. government, in spite of its democratic ideals, sometimes behaves in a manner that may be regarded as criminal. For example, while the United States was engaged in a war on drugs in the late 1980s, the CIA participated in the drug trade to help arm the right-wing Contra military forces in Nicaragua (Scott and Marshall, 1991).

In sum, white-collar crime is underreported, underdetected, underprosecuted, and underconvicted because it is the crime of the powerful and the well-to-do. The social construction of crimes against women has changed over the past half century, partly because women have become more powerful. In contrast, the social construction of white-collar crime has changed little because the upper classes are no less powerful now than they were half a century ago.

Measuring Crime

Some crimes are more common than others, and rates of crime vary over place, over time, and among different social categories. We now describe some of these variations. Then we review the main sociological explanations of crime and deviance.

First, a word about crime statistics. Since 1929, Uniform Crime Reports (UCR) have been the major source of crime statistics. Every law enforcement agency in the United States submits records of offenses and arrests to the FBI, usually through a state department of public safety or a state police organization. The results are available in the comprehensive annual publication, *Crime in the United States*. More recently, the FBI's National Incident-Based Reporting System (NIBRS) has provided more detailed records and statistics.

The UCR and NIBRS are far from perfect. First, much crime is not reported to the police. For example, many common assaults go unreported because the assailant is a friend or a relative of the victim. Similarly, many rape victims are reluctant to report the crime because they are afraid they will be humiliated and stigmatized by making it public. Second, authorities and the public decide which criminal acts to report and which to ignore. For instance, if the authorities decide to crack down on drugs, more drug-related crimes will be counted, not because more drug-related crimes occur but because more drug criminals are apprehended. Third, many crimes are not incorporated in major crime indexes published by the FBI. Excluded are many so-called **victimless crimes,** such as prostitution and illegal drug use, which involve violations of the law in which no victim steps forward and is identified. Also excluded from the indexes are most white-collar crimes.

Recognizing these difficulties, students of crime often supplement official crime statistics with other sources of information. **Self-report surveys** are especially useful. In such surveys respondents are asked to report their involvement in criminal activities, either as perpetrators or as victims. In the United States, the main source of data on victimization is the National Crime Victimization Survey, conducted by the U.S. Department of Justice twice annually since 1973 and involving a nationwide sample of about 80,000 people in 43,000 households (Rennison, 2002). Among other things, such surveys show about the same rate of serious crime (e.g., murder and non-negligent manslaughter) as official statistics but two to three times the rate of less serious crime, such as assault.

A definitive international self-report survey was conducted in 2000 in 17 countries, including the United States (van Kesteren, Mayhew, and Nieuwbeerta, 2001). It found that 38 percent of the approximately 34,000 respondents had been victims of crime in the year preceding the survey. The victimization rate ranged from a high of 58 percent in Australia to a low of 22 percent in Japan, with the United States somewhat above average at 42 percent. Examining the percentage distribution of victims within countries, the researchers found that the United States was just above average with respect to burglary and theft, just below average with respect to contact crime (robberies, sexual incidents, and assaults and threats), and considerably below average with respect to vehicular crime (▶Figure 6.1).

Survey data are influenced by people's willingness and ability to discuss criminal experiences frankly. Therefore, indirect measures of crime are sometimes used as well. For instance, sales of syringes are a good index of the use of illegal intravenous drugs. Indirect measures are unavailable for many types of crime, however.

Crime Rates

Bearing these caveats in mind, what does the official record show? *Every hour* during 2006, law enforcement agencies in the United States received verifiable reports on an average of 2 murders, 11 rapes, 50 robberies, 98 aggravated assaults, 136 motor vehicle thefts, 249 burglaries, and 750 larceny-thefts (U.S. Federal Bureau of Investigation [FBI], 2007b).

Between 1960 and 1992, the United States experienced a roughly 500 percent increase in the rate of violent crime, including murder and non-negligent manslaughter, rape, robbery, and aggravated assault. (Remember, the *rate* refers to the number of cases per 100,000 people.) Over the same period, the rate of major property crimes—motor vehicle theft, burglary, and larceny-theft—increased about 150 percent.

Although these statistics are alarming, we can take comfort from the fact that the long crime wave that began in the early 1960s and continued to surge in the 1970s

CENGAGENOW™

Learn more about **Crime Rates** by going through the Measuring Crime Rates Data Experiment.

Victimless crimes: Crimes that involve violations of the law in which no victim steps forward and is identified.

Self-report surveys: In such surveys, respondents are asked to report their involvement in criminal activities, either as perpetrators or as victims.

▶FIGURE 6.1
Victimization: Percent of Offenses by Type of Crime. Seven Countries, 2000 (percent of population victimized by all crimes).

Note: Contact crimes include robberies, sexual incidents, and assaults and threats. Horizontal lines indicate international average for each type of crime for all 17 countries in the survey. Thirty-eight percent of the population of all 17 countries were victimized in the year preceding the survey.
Source: van Kesteren, John, Pat Mayhew, Paul Nieuwbeerta (2001: 38, 401).

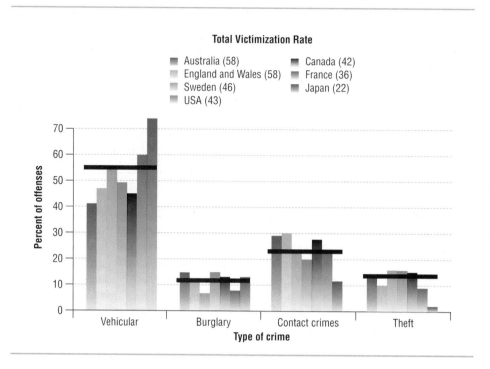

Total Victimization Rate

Australia (58)   Canada (42)
England and Wales (58)   France (36)
Sweden (46)   Japan (22)
USA (43)

eased in the 1980s and decreased in the 1990s. The good news is evident in ▶Figure 6.2 and ▶Figure 6.3, which show trends in violent and property crime between 1978 and 2006. Except for aggravated assault, the major crime rates for 1990 were about the same as or lower than the major crime rates for 1980. After about 1990, the rates for all forms of major crime began to fall significantly. The rate of murder and non-negligent manslaughter, for instance, fell 42 percent between 1991 and 2006, and the burglary rate also fell 42 percent. The results of the ongoing National Victimization Survey mirror these trends (Rennison, 2002). The 2001 criminal victimization rate was the lowest since the survey began in 1973. It fell about 50 percent between 1993 and 2001. This decrease means that there were only about half the number of crime victims per 1,000 people in the United States in 2001 as in 1993.

Why the Decline?

Sociologists usually mention four factors in explaining the decline. First, in the 1990s, governments put more police on the streets and many communities established their own systems of surveillance and patrol. This trend inhibited street crime. Second, young men are most prone to street crime, but America is aging and the proportion of young men in the population has declined. Third, the economy boomed in the 1990s. Usually, crime rates fluctuate with unemployment rates. When fewer people have jobs, more crime occurs. With an unemployment rate below 5 percent for much of the decade, economic conditions in the United States favored less crime. Finally, and more controversially, some researchers have recently noted that the decline in crime started 19 years after abortion was legalized in the United States. Beginning in 1992 the population included proportionately fewer unwanted children, and unwanted children are more crime prone than wanted children because they tend to receive less parental supervision and guidance (Donahue and Levitt, 2001; Skolnick, 1997; ▶Figure 6.4).

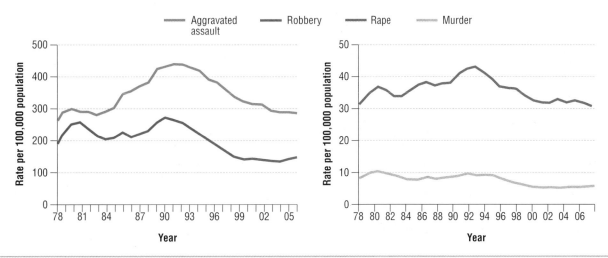

FIGURE 6.2
Violent Crime, United States, 1978–2006. Rate per 100,000 Population

Sources: U.S. Federal Bureau of Investigation (1999, 2002, 2003, 2007).

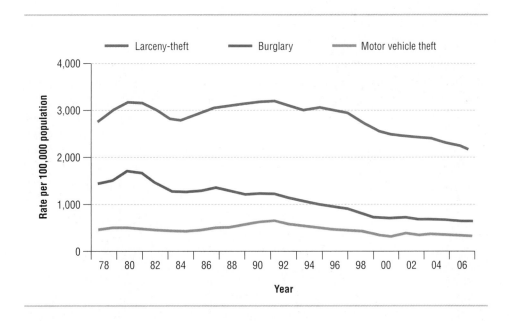

FIGURE 6.3
Property Crime, United States, 1978–2006. Rate per 100,000 Population

Sources: U.S. Federal Bureau of Investigation (1999, 2002, 2003, 2007).

Criminal Profiles

Gender and Age

According to FBI statistics 76 percent of all people arrested in the United States in 2006 were men. In the violent crime category, men accounted for 82 percent of arrests (FBI, 2007). As in most things, women, and especially teenage women, are catching up, albeit slowly. Men are still six times more likely than women to be arrested. However, with every passing decade women compose a slightly higher percentage of arrests. This change has taken place partly because, in the course of socialization, traditional social controls

▶FIGURE 6.4
**Abortions and Crime,
1973–1997**

Marguerite Holloway from "The
Aborted Crime Wave?" *Scientific
American,* 281 (6): 23–24.
Copyright 1999 Sarah Donelson.

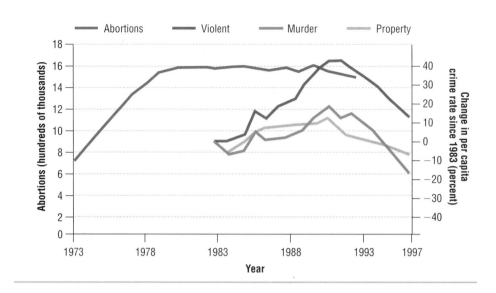

In the 1950s, a sort of "racial
profiling" was being commonly
applied to rising ethnic minorities
such as Puerto Ricans. In the
1957 classic *12 Angry Men,* the
character played by Henry Fonda
convinces the members of a jury
to overcome their prejudices,
examine the facts dispassionately,
and allow a disadvantaged minority youth accused of murdering
his father to go free.

The Everett Collection

CENGAGENOW™

Learn more about **Plea
Bargaining** by going through
the Criminal Justice System:
Plea Bargaining Video
Exercise.

and definitions of femininity are less often being imposed on women (see Chapter 10,
"Sexuality and Gender").

Most crime is committed by people who have not reached middle age. As ▶Table 6.1
shows, in 2003 Americans between the ages of 15 and 39 accounted for 73 percent of arrests. The 15- to 19-year-old age cohort is the most crime prone.

Race

Table 6.1 shows that crime also has a distinct racial distribution. Although the U.S. Census Bureau classified 75.1 percent of the U.S. population as white in 2000, whites accounted for only 69.7 percent of arrests in 2006. For African Americans, the story is reversed. They accounted for 28.0 percent of arrests but composed only 12.3 percent of the population.

Most sociologists agree that the disproportionately high arrest, conviction, and incarceration rates of African Americans are a result of three main factors: bias in the way crime statistics are collected, the low class position of blacks in American society, and racial discrimination in the criminal justice system (Hagan, 1994).

The statistical bias exists largely because of the absence of data on white-collar crimes in the official crime indexes. Because white-collar crimes are committed disproportionately by whites, official crime indexes make it seem as if blacks commit a higher proportion of all crimes than they actually do.

The low class standing of African Americans means that they experience twice the unemployment rate of whites, three times the rate of child poverty, and more than three times the rate of single motherhood. All these factors are associated with higher crime rates. The great majority of poor people are law abiding, but poverty and its associated disabilities are associated with elevated crime rates. The effect of poverty on crime rates is much the same for blacks and whites, but the problem worsened for the African American community in the last quarter of the 20th century. During this period, the U.S. economy was massively restructured and budgets for welfare and inner-city schools were drastically cut. Many manufacturing plants in or near U.S. inner cities were shut down in the 1970s and 1980s, causing high unemployment among local residents, a large number of whom were African Americans. Many young African Americans, with little prospect of getting a decent education and finding meaningful work, turned to crime as a livelihood and a source of prestige and self-esteem (Sampson and Wilson, 1995).

Finally, as Jerome Miller has convincingly shown, the criminal justice system efficiently searches out African American males for arrest and conviction (Miller, 1996: 48–88). Many white citizens are more zealous in reporting African American than white offenders. Many police officers are more eager to arrest African Americans than whites. Court officials are less likely to allow African Americans than whites to engage in plea bargaining. Fewer African Americans than whites can afford to pay fines that would prevent them from being jailed. Especially since the onset of the "war against drugs" in the 1980s, African Americans have been targeted, arrested, sentenced, and imprisoned in disproportionate numbers (Box 6.1). The fact that some 40 percent of the U.S. prison population consists of African American men is not just the result of their criminal activity. In the mid-1990s the crime rate of African American men was not much different from their

▶TABLE 6.1

Arrests by Sex, Age Cohort, and Race, United States, 2006

Sex	Percent of Population*	Percent of Arrests
Male	49.1	76.1
Female	50.9	23.9
Total	100.0	100.0
Age Cohort		
Under 10	14.0	0.1
10–14	7.3	4.4
15–19	7.1	20.5
20–24	6.8	19.5
25–29	6.8	13.8
30–34	7.2	9.9
35–39	8.2	9.4
40–44	8.1	8.8
45–49	7.2	6.7
50–54	6.1	3.7
55–59	4.8	1.8
60+	16.4	1.3
Total	100.0	99.9**
Racial Group		
White	75.1	69.7
Black	12.3	28.0
American Indian and Alaskan Native	0.9	1.3
Asian and Pacific Islander	3.7	1.1
Other***	8.0	—
Total	100.0	100.1

*According to the 2000 census.
**Does not equal 100.0 because of rounding.
****"Other" includes people who declare two or more races. The race classification used by the U.S. Census Bureau (left column) differs from that used by the FBI in its *Uniform Crime Report* (right column). Therefore, the two columns are only approximately comparable.
Sources: Calculated from U.S. Census Bureau (2003); FBI (2003, 2007).

The War on Drugs

Did your high school conduct random drug searches? Did you have to take a Breathalyzer test at your prom? Increasingly, companies are demanding that employees take urine and other tests for drug use. The war on drugs, initiated by Nancy Reagan's plea to "Just Say No" in the 1980s, continues in the United States.

One consequence of the war on drugs is the imposition of stiff penalties on drug offenders. For example, if you're caught selling one vial of crack or one bag of heroin, your sentence is 5 to 25 years, depending on which state you're in. New York drug laws are toughest. If you're caught selling 2 or more ounces of heroin or possessing 4 ounces of cocaine in New York, you will receive the maximum prison sentence of life in prison even as a first-time offender. The authorities make more than 1.5 million arrests every year for drug-related offenses, including 700,000 for the sale or possession of marijuana (Massing et al., 1999: 11–20).

Despite all of these arrests, most people think our drug control policy is ineffective. The U.S. government spends 18 times more on drug control now than it did in 1980 ($18 billion versus $1 billion). Eight times as many Americans are in jail today for drug-related offenses (400,000 versus 50,000 in 1980). Yet an estimated 4 million hardcore drug users are living in the United States (Massing et al., 1999: 32). What should we do?

Rather than continuing the war on drugs, some sociologists suggest it is time to think of alternative policies. We can, for example, estimate the effectiveness of four major policies on drug control: controlling the drug trade abroad, stopping drugs at the border, arresting drug traders and users, and implementing drug prevention and treatment. In one major government-funded study, "[t]reatment was found to be seven times more cost-effective than law enforcement, ten times more effective than interdiction [stopping drugs at the border], and twenty-three times more effective than attacking drugs at their source" (quoted in Massing et al., 1999: 14). Yet the U.S. government spends less than 10 percent of its $18 billion drug control budget on prevention and treatment. Over two-thirds of the money is spent reducing the supply of drugs (Massing et al., 1999:14).

Another more radical option is to seek limited legalization of drugs. Two arguments support this proposal. First, the United States' major foray into the control of substance abuse—the prohibition of alcohol during the 1920s and early 1930s—turned out to be a fiasco. It led to an increase in the illegal trade in alcohol and the growth of the Mafia. Second, the Netherlands, for example, has succeeded in decriminalizing marijuana use. Even after it became legal, no major increase in the use of marijuana or more serious drugs, such as heroin, took place (Massing et al., 1999: 28–9).

Clearly, the citizens of the United States need to discuss drug policy in a serious way. Just saying "no" and spending most of our drug-control budget on trying to curb the supply of illegal drugs are ineffective policies (Reinarman and Levine, 1999).

Critical Thinking

- If you were in charge of an $18 billion a year budget for the war on drugs, what proportion of the budget would you invest in controlling the drug trade abroad, stopping drugs at the border, arresting drug traders and users, and implementing drug prevention and treatment? Why?

- What groups would likely oppose the policy mix you propose? Why?

- How would you try to neutralize opposition to your proposed policy mix?

crime rate in 1980, but their imprisonment rate rose more than 300 percent during that period (Tonry, 1995).

CENGAGENOW™

Learn more about **Explaining Deviance and Crime** by going through the Perspectives on Deviance Learning Module.

Explaining Deviance and Crime

Lep: I remember your li'l ass used to ride dirt bikes and skateboards, actin' crazy an' shit. Now you want to be a gangster, huh? You wanna hang with real muthaf_____ and tear shit up, huh? . . . Stand up, get your l'il ass up. How old is you now anyway?

Kody: Eleven, but I'll be twelve in November.

—SANYIKA SHAKUR (1993: 8)

"Monster" Scott Kody eagerly joined the notorious gang the Crips in South Central Los Angeles in 1975 when he was in grade 6. He was released from Folsom Prison on parole in 1988, at the age of 24. Until about 3 years before his release, he was one of the most ruthless gang leaders in Los Angeles and the California prison system. In 1985, however, he decided to reform. He adopted the name of Sanyika Shakur, became a black nationalist, and began a crusade against gangs. Few people in his position have chosen that path. In Kody's heyday, about 30,000 gang members roamed Los Angeles County. Today there are more than 150,000. It is estimated that in 2008, there were 30,000 youth gangs in the United States, with 800,000 members (U.S. Department of Justice, 2008).

What makes the criminal life so attractive to so many young men and women? In general, why do deviance and crime occur at all? Sociologists have proposed dozens of explanations. However, we can group them into two basic types. **Motivational theories** identify the social factors that *drive* people to deviance and crime. Many motivational theories derive from functionalist ideas. **Constraint theories** identify the social factors that *impose* deviance and crime (or conventional behavior) on people. Below we examine several examples of each type of theory. Before doing so, however, we want to stress that becoming a *habitual* deviant or criminal is a learning process that occurs in a social context. Motive and lack of constraint may ignite a single deviant or criminal act, but repeatedly engaging in that act requires the learning of a deviant or criminal role.

Learning the Deviant Role: The Case of Marijuana Users

Howard S. Becker, a giant in the sociological study of deviance, analyzed this learning process in a classic study of marijuana users (Becker, 1963: 41–58). In 1948 and 1949, Becker financed his Ph.D. studies at the University of Chicago by playing piano in local jazz bands. He used the opportunity to do participant-observation research, carefully observing his fellow musicians, informally interviewing them in depth, and writing up detailed field notes after performances. All told, Becker observed and interviewed 50 jazz musicians who smoked marijuana.

Becker found that his fellow musicians had to pass through a three-stage learning process before becoming regular marijuana users. Failure to pass a stage meant failure to learn the deviant role and become a regular user. These are the three stages:

1. *Learning to smoke the drug in a way that produces real effects.* First-time marijuana smokers do not ordinarily get high. To do so, they must learn how to smoke the drug in a way that ensures sufficient dosage to produce intoxicating effects (taking deep drags and holding one's breath for a long time). This process takes practice, and some first-time users give up, typically claiming that marijuana has no effect on them or that people who claim otherwise are just fooling themselves. Others are more strongly encouraged by their peers to keep trying. If they persist, they are ready to go to stage two.

2. *Learning to recognize the effects and connect them with drug use.* Those who learn the proper smoking technique may not recognize that they are high, or they may not connect the symptoms of being high with smoking the drug. They may get hungry, laugh uncontrollably, play the same song for hours on end, and yet still fail to realize that these are symptoms of intoxication. If so, they will stop using the drug. Becker found, however, that his fellow musicians typically asked experienced users how they knew whether they were high. Experienced users identified the symptoms of marijuana use and helped novices make the connection between what they were experiencing and

Motivational theories: Theories that identify the social factors that drive people to commit deviant and criminal acts.

Constraint theories: Theories that identify the social factors that impose deviance and crime (or conventional behavior) on people.

smoking the drug. Once they made that connection, novices were ready to advance to stage three.

3. *Learning to enjoy the perceived sensations.* Smoking marijuana is not inherently pleasurable. Some users experience a frightening loss of self-control ("paranoia"). Others feel dizzy, uncomfortably thirsty, itchy, forgetful, or dangerously impaired in their ability to judge time and distance. If these negative sensations persist, marijuana use will cease. However, Becker found that experienced users typically helped novices redefine negative sensations as pleasurable. They taught novices to laugh at their impaired judgment, take special pleasure in quenching their deep thirst, and find deeper meaning in familiar music. If and only if novices learned to define the effects of smoking as pleasurable did they become habitual marijuana smokers.

So we see that becoming a regular marijuana user involves more than just motive and opportunity. In fact, learning any deviant or criminal role requires a social context like the one Becker describes. Experienced deviants or criminals must teach novices the "tricks of the trade." Bearing this fact in mind, we may now examine the two main types of theories that seek to explain deviance and crime—those that ask what motivates people to break rules and those that ask how social constraints sometimes fail to prevent rules from getting broken.

Motivational Theories

Durkheim's Functional Approach

In one of the first sociological works on deviance, Émile Durkheim (1964 [1895]) wrote that deviance is normal. What did he mean by this apparently contradictory statement?

He meant that deviance is necessary or functional, and therefore exists in all societies. What functions does deviance perform? According to Durkheim, deviance gives people the opportunity to define what is moral and what is not. Our reactions to deviance range from scorn to outrage, and our punishments from raised eyebrows to the death penalty. But all of our reactions have one thing in common. They clarify moral boundaries, allowing us to draw the line between right and wrong. This clarification is useful in two ways. First, it promotes the unity of society, or its "social solidarity." Second, by pushing against the limits of our tolerance, some deviance encourages healthy social change. Today's deviance may be tomorrow's morality, so some acts that violate norms suggest new paths for moral development. The functional necessity of deviance derives from these benefits, wrote Durkheim.

Strain Theory

Durkheim also argued that the absence of clear norms—"anomie"—can result in elevated rates of suicide and other forms of deviant behavior (see Chapter 1, "A Sociological Compass"). Robert Merton's **strain theory** (▶Concept Summary 6.1) extended Durkheim's insight (Merton, 1938).

Merton defined anomie as "the mismatch between culturally valued goals and the institutional means of achieving those goals." He argued that cultures often teach people to value material success. Just as often, however, societies do not provide enough legitimate opportunities for everyone to succeed. Therefore, some people experience strain. Most will nonetheless force themselves to adhere to social norms (Merton called this "conformity"). The rest adapt in one of four ways: They may drop out of conventional society ("retreatism"); they may reject the goals of conventional society but continue to follow its rules ("ritualism"); they may protest against convention and support alterna-

Strain theory: A theory which holds that people may turn to deviance when they experience strain. Strain results when a culture teaches people the value of material success and society fails to provide enough legitimate opportunities for everyone to succeed.

tive values ("rebellion"); or they may find alternative and illegitimate means of achieving their society's goals ("innovation"), that is, they may become criminals. The American Dream of material success starkly contradicts the lack of opportunity available to poor youths, said Merton. Therefore, poor youths sometimes engage in illegal means of attaining legitimate ends. Merton would say that "Monster" Scott Kody became an innovator at the age of 11 and a rebel at the age of 21.

		INSTITUTIONALIZED MEANS		
		Accept	**Reject**	**Create New**
	Accept	conformity	innovation	—
CULTURAL GOALS	*Reject*	ritualism	retreatism	—
	Create New	—	—	rebellion

▶CONCEPT SUMMARY 6.1
Merton's Strain Theory of Deviance

Source: Adapted from Merton (1938).

Subcultural Theory

Another type of motivational theory, known as **subcultural theory,** emphasizes that adolescents like Kody are not alone in deciding to join gangs. Many similarly situated adolescents make the same kind of decision, rendering the formation and growth of the Crips and other gangs a *collective* adaptation to social conditions. Moreover, this collective adaptation involves the formation of a subculture with distinct norms and values. Members of this subculture reject the legitimate world that they feel has rejected them (Cohen, 1955).

The literature emphasizes three features of criminal subcultures. First, depending on the availability of different subcultures in their neighborhoods, delinquent youths may turn to different types of crime. In some areas, delinquent youths are recruited by organized crime syndicates, such as the Mafia. In areas that lack organized crime networks, delinquent youths are more likely to create violent gangs. Thus, the relative availability of different subcultures influences the type of criminal activity to which one turns (Cloward and Ohlin, 1960).

A second important feature of criminal subcultures is that their members typically spin out a whole series of rationalizations for their criminal activities. These justifications make their illegal activities appear morally acceptable and normal, at least to the members of the subculture. Typically, criminals deny personal responsibility for their actions ("What I did harmed nobody"). They condemn those who pass judgment on them ("I'm no worse than anyone else"). They claim their victims get what they deserve ("She had it coming to her"). And they appeal to higher loyalties, particularly to friends and family ("I had to do it because he dissed my gang"). The creation of such justifications and rationalizations enables criminals to clear their consciences and get on with the job. Sociologists call such rationalizations **techniques of neutralization** (Sykes and Matza, 1957).

Finally, although deviants depart from mainstream culture, they are strict conformists when it comes to the norms of their own subculture. They tend to share the same beliefs, dress alike, eat similar food, and adopt the same mannerisms and speech patterns. Gangs may develop an elaborate system of hand signs to distinguish themselves from other gangs. Whether among professional thieves (Conwell, 1937) or young gang members (Short and Strodtbeck, 1965), deviance is strongly discouraged *within* the subculture. Paradoxically, deviant subcultures depend on internal conformity.

Learning Theory

Both strain and subcultural theories are problematic insofar as they tell us nothing about which adaptation someone experiencing strain will choose. Even when criminal subcultures beckon ambitious adolescents who lack opportunities to succeed in life, only a minority of adolescents join up. Most adolescents who experience strain and have the opportunity to join a gang reject a life of crime and become conformists and ritualists, to use Merton's terms. Why?

Subcultural theory: This theory argues that gangs are a collective adaptation to social conditions. Distinct norms and values that reject the legitimate world crystallize in gangs.

Techniques of neutralization: The rationalizations that deviants and criminals use to justify their activities. Techniques of neutralization make deviance and crime seem normal, at least to the deviants and criminals themselves.

As in the TV show *The Sopranos,* having family members and friends in the Mafia predisposes one to Mafia involvement.

Edwin Sutherland (1939) addressed both the class and choice problems more than 70 years ago by proposing a third motivational theory, which he called the **theory of differential association.** The theory of differential association is still one of the most influential ideas in the sociology of deviance and crime. In Sutherland's view, a person learns to favor one adaptation over another as a result of his or her life experiences or socialization. Specifically, everyone is exposed to both deviant and nondeviant values and behaviors as they grow up. If you happen to be exposed to more deviant than nondeviant experiences, chances are you will learn to become a deviant yourself. You will come to value a particular deviant lifestyle and consider it normal.

Everything depends, then, on the exact mix of deviant and conformist influences a person faces. For example, a substantial body of participant-observation and survey research has failed to discover widespread cultural values prescribing crime and violence in the inner city (Sampson, 1997: 39). Most inner-city residents follow conventional norms, which is one reason why most inner-city adolescents do not learn to become gang members. Those who do become gang members tend to grow up in very specific situations and contexts that teach them the value of crime.

Significantly, the theory of differential association holds for people in all class positions. For instance, Sutherland applied the theory of differential association in his pathbreaking research on white-collar crime. He noted that white-collar criminals, like their counterparts on the street, learn their skills from associates and share a culture that rewards rule breaking and expresses contempt for the law (Sutherland, 1949).

Constraint Theories

Motivational theories ask how some people are driven to break norms and laws. Constraint theories, in contrast, pay less attention to people's motivations. The kinds of questions constraint theorists pose include the following: How are deviant and criminal "labels" imposed on some people? How do various forms of social control fail to impose conformity on them? How does the distribution of power in society shape deviance and crime?

Labeling Theory: A Symbolic Interactionist Approach

Symbolic interactionism focuses on the meanings people attach to objects, actions, and other people in the course of their everyday lives. As we establish meanings, we put labels on things; you call the object in your hand a book and the streaker at a football game a deviant. Although labels are often convenient, the trouble with applying them to people is that they may stick irrespective of the actual behavior involved. We may persist in our belief that a person is deviant even when the person ceases to act in a deviant way. Our labeling itself may then cause more deviance. This is the chief insight of **labeling theory**—that deviance results not just from the actions of the deviant but also from the responses of others, who define some actions as deviant and other actions as normal (Becker, 1963).

For example, if an adolescent misbehaves in high school a few times, teachers and the principal may punish him. However, his troubles really begin if the school authorities and the police label him a "delinquent." Surveillance of his actions will increase. Actions that authorities would normally not notice or would define as of little consequence are more likely to be interpreted as proof of his delinquency. He may be ostracized from nondeviant cliques in the school and eventually be socialized into a deviant subculture. Over time, immersion in the deviant subculture may lead the adolescent to adopt "delinquent" as his **master status,** or overriding public identity. More easily than we may care to believe,

Differential association theory: Holds that people learn to value deviant or nondeviant lifestyles depending on whether their social environment leads them to associate more with deviants or nondeviants.

Labeling theory: Holds that deviance results not so much from the actions of the deviant as from the response of others, who label the rule breaker a deviant.

Master status: One's overriding public identity.

what starts out as a few incidents of misbehavior can get amplified into a criminal career because of labeling (Matsueda, 1988, 1992).

The important part that labeling plays in who gets caught and who gets charged with crime was demonstrated by Aaron Cicourel (1968). Cicourel examined the tendency to label rule-breaking adolescents "juvenile delinquents" if they came from families in which the parents were divorced. He found that police officers tended to use their discretionary powers to arrest adolescents from divorced families more often than adolescents from intact families who committed similar delinquent acts. Judges, in turn, tended to give more severe sentences to adolescents from divorced families than to adolescents from intact families who were charged with similar delinquent acts. Sociologists and criminologists then collected data on the social characteristics of adolescents who were charged as juvenile delinquents, "proving" that children from divorced families were more likely to become juvenile delinquents. Their finding reinforced the beliefs of police officers and judges. Thus, the labeling process acted as a self-fulfilling prophecy.

Control Theory

All motivational theories assume that people are good and require special circumstances to make them bad. A popular type of constraint theory assumes that people are bad and require special circumstances to make them good. That is because, according to **control theory,** the rewards of deviance and crime are many. Proponents of this approach argue that nearly everyone wants fun, pleasure, excitement, and profit. Moreover, they say that if we could get away with it, most of us would commit deviant and criminal acts to get more of those valued things. For control theorists, the reason most of us don't engage in deviance and crime is that we are prevented from doing so. The reason deviants and criminals break norms and laws is that social controls are insufficient to ensure their conformity.

Travis Hirschi first developed the control theory of crime (Hirschi, 1969; Gottfredson and Hirschi, 1990). He argued that adolescents are more prone to deviance and crime than adults are because they are incompletely socialized and therefore lack self-control. Adults and adolescents may both experience the impulse to break norms and laws, but adolescents are less likely to control that impulse. Hirschi went on to show that adolescents who are most prone to delinquency are likely to lack four types of social control. They tend to have few social *attachments* to parents, teachers, and other respectable role models; few legitimate *opportunities* for education and a good job; few involvements in conventional institutions; and weak *beliefs* in traditional values and morality. Because of the lack of control stemming from these sources, adolescents are relatively free to act on their deviant impulses. Other sociologists have applied control theory to gender differences in crime. They have shown that girls are less likely to engage in delinquency than boys are because families typically exert more control over girls, supervising them more closely and socializing them to avoid risk (Hagan, Simpson, and Gillis, 1987; Peters, 1994).

Labeling and control theories have little to say about why people regard certain kinds of activities as deviant or criminal in the first place. For the answer to that question, we must turn to the **conflict theory of deviance and crime,** a third type of constraint theory.

The Conflict Theory of Deviance and Crime

In 1996, JonBenét Ramsey was found strangled to death in the basement of her home in Boulder, Colorado. The police found no footprints in the snow surrounding the house and no sign of forced entry. The FBI concluded that nobody had entered the house dur-

Control theory: This theory holds that the rewards of deviance and crime are ample. Therefore, nearly everyone would engage in deviance and crime if they could get away with it, and the degree to which people are prevented from violating norms and laws accounts for variations in the level of deviance and crime.

Conflict theories of deviance and crime: A category of theories which hold that deviance and crime arise out of the conflict between the powerful and the powerless.

ing the night, when, according to the coroner, the murder took place. The police did find a ransom note saying that the child had been kidnapped. A linguistics expert from Vassar later concluded that the child's mother was the author. It was also determined that all of the materials used in the crime had been purchased by the mother. Although by no means an open-and-shut case, enough evidence was available to cast a veil of suspicion over the parents. Yet, apparently because of the lofty position the Ramseys held in their community, the police treated them in an extraordinary way. The Boulder police designated the Ramseys an "influential family" and ordered that they be treated as victims, not suspects (Oates, 1999: 32). The father was allowed to participate in the search for the child. In the process, he may have contaminated crucial evidence. The police also let him leave the house unescorted for about an hour. This led to speculation that he might have disposed of incriminating evidence. Because the Ramseys were millionaires, they were able to hire accomplished lawyers who prevented the Boulder police from interviewing them for 4 months and a public relations team that reinforced the idea that the Ramseys were victims. A grand jury decided on October 13, 1999, that nobody would be charged with the murder of JonBenét Ramsey.

Still, the way their case was treated adds to the view that the law applies differently to rich and poor. That is the perspective of conflict theory. In brief, conflict theorists maintain that the rich and the powerful impose deviant and criminal labels on the less powerful members of society, particularly those who challenge the existing social order. Meanwhile, they are usually able to use their money and influence to escape punishment for their own misdeeds.

Steven Spitzer (1980) conveniently summarizes this school of thought. He notes that capitalist societies are based on private ownership of property. Moreover, their smooth functioning depends on the availability of productive labor and respect for authority. When thieves steal, they challenge private property. Theft is therefore a crime. When so-called bag ladies and drug addicts drop out of conventional society, they are defined as deviant because their refusal to engage in productive labor undermines a pillar of capitalism. When young, politically volatile students or militant trade unionists strike or otherwise protest against authority, they also represent a threat to the social order and are defined as deviant or criminal.

Of course, says Spitzer, the rich and the powerful engage in deviant and criminal acts too. But, he adds, they tend to be dealt with more leniently. Industries can grievously harm people by damaging the environment, yet serious charges are rarely brought against the owners of industry. White-collar crimes are less severely punished than street crimes, regardless of the relative harm they cause.

And so we see that many theories contribute to our understanding of the social causes of deviance and crime. Some forms of deviance and crime are better explained by one theory than another. Different theories illuminate different aspects of the process by which people are motivated to break rules and become defined as rule breakers. Our overview should make it clear that no one theory is best. Instead, taking many theories into account allows us to develop a fully rounded appreciation of the complex processes surrounding the social construction of deviance and crime (❿Concept Summary 6.2).

Punishment

American TV viewing between July 28 and August 3, 2008, was much like that of any other week. Crime was the subject of half of the top 10 primetime network TV programs. (Nielsen Media Research, 2008). Because millions of additional viewers watched fictional

> **CONCEPT SUMMARY 6.2**
> The Main Theories of Deviance and Crime

Theory	Sociologists	Summary
MOTIVATIONAL THEORIES		Identify the social factors that *drive* people to deviance and crime
Strain theory	Merton	Derives from the functionalist tradition; societies do not provide enough legitimate opportunities for everyone to succeed, resulting in strain, one reaction to which is to find alternative and illegitimate means of achieving society's goals
Subcultural theory	Cohen; Cloward & Ohlin	Emphasizes *collective* adaptations to strain, such as the formation of gangs and organized crime, and the degree to which these collective adaptations have distinct norms and values that reject the nondeviant or noncriminal world
Learning theory	Sutherland	People become deviants or criminals—or fail to do so—because of "differential association" (i.e., they are exposed to, and therefore learn, deviant and criminal values to varying degrees)
CONSTRAINT THEORIES		Identify the social factors that impose deviance and crime (or conventional behavior) on people
Labeling theory	Becker; Matsueda; Cicourel	Derives from the symbolic interactionist tradition; deviance and crime result not just from the actions of the deviant or criminal but also from the responses of others, who define some actions as deviant and other actions as normal
Control theory	Hirschi & Gottfredson	Deviants and criminals tend to be people with few social *attachments* to parents, teachers, and other respectable role models, few legitimate *opportunities* for education and a good job, few *involvements* in conventional institutions, and weak *beliefs* in traditional values and morality; the lack of control stemming from these sources leaves them relatively free to act on their deviant impulses
Conflict theory	Spitzer	Derives from the conflict tradition; the rich and the powerful impose deviant and criminal labels on the less powerful members of society, particularly those who challenge the existing social order; they are usually able to use their money and influence to escape punishment for their misdeeds

crime shows on cable, local, daytime, and late-night TV and because the news is full of crime stories, one might reasonably conclude that the United States is a society obsessed with crime.

As one might expect in such a society, punishment is also a big issue. This fact is evident from the more than 2.1 million people in state and federal prisons and local jails—a number that is increasing by 50,000 to 80,000 per year. The United States has more people behind bars than any other country on Earth. In fact, 10 percent more people are behind bars in the United States (2007 population: 301 million) than in China and India combined (2007 population: about 2.43 billion). State prisons in California alone hold more criminals in their grip than do Japan, Germany, France, Great Britain, the Netherlands, and Singapore combined. As of 2000, the United States had the highest incarceration rate (the number of people imprisoned per 100,000 population) of any country in the world (Schlosser, 1998; The Sentencing Project, 1997, 2001; U.S. Census Bureau, 2000a, 2001a).

All societies seek to ensure that their members obey norms and laws. All societies impose sanctions on rule breakers. However, the *degree* of social control varies over time and place. *Forms* of punishment also vary. In addition to imprisonment, society deals with deviance and crime by means of medicalization, capital punishment, and rehabilitation. Let us examine each of these reactions to deviance and crime in turn.

The Medicalization of Deviance

Increasingly, we deal with deviance by medicalizing it. The **medicalization of deviance** refers to the fact that "medical definitions of deviant behavior are becoming more prevalent in . . . societies like our own" (Conrad and Schneider, 1992 [1980]: 28–9). In an earlier era, much deviant behavior was labeled evil. Deviants tended to be chastised, punished, and otherwise socially controlled by members of the clergy, neighbors, family members, and the criminal justice system. Today, however, a person prone to drinking sprees is more likely to be declared an alcoholic and treated in a detoxification center. A person predisposed to violent rages is more likely to be medicated. A person inclined to overeating is more likely to seek therapy and, in extreme cases, surgery. A heroin addict is more likely to seek the help of a methadone program. As these examples illustrate, what used to be regarded as willful deviance is now often regarded as involuntary deviance. Increasingly, what used to be defined as "badness" is defined as "sickness." As our definitions of deviance change, deviance is increasingly coming under the sway of the medical and psychiatric establishments (▶Figure 6.5).

The Spread of Mental Disorders

Many mental disorders have obvious organic causes, such as chemical imbalances in the brain. These problems can often be precisely identified and treated with drugs or other therapies. Experiments can be conducted to verify their existence and establish the effectiveness of one treatment or another. Little debate takes place over whether such ailments should be listed in the "bible" of the American Psychiatric Association, the *Diagnostic and Statistical Manual of Mental Disorders* (DSM).

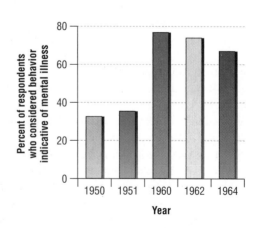

"Now here's a young woman in her twenties, let's call her Betty Smith . . . she has never had a job, and she doesn't seem to want to go out and look for one. She is a very quiet girl, she doesn't talk much to anyone—even her own family, and she acts like she is afraid of people, especially young men her own age. She won't go out with anyone, and whenever someone comes to visit her family, she stays in her own room until they leave. She just stays by herself and daydreams all the time and shows no interest in anything or anybody."

▶FIGURE 6.5

An Example of the Medicalization of Deviance

Five North American surveys conducted in the 1950s and 1960s presented respondents with the anecdote above. The graph shows the percentage of respondents who considered the behavior described in the anecdote evidence of mental illness. Notice the difference between the 1950s and the 1960s. (Nearly 100 percent of psychiatrists who evaluated the anecdote thought it illustrated "simple schizophrenia.")

Conrad and Schneider (1992 [1980]: 59).

Medicalization of deviance: The process by which medical definitions of deviant behavior are becoming more prevalent.

The organic basis for other ailments is unclear. In such cases, social values and political conflict can determine whether they are listed in the DSM. Thus, in the 1970s and 1980s, American psychiatrists fiercely debated whether "neurosis," "post-traumatic stress disorder," "homosexuality," and "self-defeating personality disorder" were real mental disorders. In the end, homosexuality was dropped from the DSM, largely in response to the efforts of liberal-minded psychiatrists, as was self-defeating personality disorder, thanks to the efforts of feminists. Neurosis was retained at the insistence of Freudians. Post-traumatic stress disorder (PTSD) was added to the DSM after a strenuous lobbying campaign by Vietnam War veterans and their supporters (Scott, 1990). These cases nicely illustrate that the medicalization of deviance is in part a social and political process.

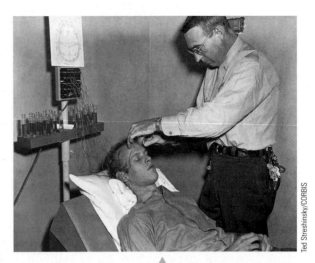

An example of the medicalization of deviance. A lobotomy is performed in Vacaville State Prison in California in 1961 to "cure" the inmate of criminality.

In the mid-19th century there was just one mental disorder recognized by the federal government: idiocy/insanity. The current DSM lists 297. As the number of mental disorders has grown, so has the proportion of Americans presumably affected by them. In the mid-19th century, few people were defined as suffering from mental disorders, but one respected survey conducted in the early 1990s found that 48 percent of Americans would suffer from a mental disorder—very broadly defined, of course—during their lifetime (Blazer, Kessler, McGonagle and Swartz, 1994; Shorter, 1997: 294).

The number and scope of mental disorders have grown partly because Americans are now experiencing more stress than ever before, due mainly to the increased demands of work and a growing time crunch. At the same time, traditional institutions for dealing with mental health problems are less able to cope with them. The weakening authority of the church and the weakening grip of the family over the individual leave the treatment of mental health problems more open to the medical and psychiatric establishments.

The cultural context also stimulates inflation in the number and scope of mental disorders. Probably more than any other people, Americans are inclined to turn their problems into medical and psychological issues, sometimes without inquiring deeply into the disadvantages of doing so.

For example, in 1980 the term "attention deficit disorder" (ADD) was coined to label hyperactive and inattentive schoolchildren, mainly boys. By the mid-1990s, doctors were writing 6 million prescriptions a year for Ritalin, an amphetamine-like compound that controls ADD. Evidence shows that some children diagnosed with ADD have problems absorbing glucose in the brain or suffer from imbalances in chemicals that help the brain regulate behavior. Yet the diagnosis of ADD is typically conducted clinically, i.e., by interviewing and observing children to see if they exhibit signs of serious "inattention," "hyperactivity," and "impulsivity." This means that many children diagnosed with ADD may have no organic disorder at all. Some cases of ADD may be due to the school system failing to capture children's imagination. Some may involve children acting out because they are deprived of attention at home. Some may involve plain, old-fashioned youthful enthusiasm. A plausible case could be made that Tom Sawyer and Winnie the Pooh suffered from ADD (Shea et al., 2000). However, once hyperactivity and inattentiveness in school are defined as a medical and psychiatric condition, officials routinely prescribe drugs to control the problem and tend to ignore possible social causes.

Finally, we have witnessed inflation in the number and scope of mental disorders because various professional organizations have an interest in it. Consider PTSD. There is no doubt that PTSD is a real condition and that many veterans suffer from it. However, once

Ted Streshinsky/CORBIS

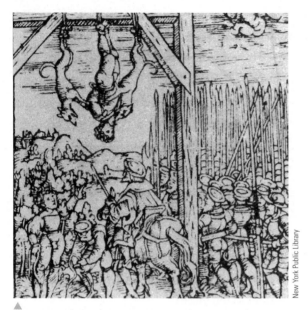

In preindustrial societies criminals who committed serious crimes were put to death, often in ways that seem cruel by today's standards. One method involved hanging the criminal with starving dogs.

the disorder was officially recognized in the 1970s, some therapists trivialized the term. By the mid-1990s some therapists were talking about PTSD "in children exposed to movies like Batman" (Shorter, 1997: 290). Some psychiatric social workers, psychologists, and psychiatrists may magnify the incidence of such mental disorders because doing so increases their stature and their patient load. Others may do so simply because the condition becomes trendy. Whatever the motive, overdiagnosis is the result.

The Prison

When he was 22, Robert Scully was sent to San Quentin Prison for robbery and dealing heroin. Already highly disturbed, he became more violent in prison. As a result, Scully was shipped off to Corcoran Prison, a maximum-security facility. He was thrown into solitary confinement. In 1990, Scully was transferred to the new "supermax" prison at Pelican Bay. There, he occupied a cell the size of a bathroom. He received food through a hatch. Even exercise was solitary. When he was released on parole in 1994, he had spent 9 years in isolation.

One night in 1995 Scully was loitering around a restaurant with a friend. The owner, fearing a robbery, called the police. Deputy Sheriff Frank Rejo, a middle-aged grandfather looking forward to retirement, soon arrived at the scene. He asked to see a driver's license. As Scully's friend searched for it, Scully pulled out a sawed-off shotgun and shot Rejo in the forehead. Scully and his friend were apprehended by police the next day.

Robert Scully was already involved in serious crime before he got to prison, but he became a murderer in San Quentin, Corcoran, and Pelican Bay—a pattern known to sociologists for a long time. Prisons are agents of socialization, and new inmates often become more serious offenders as they adapt to the culture of the most hardened, long-term prisoners (Wheeler, 1961). In Scully's case, psychologists and psychiatrists called in by the defense team said that things had gone even further. Years of sensory deprivation and social isolation had so enraged and incapacitated Scully that thinking through the consequences of his actions became impossible. He had regressed to the point where his mental state was that of an animal able to act only on immediate impulse (Abramsky, 1999).

Origins of Imprisonment

Because prison often turns criminals into worse criminals, pondering the institution's origins, development, and current dilemmas is worthwhile. In preindustrial societies, criminals were publicly humiliated, tortured, or put to death, depending on the severity of their transgression. As societies industrialized, however, imprisonment became one of the most important forms of punishment for criminal behavior (Garland, 1990; Morris and Rothman, 1995). In the industrial era, depriving criminals of their freedom by putting them in prison seemed less harsh and more "civilized" (Durkheim, 1973 [1899–1900]).

Goals of Incarceration

Some people still take a benign view of prisons, even seeing them as opportunities for *rehabilitation*. They believe that prisoners, while serving time, can be taught how to be productive citizens upon release. In the United States this view predominated in the 1960s and early 1970s, when many prisons sought to reform criminals by offering them psychological counseling, drug therapy, skills training, college education, and other programs that would help at least the less violent offenders get reintegrated into society when they were released from prison.

In 1966, 77 percent of Americans believed that the main goal of prison was to rehabilitate prisoners; by 1994 only 16 percent held that opinion (Bardes and Oldendick, 2003: 183). We have adopted a much tougher line, as the case of Robert Scully shows. Some people see prison as a means of *deterrence.* In this view, people will be less inclined to commit crimes if they know they are likely to get caught and serve long and unpleasant prison terms. Others think of prisons as institutions of *revenge.* They think that depriving criminals of their freedom and forcing them to live in poor conditions is fair retribution for their illegal acts. Still others see prisons as institutions of *incapacitation.* From this viewpoint, the chief function of the prison is simply to keep criminals out of society as long as possible to ensure that they can do no more harm (Simon, 1993; Zimring and Hawkins, 1995).

No matter which of these views predominates, two things are clear: The American public has demanded that more criminals be arrested and imprisoned, and it has gotten what it wants (Gaubatz, 1995; Savelsberg, 1994). The nation's incarceration rate rose substantially in the 1970s, doubled in the 1980s, and doubled again in the 1990s.

Moral Panic

What happened between the early 1970s and the present to so radically change the U.S. prison system? In a phrase, the United States was gripped by **moral panic.** The fear that crime posed a grave threat to society's well-being motivated wide sections of the American public, including lawmakers and officials in the criminal justice system (Cohen, 1972; Goode and Ben-Yehuda, 1994). The government declared a war on drugs, which resulted in the imprisonment of hundreds of thousands of nonviolent offenders. Sentencing got tougher, and many states passed a "three strikes and you're out" law. Such laws put three-time violent offenders in prison for life. The death penalty became increasingly popular. As ▶Figure 6.6 shows, support for capital punishment more than doubled from 38 percent to 80 percent of the population between 1965 and 1994, although it fell to 69 percent by 2007 (Figure 6.6; Box 6.2).

Moral panic could also be detected in the persistent belief that violence in the mass media has a big effect on violent criminal behavior in the real world, in spite of the fact

Moral panic: Occurs when many people fervently believe that some form of deviance or crime poses a profound threat to society's well-being.

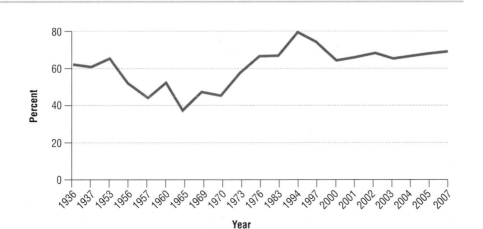

▶FIGURE 6.6
Belief in Capital Punishment

"Do you believe in capital punishment, that is, the death penalty, or are you opposed to it?" U.S.A., 1936–2007 (percent "for")

Note: Where more than one poll is available in a given year, the yearly average is shown.
Sources: Angus Reid (2007); Bardes and Oldendick (2003: 186); Bureau of Justice Statistics (2002); Maguire and Pastore (1998: 138); Newport (2000); PollingReport.com (2005).

BOX 6.2
YOU AND THE SOCIAL WORLD

Moral Panic

Recall an important fact from our discussion of recent trends in crime rates: According to FBI statistics, the moral panic of the 1980s and 1990s occurred during a period when all major crime indexes stabilized and then *decreased* dramatically. Why then the panic? Who benefits from it? We may mention several interested parties:

1. The mass media benefit from moral panic because it allows them to rake in hefty profits. They publicize every major crime because crime draws big audiences, and big audiences mean more revenue from advertisers. Fictional crime programs draw tens of millions of additional viewers to their TVs.

2. The crime prevention and punishment industry benefits from moral panic for much the same reason. Prison construction and maintenance firms, firearms manufacturers, and so forth are all big businesses that flourish in a climate of moral panic. Such industries want Americans to own more guns and imprison more people, so they lobby hard in Washington and elsewhere for relaxed gun laws and invigorated prison construction programs.

3. People in some formerly depressed rural regions have become highly dependent on prison construction and maintenance for their economic well-being. The Adirondack region of northern New York State is a case in point.

4. The criminal justice system is a huge bureaucracy with millions of employees. They benefit from moral panic because increased spending on crime prevention, control, and punishment secures their jobs and expands their turf.

5. Perhaps most important, the moral panic is useful politically. Since the early 1970s, many politicians have based entire careers on get-tough policies. Party allegiance and ideological orientation matter less than you might think. Plenty of liberal Republicans (such as former governor Nelson Rockefeller of New York) and Democrats (such as former governor Mario Cuomo of New York) have done as much to build up the prison system as have conservative Republicans (Schlosser, 1998).

Interview at least one adult member of your family about the precautions your family may have taken over the past decade to protect itself from criminal activity. Has your family installed a security system, new door or window locks or bars on basement windows? Has your family installed new lighting outside your home, a motion detector or a closed circuit camera? Has your family purchased a gun for protection? Have any members of your family been motivated to take a course in self-defense or the martial arts to protect themselves in case of attack? Once you have drawn up a list of safety precautions your family may have taken over the past decade, ask your respondent to indicate the degree to which he or she was personally victimized by crime during the past decade and during the decade before that. Answers can be given on a scale of 1 to 5, where 1 indicates no criminal victimization and 5 indicates a lot of criminal victimization. Also, ask your respondent to indicate the degree to which other family members were personally victimized by crime during the past decade and during the decade before that, again on a scale of 1 to 5.

WRITING ASSIGNMENT

Write a report based on the results of your survey. In 250–500 words address these questions:

Does the amount of criminal victimization experienced by your respondent or other family members over two decades explain the degree to which your family has taken new safety precautions over the past decade? If so, exactly how is victimization related to safety precautions? If not, how do you explain the degree to which your family has taken new safety precautions over the past decade?

---

that such a causal relationship has never been convincingly established. Evidence of the moral panic was evident in crime prevention too. For example, many well-to-do Americans had walls built around their neighborhoods, restricting access to residents and their guests. They hired private security police to patrol the perimeter and keep potential intruders at bay. Middle- and upper-class Americans installed security systems in their homes and steel bars in their basement windows. Many people purchased handguns in the belief that a firearm would enhance their personal security. The number of handguns in the United States is currently estimated at about 200 million. Some states even passed laws allowing people to conceal handguns on their person. In short, over the past few decades, Americans have prepared themselves for an armed invasion and have decided to treat criminals much more toughly than in the past.

Alternative Forms of Punishment

The two most contentious issues concerning the punishment of criminals are these: (1) Should the death penalty be used to punish the most violent criminals? (2) Should less serious offenders be incarcerated in the kinds of prisons we now have? In concluding this chapter we briefly consider each of these issues.

Capital Punishment

Although the United States has often been at the forefront of the struggle for human rights, it is one of the few industrial societies to retain capital punishment for the most serious criminal offenders (▶Figure 6.7). Yet, whether it serves as a deterrent is questionable for two reasons. First, murder is often committed in a rage, when the perpetrator is not thinking entirely rationally. In such circumstances the murderer is unlikely to coolly consider the costs and consequences of his or her actions. Second, if rational calculation of consequences does enter into the picture, the perpetrator is likely to know that very few murders result in the death sentence. More than 15,000 murders take place in the United States every year. Fewer than 200 death sentences are handed out. Thus, a murderer has a 1.25 percent chance of being sentenced to death. The chance that he or she actually will be executed is even smaller.

Because the death penalty isn't likely to deter many people unless the probability of its use is high, some people take these figures as justification for sentencing more violent offenders to death. However, one must remember that capital punishment as it is actually

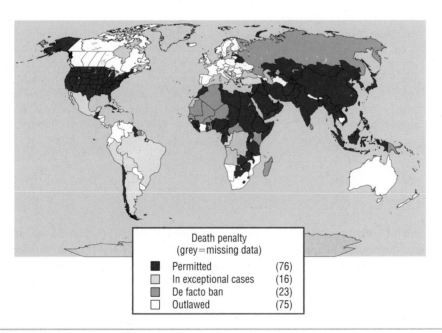

▶FIGURE 6.7
The Death Penalty Worldwide, 2005

The most controversial punishment is the death penalty, or capital punishment. Much research shows that is not an effective deterrent, and concern continues to rise regarding racial bias and wrongful conviction in its use. Despite the controversy, 48 percent of the world's countries allow capital punishment for at least some types of crimes.

Source: Infoplease (2005b).

BOX 6.3
SOCIOLOGY AT THE MOVIES

Paradise Now
(2005)

Of all the social types who populate today's world, perhaps none is more difficult to understand than the suicide attacker. Many people in the West wonder: Who in their right mind would fly a plane into a building? What kind of person do you have to be to blow yourself up in a bus full of ordinary people or a mosque full of worshippers? Somehow, the terms "deviant" and "criminal" seem inadequate to describe such people; they are widely seen by people in the West as crazy fanatics who lack all conscience and humanity.

Paradise Now, nominated for an Oscar as best foreign-language film of 2005, demonstrates that the common Western view is ethnocentric. It sketches the social circumstances that shaped the lives of two suicide bombers, showing that they are a lot like us and that if we found ourselves in similar circumstances we might turn out to be a lot like them. The film is critical of suicide bombing, but it helps us understand what makes suicide bombers tick, thereby enlightening us sociologically and politically.

Said (Kais Nashef) and Khaled (Ali Suliman) are ordinary 20-something garage mechanics and best friends. They live in the Palestinian city of Nablus, which, like the rest of the West Bank and the Gaza Strip, has been under Israeli military occupation their whole lives. As a result of the occupation, Said and Khaled have never been able to travel outside of the West Bank, they enjoy limited economic opportunities, they are bored stiff, and most importantly, they have been robbed of their dignity. Like all Palestinians, they want the Israelis out so that they can establish an independent country of their own. But their demonstrations, their rock throwing, and their armed attacks have had no effect on the powerful Israeli military. Consequently, some time before the film begins, Said and Khaled volunteered to serve as weapons of last resort: suicide bombers.

A study of all 462 suicide bombers who attacked targets worldwide between 1980 and 2003 found not a single case of depression, psychosis, past suicide attempts, or other such mental problems among them. The bombers were rarely poor and most often came from working- or middle-class families and were better educated than the populations from which they were recruited. Many of them were religious, but most of them, like Said and Khaled, were not. What they had in common was an ardent desire to liberate territory from what they regarded as foreign occupation or control (Pape, 2005). Said and Khaled are, then, quite typical suicide bombers: They are convinced by their powerlessness and their experience that they have no weapon other than suicide bombing that might help them achieve their aim of national liberation.

As *Paradise Now* opens, the two friends are informed that they have been selected for a suicide attack in 48 hours. Their mundane preparations are peppered with humor, errors, and everyday trivia that make Said and Khaled seem like very or-

practiced is hardly a matter of blind justice. This fact is particularly evident if we consider the racial distribution of people who are sentenced to death and executed. Murdering a white person is much more likely to result in a death sentence than murdering a black person. For example, in Florida in the 1970s, an African American who killed a white person was 40 times more likely to receive the death penalty than an African American who killed another African American. Moreover, a white person who murders a black person very rarely gets sentenced to death, but a black person who murders a white person is one of the types of people most likely to get the death penalty. Thus, of the 80 white people who murdered African Americans in Florida in the 1970s, not one was charged with a capital crime. In Texas, 1 out of 143 was charged with a capital crime (Tonry, 1995; Black, 1989). Given this patent racial bias, we cannot view the death penalty as a justly administered punishment.

dinary people. For example, in the middle of recording his "martyrdom tape" for TV broadcast, Khaled incongruously remembers to tell his mother, who he knows will watch the tape, that he saw a bargain on water filters at a local merchant's store. But underlying such humanizing events is a tension that gives the movie its force. Said and Khaled are ambivalent about their mission, not just because they have misgivings about dying but because they feel guilty about its inhumanity to civilians and are unsure of its ultimate political utility.

In the end, only Said manages to go through with the attack, but not before we get the full story about his ambivalence. Suha (Lubna Azabal), the woman he loves, is the daughter of a famous martyr for the Palestinian cause, but she strongly opposes suicide bombing. Said listens intently when she argues that suicide bombing is contrary to the spirit of Islam, it kills innocent victims, and it accomplishes nothing because it invites retaliation in a never-ending cycle of violence. But more compelling are the forces pushing Said to carry out the attack.

Thousands of Palestinians are paid, threatened, and blackmailed to serve as informants for the Israelis. Said's father was one of them. When he was caught, he was executed by Palestinian militants. Said has been deeply ashamed of his father's actions his whole life and angry with the Israelis for forcing his father to serve as a collaborator. His ultimate motivation for becoming a suicide bomber is retaliation against Israel for turning his father into an informant. Like most suicide bombers in the country, he is driven by the desire for revenge (Brym, 2007; Brym and Araj, 2006).

Critical Thinking

- From whose point of view are suicide bombers deviant and criminal?

- From whose point of view are suicide bombers normal?

- Must you agree with the actions of suicide bombers to understand them?

- What would you do if you were in Said's position?

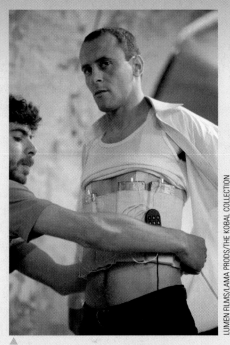

LUMEN FILMS/LAMA PRODS/THE KOBAL COLLECTION

Said and Khalef try to control their misgivings as they prepare to enter Israel for their mission.

Sometimes people favor capital punishment because they think it saves money. They argue that killing someone outright costs less than keeping the person alive in prison for the rest of his or her life. However, after trials and appeals, a typical execution costs the taxpayer up to six times more than a 40-year stay in a maximum-security prison (Haines, 1996).

Finally, in assessing capital punishment one must remember that mistakes are common. Nearly 40 percent of death sentences since 1977 have been overturned because of new evidence or a mistrial (Haines, 1996).

Incarcerating Less Serious Offenders in Violent, "No Frills" Prisons

Most of the increase in the prison population over the past 20 years is because of the conviction of nonviolent criminals. Many of them were involved in drug trafficking, and many of them are first-time offenders. The main rationale for imprisoning such offenders

Dead Man Walking, from the book by Sister Helean Prejean, an anti–death penalty activist, was made into a critically acclaimed film in 1995, starring Sean Penn and Susan Sarandon.

is that incarceration presumably deters them from repeating their offense. Supposedly, it also deters others from engaging in crime. Arguably, the streets become safer by isolating criminals from society.

Unfortunately for the hypothesis that imprisoning more people lowers the crime rate, available data show a weak relationship between the two variables. True, between 1980 and 1986 the number of inmates in U.S. prisons increased 65 percent and the number of victims of violent crime decreased 16 percent, which is what one would expect to find if incarceration deterred crime. However, between 1986 and 1991, the prison population increased 51 percent and the number of victims of violent crime *increased* 15 percent—just the opposite of what one would expect to find if incarceration deterred crime. The same sort of inconsistency is evident if we examine the relationship between incarceration and crime across states. For example, in 1992 Oklahoma had a high incarceration rate and a low crime rate, whereas Mississippi had a low incarceration rate and a high crime rate. These cases fit the hypothesis that imprisonment lowers the crime rate. However, Louisiana had a high incarceration rate and a high crime rate, whereas North Dakota had a low incarceration rate and a low crime rate, which is the opposite of what one would expect to find if incarceration deterred crime (Mauer, 1994). We can only conclude that, contrary to popular opinion, prison does not consistently deter criminals or lower the crime rate by keeping criminals off the streets.

However, prison does often teach inmates to behave more violently. The case of Robert Scully, who graduated from robbery to killing a police officer following his experiences in the California prison system, is one example. Budgets for general education, job training, physical exercise, psychological counseling, and entertainment have been cut. Brutality in the form of solitary confinement, hard labor, and physical violence is increasing. The result is a prison population that is increasingly enraged, incapacitated, lacking in job skills, and more dangerous upon release than upon entry into the system.

Former Massachusetts governor William F. Weld captured the spirit of the times when he said that prisons ought to be "a tour through the circles of hell," where inmates should learn only "the joys of busting rocks" (quoted in Abramsky, 1999). However, the new regime of U.S. prisons may have an effect just the opposite of that intended by Governor Weld. Between 1999 and 2010, an estimated 3.5 million first-time releases from U.S. prisons are expected (Abramsky, 1999). We may therefore be on the verge of a real crime wave, one that will have been created by the very get-tough policies that were intended to deter crime. According to Sgt. John Pasquarello of the Los Angeles Police Department, "Prison is basically a place to learn crime, so when these guys come out, we see many of them getting back into drug operations, and this leads to fights and killings" (quoted in Butterfield, 2001).

Rehabilitation and Reintegration

Is there a reasonable alternative to the kinds of prisons we now have? Although saying so may be unpopular, anecdotal evidence suggests that institutions designed to rehabilitate criminals and reintegrate them into society can work, especially for less serious offenders. They also cost less than the kind of prison system we have created.

Those are the conclusions some people have drawn from experience at McKean, a medium-security correctional facility opened in Bradford, Pennsylvania, in 1989. Dennis Luther, the warden at McKean, is a maverick who has bucked the trend in American corrections. Nearly half the inmates at McKean are enrolled in classes, many of them earning licenses in masonry, carpentry, horticulture, barbering, cooking, and catering that will help them get jobs when they leave. Recreation facilities are abundant, and annual surveys conducted in the prison show that inmates get into less trouble the greater their involvement in athletics. The inmates run self-help groups and teach adult continuing education. Good behavior is rewarded. If a cellblock receives high scores for cleanliness and orderliness during weekly inspection, the inmates in the cellblock get special privileges, such as the use of TV and telephones in the evening. Inmates who consistently behave well are allowed to attend supervised picnics on Family Days, which helps them adjust to life on the outside. Inmates are treated with respect and are expected to take responsibility for their actions. For example, after a few minor incidents in 1992 Luther restricted inmates' evening activities. The restriction was meant to be permanent, but some inmates asked Luther if he would do away with the restriction provided the prison was incident free for 90 days. Luther agreed, and he has never had to reimpose the restrictions.

The effects of these policies are evident throughout McKean. The facility is clean and orderly. Inmates don't carry "shanks" (homemade knives). The per-inmate cost to taxpayers is below average for medium-security facilities and 28 percent lower than the average for all state prisons, partly because relatively few guards are needed to maintain order. In McKean's first 6 years of operation, no escapes, no homicides, no sexual assaults, and no suicides occurred. Some inmates and staff members were victims of serious assault, but the *annual* number of assaults at McKean is equal to the *weekly* number of assaults at other state prisons of about the same size. Senior staff members and a local parole officer claim that McKean inmates return to prison far less often than inmates of other institutions (Worth, 1995).

Thus, a cost-effective and workable alternative to the current prison regime may exist, at least for less serious offenders. Furthermore, some aspects of the McKean approach possibly could have beneficial effects in the overcrowded, maximum-security prisons where violent offenders are housed and gangs proliferate. Dennis Luther thinks so, but we don't really know because it hasn't been tried. Nor is it likely to be tried anytime soon given the current climate of public opinion.

The Points of the Compass

When Robert Merton was looking for a term to describe deviants and criminals theoretically, he settled on "innovators." It was a revealing choice. Merton's theory is based on the idea that deviants and criminals are, to a degree, the architects of their own fate. They innovate when they create alternative and illegitimate means of achieving their society's goals. Merton recognized that certain social conditions promote innovation, but his choice of terms emphasizes the freedom of choice inherent in every deviant and criminal act. After all, in Merton's view, innovators could just as well choose to become retreatists, ritualists or rebels.

Other giants in the study of deviance and crime, especially those we have labeled "motivational" theorists, have learned Merton's lesson well. When they analyze the forces that drive some people to commit deviant and criminal acts, they stress that deviants and criminals do not respond mechanically to the conditions of their existence. Instead, considerable instruction, imagination, and daring are needed to break norms and laws, create deviant and criminal subcultures, and avoid sanctions and stay one step ahead of the law. Motivational theorists know that they wouldn't be able to sketch an accurate picture of deviance and crime if they ignored the point of the sociological compass marked "freedom."

Constraint theorists balance our appreciation of the sources of deviance and crime by stressing the opposite point of the sociological compass. They want to know things like why social control mechanisms work under some circumstances (producing conformity) and fail to work under others (producing deviance and crime). They also want to know how the distribution of power in society tends to impose deviant and criminal labels on some categories of the population but not others. By focusing on the operation or non-operation of social constraints, they add much to our understanding of how human freedom is channeled to produce particular patterns of social action, both conformist and nonconformist.

CHAPTER SUMMARY

1. What are deviance and crime? What determines how serious a deviant or criminal act is?

Deviance involves breaking a norm. Crime involves breaking a law. Both crime and deviance evoke societal reactions that help define the seriousness of the rule-breaking incident. The seriousness of deviant and criminal acts depends on the severity of the societal response to them, their perceived harmfulness, and the degree of public agreement about whether they should be considered deviant or criminal. Acts that rank lowest on these three dimensions are called social diversions. Next come social deviations and then conflict crimes. Consensus crimes rank highest.

2. Are definitions of deviance and crime the same everywhere and at all times?

No. Definitions of deviance and crime vary historically and culturally. These definitions are socially defined and constructed. They are not inherent in actions or the characteristics of people.

3. In what sense is power a key element in defining deviance and crime?

Powerful groups are generally able to create norms and laws that suit their interests. Less powerful groups are usually unable to do so. For example, the increasing power of women has led to greater recognition of crimes committed against them. However, no similar increase has occurred in the prosecution of white-collar criminals because the distribution of power between classes has not changed much in recent decades.

4. Where do crime statistics come from?

Crime statistics come from official sources, self-report surveys, and indirect measures. Each source has its strengths and weaknesses.

5. How has the rate of crime changed in the United States over the past four decades?

A crime wave occurred in the 1960s and 1970s. The crime rate began to taper off in the 1980s and decreased substantially in the 1990s because of more policing, a smaller proportion of young men in the population, a booming economy, and perhaps also a decline in the number of unwanted children resulting from the availability of abortion.

6. Why do African Americans experience disproportionately high arrest, conviction, and incarceration rates?

African Americans experience disproportionately high arrest, conviction, and incarceration rates because of bias in the way crime statistics are collected, the low social standing of the African American community, and racial discrimination in the criminal justice system.

7. What are the main types of theories of deviance and crime?

Theories of deviance and crime include motivational theories (strain theory, subcultural theory, and the theory of differential association) and constraint theories (labeling theory, control theory, and conflict theory). Motivational theories focus on the forces that drive people to commit deviant and criminal acts. Constraint theories focus on the forces that impose or fail to impose conformity on human behavior. Different theories illuminate different aspects of the process by which people are motivated to break rules and become defined as rule breakers.

8. What is the medicalization of deviance?

The medicalization of deviance refers to the fact that medical definitions of deviant behavior are becoming more prevalent in societies like ours. Deviance formerly defined as voluntary evil is now being defined as involuntary sickness and is coming under the sway of health care professionals.

9. **How important is imprisonment as a form of punishment in modern industrial societies? What do prisons accomplish?**

The prison is one of the most important forms of punishment in modern industrial societies. Since the 1980s the incarceration rate has increased in the United States. Prisons now focus less on rehabilitation than on isolating and incapacitating inmates.

10. **What is a "moral panic"?**

A moral panic occurs when many people fervently believe that some form of deviance or crime poses a profound threat to society's well-being. For example, a moral panic about crime has engulfed the United States, although crime rates have been moderating in recent decades. In all aspects of crime prevention and punishment, most Americans have taken a "get-tough" stance. Some commercial and political groups benefit from the moral panic over crime and therefore encourage it.

11. **What are some of the problems with the death penalty as a form of punishment?**

Although the death penalty ranks high as a form of revenge, its effectiveness as a deterrent is questionable. Moreover, the death penalty is administered in a racially biased manner, does not save money, and sometimes results in tragic mistakes.

12. **Does the rehabilitation of criminals ever work?**

Rehabilitative correctional facilities are cost-effective. They do work, especially for less serious offenders. However, they are unlikely to become widespread given the current political climate.

Questions to Consider

1. Has this chapter changed your view of criminals and the criminal justice system? If so, how? If not, why not?

2. Do you think that different theories are useful in explaining different types of deviance and crime? Or do you think that one or two theories explain all types of deviance and crime and that other theories are not very illuminating? Justify your answer using logic and evidence.

3. Do TV crime shows and crime movies give a different picture of crime in the United States than this chapter gives? What are the major differences? Which picture do you think is more accurate? Why?

Web Resources

CENGAGENOW™

Maximize your study time by using CengageNOW's diagnostic study plan to help you review this chapter. The Study Plan will

- help you identify areas on which you should concentrate;
- provide interactive exercises to help you master the chapter concepts; and
- provide a post-test to confirm you are ready to move on to the next chapter.

The Companion Website for *Sociology: Your Compass for a New World, The Brief Edition*, Enhanced Second Edition

www.cengage.com/sociology/brym

Supplement your review of this chapter by going to the companion website to take one of the tutorial quizzes, use flash cards to master key terms, and check out the many other study aids you'll find there. You'll also find special features such as GSS Data and Census 2000 information that will put data and resources at your fingertips to help you with that special project or help you do some research on your own.

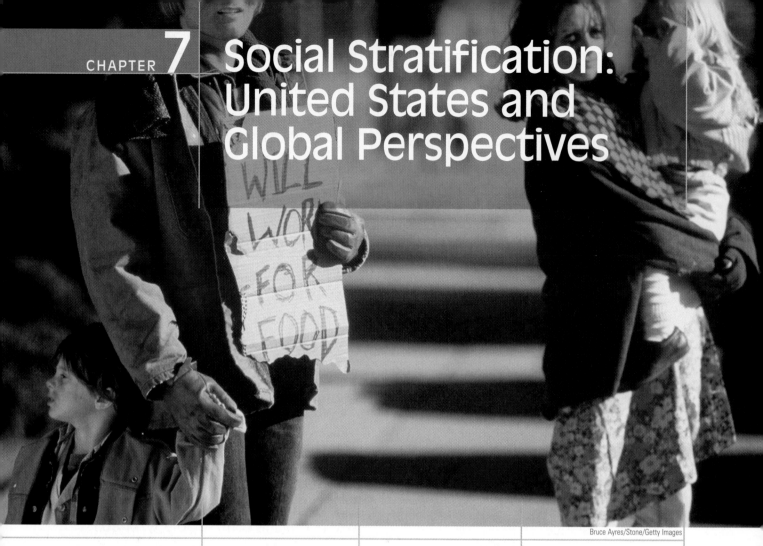

CHAPTER **7** Social Stratification: United States and Global Perspectives

In this chapter, you will learn that:

- Income inequality in the United States has been increasing since the mid-1970s.

- Income inequality is higher in the United States than in any other postindustrial society.

- As societies develop, inequality increases at first. Then, after passing the early stage of industri-alization, inequality in society declines. In the postindustrial stage of development, inequality appears to increase again in some countries.

- Most theories of social inequality focus on its economic roots.

- Prestige and power are important noneconomic sources of inequality.

- Some sociologists used to think that talent and hard work alone deter-mine one's position in the socioeconomic hierarchy. Now, many sociologists think that being a member of certain social categories limits one's opportunities for success. In this sense, social structure shapes the distribution of inequality.

Social Stratification: Shipwrecks and Inequality

Writers and filmmakers sometimes tell stories about shipwrecks and their survivors to make a point about social inequality. They use the shipwreck as a literary device. It allows them to sweep away all traces of privilege and social convention. What remains are human beings stripped to their essentials, guinea pigs in an imaginary laboratory for the study of wealth and poverty, power and powerlessness, esteem and disrespect.

The tradition began with Daniel Defoe's *Robinson Crusoe*, first published in 1719. Defoe tells the story of an Englishman marooned on a desert island. His strong will, hard work, and inventiveness turn the poor island into a thriving colony. Defoe was one of the first writers to portray capitalism favorably. He believed that people get rich if they possess the virtues of good businessmen—and stay poor if they don't.

The 1975 Italian movie *Swept Away* tells almost exactly the opposite story. In the movie, a beautiful woman, one of the idle rich, boards her yacht for a cruise in the Mediterranean. She treats the hardworking deck hands in a condescending and abrupt way. The deck hands do their jobs but seethe with resentment. Then comes the storm. The yacht is shipwrecked. Only the beautiful woman and one handsome deck hand remain alive, swept up on a desert island. Now equals, the two survivors soon have passionate sex

---

CENGAGENOW™

This icon signals when CengageNOW has important resources available for you to use in conjunction with the text. See the foldout at the front of this text for information on how to access CengageNOW.

The post–Civil War books of Horatio Alger, Jr., inspired Americans with tales of how courage, faith, honesty, hard work, and a little luck could help young people rise from rags to riches. Alger's novels lack appreciation of the social determinants of social stratification.

CENGAGENOW™

Learn more about **Social Stratification** by going through the Social Stratification in the United States Data Experiment.

and fall in love. All is well until the day of their rescue. As soon as they return to the mainland, the woman resumes her haughty ways. She turns her back on the deck hand, who is reduced again to the role of a common laborer. Thus, the movie sends the audience three harsh messages. First, it is possible to be rich without working hard, because one can inherit wealth. Second, one can work hard without becoming rich. Third, something about the structure of society causes inequality, for inequality disappears only on the desert island, without society as we know it.

Titanic is a recent movie on the shipwreck-and-inequality theme. At one level, the movie shows that class differences are important. For example, in first class, living conditions are luxurious, whereas in third class they are cramped. Indeed, on the *Titanic,* class differences spell the difference between life and death. After the *Titanic* strikes the iceberg off the coast of Newfoundland, the ship's crew prevents second- and third-class passengers from entering the few available lifeboats. They give priority to rescuing first-class passengers. Consequently, three-quarters of third-class passengers perished compared with 40 percent of first-class passengers.

As the tragedy of the *Titanic* unfolds, however, another contradictory theme emerges. Under some circumstances, we learn, class differences can be insignificant. In the movie, the sinking of the *Titanic* is the backdrop to a fictional love story about a wealthy young woman in first class and a working-class youth in the decks below. The sinking of the *Titanic* and the collapse of its elaborate class structure give the young lovers an opportunity to cross class lines and profess their devotion to one another. At one level, then, the movie *Titanic* is an optimistic tale that holds out hope for a society in which class differences matter little, a society much like that of the American Dream.

Robinson Crusoe, Swept Away, and *Titanic* raise many of the issues we address in this chapter. What are the sources of social inequality? Do determination, industry, and ingenuity shape the distribution of advantages and disadvantages in society, as *Robinson Crusoe* suggests? Or is *Swept Away* more accurate? Do certain patterns of social relations underlie and shape that distribution? Is *Titanic's* first message still valid? Does social inequality still have big consequences for the way we live? What about *Titanic's* second message? Can people act to decrease the level of inequality in society? If so, how?

To answer these questions, we first sketch the pattern of social inequality in the United States and globally. We pay special attention to change over time. We then critically review the major theories of **social stratification,** the way society is organized in layers or strata. We assess these theories in the light of logic and evidence. From time to time, we take a step back and identify issues that need to be resolved before we can achieve a more adequate understanding of social stratification, one of the fundamentally important aspects of social life.

Patterns of Social Inequality

Wealth

Social stratification: Refers to the way society is organized in layers or strata.

Your wealth is what you own. For most adults, it includes a house (minus the mortgage); a car (minus the car loan); and some appliances, furniture, and savings (minus the credit card balance). Owning a nice house and a good car and having a substantial sum of money invested securely enhances your sense of well-being. You know you have a "cushion" to fall back on in difficult times and you know you don't have to worry about paying for your children's college education or how you will make ends meet during retirement. Wealth can also give you more political influence. Campaign contributions to political parties and donations to favorite political causes increase the chance that policies you favor will become law. Wealth even improves your health. Because you can afford to engage in leisure pursuits, turn off stress, consume high-quality food, and employ superior medical services, you are likely to live a healthier and longer life than someone who lacks these advantages.

We list the 25 richest Americans in ▶Table 7.1. Their net worth ranges from $11.5 billion to $59 billion. These sums are so big that they are hard to imagine. You can begin to grasp them by considering that it would take you 3 years to spend $1 million at the rate of $1,000 a day. How long would it take you to spend $1 billion? If you spent $1,000 a day, you couldn't spend the entire sum in a lifetime. It would take nearly 3,000 years to spend $1 billion at the rate of $1,000 a day—assuming you didn't invest part to earn still more money.

Unfortunately, sociologists and other social scientists have neglected the study of wealth, partly because reliable data on the subject are hard to come by. Americans are not required to report their wealth. Therefore, wealth figures are sparse and based mainly on a few sample surveys and analyses of people who pay estate tax. The best available estimates are, however, startling. In the mid-1990s, the richest 1 percent of American households owned nearly 39 percent of all national wealth, whereas the richest 10 percent owned almost 72 percent. In contrast, the poorest 40 percent of American households owned a meager 0.2 percent of all national wealth. The bottom 20 percent had a negative net worth, which means they owed more than they owned.

Patterns of Wealth Inequality

Wealth inequality has been increasing since the early 1980s. Some 62 percent of the increase in national wealth in the 1990s went to the richest 1 percent of Americans, and fully 99 percent of the increase went to the richest 20 percent. The United States has surpassed all other highly industrialized countries in wealth inequality. Between 50 and 80 percent of the net worth of American families now derives from transfers and bequests, usually from parents (Keister, 2000; Keister and Moller, 2000; Levy, 1998; Spilerman, 2000).

Wealth inequality is also significant because only a modest positive correlation exists between income and wealth. Some wealthy people have low annual income and some people with high annual income have little accumulated wealth. Therefore, annual income

▶**TABLE 7.1**

The 25 Richest Americans, 2007

Name	Net Worth ($ billion)	Source
1. Bill Gates	59.0	Microsoft Corp.
2. Warren Buffet	52.0	Berkshire Hathaway
3. Sheldon Adelson	28.0	Casinos, hotels
4. Lawrence Joseph Ellison	26.0	Oracle Corp.
5. Sergey Brin	18.5	Google
5. Larry E. Page	18.5	Google
7. Kirk Kerkorian	18.0	Investments, casinos
8. Michael Dell	17.2	Dell Corp.
9. Charles Koch	17.0	Oil, commodities (inheritance)
10. David Koch	17.0	Oil, commodities (inheritance)
11. Paul Allen	16.8	Microsoft Corp.
12. Christy Walton	16.3	Wal-Mart stores (inheritance)
12. Jim C. Walton	16.3	Wal-Mart stores (inheritance)
12. S. Robson Walton	16.3	Wal-Mart stores (inheritance)
15. Alice L. Walton	16.1	Wal-Mart stores (inheritance)
16. Steven Ballmer	15.2	Microsoft Corp.
17. Abigail Johnson	15.0	Mutual funds (inheritance)
18. Carl Icahn	14.5	Leveraged buyouts
19. Forrest Edward Mars Jr.	14.0	Mars Inc. (inheritance)
19. Jacqueline Mars	14.0	Mars Inc. (inheritance)
19. John Franklin Mars	14.0	Mars Inc. (inheritance)
19. Jack Taylor	14.0	Enterprise Rent-a-Car
23. Donald Bren	13.0	Real estate
24. Anne Cox Chambers	12.6	Cox Enterprises (inheritance)
25. Michael Bloomberg	11.5	Bloomberg

Note: Percent who inherited their fortune: 44; percent women: 20; percent of women who inherited their fortune: 100.
Source: Forbes.com (2007).

Bill Gates, the world's richest man, lives in a house with more than 66,000 square feet of floor space. It is valued at more than $53 million.

CENGAGENOW

Learn more about **Income** by going through the Median Household Money Income Map Exercise.

may not be the best measure of a person's well-being, and policies that seek to redistribute income from the wealthy to the poor, such as income-tax laws, may not get at the root of economic inequality because income redistribution has little effect on the distribution of wealth. Income-based policies would have the least effect on black–white inequality in wealth, which is especially stark (Conley, 1999; Oliver and Shapiro, 1995).

Income

Your income is what you earn in a given period. In the United States and other societies, there is less inequality in income than inequality in the distribution of wealth. Nonetheless, income inequality is steep. Thankfully, precise and detailed information on income inequality is readily available because people must report their income to the government, and sociologists have mined income figures well. Students of social stratification often divide populations into categories of unequal size that differ in their lifestyles. These are often called "income classes." ▶Table 7.2 shows how American households were divided into income classes in 2001.

Income Classes

Sociologists often divide society's upper class into two categories, the "upper-upper class" and the "lower-upper class" (see Table 7.2). The upper-upper class, comprising 1 percent of the U.S. population, used to be described as "old money" because people in that class inherited most of their wealth. Moreover, most of it was originally earned in older industries such as banking, insurance, oil, real estate, and automobiles. Old money inhabited elite neighborhoods on the East Coast—places like Manhattan and Westchester Counties (New York); Fairfield, Somerset, and Bergen Counties (Connecticut); and Arlington (Virginia). It still does. Members of this class send their children to expensive private schools and high-prestige colleges. They belong to exclusive private clubs. They are overwhelmingly white and non-Hispanic. They live in a different world from most Americans (Baltzell, 1964).

In the past couple of decades, however, and especially in the 1990s, a substantial amount of "new money" entered the upper-upper class. Booming high-tech industries created new opportunities for entry. Among those with new money, wealth is based less on inheritance than talent. New money is concentrated in high-tech meccas in the West— in places like Silicon Valley in California and King County in Washington State (Whitman, 2000). Larry Ellison, the flamboyant CEO of Oracle Corporation (the world's leading supplier of information management software), is perhaps the outstanding example of the new breed. The adopted son of a Chicago couple of modest means, Ellison started Oracle in 1977 with $1,200 after dropping out of college. In 2007, his personal net worth was $26 billion and *Forbes* magazine ranked him the fourth richest person in the United States. Such success stories notwithstanding, one thing remains constant: New members of the upper-upper class are still overwhelmingly white and non-Hispanic (Rothman and Black, 1998).

The "middle class" consists of the nearly 65 percent of American households that earn between $20,000 and $99,999 a year. Conventionally, the middle class is divided into roughly equal thirds: the "upper middle class," the "average middle class," and the "lower middle class," or "working class" (see Table 7.2).

Over a lifetime, an individual may experience considerable movement up or down the stratification system. Sociologists call this movement **vertical social mobility.** Movement up the stratification system ("upward mobility") is a constant theme in American literature and lore (Box 7.1). Since the early 1960s, when sociologists started measuring social mobility reliably in the United States as a whole, more upward than downward mobility has occurred. However, in the early 1980s the gap between upward and downward mobility started to shrink, as about a quarter of Americans reported deterioration in their economic situation (Hauser et al., 2000; Hout, 1988; Newman, 1988: 7, 21). In general, downward mobility increases during periods of economic recession and especially during periods of economic restructuring, such as the United States experienced in the 1980s and early 1990s, and again in the first decade of the 21st century. In those years, layoffs and plant closings were common, as computerized production became widespread and well-paying factory and office jobs were lost to low-wage countries such as Mexico, China, India, and Poland. At the same time, computer technology and office reorganization allowed companies to fire many of their middle managers (see Chapter 13, "Politics, Work, and the Economy").

It was in the lower middle, or "working," class and in the lower class that the pain was experienced most sharply. Many Americans wound up working full-time, year-round for poverty-level wages doing unskilled work as Wal-Mart salespersons and the like. Sociologist and journalist Barbara Ehrenreich spent periods between 1998 and 2000 taking such jobs throughout the United States to find out what it means to be in the lowest income class. Here is how she describes her budget when she worked as a full-time restaurant server in Florida for about $6 an hour including tips:

> I earned $1,039 in one month and spent $517 on food, gas, toiletries, laundry, phone and utilities. Rent was the deal breaker. If I had remained in my $500 efficiency, I would have been able to pay the rent and have $22 left over. . . . This in itself would have been a dicey situation if I had attempted to continue for a few more months, because sooner or later I would have had to spend something on medical and dental care or drugs other than ibuprofen. But my move to the trailer park—for the purpose . . . of taking a second job—made me responsible for $625 a month in rent alone, utilities not included. Here I might have economized by giving up the car and buying a used bike (for about $50) or walking to work. Still, two jobs, or at least a job and a half, would be a necessity, and I had learned that I could not do two physically demanding jobs in the same day (Ehrenreich, 2001: 197).

In short, Ehrenreich found it impossible to live on one minimum-wage job, assuming that living requires some medical and dental care.

▶Table 7.2

Income Classes, Households, United States, 2001

Income class	Percent of Households	Annual Household Income
Upper upper	1.0	$1 million +
Lower upper	12.4	$100,000–$999,999
Upper middle	22.5	$57,500–$99,999
Average middle	18.8	$37,500–$57,499
Lower middle or working	22.7	$20,000–$37,499
Lower	22.6	$0–$19,999
Total	100.0	

Note: The U.S. Census Bureau does not provide breakdowns of incomes that are more than $100,000. Therefore, we estimated the breakpoint between the top two classes.
Source: U. S. Census Bureau (2002b).

Vertical social mobility: Movement up or down the stratification system.

BOX 7.1
SOCIOLOGY AT THE MOVIES

Sweet Home Alabama (2002)

Sweet Home Alabama is a Cinderella story with a twist: The successful heroine from humble beginnings gets the handsome prince but is not sure he is truly what she wants.

In the 7 years since Melanie Carmichael (Reese Witherspoon) left her small-town Alabama home, she has achieved impressive upward social mobility. Beginning as a daughter of the working class, she has become a world-famous fashion designer in New York City. As the film begins, the mayor's son is courting Melanie. Andrew (Patrick Dempsey) proposes to her in Tiffany's. She says yes, but before she can marry him she has to clear up a not-so-minor detail: She needs a divorce from Jake (Josh Lucas), the childhood sweetheart she left behind.

Most of the story unfolds back in rural Alabama. Melanie finds herself caught between two classes and two subcultures, and the film follows her struggle to reconcile her conflicting identities. Her dilemma will require her to acknowledge and reconnect with her mother (Mary Kay Place), who lives in a trailer park, while standing up to her future mother-in-law, the mayor of New York City (Candice Bergen).

In the end, Melanie returns to Jake, while Andrew, briefly heartbroken, pleases his mother by marrying a woman of his own class. Melanie's homecoming does not, however, require that she return to life in a trailer park. She discovers that while she was in New York, Jake transformed his life. The working class

Patrick Dempsey and Reese Witherspoon in *Sweet Home Alabama.*

"loser" built a successful business as a glass-blower. This change allows Melanie to imagine an upwardly mobile future by Jake's side.

Sweet Home Alabama sends the message that people are happiest when they marry within their own subculture. That message is comforting because it helps the audience reconcile itself to two realities.

First, although many people may want to "marry up," most Americans do not in fact succeed in doing so. We tend to marry within our own class—and within our own religion and ethnic and racial group (Kalmijn, 1998: 406–08). Second, marrying outside your subculture is likely to be unsettling insofar as it involves abandoning old norms, roles, and values, and learning new ones. It is, therefore, in some sense a relief to learn you're better off marrying within your own subculture, especially because you will probably wind up doing just that anyway.

There is an ideological problem with this message, however. Staying put in your own subculture denies the American Dream of upward mobility. *Sweet Home Alabama* resolves the problem by holding out the promise of upward mobility without having to leave home, as it were. Melanie and Jake can enjoy the best of both worlds, moving up the social hierarchy together without forsaking the community and the subculture they cherish. *Sweet Home Alabama* achieves a happy ending by denying the often difficult process of adapting to a new subculture as one experiences social mobility.

Critical Thinking

- Does upward social mobility imply that you change your community or subculture?

- Does remaining in your own community or subculture diminish your chances of upward social mobility? Why or why not?

Income Strata

We can get a summary view of how recent decades have affected the American middle class by dividing the population into a number of equal-sized statistical categories, usually called "income strata." ▶Figure 7.1 adopts this approach. It divides the country's house-

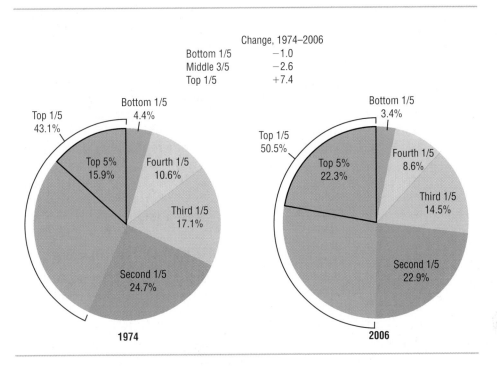

▶FIGURE 7.1
The Distribution of National Income among Households, United States, 1974 and 2006

Source: U.S. Census Bureau (2008b).

holds into five income strata: the top 20 percent of income earners, the second 20 percent, and all the way down to the bottom 20 percent. It shows how total national income was divided among each of these fifths in 1974 and 2006. It also shows the share of national income that went to the top 5 percent of income earners in these 2 years.

Patterns of Income Inequalities

Figure 7.1 illustrates three important facts. First, income inequality has been increasing in the United States for more than a third of a century. In 1974 the top fifth of households earned 9.8 times more than the bottom fifth. By 2006, the top fifth of households earned 14.9 times more than the bottom fifth. Second, in 2006, the top 20 percent of households earned more than the remaining 80 percent. Said differently, the top fifth earned more than half of all national income. Third, the middle 60 percent of income earners have been "squeezed" during the past 25 years, with their share of national income falling from 52.5 percent to 46.0 percent of the total. We conclude that for more than a third of a century, the rich have been getting relatively richer, whereas middle-income earners and the poor have been getting relatively poorer in the United States.

We can see the effects of income strata in everyday life. Think of transportation. Who rides the bus? Who drives a Mercedes or a BMW? How would you get to the airport? In New York, taking the bus from Manhattan to JFK Airport will cost you a few dollars and take 90 minutes or more. A taxi will cost $35 plus tip and take 45 minutes. Limousines, which are usually cleaner and more stylish than taxis, cost $80 or more, though they take the same time as a taxi. A helicopter ride that takes less than 10 minutes costs $155. Or consider how people save their hard-earned money. Banks now have different savings and checking plans, and the more money you have in your bank account, the more services you are entitled to, the lower the cost of writing checks, and the more interest you earn. If you are relatively wealthy, then you would be able to invest in stocks and real estate that

▶Table 7.3
United Nations Indicators of Human Development,
Top 12 and Bottom 12 Countries, 2005

Country and Overall Rank	Life Expectancy (years)	Adult Literacy (percent)	Gross Domestic Domestic Product per Capita ($ US)
1. Iceland	81.5	99.0	36,510
2. Norway	79.8	99.0	41,420
3. Australia	80.9	99.0	31,794
4. Canada	80.3	99.0	33,375
5. Ireland	78.4	99.0	38,505
6. Sweden	80.5	99.0	32,525
7. Switzerland	81.3	99.0	35,633
8. Japan	82.3	99.0	31,267
9. Netherlands	79.2	99.0	32,684
10. France	80.2	99.0	30,386
11. Finland	78.9	99.0	32,153
12. United States	77.9	99.0	41,890
166. Côte d'Ivoire	47.4	48.7	1,648
167. Burundi	48.5	59.3	699
168. Dem. Rep. Congo	45.8	67.2	714
169. Ethiopia	51.8	35.9	1,055
170. Chad	50.4	25.7	1,427
171. Cent. African Rep.	43.7	48.6	1,224
172. Mozambique	42.8	38.7	1,242
173. Mali	53.1	24.0	1,033
174. Niger	55.8	28.7	781
175. Guinea-Bissau	45.8	n.a.	827
176. Burkino Faso	51.4	23.6	1,213
177. Sierra Leone	41.8	34.8	806

Gross Domestic per Capita is calculated in terms of purchasing power.
n.a. = not available.
Source: United Nations (2008: 229, 232).

earn on average higher returns than a regular savings account. You may also acquire professional expertise in your investment decisions. Whether you think of transportation or banking, you should be able to observe different effects of income inequality.

Just as income and wealth vary widely *within* countries, so do they vary *between* countries. We now turn to an examination of global inequalities.

Global Inequality

International Differences

The United States, Canada, Japan, Australia, and a dozen or so western European countries, including Germany, France, and the United Kingdom, are the world's richest postindustrial societies. The world's poorest countries cover much of Africa, Latin America and the Caribbean, and Asia. Inequality between rich and poor countries is staggering. Nearly one-fifth of the world's population lacks adequate shelter, and more than one-fifth lacks safe water. About one-third of the world's people are without electricity, and more than two-fifths lack adequate sanitation. In the United States, there are 626 phone lines for every 1,000 people, but in Cambodia, Congo, and Afghanistan there is only 1 line per 1,000 people. Annual health expenditure in the United States is $2,765 per person, whereas the comparable figure for Vietnam is $3 per person. The average educational expenditure for an American child is $11,329 per year, compared with $57 in China (United Nations, 1998b) (▶Table 7.3). The richest 10 percent of Americans earn 10,000 times more than the poorest 10 percent of Ethiopians (Birdsall, 2005).

People living in poor countries are also more likely than people in rich countries to experience extreme suffering on a mass scale. For example, because of political turmoil in many poor countries, tens of millions of people have been driven from their homes by force in recent years (Hampton, 1998). There are still about 27 million slaves in Mozambique, Sudan, and other African countries (Bales, 1999, 2002).

When sociologists study differences in wealth or income *between* countries, they are studying **global inequality.** However, it is possible for Country A and Country B to be equally rich, whereas inside Country A the gap between rich and poor is greater than inside Country B. When sociologists study such differences *within* countries, they are studying **crossnational variations in internal stratification** (Box 7.2). We devote much of Chapter 8 ("Globalization, Inequality, and Development") to analyzing the causes, dimensions, and consequences of global inequality. Here we restrict ourselves to saying a few words about crossnational variations in internal stratification.

BOX 7.2
MASS MEDIA AND SOCIETY

The Internet and Social Stratification

Internet access mirrors both the internal stratification of the United States and global inequality. After all, the Internet requires an expensive infrastructure and people must pay for it. Consequently, access is not open to everyone. In the United States, for example, college-educated whites with above-average incomes are most likely to enjoy Internet access.

Nor is Internet access evenly distributed globally. As ▶Figure 7.2 shows, international inequalities in Internet access mirror global inequalities overall.

Critical Thinking

● Consider the relationship between Internet access and other types of social inequality. Is Internet access an independent or a dependent variable? In other words, does Internet access have an impact on other aspects of social inequality or is inequality of Internet access caused by other inequalities, such as inequality of income? Or is the relationship between Internet access and other forms of inequality reciprocal, with each type of inequality influencing the other?

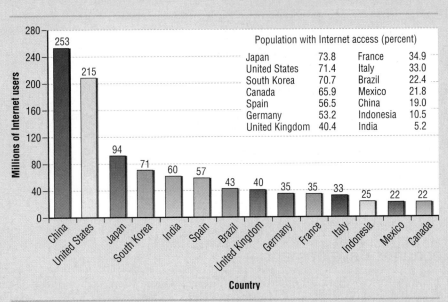

Population with Internet access (percent)

Japan	73.8	France	34.9
United States	71.4	Italy	33.0
South Korea	70.7	Brazil	22.4
Canada	65.9	Mexico	21.8
Spain	56.5	China	19.0
Germany	53.2	Indonesia	10.5
United Kingdom	40.4	India	5.2

▶FIGURE 7.2
Countries with the Most Internet Users, 2008

Source: Internet Usage Statistics (2008).

Measuring Internal Stratification

How does internal stratification differ from one country to the next? We can answer this question by first examining the **Gini index,** named after the Italian economist who invented it. The Gini index is a measure of income inequality. Its value ranges from 0 to 1. A Gini index of 0 indicates that every household in the country earns exactly the same amount of money. At the opposite pole, a Gini index of 1 indicates that a single household earns the entire national income. These are theoretical extremes. In the real world, most countries have Gini indexes between 0.2 and 0.5.

▶Figure 7.3 shows the Gini index for 30 countries using the most recent crossnational income data available. Of the 30, Denmark has the lowest Gini index (.236), whereas the United States has the third highest (.368). Only Russia's level of income inequality (.434) and Mexico's (.494) are higher than that of the United States.

Global inequality: Differences in the economic ranking of countries.

Crossnational variations in internal stratification: Differences between countries in their stratification systems.

Gini index: A measure of income inequality. Its value ranges from 0 (which means that every household earns exactly the same amount of money) to 1 (which means that all income is earned by a single household).

Household Income Inequality, 30 Countries, circa 2000

Source: Smeeding (2004).

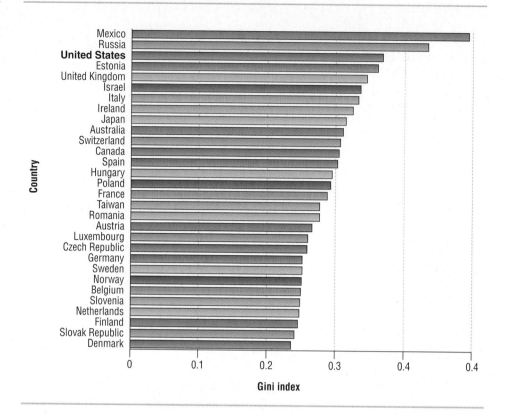

Economic Development

What accounts for crossnational differences in internal stratification, such as those described above? Later in this chapter, you will learn that *political factors* explain some of the differences. For the moment, however, we focus on how *socioeconomic development* affects internal stratification.

Over the course of human history, as societies became richer and more complex, the level of social inequality first increased, then tapered off, and then began to decline (Lenski, Nolan, and Lenski, 1995). In the most recent, postindustrial period, social inequality remained fairly stable in some countries, such as France, Germany, and Canada, but began to rise in others, such as the United Kingdom and the United States. Governments in countries where inequality remained fairly stable took a more active role in redistributing income through tax and welfare policies. ▶ Figure 7.4 illustrates the relationship between economic development and internal stratification. To account for this pattern, sociologists have analyzed how technology produces wealth and how people control that wealth in five types of societies.

Foraging Societies

For the first 90,000 years of human existence, people lived in nomadic bands of fewer than 100 people. To survive, they hunted wild animals and foraged for wild edible plants. Life was precarious. Some foragers and hunters were undoubtedly more skilled than others, but they did not hoard food. Instead, they shared food to ensure the survival of all band members. They produced little or nothing above what they required for subsistence. There were no rich people.

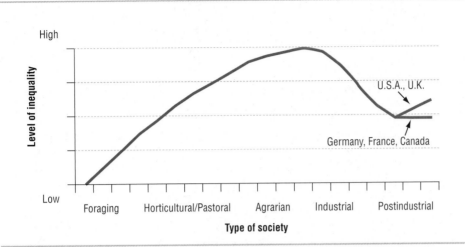

Horticultural and Pastoral Societies

About 12,000 years ago, people established the first agricultural settlements. These settlements were based on horticulture (i.e., the use of small hand tools to cultivate plants) and pastoralism (i.e., the domestication of animals). These technological innovations enabled people to produce wealth, a surplus above what they needed for subsistence. A small number of villagers controlled the surplus. Thus, significant social stratification emerged.

Agrarian Societies

About 5,000 years ago, people developed plow agriculture. By attaching oxen and other large animals to plows, farmers could increase the amount they produced. Again, thanks to technological innovation, surpluses grew. With more wealth came still sharper social stratification.

Agrarian societies developed religious beliefs justifying steeper inequality. People came to believe that kings and queens ruled by "divine right." They viewed large land-owners as "lords." Moreover, if you were born a peasant, you and your children were likely to remain peasants. If you were born a lord, you and your children were likely to remain lords. In the vocabulary of modern sociology, we say that stratification in agrarian societies was based more on **ascription** than **achievement.** That is, a person's position in the stratification system was determined more by the features he or she was born with ("ascribed characteristics") than his or her accomplishments ("achieved characteristics"). Another way of saying this is that little social mobility took place.

A nearly purely ascriptive society existed in agrarian India. Society was divided into castes—four main groups and many subgroups arranged in a rigid hierarchy. Being born into a particular caste meant that you had to work in the distinctive occupations reserved for that caste and marry someone from the same or an adjoining caste. The Hindu religion strictly reinforced the system (Srinivas, 1952). For example, Hinduism explained people's place in the **caste system** by their deeds in a previous life. If you were good, you were presumably rewarded by being born into a higher caste in your next life. If you were bad, you were presumably punished by being born into a lower caste. Belief in the sanctity of caste regulated even the most mundane aspects of life. Thus, someone from the lowest caste could dig a well for a member of the highest caste, but once the well was dug, the well

Ascription-based stratification system: A stratification system in which the allocation of rank depends on the characteristics a person is born with.

Achievement-based stratification system: A stratification system in which the allocation of rank depends on a person's accomplishments.

Caste system: An almost pure ascription-based stratification system in which occupation and marriage partners are assigned on the basis of caste membership.

Vincent Van Gogh. *The Potato Eaters* (1889). Most people in agrarian societies were desperately poor. In Ireland, potatoes were the chief staple of the peasant's diet. Most of the economic surplus wound up in the hands of royalty, the aristocracy, and religious authorities.

Art Resource, NY

digger could not so much as cast his shadow on the well. If he did, the well was considered polluted, and upper-caste people were forbidden to drink from it.

Caste systems have existed in industrial times. For example, the system of **apartheid** existed in South Africa from 1948 until 1992. The white minority enjoyed the best jobs and other privileges and consigned the large black majority to menial jobs. They also prevented marriage between blacks and whites and erected separate public facilities for members of the two races. Asians and people of "mixed race" enjoyed privileges between these two extremes. However, apartheid was an exception. For the most part, industrialism causes a decline in inequality.

Industrial Societies

The Industrial Revolution began in Britain in the 1780s. A century later, it had spread to all of western Europe, North America, Japan, and Russia. The tendency of industrialism to lower the level of social stratification was not apparent in the first stages of industrial growth. If you've ever read a Charles Dickens novel, such as *Oliver Twist,* you know that hellish working conditions and deep social inequalities characterized early industrialism.

However, improvements in the technology and social organization of manufacturing soon made it possible to produce more goods at a lower cost per unit, which raised living standards for the entire population. Moreover, birth was no longer destiny in industrial societies. Businesses required a literate, numerate, and highly trained workforce. To raise profits, they were eager to identify and hire the most talented people. They encouraged everyone to develop their talents and rewarded them for doing so by paying higher salaries. Political pressure from below also played an important role in reducing inequality. Workers struggled for the right to form and join unions and expand the vote to all adult citizens. They used union power and their growing political influence to win improvements in the conditions of their existence. Although barriers to mobility remained, social

Apartheid: A caste system based on race that existed in South Africa from 1948 until 1992. It consigned the large black majority to menial jobs, prevented marriage between blacks and whites, and erected separate public facilities for members of the two races. Asians and people of "mixed race" enjoyed privileges between these two extremes.

mobility became more widespread than ever before. Even traditional inequality between women and men began to break down because of the demand for talent and women's struggles to enter the paid workforce on an equal footing with men. Why hire an incompetent man over a competent woman when you can profit more from the services of a capable employee? Put in this way, women's demands for equality made good business sense. For all these reasons, then, stratification declined as industrial societies developed.

Postindustrial Societies

To make definitive statements about long-term trends in social inequality in postindustrial societies would be foolhardy because the postindustrial era is only a few decades old. However, in the United States and the United Kingdom, social inequality has been increasing for more than three decades. The concentration of wealth in the hands of the wealthiest 1 percent of Americans is higher today than at any time in the past 110 years. The gap between rich and poor is bigger today than it has been for 60 years.

Technological factors seem to be partly responsible for the trend toward growing inequality in the United States and the United Kingdom. Many high-tech jobs have been created at the top of the stratification system over the past few decades. These jobs pay well.

At the same time, new technologies have made many jobs routine. Routine jobs require little training, and they pay poorly. Because the number of routine jobs is growing more quickly than the number of jobs at the top of the stratification system, the overall effect of technology today is to increase the level of inequality in society.

In other postindustrial societies, governments seem to have moderated the growth of inequality. In Germany, France, and Canada, for example, governments have prevented a big transfer of income to the rich through tax and other policies. Consequently, social inequality has remained roughly stable since the mid-1970s (Centre for Economic Policy Research, 2002).

These basic patterns and trends in the history of social stratification, in the United States and globally, raise some interesting questions. Is growing inequality inevitable? Do technological factors so completely shape the stratification system that we must be resigned to a growing gap between rich and poor? These issues have concerned sociologists for more than 150 years. We next review some classical perspectives on them in an effort to shed light on our prospects today.

Is Stratification Inevitable? Three Theories

Marx

Karl Marx may fairly be regarded as the founder of conflict theory in sociology. It is ironic, therefore, that social stratification and the accompanying conflict between classes are *not* inevitable in Marx's view (Marx, 1904 [1859]; Marx and Engels, 1972 [1848]). He believed that capitalist growth would eventually produce a society in which there would be no more classes and therefore no more class conflict.

According to Marx, during the Industrial Revolution that began in late 18th-century Great Britain, industrial owners were eager to adopt new tools, machines, and production methods so they could produce more efficiently and earn higher profits. Such innovations had unforeseen consequences, however. In the first place, some owners, driven out of business by more efficient competitors, were forced to become members of the working **class.** Together with former peasants pouring into the cities from the countryside to take factory jobs, this caused the working class to grow. Second, the drive for profits motivated owners to concentrate workers in larger and larger factories, keep wages as low as possible,

Class: In Marx's sense of the term, class is determined by one's relationship to the means of production, or the *source* of income (e.g., ownership of factories vs. wage labor).

and invest as little as possible in improving working conditions. Thus, as the ownership class (or **bourgeoisie,** to use Marx's term) grew richer and smaller, the working class (or **proletariat**) grew larger and more impoverished.

Marx felt that workers would ultimately become aware of their exploitation. Their sense of **class consciousness** would, he wrote, encourage the growth of unions and workers' political parties. These organizations would eventually try to create a new "communist" society in which there would be no private wealth. Instead, under communism, everyone would share wealth, said Marx.

Critical Evaluation of Marx's Conflict Theory

Things did not work out the way Marx predicted. In the first place, industrial societies did not polarize into two opposed classes engaged in bitter conflict. Instead, a large and heterogeneous middle class of white-collar workers emerged. Some of them were nonmanual employees. Others were professionals. Many of them enjoyed higher income and status than manual workers. With a bigger stake in capitalism than propertyless manual workers, many nonmanual employees and professionals acted as a stabilizing force in society. Second, while Marx correctly argued that investment in technology makes it possible for capitalists to earn high profits, he did not expect investment in technology to also make it possible for workers to earn higher wages and toil fewer hours under less oppressive conditions. Yet that is just what happened. Their improved living standard tended to pacify workers, as did the availability of various welfare state benefits, such as unemployment insurance. Third, communism took root not where industry was most highly developed, as Marx predicted, but in semi-industrialized countries such as Russia in 1917 and China in 1948. Moreover, instead of evolving into classless societies, new forms of privilege emerged under communism. According to a Russian quip from the 1970s, "under capitalism, one class exploits the other, but under communism it's the other way around."

Functionalism: The Davis-Moore Thesis

In the mid-1900s, American sociologists Kingsley Davis and Wilbert Moore proposed a **functional theory of stratification** that, in contrast to Marx's theory, asserts the inevitability of social stratification (Davis and Moore, 1945). Davis and Moore observed that jobs differ in importance. A judge's work, for example, contributes more to society than does the work of a janitor. This presents a problem: How can the limited number of talented people be motivated to undergo the long training they need to serve as physicians, engineers, and so forth? Higher education is expensive. You earn little money while training. Long and hard study rather than pleasure seeking is essential. Clearly, incentives are needed to motivate the most talented people to train for the most important jobs. The incentives, said Davis and Moore, are money and prestige. More precisely, social stratification is necessary (or "functional") because the prospect of high rewards motivates people to undergo the sacrifices needed to obtain a higher education. Without substantial inequality, they conclude, the most talented people would have no incentive to become judges, physicians, and so forth.

Critical Evaluation of Functionalism

Although the functional theory of stratification may at first seem plausible, we can quickly uncover one of its chief flaws by imagining a society with just two classes of people—physicians and farmers. The farmers grow food. The physicians tend the ill. Then, one day,

Bourgeoisie: According to Marx, owners of the means of production, including factories, tools, and land. They do not do any physical labor. Their income derives from profits.

Proletariat: According to Marx, the working class. Members of the proletariat perform physical labor but do not own means of production. They are thus in a position to earn wages.

Class consciousness: Awareness of being a member of a class.

Functional theory of stratification: Argues that (1) some jobs are more important than others; (2) people have to make sacrifices to train for important jobs; and (3) inequality is required to motivate people to undergo these sacrifices.

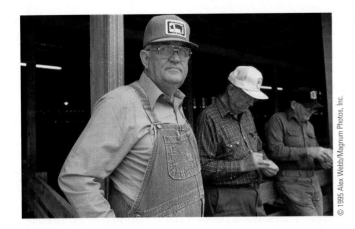

Functionalists conclude that social stratification is necessary. However, one of the problems with the functional theory of stratification is that it is difficult to establish which jobs are "important," especially when one takes a historical perspective.

a rare and deadly virus strikes. The virus has the odd property of attacking only physicians. Within weeks, there are no more doctors in our imaginary society. As a result, the farmers are much worse off. Cures and treatments for their ailments are no longer available. Soon the average farmer lives fewer years than his or her predecessors. The society is less well off, though it survives.

Now imagine the reverse. Again we have a society composed of only physicians and farmers. Again a rare and lethal virus strikes. This time, however, the virus has the odd property of attacking only farmers. Within weeks, the physicians' stores of food are depleted. After a few more weeks, the physicians start dying of starvation. The physicians who try to become farmers catch the new virus and expire. Within months, there is no more society. Who, then, does the more important work, physicians or farmers? Our thought experiment suggests that farmers do, for without them society cannot exist.

From a historical point of view, we can say that *none* of the jobs regarded by Davis and Moore as important would exist without the physical labor done by people in "unimportant" jobs. To sustain the witch doctor in a tribal society, hunters and gatherers had to produce enough for their own subsistence plus a surplus to feed, clothe, and house the witch doctor. To sustain the royal court in an agrarian society, peasants had to produce enough for their own subsistence plus a surplus to support the royal family. By using taxes, tithes, and force, government and religious authorities have taken surpluses from ordinary working people for thousands of years. Among other things, these surpluses were used to establish the first institutions of higher learning in the 13th century. Out of these, modern universities developed.

Thus, the answer to the question of which occupations are most important is not clear-cut. To be sure, physicians earn more money than farmers today and they also enjoy more prestige. But that is not because their work is more important in any objective sense of the word. (On the question of why physicians and other professionals earn more than nonprofessionals, see Chapter 12, "Religion and Education.")

Sociologists have noted other problems with the functional theory of stratification (Tumin, 1953). First, it stresses how inequality helps society discover talent, but it ignores the pool of talent lying undiscovered because of inequality. Bright and energetic adolescents may be forced to drop out of high school to help support themselves and their families. Capable and industrious high school graduates may be forced to forgo a postsecondary education because they can't afford it. Inequality may encourage the discovery of talent, but only among those who can afford to take advantage of the opportunities available to them. For the rest, inequality prevents talent from being discovered.

Second, the functional theory of stratification fails to examine how advantages are passed from generation to generation. Like Robinson Crusoe, the functional theory correctly emphasizes that talent and hard work often result in high material rewards. But it is also the case that inheritance allows parents to transfer wealth to children regardless of the latter's talent. For example, glancing back at Table 7.1, we see that 44 percent of the 25 largest personal fortunes in the United States were substantially inherited.

Weber

Like the functionalists, Max Weber argued that the emergence of a classless society is highly unlikely. Like Marx, however, he recognized that under some circumstances people can act to lower the level of inequality in society.

Writing in the early 1900s, Weber held that a person's **class** position is determined by his or her "market situation," including the possession of goods, opportunities for income, level of education, and level of technical skill. Accordingly, in Weber's view there are four main classes in capitalist societies: large property owners, small property owners, propertyless but relatively highly educated and well-paid employees, and propertyless manual workers (Weber, 1946: 180–95).

Weber also recognized that two types of groups other than classes—status groups and parties—have a bearing on the way a society is stratified (▶Figure 7.5). **Status groups** differ from one another in the prestige or social honor they enjoy and in their lifestyle. Consider members of a minority ethnic community who have recently immigrated. They may earn relatively high income but endure relatively low prestige. The longer-established members of the majority ethnic community may look down on them as vulgar "new rich." If their cultural practices differ from those of the majority ethnic group, their style of life may become a subject of scorn. Thus, the position of the minority ethnic group in

Class: In Weber's usage, class is determined by one's "market situation."

Status groups: Groups that differ from one another in terms of the prestige or social honor they enjoy and in terms of their lifestyle.

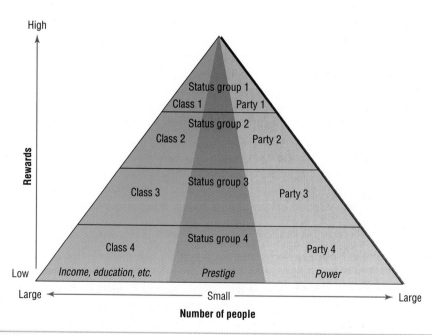

▶FIGURE 7.5
Weber's Stratification Scheme

the social hierarchy does not derive just from its economic position but also from the esteem in which it is held.

In Weber's usage, **parties** are not just political groups but also other organizations that seek to impose their will on others through the exercise of power (Weber, 1947: 152). Control over parties, especially large bureaucratic organizations, does not depend just on wealth. One can head a military, scientific, political, or other type of bureaucracy without being rich, just as one can be rich and still have to endure low prestige.

Weber argued that to draw an accurate picture of a society's stratification system one must analyze classes, status groups, and parties as somewhat independent bases of social inequality (▶Table 7.4). Each basis of stratification influences the others. For example, one political party may want to tax the rich and distribute benefits to the poor, thus increasing opportunities for upward mobility. Another political party may want to cut taxes to the rich and decrease benefits to the poor, thus decreasing opportunities for upward mobility. The class system will be affected differently depending on which party comes to power. (Recall our earlier discussion of why, in the postindustrial era, social inequality is increasing in the United States and the United Kingdom but not to the same degree in France, Germany, and Canada.) From this point of view, there is nothing inevitable about the level of social stratification in society. We are neither headed inevitably toward classlessness nor bound to endure high levels of inequality. Instead, the level of social stratification depends on the complex interplay of class, status, and party and their effects on social mobility. To further explore these themes, we now present a summary of social mobility research in the United States.

▶**TABLE 7.4**

Mean Annual Earnings, Full-Time Workers, and Prestige Scores, Selected Occupations, United States

Occupation	Median Annual Income ($)	Prestige Score
Airplane pilots	120,589	61
Physicians	117,664	86
Lawyers	99,798	75
Aerospace engineers	82,113	72
College and university professors	66,945	74
Computer programmers	59,940	61
Police officers and detectives	49,032	60
Plumbers, pipefitters, and steamfitters	46,047	45
High school teachers	45,254	66
Electrical and electronic technicians	43,856	51
Preschool teachers	31,589	55
Hairdressers and cosmetologists	26,704	36
Janitors	22,691	22
Secretaries	21,035	46
Security guards	20,804	42
Taxi drivers and chauffeurs	20,253	28
Restaurant cooks	19,107	31
Sewing machine operators	17,643	28
Waiters, waitresses, and bartenders	14,209	28

Note: Median annual income for the occupations listed above is taken from a labor force survey conducted by the federal government in 2003. Occupational prestige scores are based on the General Social Survey (GSS) for 1989. Respondents were asked to rank occupations in terms of the prestige attached to them. Prestige scores for all occupations range from 17 (miscellaneous food preparation occupations) to 86 (physicians). While median income and prestige are not perfectly correlated, as Weber would have predicted, the correlation between median income and prestige scores for the occupations listed here is strong ($r = .83$).
Source: Inter-University Consortium for Political and Social Research (1992); U.S. Department of Labor (2004).

Social Mobility

Blau and Duncan: The Status Attainment Model

The pioneering work in modern social mobility research is Peter Blau and Otis Dudley Duncan's *The American Occupational Structure* (1967). Their approach to the subject became known as the "status attainment model." Blau and Duncan set themselves the task of figuring out the relative importance of inheritance versus individual merit in determining one's place in the stratification system. To what degree is one's position based on ascription—that is, inheriting wealth and other advantages from one's family? To what degree is one's position based on achievement—that is, applying one's own talents to life's

Parties: In Weber's usage, organizations that seek to impose their will on others.

tasks? Blau and Duncan's answer was plain: Stratification in America is based mainly on individual achievement.

Blau and Duncan abandoned the European tradition of viewing the stratification system as a set of distinct groups. Marx, you will recall, distinguished two main classes by the source of their income. He was sure the bourgeoisie and the proletariat would become class conscious and take action to assert their class interests. Similarly, Weber distinguished four main classes by their market situation. He saw class consciousness and action as potentials that each of these classes might realize in some circumstances. In contrast, Blau and Duncan saw little if any potential for class consciousness and action in the United States. That is why they abandoned the entire vocabulary of class. For them, the stratification system is not a system of distinct classes at all, but a continuous hierarchy or ladder of occupations with hundreds of rungs. Each occupation—each rung on the ladder—requires different levels of education and generates different amounts of income.

To reflect these variations in education and earnings, Blau and Duncan created a **socioeconomic index (SEI) of occupational status.** Using survey data, they found the average earnings and years of education of men employed full-time in various occupations. They combined these two averages to arrive at an SEI score for each occupation. (Other researchers combined income, education, and occupational prestige data to construct an **index of socioeconomic status [SES].**)

Next, Blau and Duncan used survey data to find the SEI of each respondent's current job, first job, and father's job, as well as the years of formal education completed by the respondent and the respondent's father. They showed how all five of these variables were related (▶Figure 7.6). Their main finding was that the respondents' own achievements (years of education and SEI of first job) had much more influence on their current occupational status than did ascribed characteristics (father's occupation and years of education). Blau and Duncan concluded that the United States is a relatively open society in which individual merit counts for more than family background. This partly vindicated the functionalists.

Subsequent research on social mobility found that the rate of social mobility for men in the United States is high and that most mobility is upward (Blau and Duncan, 1967;

Socioeconomic index (SEI) of occupational status: An index developed by Blau and Duncan that combines, for each occupation, average earnings and years of education of men employed full time in the occupation.

Socioeconomic status (SES): Combines income, education, and occupational prestige data in a single index of one's position in the socioeconomic hierarchy.

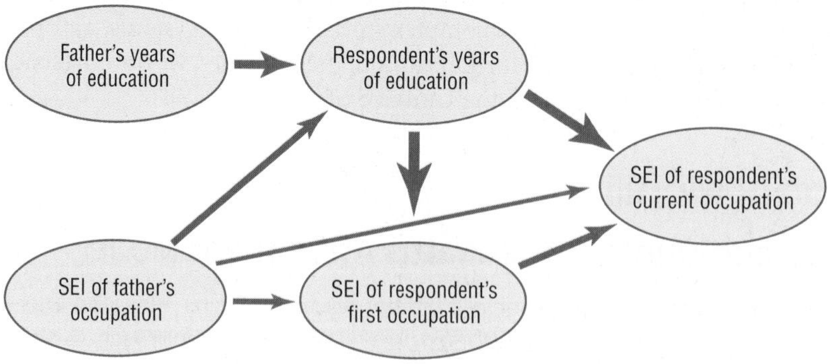

▶FIGURE 7.6
Blau and Duncan's Model of Occupational Achievement.

Note: Arrows indicate cause-and-effect relationships between variables, with the arrowheads pointing to effects. The thicker the arrow, the stronger the effect.

Featherman and Hauser, 1978; Featherman, Jones, and Hauser, 1975; Grusky and Hauser, 1984). However, since the early 1970s, substantial downward mobility has occurred. Research also revealed that mobility within a single generation (**intragenerational mobility**) is generally modest. Few people move from rags to riches or fall from the top to the bottom of the stratification system in a lifetime. On the other hand, mobility over more than one generation (**intergenerational mobility**) can be substantial.

In addition, research showed that most social mobility is the result of change in the occupational structure. One of the most dramatic changes during the late 19th and early 20th centuries was the decline of agriculture and the rise of manufacturing. This decline caused a big decrease in the number of farmers and a corresponding surge in the number of factory workers. A second dramatic change, especially apparent during the last third of the 20th century, was the decline of manufacturing and the rise of the service sector. This change caused a big drop in the number of manual workers and a corresponding surge in the number of white-collar service workers. Mobility due to such changes in the occupational structure is known as **structural mobility.**

Research also shows that there are only small differences in rates of social mobility among the highly industrialized countries. The United States does not have an exceptionally high rate of upward social mobility (Erikson and Goldthorpe, 1992; Grusky and Hauser, 1984; Lipset and Bendix, 1963). Some countries, such as Australia and Canada, apparently enjoy higher upward mobility rates than the United States (Tyree, Semyonov, and Hodge, 1979).

Group Barriers: Race and Gender

The process of status attainment is much the same for women and minorities as it is for white men. Years of schooling have a greater influence on status attainment than does father's occupation, whether one examines white men, women, African Americans, or Hispanic Americans. However, if you compare people *with the same level of education and similar family backgrounds,* women and members of minority groups tend to attain lower status than white men (Featherman and Hauser, 1976; Hout, 1988; Hout and Morgan, 1975; McClendon, 1976; Stolzenberg, 1990; Tienda and Lii, 1987). This suggests that one cannot adequately explain status attainment by examining only the characteristics of *individuals,* such as their years of education and father's occupation. One must also examine the characteristics of *groups,* such as whether some groups face barriers to mobility, regardless of the individual characteristics of their members (Horan, 1978). Such group barriers include racial and gender discrimination and being born in neighborhoods that make upward mobility unusually difficult because of poor living conditions. For instance, women and African Americans who are employed full time earn less on average than white men with the same level of education (see Chapter 9, "Race and Ethnicity," and Chapter 10, "Sexuality and Gender"). The existence of such group disadvantages suggests that American society is not as open or "meritocratic" as Blau and Duncan make it out to be. Group barriers to mobility, such as gender and race, do exist.

Could class in the Marxist or Weberian sense act like race and gender, bestowing advantages and disadvantages on entire groups of people and perhaps even helping to shape their political views? Some sociologists think so. Their research shows that parents' wealth, education, and occupation are more important determinants of a person's occupation than Blau and Duncan's research suggests (Jencks et al., 1972; Rytina, 1992). Other sociologists, dissatisfied with the Blau and Duncan model, have updated the Marxist and Weberian concepts of class to make them more relevant to the late 20th century (Erikson and Goldthorpe, 1992; Goldthorpe, Llewellyn, and Payne, 1987 [1980]; Wright, 1985;

Intragenerational mobility: Social mobility that occurs within a single generation.

Intergenerational mobility: Social mobility that occurs between generations.

Structural mobility: Social mobility that results from change in the distribution of occupations.

1997). These researchers emphasize how a person's class position tends to put limits on his or her upward social mobility.

Noneconomic Dimensions of Class

Prestige and Power

CENGAGENOW™

Learn more about **Prestige and Power** by going through the Power and Authority Learning Module.

As Weber correctly pointed out, inequality is not based on money alone. It is also based on prestige and power. These important dimensions of inequality have been somewhat neglected in recent writings on stratification.

Weber, you will recall, said status groups differ from one another in terms of their lifestyles and the honor in which they are held by others. Here we may add that members of status groups signal their rank by means of material and symbolic culture. They seek to distinguish themselves from others by displays of "taste" in fashion, food, music, literature, manners, and travel.

Status and Style

Often, rich people engage in conspicuous displays of consumption, waste, and leisure not because they are necessary, useful, or pleasurable but simply to impress their peers and inferiors (Veblen, 1899). This is evident if we consider how clothing acts as a sort of language that signals one's status to others (Lurie, 1981).

For thousands of years, certain clothing styles have indicated rank. In ancient Egypt, only people in high positions were allowed to wear sandals. The ancient Greeks and Romans passed laws controlling the type, number, and color of garments one could wear and the type of embroidery with which they could be trimmed. In medieval Europe, too, various aspects of dress were regulated to ensure that certain styles were specific to certain groups.

European laws governing the dress styles of different groups fell into disuse after about 1700. That is because a new method of control emerged as Europe became wealthier. From the 18th century on, the *cost* of clothing came to designate a person's rank. Expensive materials, styles that were difficult to care for, heavy jewelry, and superfluous trimmings became all the rage. It was not for comfort or utility that rich people wore elaborate powdered wigs, heavy damasked satins, the furs of rare animals, diamond tiaras, and patterned brocades and velvets. Such getups were often hot, stiff, heavy, and itchy. One could scarcely move in many of them. And that was just their point—to prove not only that the wearer could afford enormous sums for handmade finery but also that he or she did not have to work to pay for them.

Today, we have different ways of using clothes to signal status. Designer labels loudly proclaim the dollar value of garments. In addition, the language of status often takes the form of looking "cool." Consider jeans. Long regarded as a garment for cowboys and industrial workers, jeans have become wildly popular for just about everyone. Designer brands distinguish someone who is cool from someone who is not. Yet there are other ways of demonstrating coolness. Not wearing low-cut jeans with holes in the right places would doom a person to second-class status in many high schools.

How pervasive and important are brand names for establishing status? One indicator comes from the world of popular music. Top recording artists are much admired by young people and even act as role models. The brands they popularize help to define cool, high-status commodities. In that light, consider ▶Table 7.5, based on the top 20 songs of 2005 on the Billboard charts. The top half of Table 7.5 shows how many times the ten most frequently mentioned brands were referred to in the top 20 songs. The bottom half lists the 5 recording artists who referred to brands most frequently. The numbers tell a fascinating story. Each of the top 20 songs of 2005 mentioned brands 25.5 times on average. Assuming the average song is 3 minutes long, that works out to 1 brand mentioned every 7 seconds. From this point of view, popular music is a lot like a commercial. Status in the world of popular music—especially the music of 50 Cent—is strongly associated with driving a Mercedes, wearing Nikes, drinking Hennessy cognac, and packing an AK-47 assault rifle.

Politics and the Plight of the Poor

Power is a second noneconomic dimension of stratification that has received insufficient attention in recent work on inequality. Yet power has a profound impact on the distribution of opportunities and rewards in society. Power is exercised formally in politics, and politics can reshape the class structure by changing laws governing people's right to own property. Less radically, politics can change the stratification system by entitling people to various welfare benefits and by redistributing income through tax policies. The two main currents of American opinion on the subject of poverty correspond roughly to the Democratic and Republican positions. Broadly speaking, most Democrats want government to play an important role in helping to solve the problem of poverty. Most Republicans want to reduce government involvement with the poor so people can solve their problems themselves. At various times, each of these approaches to poverty has dominated public policy.

We can see the effect of government policy on poverty by examining fluctuations in the poverty rate over time. The **poverty rate** is the percentage of Americans who fall below the "poverty threshold." To establish the poverty threshold, the U.S. Department of Agriculture first determines the cost of an economy food budget. The poverty threshold is then set at three times that budget. It is adjusted for the number of people in the household, the annual inflation rate, whether individual adult householders are younger than 65 years of age, and whether they live in Hawaii or Alaska (where the cost of living is relatively high) or in the rest of the United States.

The Department of Health and Human Services also establishes "poverty guidelines" annually. While the poverty threshold is used for statistical purposes, poverty guidelines are used for administrative purposes, that is, to determine who is eligible for certain government services. It is not widely known that the guidelines are less generous than the thresholds. This means that some people defined as poor statistically do not receive certain welfare benefits. In 2003, the poverty guideline for individual adult householders under the age of 65 living in the 48 contiguous states or the District of Columbia was $8,980 per year. For a family of four with two children under the age of 18, the poverty guideline was $18,400.

▶Figure 7.7 shows the percentage of Americans who lived below the poverty threshold from 1961 to 2006. Between the early 1960s and the late 1970s, the poverty rate dropped dramatically from about 22 percent to around 11 percent. Then between 1980 and 1984, it jumped to about 15 percent, fluctuating in the 11 percent to 15 percent

▶**TABLE 7.5**
Brand Names in Popular Music

BRANDS MENTIONED IN TOP 20 SONGS

Brand	Number of Mentions
1. Mercedes Benz automobile	100
2. Nike sports shoes	63
3. Cadillac automobile	62
4. Bentley automobile	51
5. Rolls Royce automobile	46
6. Hennessy cognac	44
7. Chevrolet automobile	40
8. Louis Vuitton luggage	35
9. Cristal champagne	35
10. AK-47 assault rifle	33
Total	509
Mentions/song	25.5

TOP 5 BRAND-DROPPING ARTISTS

Singer	Number of Mentions
1. 50 Cent	20 brands in 7 songs
2. Ludacris	13 brands in 6 songs
2. The Game	13 brands in 2 songs
4. Ciara	10 brands in 4 songs
5. Jamie Foxx	6 brands in 1 song
5. Kanye West	6 brands in 1 song
5. Lil' Jon	6 brands in 2 songs
5. Trick Daddy	6 brands in 2 songs
Total	80 brands in 25 songs
Brands/song	3.2

Source: Agenda Inc. (2005) 4–7.

CENGAGENOW

Learn more about the **Poverty Rate** by going through the % of Persons Below the Poverty Level Map Exercise.

Poverty rate: The percentage of people living below the poverty threshold, which is three times the minimum food budget established by the U.S. Department of Agriculture.

▶FIGURE 7.7
Poverty Rate, Individuals,
United States, 1961–2006
(in percent)

Source: U.S. Census Bureau (2004;
2008c).

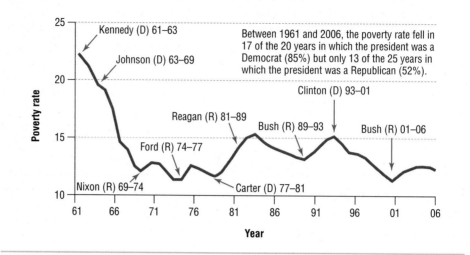

range after that. In 2006, 36.5 million Americans were living in poverty, 12.3 percent of the population.

The poverty rate among children was 17.4 percent, the highest among the world's rich countries. The poorest of the poor are homeless people. Estimates vary, but most experts seem to agree that about 750,000 Americans are homeless on a given night, fully a quarter of them children. The average annual income of a homeless person in the United States is about $3,600 a year.

Government Policy and the Poverty Rate in the United States

Fluctuations in the poverty rate are related to political events. Thus, as shown in Figure 7.7, between 1961 and 2006 the poverty rate fell in 17 of the 20 years in which the president was a Democrat (85 percent) but in only 13 of the 25 years in which the president was a Republican (52 percent). The poverty rate fluctuates as a result of economic conditions too, but these figures show that the policies of the party in power also have an important bearing on the poverty rate.

The 1930s: The Great Depression

More broadly, we can identify three policy initiatives that have been directed at the problem of poverty. The first dates from the mid-1930s. During the Great Depression (1929–39), 30 percent of Americans were unemployed, and many of the people lucky enough to have jobs were barely able to make ends meet. Remarkably, most Americans were poor in 1940 (O'Hare, 1996: 13). In the middle of the Depression, Franklin Roosevelt was elected president. In response to the suffering of the American people and the large, violent labor strikes of the era, he introduced such programs as Social Security, Unemployment Insurance, and Aid to Families with Dependent Children (AFDC) (see Chapter 15, "Collective Action and Social Movements"). For the first time, the federal government took responsibility for providing basic sustenance to citizens who were unable to do so themselves. Because of Roosevelt's "New Deal" policies and rapidly increasing prosperity in the decades after World War II, the poverty rate fell dramatically, reaching 19 percent in 1964.

The 1960s: The War on Poverty

The second antipoverty initiative dates from the mid-1960s. In 1964, President Lyndon Johnson declared a "War on Poverty." This initiative was in part a response to a new wave of social protest. Millions of southern blacks who migrated to northern and western cities in the 1940s and 1950s were unable to find jobs. In some census tracts in Detroit, Chicago, Baltimore, and Los Angeles, black unemployment ranged from 26 to 41 percent in 1960. Suffering extreme hardship, many African Americans demanded at least enough money from the government to allow them to subsist. Some helped to organize the National Welfare Rights Organization to pressure the government to give relief to more poor individuals. Others took to the streets as race riots rocked the nation in the mid-1960s. President Johnson soon broadened access to AFDC and other welfare programs (Piven and Cloward, 1993 [1971], 1977: 264–361). As a result, in 1973 the poverty rate dropped to 11.1 percent, the lowest it has ever been in this country.

The 1980s: "War against the Poor"

Finally, the third initiative aimed at the poverty problem dates from 1980. The mood of the country had shifted by the time President Ronald Reagan took office that year. Reagan assumed the presidency after the social activism and rioting of the 1960s and 1970s had died down. He was elected in part by voters born in the 1950s and 1960s. These so-called baby boomers expected their standard of living to increase as quickly as that of their parents. Many of them were deeply disappointed when things didn't work out that way. Real household income (earnings minus inflation) remained flat in the 1970s and 1980s. Even that discouraging performance was achieved thanks only to the mass entry of women into the paid labor force. Reagan explained this state of affairs as the result of too much government. In his view, big government inhibits growth. In contrast, cutting government services and the taxes that fund those services supposedly stimulates economic growth. For example, Reagan argued that welfare causes long-term dependency on government handouts, which, he claimed, worsens the problem of poverty rather than solving it. As Reagan was fond of saying, "We fought the War on Poverty and poverty won" (quoted in Rank, 1994: 7). The appropriate solution, in Reagan's view, was to reduce relief to the poor. Cut welfare programs, he said, and welfare recipients will be forced to work. Cut taxes and taxpayers will spend more, thus creating jobs.

Reagan's message fell on receptive ears. The War on Poverty was turned into what one sociologist called a "war against the poor" (Gans, 1995). Because a large proportion of welfare recipients were African Americans and Hispanic Americans, some analysts have argued that the war against the poor was fed by racist sentiment (Quadagno, 1994). The invidious stereotype of a young unmarried black woman having a baby in order to collect a bigger welfare check became common. The AFDC budget, expenditures for employee training, and many other government programs were cut sharply. Poverty rates rose. The number of homeless people jumped from 125,000 in 1980 to 402,000 in 1987–88, and after declining during the economic boom of the 1990s started to surge to record levels in 2001 (Belluck, 2002). One of the main reasons for this increase was the erosion of government support for public housing (Liebow, 1993).[1]

Dorothea Lange, "Migrant Mother, Nipomo, California, 1936." Victims of the Great Depression (1929–39).

---

[1] Just as the Reagan administration was cutting welfare, it lowered the top personal tax bracket. This change substantially increased the amount of disposable income in the hands of the wealthiest Americans (Phillips, 1990). In this way, politics helped to increase the level of inequality in American society.

Poverty Myths

Research conducted in the 1990s showed that many of the beliefs underlying the war against the poor are inaccurate:

- *Myth 1: The overwhelming majority of poor people are African or Hispanic American single mothers with children.* The fact is that while more than 20 percent of African and Hispanic Americans were poor in 2006, 44 percent of the poor were non-Hispanic whites (▶Figure 7.8). Moreover, female-headed families represented 53 percent of the poor. Another 38 percent lived in married-couple families. The remainder lived alone, with nonrelatives, or in male-headed families with no wife present (U.S. Census Bureau, 2007b: 12).

- *Myth 2: People are poor because they don't want to work.* Among poor people over the age of 15, more than 37 percent did work in 2006, nearly 12 percent of them full time. Moreover, many poor people are simply too young or too old to work, as suggested by the fact that 44 percent of poor people are under the age of 18 or over 65. Finally, many poor people are unable to work for reasons of health or disability—or because they are single parents who have to stay at home to care for their children because of the unavailability of affordable child care. The following comment of a 32-year-old, never-married mother of two is typical of welfare recipients' attitude to work: "I feel better about myself when I'm working than when I'm not. Even if I had a job and every penny went to living from payday to payday, it doesn't bother me because I feel like a better person because I am going to work" (quoted in Rank, 1994: 111).

- *Myth 3: Poor people are trapped in poverty.* In fact, the poverty population is dynamic. People are always struggling to move out of poverty. They often succeed, at least for a time. Only about 12 percent of the poor remain poor 5 or more years in a row (O'Hare, 1996: 11).

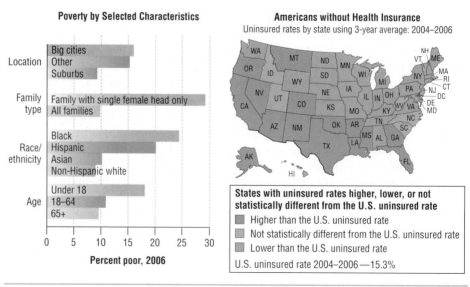

▶FIGURE 7.8
Poverty in the United States

Source: U.S. Census Bureau (2007: 11–14, 25).

● *Myth 4: Welfare encourages married women with children to divorce so they can collect welfare, and it encourages single women on welfare to have more children.* Because some welfare payments increase with the number of children in the family, some people believe that mothers on welfare give birth to more children to get more money from the government. In fact, women on welfare have a lower birthrate than women in the general population (Rank, 1994). Moreover, welfare payments are very low, and recipients therefore suffer severe economic hardship. This is hardly an incentive to go on welfare. In the words of a 51-year-old divorced mother on welfare: "I can't see anybody that would ever settle for something like this just for the mere fact of getting a free ride, because it's not worth it" (quoted in Rank, 1994: 168). As for the argument that people with children often divorce to collect welfare, the most rigorous study of welfare recipients in the United States to date found that welfare programs "have little effect on the likelihood of marriage and divorce" (Rank, 1994: 169).

● *Myth 5: Welfare is a strain on the federal budget.* "Means-tested" welfare programs require that recipients meet an income test to qualify. Such programs accounted for a mere 6 percent of the federal budget in 2001 (Executive Office, 2000). In percentage terms, this amount is substantially less than what is spent by western European governments for similar programs.

We conclude that sociological evidence does not support many of the arguments people use to justify current welfare reforms, nor are current welfare reforms enjoying unqualified success in reducing poverty (Box 7.3). Western Europe, with a poverty rate roughly half that of the United States, seems to be having more success in this regard. That is because the governments of western Europe have established job-training and child-care programs that allow poor people to take jobs with livable wages and benefits. Most of the 34.6 million Americans living in poverty are eager to work. Providing them with the required skills and the opportunity to work could possibly bring the poverty rate down to western European levels. Simply denying them welfare seems to do little to help alleviate poverty.[2]

Perception of Class Inequality in the United States

Surveys show that few Americans have trouble placing themselves in the class structure when asked to do so. The General Social Survey (GSS) has been asking Americans almost annually since 1972 whether they consider themselves "lower class," "working class," "middle class," or "upper class." By 2006, a mere 119 (0.2 percent) of 56,000 respondents said either that they didn't know which class they were in or that they were not members of any class. Slightly more than 3 percent said they were upper class, and slightly more than 5 percent said they were lower class. About 44 percent said they were working class, and about the same percentage said they were middle class. These percentages changed little from 1972 to 2006 (Jackman and Jackman, 1983; National Opinion Research Center, 2008a; Vanneman and Cannon, 1987)

If Americans see the stratification system as divided into classes, they also know that the gaps between classes are relatively large. For instance, one study compared respondents in New Haven, Connecticut, and London, England. The study revealed that the

CENGAGENOW™
Learn more about **Class Structure** by going through the American Class Structure Learning Module.

---

[2]It is unclear whether denying welfare even helps the taxpayer. To our knowledge, nobody has compared the direct tax saving gained from cutting welfare with the indirect cost of dealing with the consequences of widespread poverty, such as bigger Medicaid bills, larger budgets for police and prison services, and so forth.

BOX 7.3
SOCIAL POLICY: WHAT DO YOU THINK?

Redesigning Welfare

One of the most important experiments in American history is taking place today. Wisconsin is at the forefront of the experiment. In 1986 the state began pilot programs aimed at reducing welfare dependency and increasing the economic self-sufficiency of families. Ten years later, President Bill Clinton signed a federal welfare law replacing the old welfare program with a program of time limits and work requirements. In 1997 Wisconsin introduced a tough new plan called W-2. It requires nearly all welfare recipients to work. It also imposes a strict 5-year limit on how long one can receive welfare assistance. Especially in Wisconsin, the age of welfare has passed, and the age of "workfare" has dawned. Nationally, the welfare caseload dropped 47 percent between 1994 and 1999. In Wisconsin it dropped 91 percent.

Pointing to the drop in the welfare caseload, some observers consider the Wisconsin experiment a success. Closer inspection reveals mixed results (Massing, 1999; Newman, 1999). Roughly one-third of former AFDC recipients in Wisconsin are working and earning $9 or $10 an hour, above minimum wage. Getting by on this kind of wage is extraordinarily hard, even if it is an improvement over welfare (Ehrenreich, 2001). Another third of former AFDC recipients are working at menial jobs close to minimum wage. The bottom one-third have few, if any, skills. Many of them suffer psychological, drug,

or alcohol problems. For the most part, they have not been able to find work and many of them cannot pay rent. They live in Wisconsin's shelters and rely on handouts for food. The city's shelters have become so crowded that the Red Cross runs overflow sites in church basements during the winter. In 1999, 69 percent of mothers who had left the welfare system a year earlier said they were just barely making do. Only 16 percent enjoyed earnings above the poverty threshold (Harden, 2001).

The mixed results of the Wisconsin experiment force us to reconsider welfare policy. The results of our current get-tough policy are mixed at best. Most poor Americans without a job cannot work because they are too young, too old, or too disabled or because they have at least one young child at home and no male adult in the household. Many single mothers with children lack the skills and child-care services that would help them get a job. Thus, without more child care and job training, workfare's ability to eliminate poverty in America is questionable. Meanwhile, former welfare recipients who do find work barely manage to scrape by. Nationally in 2002, they were working a 35-hour week

at just under $8 an hour on average, giving them an annual income of $14,560 (Edelman, 2002).

Another problem is that politicians designed and implemented the current welfare policy in the mid-1990s, during an economic boom. The number of people on welfare fell nationally by 60 percent between 1996 and 2002, but then the welfare rolls started growing again because the country was in recession and low-wage jobs became scarce. As early as 2001, many states had to scrap the 5-year limit on receiving welfare benefits because so many people who could not find work were in desperate need (Associated Press, 2002; Pear, 2003). Whether a program designed for good times can survive the bad is unclear.

We conclude that the challenge Americans face in the 21st century is to develop innovative programs that can prevent welfare dependency without punishing the powerless and the destitute. How we do so is your choice.

Critical Thinking

- Can you think of any innovative program that would achieve the goal of avoiding welfare dependency without punishing the weak and the poor?

- Could there be a universal solution to this problem, that is, something that would apply around the country or even perhaps the world?

Americans accurately perceived more inequality in their society than the British did in theirs (Bell and Robinson, 1980; Robinson and Bell, 1978).

Do we think these big gaps between classes are needed to motivate people to work hard, thus increasing their own wealth and the wealth of the nation? Some Americans think so, but most do not. A survey conducted in 18 countries asked more than 22,000 respondents (including nearly 1,200 Americans) whether large differences in income are necessary for national prosperity. Americans were among the most likely to *disagree* with that view (Pammett, 1997: 77).

So we know we live in a class-divided society. Most of us think that deep class divisions are not necessary for national prosperity. Why then do we think inequality continues to exist? The 18-nation survey just cited sheds light on this issue. One of the survey

BOX 7.4
YOU AND THE SOCIAL WORLD

We expect you have had some strong reactions to our review of sociological theories and research on social stratification. You may therefore find it worthwhile to reflect more systematically on your own attitudes to social inequality and the attitudes of people unlike you. One way of doing this is to ask an acquaintance who is least like you in terms of class position the following questions, and then answer the following questions yourself. You can then compare the two sets of answers with the American averages given in the text:

- Do you consider the family in which you grew up to have been lower class, working class, middle class, or upper class?

Your Attitudes to Social Inequality

- Do you think the gaps between classes in American society are big, moderate, or small?

- How strongly do you agree or disagree with the view that big gaps between classes are needed to motivate people to work hard and maintain national prosperity? (strongly agree, agree, neither, disagree, strongly disagree)

- How strongly do you agree or disagree with the view that inequality persists because it benefits the rich and the powerful? (strongly agree, agree, neither, disagree, strongly disagree)

- How strongly do you agree or disagree with the view that inequality persists because ordinary people don't join together to eliminate it? (strongly agree, agree, neither, disagree, strongly disagree)

WRITING ASSIGNMENT

In 500 words, compare your perceptions and evaluations of the American class structure with those of your acquaintance and those of the American public in general (see text). How do you account for your views, the views of your acquaintance, and the views of the American public?

questions asked respondents how strongly they agreed or disagreed with the view that "inequality continues because it benefits the rich and powerful." Most Americans agreed with that statement. Only 23 percent disagreed with it in any way. Another question asked respondents how strongly they agreed or disagreed with the view that "inequality continues because ordinary people don't join together to get rid of it." Again, most Americans agreed. Only 30 percent disagreed in any way (Pammett, 1997: 77–8).

Government's Role in Reducing Poverty

Despite widespread awareness of inequality and considerable dissatisfaction with it, most Americans are opposed to the government playing an active role in reducing inequality.

Most of us don't want government to provide citizens with a basic income. We tend to oppose government job-creation programs. We even resist the idea that government should reduce income differences through taxation (Pammett, 1997: 81). Most Americans remain individualistic and self-reliant. On the whole, we persist in the belief that opportunities for mobility are abundant and that it is up to the individual to make something of those opportunities by means of talent and effort (Kluegel and Smith, 1986).

Significantly, however, all the attitudes summarized above vary by class position. For example, discontent with the level of inequality in American society is stronger at the bottom of the stratification system than at the top. The belief that American society is full of opportunities for upward mobility is stronger at the top of the class hierarchy than at the bottom. One finds considerably less opposition to the idea that government should reduce inequality as one moves down the stratification system. These findings permit us to conclude that if Americans allow inequality to persist, it is because the *balance* of attitudes—and of power—favors continuity over change (Box 7.4). We take up this important theme again in Chapter 13 ("Politics, Work, and the Economy"), where we discuss the social roots of politics.

The Points of the Compass

Stratification systems are opportunity structures that are more or less open to upward mobility. Their theoretical extremes are represented by the "north" and "south" points of our sociological compass (see Figure 1.5). At one extreme, people lack all opportunity. Their positions are fixed at birth. The class they are born into is the class in which they die. Because some people are born and remain privileged, while others are born and remain disadvantaged, we say that such a stratification system is characterized by inequality of opportunity.

At the other theoretical extreme, opportunities for upward mobility are evenly distributed throughout the stratification system. People born in the middle have no greater likelihood of reaching the top than people born at the bottom. People born at the top are as likely to fall to the bottom as people born in the middle. Merit and drive, not origins, determine one's eventual position in the hierarchy. This is a meritocratic system, a system of equality of opportunity.

The "American Dream" is built on an image of equality of opportunity. As we have seen, however, opportunities for upward mobility in the United States are actually no more plentiful than in other postindustrial societies relative to the size of their populations. Most of the upward mobility that takes place is due to change in the occupational structure. Mobility within a single generation is modest. For more than three decades, substantial downward mobility has taken place. Over the same period, inequality has grown. The dream is worthy, but we must keep the sociological eye open to see what's really going on.

CHAPTER SUMMARY

1. What is the difference between wealth and income? How are they distributed in the United States?

Wealth is assets minus liabilities. Income is the amount of money earned in a given period. Substantial inequality of both wealth and income exists in the United States, but inequality of wealth is greater. Both types of inequality have increased since the mid-70s. The United States leads the other highly industrialized countries in both measures of inequality.

2. How does inequality change as societies develop?

Inequality increases as societies develop from the foraging to the early industrial stage. With increased industrialization, inequality declines. In the early stages of postindustrialism, inequality has increased in some countries (e.g., the United States) but not in others, where governments take a more active role in redistributing income (e.g., France).

3. What are the main differences between Marx's and Weber's theories of stratification?

Marx's theory of stratification distinguishes between classes on the basis of their role in the productive process. It predicts inevitable conflict between the bourgeoisie and the proletariat and the birth of a communist system. Weber distinguished between classes on the basis of their market relations. His model of stratification included four main classes. He argued that class consciousness may develop under some circumstances but is by no means inevitable. Weber also emphasized prestige and power as important noneconomic sources of inequality.

4. What is the functional theory of stratification?

Davis and Moore's functional theory of stratification argues that (1) some jobs are more important than others, (2) people have to make sacrifices to train for important jobs, and (3) inequality is required to motivate people to undergo these sacrifices. In this sense, stratification is "functional."

5. **What is Blau and Duncan's theory of stratification?**

Blau and Duncan viewed the stratification system as a ladder with hundreds of occupational ranks. Rank is determined by the income and prestige associated with each occupation. On the basis of their studies, they concluded that the United States enjoys an achievement-based stratification system. However, many sociologists subsequently concluded that being a member of certain social categories limits one's opportunities for success. In this sense, social structure shapes the distribution of inequality.

6. **Is stratification based only on economic criteria?**

No. People often engage in conspicuous consumption, waste, and leisure to signal their position in the social hierarchy. Moreover, politics often influences the shape of stratification systems by changing the distribution of income, welfare entitlements, and property rights.

7. **How do Americans view the class system?**

Most Americans are aware of the existence of the class system and their place in it. They believe that large inequalities are not necessary to achieve national prosperity. Most Americans also believe that inequality persists because it serves the interests of the most advantaged members of society and because the disadvantaged don't join together to change things. However, most Americans disapprove of government intervention to lower the level of inequality.

Questions to Consider

1. How do you think the American and global stratification systems will change over the next 10 years? Over the next 25 years? Why do you think these changes will occur?

2. Why do you think most Americans oppose more government intervention to reduce the level of inequality in society? In answering this question, think about the advantages that inequality brings to many people and the resources at their disposal for maintaining inequality.

3. Compare the number and quality of public facilities such as playgrounds and libraries in various parts of your community. How is the distribution of public facilities related to the socioeconomic status of neighborhoods? Why does this relationship exist?

Web Resources

CENGAGENOW™

Maximize your study time by using CengageNOW's diagnostic study plan to help you review this chapter. The Study Plan will

- help you identify areas on which you should concentrate;
- provide interactive exercises to help you master the chapter concepts; and
- provide a post-test to confirm you are ready to move on to the next chapter.

The Companion Website for *Sociology: Your Compass for a New World,* The Brief Edition, Enhanced Second Edition

www.cengage.com/sociology/brym

Supplement your review of this chapter by going to the companion website to take one of the tutorial quizzes, use flash cards to master key terms, and check out the many other study aids you'll find there. You'll also find special features such as GSS Data and Census 2000 information that will put data and resources at your fingertips to help you with that special project or help you do some research on your own.

CHAPTER 8

Globalization, Inequality, and Development

Michael S. Yamashita/Corbis

In this chapter, you will learn that:

- People and institutions across the planet are becoming increasingly aware of, and dependent on, one another. Sociologists call this tendency "globalization."

- Globalization creates a world that is more homogeneous in some ways and more localized in others. Globalization also generates its own opposition.

- Global inequality has increased tremendously since industrialization and is still increasing in some respects today.

- Global inequality has two competing explanations. One stresses how the deficiencies of some societies contribute to their own lack of economic growth. The other stresses how the history of social relations among countries enriched some nations at the expense of others.

- For identifiable reasons, some non-Western countries have successfully industrialized.

- Globalization has both benefits and disadvantages. Various reforms can increase the benefits.

Introduction

The Creation of a Global Village

Suppose you decide to travel to Europe. You might check the Internet to buy an inexpensive ticket. You would then get your passport and perhaps buy a guidebook. Depending on the kind of person you are, you might spend a lot of time planning and preparing for the trip or you might just pack the basics—the passport, the ticket, a knapsack full of clothes, your credit card—and embark on an adventure.

How different things were just 30 years ago. Then, you probably would have gone to see a travel agent first, as most people did when they wanted airline tickets. Next, you would have had to make sure you had not only a valid passport, but also visas for quite a few countries. Obtaining a visa was a tedious process. You had to drive to an embassy or a consulate or mail in your passport. Then you had to wait days or weeks to receive the visa. Today, visas are required for fewer countries. The next step in organizing the European trip would have involved withdrawing money from your bank account. ATMs were still rare. You had to stand in line at the bank before getting to a teller. Next, you had to take the withdrawn money to the office of a company that sold traveler's checks because banks didn't sell them. When you arrived in Europe, you needed to have local currency, which you could buy only in large banks and from moneychangers. Few college students had a credit card 30 years ago. Even if you were one of the lucky few, you could use it only in large stores and restaurants in large cities. If you ran out of cash and traveler's checks, you were in big trouble. You could look for

---

CENGAGENOW™

This icon signals when CengageNOW has important resources available for you to use in conjunction with the text. See the foldout at the front of this text for information on how to access CengageNOW.

Currency conversion, then and now. ▶

Chuck Savage/CORBIS

Ariel Skelley/CORBIS

another American tourist and try to convince him or her to take your personal check. Alternatively, you could go to a special telephone for international calls, phone home, and have money wired to a major bank for you. That was time-consuming and expensive. Today, most people have credit cards and ATM cards. Even in small European towns, you can charge most of your shopping and restaurant bills on your credit card without using local currency. If you need local currency, you go to an ATM and withdraw money from your home bank account or charge it to your credit card; the ATM automatically converts your dollars to local currency.

Most European cities and towns today have many American-style supermarkets. Speakers of English are also numerous, so social interaction with Europeans is easier. You would have to try hard to get very far from a McDonald's. It is also easy to receive news and entertainment from back home on CNN and MTV. In contrast, each country you visited 30 years ago would have featured a distinct shopping experience; English speakers were rarer; and American fast-food outlets were practically nonexistent. Apart from the *International Herald-Tribune,* which was available only in larger towns and cities, American news was hard to come by. TV featured mostly local programming. You might see an American show now and then, but it would not be in English.

Clearly, the world seems a much smaller place today than it did 30 years ago. Some people go so far as to say that we have created a "global village." But what exactly does that mean? Is the creation of a global village uniformly beneficial? Or does it have a downside too? We now explore these questions in depth.

The Triumphs and Tragedies of Globalization

As suggested by our two imaginary trips to Europe, separated by a mere 30 years, people throughout the world are now linked together as never before (▶Table 8.1; ▶Figure 8.1).
Consider these facts:

- International telecommunication has become easy and inexpensive. In 1930, a 3-minute New York–London phone call cost more than $250 in today's dollars and only a minority of Americans had telephones in their homes. In 2009, the same call cost as little as 15¢ and telephones, including cell phones, seem to be everywhere.

- Between 1982 and 2006, when the world's population increased by 41 percent, the number of international tourists increased by 205 percent.

TABLE 8.1

Indicators of Globalization, 1982–2006

	1982	2006	Percent Change
International tourist arrivals (millions of people)	277	846	205
Foreign direct investment (billions of dollars)	59	1,306	2,114
Internet hosts (millions)	0	439	Undefined
Number of international organizations	14,273*	58,859	312

*1981

Sources: Internet Software Consortium (2007); Union of International Associations (2001; 2007); United Nations Conference on Trade and Development (2007: xv); United Nations World Tourism Organization (2007a; 2007b: 2).

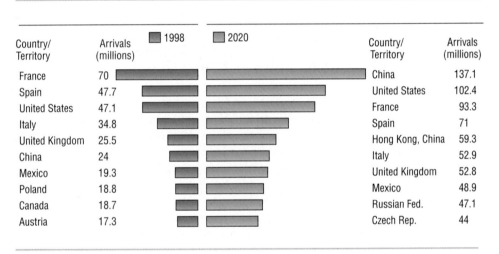

Country/Territory	Arrivals (millions)		Country/Territory	Arrivals (millions)
France	70		China	137.1
Spain	47.7		United States	102.4
United States	47.1		France	93.3
Italy	34.8		Spain	71
United Kingdom	25.5		Hong Kong, China	59.3
China	24		Italy	52.9
Mexico	19.3		United Kingdom	52.8
Poland	18.8		Mexico	48.9
Canada	18.7		Russian Fed.	47.1
Austria	17.3		Czech Rep.	44

■ 1998   ■ 2020

FIGURE 8.1

Foreign Visitors to Top Ten Visited Countries, 1998, and projected 2020 (in millions)

Source: UNESCO (1999).

CENGAGENOW™

Learn more about **Telecommunications** by going through the Mobile Telephones Map Exercise.

● International trade and investment have increased rapidly. For example, from 1982 to 2006, worldwide investment across national borders ("foreign direct investment") increased by a remarkable 2,114 percent.

● Many more international organizations and agreements now span the globe. In 1981, about 14,000 international organizations existed. By 2006, there were three-and-a-half times as many. Individual nation-states give up some of their independence when they join international organizations or sign international agreements. For example, when the United States, by far the world's most powerful country, entered the North American Free Trade Agreement (NAFTA) with Canada and Mexico in 1994, it agreed that three-country tribunals would settle disputes. The autonomy of nation-states has eroded somewhat with the creation of many such "transnational" bodies and treaties.

Technology speeds globalization. Only 125 years separate Pony Express from e-mail.

- The Internet did not exist in 1982, but in 2006 it comprised 439 million servers connecting people from around the world through e-mail, file transfers, websites, and videoconferencing.

These and other indicators point unmistakably to the *globalization* of the planet, which we defined in Chapter 1 as the process by which formerly separate economies, states, and cultures are being tied together and people are becoming increasingly aware of their growing interdependence (Giddens, 1990: 64; Guillén, 2001). Yet, not everyone is happy with globalization. Inequality between rich and poor countries remains staggering. In some respects, it is increasing. Many people also oppose globalization because it may be hurting local cultures and the natural environment. Some antiglobalization activists even suggest that globalization is a form of **imperialism,** the economic domination of one country by another. From their point of view, globalization puts the entire world under the control of powerful commercial interests. Moreover, it contributes to the "homogenization" of the world, the cultural domination of less powerful by more powerful countries. It's one thing, they say, for Indonesians and Italians to have closer ties to Americans, but is it desirable that they become *like* Americans?

In this chapter we explore what globalization is and how it affects our everyday lives. To make the impact of globalization concrete, we first trace the global movement of two commodities familiar to everyone: money and athletic shoes. This exercise illuminates the many ways in which far-flung individuals are bound together. Next, we consider the causes of globalization, emphasizing the importance of political, economic, and technological factors. We then analyze whether globalization is forcing different parts of the world to become alike. We also explore how the very process of globalization generates its own opposition.

The second major task we set ourselves is to examine the nature and causes of global inequality. We note that the gap between rich and poor countries is wide and that by some measures it is getting wider. We then discuss the major theories that seek to explain global inequality and conclude that poor countries are not doomed to remain poor. We close by considering what people can do to alleviate global inequality and poverty.

Imperialism: The economic domination of one country by another.

Globalization

Globalization in Everyday Life

Has anyone ever asked you, "What's that got to do with the price of tea in China?" The question is of course rhetorical. The person who asked it was really saying that whatever you were talking about is as *irrelevant* as the price of tea in China.

Yet, globalization implies that the price of tea in China—and the condition of the rain forest in Brazil, the outcome of Russia's war with Georgia, and the revival of traditional Celtic dance in Ireland—actually do influence your life. Everything influences everything else in a globalized world.

To explore this idea, Barbara Garson (2001) traced a small sum of money she invested in the Chase Manhattan Bank. Garson discovered that the bank almost immediately lent some of her money (along with much additional money) to Caltex, a large U.S. corporation, for the construction of an oil refinery in Thailand. Initially, Thai officials opposed the refinery, mainly because Thai fishers and farmers believed it would pollute and eventually destroy their livelihood and their villages. However, intensive lobbying by American politicians on behalf of Caltex eventually led Thai officials to relent and allow construction. Caltex secured the assistance of the politicians by using some of Garson's money for "political party contributions" (bribes). Some of Garson's money was used to help construct the oil refinery, which did contribute to the destruction of the natural environment and the displacement of farmers and fishers. Eventually, because of an economic downturn in Thailand, the refinery was shut down. When it closed, many Thai oil workers became unemployed. In short, Garson learned that her small investment, together with many other small investments, had huge implications for people's everyday lives on the other side of the planet: "Wherever my money went, it changed the landscape and it changed lives," wrote Garson (2001: 319). Garson's money got caught up in the globalization of the world.

Nike, Michael Jordan, and Global Commodity Chains

The difference between Garson and most of us is that we don't often appreciate that our actions have implications for people far away. Yet, when we buy a commodity, we often tap into a **global commodity chain,** "a [worldwide] network of labor and production processes, whose end result is a finished commodity" (Hopkins and Wallerstein, 1986: 159).

We can better understand the web of global social relations by tracing the way one commodity—athletic shoes—binds consumers and producers in a global commodity chain. Until the 1970s, most sports shoes were manufactured in the United States. Today, corporations such as Nike produce all of their shoes abroad. Manufacturing plants moved because governments eliminated many of the laws, regulations, and taxes that acted as barriers to foreign investment and trade. Consequently, Nike and other manufacturers started setting up overseas plants, where they could take advantage of low labor costs. The result was a new international division of labor. High-wage management, finance, design, and marketing services were concentrated in the United States and other advanced industrial countries; low-wage manufacturing in the less developed, industrializing countries (Fröbel, Heinrichs, and Kreyre, 1980) (see Chapter 13, "Politics, Work, and the Economy"). Not just Nike, but General Motors, General Electric, and many other large corporations closed some or all of their plants in the United States (a high-wage country) and established factories in Mexico, Indonesia, and other countries with low-wage workers.

> **Global commodity chain:** A worldwide network of labor and production processes whose end result is a finished commodity.

Michael Jordan helps globalize Nike.

The new international division of labor yielded high profits. For example, in the 1990s, "Nike spent $5.95 to make a pair of shoes in Indonesia, where workers were paid 14 cents an hour, then sold the shoes in the United States for between $49 and $125" (LaFeber, 1999: 126). Nike's Indonesian workers were not just poorly paid. They had to work as much as 6 hours a day overtime. Reports of beatings and sexual harassment by managers were common. When the workers tried to form a union to protect themselves, union organizers were fired and the military was brought in to restore order (LaFeber, 1999: 142). In 1976 Nike manufactured 70 million shoes in Indonesia but paid its 25,000 workers an average of just over $2 a day. At the same time, Michael Jordan became a spokesman for Nike and was paid a $20 million endorsement fee, more than the combined yearly wages of all the Indonesian workers who made the shoes (LaFeber, 1999: 107).

When people buy Nike athletic shoes, they insert themselves into a global commodity chain. Of course, the buyer doesn't create the social relations that exploit Indonesian labor and enrich Michael Jordan. Still, it would be difficult to deny the buyer's part, however small, in helping those social relations persist.

The Sources of Globalization

Few people doubt the impact of globalization. Although social scientists disagree on its exact causes, most of them stress the importance of technology, politics, and economics.

Technology

Technological progress has made it possible to move objects and information over long distances quickly and inexpensively. The introduction of commercial jets radically shortened the time necessary for international travel, and the cost of such travel dropped dramatically after the 1950s. Similarly, various means of communication, such as telephone, fax, and e-mail, allow us to reach people around the globe inexpensively and almost instantly. Whether we think of international trade or international travel, technological progress is an important part of the story of globalization. Without modern technology, it is hard to imagine how globalization would be possible.

Politics

Globalization could not occur without advanced technology, but advanced technology by itself could never bring globalization about. Think of the contrast between North Korea and South Korea. Both countries are about the same distance from the United States. You have probably heard of major South Korean companies like Hyundai and Samsung and may have met people from South Korea or their descendants, Korean Americans. Yet, unless you are an expert on North Korea, you will have had no contact with North Korea and its people. We have the same technological means to reach the two Koreas. Yet, although we enjoy strong relations and intense interaction with South Korea, we lack ties to North Korea. The reason is political. The South Korean government has been a close ally of the United States since the Korean War in the early 1950s and has sought greater political, economic, and cultural integration with the outside world. North Korea, in an effort to preserve its authoritarian political system and socialist economic system, has remained isolated from the rest of the world. As this example shows, politics is important in determining the level of globalization.

Economics

Finally, economics is an important source of globalization. As we saw in our discussion of global commodity chains and the new international division of labor, industrial capitalism is always seeking new markets, higher profits, and lower labor costs. Put differently, capitalist competition has been a major spur to international integration (Gilpin, 2001).

Transnational corporations—also called multinational or international corporations—are the most important agents of globalization in the world today. They are different from traditional corporations in five ways (Gilpin, 2001; LaFeber, 1999):

1. Traditional corporations rely on domestic labor and domestic production. Transnational corporations depend increasingly on foreign labor and foreign production.

2. Traditional corporations extract natural resources or manufacture industrial goods. Transnational corporations increasingly emphasize skills and advances in design, technology, and management.

3. Traditional corporations sell to domestic markets. Transnational corporations depend increasingly on world markets.

4. Traditional corporations rely on established marketing and sales outlets. Transnational corporations depend increasingly on massive advertising campaigns.

5. Traditional corporations work with or under national governments. Transnational corporations are increasingly autonomous from national governments.

Technological, political, and economic factors do not work independently in leading to globalization. For example, governments often promote economic competition to help transnational corporations win global markets. Consider Philip Morris, the company that made Marlboro cigarettes (Barnet and Cavanagh, 1994) (Philip Morris was renamed Altria in 2003). Philip Morris introduced the Marlboro brand in 1954. It soon became the country's best-selling cigarette, partly because of the success of an advertising campaign featuring the Marlboro Man. The Marlboro Man symbolized the rugged individualism of the American frontier, and he became one of the most widely recognized icons in American advertising. Philip Morris was the smallest of the country's six largest tobacco companies in 1954, but it rode on the popularity of the Marlboro Man to become the country's biggest tobacco company by the 1970s.

In the 1970s, the antismoking campaign began to have an impact, leading to slumping domestic sales. Philip Morris and other tobacco companies decided to pursue globalization as a way out of the doldrums. Economic competition and slick advertising alone did not win global markets for American cigarette makers, however. The tobacco companies needed political influence to make cigarettes one of the country's biggest and most profitable exports. To that end, the U.S. trade representative in the Reagan administration, Clayton Yeutter, worked energetically to dismantle trade barriers in Japan, Taiwan, South Korea, and other countries. He threatened legal action for breaking international trade law and said the United States would restrict Asian exports unless these countries allowed the sale of American cigarettes. Such actions were critically important in globalizing world trade in cigarettes. In 1986, the commercial counselor of the U.S. Embassy in Seoul, South Korea, wrote to the public affairs manager of Philip Morris Asia as follows: "I want to emphasize that the embassy and the various U.S. government agencies in Washington will keep the interests of Philip Morris and the other American cigarette manufacturers in the forefront of our daily concerns" (quoted in Frankel, 1996). As the case of Philip

Transnational corporations: Large businesses that rely increasingly on foreign labor and foreign production; skills and advances in design, technology, and management; world markets; and massive advertising campaigns. They are increasingly autonomous from national governments.

The Marlboro Man in Asia.

John Van Hasselt/CORBIS SYGMA

▶FIGURE 8.2
**The Size and Influence of
the U.S. Economy**

This map indicates the importance of the United States in
globalization by showing that
the economy of each U.S. state
is as big as that of a whole
country. For example, the GDP
of California is equal to that of
France, the GDP of New Jersey is
equal to that of Russia, and the
GDP of Texas is equal to that of
Canada.

Source: "The United States of the
World," *The Globe and Mail*, March
8, 2003, p. F1. Reprinted with permission from *The Globe and Mail*.

Morris illustrates, then, economics and politics typically work hand in hand to globalize
the world.

A World Like the United States?

We have seen that globalization links people around the world, often in ways that are
not obvious. We have also seen that the sources of globalization lie in closely connected
technological, economic, and political forces. Now let us consider one of the consequences
of globalization, the degree to which globalization is "homogenizing" the world and, in
particular, making the whole world look like the United States (▶Figure 8.2).

BOX 8.1
SOCIAL POLICY: WHAT DO YOU THINK?

Should the United States Promote World Democracy?

"In starting and waging a war, it is not right that matters, but victory," said Adolf Hitler (quoted in "A Survey of Human Rights Law," 1998: 10). The same mindset rationalizes state brutality today, from the Serbian attack on Bosnia and Kosovo to the genocide in Darfur in Western Sudan. Cherished ideals, such as political democracy and human rights, are trampled on daily by dictatorships and military governments.

Opinions differ as to what the U.S. government should do about this situation. One influential argument is that of Samuel Huntington (1996). He argues that the United States and other Western nations should not be ethnocentric and impose Western values on people in other countries. If these countries violate democratic principles and human rights, they also express in some way the indigenous values of those people. We should not intervene to stop nondemocratic forces and human rights abuse abroad.

Critics of Huntington argue that the ideals of democracy and human rights can be found in non-Western cultures, too. If we explore Asian or African traditions, for instance, we find "respect for the sacredness of life and for human dignity, tolerance of differences, and a desire for liberty, order, fairness and stability" (quoted in "A Survey of Human Rights Law," 1998: 10). Although Asian and African despots champion supposedly traditional values, people in Asia, Africa, and elsewhere struggle for democracy and human rights.

The United States involvement in Iraq is the most recent exemplar of the dilemma. Just as the U.S. involvement in Vietnam generated a major schism in the country a generation ago, public opinion is deeply divided over the U.S. entanglement in Iraq. A 2006 poll found that 55 percent of Americans believe the war in Iraq has increased the likelihood of terrorist attacks around the world, while only 21 percent believe it has decreased the likelihood of terrorist attacks (Oziewicz, 2006).

Critical Thinking

- What do you think the role of the United States should be in the world?

- Should the United States government promote democracy and human rights? Or should we avoid what Huntington regards as ethnocentrism?

- Because foreign aid to authoritarian regimes may help nondemocratic forces and thereby stifle human rights, should we give foreign aid to such regimes?

- Are war and violence legitimate ways to promote democracy and human rights?

Many economic and financial institutions around the world now operate in roughly the same way. For instance, transnational organizations such as the World Bank and the International Monetary Fund (IMF) have imposed economic guidelines for developing countries that are similar to those governing advanced industrial countries. In the realm of politics, the United Nations (UN) engages in global governance. Western ideas of democracy, representative government, and human rights have become international ideals (Box 8.1). In the domain of culture, American icons circle the planet: supermarkets, basketball, Hollywood movies, Disney characters, Coca-Cola, CNN, McDonald's, and others (Box 8.2).

McDonaldization

A common shorthand expression for the homogenizing effects of globalization is **McDonaldization.** George Ritzer (1996a: 1) defines McDonaldization as "the process by which the principles of the fast-food restaurant are coming to dominate more and more sectors of American society as well as of the rest of the world." The idea of McDonaldization extends Weber's concept of rationalization, the application of the most efficient means to achieve given ends (see Chapter 2, "Culture"). Because of McDonaldization, says Ritzer, the values of efficiency, calculability, and predictability have spread from the United States to the entire planet and from fast-food restaurants to virtually all spheres of life.

McDonaldization: A form of rationalization. Specifically, it refers to the spread of the principles of fast-food restaurants, such as efficiency, predictability, and calculability, to all spheres of life.

BOX 8.2
MASS MEDIA AND SOCIETY

Globalization or Cultural Imperialism?

The United States is the world's biggest exporter of mass media products: films, popular music, TV programs, and so forth. At the same time, it is among the world's smallest importers of mass media products relative to the size of its market. Some Americans relish Dutch cinema, Italian rock music, and Russian TV programs beamed in by satellite—but not many.

American cultural exporters often claim they are the vanguard of cultural globalization. They also assert that the rest of the world wants American media products. The most popular movies in Germany are invariably Hollywood blockbusters, but, media exporters remind us, that is not because anyone is forcing Germans to watch them.

Not everyone in the world is enthusiastic about American mass media products, however. Some people claim that the flood of American movies, music, and TV shows threatens distinctive national cultures and identities. They think of the flood as **media imperialism,** and they periodically call on their governments to control it.

The problem is particularly evident in Canada because the country has a relatively small population (about 32 million people), is close to the United States (more than 80 percent of Canadians live within 100 miles of the American border), and is about 75 percent English-speaking. Excluding Québec, which is largely French-speaking, pop music charts and movie offerings are virtually indistinguishable in the two countries. Private TV broadcasters dominate the Canadian market and rely mainly on American entertainment programming. The widespread use of cable and satellite dishes permits most Canadians to receive American TV programming directly from source (Brym, 2002). Canadian performing artists and media personalities are popular in the United States—think of Avril Lavigne, Lorne Michaels, James Cameron, Jim Carrey, Alanis Morissette, Anne Murray, Shania Twain, Keanu Reeves, Dan Akroyd, Mike Myers, and Céline Dion. They do not, however, export Canadian culture so much as contribute to American culture. Many movies are filmed in Canada, but they are almost all American productions eager to economize by taking advantage of the lower Canadian dollar.

The production of American films in Canada has evoked considerable opposition among some people in the American movie industry because it involves the export of jobs, particularly for technical crews and supporting actors. Resentment may have motivated the writers of *South Park* to pen their Oscar-nominated song, "Blame Canada," in 2001: "It seems that everything's gone wrong / Since Canada came along / Blame Canada / Blame Canada / They're not even a real country anyway."

Critical Thinking

- If Canada is not a "real country" for many Americans, is media imperialism partly to blame?

- Should Canadians care? Should Americans?

Media imperialism: The domination of a mass medium by a single national culture and the undermining of other national cultures.

As Ritzer shows, McDonald's has lunch down to a science. The ingredients used to prepare your meal must meet minimum standards of quality and freshness. Each food item contains identical ingredients. Each portion weighs the same and is prepared according to a uniform and precisely timed process. McDonald's expects customers to spend as little time as possible eating the food—hence the drive-through window, chairs designed to be comfortable for only about 20 minutes, and small express outlets in subways and department stores where customers eat standing up or on the run. McDonald's is even field testing self-service kiosks in which an automated machine cooks and bags French fries while a vertical grill takes patties from the freezer and cooks them to your liking (Carpenter, 2003). In short, McDonald's executives have carefully thought through every aspect of your lunch. They have turned its preparation into a model of rationality. With the goal of making profits, they have optimized food preparation to make it as fast and as inexpensive as possible. Significantly, McDonald's now does most of its business outside the United States. You can find McDonald's restaurants in nearly every country in the world. McDonaldization has come to stand for the global spread of values associated with the United States and its business culture.

Glocalization and Symbolic Interactionism

Despite the appeal of the concept of McDonaldization, anyone familiar with symbolic interactionism should be immediately suspicious of sweeping claims about the homogenizing effects of globalization. After all, it is a central principle of symbolic interactionism that people create their social circumstances, that they negotiate their identities and do not easily settle for identities imposed on them by others.

Accordingly, some analysts find fault with the view that globalization is making the world a more homogeneous place based on American values. They argue that people always *interpret* globalizing forces in terms of local conditions and traditions. Globalization, they say, may in fact sharpen some local differences. They have invented the term **glocalization** to describe the simultaneous homogenization of some aspects of life and the strengthening of some local differences under the impact of globalization (Shaw, 2000). They note, for example, that McDonald's serves different foods in different countries (Watson, 1997). Vegetarian burgers are the norm at an Indian McDonald's, as are kosher burgers at an Israeli McDonald's. The Dutch McDonald's serves the popular McKrocket, made of 100 percent beef ragout fried in batter. In Hawaii, McDonald's routinely serves Japanese ramen noodles with burgers. Although the Golden Arches may suggest that the world is becoming the same everywhere, once we go through them and sample the fare, we find much that is unique.

Regionalization

Those who see globalization merely as homogenization also ignore the **regionalization** of the world, the division of the world into different and often competing economic, political, and cultural areas. The argument here is that the institutional and cultural integration of countries often falls far short of covering the whole world. ❙Figure 8.3 illustrates one aspect of regionalization. Three main trade blocs exist—an Asian bloc dominated by Japan and, increasingly, China; a North American bloc dominated by the United States; and a European bloc dominated by Germany. These three trade blocs contain just over one-fifth of the world's countries but account for more than three-quarters of world economic activity as measured by Gross Domestic Product.[1] Most world trade takes place *within* each of these blocs. Each bloc competes against the others for a larger share of world trade. Politically, we can see regionalization in the growth of the European Union. Most European–bloc countries now share the same currency, the euro, and they coordinate economic, political, military, social, and cultural policies.

We conclude that globalization does not have a simple, one-way, and inevitable consequence. In fact, as you will now learn, its impact is often messy. Globalization has generated much criticism and opposition, unleashing a growing antiglobalization movement.

Globalization and Its Discontents: Antiglobalization and Anti-Americanism

In 1992 political scientist Benjamin Barber published an important book titled *Jihad vs. McWorld*. Barber argued that globalization (the making of what he called "McWorld") was generating an antiglobalization reaction, which he called *jihad*. *Jihad* means "striving" or "struggle" in Arabic. Traditionally, Muslims use the term to mean perseverance in achieving a high moral standard. The term can also suggest the idea of a holy war against

Glocalization: The simultaneous homogenization of some aspects of life and the strengthening of some local differences under the impact of globalization.

Regionalization: The division of the world into different and often competing economic, political, and cultural areas.

---

[1]Gross National Product (GNP) is the total dollar value of goods and services produced in a country in a year. It allocates goods and services based on the *nationality* of the owners. GDP is a similar measure, but it allocates goods and services based on the *location* of the owners. So, for example, goods and services produced overseas by foreign subsidiaries would be included in GNP but not in GDP.

▶FIGURE 8.3
Regionalization of World Trade

Source: York (2006).

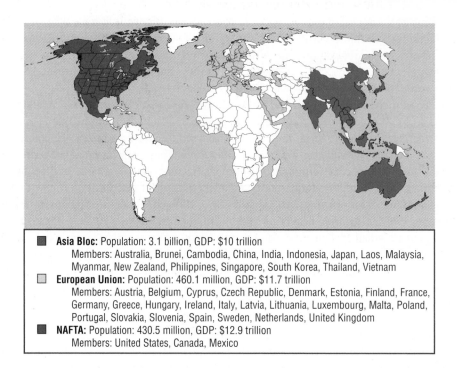

Asia Bloc: Population: 3.1 billion, GDP: $10 trillion
Members: Australia, Brunei, Cambodia, China, India, Indonesia, Japan, Laos, Malaysia, Myanmar, New Zealand, Philippines, Singapore, South Korea, Thailand, Vietnam
European Union: Population: 460.1 million, GDP: $11.7 trillion
Members: Austria, Belgium, Cyprus, Czech Republic, Denmark, Estonia, Finland, France, Germany, Greece, Hungary, Ireland, Italy, Latvia, Lithuania, Luxembourg, Malta, Poland, Portugal, Slovakia, Slovenia, Spain, Sweden, Netherlands, United Kingdom
NAFTA: Population: 430.5 million, GDP: $12.9 trillion
Members: United States, Canada, Mexico

those who harm Muslims. In the latter sense, it represents an Islamic fundamentalist reaction to globalization. The most spectacular and devastating manifestations of fundamentalist Islamic *jihad* were the September 11, 2001, jet hijackings that led to the crash of an airliner in Pennsylvania and the destruction of the World Trade Center and part of the Pentagon. About 3,000 people, the great majority Americans, lost their lives as a result of these attacks. The operatives of the al Qaeda network sought to roll back the forces of globalization by attacking what they thought symbolized the global reach of godless American capitalism.

Islamic fundamentalism is the most far-reaching and violent of many reactions against globalization throughout the world. A well-known but less violent example involves Mexican peasants in the southern state of Chiapas, who staged an armed rebellion against the Mexican government in the 1990s. The government provoked the peasants by turning over land that was long regarded as communally owned to commercial farmers so that they could increase their exports to the United States and Canada under the terms of NAFTA. The uprising involved violence and lasted several years.

Finally, we should mention the relatively nonviolent antiglobalization movement in the advanced industrial countries (Klein, 2000). In 1994, the governments of 134 countries set up the World Trade Organization (WTO) to encourage and referee global commerce. When the WTO met in Seattle in December 1999, 40,000 union activists, environmentalists, supporters of worker and peasant movements in developing countries, and other opponents of transnational corporations staged protests that caused property damage and threatened to disrupt the proceedings. The police and the National Guard replied with concussion grenades, tear gas, rubber bullets, and mass arrests.

Subsequent meetings of the WTO and allied organizations in other countries met with the same sort of protest on the part of antiglobalization forces. These protests were for the most part nonviolent, often using street drama to make their point. For example, in spring 2001, 34 heads of government from North, Central, and South America and the Caribbean gathered in Québec City to discuss the economic integration of the Americas and related matters. Among other tactics, protesters built large wooden catapults that launched volleys of miniature teddy bears at the riot police.

These examples illustrate that although globalization is far from universally welcome, the antiglobalization movement has many currents. Some are extremely violent, some nonviolent. Some reject only what they regard as the excesses of globalization, others reject globalization in its entirety. This complexity supports our view that globalization is not a simple process with predictable consequences. Beginning in earnest about 500 years ago during the era of European exploration and conquest, globalization is a multifaceted phenomenon, the outcome of which is unclear. One thing is clear, however. Some aspects of globalization have opened up a growing gap between rich and poor countries and between rich and poor people. How this came about will now be the focus of our attention.

Global Inequality

Personal Anecdote

John Lie decided to study sociology because he was concerned about the poverty and dictatorships he had read about in books and observed during his travels in Asia and Latin America. "Initially," says John, "I thought I would major in economics. In my economics classes, I learned about the importance of birth-control programs to cap population growth, efforts to prevent the runaway growth of cities, and measures to spread Western knowledge, technology, and markets to people in less economically developed countries. My textbooks and professors assumed that if only the less developed countries would become more like the West, their populations, cities, economies, and societies would experience stable growth. Otherwise, the developing countries were doomed to suffer the triple catastrophe of overpopulation, rapid urbanization, and economic underdevelopment.

"Equipped with this knowledge, I spent a summer in the Philippines working for an organization that offered farmers advice on how to promote economic growth. I assumed that, as in North America, farmers who owned large plots of land and used high technology would be more efficient and better off. Yet I found the most productive villages were those in which most farmers owned *small* plots of land. In such villages, there was little economic inequality. The women in these villages enjoyed low birthrates and the inhabitants were usually happier than the inhabitants of villages in which there was more inequality.

"As I talked with the villagers, I came to realize that farmers who owned at least some of their own land had an incentive to work hard. The harder they worked, the more they earned. With a higher standard of living, they didn't need as many children to help them on the farm. In contrast, in villages with greater inequality, many farmers owned no land but leased it or worked as farm hands for wealthy landlords. They didn't earn more for working harder, so their productivity and their standard of living were low. They wanted to have more children to increase household income.

"Few Filipino farms could match the productivity of high-tech American farms because even large plots were small by American standards. Much high-tech agricultural equipment would have been useless there. Imagine trying to use a harvesting machine in a plot not much larger than some suburban backyards.

"Thus, my Western assumptions turned out to be wrong. The Filipino farmers I met were knowledgeable and thoughtful about their needs and desires. When I started listening to them I started understanding the real world of economic development. It was one of the most important sociological lessons I ever learned."

CENGAGENOW™

Learn more about **Global Inequality** by going through the Global Stratification Data Experiment.

Let us begin our sociological discussion of economic development by examining trends in levels of global inequality. We then discuss two theories of development and underdevelopment, both of which seek to uncover the sources of inequality among nations. Next, we analyze some cases of successful development. Finally, we consider what we can do to alleviate global inequality in light of what we learn from these successful cases.

Levels of Global Inequality

We learned in Chapter 7 ("Social Stratification: United States and Global Perspectives") that the United States is a highly stratified society. If we shift our attention from the national to the global level, we find an even more dramatic gap between rich and poor. In a Manhattan restaurant, pet owners can treat their cats to $100-a-plate birthday parties. In Cairo (Egypt) and Manila (Philippines), garbage dumps are home to entire families who sustain themselves by picking through the refuse. People who travel outside the 20 or so highly industrialized countries of North America, western Europe, Japan, and Australia often encounter scenes of unforgettable poverty and misery. The UN calls the level of inequality worldwide "grotesque" (United Nations, 2002: 19).

A half-hour's drive from the center of Manila, the capital of the Philippines, an estimated 70,000 Filipinos live on a 55-acre mountain of rotting garbage, 150 feet high. It is infested with flies, rats, dogs, and disease. On a lucky day, residents can earn up to $5 retrieving scraps of metal and other valuables. On a rainy day, the mountain of garbage is especially treacherous. In July 2000 an avalanche buried 300 people alive. People who live on the mountain of garbage call it "The Promised Land."

Francis Malasig/epa/Corbis

The average income of citizens in the highly industrialized countries far outstrips that of citizens in the developing societies. Yet because poor people live in rich countries and rich people live in poor countries, these averages fail to capture the extent of inequality between the richest of the rich and the poorest of the poor. It is perhaps more revealing to note that the richest 1 percent of the world's population earns as much income as the bottom 57 percent. The top 10 percent of U.S. income earners earn as much as the poorest 2 billion people in the world (United Nations, 2002). Of the world's 6.5 billion people, around 1 billion live on less than $1 a day and 2.6 billion live on less than $2 a day. The citizens of the 20 or so rich, highly industrialized countries spend more on cosmetics or alcohol or ice cream or pet food than it would take to provide basic education, or water and sanitation, or basic health and nutrition for everyone in the world. Just 10 percent of world trade in narcotics or 5 percent of world military spending could supply these necessities to the world's desperately poor (▶Table 8.2).

▶**TABLE 8.2**

Global Priorities: Annual Cost of Various Goods and Services

Good/Service	Annual Cost (in U.S. $ billion)
Basic education for everyone in the world	6
Cosmetics in the United States	8
Water and sanitation for everyone in the world	9
Ice cream in Europe	11
Reproductive health for all women in the world	12
Perfumes in Europe and the United States	12
Basic health and nutrition for everyone in the world	13
Pet foods in Europe and the United States	17
Business entertainment in Japan	35
Cigarettes in Europe	50
Alcoholic drinks in Europe	105
Narcotic drugs in the world	400
Military spending in the world	780

Note: Items in italics represent estimates of what they would cost to achieve. Other items represent estimated actual cost.
Source: United Nations (1998b: 37).

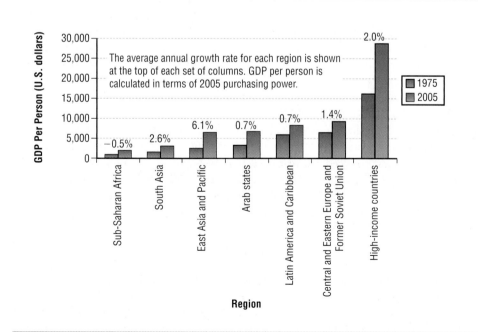

▶FIGURE 8.4

Gross Domestic Product per Person, World Regions, 1975–2005 (in 2005 U.S. dollars)

Source: From Human Development Report 2007/2008, United Nations Development Programme, p. 280. Reprinted with permission of Palgrave Macmillan.

▶TABLE 8.3

Trends in Global Inequality, 1820–1992

	1820	1870	1910	1929	1950	1970	1992
Percentage of world income going to top 10%	42.8	47.6	50.9	49.8	51.3	50.8	53.4
Percentage of world income going to bottom 20%	4.7	3.8	3.0	2.9	2.4	2.2	2.2
Percentage of people living on $1 a day or less, adjusted for inflation	3.9	75.4	65.6	56.3	54.8	35.6	23.7
Number of people living on $1 a day or less, adjusted for inflation (millions)	887	954	1128	1150	1376	1305	1294

Source: Centre for Economic Policy Research (2002: 57).

▶TABLE 8.4

Percent of People Living on Less Than $1 a Day, by Region, 1990–2015 (projected, in 1993 U.S. dollars)

Region	1990	2004	2015
Sub-Saharan Africa	46.7	41.1	31.4
East Asia and Pacific	29.8	9.0	2.8
South Asia	43.0	30.8	15.1
Latin America and Caribbean	10.2	8.6	5.1
Europe and Central Asia	0.5	0.9	0.2
Middle East and North Africa	2.3	1.5	1.2
Total	29.0	18.0	10.0

Sources: From Human Development Report 2002 by United Nations Development Programme, copyright © 2002 by the United Nations Development Programme. Used by permission of Oxford University Press; World Bank (2008).

Of the 1.3 billion people around the world living on $1 a day or less, 1 billion of them are women. Of the estimated 854 million illiterate adults in the world, 64 percent of them are women (United Nations, 2002). Moreover, racial and other minority groups often fare worse than their majority-group counterparts in the developing countries. For example, almost all South African whites are literate, compared with a literacy rate of 50 percent among blacks. The average life expectancy for whites in South Africa is 70 years, whereas the corresponding figure for blacks is 59 (United Nations, 1998b).

Trends in Global Inequality

Has global inequality increased or decreased over time? ▶Figure 8.4 helps answer that question by focusing on Gross Domestic Product (GDP) per person—the dollar value of goods and services produced in a year in each of the world's major regions divided by the number of people in that region. Between 1975 and 2005, the GDP gap between the 20 or so richest countries and the rest of the world grew enormously. GDP per person grew slowly in the Arab countries and in Latin America and the Caribbean. In sub-Saharan Africa, it actually fell. ▶Table 8.3 focuses on individual rather than regional income. It shows that the share of world income going to the top 10 percent of individuals increased from 42.8 percent in 1820 to 53.4 percent in 1992. Over that same period, the share of world income going to the bottom 20 percent of individuals fell from 4.7 percent to just 2.2 percent. That trend has continued since 1992.

On the brighter side, the actual number of people in the world living on less than $1 a day peaked in 1950 and then started declining. In percentage terms, the proportion of people living in extreme poverty fell from 83.9 percent in 1820 to 18 percent in 2004 and is projected to decline to 10 percent by 2015 (United Nations, 2007: 24; World Bank, 2008; see ▶Table 8.4). However, two regions have so far benefited little from the decline. Between 1981 and 2004, the percentage of people in Latin America and the Caribbean earning less than $1 a day declined only 1.6 percent. In sub-Saharan Africa, the percentage fell only 0.5 percent in that same period. These figures give little cause for joy.

Like all facts, statistics never speak for themselves. We need theories to interpret them. We now outline and critically assess the two main theories that seek to explain the origins and persistence of global inequality.

Theories of Development and Underdevelopment

Modernization Theory: A Functionalist Approach

Two main sociological theories claim to explain global inequality. The first, **modernization theory,** is a variant of functionalism. According to modernization theory, global inequality results from various dysfunctional characteristics of poor societies. Specifically, modernization theorists say that the citizens of poor societies lack sufficient *capital* to invest in agriculture and industry. They lack rational, Western-style *business techniques*. They lack stable, Western-style *governments* that could provide a secure framework for investment. Finally, they lack a Western *mentality:* values that stress the need for savings, investment, innovation, education, high achievement, and self-control in having children (Inkeles and Smith, 1976; Rostow, 1960). It follows that people living in rich countries can best help their poor cousins by transferring Western culture and capital to them and eliminating the dysfunctions. Only then will the poor countries be able to cap population growth, stimulate democracy, and invigorate agricultural and industrial production. Government-to-government foreign aid can accomplish some of this. Much work also needs to be done to encourage Western businesses to invest directly in poor countries and increase trade between rich and poor countries.

Dependency Theory: A Conflict Approach

Proponents of **dependency theory,** a variant of conflict theory, have been quick to point out the chief flaw in modernization theory (Baran, 1957; Cardoso and Faletto, 1979). For the last 500 years, the most powerful countries in the world deliberately impoverished the less powerful countries. Focusing on internal characteristics blames the victim rather than the perpetrator of the crime. It follows that an adequate theory of global inequality should not focus on the internal characteristics of poor countries themselves. Instead, it ought to follow the principles of conflict theory and focus on patterns of domination and submission—specifically, in this case, on the relationship between rich and poor countries. That is just what dependency theory does.

According to dependency theorists, less global inequality existed in 1500 and even in 1750 than today. However, beginning around 1500, the armed forces of the world's most powerful countries subdued and then annexed or colonized most of the rest of the world. Around 1780 the Industrial Revolution began. It enabled the western European countries, Russia, Japan, and the United States to amass enormous wealth, which they used to extend their global reach. They forced their colonies to become a source of raw materials, cheap labor, investment opportunities, and markets for the conquering nations. The colonizers

Modernization theory: Holds that economic underdevelopment results from poor countries lacking Western attributes, including Western values, business practices, levels of investment capital, and stable governments.

Dependency theory: Explains economic underdevelopment as the consequence of exploitative relations between rich and poor countries.

In 1893 leaders of the British mission pose before taking over what became Rhodesia and is now Zimbabwe. To raise a volunteer army, every British trooper was offered about 9 square miles of native land and 20 gold claims. The Matabele and Mashona peoples were subdued in a 3-month war. Nine hundred farms and 10,000 gold claims were granted to the troopers and about 100,000 cattle were looted, leaving the native survivors without a livelihood. Forced labor was subsequently introduced by the British so that the natives could pay a £2 per year tax.

thereby prevented industrialization and locked the colonies into poverty.

In the decades following World War II, nearly all of the colonies in the world became politically independent. However, dependency theorists say that exploitation by direct political control was soon replaced by new means of achieving the same end: substantial foreign investment, support for authoritarian governments, and mounting debt.

Substantial Foreign Investment

Multinational corporations invested in the poor countries to siphon off wealth in the form of raw materials and profits. True, they created some low-paying jobs in the process. But they created many more high-paying jobs in the rich countries where the raw materials were used to produce manufactured goods. They also sold part of the manufactured goods back to the poor, unindustrialized countries for additional profit.

Support for Authoritarian Governments

According to dependency theorists, multinational corporations and rich countries continued their exploitation of the poor countries in the postcolonial period by giving economic and military support to local authoritarian governments. These governments managed to keep their populations subdued most of the time. When that was not possible, Western governments sent in troops and military advisers, engaging in what became known as "gunboat diplomacy." The term itself was coined in colonial times. In 1839 the Chinese rebelled against the British importation of opium into China, and the British responded by sending a gunboat up the Yangtze River, starting the Opium War. The war resulted in Britain winning control of Hong Kong and access to five Chinese ports; what started as gunboat diplomacy ended as a rich feast for British traders. In the postcolonial period, the United States has been particularly active in using gunboat diplomacy in Central America. A classic case is Guatemala in the 1950s (LaFeber, 1993). In 1952 the democratically elected government of Guatemala began to redistribute land to impoverished peasants. Some of the land was owned by the United Fruit Company, a U.S. multinational corporation and the biggest landowner in Guatemala. Two years later, the U.S. Central Intelligence Agency (CIA) backed a right-wing coup in Guatemala, preventing land reform and allowing the United Fruit Company to continue its highly profitable business.

Mounting Debt

The governments of the poor countries struggled to create transportation infrastructures (airports, roads, harbors, etc.), build up their education systems, and deliver safe water and at least the most basic health care to their people. To accomplish these tasks, they had to borrow money from Western banks and governments. So it came about that debt—and the interest payments that inevitably accompany debt—grew every year. By 2005 the total debt of poor countries amounted to $523 billion (African countries owed $300 billion). Debt service—that is, interest payments—were $100 million a day. Bolivia—the poorest country in Latin America—spends half of its export income to service its external debt. For every African, $14 is used to service debt, while only $5 is geared toward health care. Foreign aid helps, but not very much.

For every dollar in foreign aid, poor countries pay $2.30 to service debt (Jubilee Debt Campaign, 2005).

Effects of Foreign Investment

Almost all sociologists agree that the dependency theorists are correct on one score. After about 1500, Spain, Portugal, Holland, Britain, France, Italy, the United States, Japan, and Russia treated the world's poor with brutality to enrich themselves. They rationalized their actions by claiming they were bringing "civilization" to the "savages" and inventing other such stories, such as the notion of the Dutch colonizers in early 17th-century Brazil that "there is no sin south of the equator." **Colonialism**—the political control of developing societies by more powerful, developed societies—did have a devastating economic and human impact on the poor countries of the world. In the postcolonial era, the debt burden has crippled the development efforts of many poor countries.

That said, a big question remains that research has not yet fully answered. Do foreign investment and liberalized trade policies have positive or negative effects today? Much hinges on the answer to this question. Modernization theorists want more foreign investment in poor countries and freer trade. They strongly believe that following these policies will promote economic growth and general well-being. They want trade and investment barriers to be dropped so free markets can bring prosperity to everyone. Dependency theorists diametrically oppose this strategy. They think that foreign investment drains wealth out of poor countries. Therefore, they want the poor countries to rebel against the rich countries, throw up barriers to free trade and investment, and find their own paths to economic well-being.

Over the past few decades, researchers have carefully examined the effects of free trade and foreign investment. The results of their analyses depend partly on which variables, time periods, and countries they consider and which statistical techniques they use (Bornschier and Chase-Dunn, 1985; DeSoya and Oneal, 1999; Firebaugh and Beck, 1994; Weisbrot and Baker, 2002). Not surprisingly, if you throw different countries, variables, time periods, and statistical techniques into the mix, you bake entirely different cakes. Yet, a summary of research in this area cautiously reaches two conclusions (Centre for Economic Policy Research, 2002). First, openness to international trade and foreign investment generally stimulated economic growth in the 1980s and 1990s, but not in the 1960s and 1970s. Second, openness to international trade and foreign investment usually increased inequality, but in some cases, such as Brazil and Indonesia, it did not.[2]

These findings suggest that it is a mistake to lump all periods of history and all countries together when considering the effects of openness on economic growth and inequality. After all, countries have different histories and different social structures. They may adopt a variety of economic policies that influence the effects of international trade and foreign direct investment in different ways. Consequently, international trade and foreign direct investment may have different effects in different times and places. Historical, social-structural, and policy factors matter greatly in determining how a particular country responds to international trade and foreign direct investment. This point becomes clear if we examine the different development paths taken by "core," "peripheral," and "semi-peripheral" countries.

---

[2]The effect of free trade and foreign investment on highly developed countries is similarly diverse. In the 1980s and 1990s, the United States and the United Kingdom experienced increasing inequality as a result of openness, whereas Canada, France, and Germany did not. In the latter countries, government tax and welfare policies prevented inequality from growing.

Colonialism: The political control of developing societies by more powerful, developed societies.

Core, Periphery, and Semiperiphery

Immanuel Wallerstein (1974–93) proposes a variation on this theme. He argues that capitalist development has resulted in the creation of an integrated "world system" composed of three tiers. First are the **core capitalist countries** (the United States, Japan, and Germany), which are major sources of capital and technology. Second are the **peripheral capitalist countries** (the former colonies, such as Guatemala and Angola), which are major sources of raw materials and cheap labor. Third are the **semiperipheral capitalist countries** (such as South Korea, Taiwan, and Israel), consisting of former colonies that are making considerable headway in their attempts to become prosperous. To give just one dramatic illustration of this progress, South Korea and the African country of Ghana were among the poorest nations in the world in 1960. Ghana still is. But South Korea was nine times wealthier than Ghana by 1997 (as measured by Gross National Product [GNP] per capita; calculated from World Bank, 1999: 193). Comparing the unsuccessful peripheral countries with the more successful semiperipheral countries presents us with a useful natural experiment. The comparison suggests circumstances that help some poor countries overcome the worst effects of colonialism.

The semiperipheral countries differ from the peripheral countries in four main ways (Kennedy, 1993: 193–227; Lie, 1998):

1. *Type of colonialism.* Around the turn of the 20th century, Taiwan and Korea became colonies of Japan. They remained so until 1945. However, in contrast to the European colonizers of Africa, Latin America, and other parts of Asia, the Japanese built up the economies of their colonies. They established transportation networks and communication systems. They built steel, chemical, and hydroelectric power plants. After Japanese colonialism ended, Taiwan and South Korea were thus at an advantage compared with Ghana, for example, at the time Britain gave up control of that country. South Korea and Taiwan could use the Japanese-built infrastructure and Japanese-trained personnel as springboards to development.

2. *Geopolitical position.* Although the United States was the leading economic and military power in the world by the end of World War II, it began to feel its supremacy threatened in the late 1940s by the Soviet Union and China. Fearing that South Korea and Taiwan might fall to the communists, the United States poured unprecedented aid into both countries in the 1960s. It also gave them large, low-interest loans and opened its domestic market to Taiwanese and South Korean products. Because the United States saw Israel as a crucially important ally in the Middle East, it also received special economic assistance. Other countries with less strategic importance to the United States received less help in their drive to industrialize.

3. *State policy.* A third factor that accounts for the relative success of some countries in their efforts to industrialize and become prosperous has to do with state policies. As a legacy of colonialism, the Taiwanese and South Korean states were developed on the Japanese model. They kept workers' wages low, restricted trade union growth, and maintained quasi-military discipline in factories. Moreover, by placing high taxes on consumer goods, limiting the import of foreign goods, and preventing their citizens from investing abroad, they encouraged their citizens to put much of their money in the bank. This situation created a large pool of capital for industrial expansion. The South Korean and Taiwanese states also gave subsidies, training grants, and tariff protection to export-based industries from the 1960s onward. (Tariffs are taxes on foreign goods.) These policies did much to stimulate industrial growth. Finally, the Taiwanese and South Korean states invested heavily in basic education, health care,

Core capitalist countries: Capitalist countries that are rich and are the major sources of capital and technology in the world: the United States, Japan, and Germany.

Peripheral capitalist countries: Countries that are former colonies; they are poor and are major sources of raw materials and cheap labor.

Semiperipheral capitalist countries: Countries, comprising former colonies, that are making considerable headway in their attempts to industrialize, such as South Korea, Taiwan, and Israel.

roads, and other public goods. A healthy and well-educated labor force combined with good transportation and communication systems laid solid foundations for economic growth.

4. *Social structure.* Taiwan and South Korea are socially cohesive countries. This fact makes it easy for them to generate consensus about development policies. It also allows them to get their citizens to work hard, save a lot of money, and devote their energies to scientific education.

Social solidarity in Taiwan and South Korea is based partly on the sweeping land reform both countries conducted in the late 1940s and early 1950s. By redistributing land to small farmers, both countries eliminated the class of large landowners, who usually oppose industrialization. Land redistribution got rid of a major potential source of social conflict. In contrast, many countries in Latin America and Africa have not undergone land reform. The United States often intervened militarily in Latin America to prevent land reform because U.S. commercial interests profited handsomely from the existence of large plantations (LaFeber, 1993).

Another factor underlying social solidarity in Taiwan and South Korea is that neither country suffers from internal conflicts like those that wrack Africa south of the Sahara desert. British, French, and other western European colonizers often drew the borders of African countries to keep antagonistic tribes living side-by-side in the same jurisdiction and often sought to foment tribal conflict. Keeping tribal tensions alive made it possible to play one tribe against another. That made it easier for imperial powers to rule. This policy led to much social and political conflict in postcolonial Africa. Today, the region suffers from frequent civil wars, coups, and uprisings. It is the most conflict-ridden area of the world. This high level of internal conflict acts as a barrier to economic development in sub-Saharan Africa.

In sum, certain conditions seem to permit foreign investment to have positive economic effects. Postcolonial countries that enjoy a solid industrial infrastructure, strategic geopolitical importance, strong states with strong development policies, and socially cohesive populations are in the best position to join the ranks of the rich countries in the coming decades. We may expect countries that have *some* of these characteristics to experience some economic growth and increase in the well-being of their populations in the near future. Such countries include Chile, Thailand, Indonesia, Mexico, China, India, and Brazil. In contrast, African countries south of the Sahara are in the worst position of all. They have inherited the most damaging consequences of colonialism, and they enjoy few of the conditions that could help them escape the history that has been imposed on them.

Neoliberal versus Democratic Globalization

Globalization and Neoliberalism

For some political and economic leaders, the road sign that marks the path to prosperity reads "neoliberal globalization." **Neoliberal globalization** is a policy that promotes private control of industry and minimal government interference in the running of the economy. Advocates of neoliberal globalization also support foreign investment and the removal of taxes, tariffs, and restrictive regulations that discourage the international buying and selling of goods and services. They resemble the modernization theorists of a generation ago. They believe that if the poor countries emulate the successful habits of the rich countries, they will prosper too.

Neoliberal globalization: A policy that promotes private control of industry, minimal government interference in the running of the economy, the removal of taxes, tariffs, and restrictive regulations that discourage the international buying and selling of goods and services, and the encouragement of foreign investment.

China has sustained an unprecedented economic growth rate of more than 9 percent since 1978. It is likely to become the next core capitalist country. Shanghai, shown here, is China's financial and trade center and the country's major port.

Panorama Images/The Image Works

Many social scientists are skeptical of their prescription. For example, Nobel Prize–winning economist and former chief economist of the World Bank Joseph E. Stiglitz (2002) argues that the World Bank and other international economic organizations often impose outdated policies on developing countries, putting them at a disadvantage vis-à-vis developed countries. In the African country of Mozambique, for example, foreign debt was 4.5 times GNP in the mid-1990s. This means that the amount of money Mozambique owed to foreigners was four and a half times more than the value of goods and services produced by all the people of Mozambique in a year. Facing an economic crisis, Mozambique sought relief from the World Bank and the IMF. The response of the IMF was to argue that Mozambique's government-imposed minimum wage of less than $1 a day was "excessive." The IMF also recommended that Mozambique spend twice as much as its education budget and four times as much as its health budget on interest payments to service its foreign debt (Mittelman, 2000: 104). How such crippling policies might help the people of Mozambique is unclear.

Does Neoliberalism Work?

Does historical precedent lead us to believe that neoliberalism works? To the contrary, with the exception of Great Britain, neoliberalism was *never* a successful development strategy in the early stages of industrialization. Germany, the United States, Japan, Sweden, and other rich countries became highly developed economically between the second half of the 19th century and the early 20th century. South Korea, Taiwan, and a few other semiperipheral countries became highly developed economically in the second half of the 20th century. Today, China and India are industrializing quickly. These countries did not pursue privatization, minimal government intervention in the economy, free trade, and foreign investment in the early stages of industrialization. Rather, the governments of these countries typically intervened to encourage industrialization. They protected infant industries behind tariff walls, invested public money heavily to promote national industries, and so forth. Today, China and India maintain among the highest barriers to international trade in the world (Chang, 2002; Gerschenkron, 1962).

Even the United States, the most vocal advocate of neoliberal globalization today, invested a great deal of public money subsidizing industries and building infrastructure (roads, schools, ports, airports, electricity grids, etc.) in the late 19th and early 20th centuries. It was an extremely protectionist country until the end of World War II. As late as 1930 the Smoot-Hawley Tariff Act raised tariffs on foreign goods 60 percent. Today, the United States still subsidizes large corporations in a variety of ways and maintains substantial tariffs on a range of foreign products, including agricultural goods and textiles. In the first decade of the 21st century, the cry for measures to protect American jobs grew loud as many large corporations "outsourced" hundreds of thousands of middle-class American jobs to China, India, Poland, and elsewhere. In its protectionism, the United States is little different from Japan, France, and other rich countries.

In sum, there is good reason to be skeptical about the benefits of neoliberal globalization for poor countries (Bourdieu, 1998; Brennan, 2003). Yet, as you will now see, globalization can be reformed so that its economic and technological benefits are distributed more uniformly throughout the world. Let us consider four widely discussed types of action.

Globalization Reform

Foreign Aid

Even if the United States increased its foreign aid budget by more than 400 percent to meet UN guidelines, some foreign aid as presently delivered is not an effective way of helping the developing world (Box 8.3). Foreign aid is often accompanied by high administrative and overhead costs. It is often given on condition that it be used to buy from donor countries goods that are not necessarily high-priority items for recipient countries. Some foreign aid organizations, such as Oxfam and Catholic Relief Services, waste little money on administration and overhead expenses because they are driven by high principles, pay their staffs low salaries, build partnerships with reputable local organizations, work with their partners to identify the most pressing needs of poor countries, and focus their efforts on meeting those needs (Ron, 2007). Their efforts remind us that foreign aid can be beneficial and that strict oversight is required to ensure that foreign aid is not wasted and is directed to truly helpful projects, such as improving irrigation and sanitation systems and helping people acquire better farming techniques. Increasing the amount of foreign aid and redesigning its delivery can thus help mitigate some of the excesses of neoliberal globalization.

Debt Cancellation

Many analysts argue that the world's rich countries and banks should write off the debt owed to them by the developing countries in recognition of historical injustices. They reason that the debt burden of the developing countries is so onerous that it prevents them from focusing on building economic infrastructure, improving the health and education of their populations, and developing economic policies that can help them emerge from poverty. This proposal for blunting the worst effects of neoliberal globalization is growing in popularity among politicians in the developed countries. Former British prime minister Tony Blair, former president Bill Clinton, and former Canadian prime minister Paul Martin, among others, support the idea.

Tariff Reduction

A third reform proposed in recent years involves the reduction of tariffs by the *rich* countries. Many of these tariffs prevent developing countries from exporting goods that could earn them money for investment in agriculture, industry, and infrastructure. The

BOX 8.3
YOU AND THE SOCIAL WORLD

In the film *About Schmidt* (2002), Jack Nicholson plays Warren Schmidt, a former insurance executive. Retirement leaves Schmidt with little purpose in life. His wife dies. His adult daughter has little time or respect for him. He feels his existence lacks meaning. Then, while watching TV one night, Schmidt is moved to support a poor child in a developing country. He decides to send a monthly $27 check to sponsor an orphaned Tanzanian boy named Ndugu. He writes Ndugu long letters about his life. While Schmidt's world falls apart before our eyes, his sole meaningful human bond is with Ndugu. At the end of the movie, Schmidt cries as he looks at a picture Ndugu drew for him: an adult holding a child's hand.

Foreign Aid and Personal Responsibility

It does not take a Warren Schmidt to find meaning in helping the desperately poor. Many people contribute to charities that help developing countries in a variety of ways. Many more people contribute development aid indirectly through the taxes they pay to the federal government. Many Americans think our contributions are generous.

Do you? If you happen to think that we, like all members of the rich nations, have a responsibility to compensate for centuries of injustice and that we are spending too little on foreign aid, you are in a minority. The General Social Survey (GSS) periodically asks respondents whether the United States is spending too much, too little, or about the right amount on 16 items, including foreign aid. ▶Table 8.4 shows the results for 2006. Foreign aid ranks a distant last on Americans' list of priorities. The government seems responsive to public sentiment in this regard. The UN urges the world's 22 richest countries to contribute 0.7 percent of their GDP to development aid. In 2006, only 5 countries reached that goal: Norway, Denmark, the Netherlands, Luxembourg, and Sweden. The United States ranked 20th among the 22 rich nations at 0.18 percent, about one-sixth of Sweden's percentage (Only Portugal and Greece performed worse than the United States). In 2002, a World Bank official compared (1) the subsidies rich countries gave to farms and businesses within their borders with (2) the amount of development aid they gave developing countries. He concluded that "[t]he average cow [in a rich country] is supported by three times the level of income of a poor person in Africa" (quoted in Schuettler, 2002).

WRITING ASSIGNMENT

In about 500 words, explain your views regarding foreign aid and personal responsibility.

Do you think Americans give adequate aid to poor countries as individuals or as a nation? Why do you think Americans offer proportionately less foreign aid than citizens of other rich countries, such as Japan and Sweden?

▶ TABLE 8.5

National Priorities, United States, 2006 (in percent)

Priority	Percent Answering "Too Little"
1. Improving the nation's education system	75
2. Improving and protecting the nation's health	73
3. Improving and protecting the environment	69
4. Social security	64
5. Dealing with drug addiction	62
6. Halting the rising crime rate	61
7. Assistance for child care	55
8. Solving problems of the big cities	48
9. Mass transportation	41
10. Improving the conditions of blacks	37
11. Highways and bridges	36
12. Parks and recreation	34
13. The military, armaments, and defense	25
13. Welfare	25
15. Space exploration program	15
16. Foreign aid	11

Source: National Opinion Research Center (2008b).

Bush administration proposed lifting all tariffs on textiles and apparel produced in the Western Hemisphere by 2008 (Becker, 2003). That sort of move, if broadened to include agricultural goods and the entire world, could help stimulate economic growth in the developing countries. To date, however, there is little room for optimism in this regard. In 2002 a less developed country like Mexico gave its farmers an average subsidy of $1,000 a year, while the United States gave its farmers an average subsidy of $16,000 a year. The comparable figures for western Europe and Japan were $17,000 and $27,000, respectively. International talks to lower government subsidies to Western farmers broke down in 2003.[3]

Democratic Globalization

The final reform we wish to consider involves efforts to help spread democracy throughout the developing world. A large body of research shows that democracy lowers inequality and promotes economic growth (Pettersson, 2003; Sylwester, 2002). Democracies have these effects for several reasons. They make it more difficult for elite groups to misuse their power and enhance their wealth and income at the expense of the less well-to-do. They increase political stability, thereby providing a better investment climate. Finally, because democracies encourage broad political participation, they tend to enact policies that are more responsive to people's needs and benefit a wide range of people from all social classes. For example, democratic governments are more inclined to take steps to avoid famine, protect the environment, build infrastructure, and ensure basic needs like education and health. These measures help create a population better suited to pursue economic growth.

Although democracy has spread in recent years, by 2002 only 80 countries with 55 percent of the world's population were considered fully democratic by one widely accepted measure (United Nations, 2002: 2) (see Chapter 13, "Politics, Work, and the Economy").

For its part, the United States has supported at least as many antidemocratic as democratic regimes in the developing world. Especially between the end of World War II in 1945 and the collapse of the Soviet Union in 1991, the U.S. government gave military and financial aid to many antidemocratic regimes, often in the name of halting the spread of Soviet influence. These actions often generated unexpected and undesirable consequences, or what the CIA came to call "blowback" (Johnson, 2000). For example, in the 1980s the U.S. government supported Saddam Hussein when it considered Iraq's enemy, Iran, the greater threat to U.S. security interests. The United States also funded Osama bin Laden when he was fighting the Soviet Union in Afghanistan. Only a decade later, these so-called allies turned into our worst enemies (Johnson, 2000; Kolko, 2002) (Box 8.4).

In sum, we have outlined four reforms that could change the nature of neoliberal globalization and turn it into what we would like to call "democratic globalization." These reforms include offering stronger support for democracy in the developing world, contributing more and better foreign aid, forgiving the debt owed by developing countries to the rich countries, and reducing tariffs that restrict exports from developing countries. These kinds of policies could plausibly help the developing world overcome the legacy of colonialism and join the ranks of the well-to-do.

---

[3]Farmers in the rich countries are opposed to the reduction of agricultural subsidies because many farmers would be driven out of business without them. In some rich countries, particularly Japan, France, and the United States, farmers are a politically powerful force that prevents much change on the subsidy front. One way out of the subsidy dilemma would involve the governments of rich countries compensating farmers for the reduction of farm subsidies by paying some of them to close down their farms and offering them alternative job training. Such a policy would not be cheap, but in the long run it would be cheaper than offering annual subsidies of $16,000 per farmer. Moreover, it would be more effective than foreign aid in stimulating economic development in less developed countries.

Syriana (2005)

In the 1980s, the Cold War seemed to be a struggle between the "free world" led by the United States and the "evil empire" led by the Soviet Union. Back then, CIA agent Bob Barnes (George Clooney, nominated for a 2005 Oscar for best supporting actor) operated with confidence. He could tell his friends from his enemies. In the 21st century, he is not so sure. The high-tech CIA doesn't seem to need an experienced, multilingual agent like Barnes. And the knowledge and experience Barnes acquired during the Cold War can no longer help him figure out who the good guys and the bad guys are.

That is because there *are* no good guys in *Syriana*. The CIA orders a mis-sile strike to eliminate an Arab prince who is pro-democracy but favors China over the United States in the competition for drilling rights. A poor Pakistani worker who loses his job when the Chinese take over the oil fields in the Prince's country eventually becomes radicalized and participates in the suicide bombing of a major oil refinery. The young son of energy analyst Brian Woodman (Matt Damon) dies in a freak accident in the Prince's swimming pool, and Woodman uses the accident as an opportunity to get a plum job with the Prince. With the American government's knowledge, a Washington law firm finesses a legally questionable merger between two Texas oil companies.

The storylines that swirl through *Syriana* like a sandstorm are so numerous and complex that it is almost impossible for the viewer to get the big picture. And that is precisely the aim of screenwriter and director Stephen Gaghan, whose work was nominated for best original screenplay of 2005. He wants *Syriana* to be as confusing as the real world of big oil. But he also wants to deliver a clear message: Oil corrupts everyone. As Danny D., adviser to the head of a Texas oil firm, says in the film:

> Corruption? . . . We have laws about it *precisely* so we can get away with it. Corruption is our protection. Corruption is what keeps us safe and warm. Corruption is why you and I are here in the white-hot center of things instead of fighting each other for scraps of meat in the street. Corruption is how we win.

Gaghan also wrote the screenplay for *Traffic* (2000), a film about the war on drugs that won four Oscars, and he is on record as saying that *Syriana* is about addiction too—specifically, about the corrupting influence of the world's addiction to oil.

Critical Thinking

- How are you addicted to oil?
- How does addiction to oil shape the Middle East policies of the United States and the West in general?
- What, if anything, should you do about your oil addiction and that of the West?

WARNER BROS/THE KOBAL COLLECTION

Bob Barnes (played by George Clooney) in Syriana.

The Points of the Compass

Modernization and dependency theorists stand at opposing points of the sociological compass. According to modernization theorists, less developed countries are more or less free to adopt Western traits and thereby stimulate economic growth. In contrast, dependency theorists hold that less developed countries are constrained to remain underdeveloped as long as rich countries compel them to focus on two economic processes: (1)

producing raw materials using low-wage labor and (2) consuming goods manufactured abroad by high-wage labor.

Our position is that modernization theorists exaggerate the degree to which less developed countries are free to act while dependency theorists overstate the degree to which the actions of less developed countries are constrained. As we have shown, less developed countries are not free to do as they wish, but certain social conditions and policy initiatives allow some of them to break or at least weaken the chain of dependency.

Similarly, globalization is a force that helps to shape nearly every aspect of human life. But it is no straightjacket. Public policy can fashion a new globalization that benefits humanity as a whole. We can see what is possible only by taking both constraint and freedom into account.

CHAPTER SUMMARY

1. What is globalization and why is it taking place?

Globalization is the growing interdependence and mutual awareness of individuals and economic, political, and social institutions. It is a response to many forces, some technological (e.g., the development of inexpensive means of rapid international communication), others economic (e.g., burgeoning international trade and investment), and still others political (e.g., the creation of transnational organizations that limit the sovereign powers of nation-states).

2. What are the consequences of globalization?

Globalization has complex consequences, some of which are captured by the idea of "glocalization," which denotes the homogenization of some aspects of life and the simultaneous sharpening of some local differences. In addition, globalization evokes an antiglobalization reaction.

3. What are the main trends in global inequality and poverty?

Global inequality and poverty are staggering and in some respects getting worse. The income gap between rich and poor countries and between rich and poor individuals has grown worldwide since the 19th century. In recent decades the number of desperately poor people has declined absolutely and in percentage terms worldwide, but it has increased in some less developed countries.

4. What are the main sociological theories of economic development?

Modernization theory argues that global inequality occurs as a result of some countries lacking sufficient capital, Western values, modern business practices, and stable governments. Dependency theory counters with the claim that global inequality results from the exploit-

ative relationship between rich and poor countries. An important test of the two theories concerns the effect of foreign investment on economic growth, but research on this subject is equivocal. Apparently, historical, social-structural, and policy factors matter greatly in determining how a particular country responds to international trade and foreign direct investment.

5. What are the characteristics of formerly poor countries that emerged from poverty?

The poor countries best able to emerge from poverty have a colonial past that left them with industrial infrastructures. They also enjoy a favorable geopolitical position. They implement strong, growth-oriented economic policies, and they have socially cohesive populations.

6. Can neoliberal globalization be reformed?

Neoliberal globalization can be reformed so that the benefits of globalization are more evenly distributed throughout the world. Possible reforms include offering stronger support for democracy in the developing world, contributing more and better foreign aid, forgiving the debt owed by developing countries to the rich countries, and reducing tariffs that restrict exports from developing countries.

Questions to Consider

1. How has globalization affected your life, family, and town? What would life be like in a place that has not been affected by globalization?

2. Think of a commodity you consume or use everyday—like coffee, shoes, or a cell phone—and find out where and how it was manufactured, transported, and marketed. How does your consumption of the commodity tie you into a global commodity chain? How does your consumption of the commodity affect other people in other parts of the world in significant ways?

3. Should Americans do anything to alleviate global poverty? Why or why not? If you think Americans should be doing something to help end global poverty, then what should we do?

Web Resources

CENGAGENOW™

Maximize your study time by using CengageNOW's diagnostic study plan to help you review this chapter. The Study Plan will

- help you identify areas on which you should concentrate;

- provide interactive exercises to help you master the chapter concepts; and

- provide a post-test to confirm you are ready to move on to the next chapter.

The Companion Website for *Sociology: Your Compass for a New World, The Brief Edition*, Enhanced Second Edition

www.cengage.com/sociology/brym

Supplement your review of this chapter by going to the companion website to take one of the tutorial quizzes, use flash cards to master key terms, and check out the many other study aids you'll find there. You'll also find special features such as GSS Data and Census 2000 information that will put data and resources at your fingertips to help you with that special project or help you do some research on your own.

Michael Ainsworth/Dallas Morning News/Corbis

In this chapter, you will learn that:

- Race and ethnicity are socially constructed ideas. We use them to distinguish people based on perceived physical or cultural differences, with profound consequences for their lives.

- Racial and ethnic labels and identities change over time and place. Relations between racial and ethnic groups help to shape these labels and identities.

- In the United States, members of some racial and ethnic groups are blending over time. However, this tendency is weaker among members of highly disadvantaged groups, such as African Americans and Native Americans.

- Identifying with a racial or ethnic group can be economically, politically, and emotionally advantageous for some people.

- High levels of racial and ethnic inequality are likely to persist in the United States for the foreseeable future.

Defining Race and Ethnicity

Race, Biology, and Society

People have been making biological arguments about racial differences for more than 500 years. In medieval Europe, some aristocrats saw blue veins underneath their pale skin but they couldn't see blue veins underneath the peasants' suntanned skin. They concluded the two groups must be racially distinct. The aristocrats called themselves "blue bloods." They ignored the fact that the color of blood from an aristocrat's wound was just as red as the blood from a peasant's wound.

The idea that race is rooted in biology was given what some people regarded as a scientific grounding just over 150 years ago when the most distinguished scientist in the United States, Dr. Samuel George Morton of Philadelphia, claimed to show that brain size was related to race. According to Morton, white people have the biggest brains, followed by Asians, then Native Americans, and finally African Americans. Subsequent research showed that he was wrong, although some people still cite his findings as accurate (Gould, 1996 [1981]).

Then, about 80 years ago, some Americans expressed the belief that racial differences in average IQ scores are based in biology. On average, Jews scored below non-Jews on IQ tests in the 1920s. This was used as an argument against Jewish immigration. "America

---

CENGAGENOW

This icon signals when CengageNOW has important resources available for you to use in conjunction with the text. See the foldout at the front of this text for information on how to access CengageNOW.

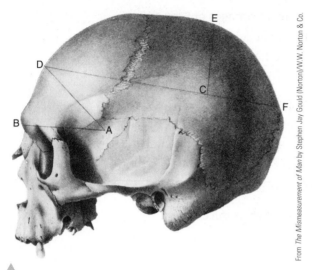

From The Mismeasurement of Man by Stephen Jay Gould (Norton)/W.W. Norton & Co.

In the 19th century, brain size was falsely held to be one of the main indicators of intellectual capacity. Average brain size was incorrectly said to vary by race. Researchers who were eager to prove the existence of such correlations are now widely regarded as practitioners of a racist quasi-science.

must be kept American," proclaimed President Calvin Coolidge as he signed the 1924 Immigration Restriction Act (quoted in Gould, 1996 [1981]: 262). More recently, African Americans have on average scored below European Americans on IQ tests. Some people say this justifies cutting budgets for schools in the inner city, where many African Americans live. Why invest good money in inner-city schooling, such people ask, if low IQ scores are rooted in biology and therefore fixed (Herrnstein and Murray, 1994)?

The people who argued against Jewish immigration and better education for poor African Americans ignored two facts. First, Jewish IQ scores rose as Jews moved up the class hierarchy and could afford better education. Second, enriched educational facilities have routinely boosted the intellectual development and academic achievement of poor African American children (Campbell and Ramey, 1994; Frank Porter Graham Child Development Center, 1999; Gould, 1996 [1981]; Steinberg, 1989 [1981]). This suggests that the social environment in which one is raised and educated has a big impact on IQ and other standardized test scores. The evidence that racial differences in IQ scores is based in biology is about as strong as evidence showing that aristocrats have blue blood (Fischer et al., 1996; see Chapter 12, "Religion and Education").[1]

If one cannot reasonably maintain that racial differences in average IQ scores are based in biology, what about differences in singing ability or athletic prowess? For example, some people insist that, for genetic reasons, African Americans are better than whites at sports. Does any evidence exist to support this belief?

At first glance, the supporting evidence might seem strong. Aren't nearly two-thirds of National Basketball Association (NBA) and National Football League (NFL) players black? Don't West African–descended blacks hold the 200 fastest 100-meter-race times, all under 10 seconds? Don't North and East Africans regularly win 40 percent of the top international distance-running honors, yet represent only a fraction of 1 percent of the world's population (Entine, 2000)? Although these facts are undeniable, the argument for the genetic basis of black athletic superiority begins to falter once we consider two additional points. First, no gene linked to general athletic superiority has been identified. Second, athletes of African descent do not perform unusually well in many sports, such as swimming, hockey, cycling, tennis, gymnastics, and soccer. The idea that people of African descent are generally superior athletes is simply untrue.[2]

Prejudice, Discrimination, and Sports

Sociologists have identified certain social conditions leading to high levels of participation in sports. These conditions operate on all groups of people, whatever their race. Specifically, people who face prejudice and discrimination often enter sports in dispro-

---

[1]Although sociologists commonly dispute a genetic basis of mean intelligence for races, evidence suggests that *individual* differences in intelligence are partly genetically transmitted (Lewontin, 1991: 19–37; Schiff and Lewontin, 1986).
[2]Genetic differences may lead some groups to have physical characteristics that lend themselves to excellence in *particular* sports, but that argument is different from the general argument we are criticizing here (Entine, 2000). Incidentally, the view among the European intellectual elite in the 19th century was that blacks are athletically *inferior*. The pioneer race theorist Arthur de Gobineau wrote that: "The negroes . . . have less muscular power. . . . In strength of fist, the English are superior to all the other European races" (quoted in Lie, 2004: 61).

portionately large numbers for lack of other ways to improve their social and economic position. For such people, other avenues of upward mobility tend to be blocked. (**Prejudice** is an attitude that judges a person on his or her group's real or imagined characteristics. **Discrimination** is unfair treatment of people because of their group membership.)

For example, prejudice and discrimination against American Jews did not begin to decline appreciably until the 1950s. Until then, Jews played a prominent role in professional sports. For instance, when the New York Knicks played their first game on November 1, 1946, beating the Toronto Huskies 68–66, the starting lineup consisted of Ossie Schechtman, Stan Stutz, Jake Weber, Ralph Kaplowitz, and Leo "Ace" Gottlieb—an all-Jewish squad (National Basketball Association, 2000). Koreans in Japan today are subject to much prejudice and discrimination. They often pursue careers in sports. In contrast, Koreans in the United States face less prejudice and discrimination. Few of them become athletes. Instead, they are often said to excel in engineering and science.

The idea that people of African descent are genetically superior to whites in athletic ability complements the idea that they are genetically inferior to whites in intellectual ability.[3] Both ideas are false, and both have the effect of reinforcing black–white inequality. Although the United States has fewer than 10,000 elite professional athletes, it has many millions of people in other interesting occupations that require higher education and offer steady employment and good pay. By promoting only the Kobe Bryants of the world as suitable role models for African American youth, the idea of "natural" black athletic superiority and intellectual inferiority in effect asks black Americans to bet on a high-risk proposition—that they will make it in professional sports. At the same time, it deflects attention from a much safer bet—that they can achieve upward mobility through academic excellence (Hoberman, 1997).

Kevork Djansezian/AP Photo

The cultural emphasis on African American sports heroes has the effect of reinforcing harmful and incorrect racial stereotypes about black athletic prowess and intellectual inferiority.

The Social Construction of Race

Many scholars believe we all belong to one human race, which originated in Africa (Cavalli-Sforza, Menozzi, and Piazza, 1994). They argue that subsequent migration, geographical separation, and inbreeding led to the formation of more or less distinct races. However, particularly in modern times, humanity has experienced so much intermixing that race as a biological category has lost nearly all meaning. Some biologists and social scientists therefore suggest we drop the term "race" from the vocabulary of science (Angier, 2000).

Most sociologists, however, continue to use the term "race" because *perceptions* of race affect the lives of most people profoundly. Everything from your wealth to your health is influenced by whether others see you as African American, white, Asian American, Native American, or something else. Race as a *sociological* concept is thus an invaluable analytical tool—if the user remembers that it refers to socially significant physical differences, such as skin color, rather than biological differences that determine behavioral traits. It is also important to note that perceptions of racial difference are socially constructed and often arbitrary. The Irish and the Jews were regarded as "blacks" by some people 100 years ago, and today many northern Italians still think

Prejudice: An attitude that judges a person on his or her group's real or imagined characteristics.

Discrimination: Unfair treatment of people due to their group membership.

---

[3]The genetic argument also belittles the athletic activity itself by denying the role of training in developing athletic skill.

"The family that produced Barack and Michele Obama is black and white and Asian, Christian, Muslim and Jewish. They speak English; Indonesian; French; Cantonese; German; Hebrew: African languages including Swahili, Luo and Igbo; and even a few phrases of Gullah, the Creole dialect of the South Carolina Low country" (Kantor, 2009). As is the case for an increasingly large number of Americans, it would be a distortion to say that Barack and Michele Obama are members of any one race or ethnic group. In this photo, Barack Obama (right) is seated with his American mother, his Indonesian step-father, and his baby half-sister.

of southern Italians from Sicily and Calabria as "blacks" (Ignatiev, 1995; Roediger, 1991). These observations allow us to define **race** as a social construct used to distinguish people in terms of one or more physical markers, usually with profound effects on their lives.

Why Race Matters

This definition raises an interesting question. If race is merely a social construct and not a useful biological term, why are perceptions of physical difference used to distinguish groups of people in the first place? Why, in other words, does race matter? Most sociologists believe race matters because it allows social inequality to be created and maintained. The English who colonized Ireland, the Europeans and Americans who went to Africa looking for slaves, and the Germans who used the Jews as a scapegoat to explain their deep economic and political troubles after World War I all set up systems of racial domination. (A **scapegoat** is a disadvantaged person or category of people whom others blame for their own problems.) Once colonialism, slavery, and concentration camps were established, behavioral differences developed between subordinates and superordinates. For example, African American slaves and Jewish concentration camp inmates, with little motivating them to work hard except the ultimate threat of the master's whip, tended to do only the minimum work necessary to survive. Their masters noticed this and characterized their subordinates as inherently slow and unreliable workers (Collins, 1982: 66–9). In this way, racial stereotypes are born. The stereotypes then embed themselves in literature, popular lore, journalism, and political debate. This reinforces racial inequalities (▶Figure 9.1). We thus see that race matters to the degree that it helps to create and maintain systems of social inequality.

Race: A social construct used to distinguish people in terms of one or more physical markers, usually with profound effects on their lives.

Scapegoat: A disadvantaged person or category of people whom others blame for their own problems.

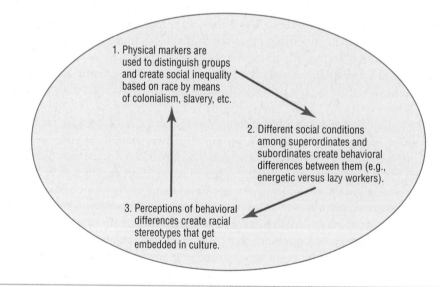

1. Physical markers are used to distinguish groups and create social inequality based on race by means of colonialism, slavery, etc.

2. Different social conditions among superordinates and subordinates create behavioral differences between them (e.g., energetic versus lazy workers).

3. Perceptions of behavioral differences create racial stereotypes that get embedded in culture.

▶FIGURE 9.1
The Vicious Circle of Racism

Ethnicity, Culture, and Social Structure

Race is to biology as ethnicity is to culture. A race is a category of people whose perceived *physical* markers are deemed socially significant. An **ethnic group** is composed of people whose perceived *cultural* markers are deemed socially significant. Ethnic groups differ from one another in terms of language, religion, customs, values, and ancestors. However, just as physical distinctions don't cause differences in the behavior of various races, cultural distinctions are often not by themselves the major source of differences in the behavior of various ethnic groups. Ethnic values and other elements of ethnic culture have less of an effect on the way people behave than we commonly believe because *social-structural* differences typically underlie cultural differences.

Thus, people often praise Jews, Koreans, and other economically successful groups for emphasizing education, family, and hard work. Their cultural values are commonly said to account for their achievements. People less commonly notice, however, that American immigration policy is highly selective. For the most part, the Jews and Koreans who arrived in the United States were literate, urbanized, and skilled. Some even came with financial assets. They confronted much prejudice and discrimination but far less than that reserved for descendants of Southern blacks. These *social-structural* conditions facilitated Jewish and Korean success in the United States. They gave members of these groups a firm basis on which to build and maintain a culture emphasizing education, family, and other middle-class virtues. As many sociologists stress, social-structural conditions often underlie ethnic values, so it is not values themselves that determine ethnic group behavior (Abelmann and Lie, 1995; Brym with Fox, 1989: 103–19; Lieberson, 1980).

We conclude that it is misleading to claim that "[r]ace and ethnicity . . . are quite different, since one is biological and the other is cultural" (Macionis, 1997 [1987]: 321). As we have seen, both race and ethnicity are rooted in social structure. The biological and cultural aspects of race and ethnicity are secondary to their sociological character. The interesting question from a sociological point of view is why social definitions of race and ethnicity change over time. We now consider that issue.

Chinese · Japanese

HOW TO TELL YOUR FRIENDS FROM THE JAPS

Of these four faces of young men (above) and middle-aged men (below) the two on the left are Chinese, the two on the right Japanese. There is no infallible way of telling them apart, because the same racial strains are mixed in both. Even an anthropologist, with calipers and plenty of time to measure heads, noses, shoulders, hips, is sometimes stumped. A few rules of thumb—not always reliable:

▶ Some Chinese are tall (average: 5 ft. 5 in.). Virtually all Japanese are short (average: 5 ft. 2 1/3 in.).

▶ Japanese are likely to be stockier and broader-hipped than short Chinese.

▶ Japanese—except for wrestlers—are seldom fat; they often dry up and grow lean as they age. The Chinese often put on weight, particularly if they are prosperous (in China, with its frequent famines, being fat is esteemed as a sign of being a solid citizen).

▶ Chinese, not as hairy as Japanese, seldom grow an impressive mustache.

▶ Most Chinese avoid horn-rimmed spectacles.

▶ Although both have the typical epicanthic fold of the upper eyelid (which makes them look almond-eyed), Japanese eyes are usually set closer together.

▶ Those who know them best often rely on facial expression to tell them apart: the Chinese expression is likely to be more placid, kindly, open: the Japanese more positive, dogmatic, arrogant.

In Washington, last week, Correspondent Joseph Chiang made things much easier by pinning on his lapel a large badge reading "Chinese Reporter–NOT Japanese—Please."

▶ Some aristocratic Japanese have thin, aquiline noses, narrow faces and, except for their eyes, look like Caucasians.

▶ Japanese are hesitant, nervous in conversation, laugh loudly at the wrong time.

▶ Japanese walk stiffly erect, hard-heeled. Chinese, more relaxed, have an easy gait, sometimes shuffle.

Chinese · Japanese

Carl Mydans, Black Star

▲ *Time* magazine explains how to make arbitrary racial distinctions, 1941.

Copyright 1941 Time, Inc./Timepix/Getty Images

Ethnic group: Composed of people whose perceived cultural markers are deemed socially significant. Ethnic groups differ from one another in terms of language, religion, customs, values, ancestors, and the like.

Race and Ethnic Relations

Labels and Identity

Personal Anecdote

John Lie moved with his family from South Korea to Japan when he was a baby. He moved from Japan to Hawaii when he was 10 years old, and again from Hawaii to the American mainland when he started college. The move to Hawaii and the move to the mainland changed the way John thought of himself in ethnic terms.

In Japan, the Koreans form a minority group. (A **minority group** is a group of people who are socially disadvantaged, though they may be in the numerical majority, like the blacks in South Africa.) Before 1945, when Korea was a colony of Japan, some Koreans were brought to Japan to work as miners and unskilled laborers. The Japanese thought the Koreans who lived there were beneath and outside Japanese society (Lie, 2001). Not surprisingly, then, Korean children in Japan, including John, were often teased and occasionally beaten by their Japanese schoolmates. "The beatings hurt," says John, "but the psychological trauma resulting from being socially excluded by my classmates hurt more. In fact, although I initially thought I was Japanese like my classmates, my Korean identity was literally beaten into me."

"When my family immigrated to Hawaii, I was sure things would get worse. I expected Americans to be even meaner than the Japanese. (By Americans, I thought only of white European Americans.) Was I surprised when I discovered that most of my schoolmates were not white European Americans, but people of Asian and mixed ancestry! Suddenly I was a member of a numerical majority. I was no longer teased or bullied. In fact, I found that students of Asian and non-European origin often singled out white European Americans (called *haole* in Hawaiian) for abuse. We even had a 'beat up *haole* day' in school. Given my own experiences in Japan, I empathized somewhat with the white Americans. But I have to admit that I also felt a great sense of relief and an easing of the psychological trauma associated with being Korean in Japan.

"As the years passed, I finished public school in Hawaii. I then went to college in Massachusetts and got a job as a professor in Illinois. I associated with, and befriended, people from various racial and ethnic groups. My Korean origin became a less and less important factor in the way people treated me. There was simply less prejudice and discrimination against Koreans during my adulthood in the United States than in my early years in Japan. I now think of myself less as Japanese or Korean than as American. When I lived in Illinois, I sometimes thought of myself as a Midwesterner. Now that I have moved to California, my self-conception may shift again; I may begin to think of myself more as an Asian American (given the large number of Asians in California), a Californian, or perhaps a Berzerkelyan (as people at Berkeley are sometimes called). Clearly, my ethnic identity has changed over time in response to the significance others have attached to my Korean origin. I now understand what the French philosopher Jean-Paul Sartre meant when he wrote that 'the anti-Semite creates the Jew' (Sartre, 1965 [1948]: 43).

The Formation of Racial and Ethnic Identities

The details of John Lie's life are unique. But experiencing a shift in racial or ethnic identity is common. Social contexts, and in particular the nature of one's relations with members of other racial and ethnic groups, shape and continuously reshape one's racial and ethnic

Minority group: A group of people who are socially disadvantaged although they may be in the numerical majority.

identity. Change your social context, and your racial and ethnic self-conception eventually changes too (Miles, 1989).

Consider Italian Americans. Around 1900, Italian immigrants thought of themselves as people who came from a particular town or perhaps a particular province, such as Sicily or Calabria. They did not usually think of themselves as Italians. Italy became a unified country only in 1861. A mere 40 years later, far from all of its citizens identified with their new nationality. In the United States, however, officials and other residents identified the newcomers as "Italians." The designation at first seemed odd to many of the new immigrants. However, over time it stuck. Immigrants from Italy started thinking of themselves as Italian Americans because others defined them that way. A new ethnic identity was born (Yancey, Ericksen, and Leon, 1976).

As symbolic interactionists emphasize, the development of racial and ethnic labels and identities is, to varying degrees, a process of negotiation. For example, members of a group may have a racial or ethnic identity, but outsiders may impose a new label on them. Group members then reject, accept, or modify the label. The negotiation between outsiders and insiders eventually results in the crystallization of a new, more or less stable ethnic identity. If the social context changes again, the negotiation process begins anew.

Case Study: The Diversity of the "Hispanic American" Community

A Cinco de Mayo celebration in the United States.

You can witness the formation of new racial and ethnic labels and identities in the United States today. Consider the terms "Hispanic American" and "Latino" (Darder and Torres, 1998). (Preferred usage seems to be "Latino" [male] and "Latina" [female] in the West and "Hispanic American" in the East. "Latino/a" is the more inclusive term because it encompasses Brazilians, who speak Portuguese, but we use "Hispanic American" here because that is the term used by the U.S. Census Bureau.) People scarcely used these terms 30 or 40 years ago. Now they are common. According to the U.S. Census Bureau, nearly 47 million Hispanic Americans lived in the United States in 2008. Because of continuing robust immigration and relatively high fertility, the Bureau predicts they will number more than 133 million in 2050. They are the second fastest growing ethnic category in the country (next to Asian Americans) and as of 2003 were the second biggest, next to non-Hispanic whites (▶Figure 9.2).

But who is a Hispanic American? ▶Table 9.1 makes it clear that Hispanic Americans form a heterogeneous population. In 2002, 67 percent of Hispanic Americans were of Mexican origin, nearly 9 percent of Puerto Rican origin, almost 4 percent of Cuban origin, and 14 percent were from El Salvador, the Dominican Republic, and other countries in Latin America. Mexican Americans are concentrated in the South and West, especially California and Texas, where they are known as "Chicanos." Puerto Ricans are found mainly in the Northeast, especially in New York. Cubans reside principally in the South, especially Miami. Other Hispanic Americans are divided fairly evenly among the Northeast, South, and West. Relatively few Hispanic Americans live in the Midwest.

Besides varying degrees of knowledge of the Spanish language, what do members of these groups have in common? One survey shows that most of them do *not* want to be called "Hispanic American." Instead, they prefer being referred to by their national origin—as Cuban Americans, Puerto Rican Americans, Mexican Americans, and so

▶FIGURE 9.2
Racial and Ethnic Composition, United States, 1970–2050 (projected)

Source: U.S. Census Bureau (1999b, 2002f).

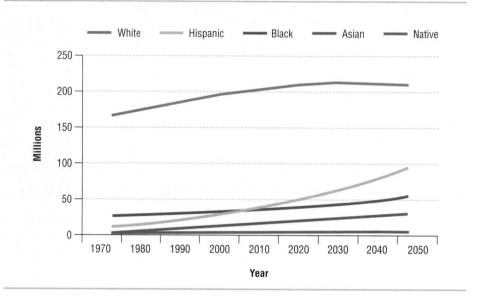

▶TABLE 9.1

Population by Hispanic Origin and Region, United States, 2002 (in percent)

	Mexican	Puerto Rican	Cuban	Other	Total
Northeast	2.4	58.0	13.3	30.2	13.3
Midwest	8.7	8.5	3.0	4.8	7.7
South	34.3	27.0	75.1	32.6	34.8
West	54.6	6.4	8.5	32.4	44.2
Total	100.0	99.9*	99.9*	100.0	100.0
Percent of all Hispanic Americans	67.0	8.6	3.7	20.7	100.0
n (in thousands)	25,074	3,222	1,376	7,765	7,438

*Due to rounding.
Source: U.S. Census Bureau (2002d).

forth. Many Hispanic Americans born in the United States want to be called simply "Americans" (de la Garza et al., 1992).

The Formation of Ethnic Enclaves

Members of various Hispanic categories also enjoy different cultural traditions, occupy different positions in the class hierarchy, and vote differently. For example, there are many more middle-class and professional people among Americans of Cuban origin than among members of other major Hispanic groups in the United States. That is because a large wave of middle-class Cubans fled Castro's revolution and arrived in the Miami area in the late 1950s and early 1960s. There they formed an **ethnic enclave.** An ethnic enclave is a geographical concentration of ethnic group members who establish businesses that serve and employ mainly members of the ethnic group and reinvest profits in community businesses and organizations (Portes and Manning, 1991). Many Cubans who arrived in subsequent waves of immigration were poor, but because they could rely on a well-

Ethnic enclave: A spatial concentration of ethnic group members who establish businesses that serve and employ mainly members of the ethnic group and reinvest profits in the businesses and organizations of the ethnic community.

established and prosperous Cuban American ethnic enclave for jobs and other forms of support, most of them soon achieved middle-class status themselves. The fact that Cuban immigrants shared strong pro-capitalist and anticommunist values with the American public also helped their integration into the larger society. Not surprisingly given their background, Cuban Americans are more likely to vote Republican than Americans of Mexican and Puerto Rican origin.

Immigrants from Mexico and Puerto Rico tend to be members of the working class who have not completed high school. Their children typically achieve educational levels similar to that of non-Hispanic whites (Bean and Tienda, 1987). However, they have not reached the average level of prosperity enjoyed by Cuban Americans because of the lower class origins of the community and its resulting weaker ethnic enclave formation. Chicanos and Puerto Rican Americans are more likely than Cuban Americans to vote Democratic.

What Unifies the Hispanic American Community?

So we see that the Hispanic American community is highly diverse. In fact, not even knowledge of the Spanish language unifies Hispanic Americans. Some people who are commonly viewed as Hispanic American do not speak Spanish. Haitians, for example, speak French or a regional dialect of French and are identified by the census as African American. Many Americans think of Brazilians as Hispanic, but they speak Portuguese. Still other people who are commonly viewed as Hispanic American in the United States reject the label. Chief among them are Mayans, indigenous Central Americans whom the Spanish colonized.[4]

Despite this internal diversity, the term "Hispanic American" is more widely used than it was 30 or 40 years ago for three main reasons:

- Many Hispanic Americans find it politically useful. Recognizing that power flows from group size and unity, Hispanic Americans have created national organizations to promote the welfare of their entire community.

- A second reason the term "Hispanic American" is becoming more common is that the government finds it useful for data collection and public policy purposes. By collecting census data on the number of people who identify themselves as Hispanic American, the government is better able to allocate funding for Spanish-language instruction in schools, ensure diversity in the workplace, and take other public policy actions that reflect the changing racial and ethnic composition of American society (Box 9.1).

- Finally, "Hispanic American" is an increasingly popular label because non-Hispanic Americans find it convenient. Central and South America are composed of about 25 countries, and many ethnic divisions exist within those countries. Lumping all Hispanic Americans together makes life easier for the majority group, although lack of sensitivity to a person's specific origins is not infrequently offensive to minority group members.

So we see that "Hispanic American" is a new ethnic label and identity. It did not spring fully formed one day from the culture of the group to which it refers. It was created out of social necessity and is still being socially constructed (Portes and Truelove, 1991). We can say the same about *all* ethnic labels and identities, even those that may seem most fixed and natural, such as "white" (Waters, 1990; Roediger, 1991).

---

[4]Similarly, particularly in the West, many indigenous Americans reject the label "Native American" as official "white" terminology and proudly call themselves "Indians."

BOX 9.1
SOCIAL POLICY: WHAT DO YOU THINK?

Bilingual Education

Ron Unz is an opponent of bilingual education. He argues that a "quarter of all the children in California public schools are classified as not knowing English. . . . Of the ones who don't know English in any given year, only five or six percent learn English. Since the goal of the system, obviously, should be to make sure that these children learn English, we're talking about a system with an annual failure rate of 95 percent. . . . Many of my friends are foreign immigrants. They came here when they were a variety of different ages. All of them agree that little children or even young teenagers can learn another language quickly, though only five percent of these children in California are learning English each year. And that's what I define as failure" (quoted in Public Broadcasting System, 1997).

In response, James Lyons of the National Association for Bilingual Education says, "It is not the case that bilingual education is failing children. There are poor bilingual education programs, just as there are poor programs of every type in our schools today. But bilingual education has made it possible for children to have continuous development in their native language, while they're in the process of learning English, something that doesn't happen overnight, and it's made it possible for children to learn math and science at a rate equal to English-speaking children while they're in the process of acquiring English" (quoted in Public Broadcasting System, 1997).

About 6 percent of all public school students were enrolled in bilingual education programs in the United States in 1997. That amounts to more than 3 million children. Bilingual education programs cost taxpayers $178 million (Public Broadcasting System, 1997). Is the expenditure worth it? Whatever the expense, is the ideal of bilingual education worth pursuing? The debate between Unz and Lyons touches on some important points concerning these issues. On the one hand, many bilingual education programs are not very effective. Furthermore, English is the main language spoken in the United States and should be taught to non-English speakers to ensure their economic progress; a less-than-fluent speaker of English is bound to do poorly not only in school but also in most workplaces. On the other hand, advocates argue that bilingual education helps nonnative speakers of English adjust to schools and keep up in other subjects. Bilingual education also recognizes the importance of learning a native language, such as Spanish, rather than simply assimilating to the dominant English-speaking culture.

Some people argue that when students value their native language skills, their self-esteem increases. Later, this improves their economic success. What do you think?

Critical Thinking

- Should we make every public school student learn only in English? What would we gain and lose by such a policy?

- Is it worthwhile keeping bilingual programs for students who wish to preserve their language skills? Should we encourage native language preservation just for large groups, such as Spanish-speaking students, or for smaller groups as well, such as students of Chinese or Russian origin?

- Perhaps in this age of globalization, everyone should participate in a bilingual education program. Would that make Americans less ethnocentric and better able to participate in global affairs?

Ethnic and Racial Labels: Choice versus Imposition

The idea that race and ethnicity are socially constructed does not mean that everyone can always choose their racial or ethnic identity freely. The degree to which people can exercise such freedom of choice varies widely from one society to the next. Moreover, in a given society at a given time, different categories of people are more or less free to choose. The people with the most freedom to choose their ethnic or racial identity are white Americans whose ancestors came from Europe more than two generations ago (Waters, 1990).

Irish Americans and Symbolic Ethnicity

For example, identifying oneself as an Irish American no longer has negative implications, as it did in, say, 1900. Then, in a city like Boston, where a substantial number of Irish immigrants were concentrated, the English-Protestant majority typically regarded working-class Irish Catholics as often drunk, inherently lazy, and born superstitious. This strong anti-Irish sentiment, which often erupted into conflict, meant the Irish found it difficult to escape their ethnic identity even if they wanted to.

Since then, however, Irish Americans have followed the path taken by many other white European groups. They have achieved upward mobility and blended into the majority. As a result, Irish Americans no longer find their identity imposed on them. Instead, they may *choose* whether to march in the St. Patrick's Day parade, enjoy the remarkable contributions of Irish authors to English-language literature and drama, and take pride in the athleticism and precision of Riverdance. For them, ethnicity is largely a *symbolic* matter, as it is for the other white European groups that have undergone similar social processes. Herbert Gans defines **symbolic ethnicity** as "a nostalgic allegiance to the culture of the immigrant generation, or that of the old country; a love for and a pride in a tradition that can be felt without having to be incorporated in everyday behavior" (Gans, 1979: 436).

Racism and Identity

At the other extreme, most African Americans lack the freedom to enjoy symbolic ethnicity. They may well take pride in their cultural heritage. However, their identity as African Americans is not an option because racism imposes it on them daily. **Racism** is the belief that a visible characteristic of a group, such as skin color, indicates group inferiority and justifies discrimination. **Institutional racism** is bias that is inherent in social institutions and is often not noticed by members of the majority group. We see institutional racism in practice when police single out African Americans for car searches, department stores tell their floorwalkers to keep a sharp eye out for African American shoplifters, and banks reject African American mortgage applications more often than applications from white Americans of the same economic standing. In his autobiography, the black leader Malcolm X poignantly noted how both individual and institutional racism can impose racial identity on people. He described one of his black Ph.D. professors as "one of these ultra-proper-talking Negroes" who spoke and acted snobbishly. "Do you know what white racists call black Ph.D.s?" asked Malcolm X. "He said something like, 'I believe that I happen not to be aware of that . . .' And I laid the word down on him, loud: 'N____!'" (Malcolm X, 1965: 284). Malcolm X's point is that it doesn't matter to a racist whether an African American is a professor or a panhandler, a genius or a fool, a saint or a criminal. Where racism is common, racial identities are compulsory and at the forefront of one's self-identity.

In sum, political and social processes structure the degree to which people are able to choose their ethnic and racial identities. Members of *ethnic* minority groups in the United States today are freer to choose their identity than members of *racial* minority groups. The contrast between Irish Americans and African Americans also suggests that relations between racial and ethnic groups can take different forms. For example, racial and ethnic groups can blend as a result of residential integration, friendship, and intermarriage or they can remain separate because of hostility. We now discuss several theories that explain why forms of racial and ethnic relations vary over time and from place to place.

Theories of Race and Ethnic Relations

Ecological Theory

Nearly a century ago, Robert Park proposed an influential theory of how race and ethnic relations change over time (Park, 1914; 1950). His **ecological theory** focuses on the struggle for territory. It distinguishes five stages in the process by which conflict between ethnic and racial groups emerges and is resolved:

Symbolic ethnicity: A nostalgic allegiance to the culture of the immigrant generation, or that of the old country, that is not usually incorporated into everyday behavior.

Racism: The belief that a visible characteristic of a group, such as skin color, indicates group inferiority and justifies discrimination.

Institutional racism: Bias that is inherent in social institutions and is often not noticed by members of the majority group.

Ecological theory: A theory of ethnic succession arguing that ethnic groups pass through five stages in their struggle for territory: invasion, resistance, competition, accommodation/cooperation, and assimilation.

1. *Invasion.* One racial or ethnic group tries to move into the territory of another. The territory may be as large as a country or as small as a neighborhood in a city.

2. *Resistance.* The established group tries to defend its territory and institutions against the intruding group. It may use legal means, violence, or both.

3. *Competition.* If the established group doesn't drive out the newcomers, the two groups begin to compete for scarce resources. These resources include housing, jobs, public park space, and political positions.

4. *Accommodation and cooperation.* Over time, the two groups work out an understanding of what they should segregate, divide, and share. **Segregation** involves the spatial and institutional separation of racial or ethnic groups. For example, the two groups may segregate churches, divide political positions in proportion to the size of the groups, and share public parks equally.

5. *Assimilation.* **Assimilation** is the process by which a minority group blends into the majority population and eventually disappears as a distinct group. Park argued that assimilation is bound to occur as accommodation and cooperation allow trust and understanding to develop. Eventually, goodwill allows ethnic groups to fuse socially and culturally. Where two or more groups formerly existed, only one remains. Park agreed with the memorable image of the United States as "God's crucible, the great Melting Pot where all the races of Europe are melting and re-forming" (Zangwill, 1909: 37).

Park's theory stimulated important and insightful research (e.g., Suttles, 1968). However, it is more relevant to some ethnic groups than to others. It applies best to whites of European origin. As Park predicted, many whites of European origin stopped thinking of themselves as Italian American, Irish American, or German American after their families were in the United States for three or four generations. Today, they think of themselves just as "whites" (Lieberson, 1991). Over time, they achieved rough equality with members of the majority group and, in the process, began to blend in with them.

However, the story does not apply to all Americans. Park's theory gives too optimistic an account of the prospects for assimilation of African Americans, Native Americans, Mexican Americans, and Chinese Americans, among others. It also fails to take into account the persistence of ethnicity among some middle-class whites of European origin into the third and fourth generation after immigration. For reasons we will now explore, many members of racial minorities and some white people of European origin seem fixed in Park's third and fourth stages (Box 9.2).

Internal Colonialism and the Split Labor Market

The main weakness of Park's theory is that it pays insufficient attention to the *social-structural* conditions that prevent some groups from assimilating. Robert Blauner examined one such condition, which he called **internal colonialism** (Blauner, 1972; Hechter, 1974). *Colonialism* involves people from one country invading another. In the process, the invaders change or destroy the native culture. They gain virtually complete control over the native population. They develop the racist belief that the natives are inherently inferior. They confine the natives to work they consider demeaning. *Internal colonialism* involves the same processes but within the boundaries of a single country. Internal colonialism prevents assimilation by segregating the colonized in terms of jobs, housing, and social contacts ranging from friendship to marriage. To varying

Segregation: Involves the spatial and institutional separation of racial or ethnic groups.

Assimilation: The process by which a minority group blends into the majority population and eventually disappears as a distinct group.

Internal colonialism: Involves one race or ethnic group subjugating another in the same country. It prevents assimilation by segregating the subordinate group in terms of jobs, housing, and social contacts.

Split labor markets: A situation in which low-wage workers of one race and high-wage workers of another race compete for the same jobs. High-wage workers are likely to resent the presence of low-wage competitors, and conflict is bound to result. Consequently, racist attitudes develop or get reinforced.

BOX 9.2
SOCIOLOGY AT THE MOVIES

Crash (2005)

Nominated for six Oscars in 2005, including best picture, *Crash* is a story about Los Angelans colliding into one another because of their racist assumptions and then, in some cases, learning that people who differ from them are as human as they are.

The movie mirrors the ethnic and racial complexities of Los Angeles by presenting many intersecting plot lines. Neighbors think an Iranian American shopkeeper (Shaun Toub) is an Arab, so they apparently feel little remorse when they loot his store. The shopkeeper thinks a Chicano locksmith (Michael Peña) is a gang member who will bring his homies in to rob him blind once he finishes the repair job. The locksmith is in fact a hardworking family man and

an exemplary father. A black police officer (Don Cheadle) has an affair with his Latina partner (Jennifer Esposito) but keeps on insulting her by not remembering what country she was born in and stopping just one step short of saying "you people all look the same to me." Ryan, a white police officer (played by Matt Dillon, who was nominated for an Oscar for best supporting actor), arbitrarily stops what he at first thinks is a white woman and a black man in an expensive car. He conducts a humiliating, overly thorough body search of the woman (who, he discovers, is actually a light-skinned African American) while her enraged husband looks on, unable to do anything because the police officer makes it clear what would happen if he tried. Later, we learn that Ryan is a compassionate man who is angry about his inability to help his dying father. Perversely, he expresses anger over his impotence by insulting blacks and making them feel powerless. Yet he partly redeems himself when he risks his life to rescue a woman from a horrible car accident—realizing part-

way through the rescue that the victim is the same black woman he had earlier body-searched.

Some critics have complained that *Crash* exaggerates the extent of racism in the United States. After all, we don't often hear explicit racist comments in public. It seems to us, however, that these critics miss the point of the movie. The apparent intention of *Crash*—and in this it succeeds admirably—is to strip away all political correctness and tell us what people are thinking to themselves or saying to members of their own ethnic or racial group about members of other groups. In that sense it may be more realistic than what we hear in public. At the same time, *Crash* offers a measure of hope that things can be better. Ryan risks his life to save the woman even after realizing that she is black. He helps us appreciate that underlying our prejudices lies a deeper humanity.

Critical Thinking

- Do you think that Americans are as racist as *Crash* makes us out to be?

- Does racism lie beneath the surface of our civility and political correctness?

- Do you sometimes rely on ethnic or racial stereotypes to account for someone's behavior?

- Do you sometimes discover that your prejudices are misconceptions? If so, under what circumstances do you make such discoveries?

- Do you believe that beneath racist sentiments lies a deeper humanity?

LIONS GATE/THE KOBAL COLLECTION

Ryan (Matt Dillon) redeems himself when he risks his life rescuing a black woman from a car accident.

degrees, Russia, China, France, Great Britain, Canada, Australia, the United States, and other countries have engaged in internal colonialism.

Edna Bonacich developed a second important theory that focuses on social-structural conditions hindering the assimilation of some groups. According to Bonacich (1972), racial identities are reinforced in **split labor markets.** Where low-wage workers of one race and high-wage workers of another race compete for the same jobs, high-wage workers are likely to resent the presence of low-wage competitors. Conflict is bound to result and racist attitudes develop or get reinforced. The effects of split labor markets and internal colonialism on racial and ethnic identity persist for some time even after these social-structural conditions cease to exist.

Let us examine how these two theories apply to the United States by considering four groups: Native Americans, Mexican Americans, African Americans, and Chinese Americans.

Native Americans

The words that best describe the treatment of Native Americans by European settlers in the 19th century are expulsion and genocide. **Expulsion** is the forcible removal of a population from a territory claimed by another population. **Genocide** is the intentional extermination of an entire population defined as a race or a people.

In 1830 the United States government passed the Indian Removal Act. It called for the relocation of all Native Americans to land set aside for them west of the Mississippi. For the next decade, white European Americans fought a series of wars against various Native American tribes. Relying on superior military technology and troop strength, the U.S. Army easily won. In one notorious incident, the "Trail of Tears," the U.S. Army rounded up all 16,000 Cherokees, held them for months in camps infested with disease, and then marched them to Oklahoma. Four thousand Cherokees died on the trek.

The effective end of the war against the Indians came in 1890 with the slaughter of hundreds of Sioux at Wounded Knee in South Dakota (Brown, 1970). Gradually, those who survived were placed on reservations under the rule of the Bureau of Indian Affairs. The reservations were segregated from the majority population. Good jobs, health facilities, and opportunities for educational advancement were scarce.

What war could not accomplish, disease and the extermination of the buffalo did. European settlers brought measles, influenza, cholera, typhoid, and malaria to North America. Native Americans had no immunity against those diseases. The settlers also killed some 15 million buffalo for meat and hides, thus destroying the Indians' most important source of food, clothing, and shelter. Between 1800 and 1900, the Native American population was cut in half.

In the late 19th century, the government adopted a policy of forced assimilation. It sold some Indian land to non-Indians and assigned some of it to individual Indians willing to farm like the settlers. This policy partly destroyed tribal life. With the help of various religious groups, the government also tried to eradicate native religions, languages, and cultures by taking Native American children from their parents and placing them in boarding schools where they could be "civilized."

The administration of Franklin D. Roosevelt adopted a more liberal policy in the 1930s and 1940s. It prohibited the further breakup of Indian lands and encouraged Native self-rule and cultural preservation. However, this policy was only a brief deviation from traditional policy. In the 1950s the government reverted to form. It proposed to end the reservation system, deny the sovereign status of the tribes, cut off all government services, and stop protecting Indian lands held in trust for the tribes.

The proposal backfired. It was never implemented because of strong resistance on the part of the Native American community. By the 1960s a full-fledged Red Power movement had emerged. It transcended tribal differences and spoke in the name of all Native Americans. The movement organized a series of occupations, sieges, sit-ins, marches, and demonstrations between 1969 and 1972. These efforts finally pushed the government to address the needs and rights of Native Americans (Cornell, 1988; Nagel, 1996).

Expulsion: The forcible removal of a population from a territory claimed by another population.

Genocide: The intentional extermination of an entire population defined as a race or a people.

Saskatchewan Archives Board, R-A8223

Saskatchewan Archives Board, R-A8223

In the late 19th and early 20th centuries, North American governments, with the help of various religious groups, tried to eradicate Native religions, languages, and cultures by taking Indian children from their parents and placing them in boarding schools where they could be "civilized." Here we see one Thomas Moore before and after such schooling in the early 20th century.

In recent decades, Native Americans have used the legal system to fight for political self-determination and the protection of their remaining lands. Their ability to do so has been enhanced by the discovery of valuable resources on reservations, including oil, natural gas, coal, and uranium. In addition, Indians have established many enterprises on reservations in recent years. Casinos are the most important of these economically. They have generated much wealth for a few tribes, but they have also created glaring inequalities between rich and poor. Small, rich tribes have used part of their casino revenue to gain political influence in Washington. Consequently, they receive the most federal aid per capita, whereas large, poor tribes receive relatively little.

Despite new sources of wealth, many Native Americans still suffer the consequences of internal colonialism. Urban Indians are less impoverished than those who live on reservations, but even in the cities they fall below the national average in terms of income, education, occupation, employment, health care, and housing (Marger, 2003: 188–93). The median family income of Native Americans is just over half the national average, and the poverty rate is nearly three times the national average. On reservations, the unemployment rate is nearly 50 percent, and in urban areas Indians often lack the skills and qualifications to secure steady jobs. Much discrimination and stereotyping continue to hamper their progress.

Chicanos

We can tell a similar story about Mexican Americans, or Chicanos. Motivated by the desire for land, the United States went to war with Mexico in 1848. The United States won. Arizona, California, New Mexico, Utah, and parts of Colorado and Texas became part of the United States. Americans justified the war in much the same way as the conquest of Native Americans. As an editorial in the *New York Evening Post* put it:

> "The Mexicans are Indians—Aboriginal Indians. . . . They do not possess the elements of an independent national existence. The Aborigines of this country have not attempted and cannot attempt to exist independently along side of us. Providence has so ordained it, and it is folly not to recognize the fact. The Mexicans are Aboriginal Indians, and they must share the destiny of their race" (quoted in Steinberg, 1989 [1981]: 22).

For the past 150 years, millions of Chicanos have lived in the U.S. Southwest (Camarillo, 1979). Specifically, more than two-thirds of Hispanic Americans are of Mexican origin and nearly 80 percent of Hispanic Americans live in the South and the West (Ramirez and de la Cruz, 2003: 2). Due mainly to discrimination, Chicanos are socially, occupationally, and residentially segregated from white European Americans. They were not forced onto reservations like Native Americans. However, until the 1970s, most Chicanos lived in ghettos, or *barrios,* far from white European American neighborhoods. Many of them still do. Many white European Americans continue to regard Chicanos as social inferiors. As a result, Chicanos interact mainly with other Chicanos. They still experience much job discrimination, and they still work mainly as agricultural and unskilled laborers with few prospects for upward mobility. (Some people find it ironic that some Mexicans who now work in California, Texas, and other states from which their ancestors were expelled are called "illegal migrants.") About half of Chicanos 25 years or older have not graduated from high school. The comparable figure for non-Hispanic whites is 11 percent. Among Hispanic Americans, Chicanos are least likely to work in managerial or professional occupations, least likely to earn $50,000 a year or more, and second most likely (next to Puerto Rican Americans) to live in poverty (Ramirez and de la Cruz, 2003: 5–6). Thus, as with Native Americans, high levels of occupational, social, and residential segregation prevent Chicanos from assimilating. Instead, especially since the 1960s, many Chicanos have taken part in a movement to renew their culture and protect and advance their rights (Gutiérrez, 1995).

African Americans

Most features of the internal colonialism model can explain the obstacles to African American assimilation too. For although the lands of Africa were not invaded and incorporated into the United States, many millions of Africans were brought here by force and enslaved. **Slavery** is the ownership and control of people. By about 1800, 24 million Africans had been captured and transported on slave ships to North, Central, and South America. As a result of violence, disease, and shipwreck, only 11 million survived the passage. Fewer than 10 percent of those 11 million arrived in the United States. By the outbreak of the Civil War, there were 4.4 million black slaves in the United States. The cotton and tobacco economy of the American South depended completely on their labor (Patterson, 1982).

Slavery kept African Americans segregated from white society. Even after slavery was legally banned in 1863, they remained a race apart. So-called Jim Crow laws kept blacks from voting, attending white schools, and in general participating equally in many social institutions. In 1896, the Supreme Court approved segregation when it ruled that separate facilities for blacks and whites were legal as long as they were of nominally equal quality (*Plessy v. Ferguson*). Most African Americans remained unskilled workers throughout this period.

In the late 19th and early 20th centuries, a historic opportunity to integrate the black population into the American mainstream presented itself. This was a period of rapid industrialization. The government could have encouraged African Americans to migrate northward and westward and get jobs in the new factories. There they could have enjoyed job training, steady employment, and better wages. But U.S. policymakers chose instead to encourage white European immigration. Between 1880 and 1930, 23 million Europeans came to the United States to work in the expanding industries. While white European immigrants made their first strides on the path to upward mobility, the opportunity to integrate the black population quickly and completely into the American mainstream was squandered (Steinberg, 1989 [1981]: 173–200).

Slavery: The ownership and control of people.

Some jobs in northern and western industries did go to African Americans, who migrated from the South in substantial numbers from the first decade of the 20th century on. They were able to compete against European immigrants in the labor market by accepting low wages. Here we see the operation of a classic split labor market of the type that Edna Bonacich analyzed. The split labor market fueled deep resentment, animosity, and antiblack riots on the part of working-class whites. This solidified racial identities, both black and white (Bonacich, 1972).

Despite this conflict, black migration northward and westward continued. That is because social and economic conditions in the South were even worse. Already by the 1920s, the world center of jazz had shifted from New Orleans to Chicago. This as much as anything signaled the permanence and vitality of the new black communities. By the mid-1960s there were about 4 million African Americans living in the urban centers of the North and the West.

The migrants from the South tended to congregate in low-income neighborhoods, where they sought inexpensive housing and low-skill jobs. Slowly—more slowly than was the case for white European immigrants—their situation improved. Many children of migrant blacks finished high school. Some finished college. Others established ethnic enterprises. Still others got jobs in the civil service. Residential segregation in poor neighborhoods decreased, and there was even some intermarriage with members of the white community (Lieberson, 1980).

In the 1960s, some sociologists observed these developments and expected African Americans to continue moving steadily up the social class hierarchy. As we will see soon, this optimism was only partly justified. Social-structural impediments, some new and some old, prevented many African Americans from achieving the level of prosperity and assimilation enjoyed by white European Americans. Thus, in the mid-1960s, about a third of African Americans lived in poverty, and the proportion is virtually unchanged today. In concluding this chapter, we carry the story of African Americans and other racial minorities forward to the present.

Chinese Americans

In 1882 Congress passed an act prohibiting the immigration of three classes of people into the United States for 10 years: lunatics, idiots, and Chinese. The act was extended for another decade in 1892, made permanent in 1907, and repealed only in 1943, when Congress established a quota of 105 Chinese immigrants per year. Earlier, the California gold rush of the 1840s and the construction of the transcontinental railroads in the 1860s had drawn tens of thousands of Chinese immigrants into the United States. The great majority of them were young men who worked as unskilled laborers. However, until 1965, fewer than 100,000 Chinese were living in the United States. They were the objects of one of the most hostile anti-ethnic movements in American history.

Extraordinary prejudice and ignorance greeted the Chinese in the United States, and the film and tourist industries did much to reinforce fear of the "yellow peril" in the first half of the 20th century. For example, in the 1920s guides would take tourists to San Francisco's Chinatown and warn them to stick together and keep their eyes peeled for Chinese hatchet men, always eager to chop the heads off unsuspecting white folk. To prove the danger, the guides paid sinister-looking Chinese men to dart in and out of the shadows of dimly lit alleys, knives and hatchets at the ready. Tourists were shown false opium dens, told phony stories about brothels populated by white women who had been enslaved by the Chinese, and misinformed that certain cuts of meat in Chinese butcher shops were rat carcasses (Takaki, 1989).

It was, however, a split labor market that caused anti-Chinese prejudice to boil over into periodic race riots and laws aimed at keeping Chinese immigrants out of the United

The anti-Chinese riot in Seattle, February 8, 1886, in front of the New England Hotel on Main and 1st Avenue.

Museum of History and Industry, Seattle

States. The American government allowed Chinese immigrants into California to do backbreaking work such as railway construction and mining with hand tools. The immigrants received wages well below those of white workers. As split labor market theory predicts, where competition for jobs between Chinese and white workers was intense, trouble brewed and ethnic and racial identities were reinforced. Recent research shows that anti-Chinese activity was especially high where white workers were geographically concentrated and successful in creating anti-Chinese organizations. San Francisco was the epicenter of anti-Chinese sentiment and activity (Fong and Markham, 2002).

Chinese Americans have experienced considerable upward mobility in the past half century. More than 30 percent of Chinese Americans now marry whites (Marger, 2003: 385). However, a social-structural factor—split labor markets—did much to prevent such mobility and assimilation until the middle of the 20th century. Similarly, our sketch of Native Americans shows that a second social circumstance—internal colonialism—helps to explain why upward mobility and assimilation are often hampered, contrary to the prediction of Park's ecological theory. The groups that have had most trouble achieving upward mobility in the United States are those, like African Americans and Native Americans, that were subjected to slavery and expulsion from their native lands. Expulsion and slavery left a legacy of racism that created social-structural impediments to assimilation, such as forced segregation in low-status jobs and low-income neighborhoods. By focusing on factors like these, we arrive at a more realistic picture of the state of race and ethnic relations in the United States than is afforded by ecological theory alone.

Some Advantages of Ethnicity

The theories of internal colonialism and split labor markets emphasize how social forces outside a racial or ethnic group force its members together, preventing their assimilation into the larger society. They focus on the disadvantages of race and ethnicity. Moreover, they deal only with the most disadvantaged minorities. The theories have less to say about the *internal* conditions that promote group cohesion and in particular about the value of group membership. Nor do they help us to understand why some white European Americans continue to participate in the life of their ethnic communities, even if their families have been in the country more than two generations.

A review of the sociological literature suggests that three main factors enhance the value of ethnic group membership for some Americans—even white European Americans—who have lived in the country for many generations. These factors are economic, political, and emotional.

Economic Advantages

The economic advantages of ethnicity are most apparent for immigrants, who comprised 12 percent of the American population in 2008 (▶Figure 9.3). Immigrants often lack extensive social contacts and fluency in English. Therefore, they commonly rely on members of their ethnic group to help them find jobs and housing. In this

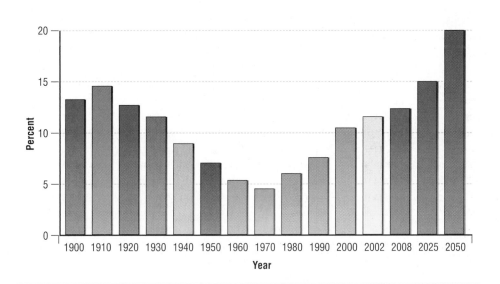

▶FIGURE 9.3
Percent Foreign-Born, United States, 1900–2008 and 2025–2050 (projected)

Sources: Roberts (2008); U.S. Census Bureau (1993: 2; 1999e; 2001a; 2002c).

way, immigrant communities become tightly knit. Community solidarity is also an important resource for "ethnic entrepreneurs." These are businesspeople who operate largely within their ethnic community. They draw on their community for customers, suppliers, employees, and credit. However, some economic advantages extend into the third generation and beyond. For example, ethnic entrepreneurs can pass on their businesses to their children, who in turn can pass the businesses on to the next generation. In this way, strong economic incentives encourage some people to remain ethnic group members, even beyond the immigrant generation (Light, 1991; Portes and Manning, 1991).

Political Advantages

Ethnic group membership may also have political advantages. Consider, for instance, the way some European Americans reacted to the Civil Rights movement of the 1960s. Civil rights legislation opened new educational, housing, and job opportunities for African Americans. It also led to the liberalization of immigration laws. Until the passage of the 1965 Hart-Celler Act, immigration from Asia and Latin America was sharply restricted. Afterward, most immigrants came from these regions (▶Table 9.2). Some white European Americans felt threatened by the improved social standing of African Americans and non-European immigrants. As a result, "racial minorities and white ethnics became polarized on a series of issues relating to schools, housing, local government, and control over federal programs" (Steinberg, 1989 [1981]: 50). Not coincidentally, many European Americans experienced renewed interest in their ethnic roots just at this time. Many sociologists believe the white ethnic revival of the 1960s and 1970s was a reaction to political conflicts with African, Asian, Native, and Hispanic Americans. Such conflicts helped to strengthen ethnic group solidarity.

Until the passage of the 1965 Hart-Celler Act, immigration from Asia, Africa, and Latin America was sharply restricted. Today, most immigrants to the United States come from Latin America and Asia.

▼

David Turnley/CORBIS

▶TABLE 9.2
Top 10 Countries of Origin of Foreign-Born Americans, 1900, 1960, and 2000
(in thousands; percent of total foreign-born in parentheses)

1900		1960		2000	
Germany	2,663 (25.8)	Italy	1,257 (12.9)	Mexico	7,418 (26.1)
Ireland	1,615 (15.6)	Germany	990 (10.2)	China	1,391 (4.9)
Canada	1,179 (11.4)	Canada	953 (9.8)	Philippines	1,222 (4.3)
Great Britain	1,167 (11.3)	Great Britain	765 (7.9)	India	1,007 (3.5)
Sweden	582 (5.6)	Poland	748 (7.7)	Cuba	952 (3.4)
Italy	484 (4.7)	Soviet Union	691 (7.1)	Vietnam	863 (3.0)
Soviet Union	423 (4.1)	Mexico	576 (5.9)	El Salvador	765 (2.7)
Poland	383 (3.7)	Ireland	338 (3.5)	Korea	701 (2.5)
Norway	336 (3.2)	Hungary	245 (2.5)	Dominican Republic	692 (2.4)
Austria	275 (2.7)	Czechoslovakia	228 (2.3)	Canada	678 (2.4)
Other	1,234 (11.9)	Other	2,947 (30.2)	Other	12,690 (44.7)
Total	10,341 (100.0)	Total	9,738 (100.0)	Total	28,379 (100.0)

Sources: Calculated from U.S. Census Bureau (1997, 2001b: 9).

Emotional Advantages

Like economic benefits, the emotional advantages of ethnicity are most apparent in immigrant communities. Speaking the ethnic language and sharing other elements of one's native culture are valuable sources of comfort in an alien environment. Even beyond the second generation, however, ethnic group membership can perform significant emotional functions. For example, some ethnic groups, such as Jews, have experienced unusually high levels of prejudice and discrimination involving expulsion and attempted genocide. For people who belong to such groups, the resulting trauma is so severe that it can be transmitted for several generations. In such cases, ethnic group membership offers security in a world still seen as hostile long after the threat of territorial loss or annihilation has disappeared (Bar-On, 1999). Another way in which ethnic group membership offers emotional support beyond the second generation is by providing a sense of rootedness. Especially in a highly mobile, urbanized, technological, and bureaucratic society such as ours, ties to an ethnic community can be an important source of stability and security (Isajiw, 1978).

In sum, ethnicity remains a vibrant force in American society for a variety of reasons. Even some white Americans whose families arrived in this country generations ago have reason to identify with their ethnic group. Bearing this in mind, what is the likely future of race and ethnic relations in the United States? We conclude by offering some tentative answers to that question.

The Future of Race and Ethnicity

At 2:30 a.m. on June 7, 1998, James Byrd, Jr., was walking home along a country road near Jasper, Texas. Three men stopped and offered Byrd a ride. But instead of taking him home, they forced Byrd out of their pickup truck. They beat him until he was unconscious. They then chained his ankles to the back of the truck and dragged him along the jagged road for nearly 3 miles. The ride tore Byrd's body into more than 75 pieces.

What was the reason for the murder? Byrd was a black man. His murderers are "white supremacists." They want the United States to be a white-only society, and they are prepared to use violence to reach their goal. The murderers expressed no remorse during their trial. Two of them wore tattoos suggesting membership in the racist Aryan Nation or the Ku Klux Klan. As such, they are part of a growing problem in the United States. More than 750 active racist and neo-Nazi organizations have sprung up in the country, with the biggest concentrations in Georgia, Texas, and California (Southern Poverty Law Center, 2000). In 2006 the Federal Bureau of Investigation recorded 7,722 **hate crimes,** or criminal incidents motivated by a person's race, religion, ethnicity, sexual orientation, or disability. Each incident may involve multiple offenses, such as assault and property damage. A total of 9,080 offenses were recorded. By far the most frequent victims of hate crimes were African Americans, who were the object of 40.6 percent of all offenses (U.S. Federal Bureau of Investigation, 2007).

White supremacists form only a tiny fraction of the American population. Many more Americans engage in subtle forms of racism. Thus, sociologists Joe Feagin and Melvin Sikes (1994) interviewed a sample of middle-class African Americans in 16 cities. They found that their respondents often had trouble hailing a cab. If they arrived in a store before a white customer, a clerk commonly served them after the white customer. When they shopped, store security often followed them around to make sure they didn't shoplift. Police officers often stop middle-class African American men in their cars without apparent reason. Blacks are less likely than whites of similar means to receive mortgages and other loans (Oliver and Shapiro, 1995). In short, African Americans continue to suffer high levels of racial prejudice and discrimination (Hacker, 1992; Shipler, 1997).

The Declining Significance of Race?

Still, sociologist William Julius Wilson (1980 [1978]) and others believe that race is declining in significance as a force shaping the lives of African Americans. Wilson argues that the Civil Rights movement helped to establish legal equality between blacks and whites. In 1954 the Supreme Court ruled against earlier decisions permitting school segregation (*Brown v. Board of Education*). The 1964 Civil Rights Act outlawed discrimination in public housing, employment, and the distribution of federal funds. It also supported school integration. The 1965 Voting Rights Act prohibited the systematic exclusion of blacks from the political process. The 1968 Civil Rights Act banned racial discrimination in housing. These reforms allowed a large black middle class to emerge, says Wilson. Today, one-third of the African American population is middle class.

Many facts support Wilson's view that the social standing of blacks has improved. For example, in 1947 median family income among blacks was only 51 percent that of whites. In 2005 it stood at nearly 64 percent (▶Figure 9.4). The proportion of whites with four or more years of college increased 235 percent from 1960 to 2002. In the same period, the proportion of blacks with four or more years of college increased 448 percent. In 2001, 0.3 percent fewer whites but 9.8 percent fewer blacks lived below the poverty line than in 1980 (U.S. Census Bureau, 1998a: 167; 2003a: 153, 456, 463). The representation of African Americans in the mass media is increasing (Box 9.3). Public opinion polls suggest that whites are becoming more tolerant of blacks (▶Figure 9.6) (Thernstrom and Thernstrom, 1997). Wilson, citing similar data, admits that the gap between blacks and whites remains substantial but is shrinking.

For Wilson, the one-third of African Americans who live below the poverty line is little different from other Americans in similar class circumstances. He therefore calls for "color-blind" public policies that aim to improve the class position of the poor, such as

Hate crimes: Criminal acts motivated by a person's race, religion, or ethnicity.

▶FIGURE 9.4
Median Family Income
Ratios, Black/White and
Hispanic/White, United
States, 1947–2005

Sources: Mishel, Bernstein, and
Schmitt (1999: 45); U.S. Census
Bureau (2004: 443; 2008e).

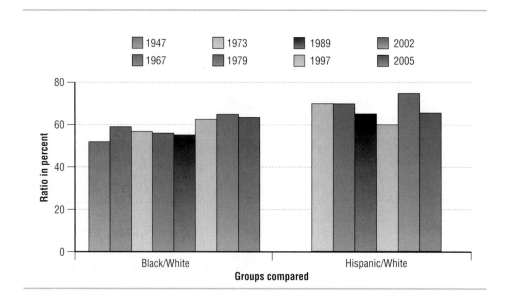

job training and health care. He opposes race-specific policies, such as **affirmative action,** a policy that gives preference to minority-group members if equally qualified people are available for a position. He feels that such policies disproportionately help middle-class African Americans while keeping poor African Americans poor (Wilson, 1996) (see Chapter 12, "Religion and Education," for an extended discussion of this subject).

Despite the points noted above, some sociologists think Wilson exaggerates the declining significance of race. For Wilson's critics, racism remains a big barrier to black progress. Their case for the continuing impact of race is strengthened by statistical analyses of data on racial differences in wages and housing patterns. They have shown that race had a *stronger* impact on wages in 1985 than in 1976, probably because the government retreated from antidiscrimination initiatives in the 1980s (Cancio, Evans, and Maume, 1996). Moreover, many African Americans continue to live in inner-city ghettos, where they experience high rates of poverty, crime, divorce, teenage pregnancy, and unemployment.

Wilson says ghettos persist not so much because of racism but for three economic and class reasons. First, since the 1970s older manufacturing industries have closed down in cities where the black working class was concentrated. This increased unemployment and poverty. Second, many middle- and working-class African Americans with good jobs moved out of the inner city. This deprived young people of successful role models. Third, the exodus of successful blacks eroded the inner-city's tax base at precisely the same time that conservative federal and state governments were cutting budgets for public services. This added to the destitution of inner-city residents (Wilson, 1996).

Although the economic and class factors discussed by Wilson undoubtedly explain much, they do not explain the persistently high level of residential segregation among the many *middle-class* blacks who have left the ghettos since the 1960s. They moved to the suburbs, yet their neighborhoods are nearly as segregated as those in the inner city. That is why people sometimes call them "ghettos with grass." White homeowners are likely to move elsewhere if "too many" blacks move into a suburban neighborhood. Meanwhile, real estate agents and mortgage lenders sometimes withhold information, refuse loans, and otherwise discourage African Americans from moving into certain areas in order to protect real estate values (Massey and Denton, 1993).

Affirmative action: A policy
that gives preference to minority-group members if equally
qualified people are available for
a position.

BOX 9.3
MASS MEDIA AND SOCIETY

Minority Representation on Television

Two studies compare the percentage of minority groups in the American population with their percentage in fictional TV roles (*Fall Colors*, 2002; Gerbner, 1998). ▶Figure 9.5 summarizes part of the studies. A score of 100 indicates that the percentage of a group in the American population is the same as its percentage in fictional TV roles. A score of more than 100 indicates the degree of overrepresentation, a score of less than 100 the degree of underrepresentation. Figure 9.5 shows that in 1994–97 and 2001–02 there were proportionately more white men in fictional TV roles than white men in the U.S. population, although their overrepresentation fell from 29 percent to 6 percent between these two periods.

Meanwhile, the representation of African Americans in fictional TV roles increased, reaching 35 percent overrepresentation in 2001–02. The claim once heard that American television does not reflect the weight of the country's black population is simply no longer true. (On the other hand, in 2001–02 there were 28 percent fewer women in fictional TV roles than in the population, 64 percent fewer Hispanics, 19 percent fewer Asians, and 99.8 percent fewer Native Americans. These figures demonstrate that TV falls far short of reflecting the diversity of American society in many respects.)

Despite overall numerical improvement, the portrayal of African Americans, other racial minorities, women, the poor, and people with disabilities still tends to reinforce traditional, mainstream, negative stereotypes. For instance, nonwhites tend to play comical or criminal characters rather than serious, heroic types. Characters of different races often interact professionally, sometimes interact socially, but are rarely romantically involved.

Certain stereotypical images of African American women recur in the mass media—for example, in the role of the welfare mother, the highly sexualized Jezebel, and the mammy. The findings reviewed here point to positive change in the way the mass media treat some minority groups, including African Americans. We have come a long way since the 1950s, when virtually the only blacks on TV were men who played butlers and buffoons. But research suggests that the mass media still have a long way to go before they cease reinforcing traditional stereotypes in American society (Dines and Humez, 1995).

Critical Thinking

- Does it matter whether the representation of minorities on TV reflects their representation in the population? If so, how? If not, why not?

- Should the government or some other body regulate TV to ensure fair representation of minorities? Why or why not?

- How, if at all, do you expect minority representation on TV to change in the next decade? If you expect no change to occur, why not? If you expect change, what do you think will cause it?

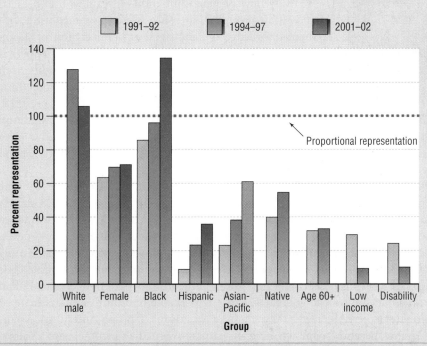

▶FIGURE 9.5

Representation of Minority Groups in Prime-Time and Daytime Television, United States, 1991–1992, 1994–1997, and 2001–2002

Note: 2001–2002 data are for prime time only. A 2001–2002 figure for Native Americans was reported but it is so small that it is not visible on the graph. For other groups, missing bars indicate missing data.
Sources: *Fall Colors* (2002: 4, 17); Gerbner (1998).

▶FIGURE 9.6
White Prejudice and Discrimination against Blacks, United States, 1972–2006

Source: National Opinion Research Center (2008b).

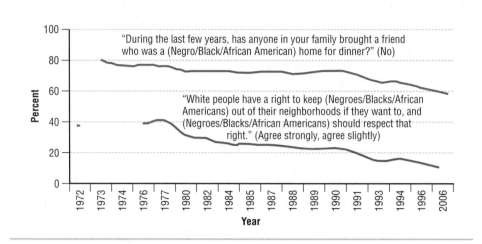

"During the last few years, has anyone in your family brought a friend who was a (Negro/Black/African American) home for dinner?" (No)

"White people have a right to keep (Negroes/Blacks/African Americans) out of their neighborhoods if they want to, and (Negroes/Blacks/African Americans) should respect that right." (Agree strongly, agree slightly)

In the late 19th and early 20th centuries, Ellis Island in New York harbor was the point of entry of more than 12 million Europeans to the United States. Today, more than one-third of all Americans can trace their origins to a person who passed through Ellis Island.

Lewis W. Hine/Getty Images

Immigration and the Renewal of Racial and Ethnic Groups

If high levels of racism and inequality ensure the persistence of racial and ethnic identity, so does immigration. A steady flow of new immigrants gives new life to racial and ethnic groups. That is because immigrants bring with them knowledge of languages, an appreciation of group culture, and a sense of community that might disappear if an ethnic or racial group were cut off from its origins. Seen in this light, we can expect many vibrant racial and ethnic communities to invigorate American life for a long time. Not since early in the 20th century has the immigration rate been so high, and not since the 1930s has such a large percentage of Americans consisted of people born in other countries (Figure 9.3 and ▶Figure 9.7).

Of all the broad racial and ethnic categories used by the U.S. Census Bureau, the fastest growing is "Asian American." Numbering 16 million people in a 2008 survey, most people in this category arrived after the mid-1960s (▶Table 9.3). That was when legislators eliminated racist selection criteria and instead designed an immigration law that emphasized the importance of choosing newcomers who could make a big economic contribution to the country. Many Asian immigrants are middle-class professionals and businesspeople. For example, nearly 60 percent of Asian-Indian American adults are college graduates, and a remarkable one-third hold graduate or professional degrees. More generally, Chinese Americans, Filipino Americans, Asian-Indian Americans, and Japanese Americans earn above median income, have a below-average poverty rate, and are more likely than non-Hispanic whites to hold a college degree.[5] Considering only the American born, one may add Korean Americans to this list (Marger, 2003: 362, 367).

---

[5]Little Japanese immigration occurred after the 1920s, however.

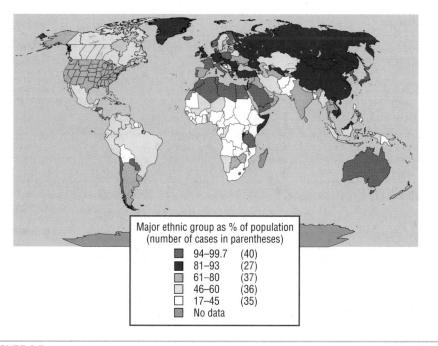

Major ethnic group as % of population
(number of cases in parentheses)

	% range	(cases)
■	94–99.7	(40)
■	81–93	(27)
■	61–80	(37)
■	46–60	(36)
□	17–45	(35)
■	No data	

▶FIGURE 9.7

Percent of Population Accounted for by Largest Ethnic Group

There are more than 5,000 ethnic groups in the world. Ethnic diversity has increased in recent years because of international migration. This map illustrates the world's ethnic diversity by showing the percentage of each country's population that is accounted for by the country's largest ethnic group. How ethnically diverse is the United States compared with other countries?

Sources: "Ethnic Groups in the World," *Scientific American.* On the World Wide Web at http://www.sciam.com/1998/0998issue/0998numbers.html (December 4, 2001); *CIA World Factbook 2002.* On the World Wide Web at http://www.cia.gov/cia/publications/factbook (February 6, 2003).

Some people hold up Asian Americans as models for other disadvantaged groups. Their formula is disarmingly simple: Emulate the Asians—work hard, keep your family intact, make sure your kids go to college—and you will surely succeed economically. There are, however, two main problems with this argument. First, some substantial Asian American groups, including several million Vietnamese, Cambodians, Hmong, and Laotians, do not fit the "Asian model." Members of these groups came to the United States as political refugees after the Vietnam War, and they are disproportionately poor and unskilled, with a poverty rate higher than that of African Americans. Thus, there is no universal Asian model. Second, most economically successful Asian Americans were selected as immigrants precisely because they possessed educational credentials, skills, or capital that could benefit the American economy. They arrived on American shores with advantages, not liabilities. Saying that unskilled Chicanos or the black descendants of slaves should follow their example ignores the very social-structural brakes on mobility and assimilation that sociologists have discovered and emphasized in their research.

▶TABLE 9.3

"Asian Alone" Americans, 2004*

Group	Number (millions)	Percent of Total
Chinese except Taiwanese	2.8	23.4
Indian	2.2	18.6
Filipino	2.1	17.8
Vietnamese	1.3	10.5
Korean	1.3	10.3
Japanese	0.8	6.9
Pakistani	0.2	1.7
Cambodian	0.2	1.6
Other	1.2	9.2
Total	12.1	100.0

*"Asian alone" refers to people who reported only Asian origin; it excludes about 4 million people who reported Asian and some other origin.
Sources: Roberts (2008); U.S. Census Bureau (2007c: 2).

▶FIGURE 9.8
Six Degrees of Separation:
Types of Ethnic and Racial
Group Relations

Source: Adapted from Kornblum
(1997 [1988]: 385).

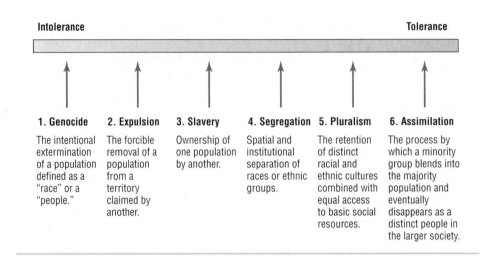

Intolerance   Tolerance

1. Genocide	2. Expulsion	3. Slavery	4. Segregation	5. Pluralism	6. Assimilation
The intentional extermination of a population defined as a "race" or a "people."	The forcible removal of a population from a territory claimed by another.	Ownership of one population by another.	Spatial and institutional separation of races or ethnic groups.	The retention of distinct racial and ethnic cultures combined with equal access to basic social resources.	The process by which a minority group blends into the majority population and eventually disappears as a distinct people in the larger society.

CENGAGENOW™

Learn more about **Genocide** by going through the Genocide: Mike Jacobs' Story Video Exercise.

A Vertical Mosaic

In 1800, the United States was a society based on slavery, expulsion, and segregation. More than two centuries later, we are a society based on segregation, **pluralism,** and assimilation. Thus, on a scale of tolerance, the United States has come a long way in the past two centuries (▶Figure 9.8).

In comparison with most other countries, too, the United States is a relatively tolerant land. In recent decades, racial and ethnic tensions in some parts of the world have erupted into wars of secession and attempted genocide. Conflict between Croats, Serbs, and other ethnic groups broke Yugoslavia apart. In Rwanda, Hutu militia and soldiers massacred many thousands of Tutsi civilians. A few years later, Tutsi soldiers massacred many thousands of Hutu civilians. A bloody war between the Chechen minority in Russia and the Russian state broke out in the 1990s. Black residents of Darfur in Western Sudan are the victims of a genocide that is supported by their own government. Comparing the United States to such poor countries may seem to stack the deck in favor of concluding that the United States is a relatively tolerant society. However, even when we compare the United States with other rich, stable, postindustrial countries, our society seems relatively tolerant by some measures (▶Figure 9.9).

Due to such factors as intermarriage and immigration, the growth of tolerance in the United States is taking place in the context of increasing ethnic and racial diversity. By the time most of today's first-year college students are 80 years old, non-Hispanic whites will form a minority of the United States population for the first time in 350 years. The United States will be even more of a racial and ethnic mosaic than it is now (▶Figure 9.10).

Contributing to this diversity is the fact that an increasing number of Americans identify themselves as biracial, multiracial, or "mixed race." According to the 2000 Census, 7.3 million Americans, 2.6 percent of the total population, think of themselves as mixed race. Just as the idea of the white race first emerged in the 19th century out of intermarriage among people of Anglo-Saxon, Teutonic, Slavic, and other origins, so in the early 21st century we are witnessing the emergence of new racial groups (Roediger, 1991).

If present trends continue, however, the racial and ethnic mosaic of American society will be vertical, with some groups, such as African Americans, Native Americans, Puerto Rican Americans, Chicanos, and some Asian American groups disproportionately

Pluralism: The retention of racial and ethnic culture combined with equal access to basic social resources.

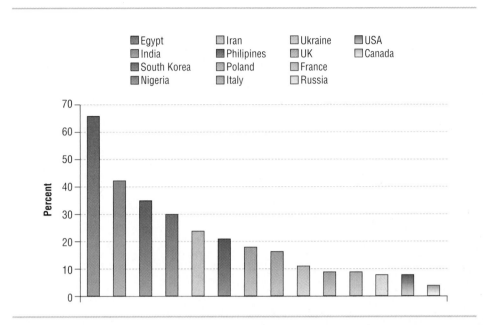

▶FIGURE 9.9
Percent Not Wanting a Neighbor of a Different Race, Selected Countries, 2000

Source: *World Values Survey* (2004).

clustered at the bottom. They will remain among the most disadvantaged groups in the country, enjoying less wealth, income, education, good housing, health care, and other social rewards than other ethnic and racial groups.

Policy initiatives could decrease the verticality of the American ethnic mosaic, thus speeding up the movement from segregation to pluralism and assimilation for the country's most disadvantaged groups. Apart from affirmative action programs, equality can be promoted by more job training, improvements in public education, and subsidized health and child care. That is because these programs would be of greatest benefit to the most disadvantaged Americans. The country may not be able to afford all of these expensive reforms at this time (see Chapter 11, "Families," and Chapter 12, "Religion and Education"), but under President Obama, some movement in their direction seems possible.

The Points of the Compass

"All that is solid melts into the air," Marx wrote. He wasn't writing about ethnicity and race in the twenty-first century, but he could have been. One of the main lessons of this chapter is that while people's ethnic and racial identities seem fixed, they are in fact flexible to varying degrees. A variety of powerful social forces constrain people's freedom of ethnic and (especially) racial choice, but people have never been less constrained to remain a member of the ethnic or racial group into which they were born.

Significantly, opportunities for upward mobility are positively correlated with freedom of ethnic and racial choice. That is, people who are relatively free to decide their ethnic and racial identity tend to enjoy more opportunities for upward mobility, while those who are less free to decide their ethnic and racial identity tend to enjoy fewer opportunities for upward mobility. To paraphrase Orwell's *Animal Farm*, it is widely believed that everyone enjoys equal opportunity, but the reality is that members of some ethnic and especially racial categories enjoy less equal opportunity than others.

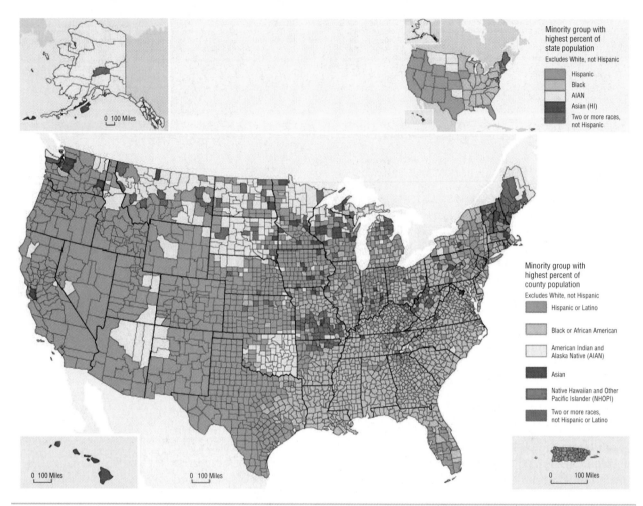

▶FIGURE 9.10
Prevalence of Hispanics and Nonwhite Minorities, United States, 2000

Source: U.S. Census Bureau (2001b).

CHAPTER SUMMARY

1. Is "race" a meaningful term?

Some biologists suggest that race is not a useful term because biological differences that distinguish races do not predict differences in social behavior. However, sociologists retain the term because *perceptions* of racial difference have important consequences for people's lives.

2. What is the difference between race and ethnicity?

A race is a category of people whose perceived *physical* markers are deemed socially significant. An ethnic group is a category of people whose perceived *cultural* markers are deemed socially significant. Just as physical distinctions don't cause differences in the behavior of races, cultural distinctions are often not by themselves the major source of differences in the behavior of various ethnic groups. *Social-structural* differences are typically the most important sources of differences in ethnic behavior.

3. What is the "social construction of race and ethnicity"?

When sociologists speak of the social construction of race and ethnicity, they mean that race and ethnicity are not fixed, and they are not inherent in people's biological makeup or cultural heritage. Rather, the way race and ethnicity are perceived and expressed depends on the history and character of race and ethnic relations in particular social contexts. These social contexts shape the way people formulate (or "construct") their perceptions and expressions of race and ethnicity. Thus, racial and ethnic labels and identities change over time and place.

4. What is Robert Park's theory of race and ethnic relations?

Robert Park's ecological theory of race and ethnic relations focuses on the way racial and ethnic groups struggle for territory and eventually blend into one another. He divides this struggle into five stages: (1) invasion, (2) resistance, (3) competition, (4) accommodation and co-operation, and (5) assimilation. The main problem with his theory is that some groups get "stuck" at stages 3 and 4, and Park offers no explanation for why this happens.

5. What are the theories of internal colonialism and split labor markets?

These theories view the persistence of ethnic and racial identities as the result of social inequalities. According to the theory of internal colonialism, immigrant settlers gain virtually complete control over a native population and change or destroy the native culture, then develop the racist belief that the natives are inherently inferior as they confine them to work they consider demeaning. This situation prevents assimilation by segregating the colonized in terms of jobs, housing, and social contacts ranging from friendship to marriage. According to split labor market theory, where low-wage workers of one race and high-wage workers of another race compete for the same jobs, high-wage workers are likely to resent the presence of low-wage competitors. Conflict is bound to result and racist attitudes develop or get reinforced.

6. Aside from the historical legacy of internal colonialism and split labor markets, do other reasons exist for the persistence of racial and ethnic identity, even among some white European Americans whose ancestors came to this country generations ago?

Identifying with a racial or ethnic group can have economic, political, and emotional benefits. These benefits account for the persistence of ethnic identity in some white European American families, even after they have been in the United States more than two generations. In addition, high levels of immigration renew racial and ethnic communities by providing them with new members who are familiar with ancestral languages, customs, and so forth.

7. What is the future of race and ethnicity in the United States?

Racial and ethnic identities and inequalities are likely to persist in the foreseeable future. In addition to affirmative action programs, we might look to more job training, improvements in public education, and subsidized health care and child care as ways to promote equality.

Questions to Consider

1. How do you identify yourself in terms of your race or ethnicity? Do conventional ethnic and racial categories "fit" your sense of who you are? Why or why not?

2. Do you think racism is becoming more serious in the United States and worldwide? Why or why not? How do trends in racism compare with trends in other forms of prejudice, such as sexism? What accounts for similarities and differences in these trends?

3. What are the costs and benefits of ethnic diversity in your college? Do you think it should adopt a policy of affirmative action to make the student body and the faculty more ethnically and racially diverse? Why or why not?

Web Resources

CENGAGENOW™

Maximize your study time by using CengageNOW's diagnostic study plan to help you review this chapter. The Study Plan will

- help you identify areas on which you should concentrate;
- provide interactive exercises to help you master the chapter concepts; and
- provide a post-test to confirm you are ready to move on to the next chapter.

The Companion Website for *Sociology: Your Compass for a New World, The Brief Edition*, Enhanced Second Edition
www.cengage.com/sociology/brym

Supplement your review of this chapter by going to the companion website to take one of the tutorial quizzes, use flash cards to master key terms, and check out the many other study aids you'll find there. You'll also find special features such as GSS Data and Census 2000 information that will put data and resources at your fingertips to help you with that special project or help you do some research on your own.

Rolf Bruderer/CORBIS

In this chapter, you will learn that:

- Whereas biology determines sex, social structure and culture largely determine gender, or the expression of culturally appropriate masculine and feminine roles.

- The social construction of gender is evident in the way parents treat babies, teachers treat pupils, and the mass media portray ideal body images.

- The social forces pushing people to assume conventionally masculine or feminine roles are compelling.

- The social forces pushing people toward heterosexuality operate with even greater force.

- The social distinction between men and women serves as an important basis of inequality in the family and the workplace.

- Male aggression against women is rooted in gender inequality.

Sex versus Gender

Is It a Boy or a Girl?

On April 27, 1966, identical 8-month-old twin boys were brought to a hospital in Winnipeg, Canada, to be circumcised. An electrical cauterizing needle—a device used to seal blood vessels as it cuts—was used for the procedure. However, because of equipment malfunction or doctor error, the needle entirely burned off one baby's penis. The parents desperately sought medical advice. No matter whom they consulted, they were given the same prognosis. As one psychiatrist summed up baby Bruce's future, "He will be unable to consummate marriage or have normal heterosexual relations; he will have to recognize that he is incomplete, physically defective, and that he must live apart" (quoted in Colapinto, 1997: 58).

One evening, more than half a year after the accident, the parents, now deeply depressed, were watching TV. They heard Dr. John Money, a psychologist from Johns Hopkins Hospital in Baltimore, say that he could *assign* babies a male or female identity. Money had been the driving force behind the creation of the world's first "sex change" clinic at Johns Hopkins. He was well known for his research on **intersexed** infants, babies born with ambiguous genitals because of a hormone imbalance in the womb or some other cause. It was Money's opinion that infants with "unfinished genitals" should be assigned a sex by surgery and hormone treatments, and reared in accordance with their newly assigned sex. According to Money, these strategies would lead to the child developing a self-identity consistent with its assigned sex.

The Winnipeg couple wrote to Dr. Money, who urged them to bring their child to Baltimore without delay. After consultation with various physicians and with Money, the

CENGAGENOW™

Learn more about **Sex versus Gender** by going through the Sex versus Gender Animation.

CENGAGENOW™

This icon signals when CengageNOW has important resources available for you to use in conjunction with the text. See the foldout at the front of this text for information on how to access CengageNOW.

Intersexed: People born with ambiguous genitals due to a hormone imbalance in their mother's womb or some other cause.

parents agreed to have their son's sex reassigned. In anticipation of what would follow, the boy's parents stopped cutting his hair, dressed him in feminine clothes, and changed his name from Bruce to Brenda. Surgical castration was performed when the twin was 22 months old.

Early reports of the child's progress indicated success. In contrast to her biologically identical brother, Brenda was said to disdain cars, gas pumps, and tools. She was supposedly fascinated by dolls, a dollhouse, and a doll carriage. Brenda's mother reported that at the age of 4½, Brenda took pleasure in her feminine clothing.

The "twins case" generated worldwide attention. Textbooks in medicine and the social sciences were rewritten to incorporate Money's reports of the child's progress (Robertson, 1987 [1977]: 316). But then, in March 1997, two researchers dropped a bombshell when they published an article showing that Bruce/Brenda had in fact struggled against his/ her imposed girlhood from the start. Brenda insisted on urinating standing up, refused to undergo additional "feminizing" surgeries that had been planned, and, from age 7, daydreamed of her ideal future self "as a twenty-one-year-old male with a moustache, a sports car, and surrounded by admiring friends" (Colapinto, 2001: 93). She experienced academic failure and rejection and ridicule from her classmates, who dubbed her "Cavewoman." At age 9, Brenda had a nervous breakdown. At age 14, in a state of acute despair, she attempted suicide (Colapinto, 2001: 96, 262).

In 1980, Brenda learned the details of her sex reassignment from her father. At age 16, she decided to have her sex reassigned once more and to live as a man rather than a woman. Advances in medical technology made it possible for Brenda, who now adopted the name David, to have an artificial penis constructed. At age 25, David married a woman and adopted her three children, but that did not end his ordeal. In May 2004, at the age of 38, David Reimer committed suicide.

Gender Identity and Gender Role

The story of Bruce/Brenda/David introduces the first big question of this chapter. What makes us male or female? Of course, part of the answer is biological. Your **sex** depends on whether you were born with distinct male or female genitals and a genetic program that released male or female hormones to stimulate the development of your reproductive system.

However, the case of Bruce/Brenda/David also shows that more is involved in becoming male or female than biological sex differences. Recalling his life as Brenda, David said: "[E]veryone is telling you that you're a girl. But you say to yourself, 'I don't *feel* like a girl.' You think girls are supposed to be delicate and *like* girl things—tea parties, things like that. But I like to *do* guy stuff. It doesn't match" (quoted in Colapinto, 1997: 66, our emphasis). As this quotation suggests, being male or female involves not just biology but also certain "masculine" and "feminine" feelings, attitudes, and behaviors. Accordingly, sociologists distinguish biological sex from sociological **gender.** One's gender is composed of the feelings, attitudes, and behaviors typically associated with being male or female. **Gender identity** is one's identification with, or sense of belonging to, a particular sex—biologically, psychologically, and socially. When you behave according to widely shared expectations about how males or females are supposed to act, you adopt a **gender role.**

The Social Learning of Gender

Contrary to first impressions, the case of Bruce/Brenda/David suggests that unlike sex, gender is not determined just by biology. Research shows that babies first develop a vague sense of being a boy or a girl at about the age of 1 year. They develop a full-blown sense of gender identity between the ages of 2 and 3 (Blum, 1997). We

---

CENGAGENOW™

Learn more about **Gender Identity and Gender Role** by going through Sex: The Biological Dimension Learning Module.

Sex: An aspect of one's biological makeup that depends on whether one is born with distinct male or female genitals and a genetic program that releases either male or female hormones to stimulate the development of one's reproductive system.

Gender: One's sense of being male or female and playing masculine and feminine roles in ways defined as appropriate by one's culture and society.

Gender identity: One's identification with, or sense of belonging to, a particular sex—biologically, psychologically, and socially.

Gender role: The set of behaviors associated with widely shared expectations about how males or females are supposed to act.

can therefore be confident that baby Bruce already knew he was a boy when he was assigned a female gender identity at the age of 22 months. He had, after all, been raised as a boy by his parents and treated as a boy by his brother for almost 2 years. He had seen boys behaving differently from girls on TV and in storybooks. He had played only with stereotypical boys' toys. After his gender reassignment, the constant presence of his twin brother reinforced those early lessons on how boys ought to behave. In short, baby Bruce's *social* learning of his gender identity was already far advanced by the time he had his sex-change operation. Many researchers believe that if gender reassignment occurs before the age of 18 months, it will usually be successful (Creighton and Mihto, 2001; Lightfoot-Klein et al., 2000).

However, once the social learning of gender takes hold, as with baby Bruce, it is apparently very difficult to undo, even by means of reconstructive surgery, hormones, and parental and professional pressure. The main lesson we draw from this story is not that biology is destiny but that the social learning of gender begins very early in life.

The first half of this chapter helps you better understand what makes us male or female. We first outline two competing perspectives on gender differences. The first perspective argues that gender is inherent in our biological makeup and that society must reinforce those tendencies if it is to function smoothly. Functionalist theory is compatible with this argument. The second perspective argues that gender is constructed mainly by social influences and may be altered to benefit society's members. Conflict, feminist, and symbolic interactionist theories are compatible with the second perspective.

In the course of our discussion we examine how people learn gender roles during socialization in the family and at school. We show how everyday social interactions and advertising reinforce gender roles. We also discuss how members of society enforce **heterosexuality**—the preference for members of the opposite sex as sexual partners. For reasons that are still poorly understood, some people resist and even reject the gender roles that are assigned to them based on their biological sex. When this occurs, negative sanctions are often applied to get them to conform or to punish them for their deviance. Members of society are often eager to use emotional and physical violence to enforce conventional gender roles.

The second half of the chapter examines one of the chief consequences of people learning conventional gender roles. Gender, as currently constructed, creates and maintains social inequality. We illustrate this in two ways. We investigate why gender is associated with the earnings gap between women and men in the paid labor force. We also show how gender inequality encourages sexual harassment and rape. In concluding our discussion of sexuality and gender, we discuss some social policies that sociologists have recommended to decrease gender inequality and improve women's safety.

Theories of Gender

Most arguments about the origins of gender differences in human behavior adopt one of two perspectives. Some analysts see gender differences as a reflection of naturally evolved tendencies and argue that society must reinforce those tendencies if it is to function smoothly. Sociologists call this perspective **essentialism** (Weeks, 1986). That is because it views gender as part of the nature or "essence" of one's biological and social makeup. Other analysts see gender differences mainly as a reflection of the different social positions occupied by women and men. Sociologists call this perspective **social constructionism.** That is because it views gender as "constructed" by social structure and culture. Conflict, feminist, and symbolic interactionist theories focus on various aspects of the social construction of gender.

Heterosexuality: The preference to have members of the opposite sex as sexual partners.

Essentialism: A school of thought that sees gender differences as a reflection of biological differences between women and men.

Social constructionism: A school of thought that sees gender differences as a reflection of the different social positions occupied by women and men.

The ceremonial dress of male Wodaabe nomads in Niger may appear "feminine" by conventional North American standards.

Essentialism

Sociobiologists and evolutionary psychologists have proposed one popular essentialist theory. They argue that humans instinctively try to ensure that their genes are passed on to future generations. However, men and women develop different strategies to achieve that goal. Presumably, women have a bigger investment than men in ensuring the survival of their offspring because women produce only a small number of eggs during their reproductive years and, at most, can give birth to about 20 children each. It is therefore in a woman's best interest to maintain primary responsibility for her genetic children and to seek out the single mate who can best help support and protect them. In contrast, men can produce as many as a billion sperm per ejaculation and this feat can be replicated frequently (Saxton, 1990: 94–5). To maximize their chance of passing on their genes to future generations, men must have many sexual partners.

According to sociobiologists and evolutionary psychologists, as men compete with other men for sexual access to many women, competitiveness and aggression emerge. Women, says one evolutionary psychologist, are greedy for money, whereas men want casual sex with women, treat women's bodies as their property, and react violently to women who incite male sexual jealousy. These are supposedly "universal features of our evolved selves" that contribute to the survival of the human species (Buss, 1998). Thus, from the point of view of sociobiology and evolutionary psychology, gender differences in behavior are based in biological differences between women and men.

Functionalism and Essentialism

Functionalists reinforce the essentialist viewpoint when they claim that traditional gender roles help to integrate society. In the family, wrote Talcott Parsons (1942), women traditionally specialize in raising children and managing the household. Men traditionally work in the paid labor force. Each generation learns to perform these complementary roles by means of *gender role socialization.*

For boys, noted Parsons, the essence of masculinity is a series of "instrumental" traits such as rationality, self-assuredness, and competitiveness. For girls, the essence of femininity is a series of "expressive" traits such as nurturance and sensitivity to others. Boys and girls first learn their respective gender traits in the family as they see their parents going about their daily routines. The larger society also promotes *gender role conformity.* It instills in men the fear that they won't be attractive to women if they are too feminine, and it instills in women the fear that they won't be attractive to men if they are too masculine. In the functionalist view, then, learning the essential features of femininity and masculinity integrates society and allows it to function properly.

A Critique of Essentialism from the Conflict and Feminist Perspectives

Conflict and feminist theorists disagree sharply with the essentialist account. They have lodged four main criticisms against it.

1. *First, essentialists ignore the historical and cultural variability of gender and sexuality.* Wide variations exist in what constitutes masculinity and femininity. Moreover, the

level of gender inequality, the rate of male violence against women, the criteria used for mate selection, and other gender differences that appear universal to the essentialists vary widely too. This variation deflates the idea that there are essential and universal behavioral differences between women and men. Three examples help illustrate the point:

- In societies with low levels of gender inequality, the tendency decreases for women to stress the good provider role in selecting male partners, as does the tendency for men to stress women's domestic skills (Eagley and Wood, 1999).

- When women become corporate lawyers or police officers or take other jobs that involve competition or threat, their production of the hormone testosterone is stimulated, causing them to act more aggressively. Aggressiveness is partly role related (Blum, 1997: 158–88).

- Hundreds of studies conducted mainly in North America show that women are developing traits that were traditionally considered masculine. Women have become considerably more assertive, competitive, independent, and analytical in the last 35 years or so (Biegler, 1999; Nowell and Hedges, 1998).

As these examples show, gender differences are not constants and they are not inherent in men and women. They vary with social conditions.

2. *Second, essentialism tends to generalize from the average, ignoring variations within gender groups.* On average, women and men do differ in some respects. For example, one of the best-documented gender differences is that men are on average more verbally and physically aggressive than women. However, when essentialists say that men are inherently more aggressive than women, they make it seem as if that is true of all men and all women. As ▶Figure 10.1 shows, it is not. When trained researchers measure verbal or physical aggressiveness, scores vary widely within gender groups. There is considerable overlap in aggressiveness between women and men. Thus, many women are more aggressive than the average man and many men are less aggressive than the average woman.

3. *Third, little or no evidence directly supports the essentialists' major claims.* For example, sociobiologists and evolutionary psychologists have not identified any of the genes

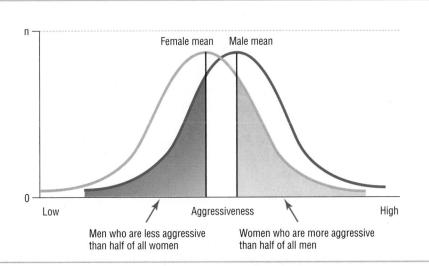

▶FIGURE 10.1
The Distribution of Aggressiveness among Men and Women

that, they claim, cause male jealousy, female nurturance, the unequal division of labor between men and women, and so forth.

4. *Finally, essentialists' explanations for gender differences ignore the role of power.* Essentialists assume that existing behavior patterns help ensure the survival of the species and the smooth functioning of society. However, as conflict and feminist theorists argue, their assumption overlooks the fact that men are usually in a position of greater power and authority than women.

Conflict theorists dating back to Marx's collaborator, Friedrich Engels, have located the root of male domination in class inequality (Engels, 1970 [1884]). According to Engels, men gained substantial power over women when preliterate societies were first able to produce more than their members needed for their own subsistence. At that point, some men gained control over the economic surplus. They soon devised two means of ensuring that their offspring would inherit the surplus. First, they imposed the rule that only men could own property. Second, by means of socialization and force, they ensured that women remained sexually faithful to their husbands. As industrial capitalism developed, Engels wrote, male domination increased because industrial capitalism made men still wealthier and more powerful while it relegated women to subordinate, domestic roles.

Feminist theorists doubt that male domination is so closely linked to the development of industrial capitalism. For one thing, they note that gender inequality is greater in agrarian than in industrial capitalist societies. For another, male domination is evident in societies that call themselves socialist or communist. These observations lead many feminists to conclude that male domination is rooted less in industrial capitalism than in the patriarchal authority relations, family structures, and patterns of socialization and culture that exist in most societies (Lapidus, 1978: 7).

Despite this disagreement, conflict and feminist theorists concur that behavioral differences between women and men result less from any essential differences between them than from men being in a position to advance their interests over the interests of women. From the conflict and feminist viewpoints, functionalism, sociobiology, and evolutionary psychology may themselves be seen as examples of the exercise of male power, that is, as rationalizations for male domination and sexual aggression.

Social Constructionism and Symbolic Interactionism

Essentialism is the view that masculinity and femininity are inherent and universal traits of men and women, whether because of biological or social necessity or some combination of the two. In contrast, social constructionism is the view that *apparently* natural or innate features of life, such as gender, are actually sustained by *social* processes that vary historically and culturally. As such, conflict and feminist theories may be regarded as types of social constructionism. So may symbolic interactionism. Symbolic interactionists, you will recall, focus on the way people attach meaning to things in the course of their everyday communication. One of the things to which people attach meaning is being a man or a woman. We illustrate the symbolic interactionist approach by first considering how boys and girls learn masculine and feminine roles in the family and at school. We then show how gender roles are maintained in the course of everyday social interaction and through advertising in the mass media.

Gender Socialization

Barbie dolls have been around since 1959. Based on the creation of a German cartoonist, Barbie is the first modern doll modeled after an adult. (Lili, the German original, became a pornographic doll for men.) Some industry experts predicted that mothers would never buy dolls with breasts for their little girls. Were *they* wrong! Mattel now sells about 10 million Barbies and 20 million accompanying outfits annually. The Barbie trademark is worth a billion dollars.

What do girls learn when they play with Barbie? The author of a website devoted to Barbie undoubtedly speaks for millions when she writes, "Barbie was more than a doll to me. She was a way of living: the Ideal Woman" (Elliott, 1995). One ideal that Barbie stimulates among many girls concerns body image. After all, Barbie is a scale model of a woman with a 40-18-32 figure (Hamilton, 1996: 197). The scales that come with Workout Barbie are fixed at a lithe 110 pounds. Researchers who compared Barbie's gravity-defying proportions with the actual proportions of several representative groups of adult women concluded that the probability of this body shape is less than 1 in 100,000 (Norton et al., 1996). (Ken's body shape is more realistic at 1 in 50.) The closets of Barbie's pink house are jammed with outfits. Bathrooms, gyms, beauty parlors, and vanity sets feature prominently among the Barbie accessories available. Presumably, this quest for physical perfection is designed to attract Ken, Barbie's boyfriend. The message Barbie conveys to girls is that the ideal woman is defined primarily by her attractiveness to men.[1]

A comparable story, with competition and aggression as its theme, could be told about how boys' toys, such as GI Joe, teach stereotypical male roles. True, a movement to market more gender-neutral toys arose in the 1960s and 1970s; there is now even a "presidential" Barbie. However, there remains a strong tendency to market toys based on gender. Typically, in the late 1990s, toy manufacturer Mattel produced a pink, flowered Barbie computer for girls with fewer educational programs than its blue Hot Wheels computer for boys (Mooney et al., 2003: 232).

Yet toys are only part of the story of gender socialization, and hardly its first or final chapter. Research conducted in the early 1970s showed that from birth, infant boys and girls who are matched in length, weight, and general health are treated differently by parents—fathers in particular. Girls tend to be identified as delicate, weak, beautiful, and cute; boys as strong, alert, and well coordinated (Rubin, Provenzano, and Lurra, 1974). Recent research shows that although parents' gender-stereotyped perceptions of newborns have declined, especially among fathers, they have not disappeared (Fagot, Rodgers, and Leinbach, 2000; Gauvain et al., 2002). One experiment found that when viewing a videotape of a 9-month-old infant, subjects tended to label its startled reaction to a stimulus as "anger" if the child had earlier been identified by the experimenters as a boy, and as "fear" if it had earlier been identified as a girl, *regardless of the infant's actual sex* (Condry and Condry, 1976).

Parents, and especially fathers, are likely to encourage their sons to engage in boisterous and competitive play and discourage their daughters from doing so. Parents tend to encourage girls to engage in cooperative, role-playing games (MacDonald and Parke, 1986). These different play patterns lead to the heightened development of verbal and emotional skills among girls and to increased concern with winning and the establishment of hierarchy among boys (Tannen, 1990). Boys are more likely than girls to be praised for assertiveness, and girls are more likely than boys to be rewarded for compliance (Kerig, Cowan, and Cowan, 1993). Given this early socialization, it seems perfectly "natural" that boys' toys stress aggres-

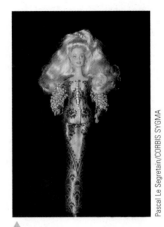

A Barbie doll.

Pascal Le Segretain/CORBIS SYGMA

The marketing of toys is still based on gender.

Brian Snyder/Reuters/CORBIS

---

[1]The Scandinavian rock group Aqua put it well in its 1997 top-10 hit, "Barbie Girl": "Make me walk / Make me talk / I can act like a star / I can beg on my knees . . . / You can touch / You can play / If you say / 'I'm always yours.'" Mattel tried to sue Aqua for its social commentary, but a Los Angeles judge tossed the case out of court in May 1998. Ironically, Lene Nystrom, the Norwegian lead singer of Aqua, had breast implants in 2000. She upset many women when she told Norway's leading daily newspaper, "I just want to be more feminine" (quoted in "Aqua Singer," 2000).

sion, competition, spatial manipulation, and outdoor activities, whereas girls' toys stress nurturing, physical attractiveness, and indoor activities (Hughes, 1995 [1991]). Still, what seems natural must be continuously socially reinforced. Presented with a choice between playing with a tool set and a dish set, preschool boys are about as likely to choose one as the other—unless the dish set is presented as a girl's toy and they think their fathers would view playing with it as "bad." Then, they tend to pick the tool set (Raag and Rackliff, 1998).

It would take someone who has spent very little time in the company of children to think they are passive objects of socialization. They are not. Parents, teachers, and other authority figures typically try to impose their ideas of appropriate gender behavior on children, but children creatively interpret, negotiate, resist, and self-impose these ideas all the time. Gender, we might say, is something that is done, not just given (Messner, 1995 [1989]; West and Zimmerman, 1987). This is nowhere more evident than in the way children play.

Gender Segregation, and Interaction

Consider the fourth- and fifth-grade classroom that sociologist Barrie Thorne (1993) observed. The teacher periodically asked the children to choose their own desks. With the exception of one girl, they always segregated *themselves* by gender. Similarly, when children played chasing games in the schoolyard, groups often *spontaneously* crystallized along gender lines. The teacher often reaffirmed such gender boundaries by pitting the boys against the girls in spelling and math contests. These contests were marked by cross-gender antagonism and expression of within-gender solidarity.

However, Thorne also observed many cases of boys and girls playing together. She also noticed quite a lot of "boundary crossing." Boundary crossing involves boys playing stereotypically girls' games and girls playing stereotypically boys' games. The most common form of boundary crossing involved girls who were skilled at soccer, baseball, and basketball, sports that were central to the boys' world. Boys and girls also interacted easily and without strong gender identities coming to the fore in activities requiring cooperation, such as group projects. Mixed-gender interaction was also more common in less public and crowded settings. Thus, boys and girls were more likely to play together and in a relaxed way in the relative privacy of their neighborhoods. In contrast, in the schoolyard, where they were under the close scrutiny of their peers, gender segregation and antagonism were more evident.

In sum, Thorne's research makes two important contributions to our understanding of gender socialization. First, children are actively engaged in the process of constructing gender roles. They are not merely passive recipients of adult demands. Second, while schoolchildren tend to segregate themselves by gender, boundaries between boys and girls are sometimes fluid and sometimes rigid, depending on social circumstances. In other words, the content of children's gendered activities is by no means fixed.

This is not to suggest that adults have no gender demands and expectations. They do, and their demands and expectations contribute significantly to gender socialization. For instance, many schoolteachers and guidance counselors still expect boys to do better in the sciences and math, and girls to achieve higher marks in English (Lips, 1999). Parents often reinforce these stereotypes in their evaluation of different activities (Eccles, Jacobs, and Harold, 1990). Although not all studies comparing mixed- and single-sex schools suggest that girls do much better in single-sex schools, most do (Bornholt, 2001; Jackson and Smith, 2000). In single-sex schools, girls typically experience faster cognitive development; higher occupational aspirations and attainment; greater self-esteem and self-confidence; and more teacher attention, respect, and encouragement; and they develop more egalitarian attitudes toward the role of women in society. Why? Because such schools place more

Boys accept girls as participants in sports if the girls are good at them.

David Young-Wolff/PhotoEdit

emphasis on academic excellence and less on physical attractiveness and heterosexual popularity. They provide more successful same-sex role models. And they eliminate gender bias in teacher–student and student–student interaction, because there are no boys around (Hesse-Biber and Carter, 2000: 99–100).

Adolescents must usually start choosing courses in school by the age of 14 or 15. By then, their **gender ideologies** are well formed. Gender ideologies are sets of interrelated ideas about what constitutes appropriate masculine and feminine roles and behavior. One aspect of gender ideology becomes especially important around grades 9 and 10: adolescents' ideas about whether, as adults, they will focus mainly on the home, paid work outside the home, or a combination of the two. Adolescents usually make course choices with gender ideologies in mind. Boys are strongly inclined to consider only their careers in making course choices. Most girls are inclined to consider both home responsibilities and careers, although a minority considers only home responsibilities and another minority considers only careers. Consequently, boys tend to choose career-oriented courses, particularly in math and science, more often than girls do. In college, the pattern is accentuated. Young women tend to choose easier courses that lead to lower-paying jobs because they expect to devote a large part of their lives to childrearing and housework (Hochschild with Machung, 1989: 15–18). The effect of these choices is to sharply restrict women's career opportunities and earnings in science and business (▶Table 10.1) (Reskin and Padavic, 2002 [1994]). We examine this problem in depth in the second half of this chapter.

The Mass Media and Body Image

The social construction of gender does not stop at the school steps. Outside school, children, adolescents, and adults continue to negotiate gender roles as they interact with the mass media.

If you systematically observe the roles played by women and men on TV programs and in ads one evening, you will probably discover a pattern noted by sociologists since the 1970s. Women will more frequently be seen cleaning house, taking care of children, modeling clothes, and acting as objects of male desire. Men will more frequently be seen

Gender ideology: A set of ideas about what constitutes appropriate masculine and feminine roles and behavior.

▶TABLE 10.1

Women and Occupations, United States, 2006

	Total Employed (1000s)	Median Weekly Earnings ($)	Women as Percent of Total	Women's Earnings as a % of Men's
Ten Most Common Occupations of Women				
Secretaries and administrative assistants	2,683	583	96.7	104.4
Elementary and middle school teachers	2,334	838	82.1	89.6
Customer service representatives	1,110	554	70.0	86.7
First-line supervisors/managers of office and administrative support	1,391	698	71.0	81.1
First-line supervisors/managers of retail sales workers	2,296	639	42.3	73.3
Bookkeeping, accounting, and auditing clerks	1,013	584	88.7	95.8
Accountants and auditors	1,448	940	61.2	72.8
Receptionists and information clerks	949	472	92.9	83.0
Retail sales persons	2,022	494	42.9	67.8
Maids and housekeeping cleaners	885	355	97.3	86.1
Average		616	74.5	84.1
Ten Highest-Earning Occupations				
Chief executives	1,040	1,875	24.8	74.6
Engineering managers	90	1,830	8.9	*
Lawyers	603	1,728	36.7	70.5
Pharmacists	189	1,640	42.3	90.6
Physicians and surgeons	558	1,602	33.7	72.0
Judges, magistrates, etc.	61	1,549	34.4	*
Aerospace engineers	97	1,508	12.4	*
Electrical and electronics engineers	362	1,386	7.7	*
Computer software engineers	799	1,371	22.0	90.2
Marketing and sales managers	805	1,316	37.5	66.5
Average		1,581	26.0	77.4

*Data not provided where fewer than 50,000 people.
Source: Department of Labor (2007).

in aggressive, action-oriented, and authoritative roles. The effect of these messages is to reinforce the normality of traditional gender roles.

Many people even try to shape their bodies after the body images portrayed in the mass media (Box 10.1). A 1997 survey of North American college graduates showed that 56 percent of women and 43 percent of men were dissatisfied with their overall appearance (Garner, 1997). Only 3 percent of the dissatisfied women, but 22 percent of the dissatisfied men, wanted to gain weight. This reflects the greater desire of men for muscular, stereotypically male physiques. Most of the dissatisfied men, and even more of the dissatisfied women (89 percent), wanted to lose weight. This reflects the societal push toward slimness, especially for women.

▶Figure 10.2 compares women's and men's attitudes toward the appearance of their stomachs. It also compares women's attitudes toward their breasts with men's attitudes toward their chests. It shows, first, that women are more concerned about their stomachs than men are. Second, it shows that by 1997 men were more concerned about their chests than women were about their breasts. Clearly, then, people's body ideals are influenced by their gender. Note also that North Americans' anxiety about their bodies increased substantially between 1972 and 1997.

BOX 10.1
MASS MEDIA AND SOCIETY

Why Thinner?

The human body has always served as a sort of personal billboard that advertises gender. However, historian Joan Jacobs Brumberg (1997) makes a good case for the view that the importance of body image to our self-definition has grown over the past century. Just listen to the difference in emphasis on the body in the diary resolutions of two typical white, middle-class American girls, separated by a mere 90 years. From 1892: "Resolved, not to talk about myself or feelings. To think before speaking. To work seriously. To be self restrained in conversation and actions. Not to let my thoughts wander. To be dignified. Interest myself more in others." From 1982: "I will try to make myself better in any way I possibly can with the help of my budget and baby-sitting money. I will lose weight, get new lenses, already got new haircut, good makeup, new clothes and accessories" (quoted in Brumberg, 1997: xxi).

As body image became more important for one's self-definition in the course of the 20th century, the ideal body image became thinner, especially for women. Thus, the first American "glamour girl" was Mrs. Charles Dana Gibson, who was famous in advertising and society cartoons in the 1890s and 1900s as the "Gibson Girl." According to the Metropolitan Museum of Art's Costume Institute, "Every man in America wanted to win her" and "every woman in America wanted to be her. Women stood straight as poplars and tightened their corset strings to show off tiny waists" (Metropolitan Museum of Art, 2000). As featured in the *Ladies Home Journal* in 1905, the Gibson Girl measured 38-27-45—certainly not slim by today's standards. During the 20th century, however, the ideal female body type thinned out. The "White Rock Girl," featured on the logo of the White Rock Beverage Company, was 5 feet 4 inches and weighed 140 pounds in 1894. In 1947 she had slimmed down to 125 pounds. By 1970 she was 5 feet 8 inches and 118 pounds (Peacock, 2000).

Why did body image become more important to people's self-definition during the 20th century? Why was slimness stressed? Part of the answer to both questions is that more Americans grew overweight as their lifestyles became more sedentary. As they became better educated, they became increasingly aware of the health problems associated with being overweight. The desire to slim down was, then, partly a reaction to bulking up. But that is not the whole story. The rake-thin models who populate modern ads are not promoting good health. They are promoting an extreme body shape that is virtually unattainable for most people. They do so because it is good business. The fitness, diet, low-calorie-food, and cosmetic surgery industries do tens of billions of dollars of business every year (Hesse-Biber, 1996). Bankrolled by these industries, advertising in the mass media blankets us with images of slim bodies and makes these body types appealing. Once people become convinced that they need to develop bodies like the ones they see in ads, many of them are really in trouble because these body images are very difficult for most people to attain.

Critical Thinking

- What is your ideal body image?
- What has influenced your ideal?
- Are you concerned about the impact of the mass media on your body image? Why or why not?

Courtesy of the White Rock Beverage Company

The "White Rock Girl" in 1894 *(left)* and 1947 *(right)*.

▶FIGURE 10.2

Body Dissatisfaction, United States, 1972–1997 (in percent, n = 4000)

Note: The n of 4,000 refers only to the 1997 survey. The number of respondents in the earlier surveys was not given.

Source: "The 1997 Body Image Survey Results" by David M. Garner, *Psychology Today*, Vol. 30, No. 1, pp. 30–44. Reprinted with permission from *Psychology Today Magazine*. Copyright © 1997 Sussex Publishers, Inc.

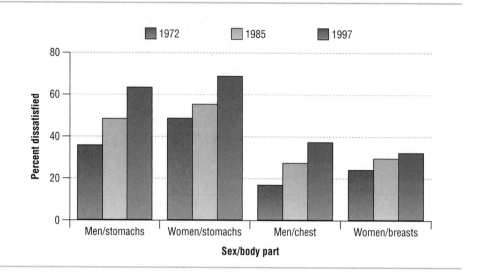

▶TABLE 10.2

The Influence of Fashion Models on Feelings about Appearance, North America (in percent; *n* = 4000)

	Men	Women	Extremely Dissatisfied Women
I always or often:			
Compare myself to models in magazines	12	27	43
Carefully study the shape of models	19	28	47
Very thin or muscular models make me:			
Feel insecure about my weight	15	29	67
Want to lose weight	18	30	67

Note: Data are for 1997.
Source: Adapted from Garner (1997).

CENGAGENOW™

Learn more about **Eating Disorders** by going through the Eating Disorders Animation.

▶Table 10.2 suggests that advertising is highly influential in creating anxiety and insecurity about appearance, particularly about body weight. Here we see that in 1997 nearly 30 percent of North American women compared themselves with the fashion models they saw in advertisements, felt insecure about their own appearance, and wanted to lose weight as a result. Among women who were dissatisfied with their appearance, the percentages were much larger, with about 45 percent making comparisons with fashion models and two-thirds feeling insecure and wanting to lose weight. It seems safe to conclude that fashion models stimulate body dissatisfaction among many North American women.

Body dissatisfaction, in turn, motivates many women to diet. Because of anxiety about their weight, 84 percent of women and 54 percent of men in North America said they had dieted in the 1997 survey. Just how important is it for people to achieve their weight goals? According to the survey, it's a "life or weight" issue: 24 percent of women and 17 percent of men said they would trade more than 3 years of their lives to achieve their weight goals.

Body dissatisfaction prompts some people to take dangerous and even life-threatening measures to reduce their weight. In the 1997 survey, 50 percent of female smokers and 30 percent of male smokers said they smoked to control their weight. Other surveys suggest that between 1 percent and 5 percent of American women suffer from anorexia, or refusal to eat enough to remain healthy. About the same percentage of American female college students suffer from bulimia, or regular self-induced vomiting. For college men, the prevalence of bulimia is between 0.2 and 1.5 percent (Averett and Korenman, 1996: 305–6). In the United Kingdom, eating disorders are just as common. However, U.K. magazine editors are taking some responsibility for the problem. They recognize that waif-thin models are likely influencing young women to feel anxious about their weight and shape. As a result, the editors recently drew up a voluntary code of conduct that urges magazine editors to monitor the body images their publications portray, impose a minimum size for models, and use models of varying shapes and sizes ("British Magazines Agree to Ban Ultra-thin Models," 2000). Whether similar measures will be adopted in the United States remains to be seen.

Male–Female Interaction

The gender roles that children learn in their families, at school, and through the mass media form the basis for their social interaction as adults. For instance, by playing team sports, boys tend to learn that social interaction is most often about competition, conflict, self-sufficiency, and hierarchical relationships (leaders versus followers). They understand the importance of taking center stage and boasting about their talents (Messner, 1995 [1989]). Because many of the most popular video games for boys exclude female characters, use women as sex objects, or involve violence against women, they reinforce some of the most unsavory lessons of traditional gender socialization (Dietz, 1998). On the other hand, by playing with dolls and baking sets, girls tend to learn that social interaction is most often about maintaining cordial relationships, avoiding conflict, and resolving differences of opinion through negotiation. They understand the importance of giving advice and not promoting themselves or being bossy.

Because of these early socialization patterns, misunderstandings between men and women are common. A stereotypical example: Harold is driving around lost. However, he refuses to ask for directions because doing so would amount to an admission of inadequacy and therefore a loss of status. Meanwhile, it seems perfectly "natural" to his passenger Sybil to want to share information, so she urges Harold to ask for directions. The result: conflict between Harold and Sybil (Tannen, 1990: 62). Gender-specific interaction styles also have serious implications for who is heard and who gets credit at work. For instance, Deborah Tannen's research discovered the typical case of the female office manager who doesn't want to seem bossy or arrogant. Eager to preserve consensus among her coworkers, she spends much time soliciting their opinions before making an important decision. But her boss perceives her approach as indecisive and incompetent. He wants to recruit leaders for upper-management positions, so he overlooks the woman and selects an assertive man for a senior job that just opened up (Tannen, 1994a: 132).

The contrasting interaction style between male and female managers can lead to women not getting credit for competent performance. That is why they sometimes complain about a **glass ceiling,** a social barrier that makes it difficult for them to rise to the top level of management. As we will see soon, factors other than interaction styles—such as outright discrimination and women's generally greater commitment to family responsibilities—also restrict women's upward mobility. But gender differences in interaction styles play an independent role in constraining women's career progress.

Homosexuality

The preceding discussion outlines some powerful social forces pushing us to define ourselves as conventionally masculine or feminine in behavior and appearance. For most people, gender socialization by the family, the school, and the mass media is compelling and is sustained by daily interactions. A minority of people, however, resist conventional gender roles.

Transgendered people defy society's gender norms and blur widely accepted gender roles. About 1 in every 5,000 to 10,000 people in North America is transgendered. Some

CENGAGENOW™

Learn more about the **Glass Ceiling** by going through the Glass Ceiling Animation.

Glass ceiling: A social barrier that makes it difficult for women to rise to the top level of management.

Transgendered: People who break society's gender norms by defying the rigid distinction between male and female. They may be heterosexual or homosexual.

transgendered people are **transsexuals.** Transsexuals are people who want to alter their gender by changing their appearance or resorting to medical intervention. Transsexuals believe they were born with the "wrong" body. They identify with, and want to live fully as, members of the opposite sex. They often take the lengthy and painful path to a sex-change operation. About 1 in every 30,000 people in North America is a transsexual (Nolen, 1999).

Homosexuals are people who prefer sexual partners of the same sex, and **bisexuals** are people who enjoy sexual partners of either sex. People usually call homosexual men *gays* and homosexual women *lesbians.* The most comprehensive survey of sexuality conducted in North America reports that 2.8 percent of American men and 1.4 percent of American women think of themselves as homosexual or bisexual. However, because of widespread animosity toward homosexuals, some people who engage in same-sex acts or want to do so do not identify themselves as gay, lesbian, or bisexual (Flowers and Buston, 2001; Herdt, 2001). Some 10.1 percent of American men and 8.6 percent of American women think of themselves as homosexual or bisexual or have had some same-sex experience or desire (▶Table 10.3) (Laumann et al., 1994: 299).

Homosexuals were not identified as a distinct category of people until the 1860s, when the term *homosexuality* was coined. The term *lesbian* is of even more recent vintage. Nevertheless, homosexual behavior has existed in every society. Some societies, such as ancient Greece, encouraged it. More frequently, homosexual acts have been forbidden.

We do not yet understand well why some people develop homosexual orientations. Some scientists think the reasons are mainly genetic, others think they are chiefly hormonal, whereas still others point to life experiences during early childhood as the most important factor. We do know that sexual orientation does not appear to be a choice. According to the American Psychological Association, it "emerges for most people in early adolescence without any prior sexual experience. . . . It is not changeable" (American Psychological Association, 1998).

In any case, sociologists are less interested in the origins of homosexuality than in the way it is socially constructed, that is, in the wide variety of ways it is expressed and repressed (Foucault, 1990 [1978]; Weeks, 1986). It is important to note in this connection that homosexuality has become less of a stigma over the past century. Two factors are chiefly responsible for this, one scientific, the other political. In the

Transsexuals: People who believe they were born with the "wrong" body. They identify with, and want to live fully as, members of the "opposite" sex, and to do so they often change their appearance or resort to medical intervention. They may be heterosexual or homosexual.

Homosexuals: People who prefer sexual partners of the same sex. People usually call homosexual men *gay* and homosexual women *lesbians.*

Bisexuals: People who prefer sexual partners of both sexes.

▶TABLE 10.3
Homosexuality in the United States (in percent)

	1994 (N = 3432)		2006 (N = 1991)	
	Men	Women	Men	Women
Identified themselves as homosexual or bisexual	2.8	1.4	—	—
Had sex with person of same sex in past 12 months	3.4	0.6	5	4
Had sex with person of same sex in past 5 years	—	—	5	5
Had sex with person of same sex at least once since puberty	5.3	3.5	—	—
Felt desire for sex with person of same sex	7.7	7.5	—	—
Had some same-sex desire or experience or identified themselves as homosexual or bisexual	10.1	8.6	—	—

Michael, Robert T., John H. Gagnon, Edward O. Laumann, and Gina Kolata. 1994. *Sex in America: A Definitive Survey,* p. 40. Boston: Little, Brown.
National Opinion Research Center. 2008b. *General Social Survey, 1972–2006.* Chicago: University of Chicago. Machine readable file.

On April 1, 2001, the Netherlands recognized full and equal marriage rights for homosexual couples.

20th century, sexologists—psychologists and physicians who study sexual practices scientifically—first recognized and stressed the wide diversity of existing sexual practices. The American sexologist Alfred Kinsey was among the pioneers in this field. He and his colleagues interviewed thousands of men and women. In the 1940s they concluded that homosexual practices were so widespread that homosexuality could hardly be considered an illness affecting a tiny minority (Kinsey, Pomeroy, and Martin, 1948).

If sexologists provided a scientific rationale for belief in the normality of sexual diversity, it was sexual minorities themselves who provided the social and political energy needed to legitimize sexual diversity among an increasingly large section of the public. Especially since the middle of the 20th century, gays and lesbians have built large communities and subcultures, particularly in major urban areas like New York and San Francisco. They have gone public with their lifestyles and have organized demonstrations, parades, and political pressure groups to express their self-confidence and demand equal rights with the heterosexual majority. This has done much to legitimize homosexuality and sexual diversity in general.

Nonetheless, opposition to people who don't conform to conventional gender roles remains strong at all stages of the life cycle. When you were a child, did you ever poke fun at a sturdily built girl who was good at sports by referring to her as a "dike"? As an adolescent or young adult, have you ever attempted to insult a man by calling him a "fag"? If so, your behavior was not unusual. Many children and young adults express the belief that heterosexuality is superior to homosexuality. "That's gay!" is used as a common expression of disapproval among teenagers.

Among adults, opposition is just as strong. What is your attitude today toward transgendered people, transsexuals, and homosexuals? Do you, for example, think that sexual relations between adults of the same sex are always, or almost always, wrong? If so, you are again not unusual. According to the 2006 General Social Survey (GSS), fully 61 percent of Americans believe that sexual relations between adults of the same sex are always, or almost always, wrong (National Opinion Research Center, 2008).

Hollandse Hoogte/Corbis Sygma

BOX 10.2
SOCIAL POLICY: WHAT DO YOU THINK?

Hate Crime Law and Homophobia

On October 7, 1998, Matthew Shepard, a gay undergraduate at the University of Wyoming, went to a campus bar in Laramie. From there, he was lured by Aaron James McKinney and Russell Henderson, both 21, to an area just outside town. McKinney and Henderson apparently wanted to rob Shepard. They wound up brutally murdering him.

One issue raised by Shepard's death concerns the definition of *hate crime.* Hate crimes are criminal acts motivated by a person's race, religion, or ethnicity. If hate motivates a crime, the law requires that the perpetrator be punished more severely than otherwise. For example, assaulting a person during an argument generally carries a lighter punishment than assaulting a person because he is an African American.

Furthermore, *federal* law permits prosecution of a hate crime only "if the crime was motivated by bias based on race, religion, national origin, or color, and the assailant intended to prevent the victim from exercising a 'federally protected right' (e.g., voting, attending school, etc.)" (Human Rights Campaign, 1999). This definition excludes crimes motivated by the sexual orientation of the victim. According to the FBI, if crimes against gays, lesbians, and bisexuals were

defined as hate crimes, they would have composed 14 percent of the total (U.S. Federal Bureau of Investigation, 2002b; Human Rights Campaign, 1999). Thirty-two states include sexual orientation in their hate crime laws.

Critical Thinking

- Do you think crimes motivated by the victim's sexual orientation are the same as crimes motivated by the victim's race, religion, or ethnicity? Why or why not?

- Do you think crimes motivated by the sexual orientation of the victim should be included in the legal definition of hate crime? Why or why not?

Antipathy to homosexuals is so strong among some people that they are prepared to back up their beliefs with force. A study of about 500 young adults in the San Francisco Bay area (probably the most sexually tolerant area in the United States) found that 1 in 10 admitted physically attacking or threatening people they believed were homosexuals. Twenty-four percent reported engaging in antigay name-calling. Among male respondents, 18 percent reported acting in a violent or threatening way and 32 percent reported name-calling. In addition, a third of those who had *not* engaged in antigay aggression said they would do so if a homosexual flirted with, or propositioned, them (Franklin, 1998).

Recent research suggests that some antigay crimes may result from repressed homosexual urges on the part of the aggressor (Adams, Wright, and Lohr, 1998). From this point of view, aggressors are **homophobic,** or afraid of homosexuals, because they cannot cope with their own, possibly subconscious, homosexual impulses. Their aggression is a way of acting out a denial of these impulses. However, although this psychological explanation may account for some antigay violence, it seems inadequate when set alongside the finding that fully half of all young male adults admitted to some form of antigay aggression in the San Francisco Bay area study previously cited. An analysis of the motivations of these San Franciscans showed that some of them did commit assaults to prove their toughness and heterosexuality. Others committed assaults just to alleviate boredom and have fun. Still others believed they were defending themselves from aggressive sexual propositions. A fourth group acted violently because they wanted to punish homosexuals for what they perceived as moral transgressions (Franklin, 1998). It seems clear, then, that antigay violence is not just a question of abnormal psychology but a broad, cultural problem with several sources.

Homophobia: Fear of homosexuals.

It would not be an exaggeration to say that Westerns—often called "Cowboy and Indian" movies—shaped a generation of Americans' expectations about gender and sexuality. John Wayne, Gary Cooper, Jimmy Stewart, and many others became role models for American men and their idea of masculinity: silent but strong, gentle toward the weak (women and children) but ferocious toward the evil (often American Indians), community-minded but ultimately lone, rugged individualists. Even today, it's hard not to be stirred and engrossed by such classic Westerns as *The Man Who Shot Liberty Valence* and *High Noon*.

Westerns, however, have not been a popular genre since the 1970s. The Civil Rights movement questioned the racial ideology of many Westerns, which presumed the superiority of the white race against the native populations. The movement against the War in Vietnam challenged the vision of the world as a place that ought to be pacified and ruled by white Americans. The feminist movement criticized the patriarchal masculine viewpoint of Westerns. The few Westerns since the 1970s have therefore deviated from classical Westerns, often parodying them.

Brokeback Mountain (2005), nominated for the 2005 best picture Oscar, traces the romantic love between two cowboys. They

Brokeback Mountain (2005)

Ennis (Heath Ledger; left) and Jack (Jake Gyllenhaal) in *Brokeback Mountain*.

fall in love in the early 60s, when both are 19 years old, long before they had heard of gay culture or even the notion of homosexual identity. They lead seemingly conventional married lives. Yet they continue to love each other and carry on their affair for two decades, periodically telling their wives that they are going on fishing trips together but raising suspicions when they

fail to bring any fish home. More than the passion, however, what the movie depicts is the high emotional cost of keeping one's sexual orientation and one's love a secret. Eventually, their marriages crumble, their social relationships suffer, and happiness and fulfillment prove elusive.

One of the reasons that Ennis (Heath Ledger, nominated for the 2005 best actor Oscar) cannot imagine the possibility of settling down with Jack (Jake Gyllenhaal, nominated for the 2005 best supporting actor Oscar) is a childhood experience. His father took him to see two men who were beaten to death, two "tough old birds" who happened to be "shacked up together." Fear of expressing his homosexuality was thus instilled early on. (In fact, both men deny their homosexuality. After their first night together, Ennis says to Jack, "You know I ain't queer." To which Jack replies, "Me neither.") Jack and Ennis's affair ends when Jack is beaten to death by homophobic men. Three grisly murders of gay men, then, provide the tragic backdrop to *Brokeback Mountain*.

Critical Thinking

● How much have things changed since the 60s, 70s, and 80s? Could *Brokeback Mountain* be set in 2009? Why or why not?

On the other hand, anecdotal evidence suggests that opposition to antigay violence is also growing in America. The 1998 murder of Matthew Shepard in Wyoming led to a public outcry. In the wake of his murder, some people called for a broadening of the definition of hate crime to include antigay violence (Box 10.2). The 1999 movie *Boys Don't Cry* also raised awareness of the problem of antigay violence, as did the 2005 movie *Brokeback Mountain* (Box 10.3).

In sum, strong social and cultural forces lead us to distinguish men from women and heterosexuals from homosexuals. We learn these distinctions throughout the socialization process, and we continually construct them anew in our daily interactions. Most people use positive and negative sanctions to ensure that others conform to conventional heterosexual gender roles. Some people resort to violence to enforce conformity and punish deviance.

Our discussion of this topic also suggests that the social construction of conventional gender roles helps to create and maintain social inequality between women and men. In the remainder of this chapter, we examine the historical origins and some of the present-day consequences of gender inequality.

Gender Inequality

The Earnings Gap Today

The earnings gap between men and women is one of the most important expressions of gender inequality today. In 2006, women over the age of 15 working full-time in the paid labor force earned only 80.8 percent of the income men earned (U.S. Department of Labor, 2007). Four main factors contribute to the gender gap in earnings. Let us review each of them in detail (Bianchi and Spain, 1996; England, 1992b).

1. *Gender discrimination persists.* In February 1985, when Microsoft, the software giant, employed about 1,000 people, it hired its first two female executives. According to a well-placed source who was involved in the hiring, both women got their jobs because Microsoft was trying to win a U.S. Air Force contract. Under the government's guidelines, Microsoft didn't have enough women in top management positions to qualify. The source quotes then–29-year-old Bill Gates, president of Microsoft, as saying: "Well, let's hire two women because we can pay them half as much as we will have to pay a man, and we can give them all this other 'crap' work to do because they are women" (quoted in Wallace and Erickson, 1992: 291).

   This incident is a clear illustration of **gender discrimination,** rewarding women and men differently for the same work. Gender discrimination has been illegal in the United States since 1964. It has not disappeared, as the previous anecdote confirms. However, antidiscrimination laws have helped to increase the **female–male earnings ratio,** that is, women's earnings as a percentage of men's earnings. The female–male earnings ratio increased 17.3 percent between 1960 and 2000. At that rate of improvement, women will be earning as much as men by about 2050, around the time most first-year college students today will be about 60 years old (calculated from Feminist. com, 1999; U.S. Department of Labor, 2000b).

2. *Heavy domestic responsibilities reduce women's earnings.* Raising children can be one of the most emotionally satisfying experiences in life. However, it is so exhausting and time-consuming and requires so many career interruptions due to pregnancy and illness that it substantially decreases the time one can spend getting training and doing paid work. Because women are disproportionately involved in childrearing, they suffer the brunt of this economic reality. Women also do more housework and spend more time caring for elderly people than men do.

   Specifically, in most countries, including the United States, women do between two-thirds and three-quarters of all unpaid child care, housework, and caring for elderly people (Boyd, 1997: 55). As a result, women devote fewer hours to paid work than men do, experience more labor-force interruptions, and are more likely than men to take part-time jobs. Part-time jobs pay less per hour and offer fewer benefits

CENGAGENOW™

Learn more about the **Origins of Gender Inequality** by going through the Gender Inequality Video Exercise.

CENGAGENOW™

Learn more about **Gender Inequality** by going through the Gender Inequality Data Experiment.

CENGAGENOW™

Learn more about **Gender Inequality and Work** by going through the Gender Inequality and Work Learning Module.

CENGAGENOW™

Learn more about **Gender Inequality and Work** by going through the Women-Owned Firms Map Exercise.

Gender discrimination: A practice that involves rewarding men and women differently for the same work.

Female–male earnings ratio: Women's earnings expressed as a percentage of men's earnings.

than full-time work. Even when they work full-time in the paid labor force, women continue to shoulder a disproportionate share of domestic responsibilities, working, in effect, a double shift (Hochschild with Machung, 1989; see Chapter 11, "Families"). This affects how much time they can devote to their jobs and careers and results in lower earnings (Mahony, 1995; Waldfogel, 1997).

3. *Women tend to be concentrated in low-wage occupations and industries.* The third factor leading to lower earnings for women is that the courses they select in high school and college tend to limit them to jobs in low-wage occupations and industries. Thus, although women have made big strides since the 1970s, especially in managerial employment, they are still concentrated in lower-paying clerical and service occupations and underrepresented in higher-paying occupations. For example, more than 96 percent of the people who provide private household services are women, compared with fewer than 9 percent of the people in "precision production, craft and repair work." Moreover, lower earnings are associated with occupations in which women are concentrated (Hesse-Biber and Carter, 2000: 114–73).

Although women have entered many traditionally "male" occupations since the 1970s, they are still concentrated in lower-paying clerical and service occupations and underrepresented in higher-paying manual occupations.

4. *Work done by women is commonly considered less valuable than work done by men because it is viewed as involving fewer skills.* Women tend to earn less than men because the skills involved in their work are often undervalued (Figart and Lapidus, 1996; Sorenson, 1994). Compare the 87.4 percent of telephone installers and repairers who were men in 2001 with the 98.3 percent of prekindergarten and kindergarten teachers who were women. The man who installed phones earned an average of $803 a week, whereas the woman who taught and interacted with 5-year-olds earned an average of $476 a week (U.S. Department of Labor, 2002b). It is, however, questionable whether it takes less training and skill to teach a young child the basics of counting and reading and cooperation and sharing than it does to install a phone. As this example suggests, we apply somewhat arbitrary standards to reward different occupational roles. In our society, these standards systematically undervalue the kind of skills needed for jobs traditionally held by women.

We thus see that the gender gap in earnings is based on several *social* circumstances rather than any inherent difference between women and men. This means that people can reduce the gender gap if they want to. Later, we discuss social policies that could create more equality between women and men. But first, to stress the urgency of such policies, we explain how the persistence of gender inequality encourages sexual harassment and rape.

Male Aggression against Women

Serious acts of aggression between men and women are common. The great majority are committed by men against women. For example, in 2006, 92,455 rapes of women were reported to the police in the United States (U.S. Federal Bureau of Investigation, 2007a).

The main source of FBI crime statistics does not even report data for male rape victims. The rate of rape is highest among young singles. Thus, in a survey of acquaintance and date rape in American colleges, 7 percent of men admitted they attempted or committed rape in the past year. Eleven percent of women said they were victims of attempted or successful rape (Koss, Gidycz, and Wisniewski, 1987).

Why do men commit more frequent, harmful acts of aggression against women than women commit against men? It is not because men on average are *physically* more powerful than women. Greater physical power is more likely to be used to commit acts of aggression only when norms justify male domination and men have much more *social* power than women. When women and men are more equal socially, and norms justify gender equality, then the rate of male aggression against women is lower. This is evident if we consider various types of aggression, including rape and sexual harassment (see also the discussion of domestic violence in Chapter 11, "Families").

Rape

Some people think that rapists suffer from a psychological disorder that compels them to achieve immediate sexual gratification, even though violence is required. Others think rape occurs because of flawed communication. They believe some rape victims give mixed signals to their assailants by, for example, drinking too much and flirting with them.

Such explanations are not completely invalid. Interviews with victims and perpetrators show that some rapists do suffer from psychological disorders. Other offenders do misinterpret signals in what they regard as sexually ambiguous situations (Hannon et al., 1995). But such cases account for only a small proportion of the total. Men who rape women are rarely mentally disturbed, and it is abundantly clear to most assailants that they are doing something their victims strongly oppose.

What then accounts for rape being as common as it is? A sociological answer is suggested by the fact that rape is sometimes not about sexual gratification at all. Some rapists cannot ejaculate. Some cannot even achieve an erection. Significantly, however, all rape involves domination and humiliation as principal motives. It is not surprising, therefore, that some rapists are men who were physically or sexually abused in their youth. They develop a deep need to feel powerful as psychological compensation for their early powerlessness. Other rapists are men who, as children, saw their mothers as potentially hostile figures who needed to be controlled or as mere objects available for male gratification. They saw their fathers as emotionally cold and distant. Raised in such an atmosphere, rapists learn not to empathize with women. Instead, they learn to want to dominate them (Lisak, 1992).

Psychological factors aside, certain social situations also increase the rate of rape. One such situation is war. In war, conquering male soldiers often feel justified in wanting to humiliate the vanquished, who are powerless to stop them. Rape is often used for this purpose, as was especially well documented in the ethnic wars that accompanied the breakup of Yugoslavia in the 1990s (Human Rights Watch, 1995).

Aggressiveness is also a necessary and important part of police work. Spousal abuse is therefore common among police officers. One U.S. study found that 37 percent of anonymously interviewed police wives reported spousal abuse. Several other surveys of police officers put the figure in the 40 percent range (Roslin, 2000). "It's a horrible, horrible problem," says Penny Harrington, former chief of police in Portland, Oregon, and now head of the Los Angeles–based National Center for Women and Policing. "Close to

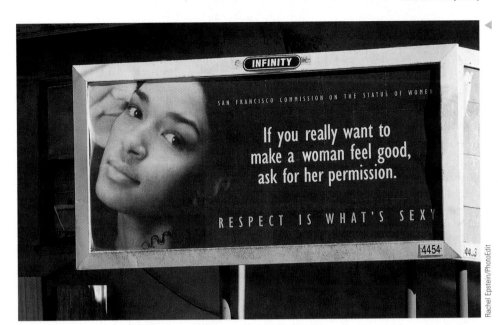

◁ A San Francisco billboard suggests that men still need reminding that no means no.

half of all 911 calls are due to family violence," says Harrington. "If the statistics are true, you've got a two-in-five chance of getting a batterer coming to answer your call" (quoted in Roslin, 2000: 46).

The relationship between male dominance and rape is also evident in research on college fraternities. Some college fraternities emphasize male dominance and aggression as a central part of their culture. Thus, sociologists who have interviewed fraternity members have shown that fraternities often try to recruit members who can reinforce a macho image and avoid any suggestion of effeminacy and homosexuality. Research also shows that fraternity houses that are especially prone to rape tend to sponsor parties that treat women in a particularly degrading way. Thus, by emphasizing a very narrow and aggressive form of masculinity, some fraternities tend to facilitate rape on college campuses (Boswell and Spade, 1996; Sanday, 1990).

Another social circumstance that increases the likelihood of rape is participation in athletics. Of course, few professional athletes are rapists. However, there are proportionately more rapists among men who participate in athletics than among nonathletes (Welch, 1997). That is because many sports embody a particular vision of masculinity in North American culture: competitive, aggressive, and domineering. By recruiting men who display these characteristics and by encouraging the development of these characteristics in athletes, sports can contribute to off-field aggression, including sexual aggression. Furthermore, among male athletes, there is a distinct hierarchy of sexual aggression. Male athletes who engage in contact sports are more prone to be rapists than other athletes. There are proportionately even more rapists among athletes involved in collision and combative sports, notably football (Welch, 1997).

Rape, we conclude, involves using sex to establish dominance. The incidence of rape is highest in situations where early socialization experiences predispose men to want to control women, where norms justify the domination of women, and where a big power imbalance between men and women exists.

Sexual Harassment

There are two types of sexual harassment. **Quid pro quo sexual harassment** takes place when sexual threats or bribery are made a condition of employment decisions (the Latin phrase *quid pro quo* means "something for something"). **Hostile environment sexual harassment** involves sexual jokes, comments, and touching that interferes with work or creates an unfriendly work setting. Research suggests that relatively powerless women are the most likely to be sexually harassed. Moreover, sexual harassment is most common in work settings that exhibit high levels of gender inequality and a culture justifying male domination of women. Specifically, women who are young, unmarried, and employed in nonprofessional jobs are most likely to become objects of sexual harassment, particularly if they are temporary workers, the ratio of women to men in the workplace is low, and the organizational culture of the workplace tolerates sexual harassment (Rogers and Henson, 1997; Welsh, 1999).

Ultimately, then, male aggression against women, including sexual harassment and rape, is encouraged by a lesson most of us still learn at home, in school, at work, through much of organized religion, and in the mass media—that it is natural and right for men to dominate women. To be sure, recent decades have witnessed important changes in the way women's and men's roles are defined. Nevertheless, in the world of paid work, in the household, in government, and in all other spheres of life, men still tend to command substantially more power and authority than women. Daily patterns of gender domination, viewed as legitimate by most people, get built into our courtship, sexual, family, and work norms. From this point of view, male aggression against women is simply an expression of male authority by other means.

This does not mean that all men endorse the principle of male dominance, much less that all men are inclined to rape or engage in other acts of aggression against women. Many men favor gender equality, and most men never rape or abuse a woman. However, the fact remains that many aspects of our culture legitimize male dominance, making it seem valid or proper. For example, much pornography, jokes at the expense of women, and whistling and leering at women might seem mere examples of harmless play. At a subtler, sociological level, however, they are assertions of the appropriateness of women's submission to men. Such frequent and routine reinforcements of male authority increase the likelihood that some men will consider it their right to assault women physically or sexually if the opportunity to do so exists or can be created. "Just kidding" has a cost. For instance, researchers have found that college men who enjoy sexist jokes are more likely than other college men to report engaging in acts of sexual aggression against women (Ryan and Kanjorski, 1998).

We thus see that male aggression against women and gender inequality are not separate issues. Gender inequality is the foundation of aggression against women. In concluding this chapter, we consider how gender inequality can be decreased in the coming decades. As we proceed, you should bear in mind that gender equality is not just a matter of justice. It is also a question of safety.

Toward 2050

The 20th century witnessed growing equality between women and men in many countries. In the United States, the decline of the family farm made it less economically useful and more costly to raise children. As a result, women started having fewer children. The industrialization of America, and then the growth of the economy's service sector,

Quid pro quo sexual harassment: Takes place when sexual threats or bribery are made a condition of employment decisions.

Hostile environment sexual harassment: Involves sexual jokes, comments, and touching that interfere with work or create an unfriendly work setting.

increased demand for women in the paid labor force (▶Figure 10.3). This gave them substantially more economic power and also encouraged them to have fewer children. The legalization and availability of contraception made it possible for women to exercise unprecedented control over their own bodies. The women's movement fought for, and won, increased rights for women on a number of economic, political, and legal fronts. All these forces brought about a massive cultural shift, a fundamental reorientation of thinking on the part of many Americans about what women could and should do in society.

One indicator of the progress of women is the Gender Empowerment Measure (GEM). The GEM of a country is computed by the United Nations. It takes into account women's share of seats in parliaments (the House of Representatives in the United States); women's share of administrative, managerial, professional, and technical jobs; and women's earning power. A score of 1.0 indicates equality with men on these three dimensions.

As ▶Figure 10.4 shows, Norway, Sweden, Finland, Denmark, and Iceland were the five most gender-egalitarian countries among the 93 on which data were available in 2005. They had GEM scores ranging from 0.91 to 0.862. This means that women in these countries are nearly 90 percent of the way to equality with men on the three measured dimensions. The United States ranked 15th, with a GEM score of 0.762.

In general, there is more gender equality in rich than in poor countries. The top-ranked countries are all rich. This suggests that gender equality is a function of economic development. However, our analysis of the GEM data suggests that there are some exceptions to the general pattern. For example, the Bahamas is not rich, but it ranks higher on the GEM (20) than the rich countries of Italy (21) and Japan (54). This finding suggests that gender equality may also be a function of government policy. Reinforcing our impression

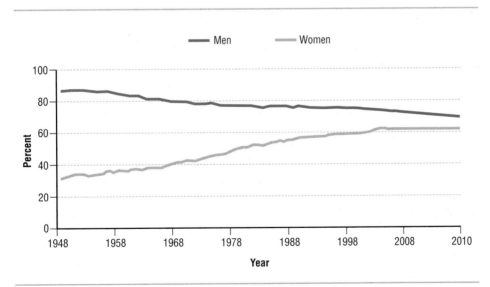

▶FIGURE 10.3
Labor Force Participation Rate by Sex, United States, 1948–2000 and 2001–2010 projected (in percent)

Note: Figures are expressed as percentage of men and women 16 years of age and older.

Source: U.S. Department of Labor (2003c).

▶FIGURE 10.4
Gender Empowerment Measure, the United States and the Top Five and Bottom Five Countries, 2005 (n = 93)

Source: United Nations (2007a).

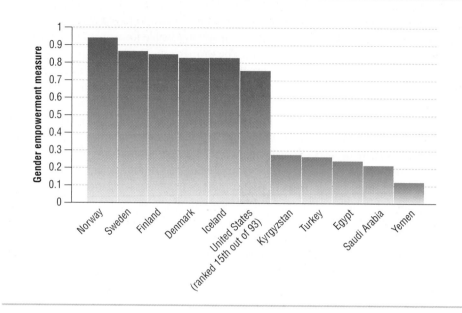

is the fact that in countries with an Islamic majority, gender inequality is *lower* than one would expect given their level of economic development. For example, Saudi Arabia ranks 92nd out of 93 countries on the GEM. We thus see that while some countries enact public policies to promote gender equality, others do the opposite.

The GEM figures suggest that American women still have a long way to go before they achieve equality with men. We have seen, for example, that the gender gap in earnings is shrinking but will not disappear until 2050—and then only if it continues to diminish at the 1960–2000 rate. That is a big *if*, because progress is never automatic. In 1963, Congress passed the Equal Pay Act. It requires equal pay for the same work. Soon after, Congress passed Title VII of the Civil Rights Act. It prohibits employers from discriminating against women. These laws were important first steps to diminishing the gender gap in earnings. However, since the mid-1960s, people in favor of closing the gender gap have recognized that we need additional laws and social programs to create gender equality.

Socializing children at home and in school to understand that women and men are equally adept at all jobs is important in motivating girls to excel in nontraditional fields. **Affirmative action,** which involves hiring more qualified women to diversify organizations, is important in helping to compensate for past discrimination in hiring.[2] However, without in any way belittling the need for such initiatives, we should recognize that their impact will be muted if women continue to shoulder disproportionate domestic responsibilities and if occupations filled by a high concentration of women continue to be undervalued in monetary terms.

Affirmative action: Involves hiring a woman if equally qualified men and women are available for a job, thus compensating for past discrimination.

[2]Affirmative action has also been applied to other groups that experience high levels of discrimination, such as African, Native, and Hispanic Americans.

Two main policy initiatives will probably be required in coming decades to bridge the gender gap in earnings. One is the development of a better child-care system. The other is the development of a policy of comparable worth. We now consider both these issues in turn.

Child Care

High-quality, government-subsidized, affordable child care is widely available in most western European countries, but not in the United States. As a result, many American women with small children are either unable to work outside the home or able to do so on only a part-time basis.

For women who have small children and work outside the home, child-care options and the quality of child care vary by social class (Annie E. Casey Foundation, 1998; Gormley, 1995; Murdoch, 1995). Affluent Americans can afford to hire nannies and send their young children to expensive day-care facilities that enjoy a stable, relatively well paid, well-trained staff and a high ratio of caregivers to children. These features yield high-quality child care. In contrast, the day-care centers, nursery schools, and preschools to which middle-class Americans typically send their children have higher staff turnover, relatively poorly paid and trained staff, and a lower ratio of caregivers to children. Fewer than one-third of American children in child care attend such facilities, however. More than two-thirds—mainly from lower-middle-class and poor families—use a day-care service operated out of a person's home or rely on the generosity of extended family members or neighbors (U.S. Census Bureau, 2008g). Overall, the quality of child care is lowest in child-care facilities run out of a person's home. A third of all day-care facilities in the United States do not meet children's basic health and safety needs (Annie E. Casey Foundation, 1998; Gormley, 1995; Murdoch, 1995). True, many companies, schools, and religious organizations in the United States provide high-quality day care. However, until the average quality and availability of child care improves, women, particularly those in the middle and lower classes, will continue to suffer economically.

Comparable Worth

In the 1980s, researchers found that women earned less than men partly because jobs in which women were concentrated were valued less than jobs in which men were concentrated. They therefore tried to establish gender-neutral standards by which they could judge the dollar value of work. These standards include such factors as the education and experience required to do a particular job and the level of responsibility, amount of stress, and working conditions associated with it. Researchers felt that by using these criteria to compare jobs in which women and men were concentrated, they could identify pay inequities. The underpaid could then be compensated accordingly. In other words, women and men would receive equal pay for jobs of **comparable worth,** even if they did different jobs.

A number of U.S. states have adopted laws requiring equal pay for work of comparable worth. Minnesota leads the country in this regard. However, the laws do not apply to most employers ("Comparable Worth," 1990). Moreover, some comparable-worth assessments have been challenged in the courts. The courts have been reluctant to agree that the devaluation of jobs in which women are concentrated is a form of discrimination (England, 1992a: 250). Only broad, new federal legislation is likely to change this state of affairs. However, no federal legislation on comparable worth is on the drawing boards.

Comparable worth: The equal dollar value of different jobs. It is established in gender-neutral terms by comparing jobs in terms of the education and experience needed to do them and the stress, responsibility, and working conditions associated with them.

Most business leaders seem opposed to such laws because their implementation would cost many billions of dollars.

The Women's Movement

Improvements in the social standing of women do not depend just on the sympathy of government and business leaders any more than they depend just on changing labor force and educational demands. Progress has always depended in part on the strength of the organized women's movement. This is likely to be true in the future too. In concluding this chapter, it is therefore fitting to consider the state of the women's movement and its prospects.

The first wave of the women's movement emerged in the 1840s. Drawing a parallel between the oppression of black slaves and the oppression of women, first-wave feminists made a number of demands, chief among them the right to vote. They finally achieved that goal in 1920, the result of much demonstrating, lobbying, organizing, and persistent educational work.

In the mid-1960s, the second wave of the women's movement started to grow. Second-wave feminists were inspired in part by the successes of the Civil Rights movement. They felt that women's concerns were largely ignored in American society despite persistent and pervasive gender inequality. Like their counterparts more than a century earlier, they held demonstrations, lobbied politicians, and formed women's organizations to further their cause. They advocated equal rights with men in education and employment, the elimination of sexual violence, and women's control over reproduction. One focus of their activities was mobilizing support for the Equal Rights Amendment (ERA)

Women's right to vote was achieved by the first wave of the women's movement.

SuperStock, Inc.

The second wave of the women's movement emerged in the mid-1960s.

Joseph Sohm/Visions of America/Corbis

to the Constitution. The ERA stipulates equal rights for men and women under the law. This amendment was approved by the House of Representatives in 1971 and the Senate in 1972. However, it fell 3 states short of the 38 needed for ratification in 1982. Since then, no further attempt has been made to ratify the ERA.

Beyond the basic points of agreement just noted, there is considerable diversity in the modern feminist movement concerning ultimate goals. For example, since the mid-1980s, *antiracist* and *postmodernist* feminists have criticized the women's movement in the United States for generalizing from the experience of white women and failing to see how women's lives are rooted in particular historical and racial experiences (hooks, 1984). These new currents have done much to extend the relevance of feminism to previously marginalized groups.

Partly as a result of the political and intellectual vigor of the women's movement, some feminist ideas have gained widespread acceptance in American society over the past three decades (▶Table 10.4). For example, the great majority of Americans approve of married women working in the paid labor force and think that women are as well suited to politics as men. In 2008, Hilary Clinton nearly became the Democratic presidential candidate. Still, many people, especially men, oppose the women's movement. In fact, in recent years several antifeminist men's groups have sprung up to defend traditional male privileges.[3] It is apparently difficult for some men to accept feminism because they feel that the social changes advocated by feminists threaten their traditional way of life and perhaps even their sexual identity.

---

[3]Profeminist men's groups, such as the National Organization for Men Against Sexism, also exist but seem to have a smaller membership (NOMAS, 2000).

▶Table 10.4
Attitudes to Women's Issues, United States, 1972–2004 (in percent)

	1972–1982	1983–1987	1996	1998	2002	2004	2006
Approve of married women working in paid labor force	70	80	83	82	—	—	—
Women suited to politics	54	63	78	77	78	75	76
Women's rights issue important/one of the most important	—	58	64	—	—	—	—
Favor preferential hiring of women	—	—	27	—	—	—	—
Think of himself/herself as a feminist	—	—	22	—	—	—	—
Women can best improve their position through women's rights groups	—	15	—	—	—	—	—

Source: National Opinion Research Center. 2008. *General Social Survey, 1972–2006*. Chicago: University of Chicago. Machine readable file.

Personal Anecdote

Our own experience suggests that traditional patterns of gender socialization weigh heavily on many men. For example, John Lie grew up in a patriarchal household. His father worked outside the home, and his mother stayed home to do nearly all the housework and child care. "I remember my grandfather telling me that a man should never be seen in the kitchen," recalls John, "and it is a lesson I learned well. In fact, everything about my upbringing—the division of labor in my family, the games I played, the TV programs I watched—prepared me for the life of a patriarch. I vaguely remember seeing members of the 'women's liberation movement' staging demonstrations on the TV news in the early 1970s. Although I was only about 11 or 12 years old, I recall dismissing them as slightly crazed, bra-burning man haters. Because of the way I grew up and what I read, heard, and saw, I assumed the existing gender division of labor was natural. Doctors, pilots, and professors should be men, I thought, and people in the 'caring' professions, such as nurses and teachers, should be women.

"But socialization is not destiny," John insists. "Entirely by chance, when I got to college I took some courses taught by female professors. It is embarrassing to say so now, but I was surprised that they seemed brighter, more animated, and more enlightening than my male high school teachers had been. In fact, I soon realized that many of my best professors were women. I think this is one reason why I decided to take the first general course in women's studies offered at my university. It was an eye opener. I soon became convinced that gender inequalities are about as natural and inevitable as racial inequalities. I also came to believe that gender equality could be as enriching for men as for women. Sociological reflection overturned what my socialization had taught me. Sociology promised—and delivered. I think many college-educated men have similar experiences today, and I hope I now contribute to their enlightenment."

The Points of the Compass

The constraints on human sexuality and gender are both natural and social. People's sex organs and hormones strongly influence their sexual identity, preferences, and behavior, while social forces—especially socialization patterns and power relations—generally reinforce biological predispositions. But strong influences and general reinforcements leave a lot of room for variation. For example, one's sex organs may not "fit" one's hormonal balance or sexual identity. Changing social requirements and conventions may allow or encourage departures from traditional gender roles. Such circumstances give those who are so inclined the freedom to escape the constraints imposed by tradition.

The sharper the distinction between masculine and feminine roles, the greater the inequality of income and opportunity between men and women. One society may regard femininity as centered on unpaid domestic work and masculinity as centered on work in the paid labor force. A second society may broaden the conventional view of femininity to include work in "helping" occupations: nurse, secretary, teacher, and the like. A third society may go still further and regard femininity as perfectly consistent with women holding the same kinds of jobs as men in the paid labor force. It may also regard the sharing of domestic responsibilities between men and women as highly desirable. As we move from the first society to the third, the distinction between masculine and feminine work roles becomes blurred and opportunities for women and men become more equal.

CHAPTER SUMMARY

1. Are sex and gender rooted in nature?

While *sex* refers to certain anatomical and hormonal features of a person, *gender* refers to the culturally appropriate expression of masculinity and femininity. Sex is rooted largely in nature, although people can change their sex by undergoing a sex-change operation and hormone therapy. In contrast, social as well as biological forces strongly influence gender. Sociologists study the way social conditions affect the expression of masculinity and femininity.

2. What are some of the major social forces that channel people into performing culturally appropriate gender roles?

Various agents of socialization channel people into performing culturally approved gender roles. The family, the school, and the mass media are among the most important of these agents of socialization. Once the sex of children is known, parents and teachers tend to treat boys and girls differently in terms of the kind of play, dress, and learning they encourage. The mass media reinforce the learning of masculine and feminine roles by making different characteristics seem desirable in boys and girls, men and women.

3. Aside from agents of socialization, are there other social forces that influence the expression of masculinity and femininity?

Yes. One of the most important nonsocialization forces that influences the expression of masculinity and femininity is the level of social inequality between men and women. High levels of gender inequality encourage

more traditional or conventional gender roles. Fewer differences in gender roles exist where low levels of gender inequality prevail. Today, we can see the influence of gender inequality on gender roles by examining male aggression against women, which tends to be high where men are much more socially powerful than women and low where there is greater gender equality.

4. What is homosexuality and why does it exist?

Homosexuals are people who prefer sexual partners of the same sex. We do not yet well understand the causes of homosexuality—whether it is genetic, hormonal, psychological, or some combination of the three. We do know that homosexuality does not appear to be a choice and that it emerges for most people in early adolescence, before they have any sexual experience. Sociologists are in any case more interested in the way homosexuality is expressed and repressed. For example, they have studied how, in the 20th century, scientific research and political movements have made the open expression of homosexuality more acceptable. Sociologists have also studied the ways in which various aspects of society reinforce heterosexuality and treat homosexuality as a form of deviance subject to tight social control.

5. How does the existence of sharply defined gender roles influence men's and women's income?

One important consequence of strict gender differentiation is the existence of a big earnings gap between women and men. The gender gap in earnings derives from outright discrimination against women, women's disproportionate domestic responsibilities, women's concentration in low-wage occupations and industries, and the undervaluation of work typically done by women.

6. **How might the gender gap in earnings be reduced or eliminated?**

Among the major reforms that could help eliminate the gender gap in earnings and reduce the overall level and expression of gender inequality are (1) the development of an affordable, accessible system of high-quality day care and (2) the remuneration of men and women on the basis of their work's actual worth.

Questions to Consider

1. By interviewing your family members and relying on your memory, compare the gender division of labor in (1) the household in which your parents grew up and (2) the household in which you grew up. Then, imagine the gender division of labor you would like to see in the household you hope to live in about 10 years from now. What accounts for change over time in the gender division of labor in these households? Do you think your hopes are realistic? Why or why not?

2. In your own case, rank the relative importance of your family, your schools, and the mass media in your gender socialization. What criteria do you use to judge the importance of each socialization agent?

3. Systematically note the roles played by women and men on TV programs and in commercials one evening. Is there a gender division of labor on TV? If so, describe it.

4. Are you a feminist? If so, why? If not, what do you find objectionable about feminism? In either case, what is the ideal form of gender relations in your opinion? Why do you think this form is ideal?

Web Resources

CENGAGENOW™

Maximize your study time by using CengageNOW's diagnostic study plan to help you review this chapter. The Study Plan will

- help you identify areas on which you should concentrate;

- provide interactive exercises to help you master the chapter concepts; and

- provide a post-test to confirm you are ready to move on to the next chapter.

The Companion Website for *Sociology: Your Compass for a New World, The Brief Edition*, Enhanced Second Edition

www.cengage.com/sociology/brym

Supplement your review of this chapter by going to the companion website to take one of the tutorial quizzes, use flash cards to master key terms, and check out the many other study aids you'll find there. You'll also find special features such as GSS Data and Census 2000 information that will put data and resources at your fingertips to help you with that special project or help you do some research on your own.

David Ellis/Digital Vision/Getty Images

In this chapter, you will learn that:

- The traditional nuclear family is less common than it used to be. Several new family forms are becoming more popular.

- The frequency of one family form or another varies by class, race and ethnicity, sexual orientation, and culture.

- Among the most important forces underlying change from the traditional nuclear family are the entry of most women into the paid labor force and the legalization of contraception. Doing paid work and having access to contraception increase women's ability to leave unhappy marriages and control whether and when they have children.

- Marital satisfaction increases (1) as one moves up the class structure, (2) where divorce laws are liberal, (3) when teenage children leave the home, (4) in families where housework is shared equally, and (5) among spouses who enjoy satisfying sexual relations.

- The worst effects of divorce on children can be eliminated if there is no parental conflict and the children's standard of living does not fall after divorce.

- A more equal division of power between spouses leads to men contributing more to domestic labor and to a decline in domestic violence.

- The decline of the traditional nuclear family is sometimes associated with a host of social problems, such as poverty, welfare dependency, and crime. However, policies have been adopted in some countries that reduce these problems.

Introduction

■ **Personal Anecdote**

One Saturday morning, the married couple who lived next door to Robert Brym and his family asked Robert for advice on new speakers they wanted to buy for their sound system. Robert volunteered to go shopping with them at a nearby mall. They told him they also wanted to buy two outdoor garbage cans at a hardware store. Robert told them he didn't mind waiting.

"After they made the purchases, we returned to their minivan in the mall's parking lot," says Robert. "The wife opened the trunk, cleared some space, and said to her husband, 'Let's put the garbage cans back here.'

"Meanwhile, the husband had opened the side door. He had already put the speakers on the back seat and was struggling to do the same with the second garbage can. 'It's okay,' he said, 'I've already got one of them partway in here.'

"'Oh,' laughed the wife, 'I can judge space better than you, and you'll never get that in there. Bring it back here.'

"'You know,' answered the husband, 'we don't always have to do things your way. I'm a perfectly intelligent person. I think there's room up here and that's where I'm going to put this thing. You can put yours back there or stick it anywhere else you like.'

CENGAGENOW™

This icon signals when CengageNOW has important resources available for you to use in conjunction with the text. See the foldout at the front of this text for information on how to access CengageNOW.

"'Why are you yelling at me?' snapped the wife.

"'I'm not yelling,' shouted the husband. 'I'm just saying that I know as well as you what fits where. There's more than one way—your way—to do things.'

"So, the wife put one garbage can in the trunk, the husband put one in the back seat (it was, by the way, a very tight squeeze) and we piled into the car for the drive home. The husband and the wife did not say a word to each other. When we got back to our neighborhood, I said I was feeling tired and asked whether I could perhaps hook up their speakers on Sunday. Actually, I wasn't tired. I just had no desire to referee round two. I went home, full of wonder at the occasional inability of presumably mature adults to talk rationally about something as simple as how to pack garbage cans into a minivan.

"However, trivializing the couple's argument in this way prevented me from thinking about it sociologically. If I had been thinking like a sociologist, I would have at least recognized that, for better or for worse, our most intense emotional experiences are bound up with our families. We love, hate, protect, hurt, express generosity toward, and envy nobody as much as our parents, siblings, children, and mates. Little wonder, then, that most people are passionately concerned with the rights and wrongs, the dos and don'ts, of family life. Little wonder that family issues lie close to the center of political debate in this country. Little wonder that words, gestures, and actions that seem trivial to an outsider can hold deep meaning and significance for family members."

CENGAGENOW™

Learn more about **Families** by going through the Family Structures Video Exercise.

Is the Family in Decline?

Because families are emotional minefields, few subjects of sociological inquiry generate as much controversy. Much of the debate centers on a single question: Is the family in decline and, if so, what should be done about it? The question is hardly new. A contributor to the *Boston Quarterly Review* of October 1859 wrote: "The family, in its old sense, is disappearing from our land, and not only our free institutions are threatened but the very existence of our society is endangered" (quoted in Lantz, Schultz, and O'Hara, 1977: 413). This alarm, or one much like it, is sounded whenever the family undergoes rapid change, and particularly when the divorce rate increases.

Today, when some people speak about the decline of the family, they are referring to the **nuclear family.** The nuclear family is composed of a cohabiting man and woman who maintain a socially approved sexual relationship and have at least one child (Box 11.1). Others are referring more narrowly to what might be called the **traditional nuclear family.** In the traditional nuclear family, the wife works in the home without pay while the husband works outside the home for money. This makes him the "primary provider and ultimate authority" (Popenoe, 1988: 1).

In the 1940s and 1950s, many sociologists and much of the American public considered the traditional nuclear family the most widespread and ideal family form. However, for reasons we examine below, the percentage of married-couple families with children living at home fell from 44 percent to just 24 percent of all households between 1960 and 2000 (▶Figure 11.1). Over the same period, the percentage of women over the age of 16 in the paid labor force increased from 38 percent to 60 percent. Consequently, only a minority of American adults live in traditional nuclear families today. Many new family forms have become popular in recent decades (▶Concept Summary 11.1).

Some sociologists, many of them functionalists, view the decreasing prevalence of the married-couple family and the rise of the "working mother" as an unmitigated disaster

Nuclear family: Consists of a cohabiting man and woman who maintain a socially approved sexual relationship and have at least one child.

Traditional nuclear family: A nuclear family in which the husband works outside the home for money and the wife works in the home without pay.

BOX 11.1
SOCIOLOGY AT THE MOVIES

Walk the Line
(2005)

When legendary country singer Johnny Cash was 12, his older brother was killed in an accident and his father screamed that "God took the wrong son," assuming, unjustly and without evidence, that Johnny was to blame for the boy's death. Burdened by the loss of his beloved brother and his father's constant rejection, Johnny Cash became a deeply troubled adult. Fame didn't help. He drank too much, popped amphetamine pills like they were Tic Tacs, neglected his children, ruined his marriage, and did time for trying to smuggle narcotics across the border from Mexico.

Redemption arrives in the form of fellow performer June Carter (Reese Witherspoon, who won the 2005 best actress Oscar). Cash (played by Joaquin Phoenix, nominated for the 2005 best actor Oscar) pursues her relentlessly for years, eventually resorting to a proposal onstage in the middle of a performance, which she accepts. From that moment, Cash's life changes. But it is not just June who rescues him with her love and support. It is the entire Carter family. The Carters display all the grace and generosity one would expect of a royal family, which is just about what they were in the country music scene. At a Thanksgiving dinner attended by the Carters and the Cashes at Johnny's new house, Johnny's father starts in on him with the usual put-downs. "So how do you like it?" Johnny asks his father, referring to the house. "Jack Benny's is bigger," snaps the

Joaquin Phoenix and Reese Witherspoon in *Walk the Line.*

FOX 2000/20TH CENTURY FOX/THE KOBAL COLLECTION

father. But Mr. Carter springs to Johnny's defense, mildly rebuking Mr. Cash by asking rhetorically, "Oh, have you been to Jack Benny's house?" Johnny is upset enough to leave the meal but Mrs. Carter encourages June to go after him and ease his pain. Later, Johnny's supplier arrives with a fresh bag of pills, but June's parents chase him away with shotguns. They integrate Johnny into their family as the beloved son he always

wanted and needed to be, and Johnny lives with June and their four girls from previous marriages happily ever after.

What is a family? A cohabiting man and woman who maintain a socially approved sexual relationship and perhaps have a child? By that standard definition, Mr. and Mrs. Cash and their children formed a family—but a pretty sorry one by any reasonable standard because their family failed to provide the emotional support that could have allowed Johnny to thrive and become a happy adult. The Carters were not part of Johnny's family according to the standard definition, but their generosity of spirit led them to treat him like a son anyway. Johnny eventually became part of their extended family, but only because they cared deeply for his welfare. The story of Johnny Cash suggests that the definition of a family as a cohabiting man and woman who maintain a socially approved sexual relationship and perhaps have a child may be too narrow. Perhaps it is appropriate to think of a family more broadly as a set of intimate social relationships that adults create to share resources so as to ensure the welfare of themselves and their dependents.

Critical Thinking

- What values are implicit in the two definitions of the family offered above?

- Which definition of family do you prefer? Why?

(e.g., Popenoe, 1988, 1996). In their view, rising rates of crime, illegal drug use, poverty, and welfare dependency (among other social ills) can be traced to the fact that so many American children are not living in two-parent households with stay-at-home mothers. They call for various legal and cultural reforms to shore up the traditional nuclear family. For instance, they want to make it harder to get a divorce, and they want people to place less emphasis on individual happiness at the expense of family responsibility.

▶FIGURE 11.1
Household Types, United States, 1960–2000 (in percent)

Source: Suzanne M. Bianchi and Lynne M. Casper, "American Families," *Population Bulletin* 55, 4. Used with permission.

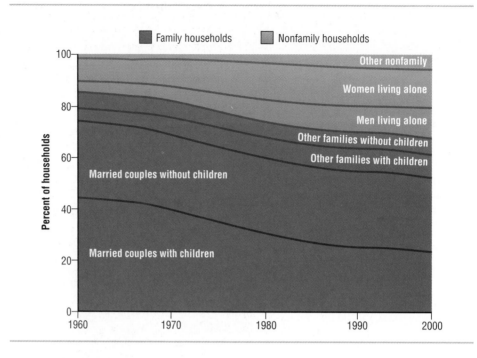

▶CONCEPT SUMMARY 11.1

The Traditional Nuclear Family and New Alternatives

Traditional Nuclear Family	New Alternatives
Legally married	Never-married singlehood, nonmarital cohabitation
With children	Voluntary childlessness
Two-parent	Single-parent (never married or previously married)
Permanent	Divorce, remarriage (including binuclear family involving joint custody, step-family or "blended" family)
Male primary provider, ultimate authority	Egalitarian marriage (including dual-career and commuter marriage)
Sexually exclusive	Extramarital relationships (including sexually open marriage, swinging, and intimate friendships)
Heterosexual	Same-sex intimate relationships or households
Two-adult household	Multi-adult households (including multiple spouses, communal living, affiliated families, and multigenerational families)

Source: Adapted from Macklin (1980: 906).

Other sociologists, influenced by conflict and feminist theories, disagree with the functionalist assessment (e.g., Coontz, 1992; Skolnick, 1991). In the first place, they argue that it is inaccurate to talk about *the* family, as if this important social institution assumed or should assume only a single form. They emphasize that families have been structured in many ways and that the diversity of family forms is increasing as people accommodate to the demands of new social pressures. Second, they argue that changing family forms do not necessarily represent deterioration in the quality of people's lives. In fact, such changes often represent *improvement* in the way people live. They believe that the decreasing prevalence of the traditional nuclear family and the proliferation of diverse family forms have benefited many men, women, and children and have not harmed other children as much as the functionalists think. They also believe that various economic and political reforms, such as the creation of an affordable nationwide day-care system, could eliminate most of the negative effects of single-parent households.

We first outline the functional theory of the family because the issues raised by functionalism are still a focus of sociological controversy (Mann et al., 1997). Borrowing from the work of conflict theorists and feminists, we next show that the nuclear family has been in decline since the 19th century and is less prevalent than is often assumed. We then explain how change in the distribution of power between husbands and wives has affected mate selection, marital satisfaction, divorce, reproductive choice, domestic labor, and wife abuse. The discussion then turns to alternative family forms—how they are structured and how their frequency varies by class, race, and sexual orientation. Finally, you will learn that although postindustrial families solve some problems, they are hardly an unqualified blessing. The chapter's concluding section considers the kinds of policies that might help alleviate some of the most serious concerns faced by families today. Let us first review the functionalist theory of the family.

Functionalism and the Nuclear Ideal
Functional Theory

For any society to survive, its members must cooperate economically. They must have babies. And they must raise offspring in an emotionally supportive environment so the offspring can learn the ways of the group and eventually operate as productive adults. Since the 1940s, functionalists have argued that the nuclear family is ideally suited to meet these challenges. In their view, the nuclear family performs five main functions: It provides a basis for regulated sexual activity, economic cooperation, reproduction, socialization, and emotional support (Murdock, 1949: 1–22; Parsons, 1955).

Functionalists cite the pervasiveness of the nuclear family as evidence of its ability to perform these functions. To be sure, other family forms exist. **Polygamy** expands the nuclear unit "horizontally" by adding one or more spouses (almost always wives) to the household. Polygamy is still legally permitted in many less industrialized countries of Africa and Asia. However, the overwhelming majority of families are monogamous, because they cannot afford to support several wives and many children. The **extended family** expands the nuclear family "vertically" by adding another generation—one or more of the spouses' parents—to the household. Extended families used to be common throughout the world. They still are in some places. However, according to the functionalists, the basic building block of the extended family (and of the polygamous family) is the nuclear unit.

George Murdock was a functionalist who conducted a famous study of 250 mainly preliterate societies in the 1940s. Murdock wrote, "Either as the sole prevailing form of the family or as the basic unit from which more complex familial forms are compounded, [the nuclear family] exists as a distinct and strongly functional group in every known society" (Murdock, 1949: 2). Moreover, the nuclear family, Murdock continued, is everywhere based on **marriage.** He defined marriage as a socially approved, presumably long-term, sexual and economic union between a man and a woman. It involves rights and obligations between spouses and between spouses and their children.

Polygamy: Expands the nuclear family "horizontally" by adding one or more spouses (usually women) to the household.

Extended family: Expands the nuclear family "vertically" by adding another generation—one or more of the spouses' parents—to the household.

Marriage: A socially approved, presumably long-term, sexual and economic union between a man and a woman. It involves reciprocal rights and obligations between spouses and between parents and their children.

Functions of the Nuclear Family

Let us consider the five main functions of marriage and the nuclear family in more detail.

1. *Sexual regulation.* The nuclear family defines the boundaries within which legitimate sexual activity is permitted, thus making an orderly social life possible. Of course, sex is readily available outside of marriage. Murdock found that only 22 percent of 250 mainly preliterate societies forbade or disapproved of premarital sex between non-relatives, and in more than half the societies a married man could legitimately have an extramarital affair with one or more female relatives (Murdock, 1949: 5–6). It is hardly news that premarital and extramarital sex are common in the United States and other postindustrial societies (especially if you believe what you see in *Desperate Housewives*). So sex is not the primary motivation for marrying.

2. *Economic cooperation.* People marry also because "a man and a woman make an exceptionally efficient cooperating unit" (Murdock, 1949: 7). Historically, pregnancy and nursing have restricted women in their activities, whereas men possess superior strength. Therefore, women have traditionally performed lighter tasks close to home while men have specialized in lumbering, mining, quarrying, land clearing, house building, hunting, fishing, herding, and trade (Murdock, 1937). Thus, "marriage exists only when the economic and the sexual are united into one relationship, and this combination occurs only in marriage" (Murdock, 1949: 8).

3. *Reproduction.* Before the invention of modern contraception, sex often resulted in the birth of a baby. Children are an investment in the future. By the age of 6 or 7, children in most societies do some chores. Their economic value to the family increases as they mature. When children become adults, they often help support their elderly parents. Thus, in most societies, there is a big economic incentive to having children.

4. *Socialization.* The investment in children can be realized only if adults rear the young to maturity. This involves not only caring for them physically but teaching them language, values, beliefs, skills, religion, and much else. Some functionalists regarded socialization as the "basic and irreducible" function of the family (Parsons, 1955: 16).

5. *Emotional support.* Functionalists note that the nuclear family universally gives its members love, affection, and companionship. In the nuclear family, it is mainly the mother who is responsible for ensuring the family's emotional well-being. It falls on the father to take on the role of earning a living outside the family (Parsons, 1955: 23). The fact that he is the "primary provider" makes him the ultimate authority.

Does this functionalist account provide an accurate picture of family relations across history? To assess the adequacy of the theory, let us discuss the families in which the early functionalists themselves lived: families in urban and suburban middle-class America in the 1950s.

The American Middle Class in the 1950s

As a description of the family patterns of white, nonpoor Americans in the 15 years after World War II, functionalism has its merits. During the Great Depression (1929–39) and the war (1939–45), millions of Americans were forced to postpone marriage due to widespread poverty, government-imposed austerity, and physical separation.

1950s TV classics such as *Father Knows Best* portrayed smoothly functioning, happy, white, middle-class, mother-householder, father-breadwinner families.

The Everett Collection

After this long and dreadful ordeal, many Americans just wanted to settle down, have children, and enjoy the peace, pleasure, and security that family life seemed to offer. Conditions could not have been better for doing just that. The immediate postwar era was one of unparalleled optimism and prosperity. Real per capita income rose 35 percent between 1945 and 1960. The percentage of Americans who owned their own homes jumped from 43 percent in 1940 to 62 percent in 1960. Government assistance in the form of the GI Bill and other laws helped to make the late 1940s and 1950s the heyday of the traditional nuclear family. This assistance took the form of guaranteed, tax-deductible mortgages, subsidized college education and health care for veterans, big income tax deductions for dependents, and massive road-building projects that opened the suburbs for commuters. People got married younger. They had more babies. They got divorced less. Increasingly, they lived in married-couple families (▶Table 11.1). Middle-class women engaged in what has been called an "orgy of domesticity" in the postwar years, devoting increasing attention to childrearing and housework. They also became increasingly concerned with the emotional quality of family life as love and companionship became firmly established as the main motivation for marriage (Coontz, 1992: 23–41; Skolnick, 1991: 49–74).

As a description of poor and nonwhite families, functionalism fares less well. For example, to support their families, some 40 percent of African American women with small children had to work outside their homes in the 1950s, usually as domestics in upper-middle-class and upper-class white households. One-fourth of these black women headed their own households. Thus, to a degree not recognized by the functionalists, the

▶**TABLE 11.1**

The Family in Numbers: The 1940s and 1950s Compared

	1940s	1950s
Percent of women age 20–24 never married	48.0	20.0
Divorce rate (per 1000 population)	4.3	2.1
Total fertility rate for white women age 20	2.6	3.1
Total fertility rate for nonwhite women age 20	3.2	3.9
Married couples as percent of all families	84.4	87.8

Note: Most figures were read from graphs and are therefore approximate.
Sources: Adapted from Cherlin (1992 [1981]: 9, 19, 21); U.S. Census Bureau (1999a).

existence of the traditional nuclear family among well-to-do whites depended in part on many black families *not* assuming the traditional nuclear form.

Moreover, as sociologist Andrew J. Cherlin meticulously shows, the immediate postwar period was in many respects a historical aberration (Cherlin, 1992 [1981]: 6–30). Trends in divorce, marriage, and childbearing show a gradual *weakening* of the nuclear family from the second half of the 19th century until the mid-1940s, and the resumption of a weakening trend after the 1950s. Specifically, throughout the 19th century, the **divorce rate** rose. The divorce rate is the number of divorces that occur in a year for every 1,000 people in the population. Meanwhile, the **marriage rate** fell. The marriage rate is the number of marriages that occur in a year for every 1,000 people in the population. The **total fertility rate** also fell. The total fertility rate is the average number of children that would be born to a woman over her lifetime if she had the same number of children as do women in each age cohort in a given year. In contrast, the divorce rate fell only between 1946 and 1958. The marriage rate took a big jump only in the two years following World War II. The fertility rate rose only for women who reached childbearing age between 1930 and the mid-1950s. By the late 1950s or early 1960s, the earlier trends had reasserted themselves. Only the peculiar historical circumstances of the postwar years, noted above, temporarily reversed them. The big picture from the 19th century until the present is that of a gradually weakening nuclear family. The early functionalists, it seems, generalized too hastily from the families they knew best—their own (▶Figure 11.2).

According to many modern-day functionalists, the nuclear family has become less prevalent since the 19th century largely because many of the traditional functions of the nuclear family have been eroded or partly taken over by other institutions. For example, the traditional division of labor, based on the physical capabilities and limitations of husband and wife, has weakened. That is because contraception and child-care services are now available, while demand for women to enter the paid labor force and pursue a higher education has increased. Women are no longer tied to the home in the way they once were. Nor are children the economic asset they were in agricultural societies that lacked a social welfare system. Quite the opposite: It is now expensive

Divorce rate: The number of divorces that occur in a year for every 1,000 people in the population.

Marriage rate: The number of marriages that occur in a year for every 1,000 people in the population.

Total fertility rate: The average number of children that would be born to a woman over her lifetime if she had the same average number of children as women in each age cohort in a given year.

▶FIGURE 11.2
Marriages and Divorces, United States, 1940–2007 (per 1,000 population)

Sources: Centers for Disease Control and Prevention (1995a, 1995b, 1998, 1999b, 2001, 2003, 2005, 2007a, 2007b, 2008).

to raise children. Meanwhile, part of the task of socialization has been taken over by schools, the mass media, and peer groups, while reproduction outside the nuclear family is possible due to the introduction of *in vitro* fertilization and other reproductive technologies. Thus, contemporary functionalists argue that the traditional nuclear family has been in decline for well over a century because other institutions perform many of the economic, reproductive, and socialization functions that were formerly reserved for the nuclear family.

Conflict and Feminist Theories

Other sociologists, influenced less by functionalism than by the conflict and feminist traditions, see the proliferation of non-nuclear families as a response to changes in power relations between women and men.

The idea that power relations between women and men explain the prevalence of different family forms was first suggested by Marx's close friend and coauthor, Friedrich Engels. Engels argued that the traditional nuclear family emerged along with inequalities of wealth. For once wealth was concentrated in the hands of a man, wrote Engels, he became concerned about how to transmit it to his children, particularly his sons. How could a man safely pass on an inheritance, asked Engels? Only by controlling his wife sexually and economically. Economic control ensured that the man's property would not be squandered and would remain his and his alone. Sexual control, in the form of enforced female monogamy, ensured that his property would be transmitted only to *his* offspring. Engels concluded that only the elimination of private property and the creation of economic equality—in a word, communism—could bring an end to gender inequality and the traditional nuclear family (Engels, 1970 [1884]: 138–9).

Engels was right to note the long history of male economic and sexual domination in the traditional nuclear family. In 1900 in the United States, any money a wife might earn typically belonged to her husband. As recently as the mid-20th century, an American wife could not rent a car, take a loan, or sign a contract without her husband's permission. It was only in 1993 that it became illegal throughout the United States for a husband to rape his wife.

However, Engels was wrong to think that communism would eliminate gender inequality in the family. Gender inequality has been as common in societies that call themselves communist as in those that call themselves capitalist. For example, the Soviet Union left "intact the fundamental family structures, authority relations, and socialization patterns crucial to personality formation and sex-role differentiation. Only a genuine sexual revolution [or, as we prefer to call it, a *gender revolution*] could have shattered these patterns and made possible the real emancipation of women" (Lapidus, 1978: 7).

Because gender inequality exists in noncapitalist (including precapitalist) societies, most feminists believe something other than, or in addition to, capitalism accounts for gender inequality and the persistence of the traditional nuclear family. In their view, *patriarchy*—male dominance and norms justifying that dominance—is more deeply rooted in the economic, military, and cultural history of humankind than the classical Marxist account allows. For them, only a "genuine gender revolution" can alter this state of affairs.

Just such a revolution in family structures, authority relations, and socialization patterns picked up steam in the United States and other rich industrialized countries about 60 years ago, although its roots extend back to the 18th century. As you will now see, the revolution is evident in the rise of romantic love and happiness as bases for marriage, the rising divorce rate, women's increasing control over reproduction through their use of contraceptives, and women's increasing participation in the system of higher education and the paid labor force, among other factors. We begin by considering the sociology of mate selection.

Power and Families

Love and Mate Selection

Most Americans take for granted that marriage ought to be based on love. Our assumption is evident, for example, in the way most popular songs in the United States celebrate love as the sole basis of long-term intimacy and marriage. In contrast, most of us view marriage devoid of love as tragic.

Yet in most societies throughout human history, love had little to do with marriage. Marriages were typically arranged by third parties, not by brides and grooms. The selection of marriage partners was based mainly on calculations intended to maximize their families' prestige, economic benefits, and political advantages.

The idea that love should be important in the choice of a marriage partner first gained currency in 18th-century England with the rise of liberalism and individualism, philosophies that stressed freedom of the individual over community welfare (Stone, 1977). The intimate linkage between love and marriage that we know today emerged only in the early 20th century, when Hollywood and the advertising industry began to promote self-gratification on a grand scale. For these new spinners of fantasy and desire, an important aspect of self-gratification was heterosexual romance leading to marriage (Rapp and Ross, 1986). Today, wherever individualism is highly prized, love has come to be defined as the essential basis for marriage. A survey of college undergraduates in the United States and 10 other countries asked, "If a man (woman) had all the qualities you desired, would you marry this person if you were not in love with him (her)?" In the 5 rich countries

Clark Gable and Vivien Leigh in *Gone with the Wind* (1939). Hollywood glamorized heterosexual, romantic love and solidified the intimate linkage between love and marriage that we know today.

The Everett Collection

plus Brazil, between 3 and 8 percent of students said they would marry someone they were not in love with if that person possessed all the qualities they were looking for in a partner. In the 5 developing countries, the comparable percentage ranged from 10 to 50 percent (Levine et al., 1995) (▶Figure 11.3).

Social Influences on Mate Selection

Still, it would be a big mistake to think that love alone determines mate selection in our society—far from it. Three sets of social forces influence whom you are likely to fall in love with and marry (Kalmijn, 1998: 398–404):

1. *Marriage resources.* Potential spouses bring certain resources with them to the "marriage market." They use these resources to attract mates and compete against rivals. These resources include financial assets, status, values, tastes, and knowledge. Most people want to maximize the financial assets and status they gain from marriage, and they want a mate who has similar values, tastes, and knowledge. As a result, who you fall in love with and choose to marry is determined partly by the assets you bring to the marriage market.

2. *Third parties.* A marriage between people from two different groups may threaten the internal cohesion of one or both groups. Therefore, to varying degrees, families, neighborhoods, communities, and religious institutions raise young people to identify with the groups they are members of and think of themselves as different from members of other groups. They may also apply sanctions to young people who threaten to marry outside the group. As a result, who you fall in love with and choose to marry is determined partly by the influence of third parties.

3. *Demographic and compositional factors.* The probability of marrying inside one's group increases with the group's size and geographical concentration. If you are a member of a small group or a group that is dispersed geographically, you stand a greater chance of having to choose an appropriate mate from outside your group. There may simply be too few "prospects" in your group from which to choose (Brym, Gillespie, and Gillis, 1985). In addition, the ratio of men to women in a group influences the degree to which members of each sex marry inside or outside the group. For instance, war and imprisonment may eliminate many male group members as potential marriage partners. This may encourage female group members to marry outside the group or forgo marriage altogether. Finally, because people usually meet potential spouses in "local marriage markets"—schools, universities and colleges, places of work, neighborhoods, bars, and clubs—the degree to which these settings are socially segregated influences mate selection. You are more likely to marry outside your group if local marriage markets are socially heterogeneous. As a result, who you fall in love with and choose to marry is determined partly by the size, geographical dispersion, and sex ratio of the groups you belong to and the social composition of the local marriage markets you frequent.

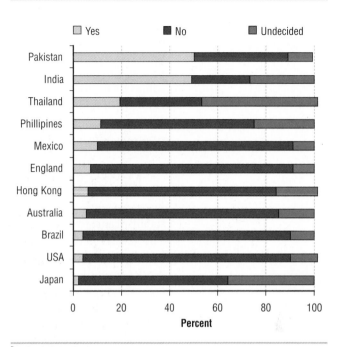

▶FIGURE 11.3

"If a Man (Woman) Had All the Other Qualities You Desired, Would You Marry this Person if You Were Not in Love with Him (Her)?"

Note: Some percentages do not equal 100 because of rounding.

Source: Levine et al. (1995: 561).

As a result of the operation of these three sets of social forces, the process of falling in love and choosing a mate is far from random. The percentage of people who marry inside their ethnic or racial group is more than 90 percent for African Americans, 75 percent for Asian Americans, 65 percent for Hispanic Americans, and 25 percent for European Americans. About 80 percent of Protestants and Jews, and 60 percent of Catholics, marry within their group. There is also a fairly strong correlation between the educational attainment of husbands and wives (Kalmijn, 1998: 406–8). We are freer than ever before to fall in love with and marry anyone we want. As in all things, however, social forces still constrain our choices to varying degrees.

Marital Satisfaction

Just as mate selection came to depend more on romantic love over the years, so marital stability came to depend more on having a happy rather than a merely useful marriage. This change occurred because women in the United States and many other societies have become more independent, especially since the 1960s. That is, one aspect of the gender revolution is that women are freer than ever to leave marriages in which they are unhappy.

One factor that contributed to women's autonomy was the introduction of the birth control pill in the 1960s. The birth control pill made it easier for women to delay childbirth and have fewer children. A second factor that contributed to their autonomy was the entry of millions of women into the system of higher education and the paid labor force (Cherlin, 1992 [1981]: 51–2, 56). Once women enjoyed a source of income independent of their husbands, they gained the means to decide the course of their own lives to a greater extent than ever before. A married woman with a job outside the home is less tied to her marriage by economic necessity than a woman who works only at home. If she is deeply dissatisfied with her marriage, she can more easily leave. Reflecting this new reality, laws were changed in the 1960s to make divorce easier and divide property between divorcing spouses more equitably. The divorce rate rose 57 percent from 1960 to 1981 and then declined 24 percent from 1981 to 2002 (see Figure 11.2). Women initiate most divorces.

The Social Roots of Marital Satisfaction

If marital stability now depends largely on marital satisfaction, what are the main factors underlying marital satisfaction? The sociological literature emphasizes five sets of forces (Collins and Coltrane, 1991: 394–406; 454–64):

1. *Economic forces.* Money issues are the most frequent subjects of family quarrels, and money issues loom larger when there isn't enough money to satisfy a family's needs and desires. Accordingly, marital satisfaction tends to fall and the divorce rate to rise as you move down the socioeconomic hierarchy. The lower the social class and the lower the educational level of the spouses, the more likely it is that financial pressures will make them unhappy and the marriage unstable. Marital dissatisfaction and divorce are also more common among groups with high poverty rates. Such groups include spouses who marry in their teens and African Americans. In contrast, the marital satisfaction of both husbands and wives generally *increases* when wives enter the paid labor force. That is mainly because of the beneficial financial effects. However, if *either* spouse spends so much time on the job that he or she neglects the family, marital satisfaction falls.

2. *Divorce laws.* Many surveys show that, on average, married people are happier than unmarried people are. Moreover, when people are free to end unhappy marriages

Andrew Benjei, *Pink Couch*, 1993. Fiberglass, 24 × 15 × 19 inches. Photo: Ron Giddings. Reproduced with permission of the artist.

◄ The U.S. divorce rate reached a historic high in 1981 and has declined since then.

and remarry, the average level of happiness increases among married people. Thus, the level of marital happiness has increased in the United States over the past few decades, especially for wives, partly because it has become easier to get a divorce. For the same reason, in countries where getting a divorce is more difficult (e.g., Italy and Spain), husbands and wives tend to be less happy than in countries where getting a divorce is easier (e.g., the United States and Canada) (Stack and Eshleman, 1998).

3. *The family life cycle.* About one-fourth of divorces take place in the first 3 years of a first marriage, and half of all divorces take place by the end of the seventh year. However, for marriages that last longer, marital satisfaction reaches a low point after about 15 to 20 years. Marital satisfaction generally starts high, falls when children are born, reaches a low point when children are in their teenage years, and rises again when children reach adulthood (Rollins and Cannon, 1974). ▶Figure 11.4 illustrates the effect of the family life cycle on marital satisfaction using survey data. Nonparents and parents whose children have left home (so-called empty nesters) enjoy the highest level of marital satisfaction. Parents who are just starting families or who have adult children living at home enjoy intermediate levels of marital satisfaction. Marital satisfaction is lowest during the "establishment" years, when children are attending school. Although most people get married at least partly to have children, it turns out that children, and especially teenagers, usually put big emotional and financial strains on families. This results in relatively low marital satisfaction.

4. *Housework and child care.* Marital happiness is higher among couples who share housework and child care. The further couples are from an equitable sharing of domestic responsibilities, the more tension there is among all family members (Hochschild with Machung, 1989). Equitable sharing tends to increase with education (Greenstein, 1996).

▶FIGURE 11.4
Family Satisfaction and the Family Life Cycle, United States

Note: Data are for 1998.

Source: Keller (2000).

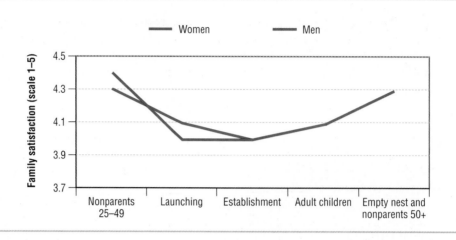

5. *Sex.* Having a good sex life is associated with marital satisfaction. Contrary to popular belief, surveys show that sex generally improves during a marriage. Sexual intercourse is also more enjoyable and frequent among happier couples. From these findings, some experts conclude that general marital happiness leads to sexual compatibility (Collins and Coltrane, 1991: 344). However, the reverse may also be true. Good sex may lead to a good marriage. After all, sexual preferences are deeply rooted in our psyches and our earliest experiences. They cannot easily be altered to suit the wishes of our partners. If spouses are sexually incompatible, they may find it hard to change, even if they communicate well, argue little, and are generally happy on other grounds. On the other hand, if a husband and wife are sexually compatible, they may work harder to resolve other problems in the marriage for the sake of preserving their good sex life. Thus, the relationship between marital satisfaction and sexual compatibility is probably reciprocal. Each factor influences the other.

Religion, we note, has little effect on level of marital satisfaction. But religion does influence the divorce rate. Thus, states with a high percentage of regular churchgoers and a high percentage of fundamentalists have lower divorce rates than other states (Sweezy and Tiefenthaler, 1996).

Let us now see what happens when low marital satisfaction leads to divorce.

CENGAGENOW™

Learn more about **Divorce** by going through the Divorce and Remarriage Learning Module.

Divorce

Economic Effects

After divorce, the most common pattern is a rise in the husband's income and a decline in the wife's. That is because husbands tend to earn more, children typically live with their mother, and support payments are often inadequate. Characteristically, one study found that in the three months after separation, 38 percent of custodial mothers but just 10.5 percent of noncustodial fathers fell below the poverty line (Bartfeld, 2000: 209). Between 1996 and 1998, the Clinton administration created a new felony offense for people who flee across state lines to avoid paying child support. It also developed a new computerized collection system to track parents across state lines, and new penalties and incentives to get states to cooperate in tracking so-called deadbeat parents (Clinton, 1998). These policies forced many delinquent parents to pay child support. Consequently, although child support payments declined in the 1970s and 1980s, they rose in the 1990s (Case, Lin, and McLanahan, 2003).

Emotional Effects

Although divorce enables spouses to leave unhappy marriages, serious questions have been raised about the emotional consequences of divorce for children, particularly in the long term. Some scholars claim that divorcing parents are simply trading the well-being of their children for their own happiness. What does research say about this issue?

Research shows that children of divorced parents tend to develop behavioral problems and do less well in school than children in intact families. They are more likely to engage in delinquent acts and to abuse drugs and alcohol. They often experience an emotional crisis, particularly in the first two years after divorce. What is more, when children of divorced parents become adults, they are less likely than children of nondivorced parents to be happy. They are more likely to suffer health problems, depend on welfare, earn low incomes, and experience divorce themselves. In one California study, almost half the children of divorced parents entered adulthood as worried, underachieving, self-deprecating, and sometimes angry young men and women (Wallerstein and Blakeslee, 1989; Wallerstein, Lewis, and Blakeslee, 2000). Clearly, divorce can have serious, long-term, negative consequences for children.

However, much of the research that seems to establish a link between divorce and long-term negative consequences for children is based on families who seek psychological counseling. Such families are a small and unrepresentative minority of the population. By definition, they have more serious emotional problems than the large majority, which does not need psychological counseling after divorce. One must be careful not to generalize from such studies. Another problem with much of this research is that some analysts fail to ask whether factors other than divorce might be responsible for the long-term distress experienced by many children of divorced parents.

Factors Affecting the Well-Being of Children

Researchers who rely on representative samples and examine the separate effects of many factors on children's well-being provide the best evidence on the consequences of divorce for children. For example, two researchers reanalyzed data from 92 relevant studies (Amato and Keith, 1991). They showed that on average the overall effect of divorce on children's well-being is not strong and is declining over time. They found that three factors account for much of the distress among children of divorce:

1. *A high level of parental conflict* creates long-term distress among children. Divorce without parental conflict does children much less harm. In fact, children in divorced families have a higher level of well-being on average than children in high-conflict *intact* families. The effect of parental conflict on the long-term well-being of children is substantially greater than the effect of the next two factors.

2. *A decline in living standards.* By itself, the economic disadvantage experienced by most children in divorced families exerts a small impact on their well-being. Nonetheless, it is clear that children of divorce who do not experience a decline in living standards suffer less harm.

3. *The absence of a parent.* Children of divorce usually lose some degree of contact with one parent as a role model, source of emotional support, practical help, and supervision. By itself, this factor also has a small effect on children's well-being, even if the child has continued contact with the noncustodial parent.

Subsequent studies confirm these generalizations and add an important observation. Many of the behavioral and adjustment problems experienced by children of divorce ex-

A high level of parental conflict creates long-term distress among children.

isted before the divorce took place. We cannot therefore attribute them to the divorce itself (Cherlin et al., 1991; Furstenberg and Cherlin, 1991; Stewart et al., 1997).

In sum, claiming that divorcing parents trade the well-being of their children for their own happiness is an exaggeration. A high level of parental conflict has serious negative consequences for children, even when they enter adulthood. In such high-conflict situations, divorce can benefit children. Increased state intervention, such as the initiatives taken by the Clinton administration, can ensure that children of divorce do not experience the decline in living standards that often has long-term negative consequences for them. By itself, the absence of a parent has a small negative effect on children's well-being. But this effect is getting smaller over time, perhaps in part because divorce is so common that it is no longer a stigma.

Reproductive Choice

We have seen that the power women gained from working in the paid labor force put them in a position to leave a marriage if it made them deeply unhappy. Another aspect of the gender revolution women are experiencing is that they are increasingly able to decide what happens in the marriage if they stay. For example, women now have more say over whether they will have children and, if so, when they will have them and how many they will have.

Children are increasingly expensive to raise. They no longer give the family economic benefits as they did, say, on the family farm. Most women want to work in the paid labor force, many of them to pursue a career. As a result, most women decide to have fewer children, to have them farther apart, and to have them at an older age. Indeed, 1 out of 20 couples does not have children at all, and among college graduates the figure is 3 out of 20.

Women's reproductive decisions not to have children are carried out by means of contraception and abortion. The United States Supreme Court struck down laws prohibiting birth control in 1965. Abortion first became legal in various states around 1970. Today, public opinion polls show that most Americans think women should be free to make their own reproductive choices. However, a substantial minority opposes abortion.

Because Americans are sharply divided on the abortion issue, *right-to-life* versus *pro-choice* activists have been clashing since the 1970s. Right-to-life activists want to repeal laws legalizing abortion. Pro-choice activists want these laws preserved. Both groups have tried to influence public opinion and lawmakers to achieve their aims. For example, as a result of pressure from the right-to-life lobby, RU-486, a drug that prevents a woman's body from producing a hormone that sustains early pregnancy, was introduced in the United States years after it was available in western Europe. A few extreme right-to-life activists (almost all men) have resorted to violence (Box 11.2).

Sociologists Randall Collins and Scott Coltrane (1991) argue that a repeal of abortion laws would likely return us to the situation that existed in the 1960s. Many abortions took place then, but because they were illegal, they were expensive, hard to obtain, and posed more dangers to women's health. If abortion laws were repealed, they predict that poor women and their unwanted children would suffer most. Taxpayers would wind up paying bigger bills for welfare and medical care.

Reproductive Technologies

For most women, exercising reproductive choice means being able to prevent pregnancy and birth by means of contraception and abortion. For some women, however, it means *facilitating* pregnancy and birth by means of reproductive technologies. Some couples are

CENGAGENOW™

Learn more about
Reproductive Technologies
by going through the
% of Population Using
Contraceptives Map Exercise.

BOX 11.2
YOU AND THE SOCIAL WORLD

The Abortion Issue

There are many shades of opinion and ambiguities in people's attitudes toward the abortion issue. At the extremes, however, we may distinguish between right-to-life and pro-choice advocates. Right-to-life advocates argue that life begins at conception. Therefore, they say, abortion destroys human life and is morally indefensible. They advocate adoption instead of abortion. In their opinion, the pro-choice option is selfish, expressing greater concern for career advancement and sexual pleasure than moral responsibility. In contrast, pro-choice advocates argue that every woman has the right to choose what happens to her own body and that bearing an unwanted child can harm not only a woman's career but the child too. For example, unwanted children are more likely to be neglected or abused. They are more likely to get in trouble with the law due to inadequate adult supervision and discipline. Furthermore, according to pro-choice advocates, religious doctrines claiming that life begins at conception are arbitrary. In any case, they point out, such ideas have no place in law because they violate the constitutionally guaranteed separation of church and state.

What are your views on abortion? To what degree are your views influenced by your social characteristics (family income, education, religiosity, etc.)? How do your views compare with those of other Americans with social characteristics similar to yours (Table 11.2, computed from the 2002 General Social Survey)? Why do certain social characteristics influence public opinion on the abortion in more or less predictable ways? What variables other than those listed in Table 11.2 might influence public opinion on the abortion issue?

WRITING ASSIGNMENT

Answer the questions above in about 500 words.

TABLE 11.2

"Please tell me whether or not you think it should be possible for a pregnant woman to obtain a legal abortion if the woman wants it for any reason," United States, 2002 (in percent)

	Yes	No	%	N
Gender				
Male	44	56	100	484
Female	41	59	100	416
Highest year of schooling completed				
0–11	31	69	100	154
12	39	61	100	258
13+	49	51	100	485
Age				
18–29	42	58	100	168
30–39	46	54	100	184
40–49	52	48	100	170
50–59	44	56	100	143
60–69	35	65	100	114
70+	34	64	100	125
Region				
New England	67	33	100	54
Middle Atlantic	52	48	100	150
South Atlantic	44	56	100	156
East North Central	39	61	100	146
West North Central	38	63	101*	72
East South Central	17	83	100	71
West South Central	28	72	100	81
Mountain	51	49	100	51
Pacific	50	50	100	119
Total annual family income				
$0–49,999	37	63	100	488
$50,000+	53	47	100	317
Vote in 2000 presidential election				
Bush	37	63	100	297
Gore	56	44	100	255
Attendance at religious services				
Less than once a month	55	45	100	495
Once a month or more	28	72	100	400
Religiously fundamentalist/moderate/liberal				
Fundamentalist	25	75	100	234
Moderate	39	61	100	317
Liberal	61	39	100	261

*Percent does not equal 100 due to rounding.
Source: National Opinion Research Center (2006).

▲
Fertilizing an egg *in vitro.*

infertile. With a declining number of desirable children available for adoption, and a persistent and strong desire by most people to have children, demand is strong for techniques to help infertile couples, some homosexual couples, and some single women have babies.

There are four main reproductive technologies. In *artificial insemination,* a donor's sperm is inserted in a woman's vaginal canal or uterus during ovulation. In *surrogate motherhood,* a donor's sperm is used to artificially inseminate a woman who has signed a contract to surrender the child at birth in exchange for a fee. In *in vitro fertilization,* eggs are surgically removed from a woman and joined with sperm in a culture dish, and an embryo is then transferred back to the woman's uterus. Finally, various *screening techniques* are used on sperm and fetuses to increase the chance of giving birth to a baby of the desired sex and to end pregnancies deemed medically problematic.

Social, Ethical, and Legal Issues

These procedures raise several sociological and ethical issues. We may mention two here (Achilles, 1993). The first problem is discrimination. Most reproductive technologies are expensive. Surrogate mothers charge $20,000 or more to carry a child. *In vitro* fertilization can cost $100,000 or more. Obviously, poor and middle-income earners who happen to be infertile cannot afford these procedures. In addition, there is a strong tendency for members of the medical profession to deny single women and homosexual couples access to reproductive technologies. In other words, the medical community discriminates not just against those of modest means but against non-nuclear families.

A second problem introduced by reproductive technologies is that they render the terms *mother* and *father* obsolete, or at least vague. Is the mother the person who donates the egg, carries the child in her uterus, or raises the child? Is the father the person who donates the sperm or raises the child? As these questions suggest, a child conceived through a combination of reproductive technologies and raised by a heterosexual couple could have as many as three mothers and two fathers! This is not just a terminological problem. If it were, we could just introduce new distinctions like "egg mother," "uterine mother," and "social mother" to reflect the new reality. The real problem is social and legal. Who has what rights and obligations to the child, and what rights and obligations the child has vis-à-vis each parent, is unclear. This lack of clarity has already caused anguished court battles over child custody. Reproductive technologies, in short, have caused people to rethink the very nature of the family (Thompson, 2005).

Public debate on a wide scale is needed to decide who will control reproductive technologies and to what ends. On the one hand, reproductive technologies may bring the greatest joy to infertile people. They may also prevent the birth of children with diseases such as muscular dystrophy and multiple sclerosis. On the other hand, reproductive technologies may continue to benefit mainly the well-to-do, reinforce traditional family forms that are no longer appropriate for many people, and cause endless legal wrangling and heartache.

Housework and Child Care

As we have seen, women's increased paid-labor-force participation, their increased participation in the system of higher education, and their increased control over reproduction transformed several areas of family life. Despite this far-ranging gender revolution, however, one domain remains resistant to change: housework, child care, and senior care. This fact was documented in detail by sociologist Arlie Hochschild. She showed that even women who work full-time in the paid labor force usually begin a "second shift" when they return home. There, they prepare meals, help with homework, do laundry, clean the toilets, and so forth (Hochschild with Machung, 1989).

To be sure, men take a more active role in the day-to-day running of the household than they used to. But the change is modest. Studies estimate that, on average, American men now do 20–35 percent of the housework and child care. Moreover, they tend to do low-stress chores that can often wait a day or a week. These jobs include mowing the lawn, repairing the car, and preparing income tax forms. They also play with their children more than they used to. In contrast, women tend to do higher-stress chores that cannot wait. These jobs include getting kids dressed and out the door to school every day, preparing dinner by 6:00 p.m., washing clothes twice a week, and the like. In short, the picture is hardly that of a revolution (Harvey, Marshall, and Frederick, 1991; Shelton and John, 1996).

The double day.

Two main factors shrink the gender gap in housework, child care, and senior care. First, the smaller the difference between the husband's and the wife's earnings, the more equal the division of household labor. Apparently, women are routinely able to translate earning power into domestic influence. Put bluntly, their increased status enables them to get their husbands to do more around the house. In addition, women who earn relatively high incomes are also able to use some of their money to pay outsiders to do domestic work.

Attitude is the second factor that shrinks the gender gap in domestic labor. The more husband and wife agree that there *should* be equality in the household division of labor, the more equality there is. Seeing eye-to-eye on this issue is often linked to both spouses having a college education (Greenstein, 1996). Thus, if there is going to be greater equality between men and women in doing household chores, two things have to happen. There must be greater equality between men and women in the paid labor force and broader cultural acceptance of the need for gender equality.

Domestic Violence

According to the U.S. Department of Justice (2007), in 2005 nearly 1 percent of women older than age 11 were assaulted, sexually assaulted, raped, or robbed by spouses, ex-spouses, boyfriends, ex-boyfriends, girlfriends, or ex-girlfriends. The comparable figure for men older than age 11 was less than one-fifth as high. Also in 2005, 1,181 women and 321 men older than age 11 were murdered by intimate partners (▶Figure 11.5). More than 70 percent of this violence occurred at the victim's home.

There are three main types of domestic violence (Johnson and Ferraro, 2000):

● *Common couple violence* occurs when partners have a specific argument and one partner lashes out physically at the other. For a couple that engages in this type of violence, violent acts are unlikely to occur often, escalate over time, or be severe. Both partners are about equally likely to engage in common couple violence, regardless of their gender.

▶FIGURE 11.5
**Intimate Partner Violence,
United States, 1993–2005**

Source: U.S. Department of Justice
(2007).

Homicide Victims Due to Intimate Partner Violence		
	Female	**Male**
1993	1,563	638
2005	1,181	329

- *Intimate terrorism* is part of a general desire of one partner to control the other. Where one partner engages in intimate terrorism, violent acts are likely to occur often, escalate over time, and be severe. Among heterosexual couples, the aggressor is usually the man.

- *Violent resistance* is the third main type of domestic violence. Among heterosexual couples, it typically involves a woman violently defending herself against a man who has engaged in intimate terrorism.

Gender Inequality and Domestic Violence

For heterosexual couples, domestic violence seems to be associated with the level of gender equality in the family and in the larger society. The higher the level of gender inequality, the greater the frequency of domestic violence. Thus, severe wife assault is more common in lower-class, less highly educated families, in which gender inequality tends to be high and men are more likely to believe that male domination is justified. Severe wife abuse is also more common among couples who witnessed their mothers being abused and who were themselves abused when they were children, although recent research suggests that these socialization factors are considerably less influential than was once believed (Gelles, 1997 [1985]; Simons et al., 1995). Still, male domination in both childhood socialization and current family organization increases the likelihood of severe wife assault.

In addition, Straus (1994) has shown that wife assault is associated with gender inequality in the larger society. He first constructed a measure of wife assault for each U.S. state using data from a national survey. The measure shows the percentage of couples in each state in which the wife was physically assaulted by her partner during the 12 months preceding the survey. He then used government data to measure gender inequality in each state. His measure of gender inequality tapped the economic, educational, political, and legal status of women. He found that as gender equality increases—as women and men become more equal in the larger society—wife assault declines. We conclude that for heterosexual couples, the incidence of domestic violence is highest where a big power imbalance between men and women exists, where norms justify the male domination of women, and, to a lesser extent, where early socialization experiences predispose men to behave aggressively toward women.

Summing up, we can say that conflict theorists and feminists have performed a valuable sociological service by emphasizing the importance of power relations in structuring family life. A substantial body of research shows that the gender revolution that has been taking place for nearly half a century has influenced the way we select mates, our reasons for being satisfied or dissatisfied with marriage, our propensity to divorce, the reproductive choices women make, the distribution of housework and child care, variations in the rate of severe domestic violence—in short, all aspects of family life. As you will now learn, the gender revolution has also created a much greater diversity of family forms.

Family Diversity

Heterosexual Cohabitation

Between 1970 and 1999, the number of American heterosexual couples who are unmarried and cohabiting (or "living together") increased more than 500 percent (▶Table 11.3). By 2004, unmarried cohabiting couples probably comprised about 5 percent of all households. Five percent may not seem like a lot. However, if we examine the number of marriages and remarriages that *begin* as cohabiting relationships, the numbers grow much larger. About 10 percent of people who married between 1965 and 1974 cohabited before marrying. For people marrying between 1990 and 1994, the figure was more than 50 percent (Smock, 2000: 4). About half of cohabiting couples have children living with them. Once considered a disgrace, cohabitation has gone mainstream.

People who disapprove of cohabitation often do so because they oppose premarital sex. Often, they cite religious grounds for their opposition. In recent decades, however, the force of religious sanction has weakened. The sexual revolution and growing individualism have allowed people to pursue intimate relationships before marriage if they so choose. Meanwhile, because women have pursued higher education and entered the paid labor force in increasing numbers, their gender roles are not so closely tied to marriage as they once were. These cultural and economic factors have all increased the rate of cohabitation.

Cohabitation is a relatively unstable relationship. Within five years of moving in together, about 55 percent of cohabiting couples marry and 40 percent split up. Moreover, marriages that begin with cohabitation are associated with a higher divorce rate than marriages that begin without cohabitation. This is true even when researchers compare couples at the same level of education and age at marriage.

Cohabitation and Marital Stability

The most often cited and best supported explanation for the association between cohabitation and marital instability is that people who cohabit before marriage differ from those who do not, and these differences increase the likelihood of divorce. Thus, people who cohabit before marriage tend to be less religious than those who do not, and religious people are less likely to divorce because they tend to believe that divorce is an unjustifiable solution to marital problems. Similarly, compared with people who do not cohabit, those who cohabit are more likely to be African American, occupy a lower class position, hold more liberal political and sexual views, and have parents who divorced. These factors are also associated with higher divorce rates (Starbuck, 2002: 239).

Sociological Significance of Cohabitation

Sociologists have debated the meaning and significance of cohabitation for decades. Some view it as a prelude to marriage or a new form of marriage. Others think cohabitation is more like being single. The latter regard it as a threat to family life, a temporary

▶**TABLE 11.3**

Unmarried Couples by Selected Characteristics, United States, 1970–1999

	1970	1980	1990	1999
Percent of households	0.8	2.0	3.1	4.3
Have children under 15 years old	37.5	27.1	31.2	33.5
Partners are under 25 years old	10.5	25.9	20.9	18.4
Partners are over 45 years old	69.6	21.3	17.0	24.7

Source: U.S. Census Bureau (2001d, 2002b).

▶TABLE 11.4

Perception and Outcome of Cohabiting Relationships

Type of Relationship, 1987–1988	Percent of Couples	OUTCOME OF RELATIONSHIP, 1992–1994, IN PERCENT			
		Still Live Together	Married	Separated	Total
Substitute for marriage*	10	39	25	35	99*
Precursor to marriage	46	17	52	31	100
Coresidential dating	49	21	33	46	100
Trial marriage	15	21	28	51	100
Total	100				

*Percent does not equal 100 due to rounding.
Source: Bianchi and Casper (2000).

relationship without commitment or responsibility. ▶Table 11.4 sheds light on this debate. Sociologists asked cohabiting couples how they think of their relationship—as a substitute for marriage, a precursor to marriage, a trial marriage, or merely as a form of serious dating. Only 29 percent of respondents saw it as a form of serious dating and 15 percent as a marital experiment, suggesting that cohabitation is viewed as a temporary relationship by a minority of cohabiting people. The researchers also determined the outcome of the relationships after 5–7 years. Significantly, about two-thirds of the couples who thought of cohabitation as a precursor to marriage or a substitute for marriage were most likely to enjoy enduring relationships after 5–7 years; they either married or were still living together. On the other hand, about half of the couples who thought of cohabitation as a more fleeting kind of relationship were still together after 5–7 years. We find this a surprisingly high number because nearly half of all recent marriages in the United States are likely to end in divorce. We conclude that although cohabitation is not seen as an enduring relationship by a substantial minority of people who cohabit, it nonetheless results in an enduring relationship for many of them. Moreover, most people see cohabitation as a prelude to marriage or a substitute for it. People who enter into a cohabiting relationship thinking of it in these ways are likely to enjoy an enduring relationship.

One of the lesbian couples who showed up at the Hawaii Department of Health in Honolulu in 1993 to apply for a marriage license. Ultimately, in 1999, the state supreme court ruled that same-sex marriages were illegal.

Serge J.F. Levy/AP Photo

Same-Sex Unions and Partnerships

In February 2004, the mayor of San Francisco, Gavin Newsom, ordered his county clerk to begin issuing marriage licenses to gay and lesbian couples. Although the laws of the state of California do not allow such marriages, Newsom argued that these laws are discriminatory and contradict protections laid out in the state constitution. Thousands of marriages between same-sex couples took place in San Francisco, many on the steps of City Hall, in a massive showing of civil disobedience that soon spread across the United States. The events in California followed closely on the heels of a Massachusetts Supreme Court decision declaring the ban on gays and lesbians marrying in that state to be unconstitutional.

Opponents of same-sex marriage quickly began legal efforts to block the issuance of marriage licenses in

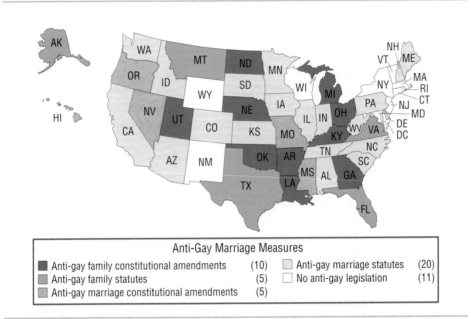

▶FIGURE 11.6
U.S. States with Laws Banning Same-Sex Marriages, 2005

Source: National Gay and Lesbian Task Force (2005).

California and to prevent same-sex marriages from taking place in their own states. The same-sex marriages in San Francisco mentioned previously were voided in August 2004 by the state supreme court. Amidst heavy lobbying from religious conservatives, President George W. Bush declared his support for an amendment to the federal constitution that would prevent same-sex marriages.

In some ways, those opposing same-sex marriage in the United States were swimming against the stream of cultural change. In 2001 the Netherlands became the first country in the world to legalize same-sex marriage. Belgium, Spain, and Canada soon followed suit. Seven other countries allow homosexuals to register their partnerships under the law in so-called civil unions. Civil unions recognize the partnerships as having some or all of the legal rights of marriage. These countries include Denmark (along with its dependency, Greenland), Hungary, Norway, Sweden, France, Iceland, and Germany. In the United States, there is more opposition to registered partnerships and same-sex marriages than in these countries. By the time Gavin Newsom was authorizing gay marriages in California, 38 states had passed laws opposing such unions (▶Figure 11.6). A nationwide poll taken in 2006 showed that 51 percent of Americans oppose same-sex marriages and 27 percent approve, with the rest taking a neutral position (National Opinion Research Center, 2008b). In 2008, four more states, including California, banned same-sex marriage. Yet, despite continuing opposition to same-sex marriage, the ultimate direction of change in many parts of the world is clear. Amid sharp controversy, the legal and social definition of "family" is being broadened to include cohabiting, same-sex partners in long-term relationships (Religious Tolerance.org, 2000).

Research shows that most homosexuals, like most heterosexuals, want a long-term, intimate relationship with one other adult (Chauncey, 2005). In fact, in Denmark, where homosexual couples can register partnerships under the law, the divorce rate for registered homosexual couples is lower than for heterosexual married couples (ReligiousTolerance. org, 2000). According to the U.S. Census, just over 600,000 gay men and just under 600,000 gay women were living together in 2000 (U.S. Census Bureau, 2002c). Educated guesses suggest that about half of these people were raising children who (1) were the offspring of previous, heterosexual marriages, (2) were adopted, or (3) resulted from artificial insemination.

Raising Children in Homosexual Families

Many people believe that children brought up in homosexual families will develop a confused sexual identity, exhibit a tendency to become homosexuals themselves, and suffer discrimination from children and adults in the "straight" community. Unfortunately, little research exists in this area. Much of the research is based on small, unrepresentative samples. Nevertheless, the research findings are consistent. They suggest that children who grow up in homosexual families are much like children who grow up in heterosexual families. For example, a 14-year study assessed 25 young adults who were the offspring of lesbian families and 21 young adults who were the offspring of heterosexual families (Tasker and Golombok, 1997). The researchers found that the two groups were equally well adjusted and displayed little difference in sexual orientation. Two respondents from the lesbian families considered themselves lesbians, whereas all of the respondents from the heterosexual families considered themselves heterosexual.

Homosexual and heterosexual families do differ in some respects. Lesbian couples with children record higher satisfaction with their partnerships than lesbian couples without children. In contrast, among heterosexual couples, it is the childless who record higher marital satisfaction (Koepke, Hare, and Moran, 1992). On average, the partners of lesbian mothers spend more time caring for children than the husbands of heterosexual mothers. Because children usually benefit from adult attention, this must be considered a plus. Homosexual couples also tend to be more egalitarian than heterosexual couples, sharing most decision making and household duties equally (Rosenbluth, 1997). That is because they tend to reject traditional marriage patterns. The fact that they tend to have the same gender socialization and earn about the same income also encourages equality (Kurdek, 1996; Reimann, 1997). In sum, available research suggests that raising children in lesbian families has no apparent negative consequences for the children. Indeed, there may be some benefits for all family members.

Single-Mother Families: Racial and Ethnic Differences

We have seen how families differ from one another because of variations in the sexual orientation of adult family heads. Now let us examine how they vary across racial and ethnic groups in terms of the number of adults who head the family (Baca Zinn and Eitzen, 1993 [1988]: 109–27; Cherlin 1992 [1981]: 91–123; Collins and Coltrane, 1991: 233–69). ▶Figure 11.7 focuses on the country's two most common family types (two-parent and single-mother) and on the three largest racial and ethnic categories (white, African American, and Hispanic American). It shows that whites have the lowest incidence of single-mother families. African Americans have the highest. In all racial and ethnic groups, the proportion of single-mother families has been increasing in recent decades, but the increase has been most dramatic among African Americans. Thus, among African Americans in 1970, there were 1.9 two-parent families for every single-mother family. The last few years of the 20th century witnessed a reversal in the trend toward more single-mother families in the African American community. Nevertheless, single-mother families still outnumber two-parent families (Harden, 2001; see also the "Social Policy: What Do You Think?" box in Chapter 7). By 2007, there were more than two single-mother families for every two-parent family.

Some single-parent families result from separation, divorce, or death. Others result from people not getting married in the first place. Marriage is an increasingly unpopular

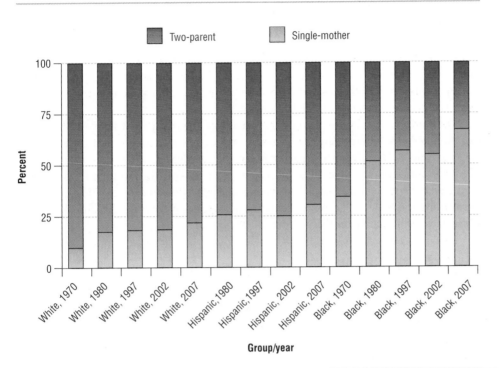

▶FIGURE 11.7
**Families with Own
Children under 18 by
Race and Hispanic Origin,
United States, Selected
Years**

Note: 1970 data on Hispanics are
not available.
Source: Baca Zinn and Eitzen (1993:
inside back cover); InfoPlease
(2005e); U.S. Census Bureau
(2008a).

institution. This is clear from statistics on births to unmarried mothers. In 2005, among non-Hispanic whites, 25.3 percent of births were to unmarried mothers. Among Hispanics, the figure was 48.0 percent. Among African Americans, it was 69.9 percent (Centers for Disease Control, 2007a).

The Decline of the Two-Parent Family among African Americans

What accounts for the decline of the two-parent family among African Americans (Cherlin, 1992 [1981])? Although some scholars trace the decline of the African American two-parent family back to slavery (Jones, 1986), rapid decline began around 1925. By then, the mechanization of the cotton economy in the South had displaced many black agricultural laborers and sharecroppers. They were forced to migrate northward. In the North, they competed fiercely for industrial jobs. Because of discrimination, however, they suffered higher rates of unemployment than any other group in America. Thus, ever since about 1925, proportionately few black men have been able to help support a family. As a result, proportionately few stable two-person families have formed. Similarly, the decline of manufacturing industries in the Northeast and the movement of many blue-collar jobs to the suburbs in the 1970s and 1980s eliminated many secure, well-paying jobs for blacks and caused their unemployment rate to rise. It is precisely in this period that the rate of increase in African American single-mother families skyrocketed.

A second factor explaining the decline of the two-parent family among African Americans is the declining ratio of eligible black men to women. This has three sources. First, largely because of the disadvantaged economic and social position of the African American community, a disproportionately large number of black men are imprisoned,

By 1997, there were more than 1.3 single-mother families for every two-parent family in the African American community.

have been murdered, and suffer from drug addiction. Second, because the armed forces represent one of the best avenues of upward mobility for African American men, a disproportionately large number of them have enlisted and been killed in action. Third, a black man is nearly twice as likely as a black woman to marry a nonblack person, and intermarriage has increased to about 10 percent of all marriages involving at least one black person. For all these reasons, there are relatively fewer black men available for black women to marry (Anderson, 1999; Wilson, 1987).

The third main factor explaining the decline of the two-parent family in the black community concerns the relative earnings of women and men. In recent decades, the average income of African American women has increased. Meanwhile, the earning power of African American men has fallen. As a result, African American women are more economically independent than ever. On average, they have less to gain in purely economic terms from marrying a black man. Economically speaking, marriage has thus become a less attractive alternative for them (Cherlin, 1992 [1981]).

Zero-Child Families

In the United States, what we prefer to call "zero-child families" are increasingly common. Our admittedly clumsy term seems necessary because the alternatives are so value laden: A "childless family" implies that a family without children lacks something it should have, while the more recent "child-free family" suggests that a family without a child is unencumbered and that a child is therefore a burden. To maintain neutrality, we resort to clumsiness.

In 1980, 10 percent of women between the ages of 40 and 44 had never given birth. In 2000, the figure was 20 percent (Lamanna and Riedmann, 2003: 369). To explain this increase we must first recognize that not having a child may be the result of circumstances beyond a couple's control. For example, one or both partners may be infertile, and some evidence suggests that infertility is a growing issue, due perhaps to chemical pollutants in the air and water. It seems that not having a child is more often a matter of choice, however, and the main reasons for the increasing prevalence of zero-child families are the rising cost of raising a child and the growth of attractive alternatives.

Just how expensive are children? About $210,000 on average. Social scientists estimate that the average child born in 2004 will cost its parents about $176,000 by the time the child reaches the age of 18 and another $34,000 by the time the child reaches the age of 34. For a family that earns more than $70,200 a year and whose child goes to a four-year college, the total cost can reach half a million dollars (Lino, 2005). That is a lot of money that could be spent on investments, the couple's own education, and other desirable things. Mothers bear most of the cost of lost economic opportunities. Usually, they are the ones whose careers are disrupted when they decide to stay home to raise children and who lose income, pension, and Social Security benefits in the process. Among rich countries, the problem of lost economic opportunities for women is most acute in the United States because we lack a system of public child care.

Couples also incur noneconomic costs when they have a child, the most important of which is stress. The birth of a child requires that couples do more work in the home, give up free time and time alone together, develop an efficient daily routine, and divide responsibilities. All this adds sources of disagreement and tension to daily life, so it is little wonder that marital satisfaction declines with a child in the house, as noted earlier.

Alternative attractions decrease the desire of some couples to have a child. People with high income, high education, and professional and managerial occupations are most likely to have zero-child families. Such people tend to place an especially high value on mobility, careers, and leisure-time pursuits. Usually, they are neither frustrated nor un-

BOX 11.3
SOCIAL POLICY: WHAT DO YOU THINK?

The Pro-Fatherhood Campaign

A TV commercial that ran a few years ago started like this: "When young bull elephants from a national park in South Africa were moved to different locations without the presence of an adult male, they began to wantonly kill other animals. When an adult male was relocated with them, the delinquent behavior stopped." For a panoramic view of elephants, the commercial switched to a basketball court where an African American man is hugging an African American boy. The voice-over said: "Without the influence of their dads, kids are more likely to get into trouble, too. Just a reminder how important it is for fathers to spend time with their children" (quoted in Davidoff, 1999: 28).

The National Fatherhood Initiative sponsored the commercial. It was part of a nationwide campaign to emphasize the importance of fatherhood to family life in particular and society in general. The 1999 Responsible Fatherhood Act pledged more than $150 million to "allow states to implement programs that promote stable and married families and support responsible fatherhood" (quoted in Davidoff, 1999: 29).

Nobody can disagree with supporting fatherhood and stable family life. However, one problem with pro-fatherhood policies is that they are often intended to replace welfare programs, which were simultaneously cut by both the federal and state governments. Moreover, critics of pro-fatherhood policies argue that what is essential for the healthy development of children is not just the father, or for that matter even a mother. As psychologists have shown, what is essential is a lasting and loving relationship with at least one adult (Silverstein and Auerbach, 1999). In other words, it is not necessarily the presence of a nuclear family that ensures healthy family life. Insofar as the Fatherhood Initiative supports only one kind of family, it devalues other forms of family life, including single-parent households, homosexual couples, and so on.

Critical Thinking

- Should we support the Fatherhood Initiative? Or does it lead us to ignore other social problems, such as poverty?

- Does the focus on fatherhood devalue other forms of family?

---

happy that they do not have a child. Despite their tendency to feel negatively stereotyped as "selfish," they tend to be more satisfied with their marriage than couples with a child (Lamanna and Riedmann, 2003: 380).

Notwithstanding the attractions of zero-child families and the high cost of having a child, there is little reason to expect that much more than 20 percent of American families will elect not to have a child in the foreseeable future. The pressure to have a child is less pronounced than it used to be, as is the negative evaluation of couples in zero-child families. But we are still socialized to want children, our friends typically expect us (and our parents often push us) to do so, and having a child continues to seem to most people to be the most natural, proper, and fulfilling thing one can do with one's life.

Family Policy

Having discussed several aspects of the decline of the traditional nuclear family and the proliferation of diverse family forms, we can now return to the big question posed at the beginning of this chapter: Is the decline of the nuclear family a bad thing for society? Said differently, do two-parent families—particularly those with stay-at-home moms—provide the kind of discipline, role models, help, and middle-class lifestyle that children need to stay out of trouble with the law and grow up to become well-adjusted, productive members of society? Conversely, are family forms other than the traditional nuclear family the main source of teenage crime, poverty, welfare dependency, and other social ills (Box 11.3)?

The answer suggested by research is clear: yes and no (Houseknecht and Sastry, 1996; Popenoe, 1988, 1991, 1992, 1993, 1996; Sandqvist and Andersson, 1992). Yes, the decline of the traditional nuclear family can be a source of many social problems. No, it doesn't have to be that way.

Crossnational Differences: The United States and Sweden

The United States is a good example of how social problems can emerge from nuclear family decline. Sweden is a good example of how such problems can be averted despite the decline of the nuclear family. Table 11.5 illustrates this. The top panel of ▶Table 11.5 shows that *with respect to most indicators of nuclear family decline, Sweden leads the United States.* In Sweden, a smaller percentage of people get married. People usually get married at a later age than in the United States. The proportion of births outside marriage is twice as high as in the United States. A much larger proportion of Swedish than American women with children under the age of 3 years work in the paid labor force.

The bottom panel of Table 11.5 shows that *with respect to most measures of children's well-being, Sweden also leads the United States.* Thus, in Sweden, children enjoy higher average reading test scores than in this country. The poverty rate in two-parent families is only one-tenth the U.S. rate, whereas the poverty rate in single-parent families is only one-twelfth as high. The rate of infant abuse is one-eleventh the U.S. rate. The rate of juvenile drug offenses is less than half as high in Sweden as in the United States. Sweden does have a higher rate of juvenile delinquency than the United States. However, the lead is slight and concerns only minor offenses. Overall, then, the decline of the traditional nuclear family has gone further in Sweden than in the United States, but children in Sweden are much better off on average. How is this possible?

One possible explanation is that Sweden has something the United States lacks: a substantial family support policy. When a child is born in Sweden, a parent is entitled to 360 days of parental leave at 80 percent of his or her salary and an additional 90 days at a flat rate. Fathers who do not take advantage of this parental leave can still take 10 days of leave with pay when the baby is born. Parents are entitled to free consultations at well-baby clinics. Like all citizens of Sweden, they receive free health care from the state-run system. Temporary parental benefits are available for parents with a sick child under the age of 12 years. One parent can take up to 60 days off per sick child per year at 80 percent of salary. All parents can send their children to heavily government-subsidized, high-quality

▶TABLE 11.5

"Decline" of the Nuclear Family and the Well-Being of Children: The United States and Sweden Compared

Indicators of Nuclear Family Decline	USA	Sweden	#1 Decline
Median age at first marriage			
Men	26.5	29.4	Sweden
Women	24.4	27.1	Sweden
Percentage of 45–49 population never married			
Men	5.7	15.4	Sweden
Women	5.1	9.1	Sweden
Nonmarital birthrate	25.7	50.9	Sweden
One-parent households with children <15 as a percent of all households with children <15	25.0	18.0	USA
Percent of mothers in labor force with children <3	51.0	84.0	Sweden
Total fertility rate	2.0	2.0	Tie
Average household size	2.7	2.2	Sweden
Indicators of Child Well-Being	**USA**	**Sweden**	**#1 Well-Being**
Mean reading performance score at 14	5.14	5.29	Sweden
Percent of children in poverty			
Single-mother households	59.5	2.2	Sweden
Two-parent households	11.1	2.2	Sweden
Death rate of infants from abuse (per 100,000)	9.8	0.9	Sweden
Suicide rate for children 15–19 (per 100,000)	11.1	6.2	Sweden
Juvenile delinquency rate (per 100,000)	11.6	12.0	USA
Juvenile drug offense rate (per 100,000)	558	241	Sweden

Source: Adapted from Houseknecht and Sastry (1996).

Painting class in a state-subsidized day-care facility in Stockholm, Sweden.

Jonathan Blair/CORBIS

day care. Finally, Sweden offers its citizens generous direct cash payments based on the number of children in each family.

Family Support Policies in the United States

Among industrialized countries, the United States stands at the other extreme. Since the Family and Medical Leave Act was passed in 1993, a parent is entitled to 12 weeks of *unpaid* parental leave. More than 45 million citizens have no health care coverage. Health care is at a low standard for an equal number. There is no system of state day care and no direct cash payments to families based on the number of children they have. The value of the dependent deduction on income tax has fallen by nearly 50 percent in current dollars since the 1940s. Thus, when an unwed Swedish woman has a baby, she knows she can rely on state institutions to maintain her standard of living and help give her child an enriching social and educational environment. When an unwed American woman has a baby, she is pretty much on her own. She stands a good chance of sinking into poverty, with all the negative consequences that has for her and her child.

In the United States, three criticisms are commonly raised against generous family support policies. First, some people say that they encourage long-term welfare dependence, illegitimate births, and the breakup of two-parent families. However, research shows that the divorce rate and the rate of births to unmarried mothers are not higher when welfare payments are more generous (Ruggles, 1997; Sweezy and Tiefenthaler, 1996). Nor is welfare dependency widespread in America. African American teen mothers are often thought to be the group most susceptible to chronic welfare dependence. Kathleen Mullan Harris (1997) studied 288 such women in Baltimore. She found that 29 percent were never on welfare. Twenty percent were on welfare only once and for a very brief time. Twenty-three percent cycled on and off welfare—off when they could find work, on when they couldn't. The remaining 28 percent were long-term welfare users. However, most of these teen mothers said they wanted a decent job that would allow them to escape from life on welfare. That is why half of those on welfare in any given year were concurrently working.

A second criticism of generous family support policies focuses on child care. Some critics say nonfamily child care is bad for children under the age of 3 years. In their view, only parents can provide the love, interaction, and intellectual stimulation infants and toddlers need for proper social, cognitive, and moral development. The trouble with this argument is that, explicitly or implicitly, it compares the quality of child care in upper-middle-class families with the quality of child care in most existing day-care facilities in the United States. Yet, as we saw in Chapter 10 ("Sexuality and Gender"), existing day-care facilities in the United States are often of poor quality. They are often characterized by high turnover of poorly paid, poorly trained staff and a high ratio of caregivers to children. When studies compare family care with day care involving a strong curriculum, a stimulating environment, plenty of caregiver warmth, low turnover of well-trained staff, and a low ratio of caregivers to children, they find that day care has no negative consequences for children older than 1 year (Clarke-Stewart, Gruber, and Fitzgerald, 1994). One study of more than 6,000 American children found that a mother's employment outside the home did have a very small negative effect on the child's self-esteem, later academic achievement, language development, and compliance. However, this effect was apparent only if the mother returned to work within a few weeks or months of giving birth. Moreover, the negative effects usually disappeared by the time the child reached the age of 5 (Harvey, 1999). Research also shows that day care has some benefits, notably an enhanced ability for the child to make friends. The benefits of high-quality day care are even more evident in low-income families, which often cannot provide the kind of stimulating environment offered by high-quality day care.

The third criticism lodged against generous family support policies is that they are expensive and have to be paid for by high taxes. That is true. Swedes, for example, are more highly taxed than the citizens of any other country. They have made the political decision to pay high taxes, partly to avoid the social problems and associated costs that emerge when the traditional nuclear family is replaced with other family forms and few institutions are available to help family members in need. The Swedish experience teaches us, then, that there is a clear trade-off between expensive family support policies and low taxes. It is impossible to have both, and the degree to which any country favors one or the other is a political choice.

 ## The Points of the Compass

Do certain functional requirements of society constrain the variety of family forms that exists and the nature of gender roles that are performed in families? Functionalists think so. In their view, sexual regulation, economic cooperation, reproduction, socialization, and emotional support are necessary for social equilibrium. Because the nuclear family is ideally suited to perform these functions, it predominates. Moreover, when women focus on providing emotional support and men focus on playing the breadwinner role, the efficiency of the family in performing its functions is supposedly maximized. Hence the gendered division of labor in the nuclear family.

Where functionalism goes wrong is in neglecting power relations between women and men in the family and the larger society. A gender revolution has mobilized many millions of women, especially since the 1960s. In most societies, women are now more economically independent and more in control of their own bodies than ever before. These and other social changes have enabled a variety of family forms to proliferate and the gendered division of labor in the family to be relaxed. Social constraints on family life have not, of course, been entirely removed. But people are now freer to constitute families and gender roles in ways that suit their individual preferences. To be sure, social problems sometimes accompany this increased freedom, but people are also free to deal creatively and responsibly with them.

CHAPTER SUMMARY

1. **What is the traditional nuclear family, and how prevalent is it compared with other family forms?**

   The traditional nuclear family consists of a father-provider, mother-homemaker, and at least one child. Today, fewer than one-fourth of American households are traditional nuclear families. Many different family forms have proliferated in recent decades, including cohabiting couples (with or without children), same-sex couples (with or without children), and single-parent families. The frequency of these forms varies by class, race, and sexual orientation.

2. **What is the functionalist theory of the family, and how accurate is it?**

   The functionalist theory holds that the nuclear family is a distinct and universal family form because it performs five important functions in society: sexual regulation, economic cooperation, reproduction, socialization, and emotional support. The theory is most accurate in depicting families in the United States and other Western societies in the two decades after World War II. Families today and in other historical periods depart from the functional model in important respects.

3. **What are the emphases of Marxist and feminist theories of families?**

   Marxists stress how families are tied to the system of capitalist ownership. They argue that only the elimination of capitalism can end gender inequality in families. Feminists note that gender inequality existed before capitalism and in communist societies. They stress how the patriarchal division of power and patriarchal norms reproduce gender inequality.

4. **What consequences does the entry of women into the paid labor force have?**

   The entry of women into the paid labor force increases their power to leave unhappy marriages and control whether and when to have children. However, it does not have a big effect on the sexual division of labor in families.

5. **What accounts for variation in marital satisfaction?**

   Marital satisfaction is lower at the bottom of the class structure, where divorce laws are strict, when children reach their teenage years, in families where housework is not shared equally, and among couples who do not have a good sexual relationship.

6. **Under what circumstances are the effects of divorce on children worst?**

   The effects of divorce on children are worst if there is a high level of parental conflict and the children's standard of living drops.

7. **Under what social circumstances is domestic violence among heterosexual couples most frequent?**

   Domestic violence is most frequent among heterosexual couples where a big power imbalance between men and women exists, where norms justify the male domination of women, and, to a lesser extent, where early socialization experiences predispose men to behave aggressively toward women.

8. **Does growing up in a household with lesbian parents have any known negative effects on children?**

   Growing up in a household with lesbian parents has no known negative effects on children.

9. **Are various social problems a result of the decline of the traditional nuclear family?**

   People sometimes blame the decline of the traditional nuclear family for increasing poverty, welfare dependence, and crime. However, some countries have adopted policies that largely prevent these problems. Therefore, the social problems are in a sense a political choice.

Questions to Consider

1. Do you agree with the functionalist view that the traditional nuclear family is the ideal family form for the United States today? Why or why not?

2. Ask your grandparents and parents how many people lived in their household when they were your age. Ask them to identify the role of each household member (e.g., mother, brother, sister, grandfather, boarder, etc.) and to describe the work done by each member inside and outside the household. Compare the size, composition, and division of labor of your household with that of your grandparents and parents. How have the size, composition, and division of labor of your household changed over three generations? Why have these changes occurred?

Web Resources

CENGAGENOW™

Maximize your study time by using CengageNOW's diagnostic study plan to help you review this chapter. The Study Plan will

- help you identify areas on which you should concentrate;
- provide interactive exercises to help you master the chapter concepts; and
- provide a post-test to confirm you are ready to move on to the next chapter.

The Companion Website for *Sociology: Your Compass for a New World, The Brief Edition,* Enhanced Second Edition

www.cengage.com/sociology/brym

Supplement your review of this chapter by going to the companion website to take one of the tutorial quizzes, use flash cards to master key terms, and check out the many other study aids you'll find there. You'll also find special features such as GSS Data and Census 2000 information that will put data and resources at your fingertips to help you with that special project or help you do some research on your own.

CHAPTER 12 Religion and Education

Charles O'Rear/CORBIS

In this chapter, you will learn that:

- Religion governs fewer aspects of many people's lives than in the past. However, a religious revival has taken place in the United States and other parts of the world in recent decades and many people still adhere to religious beliefs and practices.
- Adults who were brought up in religious families attend religious services more frequently than adults who were brought up in nonreligious families. Attendance also increases with age and varies by race.
- Schools perform important functions in society, including training and socializing the young, fostering social cohesion, transmitting culture from generation to generation, and sorting students, presumably by talent, for further training and employment.
- Schools do a far from perfect job of sorting students by talent. To a degree, they simply funnel poor and minority-group students into low-ability classes and more affluent students into high-ability classes. Eventually this results in many children occupying positions in the occupational structure similar to those occupied by their parents.
- Proposed solutions to the problems of public education in the United States include local initiatives aimed at improving schools, making schools accountable for their performance, redistributing existing resources and increasing education budgets, and substantially improving the social environment of young, disadvantaged children before and outside of school.

Religion

In 1902, psychologist William James observed that religion is the common human response to the fact that we all stand at the edge of an abyss. It helps us cope with the terrifying fact that we must die (James, 1976 [1902]: 116). It offers us immortality, the promise of better times to come, and the security of benevolent spirits who watch over us. It provides meaning and purpose in a world that might otherwise seem cruel and senseless.

The motivation for religion may be psychological, as James argued. However, the content and intensity of our religious beliefs, and the form and frequency of our religious practices, are influenced by the structure of society and our place in it. Why is religious belief more fervent at one time than another? Under what circumstances does religion act as a source of social stability and under what circumstances does it act as a force for social change? Are we becoming more or less religious? These are all questions that have

---

CENGAGENOW™

This icon signals when CengageNOW has important resources available for you to use in conjunction with the text. See the foldout at the front of this text for information on how to access CengageNOW.

occupied the sociologist of religion, and we will touch on all of them here. Note that we will have nothing to say about the truth of religion in general or the value of any religious belief or practice in particular. These are questions of faith, not science. They lie outside the province of sociology.

The cover of *Time* magazine once proclaimed "God is dead." As a sociological observation, the assertion is preposterous. In 2006, 63 percent of respondents who answered a General Social Survey (GSS) question on the subject had no doubt that God exists. Another 31 percent said they believed in God or some higher power at least some of the time. Only 4 percent said they didn't know whether God existed. A mere 2 percent said they didn't believe in God (National Opinion Research Center, 2008b). By this measure (and by other measures we will examine later), God is still very much alive in the United States. Nonetheless, as we will show, the scope of religious authority has declined in the United States and many other parts of the world. That is, religion governs fewer aspects of life than it used to. Some Americans still look to religion to deal with all of life's problems. But more and more Americans expect that religion can help them deal with only a restricted range of spiritual issues. Other institutions—medicine, psychiatry, criminal justice, and education—have grown in importance as the scope of religious authority has declined.

Foremost among these other institutions is the system of education. Organized religion used to be the main purveyor of formal knowledge and the most important agent of socialization apart from the family. Today, the education system performs that role. It is the displacement of religion by the education system that justifies our analyzing religion and education side by side in a single chapter. In the following we analyze the social functions of the education system and examine the degree to which it changes or reproduces the stratification system. We conclude by considering some of the solutions that have been proposed to what has often been called the "school crisis."

Classical Approaches in the Sociology of Religion

Durkheim: A Functionalist Approach

Somebody once said Super Bowl Sunday is second only to Christmas as a religious holiday in the United States. Aside from the first moon landing in 1969, the largest TV audience in history was recorded in 2008, when 97.5 million people watched Super Bowl XLII. The 10 most-watched regular programs in TV history are all Super Bowls. It is clear that few events attract the attention and enthusiasm of Americans as much as the annual football classic (Superbowl.com, 2004).

Apart from drawing a huge audience, the Super Bowl generates a sense of what Durkheim would have called "collective effervescence." That is, the Super Bowl excites us by making us feel part of something larger than us: the Pittsburgh Steelers, the Seattle Seahawks, the institution of American football, the competitive spirit of the United States itself. For several hours each year, Super Bowl enthusiasts transcend their everyday lives and experience intense enjoyment by sharing the sentiments and values of a larger collectivity. In their fervor, they banish thoughts of their own mortality. They gain a glimpse of eternity as they immerse themselves in institutions that will outlast them and athletic feats that people will remember for generations to come.

There is no god of the Super Bowl (although some people wanted to elevate Pittsburgh Steelers wide receiver Santonio Holmes to that position in 2008 after his game-

From a Durkheimian point of view, Super Bowl Sunday can be considered a religious holiday.

Michael Newman/PhotoEdit

winning touchdown reception with 35 seconds left in the game). Nonetheless, the Super Bowl meets Durkheim's definition of a religious experience. Durkheim said that when people live together, they come to share common sentiments and values. These common sentiments and values form a **collective conscience** that is larger than any individual. On occasion, we experience the collective conscience directly. This causes us to distinguish the secular, everyday world of the **profane** from the religious, transcendent world of the **sacred.** We designate certain objects as symbolizing the sacred. Durkheim called these objects **totems** (e.g., the team logos). We invent certain public practices to connect us with the sacred. Durkheim referred to these practices as **rituals** (e.g., the football game itself).

The effect (or *function*) of rituals and of religion as a whole is to reinforce social solidarity, said Durkheim. The ritual heightens our experience of belonging to certain groups, increases our respect for certain institutions, and strengthens our belief in certain ideas. Thus, the game is a sacred event, in Durkheim's terms. It cements society in the way Durkheim said all religions do (Durkheim, 1976 [1915]). Durkheim would have found support for his theory in research showing that the suicide rate dips during the two days preceding Super Bowl Sunday and on Super Bowl Sunday itself, just as it does for the last day of the World Series, July 4th, Thanksgiving Day, and other collective celebrations (Curtis, Loy, and Karnilowicz, 1986). This pattern is consistent with Durkheim's theory of suicide, which predicts a lower suicide rate when social solidarity increases (see Chapter 1, "A Sociological Compass").

Religion, Conflict Theory, and Feminist Theory

Durkheim's theory of religion is a functionalist account. It offers useful insights into the role of religion in society. Yet conflict and feminist theorists lodge two main criticisms against it. First, it overemphasizes religion's role in maintaining social cohesion. In reality, religion often incites social conflict. Second, it ignores the fact that when religion does increase social cohesion, it often reinforces social inequality.

Collective conscience: The common sentiments and values that people share as a result of living together.

Profane: The secular, everyday world.

Sacred: The religious, transcendent world.

Totems: Objects that symbolize the sacred.

Rituals: Public practices designed to connect people to the sacred.

▶FIGURE 12.1
The World's Predominant Religions

This map shows the religion to which more than half of a country's population adheres. Christianity predominates in 114 countries, Islam in 39, Buddhism in 8, Hinduism in 3, and Judaism in 1. A third of the world's population is Christian, a fifth is Muslim, 13 percent are Hindu, 6 percent are Buddhist, and 0.2 percent are Jewish.

Adherents.com (2001).

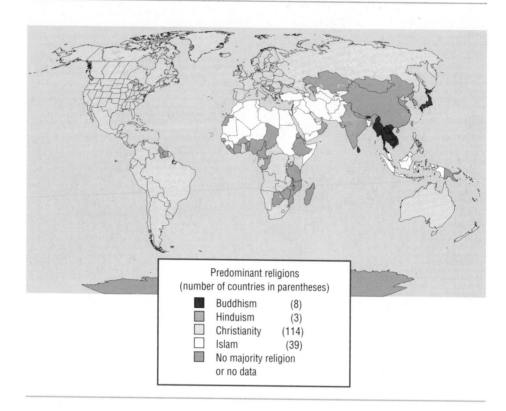

Predominant religions
(number of countries in parentheses)

- Buddhism   (8)
- Hinduism   (3)
- Christianity   (114)
- Islam   (39)
- No majority religion or no data

Religion and Social Inequality

Consider first the connection between major world religions and social inequality (▶Figure 12.1). Little historical evidence helps us understand the social conditions that gave rise to the first world religions, Judaism and Hinduism, 3,800 to 4,000 years ago. But we know enough about the rise of Buddhism, Christianity, and Islam between 2,700 and 1,500 years ago to say that the impulse to find a better world is often encouraged by adversity in this one. We also know that Moses, Jesus, Muhammad, and Buddha all had egalitarian and emancipatory messages, claiming to stand for equality and freedom. Finally, we know that over generations, the charismatic leadership of the world religions became "routinized." The routinization of charisma is Weber's term for the transformation of divine enlightenment into a permanent feature of everyday life. It involves turning religious inspiration into a stable social institution with defined roles, such as interpreters of the divine message, teachers, dues-paying laypeople, and so forth. The **routinization of charisma** typically makes religion less responsive to the needs of ordinary people, and it often supports social inequalities and injustices.

Religion and the Subordination of Women

It was Marx who first stressed how religion often tranquilizes the underprivileged into accepting their lot in life. He called religion "the opium of the people" (Marx, 1970 [1843]: 131). We can draw evidence for Marx's interpretation from many times, places, and institutions. For example, all the major world religions have traditionally placed women in a subordinate position. Catholic priests and Muslim mullahs must be men, as must Jewish

Routinization of charisma: Weber's term for the transformation of the unique gift of divine enlightenment into a permanent feature of everyday life. It involves turning religious inspiration into a stable social institution with defined roles (interpreters of the divine message, teachers, dues-paying laypeople, and so forth).

rabbis in the Conservative and Orthodox denominations. Women have been allowed to serve as Protestant ministers only since the mid-19th century and as rabbis in the more liberal branches of Judaism since the 1970s. One could also give many scriptural examples of the subordination of women:

- Corinthians in the New Testament emphasizes that "women should keep silence in the churches. For they are not permitted to speak, but should be subordinate, as even the law says. If there is anything they desire to know, let them ask their husbands at home. For it is shameful for a woman to speak in church."
- The Sidur, the Jewish prayer book, includes this morning prayer: "Blessed are you, Lord our God, King of the Universe, who did not make me a woman."
- The Qur'an, the holy book of Islam, contains a Book of Women in which it is written that "righteous women are devoutly obedient. . . . As to those women on whose part you fear disloyalty and ill-conduct, admonish them, refuse to share their beds, beat them."

Religion and Class Inequality

If religion has traditionally supported gender inequality, it has also traditionally supported class inequality once religion became routinized. In medieval and early modern Europe, Christianity promoted the view that the Almighty ordains class inequality, promising rewards to the lowly in the afterlife ("the meek shall inherit the earth"). The Hindu scriptures say that the highest caste sprang from the lips of the supreme creator, the next highest caste from his shoulders, the next highest from his thighs, and the lowest, "polluted" caste from his feet. They warn that if people attempt to achieve upward mobility, they will be reincarnated as animals. And the Qur'an says that social inequality is due to the will of Allah (Ossowski, 1963: 19–20).

In the United States today, most people do not think of social hierarchy in such rigid terms—quite the opposite. Most people celebrate the alleged *absence* of social hierarchy. This is part of what sociologist Robert Bellah calls our **civil religion,** a set of quasi-religious beliefs and practices that bind the population and justify our way of life (Bellah, 1975). When we think of America as a land of golden opportunity, a country in which everyone can realize the American Dream (regardless of race, creed, or color), a place in which individualism and free enterprise ensure the maximum good for the maximum number, we are giving voice to America's civil religion. The National Anthem, the Stars and Stripes, and great public events like the Super Bowl help to make us feel at ease with our way of life. Paradoxically, however, our civil religion may also help to divert attention from the many inequalities that persist in American society. Strong belief in the existence of equal opportunity, for instance, may lead people to overlook the lack of opportunity that remains in our society (see Chapter 7, "Social Stratification: United States and Global Perspectives"). In this manner, America's civil religion functions much like established traditional religions, although its content is markedly different.

Religion and Social Conflict

We can also find plenty of examples to illustrate religion's role in facilitating and promoting conflict. One case that springs immediately to mind is that of the African American community. In the South in the 1940s, whites sometimes allowed African Americans to sit at the back of their churches. More often, African Americans had to worship in churches of their own. These separate black churches formed the breeding

Civil religion: A set of quasi-religious beliefs and practices that bind a population together and justify its way of life.

ground of the Civil Rights movement in the 1950s and 1960s (Morris, 1984). Their impact was both organizational and inspirational. Organizationally, black churches supplied the ministers who formed the leadership of the Civil Rights movement. They also supplied the congregations within which marches, boycotts, sit-ins, and other forms of protest were coordinated. In addition, ideas from Christian doctrine inspired the protesters. Among the most powerful of these was the notion that African Americans, like the Jews in Egypt, were slaves who would be freed. It was, after all, Michael—regarded by Christians as the patron saint of the Jews—who rowed the boat ashore. Some white segregationists reacted strongly against efforts at integration, often meeting the peaceful protesters with deadly violence. But the South was never the same again. Religion had helped to promote the conflict needed to make the South a more egalitarian and racially integrated place (see also Box 12.1, p. 336).

In sum, religion can maintain social order under some circumstances, as Durkheim said. When it does so, however, it often reinforces social inequality. Moreover, under other circumstances religion can promote social conflict (Smith, 1996).

Weber and the Problem of Social Change: A Symbolic Interactionist Interpretation

If Durkheim highlighted the way religion contributes to social order, Weber stressed how it can contribute to social change. Weber captured the core of his argument in a memorable image: If history is like a train, pushed along its tracks by economic and political interests, then religious ideas are like railroad switches, determining exactly which tracks the train will follow (Weber, 1946: 280).

Weber's most famous illustration of his thesis is his short book, *The Protestant Ethic and Spirit of Capitalism.* Like Marx, Weber was interested in explaining the rise of modern capitalism. Again like Marx, he was prepared to recognize the "fundamental importance of the economic factor" in his explanation (Weber, 1958 [1904–5]: 26). But Weber was also bent on refuting any *exclusively* economic interpretation.

He did so by offering what we would today call a symbolic interactionist interpretation of religion. True, the term "symbolic interactionism" was not introduced into sociology until more than half a century after Weber wrote *The Protestant Ethic.* Yet Weber's focus on the worldly significance of the *meanings* people attach to religious ideas makes him a forerunner of the symbolic interactionist tradition.

For specifically religious reasons, wrote Weber, followers of the Protestant theologian John Calvin stressed the need to engage in intense worldly activity, to display industry, punctuality, and frugality in their everyday life. In the view of men like John Wesley and Benjamin Franklin, people could reduce their religious doubts and assure a state of grace by working diligently and living simply. Many Protestants took up this idea. Weber called it the Protestant ethic (Weber, 1958 [1904–5]: 183). According to Weber, the Protestant ethic had wholly unexpected economic consequences. Where it took root, and where economic conditions were favorable, early capitalist enterprise grew most robustly.

Subsequent research showed that the correlation between the Protestant ethic and the strength of capitalist development is weaker than Weber thought. In some places, Catholicism has coexisted with vigorous capitalist growth and Protestantism with relative economic stagnation (Samuelsson, 1961 [1957]). Nonetheless, Weber's treatment of the religious factor underlying social change is a useful corrective to Durkheim's emphasis on religion as a source of social stability. Along with Durkheim's work, Weber's contribution stands as one of the most important insights into the influence of religion on society.

Burning of Witches by Inquisition in a German Marketplace. After a drawing by H. Grobert.

The Rise, Decline, and Partial Revival of Religion

Secularization

In 1651, British political philosopher Thomas Hobbes described life as "poore, nasty, brutish, and short" (Hobbes, 1968 [1651]: 150). His description fit the recent past. The standard of living in medieval and early modern Europe was abysmally low. On average, a person lived only about 35 years. The forces of nature and human affairs seemed entirely unpredictable. In this context, magic was popular. It offered easy answers to mysterious, painful, and capricious events.

As material conditions improved, popular belief in magic, astrology, and witchcraft gradually lost ground (Thomas, 1971). Christianity substantially replaced them. The better and more predictable times made Europeans more open to the teachings of organized religion. In addition, the Church campaigned vigorously to stamp out opposing belief systems and practices. The persecution of witches in this era was partly an effort to eliminate competition and establish a Christian monopoly over spiritual life.

The Church succeeded in its efforts. In medieval and early modern Europe, Christianity became a powerful presence in religious affairs, music, art, architecture, literature, and philosophy. Popes and saints were the rock musicians and movie stars of their day. The Church was the center of life in both its spiritual and its worldly dimensions. Church authority was supreme in marriage, education, morality, economic affairs, politics, and so forth. European countries proclaimed official state religions. They persecuted members of religious minorities.

In contrast, writing at the turn of the 20th century, Weber observed that the world was becoming "disenchanted." Scientific and other forms of rationalism were replacing religious authority, he argued. His observations formed the basis of what came to be known as the **secularization thesis,** undoubtedly the most widely accepted argument in

Secularization thesis: Holds that religious institutions, actions, and consciousness are on the decline worldwide.

the sociology of religion until the 1990s. According to the secularization thesis, religious institutions, actions, and consciousness are unlikely to disappear, but they are on the decline worldwide (Tschannen, 1991).

Religious Revival

Despite the consensus about secularization that was still evident in the 1980s, many sociologists modified their judgments in the 1990s. One reason for the change was that accumulated survey evidence showed that religion was not in an advanced state of decay. Actually, in many places, such as the United States, it was in robust health (Greeley, 1989).

Consider ❯Figure 12.2, which uses data from a large 2002 survey to compare the United States with 43 other countries. It divides the countries into three groups: (1) rich countries listed by the United Nations as enjoying "high human development," (2) former communist countries, and (3) all other countries (i.e., less developed countries that were never under communist rule). The graph shows that less developed countries that were never under communist rule have a relatively high percentage of citizens who consider religion important in their lives (between 57 and 97 percent). For the highly developed countries, the percentages are considerably lower (between 11 percent and 59 percent). They are lower still for the former communist countries (between 11 percent and 36 percent). This pattern suggests that religiosity is negatively correlated with level of economic development. It also suggests that communist governments, which promoted atheism as state policy, did much to lower the level of religiosity in their countries. There is just one dramatic anomaly among the 44 countries: the United States. The United States has an unusually high level of religiosity for a rich country. Fully 59 percent of American adults considered religion important in their lives in 2002, compared with 33 percent for the United Kingdom and 30 percent for Canada, the next two countries in the "highly developed" group.

❯FIGURE 12.2
Percentage of People Who Think Religion Is Very Important, 44 Countries, 2002 (n = 38,000)

Note: Poland is a former communist country, and the UN ranks it 37th in its list of 53 countries in the "high human development" group. It is classified here as a former communist country.
Sources: Pew Research Center (2002); United Nations (2002).

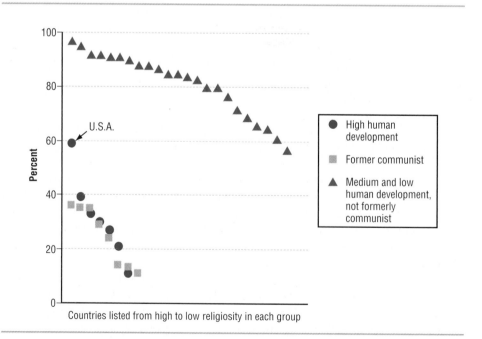

Since the 1960s, fundamentalist religious organizations have rapidly increased their membership, especially among Protestants.

A. Ramey/PhotoEdit

GSS data also show the resilience of religion in America over time. Whether we focus on the percentage of Americans who believe in God or some higher power or the percentage who claim that their religious affiliation is "strong" or "somewhat strong," we see little change over the past three decades. In 2006, 93 percent of Americans said they believed in God or some higher power. Forty-six percent attended religious services once a month or more. True, the percentage of people who frequently attended religious services fell 13 percent between 1972 and 2006. However, the percentage of people who believed in God or some higher power and who felt at least somewhat strongly affiliated to their religion did not change significantly. We conclude that although frequently attending religious services is less popular than it once was, religion is alive and well in the United States (National Opinion Research Center, 2008b).

Religious Fundamentalism in the United States

The second reason many sociologists have modified their views about secularization is that an intensification of religious belief and practice has taken place among some people in recent decades. For example, since the 1960s, fundamentalist religious organizations have increased their membership in the United States, especially among Protestants (Finke and Starke, 1992). **Fundamentalists** interpret their scriptures literally, seek to establish a direct, personal relationship with the higher being(s) they worship, are relatively intolerant of nonfundamentalists, and often support conservative social issues (Hunter, 1991).

Such social issues often spill over into political struggles, which is why religion in American politics is resurgent (Bruce, 1988). In 1988, conservative Christian Pat Robertson ran for the Republican presidential nomination, as did conservative Christian Pat Buchanan in 1992. The conservative Christian Coalition continues to lobby hard in Washington today, and Christian conservatives are a major force in the Republican party.

Fundamentalists: Religious people who interpret their scriptures literally, seek to establish a direct, personal relationship with the higher being(s) they worship, and are relatively intolerant of nonfundamentalists.

BOX 12.1
SOCIOLOGY AT THE MOVIES

The Great Debaters
(2007)

The Civil War (1861–65) outlawed slavery in the United States, but legal and violent resistance against black rights persisted for more than a century. In 1866, for example, an amendment to the Texas Constitution stipulated that all taxes paid by blacks had to be used to maintain black schools, and that it was the duty of the legislature to "encourage colored schools" ("Jim Crow Laws: Texas," 2008). In this segregationist atmosphere, the Methodist Church founded Wiley College in the northeast corner of Texas in 1873 "for the purpose of allowing Negro youth the opportunity to pursue higher learning in the arts, sciences and other professions" (Wiley College, 2007).

In 1923, Wiley hired Melvin B. Tolson as a professor of speech and English. He proceeded to build up its debating team to the point where they challenged and beat the mighty University of Southern California for the 1935 national debating championship. The victory shocked and scandalized much of the country's white population even as it instilled pride in African Americans, provided them with a shining model of academic achievement, and motivated black youth to strive to new heights. No self-fulfilling prophecy condemning black students to academic mediocrity operated at Wiley. To the contrary, Tolson worked his students hard, demanded excellence, and expected the best from them. Supported by the black community, they rose to his challenge.

The Great Debaters shows why the 1935 victory was anything but easy. Tolson (played by Denzel Washington) is harassed by the local sheriff, who brands him a troublemaker for trying to unionize local black and white sharecroppers. On one out-of-town road trip, Tolson and his debating team come across a white mob that has just lynched a black man and set his body on fire. They barely escape with their lives. The pervasive racism of the times might discourage and immobilize lesser men, but it steels Tolson and his debaters, who feel compelled to show the world what blacks are capable of achieving even in the most inhospitable circumstances.

Historically black colleges have played an important role in educating the black middle class in the United States, but since the 1960s blacks have been able to enroll in integrated colleges and universities, so many black colleges have fallen on hard times. Wiley itself was in deep financial trouble until *The Great Debaters* sparked new enrollments and endowments (Beil, 2007).

The successes of historically black colleges raise important policy issues. Can segregated black public schools benefit black youth? Should they be funded out of general tax revenue? Critics of separate black public schools argue that multiculturalism seeks to teach tolerance and respect for all cultures and that separate public schools for any minority group would therefore be a step backward. Arguably, however, integrated public schools are still the home of self-fulfilling prophecies that make it difficult for black students to excel. Their curricula do little, if anything, to instill pride in the achievements of black individuals and the black community. As a result, some black public school students dangerously identify academic excellence with "acting white," thus helping to condemn themselves to mediocre academic achievement and restricted social mobility. From this point of view, the achievements of historically black colleges like Wiley should be taken as a model of what is possible when black students are academically challenged and nourished in a nonthreatening environment. (For more on challenging students from minority groups, see pages 351–352.)

Critical Thinking

- Do black schools and colleges benefit or disadvantage black youth? How do they do so?

- Should black public schools be funded out of general tax revenue, or should they be run as private institutions? Why?

Everett Collection, Inc.

Melvin B. Tolson (Denzel Washington) coaches his team in *The Great Debaters*.

Religious Fundamentalism Worldwide

The American experience is by no means unique. Fundamentalism has spread throughout the world since the 1970s. It is typically driven by politics. Hindu nationalists formed the government in India from 1998 to 2004. Jewish fundamentalists were always important players in Israeli political life, often holding the balance of power in Israeli governments, but they have become even more influential in recent years (Kimmerling, 2001: 173–207). A revival of Muslim fundamentalism began in Iran in the 1970s. Led by the Ayatollah Khomeini, it was a movement of opposition to the repressive, American-backed regime of Shah Reza Pahlavi, which fell in 1979. Muslim fundamentalism then swept much of the Middle East, Africa, and parts of Asia. In Iran, Afghanistan, and Sudan, Muslim fundamentalists took power. Other predominantly Muslim countries' governments have begun to introduce elements of Islamic religious law (*shari'a*), either from conviction or as a precaution against restive populations (Lewis, 2002: 106). Religious fundamentalism has thus become a worldwide political phenomenon. In not a few cases it has taken extreme forms and involved violence as a means of establishing fundamentalist ideas and institutions (Juergensmeyer, 2000).

Fundamentalism and Extremist Politics in the Arab World

Personal Anecdote

In 1972, Robert Brym was finishing his B.A. at the Hebrew University of Jerusalem. One morning at the end of May, he switched on the radio to discover that a massacre had taken place at Lod (now Ben Gurion) International Airport outside Tel Aviv, just 26 miles from his apartment. Three Japanese men dressed in business suits had arrived on Air France flight 132 from Paris. They were members of the Japanese Red Army, a small, shadowy terrorist group with links to the General Command of the Popular Front for the Liberation of Palestine. Both groups wanted to help wrest Israel from Jewish rule.

After they picked up their bags, the three men pulled out automatic rifles and started firing indiscriminately. Before pausing to slip in fresh clips, they lobbed hand grenades into the crowd at the ticket counters. One man ran onto the tarmac, shot some disembarking passengers, and then blew himself up. This was the first suicide attack in modern Middle East history. Security guards shot a second terrorist and arrested the third, Kozo Okamoto. When the firing stopped, 26 people lay dead. Half were non-Jews. In addition to the two terrorists, eleven Catholics were murdered. They were Puerto Rican tourists who had just arrived on a pilgrimage to the Holy Land.

Both the Japanese Red Army and the General Command of the Popular Front for the Liberation of Palestine were strictly nonreligious organizations. Their members were atheists who quoted Bakunin and Trotsky, not Jesus or Muhammad. Yet something unexpected happened to Kozo Okamoto, the sole surviving terrorist of the Lod massacre. Israel sentenced him to life in prison but freed him in 1985 in a prisoner exchange with Palestinian forces. Okamoto wound up living in Lebanon's Bekaa Valley, the main base of the Iranian-backed Hizbollah fundamentalist organization. At some point in the late 1980s or early 1990s, he was swept up in the Middle East's Islamic revival. Okamoto the militant atheist converted to Islamic fundamentalism.

Kozo Okamoto's life tells us something important and not at all obvious about religious fundamentalism and politics in the Middle East and elsewhere. Okamoto was involved in extremist politics first and came to religion later. Religious fundamentalism became a useful way for him to articulate and implement his political views. This pattern is quite common. Religious fundamentalism often provides a convenient vehicle for framing political extremism, enhancing its appeal, legitimizing it, and providing a foundation for the solidarity of political groups (Pape, 2003; Sherkat and Ellison, 1999: 370).

Many people regard Islamic fundamentalism as an independent variable and extremist politics as a dependent variable. In this view, some people happen to become religious fanatics and then their fanaticism commands them to go out and kill their opponents. But Islamic fundamentalism has political sources (Brym, 2009b). For example, al Qaeda is strongly antagonistic to American foreign policy in the Middle East. It despises U.S. support for repressive and nondemocratic Arab governments like those of Kuwait and Saudi Arabia, which fail to distribute the benefits of oil wealth to the impoverished Arab people. It is also virulently opposed to the American position on the Israeli–Palestinian conflict, which it regards as too pro-Israeli and insufficiently supportive of Palestinian interests (to put it mildly). These political complaints are the breeding ground of support for al Qaeda in the Arab world. Thus, recent public opinion polls show that Arabs in the Middle East hold largely favorable attitudes toward American culture, democracy, and the American people, but extremely negative attitudes toward precisely those elements of American Middle East policy that al Qaeda opposes (Zogby International, 2001). Al Qaeda and other terrorist organizations in the Middle East gain in strength to the degree that these political issues are not addressed in a meaningful way. As Zbigniew Brzezinski, national security adviser to President Jimmy Carter, wrote: "To win the war on terrorism, one must . . . set two goals: first, to destroy the terrorists and, second, to begin a political effort that focuses on the conditions that brought about their emergence" (Brzezinski, 2002; Hunter, 1998). These are wise words. They are based on the sociological understanding that fundamentalism, like other forms of religion, is powerfully influenced by the social context in which it emerges.

The Revised Secularization Thesis

The spread of fundamentalist religion and the resilience and relative importance of religion in the United States led some sociologists to reject the secularization thesis in the 1990s and others to revise it. The revisionists acknowledge that religion has become increasingly influential in the lives of some individuals and groups over the past 30 years. They insist, however, that the scope of religious authority has kept on declining in most people's lives. That is, for most people, religion has less and less to say about education, family issues, politics, and economic affairs, although it continues to be an important source of spiritual belief and practice for many people. In this sense, secularization continues (Chaves, 1994; Yamane, 1997).

According to the **revised secularization thesis**—sometimes called the neo-secularization thesis—in most countries, worldly institutions have broken off, or "differentiated," from the institution of religion over time. The overall effect of the differentiation of secular institutions has been to make religion applicable only to the spiritual part of most people's lives. Because the scope of religious authority has been restricted, people look to religion for moral guidance in everyday life less often than they used to (▶Figure 12.3). Moreover, most people have turned religion into a personal and private matter rather than one imposed by a powerful, authoritative

Revised secularization thesis: Holds that worldly institutions break off from the institution of religion over time. As a result, religion governs an ever smaller part of most people's lives and becomes largely a matter of personal choice.

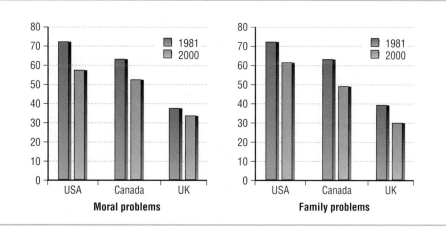

▶FIGURE 12.3
**Perceived Adequacy of
the Church, 1981–2000
(in percent)**

Note: The survey question reads:
"Generally speaking, do you think
that your church is giving, in your
country, adequate answers to: (a)
the moral problems and needs of
the individual? (b) the problems of
family life?"
Source: World Values Survey
(2003).

institution. Said differently, people feel increasingly free to combine beliefs and practices from various sources and traditions to suit their own tastes. As former supermodel Cindy Crawford said in a *Redbook* interview: "I'm religious but in my own personal way. I always say that I have a Cindy Crawford religion—it's my own" (quoted in Yamane, 1997: 116). No statement could more adequately capture the decline of religion as an authoritative institution suffusing all aspects of life.

The Structure of Religion in the United States and the World

Types of Religious Organization

The *Encyclopedia of American Religions* lists more than 2,100 religious groups that are active in the United States (Melton, 1996 [1978]). Although each of these organizations is unique in some respects, sociologists generally divide religious groups into just three types: churches, sects, and cults (Stark and Bainbridge, 1979; Troeltsch, 1931 [1923]).

Church

In the sociological sense of the term, a **church** is any bureaucratic religious organization that has accommodated itself to mainstream society and culture. Because of this accommodation, it may endure for many hundreds if not thousands of years. The bureaucratic nature of a church is evident in the formal training of its leaders, its strict hierarchy of roles, and its clearly drawn rules and regulations. Its integration into mainstream society is evident in its teachings, which are generally abstract and do not challenge worldly authority. In addition, churches integrate themselves into the mainstream by recruiting members from all classes of society.

Churches take two main forms. First are **ecclesia,** or state-supported churches. For example, Christianity became the state religion in the Roman empire in the 4th century, and Islam is the state religion in Iran and Sudan today. State religions impose advantages on members and disadvantages on nonmembers. Tolerance of other religions is low in societies with ecclesia.

Alternatively, churches may be pluralistic, allowing diversity within the church and expressing tolerance of nonmembers. Through pluralism, a church may increase its ap-

CENGAGENOW™

Learn more about **Types of
Religious Organization** by
going through the Types
of Religious Organization
Learning Module.

Church: A bureaucratic religious organization that has accommodated itself to mainstream society and culture.

Ecclesia: State-supported churches.

▶FIGURE 12.4
**Religious Affiliation,
United States, 2007 (in
percent; n = 35,009)**

Source: Pew Forum (2008).

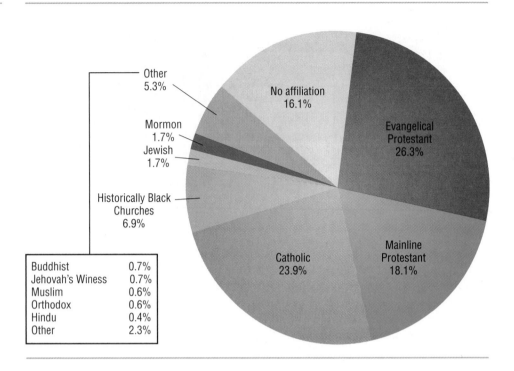

Buddhist	0.7%
Jehovah's Winess	0.7%
Muslim	0.6%
Orthodox	0.6%
Hindu	0.4%
Other	2.3%

Denominations: The various
streams of belief and practice
that some churches allow to
coexist under their overarching
authority.

Sects: Religious groups that
usually form by breaking away
from churches due to disagreement about church doctrine.
Sects are less integrated into
society and less bureaucratized
than churches. They are often
led by charismatic leaders, who
tend to be relatively intolerant
of religious opinions other than
their own.

peal by allowing various streams of belief and practice to coexist under its overarching
authority. These subgroups are called **denominations.** Baptists, Methodists, Lutherans,
Presbyterians, and Episcopalians form the major Protestant denominations in the United
States. The major Catholic denominations are Roman Catholic and Orthodox. The
major Jewish denominations are Orthodox, Conservative, Reform, Reconstructionist,
and Hasidic. The major Muslim denominations are Sunni and Shia[1]. Many of these denominations are divided into even smaller groups. ▶Figure 12.4 shows the percentage of
Americans who belonged to various religious groups in 2007. Note also the small percentages of Buddhists, Muslims, and Hindus, together totaling about 4 million people. These
religions are growing in the United States because of immigration from Asia and Africa,
and also because of conversions to Islam in the African American community and conversions to Buddhism among middle-class whites, especially on the West Coast.

Note also that, although churches draw their members from all social classes, some
churches are more broadly based than others. That is clear from ▶Figure 12.5.

Sect

Sects form by breaking away from churches as a result of disagreement about
church doctrine. Sometimes, sect members choose to separate themselves geographically, as the Amish do in their small farming communities in Pennsylvania, Ohio, and
Indiana. However, even in urban settings, strictly enforced rules concerning dress, diet,

[1]Although major Muslim subgroups are sometimes called denominations by non-Muslims, they are in some
respects more appropriately seen as sects (discussed later). That is because they often do not recognize one another as Muslim and sometimes come into violent conflict with one another.

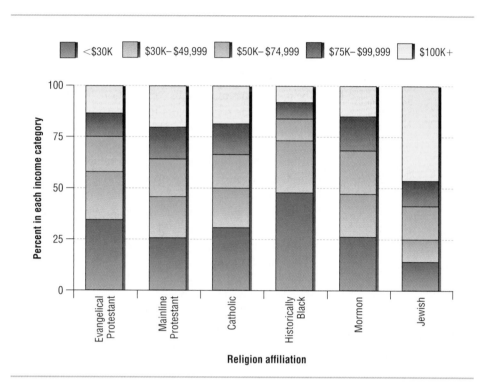

▶FIGURE 12.5
Religious Affiliation by Annual Income, United States, 2007 (in percent; n = 35,009)

Source: Pew Forum (2008).

prayer, and intimate contact with outsiders can separate sect members from the larger society. Hasidic Jews in New York and other large American cities prove the viability of this isolation strategy. Sects are less integrated into society and less bureaucratized than churches. They tend to recruit like-minded members mainly from lower classes and marginal groups. Worship in sects tends to be highly emotional and based less on abstract principles than on immediate personal experience (Stark, 1985: 314). Many sects are short-lived, but those that persist tend to bureaucratize and turn into churches. If religious organizations are to enjoy a long life, they require rules, regulations, and a clearly defined hierarchy of roles.

Cult

Cults are small groups of people deeply committed to a religious vision that rejects mainstream culture and society. Cults are generally led by charismatic individuals. Max Weber defined *charismatic leaders* as men and women who claim to be inspired by supernatural or divine powers and whose followers believe them to be so inspired. Cults also tend to be class-segregated groups. That is, a cult tends to recruit members from only one segment of the stratification system, high, middle, or low. Because they propose a radically new way of life, cults tend to recruit few members and soon disappear. There are, however, exceptions—and some extremely important ones at that. Jesus and Muhammad were both charismatic leaders of cults. They were so compelling that they and their teachings were able to inspire a large number of followers, including rulers of states. Their cults were thus transformed into churches.

Cults: Small groups of people deeply committed to a religious vision that rejects mainstream culture and society.

▶TABLE 12.1

▶**TABLE 12.1**
Social Factors Influencing How Often Americans Attend Religious Services (in percent)

ATTENDS RELIGIOUS SERVICES . . .

	Less Than Once a Month	Once a Month or More
Age, yr (N = 2743)		
18–29	61	39
30–39	54	46
40–49	53	47
50–59	53	47
60–69	44	56
70+	45	55
Race (N = 2742)		
White	56	44
Black	37	63
Mother's attendance at religious services during respondent's youth (N = 8151)		
Less than once a month	65	35
Once a month or more	41	59
Father's attendance at religious services during respondent's youth (N = 7302)		
Less than once a month	59	41
Once a month or more	38	62

Note: Race and age are for 2002. Mother's attendance and father's attendance are for 1983–1989, the only years this variable was measured in the General Social Survey.
Source: National Opinion Research Center (2006).

Religiosity: Refers to how important religion is to people.

Religiosity

We have reviewed the major classical theories of religion and society, the modern debate about secularization, and the major types of religious organization. It is now time to consider some social factors that determine how important religion is to people, that is, their **religiosity.**

We can measure religiosity in various ways. Strength of belief, emotional attachment to a religion, knowledge about a religion, frequency of performing rituals, and frequency of applying religious principles in daily life all indicate how religious a person is (Glock, 1962). Ideally, one ought to examine many measures to get a fully rounded and reliable picture of the social distribution of religiosity. For simplicity's sake, however, we focus on just one measure here: how often people attend religious services. We turn to the GSS for insights.

▶Table 12.1 divides GSS respondents into two groups: those who said they attended religious services less than once a month and those who said they attended religious services once a month or more. It then subdivides respondents by their age, race, and whether their mother and their father attended religious services frequently when the respondents were children.

Some fascinating patterns emerge from the data. First, older people attend religious services more frequently than younger people. There are two reasons for this. First, older people have more time and more need for religion. Because they are not usually in school, employed in the paid labor force, or busy raising a family, they have more opportunity than younger people to go to church, synagogue, mosque, or temple. And because elderly people are generally closer than younger people to illness and death, they are more likely to require the solace of religion. To a degree, then, attending religious services is a life-cycle phenomenon. That is, we can expect younger people to attend religious services more frequently as they age. But there is another issue at stake here, too. Different age groups live through different times, and today's elderly people reached maturity when religion was a more authoritative force in society than it is now. A person's current religiosity depends partly on whether he or she grew up in more religious times. Thus, although young people are likely to attend services more often as they age, they are unlikely ever to attend services as frequently as elderly people do today.

Second, Table 12.1 shows that frequent church attendance is more common among African Americans than whites. That is undoubtedly because of the central political and cultural role played by the church historically in helping African Americans cope with, and combat, slavery, segregation, discrimination, and prejudice.

Third, respondents whose mothers and fathers attended religious services frequently are more likely to do so themselves. Religiosity is partly a *learned* behavior. Whether parents give a child a religious upbringing is likely to have a lasting impact on the child. Table

12.1 shows that children of frequent churchgoers are more than twice as likely as children of infrequent churchgoers to become frequent churchgoers themselves.

This brief overview suggests that religiosity depends partly on opportunity, need, and learning. The people who attend religious services most often are those who were taught to be religious as children, who need organized religion for political reasons or due to their advanced age, and who have the most time to go to services. This is by no means an exhaustive list of the factors that determine frequency of attending religious services. For example, since the mid-1990s, some sociologists have stressed the "supply side" of religion (Finke, Guest, and Stark, 1996). They argue that religious organizations offer "services" and "products," and successful churches or sects rely on "religious entrepreneurs" to market and run religious organizations. Thus, a major reason for the success of U.S. fundamentalist churches is their market- and media-savvy televangelists, such as Jerry Falwell and Pat Robertson (Bruce, 1990). From this point of view, it is not just the demand for religion that influences how often people attend services, but also the nature of the supply of religious services.

The Future of Religion

Secularization is one of the dominant trends influencing religion throughout the world. We can detect secularization in survey data that track religious attitudes and practices over time. For example, between 1972 and 2006, the percentage of Americans expressing no religious preference increased from 5 to 14 percent, while the percentage of people attending religious services once a month or more fell from 57 to 46 percent (National Opinion Research Center, 2008b). The percentage of Americans who reported that religion was important in their lives fell from 75 percent in the middle of the 20th century to around 50 percent at century's end. We also know that various secular institutions are taking over some of the functions formerly performed by religion, thus robbing it of its once pervasive authority over all aspects of life. It is an exaggeration to claim, as Max Weber did, that the whole world is gradually becoming "disenchanted." But certainly part of it is.

However, we also know that even as secularization grips many people, many others in the United States and throughout the world have been caught up by a religious revival of vast proportions. Religious belief and practice are intensifying for these people, in part because religion serves as a useful vehicle for political expression. The fact that this revival was quite unexpected just a few decades ago should warn us not to be overly bold in our forecasts. It seems to us, however, that the two contradictory social processes of secularization and revival are likely to persist for some time to come, resulting in a world that is neither more religious nor more secular, but one that is certainly more polarized. The polarization of American society is also visible in other social institutions, such as the education system, to which we now turn.

Education

Despite the continuing significance of religion in American life and around the world, the revised secularization thesis is right to claim that religion does not dominate life and thought as it did even a century ago. For example, it is not religion but education that is now the dominant institution of socialization outside the family. Almost everyone goes to school, a large minority goes to college, and many people continue their education in middle age. Beyond its importance as an agent of socialization, education is also a central

CENGAGENOW™

Learn more about **World Religions** by going through the Religion Map Exercise.

determinant of opportunities for upward mobility. We care deeply about education not just because it shapes us but because it influences how well we do.

Affirmative Action and Meritocracy

In December 1996, Barbara Grutter applied to the University of Michigan Law School. Although she had a 3.8 undergraduate grade point average and an LSAT score that placed her in the 86th percentile, the Law School rejected her application for admission. Around the same time, Patrick Hamacher and Jennifer Gratz applied to the University of Michigan's College of Literature, Science and the Arts. Hamacher had a 3.0 grade point average and an ACT score of 28, Gratz a 3.8 grade point average and an ACT score of 25. Both students were likewise denied admission.

Grutter, Hamacher, and Gratz are white. Following the rejection of their applications for admission, they brought suit against the University of Michigan. They charged that the university gave unlawful preference to black, Hispanic, and Native American applicants. They also charged that as white students, they were denied equal protection under the law as guaranteed by the Constitution. Outside an immediate government interest, they argued, the Constitution prohibits the state from using race as a criterion for access to government programs and services. Their cases were heard by the Supreme Court (*Gratz and Hamacher v. Bollinger et al.*, 1997; *Grutter v. Bollinger et al.*, 1997).

At the time, a student needed 150 admission points to gain acceptance to the University of Michigan. Most points were awarded for academic achievement as signified by the student's grade point average and score on a standardized test, such as the SAT. However, black, Hispanic, and Native American applicants received an automatic 20 admission points because of their underprivileged status. That was the practice to which Grutter, Hamacher, and Gratz objected (Box 12.2).

The practice of granting underprivileged students special privileges in college admissions has a long and distinguished history in the United States. Before World War II, most colleges were the preserve of the children of a wealthy elite. In contrast, following the war many educators argued that the country would be stronger if colleges admitted capable students regardless of their ethnic or racial background and their ability to afford a higher education. Most colleges broadened recruitment efforts, found new ways to distribute information, advice, and encouragement to potential students who lacked such resources, and started offering financial support to those in need. Beginning with the GI Bill, federal and state governments eagerly assisted these efforts (Duffy and Goldberg, 1997).

A reaction against such openness and generosity has grown since the 1970s. Increasingly, white students like Grutter, Hamacher, and Gratz have argued that they are discriminated against in a country that is supposed to oppose discrimination. Such claims have led others to make the counterclaim that privileged white students also benefit from the admissions process. For example, at the University of Michigan at the time of the Grutter, Hamacher, and Gratz trials, a review committee could award up to 20 admission points to children of donors and other key supporters.

Analysts have recently detailed the privileges of class in college admissions (Avery, Fairbanks, and Zeckhauser, 2003; Steinberg, 2003; Toor, 2001). Students routinely receive admission points if they have a parent who graduated from the college to which they are applying. Such students benefit from the so-called legacy factor. A second mechanism that bestows advantages on privileged students involves parents contributing money to the colleges that their children want to attend. This is the "development" factor, so called because such gifts aid the development of the colleges that receive them.

BOX 12.2
YOU AND THE SOCIAL WORLD

Affirmative Action

Congratulations. You have just been appointed a justice of the U.S. Supreme Court. Your first case involves the complaint of Barbara Grutter, Patrick Hamacher, and Jennifer Gratz that they were the objects of discrimination when they applied to the University of Michigan (see text). Before making up your mind, please consider the arguments for and against special treatment:

1. *Advocates of affirmative action* say it compensates for historical injustices such as slavery and expulsion. Furthermore, until very recently, affirmative action benefited white over nonwhite Americans. The GI Bill after World War II that financed so many Americans' college education, for example, disproportionately helped white Americans (Katznelson, 2005). From this point of view, affirmative action helps to create a level playing field for people of all races and ethnic groups. Advocates also argue that affirmative action enriches college campuses by encouraging racial and ethnic diversity. (Incidentally, in the University of Michigan case, the Supreme Court ruled that "student body diversity is a compelling state interest that can justify the use of race in university admissions" ["Excerpts," 2003]). Finally, they say affirmative action creates a middle-class leadership group in minority communities that shows by example, instruction, and advocacy how the groups can raise their status in society. A recent study of black students who benefited from affirmative action shows that they are significantly more likely to contribute to their communities through various forms of service than are white students who attended the same colleges (Bowen and Bok, 1998).

2. *Opponents of affirmative action* contest each of these points. First, although they don't deny injustice, they emphasize its historical character. They argue that they should not have to pay for wrongs committed as long as 300 years ago. Second, they note that colleges apply affirmative action criteria to all members of selected minority groups, distributing admission points to rich and poor alike. Finally, opponents of affirmative action note that it may demean the individual achievements of minority students if people dismiss such achievements because they are presumed to derive from preferential treatment rather than talent (Carter, 1991).

3. *Advocates of special treatment for the well-to-do* argue that without the generosity of the alumni, college tuition could jump by as much as two-thirds (Steinberg, 2003). In other words, everyone who goes to college—*especially* less privileged students—benefits from the money brought in through legacy and development admissions.

4. *Advocates of **meritocracy*** support the idea of a stratification system in which equality of opportunity allows people to rise or fall to a position that matches their talent and effort. Advocates of meritocracy oppose special treatment for any group. They believe on principle that the only fair system is one in which talent alone determines college admission.

WRITING ASSIGNMENT

You must now write a 500-word opinion on the merits of the Grutter et al. complaint that deals with the following questions: Should colleges give special treatment to specific individuals or groups in admission decisions? If so, who should receive special treatment and why? If not, why not? After writing your opinion, add a brief addendum reflecting on whether and how your race, ethnicity, and class influence your judgment.

Macrosociological Processes
The Functions of Education

Awarding admission points based on cash gifts, family ties, and minority status is controversial because it strikes at the heart of a widespread belief about the American education system. Many Americans believe that we enjoy equal access to basic schooling. They think schools identify and sort students based on merit and effort. They regard the education system as an avenue of upward mobility. From their point of view, the brightest students are bound to succeed whatever their economic, ethnic, racial, or religious background. The school system is the American Dream in action. In their view, educational attainment is largely an outcome of individual talent and hard work. (**Educational attainment** refers

Meritocracy: A stratification system in which equality of opportunity allows people to rise or fall to a position that matches their talent and effort.

Educational attainment: Refers to number of years of school students complete.

Ted Horowitz/CORBIS

▲
Schools encourage the development of a separate youth culture that often conflicts with parents' values.

CENGAGENOW™

Learn more about the **Functions of Education** by going through the Functions of Education Learning Module.

to number of years of school completed. **Educational achievement** refers to how much students actually learn.)

The view that the American education system is responsible for *sorting* students based on talent and effort is a central component of the functional theory of education. The functional theory also stresses the *training* role of schools. That is, in schools, most people learn how to read, write, count, calculate, and perform other tasks essential to the workings of a modern industrial society. A third function of the education system involves the *socialization* of the young (Durkheim, 1956, 1961 [1925]). Schools teach the young to view their nation with pride, respect the law, think of democracy as the best form of government, and value capitalism. Finally, schools *transmit culture* from generation to generation, fostering a common identity and social cohesion in the process. Schools have played a particularly important role in assimilating the disadvantaged, minorities, and immigrants into American society (Fass, 1989), although in recent decades our common identity has been based increasingly on respect for the cultural diversity of American society.

Sorting, training, socializing, and transmitting culture are *manifest* functions, or positive goals that schools accomplish intentionally. But schools also perform certain *latent,* or unintended, functions too. For example, schools encourage the development of a separate youth culture that often conflicts with parents' values (Coleman et al., 1966). Especially at the college level, educational institutions bring potential mates together, thus serving as a "marriage market." Schools perform a useful custodial service by keeping children under surveillance for much of the day and freeing parents to work in the paid labor force. By keeping millions of young people temporarily out of the full-time paid labor force, colleges restrict job competition and support wage levels (Bowles and Gintis, 1976). Finally, because they can encourage critical, independent thinking, educational institutions sometimes become "schools of dissent" that challenge authoritarian regimes and promote social change (Brower, 1975; Freire, 1972).

The Effect of Economic Inequality from the Conflict Perspective

From the conflict perspective, the chief problem with the functionalist view is that it exaggerates the degree to which schools sort students by ability and thereby ensure that the most talented students eventually get the most rewarding jobs. Conflict theorists argue that, in fact, schools distribute the benefits of education unequally, allocating most of the benefits to children from upper classes and higher-status racial and ethnic groups. This means that rather than functioning as a meritocracy, schools tend to reproduce the stratification system generation after generation (Jencks et al., 1972; Lucas, 1999).

Schools reproduce the stratification system partly because, especially since the 1970s, they have varied widely in quality (Fischer et al., 1996; Sewell and Hauser, 1993). For example, Jonathan Kozol (1991) compared average spending in Chicago inner-city schools with spending in an upper-middle-class, suburban Chicago school. He found that spending per pupil was 78 percent higher in the suburban school. The suburban school offered a wide range of college-level courses and boasted the latest audiovisual, computer, photographic, and sporting equipment. Meanwhile, many schools in inner-city Chicago neighborhoods lacked adequate furniture and books. This sort of disparity repeats itself throughout the

Educational achievement: Refers to how much students actually learn.

Diane Bondareff/AP Photo

A demonstration at the New York State Supreme Court building in New York, October 12, 1999, where a coalition of public-school advocates argued in court for a change in funding formulas, saying that New York City's public school children were being cheated out of money for education.

country. Why? Because school funding is almost always based mainly on local property taxes. In wealthy communities, where property is worth a lot, people can be taxed at a lower rate than in poor communities and still generate more school funding per pupil.

Thus, wide variations in the wealth of communities and a system of school funding based mainly on local property taxes ensure that most children from poor families learn inadequately in ill-equipped schools and most children from well-to-do families learn well in better-equipped schools.

Disparities in the quality of schools go far beyond resources, however. Some schools, mainly those in poor neighborhoods, enroll a lot of students from disadvantaged homes who are likely to drop out of school or have disciplinary problems. They pay less well than schools in richer districts and therefore tend to have weaker teachers. They are therefore less conducive to learning than schools with few disadvantaged students, virtually no history of dropouts and disciplinary problems, and stronger teachers. Thus, apart from the distribution of educational resources, the kind of students who attend schools and the quality of its teachers (or the "social composition" of schools) influence the quality of education.

Standardized Tests

A second feature of schools that helps to reproduce the existing system of social stratification is the standardized test. Schools sort students into high-ability, middle-ability, and low-ability classes based on the results of intelligence-quotient (IQ) and other tests. This is called **tracking.** IQ tests are supposed to measure only innate ability, although, as we will see, whether they do is doubtful. After high school, students are sorted into colleges of varying quality based on the results of the Scholastic Assessment Test (SAT) and the American College Testing (ACT) exam. The SAT originally derived from IQ tests.

CENGAGENOW™

Learn more about **Tracking** by going through the Tracking in Education Animation.

Tracking: The procedure of sorting students into high-ability, middle-ability, and low-ability classes based on the results of IQ and other tests.

However, its sponsors now claim it measures "developed verbal and mathematical reasoning abilities related to performance in college" (quoted in Zwick, 2002: 8). In other words, the SAT focuses more on what students have achieved in terms of their verbal and math reasoning rather than their innate abilities. The ACT is supposed to be the most achievement-oriented of the three tests.

How Do IQ and Social Status Influence Academic and Economic Success?

The best research on the subject shows that, by itself, IQ contributes to academic success and to economic success later in life. This sorting by merit is what functionalists would predict. However, a number of background factors also influence success (in ▶Figure 12.6, focus for the moment on the solid black lines). This is in accordance with what conflict theorists would predict. One set of background factors derives from the home environment. Your success in school and your economic success later in life depend directly on how much money your parents earn, how many years of education they have, how much they encourage your creativity and studying, how many siblings you have, and so forth. In general, having encouraging parents with more education and higher income, and having fewer siblings, gives a person the greatest chance of success.

A second set of background factors influencing success derives from the community environment. As we have already suggested, your academic and economic success depend directly on such factors as the percentage of disadvantaged students in your school, the dropout rate in your school, and which part of the country you come from. These home and community background factors bestow privileges and disadvantages on people independent of IQ. As the solid orange lines in Figure 12.6 suggest, they also influence how many years you spend in school, whether you are placed in high-ability, medium-ability, or low-ability classes, and whether you complete college. These schooling variables influence your academic and economic success too.

Significantly, home environment, community environment, and schooling experience affect IQ test results (see the dashed black lines in Figure 12.6). Said differently, if you change a person's home environment, community environment, and schooling

▶FIGURE 12.6
How Social Background and IQ Influence Inequality

Source: Adapted from Fischer et al. (1996: 74); Sewell and Hauser (1993).

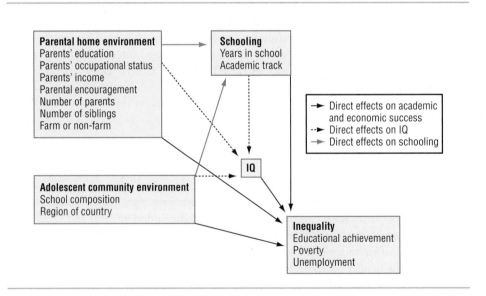

experience, you will probably change that person's IQ. A few scholars have argued that IQ is genetic in origin, that it cannot be changed, and that improving the economic circumstances and the quality of schooling of the underprivileged is therefore a waste of money (Herrnstein and Murray, 1994). However, the fact that changes in home environment, community environment, and schooling experience produce changes in IQ demonstrates that this argument must be qualified. IQ is partly genetic and partly social in origin. IQ tests measure cognitive ability *and* underlying social stratification (Schiff and Lewontin, 1986).

Are SAT and ACT Tests Biased?

Just as IQ tests sort students within schools, SAT and ACT tests sort students for college entrance, helping to determine who gets into the better colleges and who does not. These tests (along with high school grades) usefully increase the ability of colleges to predict who will do well and who will graduate. Some scholars charge the SAT and ACT tests with bias against disadvantaged minority groups. However, research shows that the biggest problem with the SAT and ACT tests is not the tests themselves (Zwick, 2002). The real problem lies in the background factors (home environment, community environment, and schooling) that determine who gets to take the test in the first place and how well prepared different groups of test-takers are (Massey et al., 2003).

The company that administers the SAT identifies various ethnic and racial groups among the test-takers. Members of three groups make it into the test room in far smaller numbers than one would expect. Compared with their representation in the population as a whole, Native American test-takers are only 43 percent as numerous as one would expect, Chicanos are just 55 percent as numerous, and Puerto Rican Americans are 71 percent as numerous (▶Table 12.2). These figures strikingly reveal the toll of background factors on who gets to take the SAT in the first place. In addition, we must bear in mind that widespread poverty, inadequate schools, tracking, and other background factors make Native Americans, Chicanos, Puerto Rican Americans, and African Americans less prepared for the SATs on average than non-Hispanic white and Asian American students. This accounts in large measure for differences between groups in test scores. Background disparities are later reflected in the proportion of people in various racial and ethnic groups who complete college, and this eventually translates into earnings disparities in the paid labor force.

▶TABLE 12.2

Average SAT Scores by Race or Ethnicity for College-Bound Seniors, 2004

Test section	RACE OR ETHNICITY						
	Native American	Asian	African	Mexican	Puerto Rican	Other Hispanic	Other White
Verbal	483	507	430	451	457	461	528
Mathematics	488	577	427	458	452	465	531
Total	971	1084	857	909	909	926	1059
Percent of all test-takers (a)	1	10	12	5	1	4	67
Ethnic or racial group as percent of population (b)	0.7	4.2	12.1	9.1	1.4	3.2	82.8
Ratio of (a) to (b)	1.43	2.38	0.99	0.55	0.71	1.25	0.81

Sources: College Entrance Examination Board (2005); Infoplease.com (2005a); U.S. Census Bureau (2005a).

We conclude that functionalists paint a rather idealized picture of the education system. They fail to emphasize sufficiently the far-reaching effects of stratified home, community, and school environments on student achievement and placement.

Case Study: Functionalist versus Conflict Theories of the American Community College

We can more fully illustrate how sociologists of education use functionalist and conflict theories by applying them to the case of the American community college system. Between the beginning and the end of the 20th century, the number of community colleges in the United States grew from zero to more than 1,400. About 5.5 million students are enrolled in American community colleges today (Cohen and Brawer, 2003 [1981]: 1, 15, 37). Aside from the general population increase, two social forces contributed most heavily to the rise of the community college system. First, the country needed skilled workers in industry and services. Second, the belief grew that higher education would contribute to upward mobility and greater equality in American society. The accuracy of that belief has become a point of contention among sociologists.

Functionalists examine the social composition of the student body in community colleges and find a disproportionate number of students from lower socioeconomic strata and minority ethnic groups. In 1997, for example, 46 percent of ethnic minority students in American higher education were enrolled in community colleges, whereas community colleges accounted for 38 percent of the total enrollment in American higher education (Cohen and Brawer, 2003 [1981]: 46). Although many community colleges are located in affluent or middle-class areas, others are located close to the neighborhoods of disadvantaged students, allowing them to live at home while studying. Community college tuition fees are lower than tuition fees in four-year colleges. Graduates of community colleges are usually able to find relatively good jobs and steady employment. These facts seem to confirm the functionalist view that the community college system creates new opportunities for disadvantaged youth who might otherwise have less rewarding jobs.

Conflict theorists deny that the growth of community colleges increases upward mobility and equality in American society. In the long run, they argue, it is the entire stratification system that is upwardly mobile. That is, the quality of nearly *all* jobs improves but the *relative* position of community college graduates versus graduates of four-year institutions remains the same. In fact, conflict theorists argue that community colleges reinforce prevailing patterns of social and class inequality by directing students from disadvantaged backgrounds away from four-year institutions and thus decreasing the probability that they will earn a four-year degree and a high-status position in society (Karabel, 1986: 18). Only about 25 to 30 percent of community college students eventually transfer to universities, and they tend to be students from the most advantaged backgrounds.

Functionalists and conflict theorists both have a point. Community colleges do create opportunities for individual upward mobility that some students would otherwise not have. Community colleges do not, however, change the overall pattern of inequality in American society. In fact, expecting community colleges or, for that matter, any part of the institution of education to change the stratification system as a whole is probably naive. Decreasing the level of inequality in society requires passing laws that change people's entitlements and the rewards they receive for doing different kinds of work, not just increasing educational opportunities.

We conclude that functionalists paint a somewhat idealized picture of the education system. Although usefully identifying the manifest and latent functions of education, they fail to emphasize sufficiently the far-reaching effects of stratified home, community, and school environments on student achievement and placement. A similar conclusion is warranted if we examine the effects of gender on education.

Gender and Education: The Feminist Contribution

In some respects, women are doing better than men in the American education system. More American women than men have graduated from high school since about 1870. Overall, women in college have higher grade point averages than men and they complete their degrees faster. The number of women enrolled as college undergraduates has exceeded the number of men since 1978. By 1984, more women than men were enrolled in graduate and professional schools. The enrollment gap between women and men is growing—and not just in the United States, but also in the UK, Canada, France, Germany, and Australia (Berliner, 2004; National Center for Educational Statistics, 2004a: 103, 115).

The facts just listed represent considerable improvement over time in the position of women in the education system. Yet feminists who have looked closely at the situation have established that women are still at a disadvantage (Spade, 2001). Consider field of study. A disproportionately large number of men earn Ph.D.s and professional degrees in the physical sciences, engineering, computer science, dentistry, medicine, and law—all relatively high-paying fields, most requiring a strong math and science background. A disproportionately large number of women earn Ph.D.s and professional degrees in home economics; area, ethnic, and cultural studies; education; English; foreign languages; and other relatively low-paying fields requiring little background in math and science. Parents and teachers are partly responsible for these choices because they tend to direct boys and girls toward what they regard as masculine and feminine fields of study. Sex segregation in the labor market also influences choice of field of study. College students know women are more likely to get jobs in certain fields than others and they make career choices accordingly (Spade, 2001) (see Chapter 10, "Sexuality and Gender"). We conclude that, like class and race, gender structures the educational experience and its consequences.

Microsociological Processes

The Stereotype Threat: A Symbolic Interactionist Perspective

Macrosociological issues such as the functions of education and the influence of class, race, and gender on educational achievement do not exhaust the interests of sociologists of education. They have also contributed much to our understanding of the face-to-face interaction processes that influence the educational process. Consider this: When black and white children begin school, their achievement test scores are similar. Yet the longer they stay in school, the more black students fall behind. By the sixth grade, blacks in many school districts are two full grades behind whites in achievement. Clearly, something happens in school to increase the gap between black and white students. Symbolic interactionists suggest that this something is the self-fulfilling prophecy, an expectation that helps bring about what it predicts.

We encountered examples of self-fulfilling prophecies in educational settings in Chapter 4 ("Social Interaction"). For instance, we discussed one famous experiment in which, at the beginning of a school year, researchers randomly identified students as high or low achievers to their teachers. At the end of the school year, they found that the students arbitrarily singled out as high achievers scored higher on an IQ test than those arbitrarily singled out as low achievers. The researchers concluded that teachers' expectations alone influenced students' performance (Rosenthal and Jacobson, 1968; Weinstein, 2002).

In general, teachers at all levels often expect African Americans, Latinos, and Native Americans to do poorly in school. Rather than being treated as a person with good prospects, a minority-group student is often under suspicion of intellectual inferiority and often feels rejected by teachers, white classmates, and the curriculum. This expectation, sometimes called a **stereotype threat,** has a negative impact on the school performance of disadvantaged groups (Massey et al., 2003; Steele, 1997).

Minority-group students often cluster together because they feel alienated from dominant groups in their school or college or perhaps even from the school or college itself. Too often, such alienation turns into resentment and defiance of authority. Many students from minority groups reject academic achievement as a goal because they see it as a goal of the dominant culture. Discipline problems, ranging from apathy to disruptive and illegal behavior, can result. The corollary of identifying one's race or ethnicity with poor academic performance is thinking of good academic performance as "selling out" to the dominant culture (Ogbu, 2003; Willis, 1984 [1977]).

In contrast, challenging students from minority groups, giving them emotional support and encouragement, giving greater recognition in the curriculum to the accomplishments of their group, creating an environment in which they can relax and achieve—all these strategies explode the stereotype threat and improve academic performance (Steele, 1992). Anecdotal evidence supporting this argument may be found in the compelling 1988 movie *Stand and Deliver,* based on the true-life story of high school math teacher Jaime Escalante. Escalante refused to write off his failing East Los Angeles Chicano pupils as "losers" and inspired them to remarkable achievements as they registered the best performance in the Advanced Placement Calculus Exam in the southern California school system (see Box 12.1).

Cultural Capital

Some students do better or worse in school than one would expect given their IQ and home, school, and community environments. That is because another variable, **cultural capital,** accounts for some differences in school performance. Cultural capital refers to "widely shared, high status cultural signals (attitudes, preferences, formal knowledge, behaviors, goals, and credentials) used for social and cultural exclusion" (Lamont and Lareau, 1988: 156). If you own a lot of cultural capital you have "highbrow" tastes in literature, music, art, dance, and even sports (rowing and fencing, for example). You behave according to established rules of etiquette. You value and pursue the goals of your school. You eventually earn a degree from one of the "right" colleges. People may earn cultural capital through socialization in high-status households or they may acquire it in school. Owning cultural capital increases one's chance of success in school and in the paid labor force.

The independent effect of cultural capital is sometimes exaggerated (Kingston, 2001). However, the most often cited American study on the subject suggests that cultural capital may be as important as measured ability (e.g., IQ) in determining grades (DiMaggio, 1982). However, the original research on cultural capital was conducted in France, and it claimed to show that possession of cultural capital is linked to being born in high-status families (Bourdieu and Passeron, 1990 [1977]). American research shows a weaker link between the status of one's family and the acquisition of cultural capital. In the United States, people acquire cultural capital mostly in school. There, students can learn and display particular tastes, styles, and understandings that make communication easier with high-status individuals. Consequently, participating in prestigious cultural activities may be a way for low-status students to achieve upward mobility (DiMaggio, 1982: 190).

Stereotype threat: The impact of negative stereotypes on the school performance of disadvantaged groups.

Cultural capital: Widely shared, high-status cultural signals (attitudes, preferences, formal knowledge, behaviors, goals, and credentials) used for social and cultural exclusion.

Education and Globalization

In Europe 300 years ago, the nobility and the wealthy usually hired personal tutors to teach their children to read and write, learn basic history, geography, and foreign languages, and study how to dress properly, conduct themselves in public, greet status superiors, and so on. Few people went to college. Only a few professions, such as theology and law, required extensive schooling. The great majority of Europeans were illiterate. As late as the 1860s, more than 80 percent of Spaniards and more than 30 percent of the French could not read (Vincent, 2000). Even as recently as a century ago, most people in the world never attended even a day of school. As late as 1950 only about 10 percent of the world's countries boasted systems of compulsory mass education (Meyer, Ramirez, and Soysal, 1992).

Today the situation is different. Compulsory mass education became a universal feature of European life by the early 20th century, and nearly universal literacy was achieved by the middle of the 20th century (Vincent, 2000). Today, every country in the world has a system of mass schooling. Mass education is related to globalization. Many of the conditions that contributed to mass education in the West now exist in the world's less developed countries. Religious authority is growing weaker, democracy is growing stronger, and new governments require the loyalty of their citizens and see education as necessary for economic development (McMahon, 1999). In addition, transnational corporations require a more literate and highly educated world population to do business, and transnational organizations such as the United Nations promote literacy and schooling. Still, this high moral principle remains a far-off goal. There are more than 860 million illiterate adults in the world, two-thirds of them women. In sub-Saharan Africa, 40 percent of primary school–age children do not attend school (UNESCO, 2002).

The United States is one of the most highly educated societies in the world. In 2007, 87 percent of Americans in the 25–29 age cohort had completed high school and nearly 30 percent had completed college (National Center for Education Statistics, 2008). These are impressive statistics. Yet the globalization of education has increased interest in comparing education in the United States with education in other countries. Such comparisons often show American students to be performing relatively poorly against some of their foreign counterparts. Consequently, many Americans believe that the U.S. school system has turned soft if not rotten. This has been true at least since the 1983 publication of *A Nation at Risk* (National Commission on Excellence in Education, 1983). Critics argue that the youth of Japan and South Korea spend long hours concentrating on the basics of math, science, and language, while American students spend fewer hours in school and study more subjects (art, music, drama, physical education, and so on) that are of little practical value. If American students do not spend more time studying core subjects, they warn, the United States will suffer declining economic competitiveness in the 21st century.

Standardized international tests support the view that American students perform significantly below average in core subjects when compared to students in other rich countries. ▶Table 12.3 reports the most recent math scores. The United States scored 35th out of 57 countries that took the test in 2006. Many of the 57 countries are not rich, but even when the United States was compared to the rich countries only, it scored significantly below average. The results for reading and science scores are not much different.

Of course, not all American schools are academically flabby. As one educator notes, "The top third of American schools are world-class, . . . the next third are okay, and the bottom third are in terrible shape" (Bracey, 1998). It would probably do students a lot of good if expectations and standards were raised in the entire school system. However, the real crisis in American education can be found not in upper-middle-class suburban

▶**TABLE 12.3**

Math Scores of 15-Year-Olds on Standardized Test, 57 Countries, 2006

Country	Score	Country	Score
Chinese Taipei (Taiwan)	549	Lithuania	486
Finland	548	Latvia	486
Hong Kong—China	547	Spain	480
Korea	547	Azerbaijan	476
Netherlands	531	Russian Federation	476
Switzerland	530	United States	474
Canada	527	Croatia	467
Macao—China	525	Portugal	466
Liechtenstein	525	Italy	462
Japan	523	Greece	459
New Zealand	522	Israel	442
Belgium	520	Serbia	435
Australia	520	Uruguay	427
Estonia	515	Turkey	424
Denmark	513	Thailand	417
Czech Republic	510	Romania	415
Iceland	506	Bulgaria	413
Austria	505	Chile	411
Slovenia	504	Mexico	406
Germany	504	Montenegro	399
Sweden	502	Indonesia	391
Ireland	501	Jordan	384
France	496	Argentina	381
United Kingdom	495	Colombia	370
Poland	495	Brazil	370
Slovak Republic	492	Tunisia	365
Hungary	491	Qatar	318
Luxembourg	490	Kyrgyzstan	311
Norway	490		

Note: Countries in black font have scores significantly above the average for rich (OECD) countries. Countries in blue font have scores significantly below the average for rich (OECD) countries. Countries in red font have scores not significantly different from the average for rich (OECD) countries.
Source: Based on Table 5, Range of rank of countries/economies on the mathematics scale, p. 53, PISA 2006: Science Competencies for Tomorrow's World Executive Summary © OECD 2007, http://www.oecd.org/pisa.

schools but in the schools that contain many disadvantaged minority students, most of them in the inner cities. We need to keep this in mind when discussing the sensitive issue of school reform.

Crisis and Reform in U.S. Schools

Because educational attainment is the single most important factor that determines income, Americans have been trying for decades to figure out how to improve the educational attainment of disadvantaged minorities. For 40 years, the main strategy has been school desegregation by busing. By trying to make schools more racially and ethnically integrated, many people hoped that the educational attainment of disadvantaged students would rise to the level of the more advantaged students.

Things did not work out as hoped. Instead of accepting busing and integration, many white families moved to all-white suburbs or enrolled their children in private schools, which are more racially and ethnically homogeneous than public schools. Meanwhile, in integrated public schools, gains on the part of students in minority groups were limited by racial tensions, competition among academically mismatched students from widely divergent family backgrounds, and related factors (Parillo, Stimson, and Stimson, 1999). Research shows that desegregation closes only 10 to 20 percent of the academic gap between black and white students (Jencks et al., 1972).

The limited success of desegregation has convinced many people that instead of pouring money into busing, a wiser course of action would be to improve the quality of traditionally underfinanced schools in predominantly minority-group areas. Many edu-

BOX 12.3
SOCIAL POLICY: WHAT DO YOU THINK?

The No Child Left Behind Act

Despair over the quality of public education in the United States is widespread. Not surprisingly, therefore, people have suggested many ways of improving schools. In the 1990s, Caroline Minter Hoxby proposed an idea that is intriguing but controversial. She believes that many problems in the education system stem from the fact that bad schools are never punished. For instance, a school's budget is unaffected if it has a high dropout rate and many of its students do poorly on their SATs. Many people feel that this is as it should be. They think that cutting the budgets of bad schools would only serve to punish their students. Hoxby has no interest in punishing students for the poor quality of their schools. Instead, she argues that public funding of schools should be cut and parents should be given school vouchers valued at $2,500 to $5,000 a year per child. Parents would be free to enroll their children in any school they want by giving the vouchers to the schools of their choice. In this way, children would be moved out of bad schools and into good ones. Schools' budgets would depend mainly on how many students enroll in them. This system, which effectively promises to privatize public education, would help children go to better schools and would give the bad schools an incentive to improve, says Hoxby. Eventually, if administrators don't improve the bad schools, they will be forced to close them for lack of funding. Hoxby notes: "It would be like restaurants. . . . New, successful schools would take over from old failing schools, and the old ones would disappear" (quoted in Cassidy, 1999: 147).

Although President Bush liked the voucher idea, the desire to build a broad consensus led him to modify it and propose the No Child Left Behind Act, which was passed in 2002. The law seeks to make schools accountable for their performance. It establishes a national system of tests, graduation rates, and other indicators that allow administrators to track and compare the performance of schools. If a school fails to reach a state-defined level of proficiency for two years running, it is subjected to escalating sanctions and interventions. Children in low-performing schools must be given extra help if they need it and they are allowed to transfer to better schools, to which the school district must provide transportation. The act also promised to provide the resources needed to place highly qualified teachers in every classroom by 2005–6.

Most Americans and their political representatives from both parties supported the No Child Left Behind Act. Yet it failed to achieve its aims. Some of the main reasons for its failure include the following:

1. The administration did not honor its funding commitments. States were saddled with noble and expensive policy objectives, but the federal government provided little money to meet them.
2. States were allowed to define their own proficiency standards. As a result, some states *lowered* their standards to make it *seem* as if they were meeting national goals. Tennessee jubilantly reported in 2005 that 87 percent of its students performed at or above the proficiency level, but when the federal government ran its own tests, only 21 percent of Tennessee students were considered proficient in math. Students from Mississippi, Oklahoma, North Carolina, Alabama, Georgia, Alaska, Texas, and more than a dozen other states did much better on state reading and math tests than on federal tests (Dillon, 2005).
3. Many schools with a high proportion of minority students, especially students who speak little English, found it difficult to reach mandated progress goals. Yet few minority students transferred to other schools because parents wanted their children to stay in the neighborhood, other schools were already overcrowded, or there were no alternatives in the area. In August 2003, 250,000 Chicago students were eligible for transfer but only 19,000 applied and a mere 1,100 went to a new school (Mathis, 2003; Schrag, 2004).

Critical Thinking

- Are the problems with the No Child Left Behind Act defects in implementation or are they inherent in the idea of making schools accountable for their performance?

- If you believe the former, how could the Act be implemented more effectively?

- If you believe the latter, what factors, in your opinion, doom a school policy based on accountability?

cators fear that ignoring integration will deny American students from different races and ethnic groups the opportunity to learn to work and live together. Nevertheless, the movement to focus on improving school quality is gaining momentum. Proposals to improve school quality fall into four main categories. Box 12.3 discusses the fourth of these. Let us consider the first three in turn.

Local Initiatives

We already noted one local initiative in our discussion of the self-fulfilling prophecy that disadvantaged students are bound to do poorly in school. By challenging minority students, giving them emotional support and encouragement, preparing a curriculum that gives more recognition to the accomplishments of their group, and creating an environment in which they can relax and achieve, they do better in school. A second local initiative is the mentoring movement. It involves community members volunteering to work with disadvantaged students in schools, church basements, community centers, and housing projects. There, the mentors tutor students, socialize with them, act as role models, and impart practical skills.

Increasing and Redistributing School Budgets

Local initiatives can go only so far to improve the quality of education in the United States. The teaching profession needs higher salaries to attract more inspiring teachers and reduce classroom size, because smaller classes have a positive, long-term impact on student achievement (Hacsi, 2002: 206). And no amount of teaching cultural diversity is going to buy desks, repair a leaky roof, or get rid of rodents scouring the school grounds for scraps of food. According to a report by the U.S. General Accounting Office, the investigative arm of Congress, a third of the country's schools need major repairs or outright replacement (Tornquist, 1998). That takes money. The second set of proposed educational reforms speaks to the need for increased investment in education and redistributing existing resources (Reich, 1991).

Where could the money come from and how could existing funds be redistributed? One possibility is that federal, state, or local governments collect school taxes and tie them at least in part to people's ability to pay. As in some other postindustrial countries, well-to-do people could be obliged to pay a higher *rate* of school tax than the less well-to-do, and funds for schools could then be distributed more equitably to communities, whatever their wealth. As things currently stand, the neediest schools in the country receive about $1,000 less annually per student than public schools with the fewest poor children. The greatest disparity is in New York State, where the gap is more than $2,100 (Schemo, 2002).

Economic Reform and Comprehensive Preschools

The problem with the first two proposed solutions for the school crisis is that attempts to implement them have met with limited success. Sociologists began to understand how little schools could do on their own to encourage upward mobility and end poverty in the 1960s, when sociologist James Coleman headed a monumental survey of American schools (Coleman et al., 1966). Coleman began his research convinced that the educational achievement of black children was due to the underfunding of their schools. What he found was that differences in the quality of schools—measured by assessments of such factors as school facilities and curriculum—accounted at most for about a third of the variation in students' academic performance. At least two-thirds of the variation in academic performance was due to inequalities imposed on children by their homes, neighborhoods, and peers. More than four decades later, little research contradicts Coleman's finding.

We conclude that programs aimed at increasing school budgets and encouraging local school reform initiatives need to be augmented by policies that improve the social environment of young, disadvantaged children *before* and *outside* of school (Hertzman, 2000). Children from disadvantaged homes do better in school if their

Head Start is insufficient in terms of improving the social environments of disadvantaged children.

Paul Conklin/Photo Edit

parents create a healthy, supportive, and academically enriched environment at home and if peers do not lead children to a life of drugs, crime, and disdain for academic achievement. Policies aimed at helping to create these conditions—job training and job creation for parents, and comprehensive child and family assistance programs that start when a child is born—would go a long way toward improving the success rate of programs that increase school budgets and encourage local reform initiatives (Hacsi, 2002; Meier, 2002; Wagner, 2002).

A few model comprehensive child and family assistance programs exist. A 1999 study of one such project analyzed 21-year-old graduates of the program who were enrolled as infants between 1972 and 1977. Ninety-eight percent of them were African American. Two decades after they first entered the preschool program, they scored higher than a control group on math and reading achievement tests. The graduates were far more likely than members of the control group to be attending an educational institution at the time of the study and far more likely to have attended a four-year college (Campbell and Ramey, 1994; Campbell et al., 2002).

Offering such programs to all poverty-level children in the United States would cost three times more than current Head Start programs, which are far inferior in quality and comprehensiveness. Effective job training and job creation programs for poor adults would also be costly. Realistically speaking, many people are likely to oppose such reforms at this time of difficult economic circumstances. After all, this is an era when some governments are cutting school budgets in the inner city. It is an era when many parents prefer to send their children to private schools or move to suburban neighborhoods with excellent public schools if they can afford it (Orfield and Eaton, 1996). On the other hand, one must remember that 75 percent of Americans in the 2006 GSS said that too little money is being spent on the nation's schools. Education was the country's number one priority, (see Chapter 8, "Globalization, Inequality, and Development," Table 8.5). This suggests that most Americans still want the education system to live up to its ideals and serve as a path to upward mobility.

The Points of the Compass

Much of the sociological study of education turns on the "opportunity" axis of the sociological compass we introduced in Chapter 1. The education system is supposed to function as a great leveler, ensuring that all children are able to realize their full potential and rise to a level of accomplishment that maximizes their rewards once they reach the job market. Opportunities are not supposed to be limited by such background factors as class, race, and gender. But they are. True, the education system affords opportunities for upward mobility; many bright children from humble origins "make it." Yet many more do not. And while some children from privileged families do poorly in school, their background typically buffers them from the threat of steep plunges down the social hierarchy. The education system remains far from the equal opportunity ideal.

Much of the sociological study of religion turns on the "freedom" axis of our sociological compass. We enjoy increased choice of religious beliefs and practices, partly because monolithic religious authority no longer exists in much of the world and also because globalization has exposed us to more religious options. Amidst this growing freedom of choice, however, a remarkable constraint imposes itself. Just four decades ago, most observers thought that religion was a weakening force. Now, in the midst of religious revivals in much of the world, they have changed or at least qualified their assessment. Religion, while by no means compulsory, is widely considered an important part of life in many countries, and has therefore proven to be more resilient than was once expected.

CHAPTER SUMMARY

1. **What is Durkheim's theory of religion and what are the main criticisms that have been lodged against it?**

Durkheim argued that the main function of religion is to increase social cohesion by providing ritualized opportunities for people to experience the collective conscience. Critics note that Durkheim ignored the ways in which religion can incite social conflict and reinforce social inequality.

2. **What is Weber's theory of religion and what are the main criticisms that have been lodged against it?**

Weber argued that religion acts like a railroad switch, determining the tracks along which history will be pushed by the force of political and economic interest. Protestantism, for example, invigorated capitalist development. Critics note that the correlation between economic development and the predominance of Protestantism is not as strong as Weber thought.

3. **What is the secularization thesis and what are the main criticisms that have been lodged against it?**

The secularization thesis holds that religious institutions, actions, and consciousness are on the decline worldwide. Critics of the secularization thesis point out that there has been a religious revival in the United States and elsewhere over the past 30 years or so.

4. **What is the revised secularization thesis?**

The revised secularization thesis recognizes the religious revival and the resilience of religion but still maintains that the scope of religious authority has declined over time. The revisionists say that religion is increasingly restricted to the realm of the spiritual; it governs fewer aspects of people's lives and is more a matter of personal choice than it used to be.

5. **What determines the frequency with which people attend religious services?**

Among other factors, the frequency of attending religious services is influenced by opportunity (how much time people have available for attending), need (whether people are in a social position that increases their desire for spiritual answers to life's problems), and learning (whether people were brought up in a religious household).

6. **What are the functions of education?**

Sorting, training, socializing, and transmitting culture are *manifest* functions, or goals that schools accomplish intentionally. Schools can perform certain *latent*, or unintended, functions too, including the development of a separate youth culture, marriage market, custodial service, and tradition of dissent.

7. **What are the arguments for and against affirmative action?**

Advocates of affirmative action say it compensates for historical injustices, encourages ethnic and racial diversity, and creates middle-class leaders in minority groups. Opponents argue that people should not have to compensate for injustices committed up to 300 years ago, that affirmative action ignores individual rights and differences, and that it diminishes the achievements of students from minority groups.

8. **What do standardized tests measure and what are their effects?**

Standardized tests are supposed to measure innate ability (IQ tests) or mathematical and reasoning abilities related to performance in college (the SAT and ACT tests). To some extent, they do. Thus, to a degree, they help to sort students by ability and aid in the creation of a meritocracy. However, they also measure students' preparedness to learn and thrive in school, and preparedness is strongly related to such background factors as a family's race and class position and the social composition of schools. Therefore, standardized tests also help to reproduce existing social inequalities.

9. **Does gender influence educational outcomes?**

Women are ahead of men in college enrollments, speed of completion of degrees, and grade point average. Still, they lag behind men substantially when it comes to the prestige and earning potential of their fields of study.

10. **How does the stereotype threat work in the education system?**

Teachers' expectations that certain students will do poorly in school often result in poor student performance. Teachers' expectations that certain students will do well in school often result in good student performance. These expectations reinforce the effects of background factors and, like background factors, help to reproduce existing patterns of inequality.

11. **What are the major reforms that have been proposed to deal with the crisis of American schools?**

The major school reforms that have been proposed in recent years include local initiatives such as mentoring, making schools accountable for their performance, redistributing and increasing school budgets, and substantially improving the social environment of young, disadvantaged children before and outside of school.

Questions to Consider

1. Does the sociological study of religion undermine one's religious faith, make one's religious faith stronger, or have no necessary implications for one's religious faith? On what do you base your opinion? What does your opinion imply about the connection between religion and science in general?

2. In your opinion, how meritocratic were the schools you attended? Did the most talented students tend to perform best? Did material advantages and parental support help the best students? Did material disadvantages and lack of parental support hinder the achievements of weaker students?

3. How would you try to solve the problem of unequal access to education? Do you favor any of the older approaches, such as busing of children from poor districts to wealthier districts or greater federal control over education budgets? What do you think about the solutions to the school crisis discussed at the end of this chapter? Do you have some suggestions of your own?

Web Resources

CENGAGENOW™

Maximize your study time by using CengageNOW's diagnostic study plan to help you review this chapter. The Study Plan will

- help you identify areas on which you should concentrate;
- provide interactive exercises to help you master the chapter concepts; and
- provide a post-test to confirm you are ready to move on to the next chapter.

The Companion Website for *Sociology: Your Compass for a New World, The Brief Edition*, Enhanced Second Edition

www.cengage.com/sociology/brym

Supplement your review of this chapter by going to the companion website to take one of the tutorial quizzes, use flash cards to master key terms, and check out the many other study aids you'll find there. You'll also find special features such as GSS Data and Census 2000 information that will put data and resources at your fingertips to help you with that special project or help you do some research on your own.

CHAPTER 13

Politics, Work, and the Economy

Chet Gordon/The Image Works

In this chapter, you will learn that:

- Political sociologists analyze the distribution of power in society and its consequences for political behavior and public policy.

- Sociological disputes about the distribution of power often focus on how social structures, especially class and state structures, influence political life.

- Enduring social inequalities limit democracy even in rich countries like the United States and often lead to warfare in less prosperous countries where democracy is weakly established.

- Three work-related revolutions—one in agriculture, one in industry, and one in the provision of services—have profoundly altered the way people sustain themselves and live. They have also increased the degree to which society is arranged in a hierarchy of jobs.

- In the past few decades, the number of "good" jobs has grown, but "bad" jobs have become even more numerous, resulting in a polarization of the occupational structure.

Politics

The Tobacco War

In the spring of 1998, the tobacco war reached a decisive stage. Congress was ready to pass a bill that would cost the tobacco companies $516 billion in damages. The bill would also raise tobacco taxes by $1.10 a pack, limit cigarette advertising, and give Washington broad new powers to regulate the tobacco industry.

The public seemed eager to support the legislation. After all, 75 percent of the people would never have to pay the new tax because only a quarter of American adults smoked. And there was widespread alarm in the land. More than three decades of educational work by governments, schools, and health professionals made it common knowledge that one out of three smokers would die prematurely and probably wretchedly as a result of illnesses caused by smoking. Well-informed citizens knew that half a million Americans died *annually* from tobacco-related illnesses, more than the *total* American casualties in

---

CENGAGE**NOW**™

This icon signals when CengageNOW has important resources available for you to use in conjunction with the text. See the foldout at the front of this text for information on how to access CengageNOW.

Chief executive officers of the major U.S. tobacco companies declare under oath at a 1994 congressional hearing that smoking is not addictive and does not cause any disease. This was a turning point in the battle against the tobacco industry.

World War II. They knew that about 90 percent of smokers started the habit by the age of 20. They knew that the percentage of grade 12 students who smoked rose from about 17 percent to nearly 25 percent between 1992 and 1997, mainly because of tobacco companies' marketing efforts.

Then, in 1998, the last straw. Documents released in a series of lawsuits against the tobacco industry revealed that tobacco companies were targeting teenagers in their ads, manipulating ammonia levels in tobacco to maximize nicotine addiction, and misrepresenting it all in public. (Some of these events were portrayed in the 1999 Oscar-winning film *The Insider*, starring Russell Crowe.) Little wonder that polls showed strong public support for the anti-tobacco bill. The United States finally seemed ready to join the other rich industrialized countries in helping to stub out one of the world's leading health hazards.

However, representatives of the tobacco industry did not sit idly in the bleachers. They mobilized their allies, including retailers and smokers, to phone and write their members of Congress expressing outrage at the anti-tobacco bill. They tripled the budget for tobacco industry lobbyists. Legions of professional arm twisters wined, dined, and cajoled members of Congress to vote against the bill. And then the industry bankrolled a last-minute $40 million national advertising blitz. The ad campaign gnawed away at traditional American sore points. According to the ads, the anti-tobacco bill was really a government tax grab. It would increase government regulation at the expense of individual freedom. It would allow anti-tobacco industry lawyers to earn exorbitant fees. And, just as Prohibition had encouraged liquor smuggling and the production of moonshine whiskey in the 1920s and early 1930s, the new law would encourage the import of contraband cigarettes.

These arguments worked. The bill was defeated in June 1998. Just before the final vote, a *Wall Street Journal*–NBC poll found that 70 percent of Americans thought the bill's real aim was to raise new revenue. Only 20 percent said its purpose was to curb teen smoking (Centers for Disease Control and Prevention, 2000; Kluger, 1996). In separate deals, the 50 states eventually decided to sign agreements with the tobacco companies worth $246 billion, less than half the amount demanded in the federal bill. The money was intended to recover the cost of treating Medicaid-eligible smokers. However, the defeat of the federal bill raises important political questions.

Politics, Social Structure, and Political Institutions

Does the outcome of the tobacco war illustrate the operation of "government of the people, by the people, for the people," as Abraham Lincoln defined democracy in the Gettysburg Address? It certainly allowed a diverse range of Americans to express conflicting views. It permitted them to influence their elected representatives. And, in the end, members of Congress did vote in line with the wishes of most American adults as expressed in public opinion polls. This suggests that Lincoln's characterization of American politics applied as well in 1998 as it did in 1863.

However, big business's access to a bulging war chest might lead one to doubt that Lincoln's definition applies. Few groups can put together, virtually overnight, $19 million for lobbyists, $3 million for political party contributions, and $40 million for public relations and advertising experts to sway the hearts and minds of the American people and their lawmakers. Should we therefore conclude that some people, especially big businessmen, are more equal than others?[1] (See Box 13.1.)

The tobacco war raises the question that lies at the heart of political sociology. What accounts for the degree to which a political system responds to the demands of all its citizens? As you will see, political sociologists have often answered this question by examining the effects of social structures, especially class structures, on politics. Although this approach contributes much to our understanding of political life, it is insufficient by itself. A fully adequate theory of democracy requires that we also examine how state institutions and laws affect political processes.

Some analysts believe that politics in the rich industrialized countries is less likely to be shaped by class inequality in the future. Our reading of the evidence is different. We argue that persistent class inequality is the major barrier to the progress of democracy in countries like the United States. We then develop this argument in two ways. First, we argue that persistent inequality among *nations* is a major cause of war, or armed conflict between politically distinct groups, usually for the purpose of protecting or increasing their control of territory. Second, we examine the roots of class inequality in the United States by analyzing the structure of work and the operation of the economy.

Power and Authority

Politics is a machine that determines "who gets what, when, and how" (Lasswell, 1936). **Power** fuels the machine. Power is the ability to control others, even against their will (Weber, 1947: 152). Having more power than others gives you the ability to get more valued things sooner. Having less power than others means you get fewer valued things later. Political sociology's key task is figuring out how power drives different types of political machines.

The use of power sometimes involves force. For example, one way of operating a system for distributing jobs, money, education, and other valued things is by imprisoning people who don't agree with the system. In that case, people obey political rules because they are afraid to disobey. More often, however, people agree with the distribution system or at least

CENGAGENOW·

Learn more about **Power and Authority** by going through the Power and Authority Learning Module.

[1]We say business*men* advisedly. In 2000, only 46 women were on the list of America's 400 richest people. Of these, a mere 6 were self-made women. This suggests where the real power lies (DiCarlo, 2000).

Power: The ability to control others, even against their will.

accept it grudgingly. Most people pay their taxes without threats from the Internal Revenue Service (IRS) and their parking tickets without serving jail time. They recognize the right of their rulers to control the political machine. When most people basically agree with how the political machine is run, raw power becomes **authority.** Authority is legitimate, institutionalized power. Power is legitimate when people regard its use as valid or justified. Power is *institutionalized* when the norms and statuses of social organizations govern its use. These norms and statuses define how authority should be used, how people can achieve authority, and how much authority is attached to each status in the organization.

Types of Authority

Max Weber (1947) wrote that authority can have one of three bases:

1. **Traditional authority.** Particularly in tribal and feudal societies, rulers inherit authority through family or clan ties. The right of a family or clan to monopolize leadership is widely believed to originate from the will of a god.

2. **Legal-rational authority.** In modern societies, authority is derived from respect for the law. Laws specify how one can achieve office. People generally believe that these laws are rational. If someone achieves office by following these laws, his or her authority is respected.

3. **Charismatic authority.** Sometimes extraordinary, "charismatic" individuals challenge traditional or legal-rational authority. They claim to be inspired by a god or some higher principle that transcends other forms of authority. Many people believe this claim. One such principle is the idea that all people are created equal. Charismatic figures sometimes emerge during a **political revolution,** an attempt by many people to overthrow existing political institutions and establish new ones. Political revolutions take place when widespread and successful movements of opposition clash with crumbling traditional or legal-rational authority.

Types of Political System

Politics takes place in all social settings. Such settings include intimate face-to-face relationships, families, and colleges. However, political sociology is mainly concerned with institutions that specialize in the exercise of power and authority. Taken together, these institutions form the **state.** The state consists of institutions that formulate and carry out a country's laws and public policies. In performing these functions, the state regulates citizens in **civil society,** the private sphere of social life (❱Figure 13.1). In turn, citizens in civil society control the state to varying degrees, depending on the type of political system in which they live (❱Figure 13.2).

Autocracies

In an **autocracy,** absolute power resides in a single person or party. Citizens in civil society exert little or no control over the state. In 2008, 22 percent of the countries in the world fit that description, down from 46 percent in 1973. Nearly all these countries are in Africa and Asia. They include China, Pakistan, Egypt, and Saudi Arabia.

Authoritarian States

In an **authoritarian** state, power is somewhat more widely shared but citizen control is still sharply restricted. Regular elections may be held, but the judiciary may not be independent of government; there may be no institutional check on presidential power;

CENGAGENOW™

Learn more about **Revolutions** by going through the Revolutions Animation.

Authority: Legitimate, institutionalized power.

Traditional authority: The norm in tribal and feudal societies, involving rulers inheriting authority through family or clan ties. The right of a family or clan to monopolize leadership is widely believed to be derived from a god's will.

Legal-rational authority: A type of authority typical of modern societies. It derives from respect for the law. Laws specify how one can achieve office. People generally believe these laws are rational. If someone achieves office by following these laws, people respect his or her authority.

Charismatic authority: Authority based on belief in the claims of extraordinary individuals to be inspired by a god or some higher principle.

Political revolution: Overthrow of political institutions by an opposition movement and replacement by new institutions.

State: The institutions responsible for formulating and carrying out a country's laws and public policies.

Civil society: The private sphere of social life.

Autocracy: Form of government in which absolute power resides in a single person or party.

Authoritarian: States that sharply restrict citizen control of government.

The three faces of authority according to Weber: traditional authority (King Louis XIV of France, circa 1670), charismatic authority (Vladimir Lenin, Bolshevik leader of the Russian Revolution of 1917), and legal-rational authority (Ronald Reagan, campaigning for the presidency of the United States).

▶FIGURE 13.1
The Institutions of State
and Civil Society

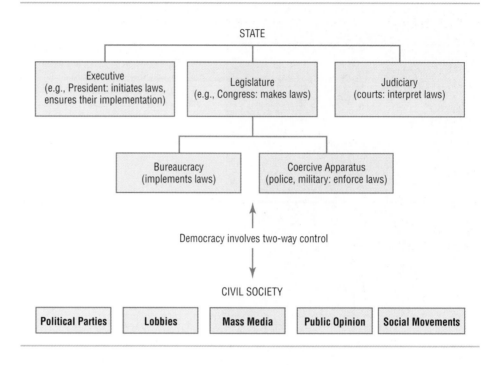

FIGURE 13.1 caption text appears to the left: The Institutions of State and Civil Society

▶FIGURE 13.2
The World's Countries by
Type of State, 1973 and
2008 (in percent)

Source: Freedom House (2004,
2008).

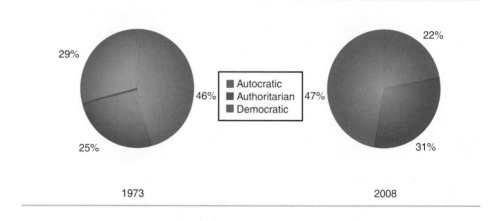

CENGAGENOW™

Learn more about **Social
Movements** by going through
the % of People Who Have
Taken Part in a Lawful
Demonstration Map Exercise.

Democracy: A political system
in which citizens exercise a
high degree of control over the
state. They do this by choosing
representatives in regular, competitive elections and enjoying
freedoms and constitutional
protections that make political
participation and competition
meaningful.

and civil liberties, such as the right of assembly and open public discussion, may be weak.
About 29 percent of the world's countries fit that description in 2004, up from 25 percent
in 1973. Nearly all of these countries are in Latin America, Africa, and Asia. Russia, Turkey,
Indonesia, and Argentina are in this category.

Democracies

In a **democracy,** citizens exert a relatively high degree of control over the state.
They not only choose representatives in regular, competitive elections but enjoy the
freedoms and constitutional protections that make political participation and competition meaningful. About 46 percent of the world's countries were democratic in 2004,

BOX 13.1
SOCIOLOGY AT THE MOVIES

The Corporation
(2003)

Indian farmers have been cultivating the neem tree ever since its valuable medicinal properties first became known 2,000 years ago. Various neem extracts kill bacteria, fungi, viruses, and insects and reduce pain and inflammation. In 1994, W. R. Grace, a large American chemical corporation, patented a fungicide derived from the neem tree. Overnight, a common and naturally occurring life form, the beneficial properties of which had been identified and nurtured by a hundred generations of Indian farmers, became the private property of a multinational corporation. The fungicide derived from the neem tree could still be manufactured and purchased—but only by paying W. R. Grace a fee.

What is a corporation? How did corporations become so powerful that they can turn nature into private property? Overall, do they do more harm than good? Vancouver filmmakers Mark Achbar, Jennifer Abbott, and Joel Bakan answer these questions in *The Corporation*, a 2003 documentary that won 26 international film awards.

Corporate ownership has a big advantage over individual ownership. It limits the legal obligations of the owners. The owners

Scene from *The Corporation*.

are not normally liable if the corporation harms consumers or goes bankrupt. Instead, the corporation is legally responsible for damage and debt. By thus limiting owners' risk, corporations are attractive investment vehicles. This is why they grew quickly.

Governments grant corporations the right to exist, but as corporations have grown, they have come to exercise more influence over governments. So, for example, corporations have for many decades impressed upon governments the importance of lowering corporate tax rates to attract business. They have also persistently reminded governments that failure to lower corporate tax rates will result in the relocation of corporations to jurisdictions where governments are more sympathetic to the interests of business. As a result, in the United States and other countries, corporations are taxed at a substantially lower rate than are individuals.

From the corporate point of view, limited liability and favorable tax laws are worth the cost to society. After all, corporations provide many useful goods and services, and competition among corporations ensures that prices are kept to a minimum. But business leaders rarely discuss the downside of the corporation. This is where Achbar, Abbott, and Bakan step in.

The Corporation argues that if corporations were people, they would be labelled psychopaths according to the standard psychiatric definition. For example:

- Psychopaths are incapable of maintaining enduring relationships. Likewise, to earn high profits, corporations routinely shut down factories in high-wage, high-tax countries like the United States, throwing millions of people out of work.

- Psychopaths display callous disregard for the feelings of others. Likewise, to earn high profits, corporations set up factories in poor countries, where women and children work long hours in horrid conditions for meager wages.

- Psychopaths display reckless disregard for the safety of others. Likewise, to earn high profits, multinational corporations routinely pollute the environment, shirk worker safety regulations, and make unsafe products.

The Corporation succeeds as a movie because it refuses to become dismal. Instead, it concludes on an optimistic note, showing how environmental activists, farmers' groups, and consumers' associations have forced corporations to behave in a more socially responsible way.

A case in point concerns the neem tree patent. In 2005, the Green Party in the European Parliament, the International Federation of Organic Agriculture, and the Research Foundation for Science, Technology, and Ecology succeeded in having W. R. Grace's patent for the neem fungicide revoked by the European Patent Office. It was the first time anyone succeeded in having a patent rejected on the grounds of "biopiracy"—corporate theft of traditional agricultural and medical knowledge and practices. Indian farmers celebrated the decision. So should we all.

Critical Thinking

- What benefits does the corporation bestow on society?

- Does characterizing the corporation as psychopathic minimize these benefits, or is the characterization justified?

- How would you reform corporations to ensure that they do not display the psychopathologies listed above?

BOX 13.2
YOU AND THE SOCIAL
WORLD

Just before the 2008 presidential election, people wondered how class, race, and age would influence voters' choices. Many citizens believed that well-to-do, white, middle-aged, and elderly people would be the biggest McCain supporters, while less well-to-do, nonwhite, young people would be the biggest Obama supporters.

Just after people voted, pollsters asked a random sample of them a series of questions that lets us test these beliefs. ▶Table 13.1 summarizes some results from one such "exit poll" conducted by MSNBC.

Who Voted for McCain and Obama in 2008?

Rick Friedman/Corbis

Critical Thinking

- Review Table 13.1. Do the exit poll results support expectations about how class, race, and age would influence voting?

- Why do you think class, race, and age influenced voting in the way they did?

- How did *your* class, race, and age influence whom you supported in the election?

AP Photo/Morry Gash

▶TABLE 13.1
Support for McCain and Obama by Social Characteristics, 2008 (in percent)

	McCain	Obama	Other	Total
2007 Total Annual Family Income				
Under $50,000	38	60	2	100
$50,000+	49	49	2	100
Race/Ethnicity				
White	55	43	2	100
Black	4	95	1	100
Hispanic/Latino	31	67	2	100
Asian	35	62	3	100
Age				
18–29	32	66	2	100
30–44	46	52	2	100
45–64	49	50	1	100
65+	53	45	2	100

Source: MSNBC (2008).

Political parties: Organizations that compete for control of government in regular elections. In the process, they give voice to policy alternatives and rally adult citizens to vote.

Lobbies: Organizations formed by special-interest groups to advise and influence politicians.

Mass media: Means of mass communication that in a democracy are supposed to help keep the public informed about the quality of government.

Public opinion: The values and attitudes of the adult population as a whole. It is expressed mainly in polls and letters to lawmakers and gives politicians a reading of citizen preferences.

Social movements: Collective attempts to change all or part of the political or social order by stepping outside the rules of normal politics.

up from 29 percent in 1973. Every continent contains democratic countries, although they are considerably less common in Africa and Asia than elsewhere. The United States, Brazil, Germany, Japan, India, Australia, and South Africa are all democracies.

Note that in modern democracies, citizens do not control the state directly. They do so through various organizations in civil society. **Political parties** compete for control of government in regular elections (Box 13.2). They put forward policy alternatives and rally adult citizens to vote. Special-interest groups and business associations form **lobbies.** They advise politicians about their members' desires. They also remind politicians how much their members' votes, organizing skills, and campaign contributions matter. The **mass media** are supposed to keep a watchful and critical eye on the state. They thus keep the public informed about the quality of government. **Public opinion** refers to the values and attitudes of the adult population as a whole. It is expressed mainly in polls and letters to lawmakers. Public opinion gives politicians a reading of citizen preferences. Finally, when dissatisfaction with normal politics is widespread, protest sometimes takes the form of **social movements.** A social movement is a collective attempt to change all or part of the political or social order by stepping outside the rules of normal politics. As Thomas Jefferson wrote in a letter to James Madison in 1787, "a little rebellion now and then is a good thing" for democracy. It helps keep government responsive to the wishes of the citizenry.

Bearing these definitions in mind, we now outline the merits and limitations of four sociological theories of democracy.

In a nationally televised address on January 17, 1961, President Eisenhower sounded much like C. Wright Mills and other elite theorists when he warned of the "undue influence" of the "military-industrial complex" in American society. An "engaged citizenry" offers the only effective defense against the "misplaced power" of the military-industrial lobby, according to Eisenhower.

Mark Richards/PhotoEdit

Theories of Democracy

Pluralist Theory

According to **pluralist theory,** democracies exist in heterogeneous societies with many competing interests and centers of power. Different classes, religious groups, ethnic and racial communities, and so forth compete against each other for state control, but none of them can dominate consistently. Sometimes one category of voters or one set of interest groups wins a political battle, sometimes another. Most often, however, politics involves negotiation and compromise among competing groups. Because no one group of people is always able to control the political agenda or the outcome of political conflicts, democracy is guaranteed, argue the pluralists (Dahl, 1961; Polsby, 1959).

Elite Theory

Elite theorists sharply disagree with the pluralist argument (Mills, 1956). They point to the existence of **elites,** small groups that occupy the command posts of a society's most influential institutions, including its biggest corporations, the executive branch of government, and the military. According to **elite theory,** the people (nearly all men) who control these institutions make important decisions that profoundly affect all members of society. Yet, according to elite theorists, they do so without much regard for elections or public opinion.

The corporate, state, and military elites are socially connected in a number of ways, according to elite theorists. People move from one elite group to another during their careers. Their children intermarry. They maintain close social contacts. They tend to be recruited from the upper-middle and upper classes. Yet the three elites are relatively independent of one another. They may see eye to eye on many issues, but each has its own sphere of influence. Conflict among elite groups is frequent (Alford and Friedland, 1985: 199; Mills, 1956: 277).

CENGAGENOW™

Learn more about **Elite Theory** by going through the Power Elite Model Animation.

Pluralist theory: Holds that power is widely dispersed, as a result of which, no group enjoys disproportionate influence, and decisions are usually reached through negotiation and compromise.

Elites: Small groups that occupy the command posts of a society's most influential institutions.

Elite theory: Holds that small groups occupying the command posts of America's most influential institutions make the important decisions that profoundly affect all members of society. Moreover, they do so without much regard for elections or public opinion.

The Elitist Critique of Pluralism

Most political sociologists today question the pluralist account of American politics because research has established the existence of large, wealth-based inequalities in political participation and influence.

Political Participation

Consider the results of the Citizen Participation Study. In the 1990s, a team of researchers surveyed a representative sample of more than 15,000 American adults. They asked respondents if they had voted in the previous presidential campaign, how many contacts they'd had with public officials, how many hours they'd worked in the election campaign, and how many dollars they'd contributed to it. Then they calculated the percentage of each political activity undertaken by people in each income group. They found that people with higher incomes were more politically active, especially in those forms of political activity that are most influential.

Political Influence and PACs

If money talks, does it speak with a single voice? If so, which political party does it support? A study of political action committees (PACs) conducted by sociologist Dan Clawson and his associates shines light on these issues (Clawson, Neustadtl, and Scott, 1992).

Winning members of Congress spend hundreds of thousands and in many cases millions of dollars on their election campaigns. PACs help them raise campaign funds by collecting money from many contributors, pooling it, and then making donations to candidates. Significantly, Clawson and his associates found that big business makes big contributions to PACs and expects contributions to buy political influence. Moreover, big business is largely unified in its political views, tending strongly to support the Republicans.

These findings are just what elite theorists would expect. However, they raise an interesting question. If the distribution of power in the United States is heavily skewed toward the wealthy, who tend to support the Republicans, why do Democrats often become president and get elected to Congress? As we will see, this question points to an important limitation of elite theory.

Power Resource Theory

In general, elite theorists believe it makes little difference whether Republicans or Democrats are in power. For them, elites always control society. Elections are little more than sideshows. Therefore, they believe, the victory of one party over another doesn't deserve much sociological attention.

We disagree. So do most political sociologists today. It matters a great deal to most citizens which party is in office because different parties support different policies. So while elite theorists are correct to claim that most power is concentrated in the hands of the wealthy, we still need a theory that accounts for the successes and failures of different parties and policies in different times and places. That is where **power resource theory** is helpful. It focuses on how long-term *variations* in the distribution of power affect the fortunes of parties and policies.

Because different parties favor different policies, they tend to be supported by different classes, religious groups, races, and other groups. Americans, for example, cluster in two main policy groups. *Liberal,* or left-wing, voters promote extensive government involvement in the economy. Among other things, they favor a strong "social safety net" of

Power resource theory: Holds that change in the distribution of power between major classes partly accounts for the successes and failures of different political parties in the long term.

health and welfare benefits to help the less fortunate members of society. As a result, liberal policies often lead to less economic inequality. In contrast, *conservative,* or right-wing, voters favor a reduced role for government in the economy. They favor a smaller welfare state and emphasize the importance of individual initiative in promoting economic growth. Thus, in the 2008 presidential election, low-income earners, African Americans, and Hispanic Americans tended to support Democrat Barack Obama while high-income earners and non-Hispanic whites tended to support Republican John McCain.

Economic issues aside, liberals and conservatives also tend to differ on social or moral issues. Liberals tend to support equal rights for women and racial and sexual minorities. Conservatives tend to support more traditional social and moral values.[2] For instance, few homosexuals and supporters of reproductive choice supported Republican John McCain in the 2008 presidential election. Most supported Democrat Barack Obama (Kaiser, 2008).

Political Parties and Class Support

In most Western democracies, the main factor that distinguishes parties is differences in *class* support (Brooks and Manza, 1997; Lipset and Rokkan, 1967; Manza, Hout, and Brooks, 1995). But the tendency for people in different classes to vote for different parties varies from one country to the next. The strength of this tendency depends on many factors. One of the most important is how socially organized or cohesive classes are (Brym with Fox, 1989: 57–91; Brym, Gillespie, and Lenton, 1989). For example, an upper class that can create PACs to support Republican candidates and lobbies to support conservative laws is more powerful than an upper class that cannot take such action. If an upper class makes such efforts while a working class fails to organize itself, right-wing candidates have a better chance of winning office. Conservative policies are more likely to become law. Similarly, a working class that can unionize many workers is more powerful than one with few unionized workers. **Unions** are organizations of workers that seek to defend and promote their members' interests. By bargaining with employers, unions have succeeded in winning improved working conditions, higher wages, and more worker participation in industrial decision making for their members. They promote worker's interests on the larger political stage as well, by collecting money for the party that is more sympathetic to their interests. They also lobby on behalf of their members and try to convince members to vote for the pro-union party. If workers become more unionized while an upper class fails to organize itself, then left-wing candidates have an improved chance of winning office. Liberal policies are more likely to become law.

Organization and Power

This, then, is the main insight of power resource theory: *Organization is a source of power. Change in the distribution of power between major classes partly accounts for the fortunes of different political parties and different laws and policies* (Esping-Andersen, 1990; O'Connor and Olsen, 1998).

We can see how power resource theory works by examining ▶Table 13.2. This table compares 18 industrialized democracies in the three decades after World War II. We divide the countries into three groups. In group 1 are countries like Sweden, where socialist parties usually control governments. (Socialist parties are more left wing than the Democrats in the United States.) In group 2 are countries like Australia, where socialist parties *sometimes* control, or share in the control of, governments. And in group 3 are

---

[2]Some people are liberal on economic issues and conservative on social issues or vice versa. Many such people call themselves moderates rather than liberals or conservatives.

Unions: Organizations of workers that seek to defend and promote their members' interests.

▶TABLE 13.2

Some Consequences of Working-Class Power in 18 Rich Industrialized Countries, 1946–1976

	Percent of Nonagricultural Workforce Unionized	Socialist Share of Government	Percent of Total National Income to Top 10% Earners	Percent Poor
Mainly socialist countries (Sweden, Norway)	68.5	High	21.8	4.3
Partly socialist countries (Austria, Australia, Denmark, Belgium, UK, New Zealand, Finland)	46.6	Medium	23.6	7.8
Mainly nonsocialist countries (Ireland, West Germany, Netherlands, USA, Japan, Canada, France, Italy, Switzerland)	28.0	Low	28.3	10.8

Note: "Socialist share of government" is the proportion of seats in each cabinet held by socialist parties weighted by the socialist share of seats in parliament and the duration of the cabinet. "Percent poor" is the average percentage of the population living in relative poverty according to Organisation for Economic Co-operation and Development (OECD) standards, with the poverty line standardized according to household size.
Source: Korpi (1983: 40, 196).

countries like the United States, where socialist parties rarely or never share control of governments. The group averages in column 1 show that socialist parties are generally more successful where workers are more unionized. The group averages in columns 3 and 4 show that there is more economic inequality in countries that are weakly unionized and have no socialist governments. In other words, by means of taxes and social policies, socialist governments ensure that the rich earn a smaller percentage of national income and the poor form a smaller percentage of the population. Studies of pensions, medical care, and other state benefits in the rich industrialized democracies reach similar conclusions. In general, where working classes are more organized and powerful, disadvantaged people are economically better off (Korpi and Palme, 2003; O'Connor and Brym, 1988; Olsen and Brym, 1996).

Other Party Differences: Religion, Race, and Gender

Class is not the only factor that distinguishes parties. In some countries, religion is an important basis of party differences, and in recent decades, race has become a cleavage factor of major and growing importance. Thus, African Americans have overwhelmingly supported the Democratic party since the 1960s and a large majority of Hispanic voters vote Democratic too (Brooks and Manza, 1997). Finally, a political gender gap exists in the United States. Men are more likely to vote Republican than women. Power resource theory focuses mainly on how the shifting distribution of power between working and upper classes affects electoral success. However, one can use the theory to analyze the electoral fortunes of parties that attract different races, gender categories, and so forth.

State-Centered Theory

There is, however, more to the story of politics than conflict between classes, religious groups, races, and so forth. Theda Skocpol and other state-centered theorists show how the state itself can structure political life, regardless of how power is distributed at a given moment (Block, 1979; Evans, Rueschemeyer, and Skocpol, 1985). The argument of **state-centered theory** is a valuable supplement to power resource theory.

To illustrate how state structures influence politics, consider a common American political practice: nonvoting. In presidential elections, voter turnout fell between the end of World War II and 1996, when it stood at 48 percent of the voting age population.[3] Turnout then increased to 56 percent by 2008. Why the upturn? The last three presidential elections were intensely competitive, and big fights tend to turn out big crowds. Even more important, technological and organizational improvements have encouraged more people to vote. Party organizers now use the Internet to solicit donations, recruit volunteers, and communicate with them. They employ census, survey, and other data to target persuadable voters. Then, they send entire armies of the party faithful out to contact persuadable voters face-to-face and encourage them to vote (CNNPolitics.com, 2008; McDonald 2008a, 2008b). However, despite these encouraging innovations, the fact remains that the United States has one of the lowest voter turnouts of any rich democracy in the world (Piven and Cloward, 1989 [1988]: 5). How can we explain this fact?

Voter Registration Laws

The high rate of nonvoting is partly a result of voter registration law, a feature of the American political structure, not of the current distribution of power. In every democracy, laws specify voter registration procedures. In some countries, citizens are registered to vote automatically when they receive state-issued identity cards at the age of 18. In other countries, state-employed canvassers go door to door before each election to register voters. Only in the United States do individual citizens have to take the initiative to go out and register themselves in voter registration centers. However, many American citizens are unable or unwilling to register. As a result, the United States has a proportionately smaller pool of eligible voters than the other democracies. Only about 70 percent of American citizens are registered to vote.

Apart from shrinking the pool of eligible voters, American voter registration law has a second important consequence. Because some *types* of people are less able and less inclined to register than others, a strong bias is introduced into the political system. Specifically, the poor are less likely to register than the better off. People without much formal education are less likely to register than the better educated. Members of disadvantaged racial minority groups, especially African Americans, are less likely to register than whites. Thus, American voter registration law is a pathway to democracy for some, a barrier to democracy for others.

American voter registration laws came into existence in the 1890s, when industrial unrest was widespread and western and southern farmers revolted against the established parties. In 1896, these rebellious forces mounted a Democratic-Populist challenge to the Republicans of the north and the wealthy Democrats of the south. Their presidential candidate, William Jennings Bryan, won nearly 48 percent of the vote in the 1896 election.

America's elites learned an important lesson from Bryan's challenge. They instituted electoral reforms—including voter registration laws—that made possible the domination of the pro-business Republican party in the north and the pro-plantation-owner Democratic party in the south. Low voter turnout and the effective disenfranchisement of many poor and black voters date from this era (Piven and Cloward, 1989 [1988]: 26–95). The political conflicts of the 1890s still influence us because, through electoral laws, they became part of the American state structure.

---

[3] The voting-age population includes noncitizens and felons ineligible to vote and excludes expatriate citizens, who can vote overseas. Other measures of voter turnout yield higher estimates (Althaus, 2005; McDonald, 2008a).

State-centered theory: Holds that the state itself can structure political life to some degree independently of the way in which power is distributed between classes and other groups at a given time.

In short, the American political system is less responsive than other rich democracies to the needs of the disadvantaged for two main reasons. First, as we saw in our discussion of power resource theory, the working class is comparatively non-unionized and therefore weak. Second, as state-centered theory suggests, the law requires citizen-initiated voter registration, one result of which is that the vote is in effect taken away from many disadvantaged people.

Summing Up

Political sociology has made good progress over the past half century. Each of the field's major schools has made a useful contribution to our appreciation of political life (▶Concept Summary 13.1). Pluralists teach us that democratic politics is about compromise and the accommodation of all group interests. Elite theorists teach us that despite compromise and accommodation, power is concentrated in the hands of high-status groups, whose interests the political system serves best. Power resource theorists teach us that despite the concentration of power in society, substantial shifts in the distribution of power do occur and that they have big effects on voting patterns and public policies. And state-centered theorists teach us that despite the influence of the current distribution of power on political life, state structures exert an important effect on politics too.

These considerations lead us to the major dilemma of American politics. Problems of economic inequality loom large, but it is doubtful that they will be addressed in a serious way unless disadvantaged Americans get more politically involved and state structures are changed to make broader political participation possible. Yet, unequal political participation shows no sign of evaporating. No mystery surrounds the reforms needed to bring more disadvantaged people into the political process. For example, comparative research has determined that removing burdensome voter registration laws would increase participation rates in the United States by 8 to 15 percent (Lijphart, 1997). There is, however, little political will to undertake such reforms now.

A solution may have to come from outside normal electoral politics, that is, from social movements (see Chapter 15, "Collective Action and Social Movements"). Social movements reoriented American public policy in the 1930s and 1960s. Perhaps we need something similar to decrease political and economic inequality in the future. The full realization of Lincoln's "government of the people, by the people, for the people" may require some of those "little rebellions" called for by Jefferson.

▶CONCEPT SUMMARY 13.1
Four Sociological Theories of Democracy Compared

	Pluralist	Elitist	Power Resource	State-Centered
How is power distributed?	Dispersed	Concentrated	Concentrated	Concentrated
Who are the main power holders?	Various groups	Elites	Upper class	State officials
On what is their power based?	Holding political office	Controlling major institutions	Owning substantial capital	Holding political office
What is the main basis of public policy?	The will of all citizens	The interests of major elites	The balance of power between classes, etc.	The influence of state structures
Do lower classes have much influence on politics?	Yes	No	Sometimes	Sometimes

Politics by Other Means

Participating in social movements is not the only way people step outside the rules of normal electoral politics to change their world. We conclude this part of our discussion by considering two others types of politics beyond the rules: war and terrorism.

War

The Costs and Types of War

War is an expensive business, and the United States spends much more than any other country financing it. With 4.5 percent of the world's population, the United States accounts for about a third of total military expenditures in the world. In addition, the United States is by far the largest exporter of arms, accounting for nearly 60 percent of world arms exports. (U.S. Census Bureau, 2001d: 327, 2002c: 860).

Wars may take place between countries (interstate wars) and within countries (civil or societal wars). A special type of interstate war is the colonial war, which involves a colony engaging in armed conflict with an imperial power to gain independence. ▶Figure 13.3 shows the magnitude of armed conflict in the world for each of these types of war from 1946 to 2002. You will immediately notice two striking features of the graph. First, after reaching a peak between the mid-1980s and early 1990s, the magnitude of armed conflict in the world dropped sharply. Second, since the mid-1950s, most armed conflict in the world has been societal rather than interstate. Today, countries rarely go to war against one another. They often go to war with themselves as contending political groups fight for state control or seek to break away and form independent states. Don't let the mass media distort your perception of global war. Wars like the ongoing U.S.–Iraq war account for little of the total magnitude of armed conflict, although they loom large in the media. Wars like the recent conflict in the Democratic Republic of Congo account for

▶FIGURE 13.3
Global Trends in Violent Conflict, 1946–2005

Note: Data are for 160 countries with populations of at least 500,000 with 500 or more deaths directly related to war between 1946 and 2005. The magnitude of armed conflict is determined by the total number of combatants and casualties, the size of the area and dislocated populations, and the extent of infrastructure damage for each year the war is active.
Source: J. Joseph Hewitt, Jonathan Wilkenfeld, and Ted Robert Gurr, Peace and Conflict 2010. Reprinted by permission.

By 2004, the civil war in the Democratic Republic of the Congo had dragged on for 6 years and registered nearly millions of deaths.

most of the total magnitude of armed conflict, yet they are rarely mentioned in the media. Thus, from 2003 to 2007, the U.S.–Iraq war killed roughly 170,000 combatants and civilians. Between 1998 and 2004, deaths due to the civil war in the Democratic Republic of Congo numbered in the millions (CBC, 2007; Coghlan et al., 2006; "Iraq Body Count," 2008; "Iraq Coalition Casualty Count," 2008).

The Risk of War

War risk varies from one country to the next, but what factors determine the risk of war on the territory of a given country? One risk factor is poverty. Poorer countries are more likely to go to war. A second risk factor is type of government. Governments that are neither democratic nor autocratic are at highest risk of war. A democratic government tends to be stable because it enjoys legitimacy in the eyes of its citizens. An autocratic government tends to be stable because an iron hand rules it. But an intermediate type of government is characterized neither by high legitimacy nor iron rule. It is therefore most prone to collapsing into societal war, with armed political groups fighting one another for state control. We conclude that economic development and democratization are the two main factors leading to less war in the world today.

In a way, this is a deeply disturbing finding. The United States allocates about 17 percent of its budget to war (or "defense") spending and less than 0.5 percent to international development and humanitarian assistance. Public opinion polls show that the American public and its leaders regard the promotion of democracy and the improvement of living standards in other countries as the least important American goal, although the cost of achieving them would be relatively low (Bardes and Oldendick, 2003: 205; Chapter 8, "Globalization, Inequality, and Development," Tables 8.2 and 8.5). It thus seems that we prefer to spend little money promoting higher living standards and democracy in other nations. This promotes more armed conflict. We then spend a lot of money dealing with the armed conflict.

Terrorism and Related Forms of Political Violence

We can learn much about the predicament of the world today by lingering a moment on the question of why societal warfare has largely replaced interstate warfare since World War II. As usual, historical perspective is useful (Tilly, 2002).

Historical Change

From the rise of the modern state in the 17th century until World War II, states increasingly monopolized the means of coercion in society. This had three important consequences:

1. As various regional, ethnic, and religious groups came under the control of powerful central states, regional, ethnic, and religious wars declined and interstate warfare became the norm.

2. Because states were powerful and monopolized the means of coercion, conflict became more deadly.

3. Civilian life was pacified because the job of killing for political reasons was largely restricted to state-controlled armed forces. Thus, even as the death toll from war rose, civilians were largely segregated from large-scale killing. As late as World War I (1914–18), civilians composed only 5 percent of war deaths.

All this changed after World War II (1939–45). Since then, there have been fewer interstate wars and more civil wars, guerilla wars, massacres, terrorist attacks, and instances of attempted ethnic cleansing and genocide perpetrated by militias, mercenaries, paramilitary groups, suicide bombers, and the like. Moreover, large-scale violence has increasingly been visited on civilian rather than military populations. By the 1990s, civilians composed fully 90 percent of war deaths. The mounting toll of civilian casualties is evident from, among other sources, U.S. Department of State data on casualties resulting from terrorist attacks (▶Figure 13.4).

Reasons for Change

Change in the form of collective violence came about for three main reasons (Tilly, 2002):

1. The number of countries in the world doubled as colonies became independent states and new states broke off from old ones. Many of the new states, especially in Africa and Asia, were too weak to control their territories effectively.

2. The United States, the Soviet Union, Cuba, and China often subsidized and sent arms to domestic opponents of regimes that were aligned against them.

3. The expansion of international trade in contraband provided rebels with new means of support. They took advantage of inexpensive international communication and travel to establish immigrant support communities abroad and export heroin, cocaine, diamonds, dirty money, and so forth.

In short, opportunities for engaging in collective violence changed after World War II in a way that favored societal warfare.

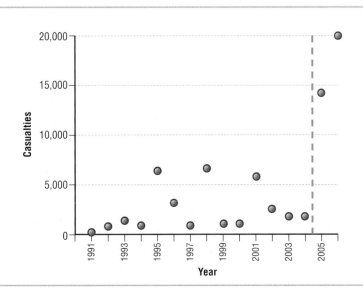

▶FIGURE 13.4

Casualties Resulting from Terrorist Attacks (1991–2004) and All Terrorist Attacks (2005–2006)

Note: In 2004, the U.S. Department of State broadened the types of terrorist attacks inluded in its calculations to include domestic acts of terror. As a result, the post-2004 figures are considerably higher than the pre-2005 figures, which are based only on international attacks. Source: U.S. Department of State (1997; 2003: 163; 2004: 178); National Counterterrorism Centre (2007: 7); Zelikow and Brennan (2005).

Al Qaeda and Contemporary Warfare

Al Qaeda is in many ways a typical creature of contemporary warfare. It originated in Afghanistan, a notoriously weak and dependent state. The United States supported its founders militarily in their struggle against the Soviet occupation of Afghanistan in the 1980s. Al Qaeda organized international heroin, diamond, and money-laundering operations. It established a network of operatives around the world. All of this was made possible by changes in the structure of opportunities for collective violence after World War II.

International terrorists of the type the U.S. Department of State collects data on typically demand autonomy or independence for some country, population, or region. For example, among al Qaeda's chief demands are Palestinian statehood and the end of U.S. support for the wealthy regimes in Saudi Arabia, Kuwait, and the Gulf States. Al Qaeda has turned to terror as a means of achieving these goals because other ways of achieving them are largely closed off. The United States considers support for the oil-rich Arab countries to be in the nation's interest. It has done little to further the cause of Palestinian statehood. Staunch opponents of American policy cannot engage in interstate warfare with the United States because they lack states of their own. At most, they are supported by states that lack the resources to engage in sustained warfare with the United States, including Iran, Syria, and the former regime of Iraq. Because the existing structure of world power closes off other possibilities for achieving political goals, terror emerges as a viable alternative for some desperate people.

In sum, social inequality powerfully structures the shape of both electoral politics and politics "by other means," such as war and terrorism. It is now time to gain a better sense of the source of class inequalities in particular. To accomplish that task, we explore the sociology of work and the economy.

Work and the Economy

Economic Sectors

The **economy** is the institution that organizes the production, distribution, and exchange of goods and services. Conventionally, analysts divide the economy into three sectors. The *primary* sector includes farming, fishing, logging, and mining. In the *secondary* sector, raw materials are turned into finished goods; manufacturing takes place. Finally, in the *tertiary* sector, services are bought and sold. These services include the work of nurses, teachers, lawyers, hairdressers, computer programmers, and so forth. Often, the three sectors of the economy are called the agricultural, manufacturing, and service sectors.

Three truly revolutionary events have taken place in the history of human labor. In each revolution, a different sector of the economy rose to dominance (Gellner, 1988; Lenski, 1966). These three revolutions were as follows:

Agriculture

Nearly all humans lived in nomadic tribes until about 10,000 years ago. Then, people in the fertile valleys of the Middle East, Southeast Asia, and South America began to herd cattle and grow plants using simple hand tools. Stable human settlements spread in these areas. About 5,000 years ago, farmers invented the plow. By attaching plows to large animals, they substantially increased the land under cultivation. **Productivity**—the amount produced for every hour worked—soared.

Economy: The institution that organizes the production, distribution, and exchange of goods and services.

Productivity: The amount of goods or services produced for every hour worked.

Manufacturing

International exploration, trade, and commerce helped stimulate the growth of markets from the 15th century on. **Markets** are social relations that regulate the exchange of goods and services. In a market, prices are established by how plentiful goods and services are (supply) and how much they are wanted (demand). About 225 years ago, the steam engine, railroads, and other technological innovations greatly increased the ability of producers to supply markets. This was the era of the Industrial Revolution. Beginning in England, the Industrial Revolution spread to western Europe, North America, Russia, and Japan within a century, making manufacturing the dominant economic sector.

Services

Service jobs were rare in preagricultural societies because nearly everyone had to do physical work for the tribe to survive. As productivity increased, however, service-sector jobs proliferated. By automating much factory and office work, the computer accelerated this shift in the last third of the 20th century. In the United States today, more than three-quarters of the labor force is employed in the service sector.

The Division and Hierarchy of Labor

Besides increasing productivity and causing shifts between sectors in employment, the agricultural, industrial, and service revolutions altered the way work was socially organized. For one thing, the **division of labor** increased. That is, work tasks became more specialized with each successive revolution. In preagricultural societies, there were four main jobs: hunting wild animals, gathering wild edible plants, raising children, and tending to the tribe's spiritual needs. In contrast, a postindustrial society like the United States boasts tens of thousands of different kinds of jobs.

Work relations also became more hierarchical—workers were divided into more sharply defined classes—as one work revolution gave way to the next. Although work used to be based on cooperation among equals, it now involves superordinates exercising authority and subordinates learning obedience. Increasingly, work hierarchies are organized bureaucratically. That is, clearly defined positions and written goals, rules, and procedures govern the organization of work.

Clearly, the increasing division of labor changed the nature of work in fundamental ways. But did the *quality* of work improve or worsen as jobs became more specialized? This is the question we now address.

The Quality of Work

We often refer to "good" jobs and "bad" jobs. What is the difference between them? Bad jobs don't pay much and require the performance of routine tasks under close supervision. Working conditions are unpleasant, sometimes dangerous. Bad jobs require little formal education. In contrast, good jobs often require higher education. They pay well. They are not closely supervised, and they encourage the worker to be creative in pleasant surroundings. Good jobs offer secure employment, opportunities for promotion, and other significant benefits. In a bad job, you can easily be fired, you receive few if any fringe benefits, and the prospects for promotion are few (Lowe, 2000). Bad jobs are often called "dead-end" jobs.

Most jobs fall between the two extremes sketched here. They have some mix of good and bad features. But what can we say about the overall mix of jobs in the United States?

CENGAGENOW

Learn more about the **Division of Labor** by going through the Division of Labor Animation.

Markets: Social relations that regulate the exchange of goods and services. In a market, the prices of goods and services are established by how plentiful they are (supply) and how much they are wanted (demand).

Division of labor: Specialization of work tasks. The more specialized the work tasks in a society, the greater the division of labor.

Are there more good than bad jobs? And what does the future hold? Are good or bad jobs likely to become more plentiful? What are *your* job prospects? These are tough questions because some conditions that influence the mix of good and bad jobs are unpredictable. Nonetheless, sociological research sheds some light on these issues.

The Deskilling Thesis

One view of how jobs are likely to develop was proposed by Harry Braverman (1974). Braverman argued that capitalists are always eager to organize work to maximize profits. Therefore, they break complex tasks into simple routines. They replace labor with machines wherever possible. They exert increasing control over workers to make sure they do their jobs more efficiently. As a result, work tends to become **deskilled** over time. In the first decade of the 20th century, for example, Henry Ford introduced the assembly line with just this aim in mind. The assembly line enabled Ford to produce affordable cars for a mass market. It also forced workers to do highly specialized, repetitive tasks requiring little skill at a pace set by their supervisors. Around the same time, Frederick W. Taylor developed the principles of **scientific management.** After analyzing the movements of workers as they did their jobs, Taylor trained them to eliminate unnecessary actions and greatly improve their efficiency. Workers became cogs in a giant machine known as the modern factory.

One problem with Braverman's deskilling thesis is that factory workers now represent only a small proportion of the labor force. The vital question may therefore be whether good jobs or bad jobs are growing in services, the sector that accounts for more than three-fourths of U.S. jobs today. Shoshana Zuboff 's analysis of office workers made it appear that Braverman's insights apply beyond the factory walls (Zuboff, 1988). She argued that the computerization of the office in the 1980s involved increased supervision of deskilled work. And she was right, at least in part. The computer did eliminate many jobs and routinize others. It allowed supervisors to monitor every keystroke, thus taking worker control to new heights. In the 1980s and 1990s, some analysts feared that good jobs in manufacturing were being replaced by bad jobs in services. From this point of view, the entire labor force was experiencing a downward slide (Bluestone and Harrison, 1982; Rifkin, 1995).

A Critique of the Deskilling Thesis

The deskilling thesis undoubtedly captures one important tendency in the development of work. However, it does not paint a complete picture. Braverman and Zuboff exaggerated the downward slide of the U.S. labor force because they underestimated the continuing importance of skilled labor in the economy. Assembly lines and computers may deskill many factory and office jobs. But if deskilling is to take place, then some members of the labor force must invent, design, advertise, market, install, repair, and maintain complex machines, including computerized and robotic systems. Most of these people have better jobs than the factory and office workers analyzed by Braverman and Zuboff. Moreover, although technological innovations kill off entire job categories, they also create entire new industries with many good jobs.

Rather than involving a downward shift in the entire labor force, it seems more accurate to think of recent changes in work as involving a declining middle or a polarization between good and bad jobs. Many good jobs are opening up at the top of the socioeco-

Deskilling: The process by which work tasks are broken into simple routines requiring little training to perform. Deskilling is usually accompanied by the use of machinery to replace labor wherever possible and increased management control over workers.

Scientific management: A system of improving productivity developed in the first decade of the 20th century by Frederick W. Taylor. After analyzing the movements of workers as they did their jobs, Taylor trained them to eliminate unnecessary actions and greatly improve their efficiency.

▶TABLE 13.3

Jobs with Largest Expected Increase in Employment, United States, 2006–2016

Occupation	Estimated New Jobs
1. Registered nurses	580,000
2. Retail salespersons	550,000
3. Customer service representatives	540,000
4. Combined food preparation & serving workers, incl. fast food	430,000
5. Office clerks, general	400,000
6. Personal & home care aides	380,000
7. Home health aides	380,000
8. Postsecondary teachers	380,000
9. Janitors & cleaners, except maids & housekeeping cleaners	320,000
10. Nursing aides, orderlies, & attendants	280,000
11. Bookkeeping, accounting, & auditing clerks	280,000
12. Waiters & waitresses	270,000
13. Child care workers	260,000
14. Executive secretaries & administrative assistants	250,000
15. Computer software engineers, applications	240,000
16. Accountants & auditors	240,000
17. Landscaping & grounds keeping workers	230,000
18. Business operation specialists, all other	220,000
19. Elementary school teachers, except special education	210,000
20. Receptionists & information clerks	200,000

Source: U.S. Department of Labor (2007b).

nomic hierarchy. Even more mediocre and bad jobs are opening up at the bottom. There are fewer new jobs in the middle (Myles, 1988).

▶Table 13.3 estimates the growth of the 20 occupations for which the U.S. Department of Labor expects demand to be highest in the period 2006–2016. Of the 20 jobs expected to grow the most, all are in the service sector and 12 require only on-the-job training. The latter include short-order cooks and servers, orderlies, gardeners, janitors, home care aides, and receptionists. Just 6 of the 20 occupations require an associate degree or higher. They include registered nurses, secondary and elementary school teachers, and software engineers. It seems evident that the bottom of the service sector is growing fastest. This pattern is consistent with the pattern of growing income inequality discussed in Chapter 7 ("Social Stratification: United States and Global Perspectives").

Worker Resistance and Management Response

If the deskilling thesis mistakes job polarization for a downward slide of the entire labor force, it also inaccurately portrays workers as passive victims of management control. In reality, workers often resist the imposition of task specialization and mechanization by managers. They form unions, go on strike, change jobs, fail to show up for work, sabotage production lines, and so forth (Burawoy, 1979; Clawson, 1980).

Worker resistance has often caused management to modify its organizational plans. For example, Henry Ford was forced to double wages to induce his workers to accept the monotony, stress, and lack of autonomy associated with assembly line production. Even so, gaining the cooperation of workers proved difficult. Therefore, beginning in the 1920s, some employers started treating their employees more like human beings than cogs in a giant machine. They hoped to improve the work environment and thus make their employees more loyal and productive.

Over the next 80 years, owners and managers of big companies in all the rich industrialized countries realized they had to make more concessions to labor if they wanted a loyal and productive workforce. These concessions included not just higher wages but, in some cases, more decision-making authority about product quality, promotion policies, job design, product innovation, company investments, and so forth. The biggest concessions to labor were made in countries with the most powerful trade union movements, such as Sweden, where about 80 percent of the nonagricultural labor force is unionized (see Chapter 15, "Collective Action and Social Movements"). At the other extreme among highly industrialized countries is the United States. Here, around 12 percent of eligible workers are members of unions. On average, Americans work more hours per week than people in most other rich industrialized countries and have fewer paid vacation days per year. This indicates the relative inability of American workers to wrest concessions from their employers.

Labor Market Segmentation

Labor market segmentation: The division of the market for labor into distinct settings. In these settings, work is found in different ways and workers have different characteristics. There is only a slim chance of moving from one setting to another.

Primary labor market: A labor market that is composed disproportionately of highly skilled or well-educated white males. They are employed in large corporations that enjoy high levels of capital investment. In the primary labor market, employment is secure, earnings are high, and fringe benefits are generous.

Secondary labor market: A labor market that contains a disproportionately large number of women and members of racial minorities, particularly African and Hispanic Americans. Employees in the secondary labor market tend to be unskilled and lack higher education. They work in small firms with low levels of capital investment. Employment is insecure, earnings are low, and fringe benefits are meager.

Related to job polarization and a relative lack of unionization in the United States is the growth of **labor market segmentation.** Especially since World War II, many large business organizations employing millions of workers have emerged while thousands of small businesses continue to exist. Different kinds of jobs are associated with small businesses and large business organizations, resulting in a *segmented* labor market—specifically a primary labor market and a secondary labor market.

Primary and Secondary Labor Markets

The **primary labor market** is composed disproportionately of highly skilled or well-educated white males, many of whom belong to unions or professional organizations. They are employed in large corporations that enjoy high levels of capital investment. In the primary labor market, employment is relatively secure, earnings are high, and fringe benefits are generous.

The **secondary labor market** contains a disproportionately large number of women and members of racial minorities, particularly African and Hispanic Americans. Employees in the secondary labor market tend to be unskilled and lack higher education. They work in small firms with low levels of capital investment. Employment is insecure, earnings are low, and fringe benefits are meager. If workers in the secondary labor market do not enjoy the high pay, job security, and benefit packages shared by workers in the primary labor market, they also find it difficult to exit the "job ghettos" of the secondary labor market.

Barriers to the Primary Labor Market

Three social barriers make the primary labor market difficult to penetrate. First, there are few entry-level positions in the primary labor market. One set of circumstances that contributes to the lack of entry-level positions is corporate "downsizing" and plant shutdowns. These took place on a wide scale in the United States throughout the 1980s and early 1990s and then again in the first decade of the 21st century.

Second, workers often lack informal networks linking them to good job openings. These informal networks of friends and acquaintances (typically of the same ethnic and racial background) are often a means of finding out about the availability of a job (Granovetter, 1995 [1974]). Recent immigrants, who compose a disproportionately large share of workers in the secondary labor market and tend to be nonwhite, are less likely than others to find out about job openings in the primary labor market, where the labor force is disproportionately white.

Third, workers usually lack the required training and certification for jobs in the primary labor market. What is more, because of their low wages and scarce leisure time, they usually cannot afford to upgrade their skills and credentials. The dollar effects of these barriers to entering the primary labor market are vividly illustrated in ▶Figure 13.5, which shows that the median weekly earnings of full-time wage and salary workers in the United States decline sharply as one moves from the core of the primary labor market (category 1) to the periphery of the secondary labor market (category 9). Notice also that men, non-Hispanic whites, and unionized workers tend to be concentrated in the primary labor market. Women, African and Hispanic Americans, and nonunion members tend to be concentrated in the secondary labor market. We conclude that the barriers to entering the primary labor market are neither color-blind nor gender neutral.

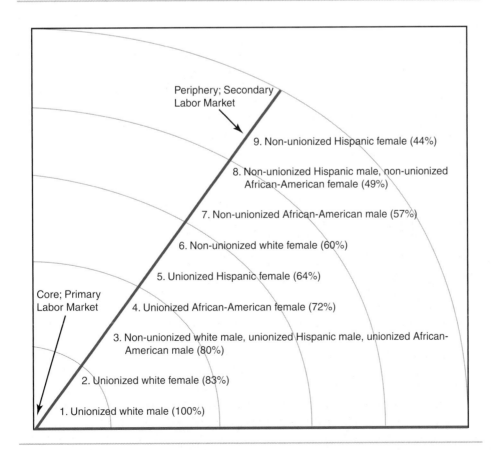

▶FIGURE 13.5
From the Primary to the Secondary Labor Market

Note: This figure shows median weekly earnings of full-time wage and salary workers in the United States by union status, sex, and race, calculated as a percentage of the earnings of white male unionized workers for 1995. Earnings decline as one moves from the core of the primary labor market (category #1) to the periphery of the secondary labor market (category #9). What happens to union status, sex, and race as one moves from core to periphery?
Source: Hesse-Biber and Carter (2000: 125).

Periphery; Secondary Labor Market

9. Non-unionized Hispanic female (44%)

8. Non-unionized Hispanic male, non-unionized African-American female (49%)

7. Non-unionized African-American male (57%)

6. Non-unionized white female (60%)

5. Unionized Hispanic female (64%)

4. Unionized African-American female (72%)

Core; Primary Labor Market

3. Non-unionized white male, unionized Hispanic male, unionized African-American male (80%)

2. Unionized white female (83%)

1. Unionized white male (100%)

Free versus Regulated Markets

We conclude that the secondary labor market is a relatively **free market,** where labor supply and demand regulate wage levels and other benefits. If supply is high and demand is low, wages fall. If demand is high and supply is low, wages rise. People who work in the secondary labor market lack much power to interfere in the operation of the forces of supply and demand. In contrast, the primary labor market is a more **regulated market.** Wage levels and other benefits are established by supply and demand and the power of workers and professionals to influence the labor market.

This suggests that the freer the market, the higher the level of social inequality. In the freest markets, many of the least powerful people are unable to earn enough to subsist. That is why the secondary labor market cannot be entirely free. For example, American governments have had to establish a legal minimum wage to prevent the price of unskilled labor from dropping too far below the point at which people are able to make a living (Polanyi, 1957 [1944]) (Box 13.3).

The dangers of weak market regulation became clear in 2007. Two guarantees should back a loan: (1) Borrowers should have collateral to cover it. (2) Lenders should have enough money to keep operating if some borrowers default. Governments are generally responsible for ensuring these guarantees, but in recent years in the United States, they encouraged financial institutions to offer mortgages with no down payments, low-interest rates, and no collateral. They failed to require that financial institutions have enough reserves to deal with defaults. By 2007, many people could not afford to renew their mortgages. Financial institutions repossessed their homes and sold them for a fraction of their former value, if at all. Soon, many financial institutions didn't have enough cash to continue operating and went bankrupt. Others received government bailouts. Credit became expensive. The stock market crashed, as millions of Americans lost their jobs, homes, and much of their retirement savings.

The question of whether free or regulated markets are better for society lies at the center of much debate in economics and politics. For many sociologists, however, that question is too abstract. First, regulation is not an either/or issue but a matter of degree. A market may be more or less regulated. Without some regulation, markets could not function. Second, markets may be regulated by different groups of people with varying degrees of power and different norms and values. Therefore, the costs and benefits of regulation may be socially distributed in many different ways, as we will now see (Lie, 1992).

Economic Systems

Capitalism

The world's dominant economic system today is **capitalism.** Capitalist economies have two distinctive features:

1. *Private ownership of property.* In capitalist economies, individuals and corporations own almost all the means of producing goods and services. Individuals and corporations are therefore free to buy and sell just about anything. Like individuals, **corporations** are legal entities. They can enter contracts and own property. However, corporations are taxed at a lower rate than individuals. Moreover, the corporation's owners typically are not liable if the corporation harms consumers or goes bankrupt. Instead, the corporation itself is legally responsible for damage and debt.

CENGAGENOW™

Learn more about **Capitalism** by going through the Capitalism versus Socialism Learning Module.

Free market: An economic arrangement in which prices are determined only by supply and demand.

Regulated market: An economic arrangement that limits the capacity of supply and demand to determine prices.

Capitalism: The dominant economic system in the world today. Capitalist economies are characterized by private ownership of property and competition in the pursuit of profit.

Corporations: Legal entities that can enter into contracts and own property. They are taxed at a lower rate than individuals, and their owners typically are not liable for the corporation's debt or any harm it may cause the public.

BOX 13.3
SOCIAL POLICY: WHAT DO YOU THINK?

The Minimum Wage

"Flipping burgers at Mickey D's is no way to make a living," a young man once told John Lie. Having tried his hand at several minimum wage jobs as a teenager, John knew the young man was right. At a little more than $5 an hour, a minimum-wage job may be fine for teenagers, many of whom are supported by their parents. However, it is difficult to live on one's own, much less to support a family, on a minimum-wage job, even if you work full-time. That is the problem with the minimum wage. It does not amount to a living wage for many people.

In 1998 dollars, the minimum wage rose from about $3 an hour to more than $7 an hour between 1938 and 1968. It fell to an inflation-adjusted $4.76 an hour by 2007 (▶Figure 13.6). Today, a single mother working full-time at the minimum wage does not make enough to lift a family of three (herself and two children) above the poverty level. Her earnings would be well below the poverty level (Bernstein, Hartmann, and Schmitt, 1999). Because the minimum wage has fallen since the late 1960s, the percentage of workers earning poverty-level wages has increased. The percentage of workers earning poverty-level wages is higher for women than men, and higher for African Americans than others.

Given the many single mothers who cannot lift themselves and their children out of poverty even if they work full-time, many scholars and policymakers suggest raising the minimum wage. Others disagree. They fear that raising the minimum wage would decrease the number of available jobs. Others disagree in principle with government interference in the economy.

Some scholars and policymakers even advocate the abolition of the minimum wage. What do you think? Should the minimum wage be raised? Should someone working full-time be entitled to live above the poverty level? Or should businesses be entitled to hire workers at whatever price the market will bear?

In thinking about this question, you should bear in mind what happened between 1996 and 1999. In late 1996 and 1997, the minimum wage increased. In the next couple of years, the employment rate of low-wage workers, and particularly single mothers, followed suit. Because of the booming economy, the percentage of low-wage workers rose dramatically (Bernstein, Hartmann, and Schmitt, 1999).

Critical Thinking

- What does the rise in the percentage of low-wage workers in times of economic boom say about the relationship between the minimum wage and the employment rate of low-wage workers?

- If you were in charge of setting the minimum wage, what would you do? Why?

▶FIGURE 13.6
Value of the Federal Minimum Wage, United States, 1938–2007 (in 1998 dollars)

Source: "U.S. Inflation Rate" (2008); U.S. Department of Labor (2005a).

2. *Competition in the pursuit of profit.* The second hallmark of capitalism is that producers compete to offer consumers desired goods and services at the lowest possible price. In a purely capitalist economy the government does not interfere in the operation of the economy. Presumably, everyone benefits; the most efficient producers make profits while consumers can buy at low prices.

In reality, however, no economy is perfectly free. The state had to intervene heavily to create markets in the first place. For example, 500 years ago the idea that land was a commodity that could be bought, sold, and rented on the free market was utterly foreign to the Native Americans who lived in the territory that is now North America. To turn the land into a marketable commodity, European armies had to force Native Americans off the land and eventually onto reservations. Governments had to pass laws regulating the ownership, sale, and rent of land. Without the military and legal intervention of government, no market for land would exist.

Today, governments must also intervene in the economy to keep the market working effectively. For instance, governments create and maintain roads and ports to make commerce possible. They pass laws governing the minimum wage, occupational health and safety, child labor, and industrial pollution to protect workers and consumers from the excesses of corporations. If very large corporations get into financial trouble, they can expect the government to bail them out with various forms of "corporate welfare," rationalizing the policy by claiming that their bankruptcy would be devastating to the economy. The American government also plays an influential role in establishing, promoting, and supporting many leading industries, especially those that require large outlays for research and development.

Communism

Communism is the name Karl Marx gave to the classless society that, he said, is bound to develop out of capitalism. Socialism is the name usually given to the transitional phase between capitalism and communism. No country in the world is or ever has been communist in the pure sense of the term. About two dozen countries in Asia, South America, and Africa consider themselves socialist. These include China, North Korea, Vietnam, and Cuba. As an ideal, however, communism is an economic system with two distinct features:

1. *Public ownership of property.* Under communism, the state owns almost all the means of producing goods and services. Private corporations do not exist. Individuals are not free to buy and sell goods and services. The stated aim of public ownership is to ensure that all individuals have equal wealth and equal access to goods and services.

2. *Government planning.* Five-year state plans establish production quotas, prices, and most other aspects of economic activity. The political officials who design the state plans, not the forces of supply and demand, determine what is produced, in what quantities, and at what prices. A high level of control is required to implement these rigid state plans. As a result, democratic politics is not allowed to interfere with state activities. Only one political party exists—the Communist party. Elections are held regularly, but only members of the Communist party are allowed to run for office (Zaslavsky and Brym, 1978).

Until recently, the countries of central and eastern Europe and central Asia were single-party, socialist societies. The most powerful of these countries was the Soviet Union, which was composed of Russia and 14 other socialist republics. In perhaps the most surprising and sudden change in modern history, the countries of the region began introducing capitalism and holding multiparty elections in the late 1980s and early 1990s.

The collapse of socialism in central and eastern Europe and central Asia was attributable to several factors. For one thing, the citizens of the region enjoyed few civil rights. For another, their standard of living was only about half as high as that of people in the rich

Communism: A political and economic system characterized by public ownership of property and government planning of the economy.

industrialized countries of the West. The gap between East and West grew as the arms race between the Soviet Union and the United States intensified in the 1980s. The standard of living fell as the Soviet Union mobilized its economic resources to try to match the quantity and quality of military goods produced by the United States. Dissatisfaction was widespread and expressed itself in many ways, including strikes and political demonstrations. It grew as television and radio signals beamed from the West made the gap between socialism and capitalism more apparent to the citizenry. Eventually, the Communist parties of the region felt they could no longer govern effectively and so began to introduce reforms.

Democratic Socialism

Several prosperous and highly industrialized countries in northwestern Europe, such as Sweden, Denmark, and Norway, are democratic socialist societies. So are France and Germany, albeit to a lesser degree. Such societies have two distinctive features (Olsen, 2002):

1. *Public ownership of certain basic industries.* In democratic socialist countries, the government owns certain basic industries entirely or in part. These industries have included telecommunications, electricity, railways, airlines, and steel. Still, as a proportion of the entire economy, the level of public ownership is not high—far lower than the level of public ownership in socialist societies. The great bulk of property is privately owned, and competition in the pursuit of profit is the main motive for business activity, just as in capitalist societies.

2. *Substantial government intervention in the market.* As the term **democratic socialism** implies, these countries enjoy regular, free, multiparty elections, just like the United States. However, unlike the United States, political parties backed by a strong trade union movement have formed governments in democratic socialist countries for much of the post–World War II period. The governments that these unions back intervene strongly in the operation of markets for the benefit of ordinary workers. Taxes are considerably higher than those in capitalist countries. Consequently, social services are more generous, and workers earn more, work fewer hours, and enjoy more paid vacation days. Since the 1980s, the democratic socialist countries have moved in a somewhat more capitalist direction. In particular, they have privatized some previously government-owned industries and services. Still, these countries retain their distinct approach to governments and markets, which is why democratic socialism is sometimes called a "third way" between capitalism and socialism.

The Corporation

If markets are constrained by governments to varying degrees, they are also constrained by big corporations. When just a few corporations dominate an economic sector, they can influence prices, thus forcing consumers to pay more for goods and services. They can also exercise excessive influence on governments.

In the United States and other Western countries, antitrust laws limit the growth of corporations. The 1890 Sherman Antitrust Act and the 1914 Clayton Act are the basic U.S. antitrust laws. However, they have been only partly effective in stabilizing the growth of giant corporations. For instance, the government managed to break AT&T's stranglehold on the telecommunications market in the 1980s, but its efforts to break Microsoft into two

Democratic socialism: A political system in which democratically elected governments own certain basic industries entirely or in part and intervene vigorously in the market to redistribute income.

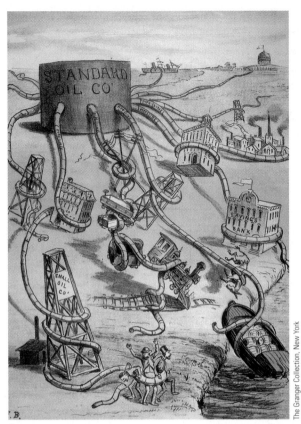

The Granger Collection, New York

"The Monster Monopoly," an 1884 cartoon attacking John D. Rockefeller's Standard Oil Company. One of the most famous antitrust cases ever to reach the U.S. Supreme Court resulted in the breakup of Standard Oil in 1911. The Court broke new ground in deciding to dissolve the company into separate geographical units.

smaller corporations failed. Moreover, it is hard to deny that corporations today are enormously powerful. The top 500 corporations in the United States control more than two-thirds of business resources and profit. This is a world apart from the early 19th century, when most business firms were family owned and served only local markets.

It is also noteworthy that an important effect of U.S. antitrust law has been to encourage big companies to diversify. That is, rather than increasing their share of control in their own industry, corporations often move into new industries. Big companies that operate in several industries at the same time are called **conglomerates.** Conglomerates are growing rapidly in the United States. Big companies are swallowed up by still bigger ones in wave after wave of corporate mergers (Mizruchi, 1982, 1992).

Outright ownership of a company by a second company in another industry is only one way that corporations may be linked. **Interlocking directorates** are another. Interlocking directorates are formed when an individual sits on the board of directors of two or more noncompeting companies. (Antitrust laws prevent an individual from sitting on the board of directors of a competitor.) Such interlocks enable corporations to exchange valuable information and form alliances for their mutual benefit. They also create useful channels of communication to, and influence over, government (Mintz, 1989; Mintz and Schwartz, 1985).

Of course, small businesses are plentiful (Granovetter, 1984). In the United States, 85 percent of businesses have fewer than 20 employees. Fully 40 percent of the labor force works in firms with fewer than 100 employees. Small firms are particularly important in the service sector. However, compared with large firms, profits in small firms are typically low. Bankruptcies are common. Small firms usually use outdated production and marketing techniques. Jobs in small firms often offer low wages and meager benefits.

Most of the U.S. labor force now works in large corporations. Specifically, about a third of the labor force is employed in the 1,500 largest industrial, financial, and service firms. In the service sector, the biggest employer is Wal-Mart, with 1.8 million employees in 2005. In manufacturing, the largest employer is General Motors, with 335,000 employees in the United States in 2005 (Forbes.com, 2006). As we will now see, however, even these figures underestimate the global reach and influence of the biggest corporations (see also Chapter 8, "Globalization, Inequality, and Development").

Globalization

In the 1980s and early 1990s, the United States was hit by a wave of corporate "downsizing" (Dudley, 1994; Gordon, 1996). Especially in the older manufacturing industries of the Northeast and Midwest (sometimes called the "rust belt"), hundreds of thousands of blue-collar workers and middle managers were fired. In places like Flint, Michigan, and Racine, Wisconsin, the consequences were devastating. Unemployment soared. Social problems such as alcoholism and wife abuse became acute.

Conglomerates: Large corporations that operate in several industries at the same time.

Interlocking directorates: Structures formed by one or more individuals sitting on the board of directors of two or more noncompeting companies.

Some people blamed government for the plant shutdowns. They said taxes were so high, big corporations could no longer make decent profits. Others blamed the unemployed themselves. They said powerful unions drove up the hourly wage to the point where companies like General Motors and Ford were losing money. Still others blamed the corporations. As soon as they closed plants in places like Racine and Flint, they opened new ones in places like northern Mexico. Mexican workers were happy to earn only one-sixth or one-tenth as much as their American counterparts. The Mexican government was delighted to make tax concessions to attract the new jobs.

In the 1980s, workers, governments, and corporations got involved as unequal players in the globalization of the world economy. Japan and Germany had fully recovered from the devastation of World War II. With these large and robust industrial economies now firing on all cylinders, American-based multinationals were forced to cut costs and become more efficient to remain competitive. On a scale far larger than ever before, they began to build branch plants in many countries to take advantage of inexpensive labor and low taxes. Multinational corporations based in Japan and other highly industrialized countries did the same.

Although multinational corporations could easily move investment capital from one country to the next, workers were rooted in their communities and governments were rooted in their nation-states. Multinationals thus had a big advantage over the other players in the globalization game. They could threaten to move plants unless governments and workers made concessions. They could play one government off another in the bidding war for new plants. And they could pick up and leave when it became clear that relocation would do wonders for their bottom line.

Today, three decades after the globalization game began in earnest, it is easier to identify the winners than the losers. The clear winners are the stockholders of the multinational corporations, whose profits have soared. The losers, at least initially, were American blue-collar workers. To cite just one example, between 1980 and 1993, General Motors cut its labor force by more than 30 percent. Between 1993 and 1999, the number of Americans employed by General Motors fell another 20 percent.

Even while these cuts were being made, however, some large American manufacturers were hiring. For instance, employment at Boeing grew more than 65 percent between 1993 and 1999. In the service sector, employment soared. For example, Wal-Mart employed twice as many people in 1999 as in 1993 ("Forbes 500," 2000; Hodson and Sullivan, 1995 [1990]: 393). In 2000, unemployment in the United States hit a 38-year low. As a result, many analysts believed that the 1980s was a period of extremely difficult economic restructuring rather than the beginning of the decline of the American economy, as some people warned at the time.

New worries surfaced by 2003, however, some linked to the rise of China as an economic powerhouse. Since 1979, Chinese economic growth has averaged about 10 percent a year, transforming China into the world's seventh largest economy and one of the world's major exporters. Americans now eagerly buy a quarter of China's exports. Why? Chinese wages are low, so Chinese manufactured goods are inexpensive, and American consumers like a bargain. The downside is that inexpensive Chinese goods have driven many American manufacturers out of business and left many American workers without jobs. Other American manufacturers have reduced operations in the United States and established Chinese branch plants, effectively exporting American jobs in the process. Manufacturing employment fell to 13 percent of total employment in the United States in 2000, half of what it was in 1970.

Defenders of free trade argue that most of the decline in manufacturing employment is not due to Chinese competition but to the increased productivity of American work-

Beth A. Keiser/AP Photo

Some people in the rich, industrialized countries oppose the globalization of commerce. For example, the World Trade Organization (WTO) was set up by the governments of 134 countries in 1994 to encourage and referee global commerce. When the WTO met in Seattle in December 1999, 40,000 union activists, environmentalists, supporters of worker and peasant movements in developing countries, and other opponents of multinational corporations staged protests. Similar protests have taken place at subsequent WTO meetings in other countries.

ers (Mankiw, 2003). From their point of view, an American worker can produce a lot more today than 30 years ago because of improved technology, so fewer workers are need to manufacture more goods. This argument is accurate but it ignores that increased productivity itself is in part a response to competition from abroad; we invest more in technology to help overcome wage competition. Free trade supporters also note that most displaced workers eventually find other jobs. Again true. Yet, more often than not, the new jobs are inferior to the jobs that are lost. Recent research shows that the overall quality of American jobs (as measured by job stability, wages, and part-time vs. full-time employment) is declining (Tal, 2004). An American worker in a manufacturing plant may lose her job because of cheap Chinese imports and then find a new job at a Wal-Mart checkout, but the new job is more likely to be part-time, pay less, and offer fewer benefits. (Ironically, the checkout clerk will wind up scanning Chinese manufactured goods, since Wal-Mart accounts for more than 10 percent of all sales of Chinese imports in the United States.)

Another issue ignored by supporters of free trade is that it is not just manufacturing jobs that are being lost to low-wage countries like China. In 2004, the *International Herald Tribune* reported that in the next three years major New York securities firm plans to replace its team of American software engineers (annual wage: $150,000) with equally competent engineers in India (annual wage: $20,000). Between 2004 and 2009, the number of radiologists in the United States is expected to decline "significantly" because MRI data can be sent to Asia over the Internet where diagnoses can be delivered at a fraction of the cost (Schumer and Roberts, 2004). These and many other examples of outsourcing point to a growing trend for high-wage, technical jobs to be lost to highly educated workers in India, Poland, and elsewhere. As Nobel-prize winning economist Paul A. Samuelson recently noted, many mainstream economists prefer to ignore the negative effects of free trade on average income and class inequality in the United States (Samuelson, 2004; Public Citizen, 2004).

Globalization and the Less Developed Countries

In the globalization game, there are both winners and losers among the governments and citizens of the less developed countries too. On the one hand, it is hard to argue with the assessment of the rural Indonesian woman interviewed by Diane Wolf. She prefers the regime of the factory to the tedium of village life. In the village, the woman worked from dawn till dusk doing household chores, taking care of siblings, and feeding the family goat. In the factory, she earns less than a dollar a day sewing pockets on men's shirts. Yet because work in the factory is less arduous, pays something, and holds out the hope of even better work for future generations, the woman views it as nothing less than liberating (Wolf, 1992). Many workers in other regions of the world where branch plants of multinationals have sprung up in recent decades feel much the same way. A wage of $3 an hour is good pay in Mexico, and workers rush to fill jobs along Mexico's northern border with the United States.

Yet the picture is not all bright. The governments of developing countries attract branch plants by imposing few if any pollution controls on their operations. This has dangerous effects on the environment. Typically, fewer jobs are available than the number of workers who are drawn from the countryside to find work in the branch plants. This results in the growth of urban slums suffering from high unemployment and unsanitary conditions. High-value components are often imported. Therefore, the branch plants create few good jobs involving design and technical expertise. Finally, some branch plants—particularly clothing and shoe factories in Asia—exploit children and women, requiring them to work long workdays at paltry wages and in unsafe conditions. Such cases suggest that the benefits of foreign investment are unlikely to be uniformly beneficial for the residents of developing countries.

The Future of Work and the Economy

Although work and the economy have changed enormously over the years, one thing has remained constant for centuries. Businesses have always looked for ways to cut costs and boost profits. Two of the most effective means they have adopted for accomplishing these goals involve introducing new technologies and organizing the workplace in more efficient ways. Much is uncertain about the future of work and the economy. However, it is a pretty good bet that businesses will continue to follow these established practices.

Just how these practices will be implemented is less predictable. One option is to use technology and improved work organization to increase productivity by complementing the abilities of skilled workers. Worldwide, the automotive, aerospace, and computer industries have tended to adopt this approach. They have introduced automation and robots on a wide scale. They constantly upgrade the skills of their workers. And they have proved the benefits of small autonomous work groups for product quality, worker satisfaction, and therefore the bottom line.

A second option is to use new technology and more efficient work organization to replace workers, downsize plants, deskill jobs, and employ low-cost labor on a large scale. The main sources of low-cost labor are women, minority-group members, and low-wage workers outside the United States. Women are entering the labor force at a faster rate than men. Hispanic, Asian, and African American workers are entering the labor force at a much faster rate than whites. Competition from low-wage industries abroad remains intense. Just in the last few years, hundreds of thousands of American jobs, including a growing number of white-collar jobs such as computer programming, have been exported to China, India, Russia, Poland, and other countries by large American corporations.

Our analysis suggests that the polarization of the labor force between good jobs in the primary sector and bad jobs in the secondary sector is likely to continue in the near future. However, workplace struggles have a bearing on how technologies are implemented and work is organized. To a degree, therefore, the future of work and the economy is up for grabs.

The Points of the Compass

In this chapter we have examined two of society's most important institutions—the state and the economy—and some of their interactions. Two paradoxes emerged. First, while completely free markets expand opportunities to accumulate wealth they also increase social inequality, thus limiting opportunities for social mobility and democratic participation by people at the bottom of the stratification order. Second, while states often act to decrease social inequality, excessive state involvement in the economy limits mobility opportunities and democratic participation. Politics in any society involves struggles over the degree to which markets should be free and the state should intervene in the economy. At root, however, both struggles involve finding a legitimized point of balance on the sociological compass between equality and inequality of opportunity.

CHAPTER SUMMARY

1. What accounts for the level of democracy in a society?

The level of democracy in a society depends on the distribution of power. When power is concentrated in the hands of few people, society is less democratic.

2. What are the major sociological theories of democratic politics?

Pluralists correctly note that democratic politics is about negotiation and compromise among many interests. However, they fail to appreciate that economically advantaged groups have more power than disadvantaged groups. *Elite theorists* correctly note that power is concentrated in the hands of advantaged groups. However, they fail to appreciate how variations in the distribution of power influence political behavior and public policy. *Power resource theorists* usefully focus on changes in the distribution of power in society and their effects. However, they fail to appreciate what *state-centered theorists* emphasize—that state institutions and laws also independently affect political behavior and public policy.

3. What are the main causes of war?

The risk of war declines as a country becomes more prosperous and democratic.

4. How has the nature of the state affected patterns of warfare?

The rise of the modern state in the 17th century led to the monopolization of the means of coercion in society. Once centralized state armies became the major military force in society, interstate warfare became the norm, warfare became more deadly, and few civilians died in war. However, the emergence of many weak states after World War II encouraged the outbreak of societal or civil wars, which are now the norm. Civilian deaths now account for most war deaths.

Societal wars gain impetus when hostile outside powers get involved and rebels take advantage of increased opportunities to engage in illegal trade and establish support communities abroad. International terrorism has benefited greatly from the combination of weak states, outside support, and new ways of mobilizing resources.

5. What are the major work-related revolutions in human history?

The first work-related revolution (the Agricultural Revolution) began about 10,000 years ago when people established permanent settlements and started herding and farming. The second work-related revolution (the Industrial Revolution) began about 225 years ago when various mechanical devices such as the steam engine greatly increased the ability of producers to supply markets. The third revolution in work (the Postindustrial Revolution) was marked by growth in the provision of various services. It accelerated in the last decades of the 20th century with the widespread use of the computer. Each revolution in work increased productivity and the division of labor, caused a sectoral shift in employment, and made work relations more hierarchical.

6. What are "good" and "bad" jobs, and which type of job is becoming more plentiful?

"Bad" jobs pay little and require the performance of routine tasks under close supervision. Working conditions are unpleasant and sometimes dangerous. Bad jobs require little formal education. In contrast, "good" jobs often require higher education. They pay well, are not closely supervised, and encourage the worker to be creative in pleasant surroundings. Good jobs offer secure employment, opportunities for promotion, health insurance, and other fringe benefits. In a bad job, you can easily be fired, you receive few if any fringe benefits, and the prospects for promotion are few.

Deskilling and the growth of part-time jobs are two of the main trends in the workplace in the 20th century. However, skilled labor has remained important. Good jobs are becoming more plentiful, but the number of bad jobs is growing even more rapidly. The result is polarization or segmentation of the labor force into primary and secondary labor markets. Various social barriers limit mobility from the secondary to the primary labor market.

7. **What are the main types of markets?**

Markets are free or regulated to varying degrees. No market that is purely free or completely regulated could function for long. A purely free market would create unbearable inequalities, and a completely regulated market would stagnate.

8. **What are the main differences between capitalism, communism, and social democracy?**

Private ownership of property and competition in the pursuit of profit characterize capitalism. Public ownership of property and government planning characterize communism. Public ownership of certain basic industries and substantial government intervention in the market characterize democratic socialism.

9. **What are corporations?**

Corporations are legal entities that can enter into contracts and own property. They are taxed at a lower rate than individuals, and their owners typically are not liable for the corporation's debt or any harm it may cause the public. Corporations are the dominant economic players in the world today. They exercise disproportionate economic and political influence by forming giant corporations, conglomerates, and interlocking directorates.

Questions to Consider

1. Younger people are less likely to vote than older people. How would power resource theory explain this?

2. Do you think the United States will become a more democratic country in the next 25 years? Will a larger percentage of the population vote? Will class and racial inequalities in political participation decline? Will public policy more accurately reflect the interests of the entire population? Why or why not?

3. The computer is widely regarded as a laborsaving device and has been adopted on a wide scale. Yet, many Americans work more hours per week now than they did 20 or 30 years ago. How do you explain this paradox?

Web Resources

CENGAGENOW™

Maximize your study time by using CengageNOW's diagnostic study plan to help you review this chapter. The Study Plan will

- help you identify areas on which you should concentrate;
- provide interactive exercises to help you master the chapter concepts; and
- provide a post-test to confirm you are ready to move on to the next chapter.

The Companion Website for *Sociology: Your Compass for a New World, The Brief Edition,* Enhanced Second Edition

www.cengage.com/sociology/brym

Supplement your review of this chapter by going to the companion website to take one of the tutorial quizzes, use flash cards to master key terms, and check out the many other study aids you'll find there. You'll also find special features such as GSS Data and Census 2000 information that will put data and resources at your fingertips to help you with that special project or help you do some research on your own.

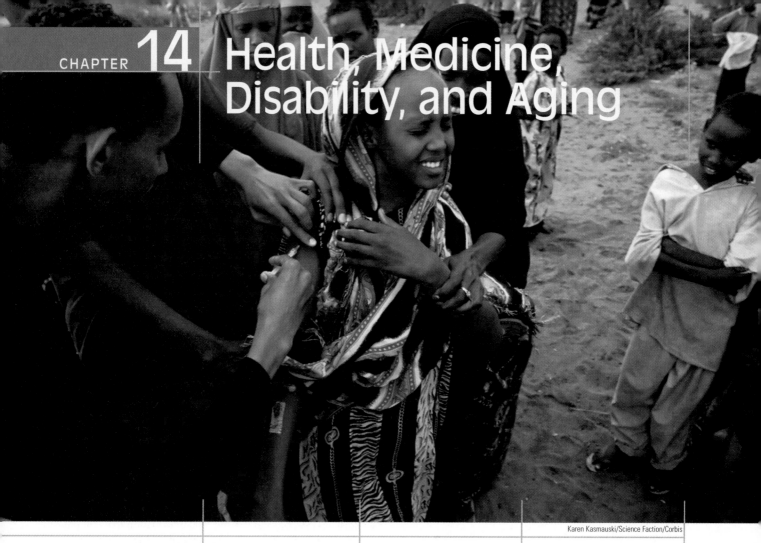

Karen Kasmauski/Science Faction/Corbis

In this chapter, you will learn that:

- Health risks are unevenly distributed in human populations. Men and women, upper and lower classes, rich and poor countries, and privileged and disadvantaged racial and ethnic groups are exposed to health risks to varying degrees.

- The average health status of Americans is lower than the average health status of people in other rich postindustrial countries. That is partly because the level of social inequality is higher in the United States and partly because the health-care system makes it difficult for many people to receive adequate care in this country.

- The dominance of medical science is attributable to its successful treatments and the way doctors excluded competitors and established control over their profession and their clients.

- Patient activism, alternative medicine, and holistic medicine promise to improve the quality of health care in the United States and worldwide.

- People have defined and dealt with disability in different ways in different times and places.

- Age is an important basis of social stratification.

- Although prejudice and discrimination against older people are common in the United States, elderly people have wielded increasing political power in recent decades.

- The way people die reflects the nature of the society in which they live. This is evident in our attitudes toward death, euthanasia, and funerals.

Health and Medicine

The Black Death

In 1346, rumors reached Europe of a plague sweeping the East. Originating in Asia, the epidemic spread quickly along trade routes to China and Russia. A year later, 12 galleys sailed from southern Russia to Italy. Diseased sailors were aboard. Their lymph nodes were terribly swollen and eventually burst, causing painful death. Anyone who came into contact with the sailors was soon infected. As a result, their ships were driven out of several Italian and French ports in succession. Still, the disease spread relentlessly, again moving along trade routes to Spain, Portugal, and England. Within two years, the Black Death, as it came to be known, killed a third of Europe's population. More than six hundred and

CENGAGENOW

This icon signals when CengageNOW has important resources available for you to use in conjunction with the text. See the foldout at the front of this text for information on how to access CengageNOW.

The Black Death.

fifty years later, the plague still ranks as the most devastating catastrophe in human history (Herlihy, 1998; McNeill, 1976).

Today we know that the cause of the plague was a bacillus that spread from lice to rats to people. It spread so efficiently because many people lived close together in unsanitary conditions. In the middle of the 14th century, however, nobody knew anything about germs.

Therefore, Pope Clement VI sent a delegation to Europe's leading medical school in Paris to discover the cause of the plague. The learned professors studied the problem. They reported that a particularly unfortunate conjunction of Saturn, Jupiter, and Mars in the sign of Aquarius had occurred in 1345. The resulting hot, humid conditions caused the Earth to emit poisonous vapors. To prevent the plague, they said, people should refrain from eating poultry, waterfowl, pork, beef, fish, and olive oil. They should not sleep during the daytime or engage in excessive exercise. Nothing should be cooked in rainwater. Bathing should be avoided at all costs.

We do not know whether the pope followed the professors' advice. We do know he made a practice of sitting between two large fires to breathe pure air. Because the plague bacillus is destroyed by heat, the practice may have saved his life. Other people were less fortunate. Some rang church bells and fired cannons to drive the plague away. Others burned incense, wore charms, and cast spells. But, apart from the pope, the only people to have much luck in avoiding the plague were the well-to-do (who could afford to flee the densely populated cities for remote areas in the countryside) and the Jews (whose religion required that they wash their hands before meals, bathe once a week, and conduct burials soon after death).

Sociological Issues of Health, Medicine, Disability, and Aging

Some of the main themes of the sociology of health, medicine, disability, and aging are embedded in the story of the Black Death. First, recall that some groups were more likely to die of the plague than others. This is a common pattern. Health risks are always unevenly distributed. Women and men, upper and lower classes, rich and poor countries, and privileged and disadvantaged racial and ethnic groups are exposed to health risks to varying degrees. This suggests that health is not just a medical question but also a sociological issue. The first task we set for ourselves in this chapter is to examine the sociological factors that account for the uneven distribution of health in society.

Second, the story of the Black Death suggests that health problems change over time. Epidemics still break out, but there can be no Black Death where sanitation and hygiene prevent the spread of disease.[1]

Today we are able to cure many infectious diseases thanks to the discoveries of modern medical science. As a result of such advances, people live longer on average; in the United States, **life expectancy** (the average number of years a person can expect to live) rose from 47 years in 1900 to 78 years in 2008. Note, however, that longer life expectancy gives

CENGAGENOW™

Learn more about **Life Expectancy** by going through the Average Life Expectancy Map Exercise.

Life expectancy: The average number of years a person can expect to live.

[1]One case that may approximate the Black Death in the 21st century is the spread of acquired immune deficiency syndrome (AIDS) in sub-Saharan Africa.

degenerative conditions such as cancer and heart disease an opportunity to develop in a way that was not possible a century ago (▶Table 14.1, column 1). This places a substantial strain on the health care system. It also leads to other social problems associated with a rapidly aging population, such as an increase in the prevalence of **disability,** or the inability of people to perform within the range of what is considered normal human activity. Our second task in this chapter is to examine how health issues and the social problems associated with disability and a rapidly aging population change over time.

Third, the story of the Black Death highlights the superstition and ignorance surrounding the treatment of the ill in medieval times. Remedies were often herbal but also included earthworms, urine, and animal excrement. People believed it was possible to maintain good health by keeping body fluids in balance. Therefore, cures that released body fluids were common. These included hot baths, laxatives, and diuretics, which increase the flow of urine. If these treatments didn't work, bloodletting was often prescribed. No special qualifications were required to administer medical treatment. Barbers doubled as doctors.

Yet the backwardness of medieval medical practice, and the advantages of modern scientific medicine, can easily be exaggerated. For example, medieval doctors stressed the importance of prevention, exercise, a balanced diet, and a congenial environment in maintaining good health. We now know that this is sound advice. On the other hand, one of the great shortcomings of modern medicine is its emphasis on high-tech cures rather than preventive and environmental measures. Therefore, in this chapter we investigate not just the many wonderful cures and treatments brought to us by modern scientific medicine but also some of its shortcomings. We also examine how the medical professions gained substantial control over health issues and promoted their own approach to well-being.

▶**TABLE 14.1**

Leading Causes of Death, United States, 1900 and 2005

	Deaths per 100,000 Population	Percentage of Deaths
1900		
1. Pneumonia/influenza	202.2	11.8
2. Tuberculosis	194.4	11.3
3. Diarrhea/other intestinal	142.7	8.3
4. Heart disease	137.4	8.0
5. Stroke	106.9	6.2
6. Kidney disease	88.6	5.2
7. Accidents	72.3	4.2
8. Cancer	64.0	3.7
9. Senility	50.2	2.9
10. Bronchitis	40.3	2.3
All other causes	620.1	36.1
Total	1719.1	100.0
2005		
1. Heart disease	220.0	26.6
2. Cancer	188.7	22.8
3. Stroke	48.4	5.9
4. Chronic lung disease	44.4	5.3
5. Accidents	39.7	4.8
6. Diabetes	25.3	3.1
7. Alzheimer's disease	24.2	2.9
8. Pneumonia/influenza	21.3	2.6
9. Kidney disease	14.8	1.8
10. Blood poisoning	11.5	1.4
11. Suicide	11.0	1.3
12. Liver diseases	9.3	1.0
13. High blood pressure	8.4	1.0
14. Parkinson's disease	6.6	0.8
15. Homicide	6.1	0.7
All other causes	146.4	17.7
Total	825.9	100.0

Sources: National Center for Health Statistics (2008); National Office of Vital Statistics (1947).

Defining and Measuring Health

When sociologists measure the health of a population, they typically examine rates of illness and death. They reason that healthy populations experience less illness and longer life than unhealthy populations. That is the approach we follow here.

Assuming ideal conditions, how long can an individual live? So far, the record is held by Jeanne Louise Calment, a French woman who died in 1997 at the age of 122. (Other people claim to be older, but they lack authenticated birth certificates or other proof.) Calment was an extraordinary individual. She took up fencing at 85, rode a bicycle until she was 100, gave up smoking at 120, and released a rap CD at 121 (Matalon, 1997). In

Disability: The inability of people to perform within the range of what is widely regarded as normal human activity.

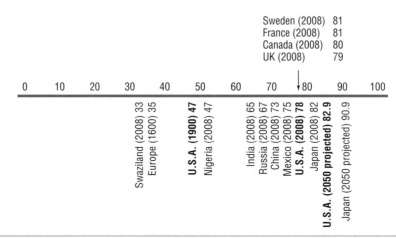

▶FIGURE 14.1
Life Expectancy, Selected Countries and Years

Sources: Population Reference Bureau (2008); Tuljapurkar, Li, and Boe (2000).

Jeanne Louise Calment, a French woman who died in 1997 at the age of 122, is the oldest person who ever lived whose age has been confirmed.

contrast, only 1 in 100 people in the world's rich countries now lives to be 100. Medical scientists tell us that the **maximum average human life span**—the average age of death for an entire population *under ideal conditions*—is likely to increase in this century. Now it is about 85 years (Olshansky, Carnes, and Desesquelles, 2001).

Unfortunately, conditions are nowhere ideal. Throughout the world, life expectancy is less than 85 years. ▶Figure 14.1 shows life expectancy in selected countries. Leading the list is Japan, where life expectancy was 82 years in 2008. Among the world's 20 or so rich countries, the United States had the lowest life expectancy at 78 years. In India, life expectancy was only 65 years. The poor African country of Swaziland suffered the world's lowest life expectancy at just 33 years (Population Reference Bureau, 2004b).

Accounting for the difference between the maximum average human life span and life expectancy is one of the main tasks of the sociologist of health. For example, although the maximum average human life span is 85 years, life expectancy in the United States is 78 years. This implies that, on average, Americans are being deprived of 7 years of life because of avoidable social causes ($85 - 78 = 7$). Avoidable social causes deprive the average citizen of Swaziland of 52 years of life ($85 - 33 = 52$). Clearly, social causes have a big—and variable—impact on illness and death. We must therefore discuss them in detail.

The Social Causes of Illness and Death

People get sick and die partly because of natural causes. One person may have a genetic predisposition to cancer. Another may come in contact with the deadly Ebola virus in the environment. However, over and above such natural causes of illness and death, we can single out three types of social causes.

Human–Environmental Factors

The environment constructed by humans poses major health risks. For example, more than 100 oil refineries and chemical plants are concentrated in a 75-mile strip between New Orleans and Baton Rouge. The area is commonly known as "Cancer Alley," because the

Maximum average human life span: The average age of death for a population under ideal conditions. It is currently about 85 years.

petrochemical plants spew cancer-causing pollutants into the air and water. Local residents, overwhelmingly African American, are more likely than other Americans to get cancer because they breathe and drink high concentrations of these pollutants (Bullard, 1994 [1990]). Cancer Alley is a striking illustration of how human–environmental conditions can cause illness and death.

Lifestyle Factors

Smoking cigarettes, excessive use of alcohol and drugs, poor diet, lack of exercise, and social isolation are among the chief lifestyle factors associated with poor health and premature death. For example, a third of the people who smoke are likely to die prematurely from smoking-related illnesses. This amounts to about half a million Americans annually. About 30 percent of all cancer deaths in the United States result from tobacco use. About 35 percent result from poor diet (Remennick, 1998: 17). Social isolation, too, affects one's chance of becoming ill and dying prematurely. Thus, unmarried people have a greater chance than married people of dying prematurely. At any age, the death of a spouse increases one's chance of dying, whereas remarrying decreases one's chance of dying (Helsing, Szklo, and Comstock, 1981). Social isolation is particularly problematic among elderly people who retire, lose a spouse and friends, and cannot rely on family members or state institutions for social support. Such people are prone to fall into a state of depression that contributes to ill health. And when catastrophe hits—from the great Chicago heat wave of 1995 to hurricane Katrina a decade later—the isolated elderly are the least likely to get help and the most likely to die.

The Public Health and Health Care Systems

Finally, the state of a nation's health depends partly on public and private efforts to improve people's well-being and treat their illnesses. The **public health system** is composed of government-run programs that ensure access to clean drinking water, basic sewage and sanitation services, and inoculation against infectious diseases. The absence of a public health system is associated with high rates of disease and low life expectancy. The **health care system** is composed of a nation's clinics, hospitals, and other facilities responsible for ensuring health and treating illness. The absence of a system that ensures citizens access to a minimum standard of health care is also associated with high rates of disease and low life expectancy.

Exposure to all three sets of social causes of illness and death is strongly related to country of residence, class, race, and gender. We now consider the impact of these factors, beginning with country of residence.

Global Health Inequalities

Acquired immune deficiency syndrome (AIDS) is the leading cause of death in the poverty-stricken part of Africa south of the Sahara desert. ▌Figure 14.2 shows that in December 2007, 7.4 percent of sub-Saharan Africans—25.4 million people—were living with HIV/AIDS. In contrast, 0.6 percent of North Americans and 0.3 percent of western Europeans were living with HIV/AIDS. This means that HIV/AIDS is 12 times more common in sub-Saharan Africa than in North America and 24 times more common than in western Europe. Despite the much greater prevalence of HIV/AIDS in sub-Saharan Africa, however, spending on research and treatment is concentrated overwhelmingly in the rich countries of North America and western Europe. As the case of HIV/AIDS illustrates, global inequality influences people's exposure to different health risks.

Public health system: Composed of government-run programs that ensure access to clean drinking water, basic sewage and sanitation services, and inoculation against infectious diseases.

Health care system: Composed of a nation's clinics, hospitals, and other facilities for ensuring health and treating illness.

Biomedical advances increase life expectancy, but the creation of a sound public health system has even more dramatic effects.

A health worker at Nazareth House in Cape Town, South Africa, lavishes care and attention on some of the 41 infected children in her care. Nearly one-fifth of South Africa's adult population is infected with HIV/AIDS.

▶FIGURE 14.2
Number of People with HIV/AIDS, December 31, 2007 (adult prevalence in parentheses)

Source: World Health Organization (2007)

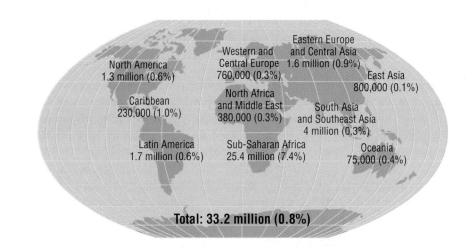

North America
1.3 million (0.6%)

Western and
Central Europe
760,000 (0.3%)

Eastern Europe
and Central Asia
1.6 million (0.9%)

East Asia
800,000 (0.1%)

Caribbean
230,000 (1.0%)

North Africa
and Middle East
380,000 (0.3%)

South Asia
and Southeast Asia
4 million (0.3%)

Latin America
1.7 million (0.6%)

Sub-Saharan Africa
25.4 million (7.4%)

Oceania
75,000 (0.4%)

Total: 33.2 million (0.8%)

You might think that prosperity increases health because of biomedical advances, such as new medicines and diagnostic tools. If so, you are only partly correct. Biomedical advances do increase life expectancy. In particular, vaccines against infectious diseases have done much to improve health and ensure long life. However, the creation of a sound public health system is even more important in this regard. If a country can provide its citizens with clean water and a sewage system, epidemics decline in frequency and severity and life expectancy soars.

The industrialized countries started to develop their public health systems in the mid-19th century. Social reformers, concerned citizens, scientists, and doctors joined industrialists and politicians in urging governments to develop health policies that would help create a healthier labor force and citizenry (Goubert, 1989 [1986]; McNeill, 1976). But what was possible in North America and western Europe 150 years ago is not possible in many of the developing countries today. Most of us take clean water for granted. In contrast, more than 1 billion of the world's 6.7 billion people do not have access to a sanitary water supply (de Villiers, 1999).

▶TABLE 14.2

Health Indicators, Selected Countries, circa 2004

	Health Expenditure per Capita ($US)	Physicians/ 100,000 Population	Nurses/ 100,000 Population	Infant Mortality/ 1,000 Live Births	Children Immunized against Measles (%)
U.S.	5271	548.9	772.6	6.5	93
Canada	2931	209.5	1009.9	4.8	95
Japan	2133	201.4	820.6	3.3	99
Mexico	550	171.5	221.4	20.9	96
Zambia	51	6.9	113.1	88.3	84

Sources: World Health Organization (2002, 2005); Infoplease.com (2005d); Central Intelligence Agency (2005); United Nations (2005).

We show other indicators of health inequality for selected countries in ▶Table 14.2. We see immediately that there is a positive correlation between national wealth and good health. The United States, Japan, and Canada are rich countries. They spend a substantial part of their wealth on health care. Many physicians and nurses service their populations. As a result, **infant mortality** (the annual number of deaths before the age of 1 year for every 1,000 live births) is low. As noted previously, rich countries also enjoy high life expectancy. Mexico, however, is poorer than the United States, Japan, and Canada and spends much less per capita on health care. Accordingly, its population is less healthy in several respects. Sub-Saharan Zambia is one of the poorest countries in the world. It spends little on health care, has few medical personnel, and suffers a very high infant mortality rate.

Closer inspection of Table 14.2 reveals an anomaly, however. The United States spends two and a half times as much per person on health care as Japan and 80 percent more than Canada. On average, Americans work nearly two months a year just to pay their medical bills. Moreover, the United States has 162 percent more doctors per 100,000 people than Canada and 172 percent more than Japan. Yet the United States has a lower life expectancy than Canada and Japan, it immunizes a smaller percentage of its children against measles, and it has a higher rate of infant mortality. On one measure—immunization of children against measles—the United States falls behind Mexico. The American case shows that spending more money on health care does not always improve the health of a nation.

Class Inequalities and Health Care

What accounts for the American anomaly? Why do we spend far more on health care than any other country in the world yet wind up with a population that, on average, is less healthy than the population of other rich countries? Part of the answer is that the gap between rich and poor is greater in the United States than in Japan, Sweden, Canada, France, and other rich countries. In general, the higher the level of inequality in a country, the more unhealthy its population (Wilkinson, 1996). Because the United States contains a higher percentage of poor people than do other rich countries, its average level of health is lower. Moreover, because income inequality has widened in the United States since the early 1970s, health disparities between income groups have grown (Williams and Collins, 1995).

Health inequality manifests itself in many ways. For example, poor people have higher infant mortality rates and lower life expectancy than people who are not poor. One reason for this disparity is that the poor are more likely than others to be exposed to violence,

Infant mortality: The number of deaths before the age of 1 year for every 1,000 live births in a population in 1 year.

high-risk behavior, and environmental hazards and they are more likely to do physical labor in which accidents are common. A second reason why the poor are less healthy than the well-to-do is that they cannot afford adequate, and in some cases even minimal, health care. We discuss this issue in more detail later. Despite Medicaid, most poor people are inadequately served. Only about half the poor receive Medicaid assistance. Furthermore, poor people typically live in areas where medical treatment facilities are inadequate. This has been especially true in recent decades, when many public hospitals that served the poor were closed as a result of government budget cuts (Albelda and Folbre, 1996).

If poor people have less access to doctors and hospitals than the well-to-do, they also tend to have less knowledge about healthful lifestyles. For example, they are less likely to know what constitutes a nutritious diet. That, too, contributes to their propensity to illness. The overconsumption of fat and sugary foods is causing obesity and diabetes epidemics that disproportionately affect the poor (Critser, 2003). Illness, in turn, makes it more difficult for poor people to escape poverty (Abraham, 1993).

Increases in income have a bigger positive health impact on below-median income earners than on above-median income earners. But inequality is not simply a matter of differential access to resources such as medical care and knowledge. Even among people who have the same access to medical resources, people of higher rank tend to live more healthful and longer lives. Why? Researchers in the United States, the UK, and Canada have argued that people of high rank experience less stress because they are more in control of their lives. If you can decide when to work, how to work, and what to work on, if you can exercise autonomy and creativity at work, you are likely to be healthier than someone who lacks these freedoms. You not only have the resources to deal with stress, you also have the ability to turn it off. In contrast, subordinates in a hierarchy have little control over their work environment. They experience a continuous sense of vulnerability that results in low-level stress. Continuous low-level stress, in turn, results in reduced immune function, increased hardening of the arteries, increased risk of heart attack, and other ailments. In short, if access to medical resources is associated with improved health, so is lower stress—and both are associated with higher positions in the socioeconomic hierarchy (Epstein, 1998; Evans, 1999).

Racial and Ethnic Inequalities in Health Care

Partly because poverty is relatively widespread among some racial and ethnic groups—especially African Americans, Hispanic Americans, and Native Americans—health status is also correlated with race. For example, the infant mortality rate in Harlem, New York City's main African American district, is higher than that in Bangladesh (Shapiro, 1992).

The effects of economic inequality are also evident in the way causes of death differ between relatively poor and relatively advantaged racial and ethnic groups. ▶Table 14.3 shows that in general, non-Hispanic whites have a relatively high mortality rate for degenerative diseases associated with old age (such as heart disease, cancer, stroke, and Alzheimer's disease). In contrast, many African Americans, Hispanic Americans, and Native Americans do not live long enough to die from degenerative diseases associated with old age. Instead, they are much more likely than non-Hispanic whites to die from accidents, infant diseases, homicide, and HIV/AIDS. This pattern reflects their relatively low class position.

Racial disparities in health status are not entirely attributable to economic differences between racial groups. Thus, the health status of African Americans is somewhat lower than that of European Americans *even within the same income category.* This suggests that

▶TABLE 14.3

Leading Causes of Death: Ratios for Sex, Race, and Ethnicity, 2000

Cause	RATIO				
	Female: Male	African American: White	Hispanic American: White	Asian American*: White	Native American: White
Heart disease	1.02	0.90	0.80	0.87	0.71
Cancer	0.90	0.94	0.84	1.14	0.72
Stroke	1.53	0.96	0.82	1.34	0.71
Lung disease	1.00	0.50	0.45	0.59	0.70
Accidents	0.52	1.08	2.16	1.20	2.98
Influenza/ pneumonia	1.2	0.75	0.86	1.14	0.89
Diabetes	1.15	1.56	1.92	1.19	2.00
Alzheimer's disease	2.42	0.45	0.48	0.36	0.36
Kidney disease	1.07	1.71	1.07	1.07	1.36
Suicide	0.25	0.54	1.30	1.38	2.00
Liver disease	0.53	0.91	3.00	0.82	4.27
Blood poisoning	1.27	n.a.	n.a.	n.a.	n.a.
Infant diseases	n.a.	4.50	6.67	2.75	2.75
Homicide	n.a.	7.00	9.00	2.50	4.50
HIV/AIDS	n.a.	9.00	9.00	0.67	1.67

n.a = not available because of the way the Centers for Disease Control constructs its tables. *Includes Pacific Islanders.
We calculated the ratios by dividing the percent of total deaths due to each cause (heart disease, etc.) for population categories (female versus male, etc.).
Source: Anderson (2002: 8, 9).

racism affects health. It does so in three ways. First, income and other rewards do not have the same value across racial groups. For instance, because of discrimination, each year of education completed by an African American results in smaller income gains than it does for white Americans. Because, as we have seen, income is associated with good health, blacks tend to be worse off than whites at the same income level. Second, racism affects access to health services. That is because African Americans at all income levels tend to live in racially segregated neighborhoods with fewer health-related facilities. Third, the experience of racism induces psychological distress that has a negative effect on health status. For example, racism increases the likelihood of drug addiction and engaging in violence (Williams and Collins, 1995). Similar patterns hold for Hispanic and Native Americans.

Gender Inequalities in Health Care: The Feminist Contribution

Feminist scholars have brought health inequalities based on gender to the attention of the sociological community in recent decades. In a review of the relevant literature in the *New England Journal of Medicine,* one researcher concluded that such gender inequalities are substantial (Haas, 1998). Specifically:

● Gender bias exists in medical research. Thus, more research has focused on "men's diseases" (such as cardiac arrest) than on "women's diseases" (such as breast cancer). Similarly, medical research is only beginning to explore the fact that women may react differently than men to some illnesses and may require different treatment regimes.

● Gender bias also exists in medical treatment. For example, women undergo fewer kidney transplants, various cardiac procedures, and other treatments than men.

● Because women live longer than men, they experience greater lifetime risk of functional disability and chronic illness and have a greater need for long-term care. Yet more is spent on men's than women's health care in this country. (In contrast, Canadian health care spending for women and men, excluding expenditures related to childbirth, is about equal. This is because Canada, unlike the United States, has a system of universal health insurance for a comprehensive range of health care services [Mustard et al., 1998]. We analyze the American health care system later.)

● There are 40 percent more poor women than poor men in the United States (Casper, McLanahan, and Garfinkel, 1994: 597). Because, as we have seen, poverty contributes to ill health, we could expect improvements in women's economic standing to be reflected in improved health status for women.

In sum, although women live longer than men, gender inequalities have a negative impact on women's health. Women's health is negatively affected by differences between women and men in access to gender-appropriate medical research and treatment as well as the economic resources needed to secure adequate health care (Table 14.3, column 1).

Health and Politics: The United States from Conflict and Functionalist Perspectives

Earlier we noted the existence of an American anomaly. We spend more on health care than any other country, yet all the other rich postindustrial societies have healthier populations. One reason for this anomaly, as we have seen, is the relatively high level of social inequality in the United States. A second reason, which we will now examine, is the nature of the American health care system.

You will recall from our discussion in Chapter 1 ("A Sociological Compass") and elsewhere that conflict theory is concerned mainly with the question of how privileged groups seek to maintain their advantages and subordinate groups seek to increase theirs. As such, conflict theory is an illuminating approach to analyzing the American health care system. We can usefully see health care in the United States as a system of privilege for some and disadvantage for others. It therefore contributes to the poor health of less well-to-do Americans (Box 14.1).

Consider, for example, that the United States lacks a system of health insurance that covers the entire population. Only elderly people, some of the poor, and some veterans receive medical benefits from the government under the Medicare, Medicaid, and military health care programs. All told, the American government pays about 45 percent of all medical costs out of taxes. In the United Kingdom, Sweden, and Denmark, the comparable figure is about 85 percent; in Japan and Germany it is around 80 percent; and in France, Canada, Italy, and Australia it is around 70 percent. The governments of Germany, Italy, Belgium, Denmark, Finland, Greece, Iceland, Luxembourg, Norway, and Spain cover almost all health care costs, including drugs, eyeglasses, dental care, and prostheses. About 47 million Americans lack health insurance. An equal number lacks adequate coverage (Anderson, Reinhardt, Hussey, and Petrosyan, 2003; "Health Care Systems," 2001; Schoen, Doty, Collins, and Holmgren, 2005; Starr, 1994 [1992]; Box 14.3).

CENGAGENOW™

Learn more about the
American Health-Care System
by going through the Health
Care in the United States
Learning Module.

BOX 14.1
SOCIAL POLICY: WHAT DO YOU THINK?

The High Cost of Prescription Drugs

Americans pay more for prescription drugs than anyone else in the world. In 2002, prescription drug prices in other rich countries were 37 percent to 53 percent below American prices (Figure 14.3). Between 1998 and 2002, the price of prescription drugs in the United States increased three times faster than the rate of inflation and faster than any other item in the nation's health care budget. Elderly people and people with chronic medical conditions such as diabetes feel the burden most acutely because they are the biggest prescription drug users.

Other rich countries keep prescription drug prices down through some form of government regulation. For example, since 1987, Canadian drug companies have not been able to increase prices of brand-name drugs above the inflation rate. New brand-name drugs cannot exceed the highest Canadian price of comparable drugs used to treat the same disease. For new brand-name drugs that are unique and have no competitors, the price must be no higher than the median price for that drug in the United Kingdom, France, Italy, Germany, Sweden, Switzerland, and the United States. If a company breaks the rules, the government requires a price adjustment. If the government deems that a company has deliberately flouted the law, it imposes a fine (Patent Medicine Prices Review Board, 2002). Not surprisingly, more than 1 million Americans now regularly buy their brand-name prescription drugs directly from Canadian pharmacies.

American drug manufacturers justify their high prices by claiming they need the money for research and development (R&D). The American public benefits from R&D, they say, while lower drug prices impair R&D in other countries.

Their argument would be more convincing if evidence showed that price curbs actually hurt R&D. However, in the UK, where the government regulates prescription drug costs, drug companies spend 20 percent of their sales revenue on R&D. In the United States, the figure is just 12.5 percent. In Canada, expenditure on R&D has increased 1,500 percent since the beginning of government regulation (1987–2002). This hardly suggests that price regulation hurts R&D (Barry, 2002c; Patent Medicine Prices Review Board, 2002: 49).

What we can say with confidence is that the American pharmaceutical industry is by far the most profitable industry in the country. In 2001, profit as a percentage of revenue was 18.5 percent—four times higher than that of all other industries combined. We also know that drug companies spend about half as much on advertising and promotions as they do on R&D. This drives up drug prices. Finally, we know that the pharmaceutical industry spends more on lobbying and political campaign contributions than any other industry. Spending $197 million in 1999–2000, it hired 625 Washington lobbyists, more than one for each member of Congress. Most of the lobbying effort is aimed at influencing members of Congress to maintain a free market in drug prices (Barry, 2002a, 2002b, 2002c).

The drug companies' lobbying efforts have proved only partly successful (Gearon, 2002; Saunders, 2003). Various states have formed purchasing pools so they can buy Medicaid drugs in bulk and save money. Governors and city officials in several states have said they want to import less expensive medicines from Canada to save their state budgets and their citizens millions of dollars. The drug companies, backed by the U.S. Food and Drug Administration (FDA), are fighting such maneuvers. The struggle over prescription drug prices has become a major policy debate focused squarely on the advisability of allowing a free market to operate unchallenged in the health field.

Critical Thinking

- What are the advantages and disadvantages of having the government regulate the cost of prescription drugs?

- Weighing the costs and benefits of a free market versus government regulation, which do you favor?

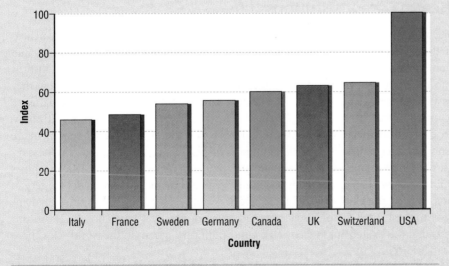

▶FIGURE 14.3

Prescription Drug Costs in Eight Rich Countries, 2002 (Index, United States = 100)

Source: Patent Medicine Prices Review Board (2002: 23).

Problems with Private Health Insurance and Health Maintenance Organizations

Private insurance programs run by employers and unions cover most Americans, although some people buy private coverage. About 85 percent of employees receive their health coverage through health maintenance organizations (HMOs) (Gorman, 1998). HMOs are private corporations that collect regular payments from employers and employees. When an employee needs medical treatment, an HMO administers it.

Like all corporations, HMOs pursue profit. They employ four main strategies to keep their shareholders happy. Unfortunately, all four strategies lower the average quality of health care in the United States (Kuttner, 1998a, 1998b):

1. Some HMOs avoid covering sick people and people who are likely to get sick. This keeps their costs down. For example, if an HMO can show that you had a medical condition before you came under its care, the HMO won't cover you for that condition.

2. HMOs try to minimize the cost of treating sick people they can't avoid covering. Thus, HMOs have doctor-compensation formulas that reward doctors for withholding treatments that are unprofitable.

3. There have been allegations that some HMOs routinely inflate diagnoses to maximize reimbursements. In 2000, Columbia/HCA, the largest for-profit hospital chain in the nation, agreed to pay the federal government $745 million to settle a federal billing fraud investigation (Galewitz, 2000).

4. HMOs keep overhead charges high. Administrative costs are higher in the private sector of the health care system than in the public sector in almost every country for which data are available. Administrative costs are highest in the private sector of the American health care system. Administrative costs in Medicare and Medicaid are only 37 percent as high as administrative costs in the private sector of American health care ("Health Care Systems," 2001: 8).

Advantages of Private and For-Profit Health Care Institutions

Despite these drawbacks, running HMOs and other health care institutions such as hospitals as for-profit organizations has one big advantage, which functionalists would undoubtedly highlight in their tendency to emphasize the contribution of social institutions to the smooth operation of society. Health organizations are so profitable that they can invest enormous sums in R&D, the latest diagnostic equipment, and high salaries to attract many of the best medical researchers and practitioners on the planet. Significantly, for people with adequate coverage, waiting times to see doctors and receive treatment are very short by international standards. Compare the United States with Canada in these respects. The United States has twice as many magnetic resonance imaging (MRI) machines per million people than Canada. The extended waiting time for nonemergency surgery in Canada has become a hot political issue, and it is not unusual for well-to-do Canadians to travel to the United States for elective surgery and pay for it here (Box 14.2). All this suggests that the United States enjoys the best health care system in the world—for those who can afford it.

The main supporters of the current U.S. health care system are the stockholders of the 1,500 private health-insurance companies and the physicians and other health professionals who get to work with the latest medical equipment, conduct cutting-edge research,

BOX 14.2
YOU AND THE SOCIAL WORLD

What Kind of Health System Do You Prefer?

A recent survey asked nearly 9,000 American and Canadian adults to evaluate their respective health care systems. Among other things, they were asked if, over the past year, they did not receive a health care service when they felt they needed it. If they did not, they were counted as having an "unmet health care need."

Table 14.4 shows the percentage of four categories of respondents with an unmet health care need: all Americans, Americans with health insurance, Americans without health insurance, and all Canadians (all of whom have state health insurance). Please inspect the table.

Is there a meaningful difference between Canadians and Americans? If so, why? If not, why not?

WRITING ASSIGNMENT

Equipped with the conclusions you draw from Table 14.4 and from the discussion of health care systems in the text, in about 500 words explain why you favor a largely private health care system like that of the United States or a state-managed system like that of Canada. In framing your answer, you may wish to consult the brief comparison of American, Canadian, Japanese, and German health care systems at http://www.context.org/ICLIB/IC39/CoopTalr.htm.

TABLE 14.4
Individuals Reporting an Unmet Health Care Need, United States and Canada, 2002–03 (in percent; n = 8,688)

	Percent with Unmet Health Care Need	Main Reason for Unmet Health Care Need
Canada	10.7	Waiting time
United States	13.1*	Cost
Insured Americans	11.3**	Cost
Uninsured Americans	40.0***	Cost

* Statistically significant difference between Canadians and Americans. This means that the sample difference between Canadians and Americans is probably meaningful; the chance that the difference does not exist in the population is less than 5 percent.
** No statistically significant difference between Canadians and insured Americans. This means that the sample difference between Canadians and insured Americans is probably not meaningful; the chance that the difference does not exist in the population is 5 percent or *greater*.
*** Statistically significant difference between Canadians and uninsured Americans. This means that the sample difference between Canadians and uninsured Americans is probably meaningful; the chance that the difference does not exist in the population is less than 5 percent.
Source: Sanmartin et al. (2004: 18, 30).

and earn high salaries. Thus, HMOs and the American Medical Association (AMA) have been at the forefront of attempts to convince Americans that the largely private system of health care serves the public better than any state-run system could. Their efforts have been only partly successful. The 1998 General Social Survey (GSS) asked a nationwide sample of Americans whether HMOs improved the quality of medical care. Only 22 percent of Americans agreed or strongly agreed that they do. In contrast, 41 percent disagreed or strongly disagreed. Nearly twice as many Americans disapproved of HMOs as approved of them (National Opinion Research Center, 2006).

A National System of Health Care for the United States?

Despite this overall negative evaluation of the private health care system, attempts to create a national system of health care in which everyone is covered regardless of his or her employment status or income level have failed (Hacker, 1997; Marmor, 1994). Most recently, Congress rejected President Clinton's 1993–94 Health Security proposal. Clinton was unable to unify political and public support for his proposal, partly because of the massive media campaign bankrolled by health-insurance companies and Clinton's political opponents (Skocpol, 1996).

Summing up, we may say that the apparently natural processes of health and illness are in fact deeply social processes. Social circumstances account for variations in life expectancy and rates of mortality resulting from various causes. These social circumstances include a country's standard of living, level of inequality, and type of health care system, as well as a person's gender, class, race, and ethnicity.

The Professionalization of Medicine

In 1850, the practice of medicine was in a chaotic state. Herbalists, faith healers, midwives, druggists, and medical doctors vied to meet the health needs of the American public. A century later, the dust had settled. Medical science was victorious. Its first series of breakthroughs involved identifying the bacteria and viruses responsible for various diseases and then developing effective procedures and vaccines to combat them. These and subsequent triumphs in diagnosis and treatment convinced most people of the superiority of medical science over other approaches to health. Medical science worked more effectively and more often than other therapies.

CENGAGENOW™

Learn more about **Physicians** by going through the # of Physicians per 100,000 Map Exercise.

It would be wrong, however, to think that scientific medicine came to dominate health care only because it produced results. A second, sociological reason for the rise and dominance of scientific medicine is that doctors were able to professionalize. A *profession* is an occupation requiring extensive formal education. Professionals regulate their own training and practice. They restrict competition within the profession, mainly by limiting the recruitment of practitioners. They maximize competition with some other professions, partly by laying exclusive claim to a field of expertise. Professionals are usually self-employed. They exercise considerable authority over their clients. And they profess to be motivated mainly by the desire to serve their community, although they earn a lot of money in the process. **Professionalization,** then, is the process by which people gain control and authority over their occupation and their clients. It results in professionals enjoying high occupational prestige and income and considerable social and political power (Freidson, 1986; Starr, 1982).

The American Medical Association

The professional organization of American doctors is the AMA, founded in 1847. It quickly set about broadcasting the successes of medical science and criticizing alternative approaches to health as quackery and charlatanism. By the early years of the 20th century, the AMA had convinced state licensing boards to certify only doctors who had been trained in programs recognized by the AMA. Soon, schools teaching other approaches to health care were closing down across the country. Doctors had never earned much. In the 18th century it was commonly said that "few lawyers die well, few physicians live well" (Illich, 1976: 58). But once it was possible to lay virtually exclusive claim to health care, big financial rewards followed. Today, American doctors in private practice earn on average more than $200,000 a year, although income varies substantially by specialty.

The Rise of Modern Hospitals

The modern hospital is the institutional manifestation of the medical doctor's professional dominance. Until the 20th century, most doctors operated small clinics and visited patients in their homes. Medicine's scientific turn in the mid-19th century guaranteed the rise of the modern hospital. Expensive equipment for diagnosis and treatment had to be shared by many physicians. This required the centralization of medical facilities in large,

Professionalization: The process by which people gain control and authority over their occupation and clients.

bureaucratically run institutions that strongly resisted deviations from professional conduct. Practically nonexistent until the Civil War, hospitals are now widespread.

Recent Challenges to Traditional Medical Science

Patient Activism

By the mid-20th century, the dominance of medical science in the United States was virtually complete. Any departure from the dictates of scientific medicine was considered deviant. Thus, when sociologist Talcott Parsons defined the **sick role** in 1951, he first pointed out that illness suspends routine responsibilities and is not deliberate. Then he stressed that people playing the sick role must want to be well and must seek competent help, cooperating with health-care practitioners at all times (Parsons, 1951: 428ff.). Must they? By Parsons's definition, a competent person suffering from a terminal illness cannot reasonably demand that doctors refrain from using heroic measures to prolong his or her life. And by his definition, a patient cannot reasonably question doctors' orders, no matter how well educated the patient and how debatable the effect of the prescribed treatment. Although Parsons's definition of the sick role may sound plausible to many people born before World War II, it probably sounds authoritarian and foreign to most younger people. Today, it corresponds best to elderly people and to patients in intensive care units who are too weak and disoriented to take a more active role in their own care (Rier, 2000).

This is because things have changed. The American public is more highly educated now than it was in the 1950s. Many people now possess the knowledge, the vocabulary, the self-confidence, and the political organization to participate in their own health care rather than passively accepting whatever experts tell them. Increasingly, patients are taught to perform simple, routine medical procedures themselves. Many people now use the Internet to seek information about various illnesses and treatments. Increasingly, they are uncomfortable with doctors acting like all-knowing parents and patients like dutiful children. Doctors now routinely seek patients' informed consent for some procedures rather than deciding what to do on their own. Similarly, most hospitals have established ethics committees, which were unheard of only two decades ago (Rothman, 1991). These are responses to patients wanting a more active role in their own care.

Some recent challenges to the authority of medical science are organized and political. For example, when AIDS activists challenge the stereotype of AIDS as a "gay disease" and demand more research funding to help find a cure, they changed research and treatment priorities in a way that could never have happened in, say, the 1950s or 1960s (Epstein, 1996). Similarly, when feminists support the reintroduction of midwifery and argue against medical intervention in routine childbirth, they are challenging the wisdom of established medical practice. The previously male-dominated profession of medicine considered the male body the norm and paid relatively little attention to women's diseases, such as breast cancer, and women's issues, such as reproduction. This, too, is now changing thanks to feminist intervention (Boston Women's Health Book Collective, 1998; Rothman, 1982, 1989). And although doctors and the larger society traditionally treated people with disabilities like incompetent children, various movements now seek to empower them (Charlton, 1998; Zola, 1982). As a result, attitudes toward people with disabilities are changing.

Sick role: According to Talcott Parsons, involves (1) the nondeliberate suspension of routine responsibilities, (2) wanting to be well, (3) seeking competent help, and (4) cooperating with health care practitioners at all times.

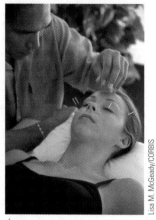

Acupuncture is one of the most widely accepted forms of alternative medicine.

Alternative Medicine

Other challenges to the authority of medical science are less organized and political than those just mentioned. Consider, for example, alternative medicine. The most frequently used types of alternative medicine are chiropractic therapy, acupuncture, massage therapy, and various relaxation techniques. Alternative medicine is used mostly to treat back problems, chronic headache, arthritis, chronic pain, insomnia, depression, and anxiety. Especially popular in the western states, alternative medicine is most often used by highly educated, upper-income white Americans in the 25- to 49-year age cohort. A nationwide poll conducted in 1990 showed that 34 percent of Americans tried alternative medicine in the year before the survey. Most of them had *not* lost faith in traditional medical science. Thus 83 percent of them tried alternative medicine in conjunction with treatment from a medical doctor (Eisenberg et al., 1993). Two surveys conducted in 1998 show that demand for alternative care is rising (American Chiropractic Association, 1999).

Despite the growing popularity of alternative medicine, many medical doctors met it with hostility until recently. They lumped together all alternative therapies and dismissed them as unscientific (Campion, 1993). By the late 1990s, however, a more tolerant attitude was evident in many quarters. For certain ailments, physicians began to recognize the benefits of at least the most popular forms of alternative medicine. For example, a 1998 editorial in the respected *New England Journal of Medicine* admitted that the beneficial effect of chiropractic therapy on low back pain is "no longer in dispute" (Shekelle, 1998). This change in attitude resulted in part from new scientific evidence showing that spinal manipulation is a relatively effective and inexpensive treatment for low back pain (Manga, Angus, and Swan, 1993).

The medical profession's grudging acceptance of chiropractic therapy in the treatment of low back pain indicates what we can expect in the uneasy relationship between scientific and alternative medicine in coming decades. Doctors will for the most part remain skeptical about alternative therapies unless properly conducted experiments demonstrate their beneficial effects. Most Americans probably agree with this cautious approach.

Holistic Medicine

Medical doctors understand that a positive frame of mind often helps in the treatment of disease. For example, research shows that strong belief in the effectiveness of a cure can by itself improve the condition of about a third of people suffering from chronic pain or fatigue (Campion, 1993). This is the **placebo effect.** Doctors also understand that conditions in the human environment affect people's health. There is no dispute, for example, about why so many people in Cancer Alley develop malignancies.

Despite their appreciation of the effect of mind and environment on the human body, traditional scientific medicine tends to respond to illness by treating disease symptoms as a largely physical and individual problem. Moreover, scientific medicine keeps subdividing into more specialized areas of practice that rely more and more heavily on drugs and high-tech machinery. Most doctors are less concerned with maintaining and improving health by understanding the larger mental and social context within which people become ill.

Traditional Indian and Chinese medicine takes a different approach. India's Ayurvedic medical tradition sees people in terms of the flow of vital fluids, or "humors," and their health in the context of their environment. In this view, maintaining

Placebo effect: The positive influence on healing of strong belief in the effectiveness of a cure.

good health requires not only balancing fluids in the individual but also balancing the relationship between people and the world around them (Zimmermann, 1987 [1982]). Despite significant differences, the outlook is similar in traditional Chinese medicine. Chinese medicine and its remedies, ranging from acupuncture to herbs, seek to restore people's internal balance, as well as their relationship to the outside world (Unschuld, 1985). Contemporary **holistic medicine,** the third and final challenge to traditional scientific medicine we will consider, takes a similar approach to these "ethnomedical" traditions. Practitioners of holistic medicine argue that good health requires maintaining a balance between mind and body and between the individual and the environment.

Most holistic practitioners do not reject scientific medicine. However, they emphasize disease *prevention.* When they treat patients, they take into account the relationship between mind and body and between the individual and his or her social and physical environment. Holistic practitioners thus seek to establish close ties with their patients and treat them in their homes or other relaxed settings. Rather than expecting patients to react to illness by passively allowing a doctor to treat them, they expect patients to take an active role in maintaining their good health. And, recognizing that industrial pollution, work-related stress, poverty, racial and gender inequality, and other social factors contribute heavily to disease, holistic practitioners often become political activists (Hastings, Fadiman, and Gordon, 1980).

In sum, patient activism, alternative medicine, and holistic medicine represent the three biggest challenges to traditional scientific medicine today. Few people think of these challenges as potential replacements for scientific medicine. Many people believe that, together with traditional scientific approaches, these challenges will help improve the health status of people in the United States and throughout the world in the 21st century.

Disability

We have seen how health issues and medical treatments have changed over time. We now examine parallel changes in the way people have defined and developed strategies for dealing with disabilities. Among other things, we show that the dominant treatment tendency since the 19th century has involved the rehabilitation and integration of people with disabilities into so-called normal society. Then, in the early 20th century, some governments tried to eliminate disabled people altogether. Finally, in the late 20th century, disabled people began to assert their dignity and normality as never before. One consequence of this new attitude has been a vigorous move toward self-help and the establishment of independent communities of people with disabilities.

The Social Construction of Disability

Pity the poor "lefty," for centuries considered inferior. About 400 years ago, the Catholic Church declared left-handed people servants of the Devil. It burned some of them at the stake. In later years, it forced them to become right-handed in school. In Japan as recently as the early 20th century, left-handedness in a wife was grounds for divorce.

Almost universally, people have considered left-handedness a handicap, so much so that the sentiment has been embedded in many languages. In Russian, to do something *na levo* means to do it under the table or illegally, but the phrase literally means "on the left."

Holistic medicine: Emphasizes disease prevention. Holistic practitioners treat disease by taking into account the relationship between mind and body and between the individual and his or her social and physical environment.

In English, the word *left* derives from an Old English word that means "weak" or "worthless." In Latin, "right" is *dexter* (as in the English *dexterous*, a laudable trait), and "left" is *sinister*, which means "evil" in English.

To us, negative attitudes toward left-handedness seem like so much nonsense. We don't think of left-handed people—roughly 10 percent of the population—as **impaired** or deficient in physical or mental capacity. Nor do we think of them as disabled or incapable of performing within the range of normal human activity. The fact that so many people once thought otherwise suggests that definitions of disability are not based on self-evident biological realities. Instead, they vary socially and historically. Note also that some people, but not others, consider a 4-foot-tall person disabled and that most people must be convinced by advertising that erectile dysfunction in a 75-year-old man is a disability. These examples suggest not only that definitions of disability differ across societies and historical periods but also that in any one time and place people may disagree over these definitions.

Rehabilitation and Elimination

Modern Western approaches to disability emerged in the 19th century. All scientists and reformers of the time viewed disability as a self-evident biological reality. Some scientists and reformers sought the **rehabilitation** of people with disabilities. Rehabilitation involves curing disabilities to the extent possible through medical and technological intervention. It also involves trying to improve the lives of those with disabilities by means of care, training, and education. Finally, it involves integrating people with disabilities into "normal" or mainstream society (Stiker, 1999 [1982]; Terry and Urla, 1995). The desire for rehabilitation motivated the establishment of schools for the blind, the widespread use of prosthetics, the construction of wheelchair-accessible buildings, and so forth. It prompted the passage of laws that have benefited people with disabilities. In the United States, the Architectural Barriers Act (1968) ensures that all federally funded buildings are accessible to disabled people. The Americans with Disabilities Act (1990) prohibits discrimination and ensures equal opportunity for people with disabilities in employment, state and local government services, public accommodations, commercial facilities, and transportation. These laws have done much to help integrate disabled people into "normal" society.

Other scientists and reformers took a different tack. They sought to eliminate disability altogether by killing people with disabilities or sterilizing them and preventing them from having offspring. The Nazis adopted this approach in Germany beginning in 1933. They engineered the sterilization and killing of those they considered mentally deficient and physically "deviant," including the blind and the deaf (Proctor, 1988).

To justify Nazi policies, Adolf Hitler noted that governments in the United States and Canada had funded the forced sterilization of native North Americans, most of them women, beginning in the 1920s. The "disability" that these women were alleged to have was that they were native North Americans and were deemed by physicians to be having too many babies. Tubal ligations and hysterectomies were performed as a form of birth control on many thousands of native North Americans, some of them minors, without their informed consent. In two cases, doctors told 15-year-old girls that they were having their tonsils removed and then proceeded to remove their ovaries. It was only in 1975 that Congress passed laws prohibiting the use of federal funds to force women to undergo abortion or sterilization. By then, however, tremendous

Impaired: A description of people considered deficient in physical or mental capacity.

Rehabilitation: Curing disabilities to the extent possible through medical and technological intervention; trying to improve the lives of those with disabilities by means of care, training, and education; and integrating them into mainstream society.

damage had been inflicted on the Native American population. By 1982, when 15 percent of white American women of childbearing age had been sterilized, the figure for Native American women was about 40 percent (DeFine, 1997; Johansen, 1998).

Ablism

Perhaps a tenth of the world's people identify themselves as disabled or are characterized as such by others (Priestly, 2001). Because the human environment is structured largely around the norms of the able-bodied, disabled people suffer many disadvantages. Their deprivations are still greater if they are elderly, women, or members of a lower class or a disadvantaged racial or ethnic group.

Specifically, people routinely stigmatize disabled people, negatively evaluating them because of a visible characteristic that supposedly sets them apart from others. People also routinely employ stereotypes when dealing with those with disabilities, expecting them to behave according to a rigid and often inaccurate view of how everyone with their disability acts. The resulting prejudice and discrimination against disabled people is called **ablism.** A historical example of ablism is the widespread belief among 19th-century Western educators that blind people were incapable of high-level or abstract thought. Because of this prejudice, blind people were systematically discouraged from pursuing intellectually challenging tasks and occupations. Similarly, an 1858 article in the *American Annals of the Deaf and Dumb* held that "the deaf and dumb are guided almost wholly by instinct and their animal passions. They have no more opportunity of cultivating the intellect and reasoning facilities than the savages of Patagonia or the North American Indians" (quoted in Groce, 1985: 102). Racists think of racial minorities as naturally and incurably inferior. Ablists think of disabled people in the same way. As the preceding quotation suggests, racists and ablists were often the same people.

Ablism involves more than active prejudice and discrimination. It also involves the largely unintended neglect of the conditions of disabled people. This point should be clear to anyone who must rely on a wheelchair for mobility. Many buildings were constructed without the intention of discriminating against people in wheelchairs, yet they are extremely inhospitable to them. Impairment becomes disability when the human environment is constructed largely on the basis of ablism. Ablism exists through both intention and neglect; but in recent decades, as you will now see, it has increasingly come under attack.

Challenging Ablism: The Normality of Disability

In 1927, science fiction writer H. G. Wells published a short story called "The Country of the Blind" (Wells, 1927). It provocatively reversed the old saying that "in the land of the blind, the one-eyed man is king." In the story, the protagonist, Nuñez, survives an avalanche high in the Andes. When he revives in a mountain valley, he discovers he is on the outskirts of an isolated village whose members are all blind from a disease that struck 14 generations earlier. For them, words like *see*, *look*, and *blind* have no meaning.

The social environment turns an impairment into a disability. Architecture and urban planning that neglect nonstandard modes of mobility make life difficult for people who depend on wheelchairs.

Lightscapes Photography, Inc./CORBIS

Ablism: Prejudice and discrimination against disabled people.

Because he can see, Nuñez feels vastly superior to the villagers; he thinks he is their "Heaven-sent King and master." Over time, however, he realizes that his sight places him at a disadvantage vis-à-vis the villagers. Their sense of hearing and touch are more highly developed than his, and they have designed their entire community for the benefit of people who cannot see. Nuñez stumbles where his hosts move gracefully, and he constantly rants about seeing—which only proves to his hosts that he is out of touch with reality. The head of the village concludes that Nuñez is "an idiot. He has delusions; he can't do anything right." In this way, Nuñez's vision becomes a disability. He visits a doctor, who concludes there is only one thing to do. Nuñez must be cured of his ailment. As the doctor says:

> Those queer things that are called eyes . . . are diseased . . . in such a way as to affect his brain. They are greatly distended, he has eyelashes, and his eyelids move, and consequently his brain is in a state of constant irritation and distraction. . . . I think I may say with reasonable certainty that, in order to cure him complete, all that we need to do is a simple and easy surgical operation—namely, to remove these irritant bodies.

Thus, Wells suggests that in the land of the blind, the man who sees must lose his vision or be regarded as a raving idiot.

Wells's tale is noteworthy because it makes blindness seem utterly normal. Its depiction of the normality of blindness comes close to the way many disabled people today think of their disabilities—not as a form of deviance but as a different form of normality. As one blind woman wrote: "If I were to list adjectives to describe myself, blind would be only one of many, and not necessarily the first in significance. My blindness is as intrinsically a part of me as the shape of my hands or my predilection for salty snacks. . . . The most valuable insight I can offer is this: blindness is normal to me" (Kleege, 1999: 4).

The idea of the normality of disability has partly supplanted the rehabilitation ideal that, as we saw, originated in the 19th century. Able-bodied reformers led the rehabilitation movement. They represented and assisted disabled people. Disabled people themselves participated little in efforts to improve the conditions of their existence. This situation began to change in the 1960s. Inspired by other social movements of the era, notably the Civil Rights movement, disabled people began to organize themselves (Campbell and Oliver, 1996; Shapiro, 1993). The founding of the Disabled Peoples' International in 1981 and inclusion of the rights of people with disabilities in the United Nations Universal Declaration of Human Rights in 1985 signified the growth—and growing legitimacy—of the new movement, not just in the United States but globally. Since the 1980s, disabled people have begun to assert their autonomy and the "dignity of difference" (Charlton, 1998; Oliver, 1996). Rather than requesting help from others, they insist on self-help. Rather than seeing disability as a personal tragedy, they see it as a social problem. Rather than regarding themselves as deviant, they think of themselves as inhabiting a different but quite normal world.

The deaf community typifies the new challenge to ablism. Increasingly, deaf people share a "collective identity" with all other deaf people (Becker, 1980: 107). Members of the deaf community have a common language and culture, and they tend to marry other deaf people (Davis, 1995: 38). Rather than feeling humiliated by the seeming disadvantage of deafness, they take pride in their condition. Indeed, many people in the deaf community are eager to remain deaf even if medical treatment can "cure" them (Lane, 1992). As Roslyn Rosen, former president of the National Association of the Deaf, put it: "I'm happy with who I am. . . . I don't want to be 'fixed.' . . . In our society everyone agrees that whites have an easier time than blacks. But do you think a black person would undergo operations to become white?" (quoted in Dolnick, 1993: 38).

BOX 14.3
SOCIOLOGY AT THE MOVIES

Sicko (2007)

Roughly a sixth of Americans have no access to health care and another sixth lack adequate coverage. It would be too easy to tell horror stories about the former, so Michael Moore's *Sicko* does not dwell on them. Instead, his widely acclaimed documentary tells viewers how ordinary Americans who have health care are routinely shocked to discover just how inadequate their coverage is. Here are three cases in point:

© Lions Gate/Courtesy Everett Collection

- A woman faints on a sidewalk and is taken to the hospital by ambulance, but her insurer bills her for the trip because she didn't have it pre-authorized. "How could I have it pre-authorized when I was unconscious?" she asks.

- When the World Trade Center was attacked in 2001, some brave souls volunteered to help rescue people. Many of them later developed respiratory and other problems, but their insurers refused to cover their medical and drug expenses because they voluntarily put themselves at risk.

- A life of hard work enabled Larry and Donna to own their own house and put all six of their children through college. Now retired, and with Larry in poor health, they must sell their house to pay for medical fees not covered by their insurer. They are forced to move into a small room in the home of one of their adult children.

This is what happens when health care becomes a profit-making enterprise. People are forced to visit only the doctors and hospitals designated by their health maintenance organizations (HMOs)—privately owned companies that administer medical treatment in return for a fee paid by individuals, unions, and employers. HMOs give bonuses to claims investigators and doctors for denying claims and avoiding expensive procedures. Fine print denies treatment for medical conditions that existed prior to signing up with an HMO. These mechanisms help make HMOs profitable, but they lower life expectancy in the United States below the level of life expectancy in other rich countries.

Moore visits Canada, France, the UK, and Cuba and makes the health care systems of these countries seem perfect. They are not. For example, Canadians know all too well that governments and the medical community are working hard (and with some success) to shorten waiting times for elective surgery and diagnostic procedures, increase the availability of expensive imaging equipment, and so on. But whatever the shortcomings of universal medical care, *Sicko* serves as a cautionary tale for those who sing the praises of privatization. As Moore says, "If you want to stay healthy in America, don't get sick." (For more on health and politics, see pages 404–408.)

Critical Thinking

- What are the potential advantages of "socialized medicine," such as exists in Canada and Western Europe?

- What are the potential disadvantages of socialized medicine?

Aging

Disability affects some people. Aging affects us all. Many people think of aging as a natural process that inevitably thwarts our best attempts to delay death. Sociologists, however, see aging in a more complex light. For them, aging is also a process of socialization, or learning new roles appropriate to different stages of life. It is also a basis for social stratification.

CENGAGENOW™

Learn more about the **Sociology of Aging** by going through Then and Now: Aging in the Movies.

Age Stratification

Sociologists call a category of people born in the same range of years an **age cohort.** For example, all Americans born between 1980 and 1989 form an age cohort. **Age stratification** refers to social inequality among age cohorts. It exists in all societies, and we can observe it in everyday social interaction. For example, there is a clear status hierarchy in most high schools. On average, seniors enjoy higher status than sophomores, and sophomores enjoy higher status than freshmen.

The very young are often at the bottom of the stratification system. In preindustrial societies, people sometimes killed infants so that populations would not grow beyond the environment's ability to support them. Facing poverty and famine, parents sometimes abandoned children. Many developing countries today are overflowing with orphans and "street" children. During the early stages of Western industrialization, adults brutally exploited children. For instance, the young chimney sweeps in *Mary Poppins* may look cute, but during the Industrial Revolution, skinny "climbing boys" as young as 4 were valued in Britain because they could squeeze up crooked chimney flues no more than a foot or two in diameter 12 hours a day. The first description of job-related cancer appeared in an article on chimney sweeps published in 1775 (Nuland, 1993: 202–5).

Even in rich countries, poverty is more widespread among children than adults. According to the 2000 U.S. Census, for example, childhood poverty exceeds adult poverty by 71 percent (U.S. Department of Health and Human Services, 2002). The United States is also distinguished by having the highest child poverty rate among the world's two dozen richest countries (Bradbury and Jäntti, 2001).

Gerontocracy

If young people are often at the bottom of the stratification system, are elderly people often at the top? Some people believe that ancient China and other preindustrial societies were **gerontocracies,** or societies in which elderly men ruled, earned the highest income, and enjoyed the most prestige. Even today, people in some industrialized countries pay more attention to age than Americans do. In South Korean corporations, for instance, when a new manager starts work, everyone in the department who is older than the new manager may resign or be reassigned. Given the importance of age seniority in South Korea, it is considered difficult for a manager to hold authority over older employees. Older employees in turn find it demeaning to be managed by a younger boss (Lie, 1998).

Although some societies may approximate the gerontocratic model, its extent has been exaggerated. Powerful, wealthy, and prestigious leaders are often mature, but not the oldest, people in a society. The United States today is typical of most societies, past and present, in this regard. For example, in the United States, median income gradually rises with age, reaching its peak in the 45- to 54-year age cohort. Median income then declines for the oldest age cohorts (U.S. Census Bureau, 2006b). Prestige and power follow the same course. A similar pattern is evident in South Korea.

Just as true gerontocracy is uncommon, so is rule by youth. True, relatively young age cohorts sometimes supply most of a country's political leadership. This happened in revolutionary France in the late 18th century, revolutionary Russia in the early 20th century, and revolutionary China in the mid-20th century. However, youthful ruling cadres

Age cohort: A category of people born in the same range of years.

Age stratification: Social inequality among age cohorts.

Gerontocracy: A society ruled by elderly people.

often become gerontocracies in their own right, especially in nondemocratic societies. This was the case with the Russian Communist leadership in the 1980s and the Chinese Communist leadership in the 1990s. The young generation that grabbed power half a century earlier still clung on as senility approached.

Theories of Age Stratification

The Functionalist View

How can we explain age stratification? Functionalists observe that in preindustrial societies, family, work, and community were tightly integrated (Parsons, 1942). People worked in and with their family, and the family was the lifeblood of the community. Industrialization, however, separated work from family. It also created distinct functions for different age cohorts. Thus, whereas traditional farming families lived and worked together on the farm, the heads of urban families work outside the home. Children worked for their parents in traditional farming families, but in urban settings they attend schools. At the same time, industrialization raised the standard of living and created other conditions that led to increased life expectancy. The cohort of retired elderly people thus grew. And so it came about that various age cohorts were differentiated in the course of industrialization.

At least in principle, social differentiation may exist without social stratification. But, according to the functionalists, age stratification developed in this case because different age cohorts performed functions of differing value to society. For example, in preindustrial societies, elderly people were important as a storehouse of knowledge and wisdom. With industrialization, their function became less important, so their status declined. Age stratification, in the functionalist view, reflects the importance of each age cohort's current contribution to society, with children and elderly people distinctly less important than adults employed in the paid labor force. Moreover, all societies follow much the same pattern. Their systems of age stratification converge under the force of industrialization.

Conflict Theory

Conflict theorists agree with the functionalists that the needs of industrialization generated distinct categories of youth and the elderly. They disagree, however, on two points. First, they dispute that age stratification reflects the functional importance of different age cohorts (Gillis, 1981). Instead, they say, age stratification stems from competition and conflict. Young people may participate in a revolutionary overthrow and seize power. Elderly people may organize politically to decrease their disadvantages and increase their advantages. In other words, power and wealth do not necessarily correlate with the roles the functionalists regard as more or less important. Competition and conflict may redistribute power and wealth among age cohorts.

The second criticism lodged by conflict theorists concerns the issue of convergence. Conflict theorists suggest that political struggles can make a big difference in how much age stratification exists in a society. We saw, for example, that child poverty is higher in the United States than in other rich countries. That is because in other rich countries, particularly in continental western Europe, successful working-class political parties have struggled to implement more generous child welfare measures and employment policies that lower the poverty level. This suggests that the fortunes of age cohorts are shaped by other forms of inequality, such as class stratification (Gillis, 1981; Graff, 1995).

Symbolic Interactionist Theory

Symbolic interactionists focus on the meanings people attach to age-based groups and age stratification. They stress that the way in which people understand aging is always a matter of interpretation. Symbolic interactionists have done especially important research in community studies of elderly people. They have also helped us better understand the degree and nature of prejudice and discrimination against elderly people. For example, one study examined how movies from the 1940s to the 1980s contributed to the negative stereotyping of elderly individuals, particularly women. Among other things, it found that young people were overrepresented numerically in the movies (as compared with their representation in the general population) and tended to be portrayed as leading active, vital lives. Elderly women were underrepresented numerically and tended to be portrayed as unattractive, unfriendly, and unintelligent (Brazzini et al., 1997).

Social Problems of Elderly People

If you've been to South Florida lately, you have a good idea of what the age composition of the United States will look like in 2050. ❭Figure 14.4 shows how the elderly have grown as a percentage of the United States population since 1900 and how this age cohort is expected to grow until 2050. In 1900, only about 4 percent of the U.S. population was 65 and older. Today, the figure is more than 13 percent. By 2040, nearly 21 percent of Americans will be elderly. Thereafter, their influence in the U.S. population will start to decline.

Many sociologists of aging refer to elderly people who enjoy relatively good health—usually people between the ages of 65 and 74—as the "young old" (Neugarten, 1974; Laslett, 1991 [1989]). They refer to people 85 and older as the "old old." Figure 14.4 shows that the young old are expected to decline as a percentage of the American population after 2030. In contrast, the proportion of the old old is expected to continue increasing.

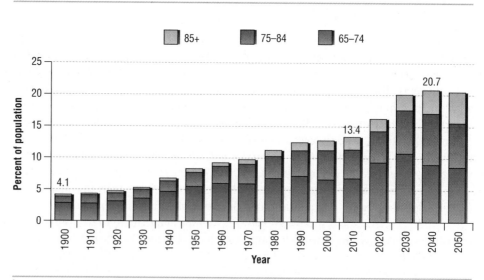

❭FIGURE 14.4
Elderly as Percentage of U.S. Population, 1900–2050 (projected)

Source: U.S. Administration on Aging (1999).

The reasons for the rising proportion of elderly people are clear. On one hand, fertility rates have been declining in virtually all industrial societies. That is, women are having fewer babies and population growth has slowed, if not actually declined, in rich societies (see Chapter 16, "Population, Urbanization, and the Environment"). On the other hand, life expectancy has been increasing because of medical advances, better welfare provisions, and other factors.

Aging and Poverty

The rising number of elderly people concerns many observers because this age cohort is most likely to suffer general physiological decline, life-threatening diseases, social isolation, and poverty. It is also significant that the sex ratio (the number of men divided by the number of women) falls with age. That is, because women live longer than men on average, there are more elderly women than elderly men. This imbalance is most marked in the oldest age cohorts. In large part, therefore, poverty and related problems among the oldest Americans are partly gender issues.

Economic inequality between elderly women and men is largely the result of women's lower earning power when they were young. Women are entering the paid labor force in increasing numbers, but there are still more women than men who are homemakers and do not work for a wage. Therefore, fewer women than men receive employer pensions when they retire. Moreover, as we saw in Chapter 10 ("Sexuality and Gender"), women who are in the paid labor force tend to earn less than men. When they retire, their employer pensions are generally smaller. As a result, the people most in need—the most elderly women—receive the fewest retirement benefits.

In addition to the old old and women, the categories of elderly people most likely to be poor include African Americans, people living alone, and people living in rural areas (Siegel, 1996). But declining income and poverty are not the only social problems faced by elderly people. In addition, elderly people are sometimes socially segregated in nursing homes, seniors' apartment buildings, and subdivisions with a high proportion of retired people.

CENGAGENOW™

Learn more about the **Aging Population** by going through the Aging Population Data Experiment.

A Shortage of Caregivers

Another problem facing elderly people is the looming shortage of caregivers. In 2001, home-care agencies and institutional care settings such as nursing homes employed 2.1 million caregivers in the United States. The U.S. Bureau of Labor Statistics expected a 58 percent rise in demand for such workers between 1998 and 2008. However, such workers are increasingly hard to find and increasingly hard to keep on the job because the work is difficult and pays little. You might think new workers could easily be recruited from the ranks of former welfare recipients. The problem is that the government requires two weeks of pre-employment training for direct-care aides, and this runs afoul of Congress's 1996 welfare reform, which discourages such training for former welfare recipients (DeFrancis, 2002). Thus, along with the increasing strain on Social Security, Medicare, and Medicaid, the scarcity of caregivers has become a major concern in our aging society.

Ageism

Especially in a society that puts a premium on vitality and youth, such as the United States, being elderly is a social stigma. **Ageism** is prejudice and discrimination against people based on their age. Ageism is evident, for example, when elderly men are stereotyped as

Ageism: Prejudice and discrimination against people based on their age.

Often, elderly people do not conform to the negative stereotypes applied to them.

Ron Dahlquist/Stone/Getty Images

"grumpy." Ageism affects women more than men. Thus, the same person who considers some elderly men "distinguished looking" may disparage elderly women as "haggard" (Banner, 1992).

Often, however, elderly people do not conform to the negative stereotypes applied to them. In the United States, 65 is usually taken to be the age when people become "elderly." (Sixty-five used to be the mandatory retirement age.) But just because someone is 65 or older does not mean he or she is decrepit and dependent. On the contrary, most people who retire from an active working life are far from being a tangle of health problems and a burden on society. That is because of the medical advances of recent decades and the more healthful lifestyles and improved financial status of elderly people.

Specifically, the housing arrangements of elderly people are not usually desolate and depressing (Hochschild, 1973; Myerhoff, 1978). Fewer than 5 percent of Americans 65 years and older lived in nursing homes in 2000, and many of these were of high quality. For people 85 years and older, the figure was more than 18 percent (AARP, 2001: 7). In 2000, fully 70 percent of Americans 75 years and older lived in single-family detached homes. Moreover, surveys show that most Americans want to stay in their own home as long as possible. This desire is strongest among the oldest Americans and is increasing over time. More than 80 percent of Americans 45 years and older say they would prefer to modify their homes and have help at home should such assistance become necessary (Bayer and Harper, 2000).

French social critic Simone de Beauvoir argued that "[t]here is only one solution if old age is not to be an absurd parody of our former life, and that is to go on pursuing ends that give our existence meaning—devotion to individuals, to groups or to causes, social, political, intellectual, or creative work" (Beauvoir, 1972 [1970]: 540). Indeed, that is precisely what many elderly people are doing now, as they work, pursue education and training, enjoy travel and leisure, and maintain ties with their family members and fellow senior citizens while living on their own.

Many elderly people are able to enjoy their retirement because they own assets aside from their home, such as investments. Most elderly people receive private and public pensions. Nearly 13 percent of Americans older than age 65 work in the paid labor force, nearly half of them full-time (AARP, 2001: 11). As a result, although the poverty rate does increase somewhat for people older than age 54, the poverty rate among people 65 and older is only about half the poverty rate of people in the 15- to 24-year age cohort. Poverty among elderly people has fallen sharply since the 1960s. Finally, compared with other age cohorts, elderly people are better served by the social welfare system. Social Security and other programs geared to the elderly are relatively generous. Elderly people are quite well covered by Medicare or health plans tied to the pension plan of their former union or employer.

One reason for the relative economic security of elderly people is that they are well organized politically. Their voter participation rate is above average, and they are overrepresented among those who hold positions of political, economic, and religious power. Many groups seek to improve the status of elderly people, the Gray Panthers being perhaps the best known among them. AARP is an effective lobby in Washington, D.C., for elderly people (Morris, 1996). In part because of the activism of elderly people, discrimination based on age has become illegal in the United States. In fact, activism on the part of elderly people may have led to a redistribution of resources away from young people. For example, educational funding has declined, but funding has increased for medical research related to diseases disproportionately affecting those who are elderly.

Death and Dying

It may seem odd to say so, but the ultimate social problem that elderly people must face is their own demise. Why are death and dying *social* problems and not just religious, philosophical, and medical issues? For one thing, attitudes toward death vary widely across time and place. So do the settings within which death typically takes place. Although people have always dreaded death, in most traditional societies, such as Europe until early modern times, most people accepted it (Ariès, 1982). That is partly because most people apparently believed in life after death, whether in the form of a continuation of life in heaven or in cyclical rebirth. What also made death easier to accept was that the dying were not isolated from the living. They continued to interact with household members and neighbors, who offered them continuous emotional support. Finally, because the dying had previous experience giving emotional support to other dying people, they could more easily accept death as part of everyday life.

CENGAGENOW

Learn more about **Death and Dying** by going through the Death and Dying Animation.

In contrast, in the United States today, dying and death tend to be separated from everyday life. Most terminally ill patients want to die peacefully and with dignity at home, surrounded by their loved ones. Yet about 80 percent of Americans die in hospitals. Often, hospital deaths are sterile, noiseless, and lonely (Nuland, 1993). Dying used to be public. It is now private. The frequent lack of social support makes dying a more frightening experience for many people (Elias, 1985 [1982]). In addition, our culture celebrates youth and denies death (Becker, 1973). We use diet, fashion, exercise, makeup, and surgery to prolong youth or at least the appearance of youth. This makes us less prepared for death than our ancestors were.

Psychiatrist Elisabeth Kübler-Ross's analysis of the stages of dying in contemporary America also suggests how reluctant we are to accept death (Kübler-Ross, 1969). She based her analysis on interviews with patients who were told they had an incurable disease. At first, the patients went into denial, refusing to believe their death was imminent. Then they expressed anger, seeing their demise as unjust. Negotiation followed; they pled with God or with fate to delay their death. Then came depression, when they resigned themselves to their fate but became despondent. Only then did the patients reach the stage of acceptance, when they put their affairs in order, expressed regret over not having done certain things when they had the chance, and perhaps spoke about going to heaven.

Euthanasia

The reluctance of many Americans to accept death is clearly evident in the debate over euthanasia, also known as mercy killing or assisted suicide (Rothman, 1991). The very definitions of life and death are no longer clear-cut (Lock, 2002). Various medical technologies, including machines able to replace the functions of the heart and lungs, can prolong life beyond the point that was possible in the past. This raises the question of how to deal with people who are near death. In brief, is it humane or immoral to hasten the death of terminally ill patients?

The AMA's Council on Ethical and Judicial Affairs (AMA-CEJA) says it is the duty of doctors to withhold life-sustaining treatment if that is the wish of a mentally competent patient. The AMA-CEJA also endorses the use of effective pain treatment even if it hastens death. As a result, doctors and nurses make decisions every day about who will live and

John Hillary/Reuters/Corbis

▲
Dr. Jack Kevorkian is the most prominent advocate of euthanasia in the United States.

who will die (Zussman, 1992, 1997). Public opinion polls show that about three-fourths of Americans favor this practice (Benson, 1999).

Euthanasia involves a doctor prescribing or administering medication or treatment that is intended to end a terminally ill patient's life. It is therefore a more active form of intervention than those noted in the preceding paragraph. Public opinion polls show that about two-thirds of Americans favor physician-assisted euthanasia (Benson, 1999). Between 33 percent and 60 percent of American doctors (depending on the survey) say they would be willing to perform euthanasia if it were legal. Nearly 30 percent of American doctors have received a euthanasia request, but only 6 percent say they have ever complied with such a request (Finsterbusch, 2001; Meier et al., 1998). The AMA-CEJA, the Catholic Church, some disabled people, and other groups oppose euthanasia.

Euthanasia is legal in the Netherlands and may become legal in some other countries in the next decade. In Oregon, a physician-assisted suicide law, the Death with Dignity Act, took effect in October 1997. It allows doctors to prescribe a lethal dose of drugs to terminally ill patients who choose not to prolong their suffering. The law stipulates that before a doctor can give a patient barbiturates to end his or her life, two physicians must concur that the patient is terminally ill and has less than 6 months to live. Patients must request euthanasia three times, both orally and in writing, and must swallow the barbiturates themselves. In a little more than 6 years of operation (to the end of 2003), only 171 people took advantage of Oregon's physician-assisted suicide law. The U.S. Department of Justice appealed to the Supreme Court to have physician-assisted suicide made illegal in Oregon, but the appeal was rejected in 2005.

Euthanasia is bound to become a major political issue in coming decades as medical technologies for prolonging life improve, the number of elderly people increases, and the cost of medical care skyrockets. Extending the lives of terminally ill patients by all means possible will be upheld as an ethical imperative by some people. Others will regard it as immoral because it increases suffering and siphons scarce resources away from other pressing medical needs.

The Business of Dying

In every society, a ceremonial rite of passage surrounds death. We pay our last respects to the departed, soothe the pain of our loss, and affirm our resolve to carry on. People have a deep emotional need to bury or cremate the dead, which is why we go to extraordinary lengths to recover bodies even under difficult and dangerous circumstances, including war and natural disaster.

The way we die reflects the nature of our society and culture. The United States is a capitalist, business-oriented society. Not surprisingly, therefore, funerals are big business—a more than $20-billion-a-year industry (Wiegand and Gibson, 1999). The average undertaker's bill in 2008 was about $5,500. Adding cemetery charges, the average funeral and burial bill grew to more than $8,000 ("Funeral Help," 2008).

There are two main reasons why funerals are so expensive. First, big corporations have supplanted small family operations in the funeral industry. The undisputed giant in this field, Services Corp. International (SCI), now controls about 13 percent of the U.S. funeral industry (along with 15 percent in the UK and 25 percent in Australia). Concentration of ownership lowers competition and results in higher prices, as a New York City report documented (New York City Department of Consumer Affairs, 2001). The second main reason why funerals cost so much is that people are vulnerable when their loved ones die, and much of the funeral industry takes advantage of their vulnerability. In journals such as *Mortuary Management,* funeral directors can learn how to make the bereaved feel that

Euthanasia: Involves a doctor prescribing or administering medication or treatment that is intended to end a terminally ill patient's life.

they can make up for any real or imagined neglect of the deceased by spending lavishly on the funeral. We conclude that funerals, no less than other social processes involving the human body, bear the imprint of the society in which they take place.

 ## The Points of the Compass

Identifiable social constraints increase the likelihood of ill health among certain categories of the population and the experience of prejudice and discrimination among disabled and elderly people. Underprivileged countries, classes, and races experience more ill health than their privileged counterparts. Disabled and elderly people experience more prejudice and discrimination than the able-bodied and the young when institutions and ideologies are designed without due regard for the needs of the former.

Ultimately, there is no escaping illness, disability, old age, and death. Still, social, technological, and medical advances have greatly improved the capabilities and longevity of the human body, and they will undoubtedly continue to do so. This trend suggests that while complete independence from the dictates of nature is unattainable, we can move closer to the "freedom" point of the sociological compass by loosening the social constraints on our physical potential.

CHAPTER SUMMARY

1. Are all causes of illness and death biological?

Ultimately, yes. However, variations in illness and death rates often stem from social causes. The social causes of illness and death include human–environmental factors, lifestyle factors, and factors related to the public health and health care systems. All three factors are related to country of residence, class, race, and gender. Specifically, health risks are lower among upper classes, rich countries, and privileged racial and ethnic groups than among lower classes, poor countries, and disadvantaged racial and ethnic groups. In some respects related to health, men are in a more advantageous position than women are.

2. Does the United States have the world's best health-care system?

In some ways the United States does have the world's most advanced health-care system. Cutting-edge research, abundant high-tech diagnostic equipment, and exceptionally well-trained medical practitioners help make it so. However, the average health status of Americans is lower than the average health status of people in other rich postindustrial countries. That is partly because the level of social inequality is higher in the United States and partly because the private health care system in this country makes it difficult for many people to receive adequate care.

3. What are the main challenges and alternatives to traditional medicine?

Several challenges to traditional scientific medicine promise to improve the quality of health care in the United States and worldwide. These include patient activism, alternative medicine, and holistic medicine.

4. Are disabilities defined similarly everywhere and at all times? Have disabilities always been handled in the same way?

The definition of *disability* varies over time and place. For example, some people used to consider left-handedness and being a Native American disabilities, but we no longer share that view. As far as treatment is concerned, we also see much variation. Disabled people have traditionally suffered much prejudice and discrimination, but attempts were made from the 19th century on to integrate and rehabilitate them. Some governments sought to eliminate disabled people from society in the 20th century. Recently, disabled people have begun to organize themselves, assert the normality of disability, and form communities of disabled people.

5. Is there a positive correlation between age and status?

Although it is true that young people have been, and still are, disadvantaged in many ways, it is rarely true that the oldest people in society are the best off. In most societies, including the United States, people of middle age have the most power and economic clout.

6. What are the main approaches to age stratification?

Functionalist theory emphasizes that industrialization led to the differentiation of age cohorts and the receipt of varying levels of reward by each age cohort based on its functional importance to society. This supposedly results in the convergence of age stratification systems in all industrialized societies. Conflict theory stresses the way competition and conflict can result in the redistribution of rewards between age cohorts and the divergence of age stratification systems. Symbolic interactionists focus not on these macrosociological issues but on the meanings people attach to different age cohorts.

7. How is the United States aging?

The population of the United States is aging rapidly. By 2040 more than one-fifth of Americans will be 65 or older. The fastest-growing age cohort among elderly people is composed of people 85 years and older. The ratio of men to women falls with age.

8. How are elderly people faring in the United States?

Economically speaking, elderly Americans are faring reasonably well, partly because they have considerable political power. For example, poverty is less widespread among people older than 65 than among people younger than 45. Among elderly people, poverty is most widespread for those 85 and older, women, African Americans, people living alone, and people living in rural areas. Elderly Americans also enjoy considerable political influence.

9. If elderly people in the United States are doing reasonably well economically and politically, then does this mean that they don't face significant problems in our society?

Elderly Americans still face much prejudice and discrimination. Moreover, there exist crises in the provision of adequate care to elderly people and in the pension system.

10. What is sociological about death and dying?

Different cultures attach different meanings to death and dying. Norms and commercial interests affect how we deal with these processes.

Questions to Consider

1. Do you believe that patient activism and alternative medicine improve health care or detract from the efforts of scientifically trained physicians and researchers to do the best possible research and administer the best possible treatment? Because patient activists may not be scientifically trained and because alternative therapies may not be experimentally proven, are there dangers inherent in these challenges to traditional medicine? On the other hand, do biases in traditional medicine detract from health care by ignoring the needs of patient activists and the possible benefits of alternative therapies?

2. If you do not already use a wheelchair, borrow one and try to get around campus for a few hours. If you cannot borrow a wheelchair, pretend you are in one. Draw up an inventory of difficulties you face. How would the campus have to be redesigned to make access easier?

Web Resources

CENGAGENOW

Maximize your study time by using CengageNOW's diagnostic study plan to help you review this chapter. The Study Plan will

- help you identify areas on which you should concentrate;
- provide interactive exercises to help you master the chapter concepts; and
- provide a post-test to confirm you are ready to move on to the next chapter.

The Companion Website for *Sociology: Your Compass for a New World*, *The Brief Edition*, Enhanced Second Edition

www.cengage.com/sociology/brym

Supplement your review of this chapter by going to the companion website to take one of the tutorial quizzes, use flash cards to master key terms, and check out the many other study aids you'll find there. You'll also find special features such as GSS Data and Census 2000 information that will put data and resources at your fingertips to help you with that special project or help you do some research on your own.

CHAPTER 15

Collective Action and Social Movements

Mark Peterson/Corbis

In this chapter, you will learn that:

- People sometimes lynch, riot, and engage in other forms of nonroutine group action to correct perceived injustices. Such events are rare, short-lived, spontaneous, and often violent. They subvert established institutions and practices. Nevertheless, most nonroutine collective action requires social organization, and people who take part in collective action often act in a calculated way.

- Collective action can result in the creation of one or more formal organizations or bureaucracies to direct and further the aims of its members. The institutionalization of protest signifies the establishment of a social movement.

- People are more inclined to rebel against existing conditions when strong social ties bind them to many other people who feel similarly wronged; when they have the time, money, and other resources needed to protest; and when political structures and processes give them opportunities to express discontent.

- For social movements to grow, members must make the activities, goals, and ideology of the movement consistent with the interests, beliefs, and values of potential recruits.

- The history of social movements is a struggle for the acquisition of constantly broadening citizenship rights—and opposition to those struggles.

How to Spark a Riot

▋ Personal Anecdote

Robert Brym almost sparked a small riot once. "It happened in grade 11," says Robert, "shortly after I learned that water combined with sulfur dioxide produces sulfurous acid. The news shocked me. To understand why, you have to know that I lived 60 miles east of the state of Maine and about 100 yards downwind of one of the largest pulp and paper mills in Canada. Waves of sulfur dioxide billowed day and night from the mill's smokestacks. The town's pervasive rotten-egg smell was a long-standing complaint in the area. But, for me, disgust turned to upset when I realized the fumes were toxic. Suddenly it was clear why many people I knew—especially people living near the mill—woke up in the morning with a kind of 'smoker's cough.' By the simple act of breathing we were causing the gas to mix with the moisture in our bodies and form an acid that our lungs tried to expunge, with only partial success.

"Twenty years later, I read the results of a medical research report showing that area residents suffered from rates of lung disease, including emphysema and lung cancer, significantly higher than the North American average. But even in 1968 it

---

was evident my hometown had a serious problem. I therefore hatched a plan. Our high school was about to hold its annual model parliament. The event was notoriously boring, partly because, year in, year out, virtually everyone voted for the same party, the Conservatives. But here was an issue, I thought, that could turn things around. A local man, K. C. Irving, owned the pulp and paper mill. *Forbes* business magazine ranked him as one of the richest men in the world. I figured that when I told my fellow students what I had discovered, they would quickly demand the closure of the mill until Irving guaranteed a clean operation.

"Was *I* naive. As head of the tiny Liberal party, I had to address the entire student body during assembly on election day to outline the party platform and rally votes. When I got to the part of my speech explaining why Irving was our enemy, the murmuring in the audience, which had been growing like the sound of a hungry animal about to pounce on its prey, erupted into loud 'boos.' A couple of students rushed the stage. The principal suddenly appeared from the wings and commanded the student body to settle down. He then took me by the arm and informed me that, for my own safety, my speech was finished. So, I discovered on election day, was our high school's Liberal party. And so, it emerged, was my high school political career.

"This incident troubled me for many years, partly due to the embarrassment it caused, partly due to the puzzles it presented. Why did I almost spark a small riot? Why didn't my fellow students rebel in the way I thought they would? Why did they continue to support an arrangement that was enriching one man at the cost of a community's health? Couldn't they see the injustice? Other people did. Nineteen sixty-eight was not just the year of my political failure in high school. It was also the year that student riots in France nearly toppled that country's government. In Mexico, the suppression of student strikes by the government left dozens of students dead. In the United States, students at Berkeley, Michigan, and other colleges demonstrated and staged sit-ins with unprecedented vigor. They supported free speech on their campuses, an end to American involvement in the war in Vietnam, increased civil rights for American blacks, and an expanded role for women in public affairs. It was, after all, the Sixties."

The Study of Collective Action and Social Movements

Robert didn't know it at the time, but by asking why students in Paris, Mexico City, and Berkeley rebelled whereas his fellow high school students did not, he was raising the main question that animates the study of collective action and social movements. Under what social conditions do people act in unison to change, or resist change to, society? That is the main issue we address in this chapter.

We have divided the chapter into three sections:

1. We first discuss the social conditions leading to the formation of lynch mobs, riots, and other types of nonroutine **collective action.** When people engage in collective action, they act in unison to bring about or resist social, political, and economic change (Schweingruber and McPhail, 1999: 453). Some collective actions are "routine." Others are "nonroutine" (Useem, 1998: 219). Routine collective actions are usually nonviolent and follow established patterns of behavior in bureaucratic social structures. For instance, when Mothers Against Drunk Driving (MADD) lobbies

Collective action: Occurs when people act in unison to bring about or resist social, political, and economic change.

for tougher laws against driving under the influence of alcohol, when members of a community organize a campaign against abortion or for freedom of reproductive choice, and when workers decide to form a union, they are engaging in routine collective action. Sometimes, however, "usual conventions cease to guide social action and people transcend, bypass, or subvert established institutional patterns and structures" (Turner and Killian, 1987 [1957]: 3). On such occasions, people engage in nonroutine collective action, which is often short-lived and sometimes violent. They may, for example, form lynch mobs and engage in riots. Until the early 1970s, it was widely believed that people who engage in nonroutine collective action lose their individuality and capacity for reason. Lynch mobs and riots were often seen as wild and uncoordinated affairs, more like stampedes of frightened cattle than structured social processes. As you will see, however, sociologists later showed that this portrayal is an exaggeration. It deflects attention from the social organization and inner logic of extraordinary sociological events.[1]

2. We next outline the conditions underlying the formation of **social movements.** Social movements are enduring and usually bureaucratically organized collective attempts to change (or resist change to) part or all of the social order. This is achieved by rioting, petitioning, striking, demonstrating, and establishing lobbies, unions, and political parties. We will see that an adequate explanation of institutionalized protest also requires the introduction of a set of distinctively sociological issues. These concern the distribution of power in society and the framing of political issues in ways that appeal to many people.

3. Finally, we make some observations about the changing character of social movements. We argue that the history of social movements is the history of attempts by underprivileged groups to broaden their members' citizenship rights and increase the scope of protest from the local to the national to the global level.

We begin by considering the lynch mob, a well-studied form of nonroutine collective action.

Nonroutine Collective Action

The Lynching of Claude Neal

On October 27, 1934, a black man was lynched near Greenwood, a town in Jackson County, Florida. Claude Neal, 23, was accused of raping and murdering 19-year-old Lola Cannidy, a pretty white woman and the daughter of his employer. The evidence against Neal was not totally convincing. Some people thought he had confessed under duress. But Neal's reputation in the white community as a "mean n_____," "uppity," "insolent," and "overbearing" helped to seal his fate (McGovern, 1982: 51). He was apprehended and jailed. Then, for his own safety, he was removed to the jailhouse in Brewton, Alabama, about 120 miles northwest of the crime scene.

When the white residents in and around Greenwood found that Neal had been taken from the local jail, they quickly formed a lynch mob to find him. Once word mysteriously leaked out that Neal was in Brewton, 15 men in three cars headed west. They got the

CENGAGENOW™

Learn more about **Demonstrations** by going through the % of People Who Have Taken Part in a Lawful Demonstration Map Exercise.

Social movements: Collective attempts to change all or part of the social order by stepping outside the rules of normal politics and rioting, petitioning, striking, demonstrating, and establishing lobbies, unions, and political parties.

---

[1]Reflecting new research and theoretical perspectives, the older term, *collective behavior,* fell into disfavor in the 1990s. That is because *behavior* suggests a relatively low level of consciousness of self and therefore conduct that is not entirely rational. Following Weber (1947), *action* denotes greater consciousness of self and therefore more rationality.

The National Association for the Advancement of Colored People (NAACP) took out this full-page ad in the *New York Times* on November 23, 1922, to encourage people to support passage of the Dyer anti-lynching bill in Congress. The bill was passed in the House of Representatives but defeated in the Senate. Despite the NAACP's vigorous efforts throughout the 1920s and 1930s, Congress never outlawed lynching.

sheriff out of the Brewton jail by sending him on a wild goose chase. Then, entering the jail holding guns and dynamite, they threatened to blow up the place if the lone jailer did not hand over Neal. He complied. They then tied Neal's hands with a rope. Finally, they dumped him in the back seat of a car for the ride back to Jackson County. There, a mob of two or three thousand people soon gathered near the Cannidy house.

The mob was in a state of violent agitation. Drinking moonshine whiskey and shouting, "We want the n_____," many of them "wanted to get their hands on [Neal] so bad they could hardly stand it," according to one bystander. However, the jail raiders feared the mob was uncontrollable and its members might injure each other in the frenzy to get at Neal. So they led their prisoner into the woods, where he was tortured to death. "From time to time during the torture," continued the investigator, "a rope would be tied around Neal's neck and he was pulled up over a limb and held there until he almost choked to death[,] then he would be let down and the torture [would] begin all over again" (McGovern, 1982: 80).

Having thus disposed of Neal, the jail raiders tied a rope around his body. They attached the rope to a car and dragged the body several miles to the mob in front of the Cannidy house. There, several people drove knives into the corpse, "tearing the body almost to shreds" according to one report (McGovern, 1982: 81). Lola Cannidy's grandfather took his .45 and pumped three bullets into the corpse's forehead. Some people started kicking the body. Others drove cars over it. Children were encouraged to take sharpened sticks and drive them deep into the flesh of the dead man. Then some members of the crowd rushed to a row of nearby shacks inhabited by blacks and burned the dwellings to the ground. Others took the nude and mutilated body of Claude Neal to the lawn of the Jackson County courthouse, where they strung it up on a tree. Justice, they apparently felt, had now been served. Later, they sold a photograph of Neal's hanging body as a postcard.

Breakdown Theory

Until about 1970, most sociologists believed that at least one of three conditions had to be met for nonroutine collective action, such as Claude Neal's lynching, to emerge. First, a group of people must be economically deprived or socially rootless. Second, their norms must be strained or disrupted. Third, they must lose their capacity to act rationally by getting caught up in the supposedly inherent madness of crowds. Following Charles Tilly and his associates, we may group these three factors together as the **breakdown theory** of collective action. That is because all three factors assume that collective action results from the disruption or breakdown of traditional norms, expectations, and patterns of behavior (Tilly, Tilly, and Tilly, 1975: 4–6). At a more abstract level, breakdown theory may be seen as a variant of functionalism, for it regards collective action as a form of social imbalance that results from various institutions functioning improperly.

Deprivation, Crowds, and the Breakdown of Norms

Most pre-1970 sociologists would have said that Neal's lynching was caused by one or more of the following factors:

1. *A background of economic deprivation experienced by impoverished and marginal members of the community.* The very year of Neal's lynching signals deprivation: 1934, the midpoint of the Great Depression of 1929–39. Blacks may have become the collective target of white frustration because fully one-fourth of all black farmers in Jackson County owned their own land and received government aid from the Farm Credit Administration. In contrast, many whites were landless migrants from other states or dispossessed sharecroppers who may have resented blacks receiving federal funds (McGovern, 1982: 39–41).

   Often, say proponents of breakdown theory, it is not grinding poverty, or **absolute deprivation,** that generates collective action so much as relative deprivation. **Relative deprivation** refers to the growth of an intolerable gap between the social rewards people expect to receive and those they actually receive. Social rewards are widely valued goods, including money, education, security, prestige, and so forth. Accordingly, people are most likely to rebel when rising expectations (brought on by, say, rapid economic growth and migration) are met by a sudden decline in received social rewards (due to, say, economic recession or war) (Davies, 1969; Gurr, 1970).

Breakdown theory: Holds that social movements emerge when traditional norms, expectations, and patterns of social organization are disrupted.

Absolute deprivation: A condition of extreme poverty.

Relative deprivation: An intolerable gap between the social rewards people expect to receive and the social rewards they actually receive.

CENGAGENOW™

Learn more about **Crowd Behavior** by going through the Crowd Behavior Learning Module.

From this point of view, the rapid economic growth of the Roaring Twenties, followed by the economic collapse of 1929, would likely have caused widespread relative deprivation in Jackson County.

2. *The inherent irrationality of crowd behavior* is a second factor likely to be stressed in any pre-1970 explanation of the Neal lynching. Gustave Le Bon, an early interpreter of crowd behavior, wrote that an isolated person may be a cultivated individual. But in a crowd, the individual is transformed into a "barbarian," a "creature acting by instinct" possessing the "spontaneity, violence, [and] ferocity" of "primitive beings" (Le Bon, 1969 [1895]: 28). Le Bon argued that this transformation occurs because people lose their individuality and willpower when they join a crowd. Simultaneously, they gain a sense of invincible group power that derives from the crowd's sheer size. Their feeling of invincibility allows them to yield to instincts they would normally hold in check. Moreover, if people remain in a crowd long enough, they enter something like a hypnotic state. This makes them particularly open to the suggestions of manipulative leaders and ensures that extreme passions spread through the crowd like a contagious disease. (Sociologists call Le Bon's argument the **contagion** theory of crowd behavior.) For all these reasons, Le Bon held, people in crowds are often able to perform extraordinary and sometimes outrageous acts. "Extraordinary" and "outrageous" are certainly appropriate terms for describing the actions of the citizens of Jackson County in 1934.

3. The *serious violation of norms* is the third factor that pre-1970s sociologists would likely have stressed in trying to account for the Neal lynching. In the 1930s, intimate contact between blacks and whites in the South was strictly forbidden. In that context, black-on-white rape and murder were not just the most serious of crimes but the deepest possible violation of the region's norms. Neal's alleged crimes were therefore bound to evoke a strong reaction on the part of the dominant race. In general, before about 1970, sociologists highlighted the breakdown in traditional norms that preceded group unrest, sometimes referring to it as an indicator of **strain** (Smelser, 1963: 47–48, 75).

Assessing Breakdown Theory

Can deprivation, contagion, and strain really explain what happened in the backwoods of Jackson County in the early hours of October 27, 1934? Can breakdown theory adequately account for collective action in general? The short answer is no. Increasingly since 1970, sociologists have uncovered flaws in all three elements of breakdown theory. They have proposed alternative frameworks for understanding collective action. To help you appreciate the need for these alternative frameworks, let us reconsider the three elements of breakdown theory in the context of the Neal lynching.

Deprivation

Research shows no clear association between fluctuations in economic well-being (as measured by, say, the price of cotton in the South) and the number of lynchings that took place each year between the 1880s and the 1930s (Mintz, 1946). Moreover, in the case of the Neal lynching, the main instigators were not especially economically deprived. The men who seized Neal from the Brewton jail were middle- to lower-middle-class farmers, merchants, salesmen, and the like. They were economically solvent, even at the height of the Great Depression, with enough money, cars, and free time to take a couple of days off work to organize a lynching. Nor were they socially marginal "outside agitators" or

Contagion: The process by which extreme passions supposedly spread rapidly through a crowd like a contagious disease.

Strain: Breakdown in traditional norms that precede collective action.

rootless, recent migrants to the region. They enjoyed good reputations in their communities as solid citizens, churchgoing men with a well-developed sense of civic responsibility. Truly socially marginal individuals did not take part in the lynching at all (McGovern, 1982: 67–8, 85). This fits a general pattern. In most cases of collective action, leaders and early joiners are well-integrated members of their communities, not outsiders (Brym, 1980; Brym and Economakis, 1994; Economakis and Brym, 1995; Lipset, 1971 [1951]). Levels of deprivation, whether absolute or relative, are not commonly associated with the frequency or intensity of outbursts of collective action (McPhail, 1994).

A demonstration in Jakarta, Indonesia, during which a crowd burns the flag of an Islamic opposition party.

Contagion

Despite its barbarity, the Neal lynching was not a spontaneous and unorganized affair. Sophisticated planning went into the Brewton jail raid. For example, decoying the sheriff took much cunning. Even the horrific events in front of the Cannidy home did not just erupt suddenly because of the crowd's "madness." For example, before Neal's body was brought to the Cannidy home, some adults got the idea of sharpening some long sticks, stacking them, and instructing children to use them to pierce the body. As this example shows, and as research on riots, crowds, and demonstrations has consistently confirmed, nonroutine collective action may be wild but it is usually structured. In the first place, nonroutine collective action is structured by ideas and norms that emerge in the crowd itself, such as the idea of preparing sharp sticks in the Neal lynching (Turner and Killian, 1987 [1957]). Second, nonroutine collective action is structured by the predispositions that unite crowd members and predate their collective action. The participants in the Neal lynching, for instance, were all predisposed to take part in it by racist attitudes. If they had not been similarly predisposed, they would never have assembled for the lynching in the first place (Berk, 1974; McPhail, 1991). Third, nonroutine collective action is structured by the *degree* to which different types of participants adhere to emergent and preexisting norms. Leaders, rank-and-file participants, and bystanders adhere to such norms to varying degrees (Zurcher and Snow, 1981). Fourth, preexisting social relationships among participants structure nonroutine collective action. For instance, relatives, friends, and acquaintances are more likely than strangers to cluster together and interact in crowds, riots, demonstrations, and lynchings (McPhail, 1991; McPhail and Wohlstein, 1983).

Strain

The alleged rape and murder of Lola Cannidy by Claude Neal did violate the deepest norms of the Old South in a pattern that was often repeated. Thus, data exist on 4,752 lynchings that took place in the United States between 1882 and 1964, when the last lynching was recorded. Three-quarters of them were white lynchings of blacks. Nearly two-thirds were motivated by alleged rapes or murders (calculated from Williams, 1970: 12–15).

However, lynching had deeper roots than the apparent violation of norms governing black–white relations. Significantly, it was a means by which black farmworkers were disciplined and kept tied to the southern cotton industry after the abolition of slavery threatened to disrupt the industry's traditional, captive labor supply.

▶FIGURE 15.1
Frequency of Lynching,
United States, 1882–1935

Source: Williams (1970: 8–11).

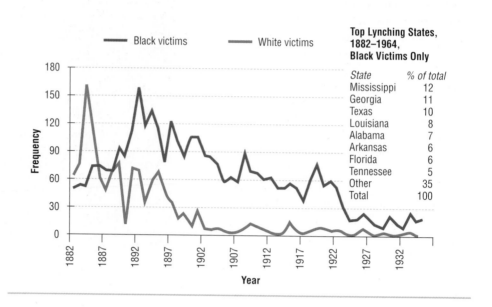

Figure 15.1, which contains data on the annual frequency and geographical distribution of lynching, supports this interpretation. Note first that there were more white than black lynching victims in the first half of the 1880s. That is because, originally, lynching was not just an expression of a racist system of labor control. It was also a means by which people sought quick and brutal justice in areas with little government or police, whatever the alleged criminal's race. Only in 1886 did the number of black victims exceed the number of white victims for the first time. After that, as state control over criminal justice became more widespread, the number of white lynchings continued to decline. The practice was soon used almost exclusively to control blacks.

Second, notice that nearly two-thirds of all lynchings took place in just eight contiguous southern states that formed the center of the cotton industry. Other data show that the great majority of lynchings took place in rural areas, where, of course, cotton is farmed (McAdam, 1982: 89–90). Where cotton was king, lynching was its handmaiden.

Third, observe how the annual number of lynchings rose when the cotton industry's labor supply was most threatened. The peak in black lynchings occurred between 1891 and 1901: an annual average of 112. These were the years when the Populist Party, a coalition of black and white farmers, threatened to radically restructure southern agriculture and eliminate many of the white plantation owners' privileges. More lynching was one reaction to this danger to the traditional organization of agricultural labor. Finally, note that lynching disappeared as a form of collective action when the cotton industry lost its economic significance and its utter dependence on dirt-cheap black labor. Specifically, the organization of the southern cotton industry began to change after 1915 due to mechanization, the mass migration of black workers to jobs in northern industry, and other factors. In 1935, when the cotton industry's economic significance had substantially declined, "only" 18 lynchings of blacks took place. After that, the figure never again reached double digits, finally dropping to zero in 1965.

We conclude that lynching was a two-sided phenomenon. Breakdown theory alerts us to one side. Lynching was partly a reaction to the apparent violation of norms that threatened to *disorganize* traditional social life in the South. However, breakdown theory deflects attention from the other side of collective action. Lynching was also a form of collective action that grew out of, and was intended to maintain, the traditional *organization* of the South's cotton industry. Without that organization, there was no lynching (Soule, 1992; Tolnay and Beck, 1995).

Social Organization and Collective Action

Social disorganization, or the threat of social disorganization, typically accompanies *all* forms of short-lived collective action, not just lynchings. For example, prison riots tend to occur under certain circumstances:

- Government officials make new demands of prison administrators without providing resources to implement them.
- Corrections staff oppose administrative reforms.
- Prison administrators take actions that inmates perceive as unjust or ineffective.
- Inmates develop the belief that living conditions should be better and that rioting will draw public attention to those conditions (Useem and Goldstone, 2002).

These circumstances cause a breakdown in the prison's social order. Riots often result. Yet the study of riots, lynching, and other forms of short-lived collective action also shows that social *organization* underlies all collective action, even its apparently most fleeting and unstructured forms. The sociological study of rumors illustrates the point.

Case Study: Rumors and the Los Angeles Riot

Rumors are claims about the world that are not supported by authenticated information. They are a form of communication that takes place when people try to construct a meaningful interpretation of an ambiguous situation. They are often short-lived, although they may recur (Shibutani, 1966: 17).

Although rumor transmission is a form of collective action in its own right, it typically intensifies just before and during riots. That is because tension and uncertainty about the near future mount at such times. In turn, increased rumor transmission often incites more rioting. Thus, rumors significantly aggravated tensions in about two-thirds of the roughly 300 race riots that rocked American cities between 1964 and 1968. Similarly, rumors inflamed the three-day riot that broke out in Los Angeles in April 1992, when four white police officers from the Los Angeles Police Department were acquitted of the videotaped beating of Rodney King, an unarmed black motorist. The LA riot involved about 45,000 active participants and 100,000 onlookers. Forty-five people were killed and 2,400 were injured. Thirteen thousand police officers arrested 10,000 blacks and Latinos. Insured damage alone totaled $1 billion. Public fears were stoked and rioting intensified when the extent of the violence was initially exaggerated, when word spread that the authorities were using the riot as an excuse for cracking down on illegal immigrants, when firefighters were said to be saving only nonblack businesses, when poor people heard rumors of looting and decided they didn't want to miss the opportunity, and when they heard the police were not responding to the looting (Fine and Turner, 2001: 29–39, 55, 58–9).

Recent analyses link rumors to hope, fear, and anger. *Hope* gives rise to "pipe dreams," a sort of public wish fulfillment. Rumors of the death of Black Muslim leader Louis Farrakhan might serve as a pipe dream for some white Americans. *Fear* gives rise to "bogey rumors." Claims of Farrakhan's death that might circulate in the African American

Rumors: Claims about the world that are not supported by authenticated information. They are a form of communication that takes place when people try to construct a meaningful interpretation of an ambiguous situation. They are often short-lived, although they may recur.

▶FIGURE 15.2
The Social Determinants of Rumors

Source: Adapted from Fine and Turner (2001: 79).

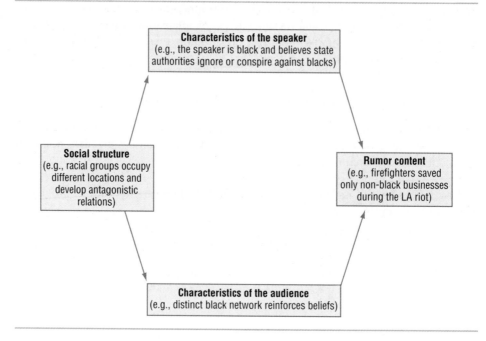

community would qualify as bogey rumors. *Anger* gives rise to "wedge-driving rumors," which divide populations into antagonistic groups. The assertion that Farrakhan's death was due to his being poisoned by white doctors under government orders would constitute a wedge-driving rumor (Fine and Turner, 2001: 64).

Rumors are often false or unverifiable. They seem credible to insiders but preposterous to outsiders. Yet nobody should dismiss them as frivolous. For just as x-rays can reveal flaws in the structure of a bridge, so can a sociological understanding of rumors reveal the distribution of hope, fear, and anger in society and the structural flaws that lie beneath these emotions. For example, there is no evidence to corroborate the rumor that firefighters saved only nonblack businesses during the LA riot. Yet the rumor is a faithful expression of three underlying social facts (▶Figure 15.2). First, blacks and whites occupy different structural locations in American society and, to varying degrees, have developed antagonistic relations (see Chapter 9, "Race and Ethnicity"). Second, antagonism has given rise to the belief among some members of the African American community that white-dominated corporations and state institutions ignore or conspire against them. A third reality reinforces that view: There is little overlap between black and white networks of communication. The absence of much candid talk between the two communities reinforces the beliefs of each community about the other. In the context of these three undeniable social facts, the rumor that firefighters saved only nonblack businesses during the LA riot gained credibility in the African American community, even if it was factually inaccurate.

Summing Up

Our discussion of lynching led us to conclude that collective action is usually more than just a short-term reaction to disorganization and deprivation. Instead, it is often part of a long-term attempt to correct perceived injustice that requires a sound social organizational basis. We now see that a second form of collective action—rumor transmission—is also rooted in the hard facts of social organization. We thus arrive at the starting point of post-1970 theories of collective action and social movements. For more than 30 years, most students of the subject have recognized that we can best understand collective action by focusing on its social-organizational roots.

Social Movements

According to breakdown theory, people usually rebel soon after social breakdown occurs. In this view, rapid urbanization, industrialization, mass migration, unemployment, and war often lead to the buildup of deprivations or the violation of important norms. Under these conditions, people soon take to the streets.

In reality, however, people often find it difficult to turn their discontent into an enduring social movement. Social movements emerge from collective action only when the discontented succeed in building up a more or less stable membership and organizational base. Once that is accomplished, they typically move from an exclusive focus on short-lived actions such as demonstrations to more enduring and routine activities. Such activities include establishing a publicity bureau, founding a newspaper, and running for public office. These and similar endeavors require hiring personnel to work full time on various movement activities. Thus, the creation of a movement bureaucracy takes time, energy, and money. On these grounds alone, one should not expect social breakdown to quickly result in the formation of a social movement.

Solidarity Theory

Research conducted since 1970 shows that, in fact, social breakdown often does not have the expected short-term effect. That is because several social-structural factors modify the effects of social breakdown on collective action. For example, research on strikes, demonstrations, and acts of collective violence in France from 1830 to 1930 shows that episodes of collective action were not correlated with various measures of social breakdown, such as the rate of urban growth and the rate of major crime (Tilly, 1979a; Tilly, Tilly, and Tilly, 1975). Instead, three other variables were associated with episodes of collective action. These three variables hint at the three fundamental lessons of the **solidarity theory** of social movements, a variant of conflict theory (see Chapter 1, "A Sociological Compass") and the most influential approach to the subject since the 1970s.

Resource Mobilization
Collective violence in France increased when the number of union members rose. It decreased when the number of union members fell. Why? Because union organization gave workers more power, and that power increased their capacity to pursue their aims—if necessary, by demonstrating, striking, and engaging in collective violence. We can generalize from the French case as follows: Most collective action is part of a power struggle. The struggle usually intensifies as groups whose members feel disadvantaged become more powerful relative to other groups. How do disadvantaged groups become more powerful? By gaining new members, becoming better organized, and increasing their access to scarce resources, such as money, jobs, and means of communication (Bierstedt, 1974). French unionization is thus only one example of **resource mobilization,** a process by which groups engage in more collective action as their power increases because of their growing size and increasing organizational, material, and other resources (Gamson, 1975; Zald and McCarthy, 1979).

CENGAGENOW™

Learn more about **Unions** by going through the % of Workers That Are Unionized Map Exercise.

Solidarity theory: Holds that social movements are social organizations that emerge when potential members can mobilize resources, take advantage of new political opportunities, and avoid high levels of social control by authorities.

Resource mobilization: The process by which social movements crystallize due to increasing organizational, material, and other resources of movement members.

Political Opportunities

There was somewhat more collective violence in France when national elections were held. Again, why? Because elections gave people new political opportunities to protest. By providing a focus for discontent and a chance to put new representatives with new policies into positions of authority, election campaigns often serve as invitations to engage in collective action. When else do new political opportunities open up for the discontented? Chances for protest also emerge when influential allies offer support, when ruling political alignments become unstable, and when elite groups are divided and come into conflict with one another (Tarrow, 1994: 86–9; Useem, 1998). Said differently, collective action takes place and social movements crystallize not just when disadvantaged groups become more powerful but when privileged groups and the institutions they control are divided and therefore become weaker. This second important insight of solidarity theory links the timing of collective action and social-movement formation to the emergence of new **political opportunities** (McAdam, 1982; Tarrow, 1994).

Social Control

The frequency of collective violence in France fell when governments threw more people into jail for longer periods. This regularity hints at the third main lesson of solidarity theory: Government reactions to protest influence subsequent protest (Box 15.1). In general, governments can try to influence the frequency and intensity of protest by taking various **social control** measures (Oberschall, 1973: 242–83). These measures include making concessions to protesters, co-opting the most troublesome leaders (for example, by appointing them advisers), and violently repressing collective action. In France, more violent protest often resulted in more state repression. The firm and decisive use of force usually stopped protest, but the moderate or inconsistent use of force often backfired. That is because unrest typically intensifies when protesters are led to believe that the government is weak or indecisive (Piven and Cloward, 1977: 27–36; Tilly, Tilly, and Tilly, 1975: 244).

Discussions of strain, deprivation, and contagion dominated analyses of collective action and social movements before 1970. Afterward, analyses of resource mobilization, political opportunities, and social control dominated the field. Let us now make the new ideas more concrete. We do so by analyzing the ups and downs of one of the most important social movements in 20th-century America, the union movement, and its major weapon, the strike.

Case Study: Strikes and the Union Movement in the United States

Workers have traditionally drawn three weapons from the arsenal of collective action to advance their interests: unions, political parties, and strikes. Unions enable groups of workers to speak with one voice and thus to bargain more effectively with their employers for better wages, working conditions, and benefits. The union movement brought us many things we take for granted today, such as the eight-hour day, two-day weekends, health insurance, and pensions. In most of the advanced industrial democracies (although, as we saw in Chapter 13, "Politics, Work, and the Economy," not in the United States), workers have also created and supported labor or socialist parties. Their hope has been that by gaining political influence, they can get laws passed that favor their interests. Finally, when negotiation and political influence get them nowhere, workers have tried to

Political opportunities: Chances for collective action and social-movement growth that emerge during election campaigns, when influential allies offer insurgents support, when ruling political alignments become unstable, and when elite groups become divided and conflict with one another.

Social control: The containment of collective action by co-optation, concessions, and coercion.

BOX 15.1
SOCIAL POLICY: WHAT DO YOU THINK?

Government Surveillance of Social Movements

A public policy debate has emerged over whether the U.S. government should have a free hand to spy on the activities of social movements. The debate was provoked by Osama bin Laden's terrorist network, al Qaeda. Al Qaeda originated in Afghanistan in the 1980s, where it helped radical anti-Western Muslim fundamentalists wage a successful war against the Soviet Union ("Hunting bin Laden," 1999). By 2000, bin Laden had operatives in 60 countries. He often used a satellite phone to communicate with them—until U.S. law enforcement officials revealed that they were tapping his calls. Once he learned of these taps, bin Laden increased his use of another, more effective means of communication: sending messages via the Internet that are easily encrypted but difficult to decode (Kelley, 2001; McCullagh, 2000a). Such messages may have been used to help plan and coordinate the complex, almost simultaneous jet hijackings that resulted in the crash of an airliner in Pennsylvania and the destruction of the World Trade Center and part of the Pentagon on September 11, 2001.

Hiding messages in innocent-looking packages is an old practice made easier by computers (Johnson and Jajodia, 1998). For example, using programs freely available on the Web, one can hide messages inside photographs or MP3 files and then place the files on a publicly accessible website, where they can be downloaded by operatives ("MP3stego," 2001). Such messages have been found in files posted in sports chat rooms and pornography sites, for example.

From the point of view of law enforcement officials, the problem is figuring out how to decode the messages. Supercomputers can be used, but they can take months to decode a single message. That is why some people think we need more government regulation, such as laws requiring that all encryption programs be built with a "backdoor," or an encryption key that would allow officials to read coded messages quickly and easily.

Right-wing free-market organizations oppose this idea. They are wary of giving the government more power to invade people's privacy (McCullagh, 2000b). Opposition may be found on the left, too, because many liberals know that the government has a history of surveillance of popular social movements. For example, the Civil Rights movement, led by Dr. Martin Luther King, Jr., and others, was under constant surveillance by the Federal Bureau of Investigation (FBI) and other law enforcement agencies. Many people now decry the government's attempt to control and even suppress the Civil Rights movement. They worry that government access to backdoors and encryption keys will only enhance its ability to spy on popular American movements and suppress them. Here, then, we face one of democracy's great dilemmas: Democracy empowers both its citizens and its enemies.

Critical Thinking

- Should the government be allowed to increase its surveillance of social movements?

- Increasing government surveillance in general is likely to harm both the enemies of democracy and its champions. But failing to increase government surveillance is likely to help democracy's enemies. How can this dilemma be resolved?

The remains of the twin towers of the World Trade Center, destroyed by terrorists on September 11, 2001.

Neville Elder/CORBIS

North Carolina mill workers on strike, 1934.

AP Photo

extract concessions from employers by withholding their labor. That is, they have gone on strike.

2 July:

Seven hundred police officers storm San Francisco dockworkers who have been on strike for 45 days. Twenty-five people are hospitalized. Two days later, the police charge again, hospitalizing 155 people and killing 2. The National Guard is called in to restore order. An eyewitness describes the funeral procession for the slain strikers as follows:

> *In solid ranks, eight to ten abreast, thousands of strike sympathizers . . . Tramp-tramp-tramp. No noise except that. The band with its muffled drums and somber music . . . On the marchers came—hour after hour—ten, twenty, thirty thousand of them . . . A solid river of men and women who believed they had a grievance and who were expressing their resentments in this gigantic demonstration (quoted in Piven and Cloward, 1977: 125).*

1 September:

More than 375,000 textile workers are on strike. Employers hire armed guards who, with the National Guard, keep the mills open in Alabama, Mississippi, Georgia, and the Carolinas. The governor of Georgia declares martial law and sets up a detention camp for 2,000 strikers. Six strikers are killed in clashes with police in South Carolina. Another 9 are killed elsewhere in the country. This brings the annual total of slain strikers to at least 40. Riots break out in Rhode Island, Connecticut, and Massachusetts, and National Guardsmen are on duty throughout New England.

It was 1934, one of the bloodiest years of collective violence in American history. What spurred the mass insurgency? As we might suspect from our knowledge of resource mobilization theory, an important underlying cause was the rapid growth of the industrial working class over the preceding half century. By 1920, industrial workers made up 40 percent of the American labor force and were central to the operation of the economy. As a result, strikes were never more threatening to political and industrial leaders. On the other hand, workers were not well organized. Until 1933, they did not have the right to bargain collectively with their employers, so fewer than 12 percent of America's nonfarm workers were union members. And they were anything but well-to-do. The economic collapse that began in 1929 brought unemployment to a full third of the workforce and severely depressed the wages of those lucky enough to have jobs.

More than their ability to mobilize organizational and material resources, it was a new law that galvanized industrial workers by opening vast political and economic opportunities for them. In 1932, a nation in despair swept Franklin Delano Roosevelt into the White House. He forged his "New Deal" legislation aimed at ending the Great Depression. One of his early laws was the 1933 National Industrial Recovery Act (NIRA). Section 7(a) of the NIRA specified workers' minimum wages and maximum hours of work. It also gave them the right to form unions and bargain collectively with their employers. Not surprisingly, industrial workers hailed the NIRA as a historic breakthrough. But employers challenged the law in the courts. And so the seesaw was set in motion. First the U.S. Supreme Court invalidated the NIRA. Then Congress reinstated the basic terms of the NIRA by passing the Wagner Act in 1935. Then the Wagner Act was largely ignored in practice. Finally, in 1937, the Supreme Court ruled the Wagner Act constitutional. In the interim, from 1933 to 1937, the promise of the new pro-union laws gave industrial workers new hope and determination. The workers thus armed, open class war rocked America.

From 1933 until the end of World War II, many millions of American workers joined unions. In 1945, unionization reached its historic peak. In that year, 35.5 percent of non-farm employees were union members. Then the figure began to drop. **Union density** (union members as a percentage of nonfarm workers) remained above 30 percent until the early 1960s. By 2007, it stood at a mere 12.1 percent (U.S. Department of Labor, 2000b, 2008b). Today, the United States has the lowest union density of any rich industrialized country. What accounts for the post-1945 drop? Focusing on resource mobilization and political opportunities takes us a long way toward answering that question.

Strikes and Resource Mobilization

The post-1945 drop in union density is partly a result of changes in America's occupational structure. The industrial working class has shrunk and therefore become weaker (Troy, 1986). In 1900, there was roughly one blue-collar (goods-producing) job in America for every white-collar (service-producing) job. By 2000, the blue-collar/white-collar ratio had dropped to about 1:3. These figures show that blue-collar workers are an increasingly rare species. Yet, it is precisely among blue-collar workers that unionism is strongest. True, unionization has increased among government workers. Since the early 1960s, they have enjoyed limited union rights. But this gain has not offset losses due to decline in the size of the industrial working class. Meanwhile, unions have scarcely penetrated the rapidly growing ranks of white-collar workers in the private sector. Usually better educated and higher paid, and with more prestige attached to their occupations than blue-collar workers, American private sector white-collar workers have traditionally resisted unionization.

The industrial working class has also been weakened by globalization and employer hostility to unions. As we saw in Chapter 13 ("Politics, Work, and the Economy"), the globalization of production that began in the 1970s put American blue-collar workers in direct competition for jobs with overseas workers. Employers could now close American

Union density: Union members as a percent of nonfarm workers.

An abandoned factory in East St. Louis. The globalization of production that began in the 1970s put American workers in direct competition for jobs with overseas workers. Employers could relocate factories in Mexico, China, and other countries unless American workers accepted lower wages, fewer benefits, and less job security.

factories and relocate them in Mexico, China, and other countries unless American workers were willing to work for lower wages, fewer benefits, and less job security. American plant closings became increasingly common in the 1970s and 1980s, and unions were often forced to make concessions on wages and benefits. Growing ineffectiveness weakened unions and made them less popular among some workers. In addition, beginning in the 1970s, many American employers began to contest unionization elections legally. They also hired consulting firms in anti-union "information" campaigns aimed at keeping their workplaces union free. In some cases, they used outright intimidation to prevent workers from unionizing. Thus, a decline in organizational resources available to industrial workers was matched by an increase in anti-union resources mobilized by employers (Clawson and Clawson, 1999: 97–103).

Strikes and Political Opportunities

Apart from the erosion of the union movement's mass base, government action has limited opportunities for union growth since the end of World War II. This was evident as early as 1947, when Congress passed the Taft-Hartley Act in reaction to a massive post–World War II strike wave. Unions were no longer allowed to force employees to become members or to require union membership as a condition of being hired. The Taft-Hartley Act also allowed employers to replace striking workers. Unions thus became less effective—and therefore less popular—as vehicles for achieving workers' aims. Taft-Hartley remains the basic framework for industrial relations in the United States.

Resource mobilization theory teaches us that social organization usually facilitates collective action. The opposite also holds. Less social organization typically means less protest. We can see this by examining the frequency of strikes over time.

Comparing historical periods, we see that unusually low union density has helped to virtually extinguish the strike as a form of collective action in the United States.[2] That is apparent from ▶Figure 15.3, which shows the annual number of strikes involving 1,000 or more workers from 1947 to 2007. Between 1947 and 1983, an annual average of 277 big strikes took place. Between 1984 and 2007, an annual average of only 37 big strikes took place. This indicates a major historical shift.

Over the short term, strikes have usually been more frequent during economic booms and less frequent during economic busts (Kaufman, 1982). That is the main reason we see year-to-year fluctuations in strike frequency in Figure 15.3. With more money, more job opportunities, and bigger strike funds in good times, workers can better afford to go out on strike to press their claims than during periods of high unemployment.

However, ▶Figure 15.4 shows that the relationship between unemployment and strike frequency changed after 1983. Thus, the dots representing the years 1948–83 slope downward. This means that whenever unemployment increased, big strikes were less common. In contrast, for the period 1984–2007, a flat line replaces the downward slope. This means that even in good times, workers avoided striking. It seems that, due partly to weak unions, many workers are now unable to use the strike weapon

---

[2]Note, however, that strike activity also tends to be low in countries with *high* levels of unionization. Sweden, for example, has the world's highest union density. Its strike rate is low, because workers and their representatives have been involved in government policymaking since World War II. Decisions about wages and benefits tend to be made in negotiations among unions, employer associations, and governments rather than on the picket line. We conclude that strike activity is highest in countries with intermediate levels of unionization.

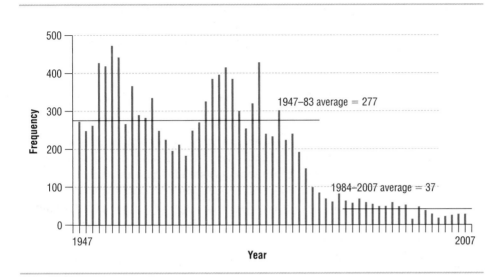

▶FIGURE 15.3
Frequency of Strikes with 1,000+ Workers, United States, 1947–2007

Source: U.S. Department of Labor (2008b).

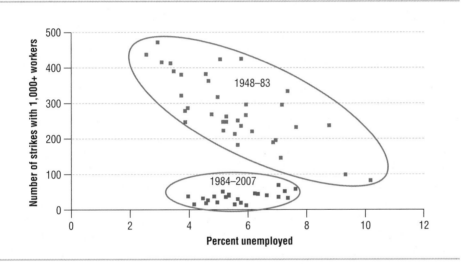

▶FIGURE 15.4
Unemployment and the Frequency of Strikes with 1,000+ Workers, United States, 1948–2007

Source: U.S. Department of Labor (2004b, 2008a, 2008b).

as a means of improving their wages and benefits (Brym, 2009a; Cramton and Tracy, 1998).[3]

Since the mid-1990s, the American Federation of Labor–Congress of Industrial Organizations (AFL-CIO), the largest union umbrella organization in the United States, has sought to reverse the trends in unionization described above. Specifically, it has tried to organize immigrants, introduce more feminist issues into its program in a bid to attract more women, and develop new forms of employee organization and representation that are more appropriate to a postindustrial society. The latter include coalitions with other social movements and councils that bring together all the unions in a city or other

[3]Other important factors making strikes less sensitive to the business cycle since the early 1980s include (1) the willingness of employers to fire strikers and replace them with other workers, thus rendering strikes riskier from the worker's viewpoint (using replacement workers—a practice outlawed in much of western Europe and some Canadian provinces—was legalized in 1938 by the Supreme Court and became widespread after President Ronald Reagan fired the nation's striking air traffic controllers in 1980) and (2) the workers' perception of strikes as riskier since the 1980s, because income-replacing social welfare benefits have been cut.

geographical area (Clawson and Clawson, 1999: 112–15). Whether these strategies will succeed in revitalizing the American union movement is unclear. Figures on union density up to 2007 suggest that they have not yet reversed the downward slide of the union movement.

Framing Discontent

As we have seen, solidarity theory helps explain the emergence of many social movements. Still, the rise of a social movement sometimes takes strict solidarity theorists by surprise. So does the failure of an aggrieved group to press its claims by means of collective action. It seems, therefore, that something lies between (a) the capacity of disadvantaged people to mobilize resources for collective action, and (b) the recruitment of a substantial number of movement members. That "something" is **frame alignment** (Benford, 1997; Goffman, 1974; Snow et al., 1986; Valocchi, 1996). Frame alignment is the process by which social-movement leaders make their activities, ideas, and goals congruent with the interests, beliefs, and values of potential new recruits to their movement. Thanks to the efforts of scholars operating mainly in the symbolic interactionist tradition (see Chapter 1, "A Sociological Compass"), frame alignment has recently become the subject of sustained sociological investigation.

Examples of Frame Alignment

Frame alignment can be encouraged in several ways. First, social-movement leaders can reach out to other organizations that, they believe, contain people who may be sympathetic to their movement's cause. For example, leaders of an antinuclear movement may use the mass media, telephone campaigns, and direct mail to appeal to feminist, antiracist, and environmental organizations. In doing so, they assume that these organizations are likely to have members who would agree at least in general terms with the antinuclear platform.

Second, movement activists can stress popular values that have so far not featured prominently in the thinking of potential recruits. They can also elevate the importance of positive beliefs about the movement and what it stands for. For instance, in trying to win new recruits, movement members might emphasize the seriousness of the social movement's purpose. They might analyze the causes of the problem the movement is trying to solve in a clear and convincing way. Or they might stress the likelihood of the movement's success. By doing so, they can increase the movement's appeal to potential recruits and perhaps win them over to the cause.

Third, social movements can stretch their objectives and activities to win recruits who are not initially sympathetic to the movement's original aims. This may involve a "watering down" of the movement's ideals. Alternatively, movement leaders may decide to take action calculated to appeal to nonsympathizers on grounds that have little or nothing to do with the movement's purpose. When rock, punk, or reggae bands play at nuclear disarmament rallies or gay liberation festivals, it is not necessarily because the music is relevant to the movement's goals. Nor do bands play just because movement members want to be entertained. The purpose is also to attract nonmembers. Once attracted by the music, however, nonmembers may make friends and acquaintances in the movement and then be encouraged to attend a more serious-minded meeting.

As we see, then, there are many ways in which social movements can make their ideas more appealing to a larger number of people. However, movements must also confront the fact that their opponents routinely seek to do just the opposite. That is, whereas movements seek to align their goals, ideas, and activities with the way in which potential

Frame alignment: The process by which individual interests, beliefs, and values are made congruent and complementary with the activities, goals, and ideology of a social movement.

The "Human Rights Now" tour, Los Angeles, 1988. When musicians play at protest rallies, it is not just for entertainment or because the music is relevant to a social movement's goals. It is also a way of framing the movement's goals to make them appealing to nonmembers.

Henry Diltz/CORBIS

recruits frame theirs, their adversaries seek to *disalign* the way issues are framed by movements and potential recruits (Doyle, Elliott, and Tindall, 1997 [1992]) (Box 15.2). Frame alignment should therefore be viewed as a conflict-ridden process in which social-movement partisans and their opponents use all the resources at their disposal to compete for the way in which potential recruits and sympathizers view movement issues.

An Application of Frame Alignment Theory: Back to 1968

Frame alignment theory stresses the face-to-face interaction strategies employed by movement members to recruit nonmembers who are like-minded, apathetic, or even initially opposed to the movement's goals. Resource mobilization theory focuses on the broad social-structural conditions that facilitate the emergence of social movements. One theory usefully supplements the other.

The two theories certainly help clarify the 1968 high school incident described at the beginning of this chapter. In light of our discussion, it seems evident that two main factors prevented Robert Brym from influencing his classmates when he spoke to them about the dangers of industrial pollution from the local pulp and paper mill. First, he lived in a poor and relatively unindustrialized region of Canada where people had few resources they could mobilize on their own behalf. Per capita income and the level of unionization were among the lowest of any state or province in North America. The unemployment rate was among the highest. In contrast, K. C. Irving, who owned the pulp and paper mill, was so powerful that most people in the region could not even conceive of the need to rebel against the conditions of life that he created for them. He owned most of the industrial establishments in the province. Every daily newspaper, most of the weeklies, all of the TV stations, and most of the radio stations were his too. Little wonder one rarely heard a critical word about his operations. Many people believed that Irving could make or break local governments single-handedly. Should one therefore be surprised that mere high school students refused to take him on? In their reluctance, Robert's fellow students were only mimicking their parents, who, on the whole, were as powerless as Irving was mighty (Brym, 1979).

BOX 15.2
SOCIOLOGY AT THE MOVIES

The Day after Tomorrow (2004)

Most summers, Hollywood releases a disaster movie in which a highly implausible catastrophe serves as the backdrop for heroism and hope. Audiences return home momentarily frightened but ultimately safe in the knowledge that the chance of any such cataclysm is vanishingly remote.

The Day after Tomorrow follows the usual script. The movie opens with a sequence of bizarre meteorological events. A section of ice the size of Rhode Island breaks off the Antarctic ice cap. Snow falls in New Delhi. Hail the size of grapefruits pounds Tokyo. Enter Jack Hall (Dennis Quaid), a scientist whose research suggests an explanation: Sudden climate change is a very real possibility. The idea becomes a political football when it is ridiculed by the vice president of the United States, but once torrential rains and a tidal wave flood New York City, Hall's theories are vindicated. In a matter of days, temperatures plummet—at one point, they fall 10 degrees a minute to 150 below zero Fahrenheit. The entire Northern Hemisphere is plunged into a new ice age. Almost everyone freezes to death in the northern United States, while millions of desperate southerners flee to Mexico.

Although it seems like standard fare, *The Day after Tomorrow* is a Hollywood disaster movie with a difference, for it is based on a three-part idea with considerable scientific support. Everyone agrees on part 1: Since the Industrial Revolution, humans have released increasing quantities of carbon dioxide into the atmosphere as we burn more and more fossil fuels to operate our cars, furnaces, and factories. Most scientists agree with part 2: The accumulation of carbon dioxide allows more solar radiation to enter the atmosphere and less heat to escape. This contributes to global warming. As temperatures rise, more water evaporates and the polar ice caps begin to melt. This causes more rainfall, bigger storms, and more flooding. Part 3 is the most recent and controversial part of the argument: The melting of the polar ice caps may be adding enough fresh water to the oceans to disrupt the flow of the Gulf Stream, the ocean current that carries warm water up the east coast of North America and the west coast of Europe. Computer simulations suggest that decreased salinity could push the Gulf Stream southward, causing average winter temperatures to drop by 10 degrees Fahrenheit in the northeastern United States and other parts of the Northern Hemisphere. A recent Pentagon study suggests that such climate change could cause droughts, storms, flooding, border raids, large-scale illegal migration from poor regions, and even war between nuclear powers over scarce food, drinking water, and energy (Joyce and Keigwin, 2004; Stipp, 2003). *The Day after Tomorrow* greatly exaggerates the suddenness and magnitude of what scientists mean by abrupt climate change. "Abrupt" can mean centuries to climatologists, and temperature drops of 10 degrees a minute are pure fantasy. Still, at

Second, many of Robert's classmates did not share his sense of injustice. Most of them regarded Irving as the great provider. They thought his pulp and paper mill, as well as his myriad other industrial establishments, gave many people jobs. They regarded that fact as more important for their lives and the lives of their families than the pollution problem Robert raised. Frame alignment theory suggests that Robert needed to figure out ways of building bridges between their understanding and his. He did not. Therefore, he received an unsympathetic hearing (Box 15.3).

The Future of Social Movements

We can summarize what we have learned about the causes of collective action and social-movement formation with the aid of ▶Figure 15.5 (McAdam, McCarthy, and Zald, 1996; Tarrow, 1994). Breakdown theory partly answers the question of *why* dis-

the movie's core lies an ominous and real possibility.

The Day after Tomorrow also teaches us an important sociological lesson about the framing of issues by social movements and their opponents. Environmental problems do not become social issues spontaneously. They are socially constructed in what might be called a "framing war." Just as Jack Hall and the vice president spar over the credibility of Hall's prediction of sudden climate change, so do groups with different interests dispute all environmental problems, framing them in different ways so as to win over public opinion.

Before environmental issues can enter the public consciousness, policy-oriented scientists, the environmental movement, the mass media, and respected organizations must discover and promote them. Members of the public also have to connect real-life events to the information learned from these groups. On the other hand, some scientists, industrial interests, and politicians inevitably dispute the existence of environmental threats. For example, the big oil-producing states, oil companies, and coal producers deny that global warming is a problem and hire scientists to help them make their case. Consequently, some members of the public have begun to question whether global warming is really an issue. Part of the environmentalists' response involved piggybacking their message on *The Day after Tomorrow.* In the months leading up to the release of the movie, they bombarded journalists with e-mails explaining global warming and offering interviews with leading scientists on the subject. Newspapers and magazines around the world subsequently carried stories on the issue. Environmentalists then distributed flyers to moviegoers leaving theaters (Houpt, 2004). In this way, *The Day after Tomorrow* became not just another disaster movie but part of the framing war around one of the major environmental issues of the day.

The Day after Tomorrow (2004).

20TH CENTURY FOX/THE KOBAL COLLECTION

Critical Thinking

- How important are movies in "framing" social problems and social movements?

- Are people motivated to engage in social or political action by viewing movies?

- How, if at all, have your views been changed by the movies you've seen?

content is sometimes expressed collectively and in nonroutine ways. Industrialization, urbanization, mass migration, economic slowdown, and other social changes often cause dislocations that engender feelings of strain, deprivation, and injustice. Solidarity theory focuses on *how* these social changes may eventually facilitate the emergence of social movements. They may cause a reorganization of social relations, shifting the balance of power between disadvantaged and privileged groups. Solidarity theory also speaks to the question of *when* collective action erupts and social movements emerge. The opening and closing of political opportunities, as well as the exercise of social control by authorities, helps to shape the timing of collective action. Finally, by analyzing the day-to-day strategies employed to recruit nonmembers, frame alignment theory directs our attention to the question of *who* is recruited to social movements. Altogether, then, the theories we have considered provide a comprehensive picture of the why, how, when, and who of collective action and social movements.

Organizing for Change

Try applying solidarity and frame alignment theories to times when *you* felt a deep sense of injustice against an institution such as a school, an organization, a company, or a government.

If you've never been involved in collective action to correct a perceived injustice, try analyzing a movie about collective action using insights gleaned from solidarity and frame alignment theories. A classic is *Norma Rae* (1979), starring Sally Field. Field won the best actress Oscar for her performance as a Southern textile worker who joins with a labor organizer to unionize her mill. Alternatively, see *North Country* (2005), starring Charlize Theron (nominated for the 2005 best actress Oscar), which tells the true story of Lois Jenson, a mineworker who, against much resistance, lodged a successful sexual harassment suit against Eveleth Mines.

WRITING ASSIGNMENT

Write a 500-word essay explaining how you felt at a time when you were moved by a sense of injustice and what actions you took. Did you do anything about your upset? If not, why not? If so, what did you do? Why were you able to act in the way you did? Did you try to get other people to join you in your action? If not, why not? If so, how did you manage to recruit them? Did you reach the goal you set out to achieve? If not, why not? If so, what enabled you to succeed? Alternatively, answer these questions by putting yourself in the place of the heroines in *Norma Rae* or *North Country*.

▶FIGURE 15.5
Determinants of Collective Action and Social-Movement Formation

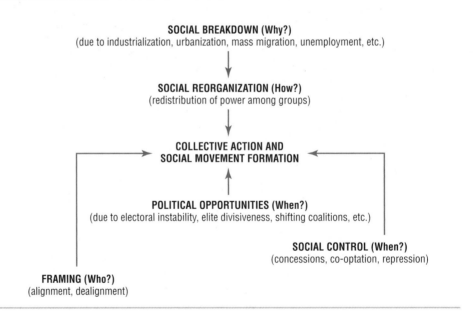

Bearing this summary in mind, we can now turn to this chapter's final goal: sketching the prospects of social movements in broad, rapid strokes. Over the past 300 years, social movements have grown. They first increased in scope from the local to the national level. On the whole, they became less violent. Often, they struggled to expand the rights of citizens, fighting at first for the right to free speech, freedom of religion, and justice before the law; next for the right to vote and run for office; and then, in the twentieth century, for the right to a certain minimum level of economic security and full participation in social

In medieval Europe, social movements were small, localized, and violent. This painting depicts a spontaneous uprising against the nobility in the Beauvais region of France in the mid-14th century.

Bibliotheque Nationale, Paris/SuperStock

life (Marshall, 1965; Tilly, 1979a, 1979b). Other social movements reacted against these attempts to expand the rights of citizens by restricting citizenship rights.

In the 1970s, new social movements set still broader goals, attracted new kinds of participants, and became global in scope (Melucci, 1980, 1995). Let us consider each of these issues in turn.

Goals of New Social Movements

Some new social movements promote the rights not of specific groups but of humanity as a whole to peace, security, and a clean environment. Such movements include the peace movement, the environmental movement, and the human rights movement. Other new social movements, such as the women's movement and the gay rights movement, promote the rights of particular groups that have been excluded from full social participation. Accordingly, gay rights groups have fought for laws that eliminate all forms of discrimination based on sexual orientation. They have also fought for the repeal of laws that discriminate on the basis of sexual orientation, such as anti-sodomy laws and laws that negatively affect parental custody of children. Since the 1960s, the women's movement has succeeded in getting admission practices altered in professional schools, winning more freedom of reproductive choice for women, and opening up opportunities for women in the political, religious, military, educational, medical, and business systems. The emergence of the peace, environmental, human rights, gay rights, and women's movements involves the extension of citizenship rights to all adult members of society and to society as a whole (Roche, 1995; Turner, 1986: 85–105).

Membership in New Social Movements

New social movements are also novel in that they attract a disproportionately large number of highly educated, relatively well-to-do people from the social, educational, and cultural fields. Such people include teachers, professors, journalists, social workers, artists, and student apprentices to these occupations. For several reasons, people in these occupations are more likely to participate in new social movements than are people in other occupations. Their higher education exposes them to radical ideas and makes those ideas appealing. They tend to hold jobs outside the business community, which often opposes their values. And they often become personally involved in the problems of their clients and audiences, sometimes even becoming their advocates (Brint, 1984; Rootes, 1995).

Globalization Potential of New Social Movements

Finally, new social movements increased the scope of protest beyond the national level. For example, members of the peace movement viewed federal laws banning nuclear weapons as necessary. Environmentalists felt the same way about federal laws protecting the environment. However, environmentalists also recognized that the condition of the Brazilian rain forest affects climactic conditions worldwide. Similarly, peace activists understood that the spread of weapons of mass destruction could destroy all of humanity. Therefore, members of the peace and environmental movements pressed for *international* agreements binding all countries to protect the environment and stop the spread of nuclear weapons. Social movements went global.

Inexpensive international travel and communication facilitated the globalization of social movements. New technologies made it easier for people in various national movements to work with like-minded activists in other countries. In the age of CNN, inexpensive jet transportation, fax machines, websites, and e-mail, it was possible not only to see the connection between apparently local problems and their global sources, but to act both locally and globally (Box 15.4).

An Environmental Social Movement

Greenpeace is a highly successful global environmental movement that originated in Vancouver in the mid-1970s and now has offices in 41 countries. Here, Greenpeace activists try to stop a whaling ship.

Consider the case of Greenpeace. Greenpeace is a highly successful environmental movement that originated in Vancouver in the mid-1970s. It now has offices in 41 countries, with its international office in Amsterdam (Greenpeace, 2000). Among many other initiatives, it has mounted a campaign to eliminate the international transportation and dumping of toxic wastes. Its representatives visited local environmental groups in Africa. They supplied the Africans with organizing kits to help them tie their local concerns to global political efforts. They also published a newsletter to keep activists up-to-date on legal issues. Thus, Greenpeace coordinated a global campaign that enabled weak environmental organizations in developing countries to act more effectively. Their campaign also raised the costs of continuing the international trade in toxic waste.

Greenpeace is hardly alone in its efforts to go global. In 1953, 110 international social movement organizations spanned the globe. By 1993, there were 631. About one-fourth were human rights organizations and about one-seventh were environmental organizations. The latter are by far the fastest-growing organizational type (Smith, 1998: 97).

The globalization of social movements can be further illustrated by coming full circle and returning to the anecdote with which we began this chapter. In 1991, Robert Brym visited his hometown. He hadn't been back in years. As he entered the city he vaguely sensed that something was different. "I wasn't able to identify the change until I reached

BOX 15.4
MASS MEDIA AND SOCIETY

Even "old" social movements can go global owing to changes in the technology of mobilizing supporters. In 1994, for example, the peasants of Chiapas, a southern Mexican province, started an uprising against the Mexican government. Oppressed by Europeans and their descendants for nearly 500 years, the poor, indigenous people of southern Mexico were now facing a government edict preventing them from gaining access to formerly communal farmland. They wanted the land for subsistence agriculture. But the government wanted to make sure the land stayed in the hands of large, Hispanic ranchers and farmers, who could earn foreign revenue by exporting goods to the United States and Canada under the terms of the new North American Free Trade Agreement. The peasants seized a large number of ranches and farms. A mysterious masked man known as "Subcomandante Marcos" was their leader. Effectively using the Internet and the international mass media as his secret weapon against the Mexican government,

"The First Postmodern Revolution"

Marcos led what the *New York Times* called "the first postmodern revolution," combining a peasant uprising with the World Wide Web, shortwave radio, and photo spreads in *Marie Claire*. By ingeniously keeping the movement in the international public eye using modern forms of communication, Marcos mobilized support abroad and limited the retaliatory actions of the Mexican government (*A Place Called Chiapas*, 1998; Jones, 1999).

Critical Thinking

- As the number of Internet users increases worldwide, and as personal computers,

Subcomandante Marcos

cellphones, Blackberries, and other network devices proliferate, do opportunities for social movement recruitment, organizing, fundraising, and publicity increase? Or does Internet connectedness tend to distract people from participation in movements for change?

the pulp and paper mill," says Robert. "Suddenly, it was obvious. The rotten egg smell was virtually gone. I discovered that in the 1970s a local woman whose son developed a serious case of asthma took legal action against the mill and eventually won. The mill owner was forced by law to install a 'scrubber' in the main smokestack to remove most of the sulfur dioxide emissions. Soon, the federal government was putting pressure on the mill owner to purify the polluted water that poured out of the plant and into the local river system."

Apparently, local citizens and the environmental movement had caused a deep change in the climate of opinion. This influenced the government to force the mill owner to spend millions of dollars to clean up his operation. It took decades, but what was political heresy in 1968 became established practice by 1991. That is because environmental concerns had been amplified by the voice of a movement that had grown to global proportions. In general, as this case illustrates, globalization helps ensure that many new social movements transcend local and national boundaries and promote universalistic goals.

 ## The Points of the Compass

Although some forms of collective action may seem to break out spontaneously and develop in a free and unstructured way, sociologists have shown that even lynch mobs and riots are constrained by social forces that give them shape and momentum. Social movements are to varying degrees bureaucratized, and pre-existing social ties, patterns of resource distribution, the structure of political opportunities, social control efforts on the part of authorities, and framing efforts on the part of movement members explain much about the course of their development. We also see the constraining pressures of society when examining the history of social movements. The development of social movements from small, localized affairs to national and eventually worldwide phenomena reflects the growth of the state and the globalization of the world. As the social constraints on protest have broadened, so has protest itself.

CHAPTER SUMMARY

1. **Common sense and some sociological theory suggest that lynch mobs, riots, and other forms of collective action are irrational and unstructured actions that take place when people are angry and deprived. Is this view accurate?**

   Deprivation and strain due to rapid social change are generally *not* associated with increased collective action and social-movement formation. Mobs, riots, and other forms of collective action may be wild and violent but social organization and rationality underlie much crowd behavior.

2. **Which aspects of social organization facilitate rebellion against the status quo?**

   People are more inclined to rebel against the status quo when social ties bind them to many other people who feel similarly wronged and when they have the time, money, organization, and other resources needed to protest. In addition, collective action and social-movement formation are more likely to occur when political opportunities allow them. Political opportunities emerge due to elections, increased support by influential allies, the instability of ruling political alignments, and divisions among elite groups.

3. **How do the attempts of authorities to control unrest affect collective action?**

   Authorities' attempts to control unrest influence the timing of collective action. They may offer concessions to insurgents, co-opt leaders, and employ coercion.

4. **What is "framing"?**

   For social movements to grow, members must make the activities, goals, and ideology of the movement congruent with the interests, beliefs, and values of potential new recruits. Doing so is known as "framing."

5. **How have social movements changed in the past three centuries?**

   In 1700, social movements were typically small, localized, and violent. By the mid-20th century, social movements had become typically large, national, and less violent. In the late 20th century, new social movements developed broader goals, recruited more highly educated people, and developed global potential for growth.

6. **How is the history of social movements tied to the struggle for the acquisition of citizenship rights?**

   The history of social movements is a struggle for the acquisition of constantly broadening citizenship rights. These rights include the right to free speech, religion, and justice before the law, the right to vote and run for office, the right to a certain level of economic security and full participation in the life of society, the right of marginal groups to full citizenship, and the right of humanity as a whole to peace and security.

Questions to Consider

1. How would you achieve a political goal? Map out a detailed strategy for reaching a clearly defined aim, such as a reduction in income tax or increased government funding of colleges. Who would you try to recruit to help you achieve your goal? Why? What collective actions do you think would be most successful? Why? To whose attention would these actions be directed? Why? Write a manifesto that frames your argument in a way that is culturally appealing to potential recruits.

2. Do you think that social movements will be more or less widespread in the 21st century than they were in the 20th century? Why or why not? What kinds of social movements are likely to predominate?

Web Resources

CENGAGENOW™

Maximize your study time by using CengageNOW's diagnostic study plan to help you review this chapter. The Study Plan will

- help you identify areas on which you should concentrate;
- provide interactive exercises to help you master the chapter concepts; and
- provide a post-test to confirm you are ready to move on to the next chapter.

The Companion Website for *Sociology: Your Compass for a New World, The Brief Edition*, Enhanced Second Edition

www.cengage.com/sociology/brym

Supplement your review of this chapter by going to the companion website to take one of the tutorial quizzes, use flash cards to master key terms, and check out the many other study aids you'll find there. You'll also find special features such as GSS Data and Census 2000 information that will put data and resources at your fingertips to help you with that special project or help you do some research on your own.

CHAPTER 16

Population, Urbanization, and the Environment

Paul A. Souders/CORBIS

In this chapter, you will learn that:

- Many people think that only natural conditions influence human population growth. However, social forces are important influences too.

- In particular, sociologists have focused on two major social determinants of population growth: industrialization and social inequality.

- Industrialization also plays a major role in causing the movement of people from countryside to city.

- Cities are not as anonymous and alienating as many sociologists once believed them to be.

- The spatial and cultural forms of cities depend largely on the level of development of the societies in which they are found.

- Widespread environmental degradation is the main negative consequence of technological development.

- Policy-oriented scientists, the environmental movement, the mass media, and respected organizations have to discover and promote environmental issues if they are to be framed as social problems. In addition, the public must connect the information learned from these groups to real-life events.

- Economically disadvantaged groups experience more environmental risks than economically advantaged groups.

- Most Americans are not prepared to pay the price of creating a safe environment, but repeated environmental catastrophes could change their minds.

- By helping to make the public aware of environmental and other choices we face in the 21st century, sociology can play an important role in the evolution of human affairs.

The City of God

Rio de Janeiro, Brazil, is one of the world's most beautiful cities. Along the warm, blue waters of its bays lie flawless beaches, guarded by four- and five-star hotels and pricey shops. Rising abruptly behind them is a mountain range, partly populated, partly covered by luxuriant tropical forest. The climate seems perpetually balanced between spring and summer. The inner city of Rio is a place of great wealth and beauty, devoted to commerce and the pursuit of leisure.

Rio is also a large city. With a metropolitan population of more than 12 million people in 2007, it is the 21st biggest metropolitan area in the world, larger than Chicago, Paris, and London (Brinkhoff, 2007). Not all of its 12 million inhabitants are well off, however. Brazil is characterized by more inequality of wealth than almost any other country in the world. Slums started climbing up the hillsides of Rio about a century ago. Fed by a high birthrate and the migration of people from the surrounding countryside in search of a better life, slums are now home to about 20 percent of the city's inhabitants (Jones, 2003).

CENGAGENOW™

This icon signals when CengageNOW has important resources available for you to use in conjunction with the text. See the foldout at the front of this text for information on how to access CengageNOW.

One of Rio de Janeiro's biggest slums.

Some of Rio's slums began as government housing projects designed to segregate the poor from the rich. One such slum, as famous in its own way as the beaches of Copacabana and Ipanema, is Cidade de Deus (the "City of God"). Founded in the 1960s, it became one of the most lawless and dangerous parts of Rio by the 1980s. It is a place where some families of four live on $50 a month in houses made of discarded scraps of wood and tin, a place where roofs leak and rats run freely. For many inhabitants, crime is survival. Drug traffickers wage a daily battle for control of territory, and children as young as 6 perch in key locations with walkie-talkies to feed information to their bosses on the comings and goings of passersby.

Cidade de Deus is a depressing reminder that the closely related problems of population growth and urbanization are more serious now than ever. Brazil's 41 million people in 1940 multiplied to about 180 million in 2004. The country is now more urbanized than the United States, with more than three-quarters of its population living in urban areas (estimated from Lahmeyer, 2003; Ministério de Ciência e Tecnologia Brasil, 2002).

Rapid urbanization and industrialization come with a steep price. In Brazil's case, the steepest price of all is being paid by the country's rain forests, the biggest in the world. The rain forests are sometimes called the world's lungs because they produce so much oxygen and remove so much carbon dioxide from the atmosphere. They are the source of unique species of plants from which many of the world's wonder drugs are derived. The ancient way of life of many aboriginal peoples depends on the rain forests. Yet miners, ranchers, loggers, hydroelectric projects, and the spread of cities are rapidly destroying the rain forests. As their means of existence disappear, the aboriginal peoples of Brazil have become among the most suicide-prone people in the world (Hamlin and Brym, 2006).

This chapter tackles the closely connected problems of population growth, urbanization, and the environment. We first show that population growth is a process governed less by natural laws than by social forces. We argue that these social forces are not related exclusively to industrialization, as social scientists commonly believed just a few decades ago. Social inequality also plays a major role in shaping population growth. We next turn to the problem of urbanization. Today, population growth is typically accompanied by the increasing concentration of the world's people in urban centers. As recently as 40 years ago, sociologists typically believed that cities were alienating and anomic (or normless). We argue that this view is an oversimplification. We also outline the social roots of the city's physical and cultural evolution from preindustrial to postindustrial times. We then outline the main forms of environmental degradation, show how people socially construct environmental problems, and analyze how different classes, race, and nations experience such problems. We conclude by discussing the two major approaches to solving the environmental crisis.

CENGAGENOW™

Learn more about **Population** by going through the Population per Square Mile of Land Map Exercise.

Population

The Population "Explosion"

Ten thousand years before the birth of Christ there were only about 6 million people in the world. By the time Christ was born, world population had risen to 250 million, and it increased to some 760 million by 1750. After that, world population skyrocketed. The number of humans reached 1 billion in 1804 and 5 billion in 1987 (▶Figure 16.1). On July 1, 2008, there were 6.7 billion people in the world according to the U.S. Census Bureau (2008f). Where 1 person stood 12,000 years ago, there are now 1,116 people; statistical projections suggest that by 2100, there will be about 1,667 people. Of those 1,667, 250 will be standing in the rich countries of the world. More than 1,400 of them will be in the developing countries of South America, Asia, and Africa.

Many analysts project that after passing the 10 billion mark around 2100, world population will level off. Indeed, women in North America and Europe are already having fewer babies than are needed to replace the aging populations of those continents, and women in China, Brazil, and other industrializing countries are in the same position (Population Reference Bureau, 2004: 10; Box 16.1). But given the numbers cited previously, is it any wonder that some population analysts say we're now in the midst of a population "explosion"? Explosions are horrifying events. They cause widespread and severe damage. They are fast and unstoppable. And that is exactly the imagery some population analysts, or **demographers,** wish to convey (Ehrlich, 1968; Ehrlich and Ehrlich, 1990) (▶Figure 16.2). Some demographers are frightened enough to refer to overpopulation as catastrophic. They link it to recurrent famine, brutal ethnic warfare, and other massive and seemingly intractable problems.

A "population explosion"? Hong Kong is one of the most densely populated places on Earth.

World population			
1804	1 billion	1999	6 billion
1927	2 billion	2012	7 billion
1960	3 billion	2025	8 billion
1974	4 billion	2040	9 billion
1987	5 billion	2100	10 billion

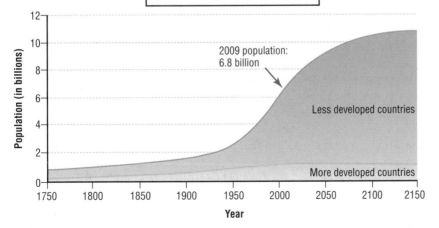

CENGAGENOW™

Learn more about **Demographics** by going through the Three Basic Demographic Processes Animation.

▶FIGURE 16.1
World Population, 1750–2150 (in billions, projected)

Sources: Livi-Bacci (1992: 31); Population Reference Bureau (2008).

Demographers: Social-scientific analysts of human population.

BOX 16.1
SOCIAL POLICY: WHAT DO YOU THINK?

Two main factors are causing the rate of world population growth to fall: economic development and the emancipation of women. Agricultural societies need many children to help farm, but industrial societies require fewer children. Because many countries in the so-called Third World are industrializing, the rate of world population growth is falling apace. The second main factor responsible for the declining growth rate is the improving economic status and education of women. Once women become literate and enter the nonagricultural paid labor force, they quickly recognize the advantages of having few children. The birthrate plummets. In many Third World countries, that is just what is happening. In other Third World countries, the position of women is less satisfactory. We can see this by examining the ratio of women to men, or the **sex ratio** (United Nations, 2000).

In the United States in 2000, the sex ratio was about 1.03; there were 103 women for every 100 men. This is about average for a highly developed country. The surplus of women reflects the fact that men are more likely than women to be employed in occupations that jeopardize their health, consume a lot of cigarettes and alcohol, and engage in riskier and more violent behavior, whereas women are the hardier sex, biologically speaking.

In the world as a whole, the picture is reversed. There were just 98 women for every 100 men in 2000. In India and China,

How Can We Find 100 Million Missing Women?

there were only 94 women for every 100 men. Apart from Asia, North Africa is the region that suffers most from a deficit of women.

What accounts for variation in the sex ratio? According to Amartya Sen (1990, 2001), the sex ratio is low where women have less access to health services, medicine, and adequate nutrition than do men. These factors are associated with high female mortality. Another factor is significant in China and India. In those countries, some parents so strongly prefer sons over daughters that sex-selective abortion contributes to the low sex ratio. Parents who strongly prefer sons over daughters are inclined to abort female fetuses. In contrast, in highly developed countries, women and men have approximately equal access to health services, medicine, and adequate nutrition, and sex-selective abortion is rare. Therefore, there are more women than men. By this standard, the world as a whole is "missing" about 5 women for every 100 men (because 103 − 98 = 5). This works out to about 100 million missing women in 2000.

We can "find" many of the missing 100 million women partly by eliminat-

ing gender inequalities in access to health services, medicine, and adequate nutrition. Increased female literacy and employment in the paid labor force are the most effective paths to eliminating such gender inequalities. That is because literate women who work in the paid labor force are in a stronger position to demand equal rights.

The question of how to eliminate sex-selective abortion is more difficult. Economic factors do not account for variations in sex-selective abortion. In some parts of Asia with high levels of female education and economic participation, sex-selective abortion is relatively common. In other parts of Asia with low levels of female education and economic participation, sex-selective abortion is relatively rare. The best explanation for variations in sex-selective abortion seems to be that preference for sons is a strong *cultural* tradition in some parts of Asia. In India, for example, it may not be coincidental that sex-selective abortion is most widespread in the North and the West, where the nationalist and fundamentalist-Hindu BJP (Bharatiya Janata party) is most popular. Hindu nationalism and religious fundamentalism may feed into a strong preference for sons over daughters.

Critical Thinking

● Bearing in mind that cultural and religious traditions do not easily give way to economic forces, can reformers inside and outside the region rectify the situation? If so, how?

Sex ratio: The ratio of women to men in a geographical area.

If this imagery makes you feel that the world's rich countries must do something about overpopulation, you're not alone. In fact, concern about the population "bomb" is as old as the social sciences. In 1798, Thomas Robert Malthus, a British clergyman of the Anglican faith, proposed a highly influential theory of human population (Malthus, 1966 [1798]). As you will soon see, contemporary sociologists have criticized, qualified, and in part rejected his theory. But because much of the sociological study of population is, in effect, a debate with Malthus's ghost, we must confront the man's ideas squarely.

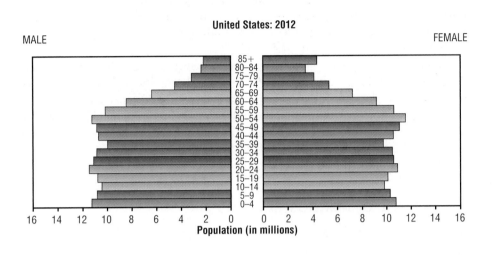

United States: 2012

MALE   FEMALE

Population (in millions)

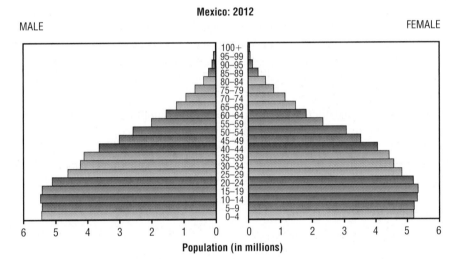

Mexico: 2012

MALE   FEMALE

Population (in millions)

▶FIGURE 16.2
How Demographers Analyze Population Change and Composition

The main purpose of demography is to figure out why the size, geographical distribution, and social composition of human populations change over time. The basic equation of population change is $P2 = P1 + B - D + I - E$, where P2 is population size at a given time, P1 is population size at an earlier time, B is the number of births in the interval, D is the number of deaths in the interval, I is the number of immigrants arriving in the interval, and E is the number of emigrants leaving in the interval. One basic tool for analyzing the composition of a population is the "age-sex pyramid," which shows the number of males and females in each age cohort of the population at a given point in time. Age-sex pyramids for the U.S. and Mexico are shown here, projected by the U.S. Census Bureau for 2012. Why do you think they look so different? Compare your answer to that of the theory of the demographic transition, discussed in the text.

Source: U.S. Census Bureau (2008d).

Theories of Population Growth

The Malthusian Trap

Malthus's theory rests on two undeniable facts and a questionable assumption. The facts: People must eat, and they are driven by a strong sexual urge. The assumption: Whereas food supply increases slowly and arithmetically (1, 2, 3, 4, etc.), population size grows quickly and geometrically (1, 2, 4, 8, etc.). Based on these ideas, Malthus concluded that "the superior power of population cannot be checked without producing misery or vice" (Malthus, 1966 [1798]: 217–18.) Specifically, only two forces can hold population growth in check. First are "preventive" measures, such as abortion, infanticide, and prostitution. Malthus called these "vices" because he morally opposed them and thought everyone else should too. Second are "positive checks" such as war, pestilence, and famine. Malthus recognized that positive checks create much suffering. Yet he felt that they are the only forces that can be allowed to control population

Albrecht Dürer, *The Four Horsemen of the Apocalypse* (woodcut, 1498). According to Malthus, only war, pestilence, and famine can keep population growth in check.

Scala/Art Resource, NY

CENGAGENOW™

Learn more about the **Malthusian Trap** by going through the Malthusian Perspective Learning Module.

growth. Here, then, is the so-called **Malthusian trap:** a cycle of population growth followed by an outbreak of war, pestilence, or famine that keeps population growth in check. Population size might fluctuate, said Malthus, but it has a natural upper limit that western Europe has reached.

Although many people supported Malthus's theory, others reviled him as a misguided prophet of doom and gloom (Winch, 1987). For example, people who wished to help the poor disagreed with Malthus. He felt that such aid was counterproductive. Welfare, he said, would enable the poor to buy more food. With more food, they would have more children. And having more children would only make them poorer than they already were. Better leave them alone, said Malthus. That will reduce the sum of human suffering in the world.

A Critique of Malthus

Although in some respects compelling, events have cast doubt on several of Malthus's ideas.

- Since Malthus proposed his theory, technological advances have allowed rapid growth in how much food is produced for each person on the planet. This is the opposite of the slow growth Malthus predicted. Moreover, except for Africa south of the Sahara, the largest increases in the food supply are taking place in the developing countries (Sen, 1994).

- If, as Malthus claimed, there is a natural upper limit to population growth, it is unclear what that limit is. Malthus thought that the population couldn't grow much larger in late 18th-century western Europe without "positive checks" coming into play. Yet the western European population increased from 187 million people in 1801 to 321 million in 1900. It has now stabilized at about half a billion (McNeill, 1990). The western European case suggests that population growth has an upper limit far higher than that envisaged by Malthus.

- Population growth does not always produce misery. For example, despite its rapid population increase over the past 200 years, western Europe is one of the most prosperous regions in the world.

- Helping the poor does not generally result in the poor having more children. For example, in western Europe, social welfare policies (unemployment insurance, state-funded medical care, paid maternity leave, pensions, etc.) are the most generous on the planet. Yet the size of the population is quite stable. In fact, as you will learn in the following, some forms of social welfare produce rapid and large decreases in population growth, especially in the poor, developing countries.

- Although the human sexual urge is as strong as Malthus thought, people have developed contraceptive devices and techniques to control the consequences of their sexual activity (Szreter, 1996). There is no necessary connection between sexual activity and childbirth.

The developments listed here all point to one conclusion. Malthus's pessimism was overstated. Human ingenuity seems to have enabled us to wriggle free of the Malthusian trap, at least for the time being.

We are not, however, home free. Today there are renewed fears that industrialization and population growth are putting severe strains on the planet's resources. We must take

Malthusian trap: A cycle of population growth followed by an outbreak of war, pestilence, or famine that keeps population growth in check.

these fears seriously. It is encouraging to learn that the limits to growth are as much social as natural, and therefore avoidable rather than inevitable. However, as you will see, the environmental issues we face are so serious that our ability to avoid the Malthusian trap in the 21st century will require all the ingenuity and self-sacrifice we can muster.

Demographic Transition Theory

The second main theory of population growth is the theory of the demographic transition. According to **demographic transition theory,** the main factors underlying population dynamics are industrialization and the growth of modern cultural values (Chesnais, 1992 [1986]; Coale, 1974) (▶Figure 16.3). The theory is based on the observation that the European population developed in four distinct stages.

The Preindustrial Period

In the first, preindustrial stage of growth, a large proportion of the population died every year due to inadequate nutrition, poor hygiene, and uncontrollable disease. In other words, the crude deathrate was high. The **crude deathrate** is the annual number of deaths (or *mortality*) per 1,000 people in a population. During this period, the crude birthrate was high too. The **crude birthrate** is the annual number of live births per 1,000 people in a population. In the preindustrial era, most people wanted to have as many children as possible. That was partly because relatively few children survived until adulthood. In addition, children were considered a valuable source of agricultural labor and a form of old age security in a society consisting largely of peasants and lacking anything resembling a modern welfare state.

The Early Industrial Period

The second stage of European population growth was the early industrial, or transition, period. At this stage, the crude deathrate dropped. People's life expectancy, or average life span, increased because economic growth led to improved nutrition and hygiene.

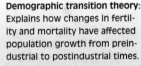

Demographic transition theory: Explains how changes in fertility and mortality have affected population growth from preindustrial to postindustrial times.

Crude deathrate: The annual number of deaths per 1,000 people in a population.

Crude birthrate: The annual number of live births per 1,000 women in a population.

▶FIGURE 16.3
Demographic Transition Theory

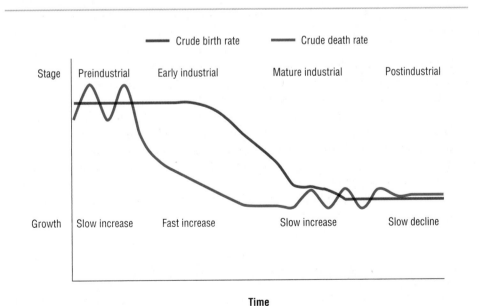

However, the crude birthrate remained high. With people living longer and women having nearly as many babies as in the preindustrial era, the population grew rapidly. Malthus lived during this period of rapid population growth, and that accounts in part for his alarm.

The Mature Industrial Period

The third stage of European population growth was the mature industrial period. At this stage, the crude deathrate continued to fall. The crude birthrate fell even more dramatically because economic growth eventually changed people's traditional beliefs about the value of having many children. Having lots of children made sense in an agricultural society, where children were a valuable economic resource. In contrast, children were more of an economic burden in an industrial society, because breadwinners worked outside the home for a wage or a salary and children contributed little if anything to the economic welfare of the family. Note, however, that the crude birthrate took longer to decline than the crude deathrate did. That is because people's values often change more slowly than their technologies. People can put in a sewer system or a water purification plant to lower the crude deathrate faster than they can change their minds about something as fundamental as how many children to have.

Eventually, however, the technologies and outlooks that accompany modernity led people to postpone getting married and to use contraceptives and other birth-control methods. As a result, population stabilized during the mature industrial period. This demonstrates the validity of one of the demographer's favorite sayings: "Economic development is the best contraceptive."

The Postindustrial Period

The **total fertility rate** is the average number of children that would be born to a woman over her lifetime if she had the same number of children as women in each age cohort in a given year. In the last decades of the 20th century, the total fertility rate continued to fall. In fact, it fell below the replacement level in some countries. The **replacement level** is the number of children each woman must have on average for population size to remain stable. Ignoring any inflow of settlers from other countries (**immigration,** or **in-migration**) and any outflow to other countries (**emigration,** or **out-migration**), the replacement level is 2.1. This means that on average, each woman must give birth to slightly more than the two children needed to replace her and her mate. Slightly more than two children are required because some children die before they reach reproductive age.

By the 1990s, some Europeans were worrying about declining fertility and its possible effects on population size. Dozens of countries, most of them in Europe, now have fertility rates below 1.5, and nearly half the world's population lives in countries with fertility rates below the replacement level. The United States is among them, with a fertility rate of 2.1 in 2008. Because of the proliferation of low-fertility societies, some countries have now entered a fourth, postindustrial stage of population development. In this fourth stage of the demographic transition, the number of deaths per year exceeds the number of births (Van de Kaa, 1987).

A Critique of Demographic Transition Theory

As outlined earlier, demographic transition theory provides a rough picture of how industrialization affects population growth. However, research has revealed a number of inconsistencies in the theory, most of them due to its overemphasis on industrialization

Total fertility rate: The average number of children that would be born to a woman over her lifetime if she had the same average number of children as women in each age cohort in a given year.

Replacement level: The number of children that each woman must have on average for population size to remain stable. Ignoring any inflow of population from other countries and any outflow to other countries, the replacement level is 2.1.

Immigration: Or in-migration; the inflow of people into one country from one or more other countries and their settlement in the destination country.

Emigration: Or out-migration; the outflow of people from one country and their settlement in one or more other countries.

as the main force underlying population growth (Coale and Watkins, 1986). For example, demographers have found that reductions in fertility sometimes occur when standards of living stagnate or decline, not just when they improve due to industrialization. Thus, in Russia and some developing countries today, declining living standards have led to a deterioration in general health and a subsequent decline in fertility. Because of such findings, many scholars have concluded that an adequate theory of population growth must pay more attention to social factors other than industrialization, and in particular to the role of social inequality.

Population and Social Inequality

Karl Marx

One of Malthus's staunchest intellectual opponents was Karl Marx, who argued that the problem of overpopulation is specific to capitalism (Meek, 1971). In his view, overpopulation is not a problem of too many people. Instead, it is a problem of too much poverty. Do away with the exploitation of workers, said Marx, and poverty will disappear. If a society is rich enough to eliminate poverty, then by definition its population is not too large. By eliminating poverty, one also solves the problem of overpopulation in Marx's view.

Marx's analysis makes it seem that capitalism can never generate enough prosperity to solve the overpopulation problem. He was evidently wrong. Overpopulation is not a serious problem in the United States or Japan or Germany today.[1] It *is* a problem in most of Africa, where capitalism is weakly developed and the level of social inequality is much higher than in the postindustrial societies. Still, a core idea in Marx's analysis of the overpopulation problem rings true. As some contemporary demographers argue, social inequality is a main cause of overpopulation. In the following, we illustrate this argument by first considering how gender inequality influences population growth. Then we discuss the effects of class inequality on population growth.

Gender Inequality and Overpopulation

The effect of gender inequality on population growth is well illustrated by the case of Kerala (pronounced "CARE-a-la"), a state in India with more than 30 million people. Kerala had a total fertility rate of 1.8 in 1991, half of India's national rate and less than the replacement level of 2.1. How did Kerala achieve this remarkable feat? Is it a highly industrialized oasis in the midst of a semi-industrialized country, as one might expect given the arguments of demographic transition theory? To the contrary, Kerala is not highly industrialized. In fact, it is among the poorer Indian states, with a per capita income less than the national average. Has the government of Kerala enforced a state childbirth policy similar to China's? The Chinese government strongly penalizes families that have more than one child—second children are not allowed to attend university, for example—and it allows abortion when a woman is 8½ months pregnant (Wordsworth, 2000). As a result, China had a total fertility rate of just 2.0 in 1992 and 1.7 in 2003. In Kerala, however, the government keeps out of its citizens' bedrooms. The decision to have children remains a strictly private affair.

The women of Kerala achieved a low total fertility rate because their government purposely and systematically raised their status over a period of decades (Franke and

---

[1] However, because Americans in particular consume so much energy and other resources, we have a substantial negative impact on the global environment. (Americans comprise about 4 percent of the world's population and consume nearly one-fourth of its natural resources.)

Chasin, 1992; Sen, 1994). The government helped to create a realistic alternative to a life of continuous childbearing and child rearing and helped women understand that they could achieve that alternative if they wanted to. In particular, the government organized successful campaigns and programs to educate women, increase their participation in the paid labor force, and make family planning widely available. These government campaigns and programs resulted in Keralan women enjoying the highest literacy rate, labor force participation rate, and rate of political participation in India. Given their desire for education, work, and political involvement, most Keralan women want small families, so they use contraception to prevent unwanted births. Thus, by lowering the level of gender inequality, the government of Kerala solved its overpopulation problem. In general:

> [where] women tend to have more power[, their society has] low rather than high mortality and fertility. Education and employment, for example, often accord women wider power and influence, which enhance their status. But attending school and working often compete with childbearing and child rearing. Women may choose to have fewer children in order to hold a job or increase their education (Riley, 1997).

Class Inequality and Overpopulation

Unraveling the Keralan mystery is an instructive exercise. It establishes that population growth depends not just on a society's level of industrialization but also on its level of gender inequality. *Class* inequality influences population growth too. We turn to the South Korean case to illustrate this point.

In 1960 South Korea had a total fertility rate of 6.0. Yet by 1989, South Korea's total fertility rate had dropped to a mere 1.6. By 2003 it fell to 1.3. Why? The first chapter in this story involves land reform, not industrialization. The government took land from big landowners and gave it to small farmers. Consequently, the standard of living of small farmers improved. This eliminated a major reason for high fertility. Once economic uncertainty decreased, so did the need for child labor and support of elderly parents by adult offspring. Soon, the total fertility rate began to fall. Subsequent declines in the South Korean total fertility rate were due to industrialization, urbanization, and the higher educational attainment of the population. But a decline in class inequality in the countryside first set the process in motion (Lie, 1998).

The reverse is also true. Increasing social inequality can lead to overpopulation, war, and famine. For example, in the 1960s the governments of El Salvador and Honduras encouraged the expansion of commercial agriculture and the acquisition of large farms by wealthy landowners. The landowners drove peasants off the land. The peasants migrated to the cities. There they hoped to find employment and a better life. Instead, they often found squalor, unemployment, and disease. Suddenly, two countries with a combined population of less than 5 million people had a big "overpopulation" problem. Competition for land increased and contributed to rising tensions. This eventually led to the outbreak of war between El Salvador and Honduras in 1969 (Durham, 1979).

Summing Up

A new generation of demographers has begun to explore how class and gender inequality affect population growth (Seccombe, 1992; Szreter, 1996). Their studies drive home the point that population growth and its negative consequences do not stem from natural causes (as Malthus held). Nor are they only responses to industrialization and modernization (as demographic transition theory suggests). Instead, population growth is influenced by a variety of social causes, social inequality chief among them.

Some undoubtedly well-intentioned Western analysts continue to insist that people in the developing countries should be forced to stop multiplying at all costs. Some observers even suggest diverting scarce resources from education, health, and industrialization into various forms of birth control, including, if necessary, forced sterilization (Riedmann, 1993). They regard the presumed alternatives—poverty, famine, war, ethnic violence, and the growth of huge, filthy cities—as too horrible to contemplate. However, they fail to see how measures that lower social inequality help to control overpopulation and its consequences. Along with industrialization, lower levels of social inequality cause total fertility rates to fall.

Urbanization

We have seen that overpopulation remains a troubling problem due to lack of industrialization and too much gender and class inequality in much of the world. We may now add that overpopulation is in substantial measure an *urban* problem. Driven by lack of economic opportunity and by political unrest and other factors in the countryside, many millions of people flock to big cities in the world's poor countries every year. Thus, most of the fastest-growing cities in the world today are in semi-industrialized countries where the factory system is not highly developed. As ▶Table 16.1 shows, in 1900, 9 of the 10 biggest cities in the world were in industrialized Europe and the United States. By 2015, 6 of the world's 10 biggest cities will be in Asia, 2 will be in Africa, and 2 will be in Latin America. Only 1 of the 10 biggest cities—Tokyo—will be in a highly industrialized country. Clearly, the developing countries are urbanizing at a faster rate than the highly industrialized countries (United Nations, 1997; ▶Figure 16.4).

◀ Mexico City during one of its frequent smog alerts.

Christopher Morris/Black Star Publishing

▶TABLE 16.1

World's 10 Largest Metropolitan Areas, 1900 and 2015,
Projected (in millions)

1900		2015	
London, England	6.5	Tokyo, Japan	28.7
New York, USA	4.2	Mumbai (Bombay), India	27.4
Paris, France	3.3	Lagos, Nigeria	24.4
Berlin, Germany	2.4	Shanghai, China	23.4
Chicago, USA	1.7	Jakarta, Indonesia	21.2
Vienna, Austria	1.6	São Paulo, Brazil	20.8
Tokyo, Japan	1.5	Karachi, Pakistan	20.6
Saint Petersburg, Russia	1.4	Beijing, China	19.4
Philadelphia, USA	1.4	Dhaka, Bangladesh	19.0
Manchester, England	1.3	Mexico City, Mexico	18.8

Sources: Department of Geography, Slippery Rock University (1997, 2003).

From the Preindustrial to the Industrial City

To a degree, urbanization results from industrialization. Many great cities of the world grew up along with the modern factory, which drew hundreds of millions of people out of the countryside and transformed them into urban, industrial workers. Industrialization is not, however, the whole story behind the growth of cities. As we have just seen, the connection between industrialization and urbanization is weak in the world's less developed countries today. Moreover, cities first emerged in Syria, Mesopotamia, and Egypt 5,000 or 6,000 years ago, long before the growth of the modern factory. These early cities served as centers of religious worship and political administration. Similarly, it was not industry but international trade in spices, gold, cloth, and other precious goods that stimulated the growth of cities in preindustrial Europe and the Middle East. Thus, the correlation between urbanization and industrialization is far from perfect (Bairoch, 1988 [1985]; Mumford, 1961).

Preindustrial cities differed from those that developed in the industrial era in several ways. Preindustrial cities were typically smaller, less densely populated, built within protective walls, and organized around a central square and places of worship. The industrial cities that began to emerge at the end of the 18th century were more dynamic and com-

▶FIGURE 16.4

Population Distribution in the United States

If you were circling the Earth in a satellite on a clear night, the United States would look like this map, in which each dot of light represents 7,500 people. The dense clusters of light are the most urbanized areas.

Source: U.S. Census Bureau (2003b).

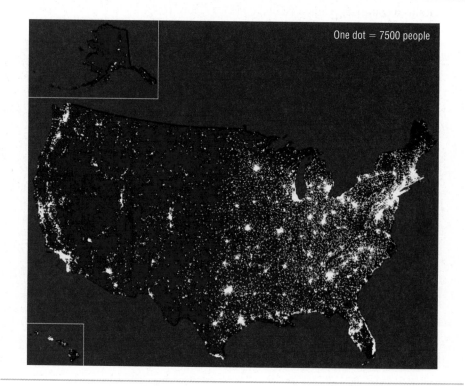

One dot = 7500 people

plex social systems requiring new means of mass communication. A host of social problems, including poverty, pollution, and crime, also accompanied the growth of the industrial city. The complexity, dynamism, and social problems of the new city were all evident in Chicago at the turn of the 20th century. Not surprisingly, therefore, it was at the University of Chicago that American urban sociology was born.

Carcassonne, France, a medieval walled city.

The Chicago School and the Industrial City

From the first decade of the 20th century to the 1930s, the members of the **Chicago school** of sociology distinguished themselves by their vividly detailed descriptions and analyses of urban life, backed up by careful in-depth interviews, surveys, and maps showing the distribution of various features of the social landscape, all expressed in plain yet evocative language (Lindner, 1996 [1990]). Three of its leading members, Robert Park, Ernest Burgess, and Roderick McKenzie, proposed a theory of **human ecology** to illuminate the process of urbanization (Park, Burgess, and McKenzie, 1967 [1925]). Borrowing from biology and ecology, the theory highlights the links between the physical and social dimensions of cities and identifies the dynamics and patterns of urban growth.

The Concentric Zone Model

The theory of human ecology, as applied to urban settings, holds that cities grow in ever-expanding concentric circles. It is sometimes called the "concentric zone model" of the city. Three social processes animate this growth (Hawley, 1950). **Differentiation** is the process by which urban populations and their activities become more complex and heterogeneous over time. For instance, a small town may have a diner, a pizza parlor, and a Chinese restaurant. But if that small town grows into a city, it will likely boast a variety of ethnic restaurants reflecting its more heterogeneous population. Moreover, in a city, members of different ethnic and racial groups and socioeconomic classes may enter into **competition** with one another for dominance in particular areas. For instance, businesses may try to push residents out of certain areas to establish commercial zones. Finally, **ecological succession** takes place when a distinct group of people moves from one area to another and another group moves into the old area to replace the first group. For example, a recurrent pattern of ecological succession involves members of the middle class moving to the suburbs, with working-class and poor immigrants moving into the inner city from the countryside, other regions, or abroad. In Chicago in the 1920s, differentiation, competition, and ecological succession resulted in the zonal pattern illustrated by ▶Figure 16.5.

Urbanism: A Way of Life

For members of the Chicago school, the city was more than just a collection of socially segregated buildings, places, and people. It also involved a way of life they called **urbanism.** They defined urbanism as "a state of mind, a body of customs[,] . . . traditions, . . . attitudes and sentiments" specifically linked to city dwelling (Park, Burgess, and McKenzie, 1967 [1925]: 1). Louis Wirth (1938) developed this theme, building on the work of 19th-century German sociologist Ferdinand Tönnies (1988 [1887]). Tönnies had distinguished community from society (in German, *Gemeinschaft* and *Gesselschaft,* respectively). In his view, communities are bound together by emotionally rich, intimate social ties, while societies are bound together mainly by self-interest.

Chicago school: Group of researchers in the first decades of the 20th century who founded urban sociology in the United States. Its members distinguished themselves by their vivid and detailed descriptions and analyses of urban life and their development of the theory of human ecology.

Human ecology: A theoretical approach to urban sociology that borrows ideas from biology and ecology to highlight the links between the physical and social dimensions of cities and identify the dynamics and patterns of urban growth.

Differentiation: In human-ecology theory, the process by which urban populations and their activities become more complex and heterogeneous over time.

Competition: In human-ecology theory, the struggle by different groups for optimal locations in which to reside and set up their businesses.

Ecological succession: In human-ecology theory, the process by which a distinct urban group moves from one area to another and a second group comes in to replace the group that has moved out.

Urbanism: A way of life that, according to Louis Wirth, involves increased tolerance but also emotional withdrawal and specialized, impersonal, and self-interested interaction.

▶FIGURE 16.5
The Concentric Zone Model of Chicago, about 1920

Source: From "The Growth of the City: An Introduction to a Research Project," Ernest W. Burgess, pp. 47–62 in *The City* by Robert E. Park et al. Copyright © 1967 University of Chicago Press. Used with permission.

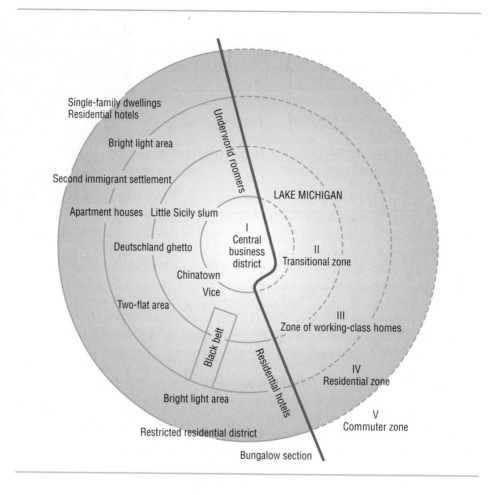

Similarly, Wirth held that rural community life involves frequent face-to-face inter-action among few people. Most of these people are familiar with each other, share common values and a collective identity, and strongly respect traditional ways of doing things. Urban life, in contrast, involves the absence of community and of close personal relationships. Extensive exposure to many socially different people leads city dwellers to become more tolerant than rural folk are, said Wirth. However, urban dwellers also withdraw emotionally and reduce the intensity of their social interaction with others. In Wirth's view, interaction in cities is therefore superficial and impersonal and is focused on specific goals. People become more individualistic. Weak social con-trol leads to a high incidence of deviance and crime.

After Chicago: A Critique

The Chicago school dominated American urban sociology for decades. It still inspires much interesting research (e.g., Anderson, 1991). However, three major criticisms of this approach to understanding city growth have gained credibility over the years.

One criticism focuses on Wirth's characterization of the "urban way of life." Research shows that social isolation, emotional withdrawal, stress, and other problems may be just as common in rural as in urban areas (Crothers, 1979; Webb and Collette, 1977, 1979). After all, in a small community a person may not be able to find anyone with whom to

The Mass Media and the Establishment of Community

Since their origins, the mass media have been used to help turn individuals into communities—first urban, then national, and most recently virtual.

As societies urbanized, the number of institutions, roles, and people increased. Face-to-face interaction became less viable as a means of communication. New ways of coordinating the operation of the various parts of society were required. People in Maine must have at least a general sense of what is happening in California and they need to share certain basic values with Californians if they are going to feel that they are citizens of the same country. The nationwide distribution of newspapers, magazines, movies, and TV shows binds together the large,

socially diverse, and geographically dispersed population of the United States. Fundamentally, the nation is an imagined community, and the mass media make it possible for us to imagine it (Anderson, 1990).

The Internet lifted community out of its geographical context, allowing the formation of various types of associations—chat rooms, discussion groups, multiple-user dimensions, and so forth—on the basis of interest rather than physical proximity. New forms of community have thus been layered on top of old ones as the mass media have conquered space and time.

Critical Thinking

- How are traditional communities the same as, and different from, virtual communities on the Internet?

- In light of these similarities and differences, do you think it is fair to say that, overall, Americans' involvement in community life has weakened over time? Why or why not?

---

share a particular interest or passion. Moreover, farmwork can be every bit as stressful as work on an assembly line. Research also shows that urban life is less impersonal, anomic, and devoid of community than the Chicago sociologists made it appear. True, newcomers (of whom there were admittedly many in Chicago in the 1920s) may find city life bewildering, if not frightening. Neighborliness and friendliness to strangers are less common in cities than in small communities (Fischer, 1981). However, even in the largest cities, most residents create social networks and subcultures that serve functions similar to those performed by the small community. Friendship, kinship, ethnic and racial ties, as well as work and leisure relations, form the bases of these urban networks and subcultures (Fischer, 1984 [1976]; Wellman, 1979). Cities, it turns out, are clusters of many different communities. Sociologist Herbert Gans found such a rich assortment of close social ties in his research on Italian Americans that he was prompted to call them "urban villagers" (Gans, 1962; Box 16.2).

A second major criticism of the Chicago school's approach to urban sociology focuses on the concentric zone model. The specific patterns discovered by the Chicago sociologists are most applicable to American industrial cities in the first quarter of the 20th century. After the automobile became a major means of transportation, some American cities expanded not in concentric circles but in wedge-shaped sectors along natural boundaries and transportation routes (Hoyt, 1939). Others grew up around not one but many nuclei, each attracting similar kinds of activities and groups (Harris and Ullman, 1945). Recent models of urban growth emphasize the expansion of services from the city core to the city periphery, aided by the construction of radial highways (Harris, 1997; ▶Figure 16.6).

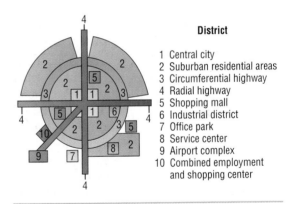

District

1 Central city
2 Suburban residential areas
3 Circumferential highway
4 Radial highway
5 Shopping mall
6 Industrial district
7 Office park
8 Service center
9 Airport complex
10 Combined employment and shopping center

▶FIGURE 16.6
The Peripheral Model of Cities

Source: Harris (1997).

The *corporate* city: New York.

The third main criticism of the human ecology approach is that it presents urban growth as an almost natural process, slighting its historical, political, and economic foundations in capitalist industrialization. The Chicago sociologists' analysis of competition in the transitional zone came closest to addressing this criticism. However, their discussions of differentiation and ecological succession made the growth of cities seem almost like a force of nature rather than a process rooted in power relations and the urge to profit.

The Conflict View and New Urban Sociology

The so-called **new urban sociology,** heavily influenced by conflict theory, sought to correct this problem (Gottdiener and Hutchison, 2000 [1994]; Zukin, 1980). For new urban sociologists, urban space is not just an arena for the unfolding of social processes like differentiation, competition, and ecological succession. Instead, they see urban space as a set of *commodified* social relations. That is, urban space, like all commodities, can be bought and sold for profit. As a result, political interests and conflicts shape the growth pattern of cities. John Logan and Harvey Molotch (1987), for example, portray cities as machines fueled by a "growth coalition." This growth coalition comprises investors, politicians, businesses, property owners, real estate developers, urban planners, the mass media, professional sports teams, cultural institutions, labor unions, and universities. All these partners try to obtain government subsidies and tax breaks to attract investment dollars. Reversing the pattern identified by the Chicago sociologists, this investment has been used to redevelop decaying downtown areas in many American cities since the 1950s.

According to Logan and Molotch, members of the growth coalition present redevelopment as a public good that benefits everyone. This tends to silence critics, prevent discussions of alternative ideas and plans, and veil the question of who benefits from redevelopment and who does not. In reality, the benefits of redevelopment are often unevenly distributed. Most redevelopments are "pockets of revitalization surrounded by areas of extreme poverty" (Hannigan, 1998a: 53). That is, local residents often enjoy few if any direct benefits from redevelopment. Indirectly, they may suffer when budgets for public schooling, public transportation, and other amenities are cut to help pay for development subsidies and tax breaks.

New urban sociology: Emerged in the 1970s and stresses that city growth is a process rooted in power relations and the urge to profit.

Corporate city: The growing post–World War II perception and organization of the North American city as a vehicle for capital accumulation.

Suburbanism: A way of life outside city centers that is organized mainly around the needs of children and involves higher levels of conformity and sociability than life in the central city.

The Corporate City

As a result of the efforts of the growth coalition, the North American industrial city, typified by Chicago in the 1920s, gave way after World War II to the **corporate city.** Sociologist John Hannigan defines the corporate city as "a vehicle for capital accumulation—that is, . . . a money-making machine" (Hannigan, 1998b [1995]: 345).

The Growth of Suburbs

In the suburbs—urbanized areas outside the political boundaries of cities—developers built millions of single-family detached homes for the corporate middle class. These homes boasted large backyards and a car or two in every garage. A new way of life developed, which sociologists, appropriately enough, dubbed **suburbanism.** Every bit as distinctive as urbanism, suburbanism organized life mainly around the needs of children. It also involved higher levels of conformity and sociability than life in the central city (Fava, 1956). Suburbanism became fully entrenched as developers built shopping malls to serve the needs of the suburbanites. This reduced the need to travel to the central city for consumer goods.

The suburbs were at first restricted to the well-to-do. However, following World War II, brisk economic growth and government assistance to veterans put the suburban lifestyle within the reach of middle-class Americans. The lack of housing in city cores, extensive road-building programs, the falling price of automobiles, and the baby boom that began in 1946 also stimulated mushroom-like suburban growth. By 1970, more Americans lived in suburbs than in urban core areas. That remains the case today.

Gated Communities, Exurbs, and Edge Cities

Owing to the expansion of the suburbs, urban sociologists today often focus their attention not on cities but on entire **metropolitan areas.** Metropolitan areas include downtown city cores and their surrounding suburbs. They also include three recent developments the growth of which indicates the continued decentralization of urban America: **gated communities,** in which upper-middle-class residents pay high taxes to keep the community patrolled by security guards and walled off from the outside world; **exurbs,** or rural residential areas within commuting distance of the city; and **edge cities,** or exurban clusters of malls, offices, and entertainment complexes that arise at the convergence points of major highways (Garrau, 1991).

The spread of gated communities is motivated above all by fear of urban crime. The growth of exurban residential areas and edge cities since the 1970s has been motivated mainly by the mounting costs of operating businesses in city cores and the growth of new telecommunication technologies that allow businesses to operate in the exurbs. Home offices, mobile employees, and decentralized business locations are all made possible by these technologies. Some sociologists, urban and regional planners, and others lump all these developments together as indicators of **urban sprawl,** the spread of cities into ever larger expanses of the surrounding countryside.

City cores continued to decline as the middle class fled, pulled by the promise of suburban and exurban lifestyles and pushed by racial animosity and crime. Many middle-class people went farther afield, abandoning the snowbelt cities in America's traditional industrial heartland and migrating to the burgeoning cities of the American sunbelt in the South and the West (▶Table 16.2). As a result, particularly in northeastern and Midwestern cities, tax revenues in the city core fell, even as more money was needed to sustain social welfare programs for the poor.

Urban Renewal

In a spate of urban renewal in the 1950s and 1960s, many homes in low-income and minority-group areas were torn down and replaced by high-rise apartment buildings and office towers in the city core. In the 1970s and 1980s, some middle-class people moved into rundown areas and restored them in a process called **gentrification.** Still, large residential sections of downtown Detroit, Baltimore, Cleveland, and other cities remained in a state of decay. The number of Americans living in high-poverty neighborhoods doubled as recessions and economic restructuring closed factories in inner cities. The situation

▶**TABLE 16.2**
The 20 Largest Cities in the United States, 2006

Rank	City	Population
1	New York, NY	8,214,426
2	Los Angeles, CA	3,849,378
3	Chicago, IL	2,833,321
4	Houston, TX	2,144,491
5	Phoenix, AZ	1,512,986
6	Philadelphia, PA	1,448,394
7	San Antonio, TX	1,296,682
8	San Diego, CA	1,256,951
9	Dallas, TX	1,232,940
10	San Jose, CA	929,936
11	Detroit, MI	871,121
12	Jacksonville, FL	794,555
13	Indianapolis, IN	785,597
14	San Francisco, CA	744,041
15	Columbus, OH	733,203
16	Austin, TX	709,893
17	Memphis, TN	670,902
18	Fort Worth, TX	653,320
19	Baltimore, MD	631,366
20	Charlotte, NC	630,478

Note: Figures are for incorporated cities, not metropolitan areas.
Source: U.S. Census Bureau (2007a).

Metropolitan areas: Downtown city cores and their surrounding suburbs.

Gated communities: Expensive, upper middle-class residential developments patrolled by security guards and walled off from the outside world.

Exurbs: Rural residential areas within commuting distance of a city.

Edge cities: Exurban clusters of malls, offices, and entertainment complexes that arise at the convergence point of major highways.

Urban sprawl: The spread of cities into ever-larger expanses of the surrounding countryside.

Gentrification: The process of middle-class people moving into rundown areas of the inner city and restoring them.

BOX 16.3
SOCIOLOGY AT THE MOVIES

8 Mile (2002)

8 Mile Road is a depressing stretch of rundown buildings, gas stations, fast-food outlets, and strip malls that separates the rich and poor areas of Detroit, the most racially segregated city in the country. South of 8 Mile Road, Detroit is overwhelmingly African American. The suburbs north of 8 Mile Road are overwhelmingly European American.

Jimmy "Rabbit" Smith (Eminem) is a member of the white minority in the poor area. He and his family live in a trailer park near 8 Mile Road. Rabbit slouches and keeps a beanie pulled low over his head, as if hiding from the world or keeping it at bay. His close friends think he is a gifted rap artist but his more numerous enemies think a white boy rapping is a travesty. They ridicule Rabbit and call him Elvis. He meets Alex (Brittany Murphy), a beautiful young woman who discerns his talent, but she betrays him. No wonder Rabbit is sullen and angry.

Two rap competitions bracket the movie. In the first, Rabbit has 45 seconds to out-insult his opponent. Instead, he freezes and the audience laughs and boos him off the stage. In the second session, near the end of the movie, he has 90 seconds to prove his mettle. This time, he succeeds brilliantly.

The lyrics in the second rap session are worth heeding for their sociological implications. Rabbit first anticipates the attack of his African American opponent, Papa Doc, by listing his own deficiencies: I'm a white rapper, I'm a bum, I live in a trailer with my mom, my girlfriend betrayed me, and so forth. "Tell these people something they *don't* know about me," Rabbit taunts. After taking the wind out of his opponent's sails, he dissects Papa Doc with the following words:

> But I know something about you:
> You went to Cranbrook, that's a private school.
> What's the matter dawg, you embarrassed?
> This guy's a gangster?
> His real name's Clarence.
> And Clarence lives at home with both parents.
> And Clarence's parents have a real good marriage.

Cranbrook is a prep school in Bloomfield Hills, a Detroit suburb north of 8 Mile Road. Clarence, it turns out, is not quite the streetwise gang member from a single-parent family he makes himself out to be.

Clarence, however, reflects a trend that is big news. Between 1970 and 1990, the number of Americans living in high-poverty neighborhoods (where the poverty rate is 40 percent or higher) doubled. During the economic boom of the 1990s, the process of poverty concentration went into reverse. Two and a half million Americans moved out of high-poverty neighborhoods and mostly into less impoverished, older, inner-ring

Eminem and Brittany Murphy in *8 Mile*.

of the inner cities improved during the economic boom of the 1990s, but it is unclear whether the improvement will last (Box 16.3).

The Postmodern City

Postmodern city: A new urban form that is more privatized, socially and culturally fragmented, and globalized than the corporate city.

Many of the conditions that plagued the industrial city—poverty, inadequate housing, structural employment—are still evident in cities today. However, since about 1970, a new urban phenomenon has emerged alongside the legacy of old urban forms: the **postmodern city** (Hannigan, 1995a). The postmodern city has three main features:

▶FIGURE 16.7
The Distribution of Poverty in Detroit, 1970–2000

Source: From Paul A. Jargowsky, *Stunning Progress, Hidden Problems*, p. 7. © 2003 The Brookings Institution. Reprinted with permission.

suburbs around major metropolitan areas. Nowhere was the reversal more dramatic than in Detroit (Jargowsky, 2003) (▶Figure 16.7).

The phenomenon represented by Clarence is encouraging yet fraught with danger. On the one hand, poor people are better off if they are widely dispersed rather than spatially concentrated. Spatially concentrated poor people have to deal not only with their own poverty but also with a violent environment, low-performing schools, and a lack of positive role models. Thus, the exodus from the inner city is a positive development because it puts poor people in neighborhoods where poverty is less concentrated. On the other hand, the exodus increases the percentage of poor people in many of the older, inner-ring suburbs around major metropolitan areas. During the next economic slowdown, this may result in the migration of many of the social ills of the inner city into the inner suburbs. If Clarence's children grow up where he did, they may be less susceptible to the ridicule of an Eminem.

Critical Thinking

- Do you think the concentration of urban poverty in the United States as a whole will increase or decrease between 2000 and 2010? On what grounds do you hold this opinion?

- Do you think that certain regions or states are more likely to witness increased or decreased concentration of urban poverty between 2000 and 2010? If so, which regions? If not, why not? Why do you hold this opinion?

1. The postmodern city is more *privatized* than the corporate city because access to formerly public spaces is increasingly limited to those who can afford to pay. Privatization is evident in the construction of closed-off gated communities in the suburbs. In downtown cores, gleaming office towers and shopping areas are built beside slums. Yet the two areas are separated by the organization of space and access. For instance, a series of billion-dollar, block-square structures have been built around Bunker Hill in Los Angeles. Nearly all pedestrian linkages to the surrounding poor immigrant neighborhoods have been removed. Barrel-shaped, "bum-proof" bus benches prevent homeless people from sleeping on them. Trash cans are designed

to be "bag-lady proof." Overhead sprinklers in Skid Row Park discourage overnight sleeping. Public toilets and washrooms have been removed in areas frequented by vagrants (Davis, 1990).

2. The postmodern city is also more *fragmented* than the corporate city. It lacks a single way of life, such as urbanism or suburbanism. Instead, a great variety of lifestyles and subcultures proliferate in the postmodern city. They are based on race, ethnicity, immigrant status, class, sexual orientation, and so forth.

3. The third characteristic of the postmodern city is that it is more *globalized* than the corporate city. According to Saskia Sassen (1991), New York, London, and Tokyo epitomize the global city. They are world centers of economic and financial decision making. They are also sites of innovation, where new products and fashions originate. In short, they have become the command posts of the globalized economy and its culture.

The processes of privatization, fragmentation, and globalization are evident in the way the postmodern city has come to reflect the priorities of the global entertainment industry. The postmodern city gets its distinctive flavor from its theme parks, restaurants and night clubs, waterfront developments, refurbished casinos, giant malls, megaplex cinemas, IMAX theaters, virtual-reality arcades, ride simulators, sports complexes, book and CD megastores, aquariums, and hands-on science "museums." In the postmodern city, nearly everything becomes entertainment or, more accurately, combines entertainment with standard consumer activities. This produces hybrid activities like "shoppertainment," "eatertainment," and "edutainment."

John Hannigan has shown how the new venues of high-tech urban entertainment manage to provide excitement—but all within a thoroughly clean, controlled, predictable, and safe environment (Hannigan, 1998a). For example, entertainment developments often enforce dress codes, teenager curfews, and rules banning striking workers and groups espousing social or political causes from their premises. The most effective barriers to potentially disruptive elements, however, are affordability and access. User surveys show that the new forms of urban entertainment tend to attract middle- and upper-middle-class patrons, especially whites. That is because they are pricey, and many of them are in places that lack public transit and are too expensive for most people to reach by taxi.

Referring to the major role played by the Disney corporation in developing the new urban entertainment complexes, an architect once said that our downtowns would be "saved by a mouse" (quoted in Hannigan, 1998a: 193). But do the new forms of entertainment that dot the urban landscape increase the economic well-being of the communities in which they are established? Not much beyond creating some low-level, dead-end jobs (security guard, waiter, janitor). Do they provide ways of meeting new people, seeing old friends and neighbors, and in general improving urban sociability? Not really. You visit a theme park with family or friends, but you generally stick close to your group and rarely have chance encounters with other patrons or bump into acquaintances. Does the high-tech world of globalized urban entertainment enable cities and neighborhoods to retain and enhance their distinct traditions, architectural styles, and ambience? It would be hard to destroy the distinctiveness of New York, San Francisco, or Vancouver, but many large North American cities are becoming homogenized as they provide the same entertainment services—and the same global brands—as Tokyo, Paris, and Sydney. If the mouse is saving our cities, perhaps he is also gnawing away at something valuable in the process.

The Environment

Environmental Degradation

In the 20th century, the world's population increased by 375 percent. Much of the increase took place in cities. By 2030, 60 percent of the world's people will be urban residents. Such growth places extraordinary demands on the natural environment. In fact, feeding, housing, and transporting so many people causes widespread environmental damage. Environmental degradation takes three main forms: global warming, industrial pollution, and the decline of biodiversity. Let us consider each of these in turn.

Global Warming

Since the Industrial Revolution, humans have been burning increasing quantities of fossil fuels (coal, oil, gasoline, natural gas, etc.) to drive their cars, furnaces, and factories. Burning these fuels releases carbon dioxide into the atmosphere. The accumulation of carbon dioxide allows more solar radiation to enter the atmosphere and less heat to escape.

This is the so-called **greenhouse effect.** Surveys show that most climate scientists believe that the greenhouse effect contributes to **global warming,** a gradual increase in the world's average surface temperature (Bray and Storch, 2005; Oreskes, 2004). ▶Figure 16.8 graphs the world's annual average surface air temperature and the concentration of carbon dioxide in the atmosphere from 1866 to 2007. The graph shows a warming trend that mirrors the increased concentration of carbon dioxide in the atmosphere. It also shows that the warming trend began in the last third of the 20th century.

Many scientists believe that global warming is already producing serious climatic change, for as temperatures rise, more water evaporates. This causes more rainfall and bigger storms, which leads to more flooding and soil erosion, which in turn leads to less cultivable land. People suffer and die all along the causal chain. This was tragically evident in 2005, when hurricanes Katrina and Rita delivered knockout punches to coastal Louisiana, Alabama, Mississippi, and Texas, killing more than a thousand people and causing hundreds of billions of dollars of damage. Hurricane intensity and duration have increased over the past 30 years (Emanuel, 2005).

CENGAGENOW

Learn more about **Technology and Change** by going through the Technology and Change Learning Module.

CENGAGENOW

Learn more about the **Greenhouse Effect** by going through the Share of Global Emissions Map Exercise.

Greenhouse effect: The accumulation of carbon dioxide in the atmosphere that allows more solar radiation to enter the atmosphere and less solar radiation to escape.

Global warming: The gradual worldwide increase in average surface temperature.

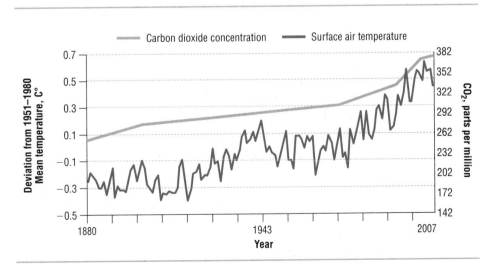

▶FIGURE 16.8
Annual Mean Global Surface Air Temperature and Carbon Dioxide Concentration, 1880–2007

Sources: Goddard Institute for Space Studies (2008); Karl and Trenberth (1999: 102); Quaschning (2003); U.S. Department of Commerce, National Oceanic and Atmospheric Administration (2008).

▶FIGURE 16.9
Worldwide Insured Losses Due to Natural and Human Catastrophes, 1970–2006 (in 2005 $US billions)

Source: Swiss Re (2003: 8; 2004: 7; 2005: 5; 2007: 7); U.S. Department of Labor (2009).

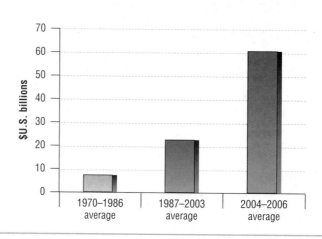

▶Figure 16.9 graphs the worldwide dollar cost of damage due to natural and human catastrophes from 1980 to 2005. (Recall that an increasingly large number of meteorological events deemed "natural" are rendered extreme by human action.) Clearly, the damage caused by extreme meteorological events is on the upswing. This, however, may be only the beginning. It seems that global warming is causing the oceans to rise. That is partly because warmer water expands and partly because the partial melting of the polar ice caps puts more water in the oceans. In the 21st century, this may result in the flooding of some heavily populated coastal regions throughout the world.

Industrial Pollution

Industrial pollution is the emission of various impurities into the air, water, and soil due to industrial processes. It is the second major form of environmental degradation. Every day, we release a witch's brew into the environment, the more common ingredients of which include household trash, scrap automobiles, residue from processed ores, agricultural runoff containing dangerous chemicals, lead, carbon monoxide, carbon dioxide, sulfur dioxide, ozone, nitrogen oxide, various volatile organic compounds, chlorofluorocarbons (CFCs), and various solids mixed with liquid droplets floating in the air. Most pollutants are especially highly concentrated in the U.S. Northeast and around the Great Lakes. These densely populated areas are identified with old, heavy, dirty industries (United States Environmental Protection Agency, 2000).

Pollutants may affect us directly. For example, they seep into our drinking water and the air we breathe, causing a variety of ailments, particularly among the young, the elderly, and the ill. A dramatic natural experiment demonstrating the direct effect of air pollution on health occurred during the 1996 Atlanta Olympics. For the 17 days of the Olympics, asthma attacks among children in the Atlanta area plummeted 42 percent. When the athletes went home, the rate of asthma attacks among children immediately bounced back to "normal" levels. Epidemiologists soon figured out why. During the Olympics, Atlanta closed the downtown to cars and operated public transit around the clock. Vehicle exhaust fell, with an immediate benefit to children's health. Children's health deteriorated as soon as normal traffic resumed (Mittelstaedt, 2001).

Pollutants may also affect us indirectly. For instance, sulfur dioxide and other gases are emitted by coal-burning power plants, pulp and paper mills, and motor-vehicle exhaust. They form **acid rain.** This is a form of precipitation whose acidity eats away at, and eventually destroys, forests and the ecosystems of lakes. Another example: Until recently CFCs were used in industry and by consumers, notably in refrigeration equipment. They contain chlorine, which is responsible for the depletion of the **ozone layer** 5 to 25 miles above the Earth's surface. Ozone is a form of oxygen that blocks ultraviolet radiation from the sun. Let more ultraviolet radiation reach ground level and, as we are now witnessing, rates of skin cancer increase.

The Decline of Biodiversity

The third main form of environmental degradation is the decline in **biodiversity,** the enormous variety of plant and animal species inhabiting the Earth. Biodiversity changes as new species emerge and old species die off because they cannot adapt to their environment. This is all part of the normal evolutionary process. However, in recent decades the environment has become so inhospitable to so many species that the rate of extinction has greatly accelerated.

The extinction of species is impoverishing in itself, but it also has practical consequences for humans. For example, each species of animal and plant has unique properties. When scientists discover that a certain property has a medically useful effect, they synthesize the property in the laboratory. Treatments for everything from headaches to cancer have been found in this way. Indeed, about a quarter of all drugs prescribed in the United States today (including 9 of the top 10 in sales) include compounds first found in wild organisms. The single richest source of genetic material with pharmaceutical value is found in the world's rain forests, particularly in Brazil, where more than 30 million species of life exist. However, the rain forests are being rapidly destroyed by strip mining, the construction of huge pulp and paper mills and hydroelectric projects, and the deforestation of land by farmers and cattle grazers.

Similarly, fleets of trawlers belonging to the highly industrialized countries are now equipped with sonar to help them find large concentrations of fish. Some of these ships use fine-mesh nets to increase their catch. They have been enormously "successful." Trawlers have depleted fish stocks in some areas of the world. In North America, for example, the depletion of cod, salmon, bluefin tuna, and shark stocks has devastated fishing communities and endangered one of the world's most important sources of protein. All told, 11 of the world's 15 main fishing grounds and 69 percent of the world's main fish species are in decline (McGinn, 1998: 60; Myers and Worm, 2003).

Global warming, industrial pollution, and the decline of biodiversity threaten everyone. However, as you will now see, the degree to which they are perceived as threatening depends on certain social conditions being met. Moreover, the threats are not evenly distributed in society.

The Social Construction of Environmental Problems

Environmental problems do not become social issues spontaneously. Before they can enter the public consciousness, policy-oriented scientists, the environmental movement, the mass media, and respected organizations must discover and promote them. People have to connect real-life events to the information learned from these groups. Because some scientists, industrial interests, and politicians dispute the existence of environmental threats, the public can begin to question whether environmental issues are in fact social

Acid rain: Precipitation whose acidity destroys forests and the ecosystems of lakes. It is formed by sulfur dioxide and other gases emitted by coal-burning power plants, pulp and paper mills, and motor-vehicle exhaust.

Ozone layer: Lies 5 to 25 miles above the Earth's surface. It is depleted by CFCs. The depletion of the ozone layer allows more ultraviolet light to enter the Earth's atmosphere, increasing the rate of skin cancer.

Biodiversity: The enormous variety of plant and animal species inhabiting the Earth.

problems that require human intervention. We must not, then, think of environmental issues as inherently problematic. Rather, they are contested phenomena. They can be socially constructed by proponents. They can be socially demolished by opponents. This is the key insight of the school of thought known as *social constructionism* (Hannigan, 1995b).

The Case of Global Warming

The controversy over global warming is a good example of how people create and contest definitions of environmental problems (Gelbspan, 1999; Ungar, 1999). The theory of global warming was first proposed about a century ago. However, an elite group of scientists began serious research on the subject only in the late 1950s. They attracted no public attention until the 1970s. That is when the environmental movement emerged. It gave new legitimacy and momentum to scientific research and helped secure public funding for it. Respected and influential scientists now began to promote the issue of global warming.

The mass media, always thirsting for sensational stories, were highly receptive to these efforts. Newspaper and television reports about the problem began to appear in the late 1970s. They proliferated in the mid- to late-1980s. The summer of 1988 brought the worst drought in half a century to North America. Respected organizations outside the scientific community, the mass media, and the environmental movement began expressing concern about the effects of global warming. By the early 1990s, public opinion polls showed that most North Americans with an opinion on the subject thought that using coal, oil, and gas contributes to global warming.

However, some industrialists, politicians, and scientists soon began to question whether global warming was, in fact, taking place. This group included coal and oil companies, the member states of the Organization of Petroleum Exporting Countries (OPEC), other coal- and oil-exporting nations, and right-wing think tanks, some of which were subsidized in part by major oil companies. (Years earlier, at least one of the leading global warming skeptics in the scientific community worked for big tobacco companies, arguing that smoking does not cause cancer.) "[B]ad scientific reporting, bad economics and bad judgment" is how one such think tank summarized the analyses of those who regarded global warming as a serious issue requiring immediate action (Jones, 1997). Largely because of this onslaught, public concern about global warming began to falter.

Yet the evidence that global warming was substantial, dangerous, and caused by human activity continued to accumulate. In the United States, for example, ordinary people experienced firsthand ongoing drought in areas of the South and the West, falling water levels in the Great Lakes, the melting of glaciers in Alaska, and the collapse of fish stocks on the East Coast. Al Gore's 2006 film, *An Inconvenient Truth,* vividly portrayed the scope and danger of climate change to a large audience in the United States and abroad. The movie alarmed many people, and when Gore received the Nobel Peace Prize in 2007 for his work on climate change, it drew additional attention to the problem. Also in 2007, the Intergovernmental Panel on Climate Change (IPCC) issued a definitive report to much fanfare. The World Meteorological Organization and the United Nations Environment Programme set up the IPCC. It organizes hundreds of leading climate scientists from around the world to review all relevant research and write periodic reports summarizing the state of knowledge about climate change. The 2007 report found strong evidence for a warming world climate (especially in the North), the substantial contribution of human activity to climate change, and the devastating consequences of climate change for life on the planet. It showed that global warming is real, dangerous, and stoppable through human intervention (Intergovernmental Panel on Climate Change, 2007). The public mood shifted again. Both candidates in the 2008 presidential election adopted "green" platforms that promised swift and effective action. We conclude that environmental issues become social problems only when social, political, and scientific circumstances allow them to be defined as such.

As you will now see, in addition to being socially defined, environmental problems are socially distributed. That is, environmental risks are greater for some groups than for others.

The Social Distribution of Environmental Risk

You may have noticed that after a minor twister touches down on some unlucky community in Texas or Kansas, TV reporters often rush to interview the surviving residents of trailer parks. The survivors stand amid the rubble that was their lives. They heroically remark on the generosity of their neighbors, their good fortune in still having their family intact, and our inability to fight nature's destructive forces. Why trailer parks? Small twisters aren't particularly attracted to them, but reporters are. That is because trailers are pretty flimsy in the face of a small tornado. They often suffer a lot of damage from twisters. They therefore make a more sensational story than the minor damage typically inflicted on upper-middle-class homes with firmly shingled roofs and solid foundations. This is a general pattern. Whenever disaster strikes—from the sinking of the *Titanic* to the fury of hurricane Katrina—economically and politically disadvantaged people almost always suffer most. That is because their circumstances render them most vulnerable.

Environmental Racism

In fact, the advantaged often consciously put the disadvantaged in harm's way to avoid risk themselves. For example, toxic dumps, garbage incinerators, and other environmentally dangerous installations are more likely to be built in poor communities with a high percentage of African Americans or Hispanic Americans than in more affluent, mainly white communities. That is because disadvantaged people are often too politically weak to oppose such facilities, and some may even value the jobs they create (Stretesky and Hogan, 1998; Szasz and Meuser, 1997: 100). Similarly, the 75-mile strip along the lower Mississippi River between New Orleans and Baton Rouge has been nicknamed "Cancer Alley" because the largely black population of the region suffers from unusually high rates of lung, stomach, pancreatic, and other cancers. The main reason? This small area is the source of fully one-quarter of the petrochemicals produced in the country, containing more than 100 oil refineries and chemical plants (Bullard, 1994 [1990]). Here again we see the recurrent pattern of what some analysts call **environmental racism** (Bullard, 1994 [1990]). This is the tendency to heap environmental dangers on the disadvantaged, and especially on disadvantaged racial minorities.

Hurricane Katrina

One of the biggest disasters of recent years was hurricane Katrina, which hit the American Gulf Coast on August 29, 2005. Its effect was especially devastating in New Orleans, where environmental racism transformed the face of the city (Brym, 2009:53–81).

Environmental racism: The tendency to heap environmental dangers on the disadvantaged, especially on disadvantaged racial minorities.

A makeshift grave near New Orleans following Hurricane Katrina in 2005.

Dave Martin/AP Photo

Before Katrina hit, New Orleans was two-thirds African American and one-quarter non-Hispanic white. Black–white income inequality was substantially greater than in the United States as a whole. Two-thirds of the public schools were deemed to be "academically unacceptable" by the U.S. Department of Education, and the city's homicide rate was among the highest of any city in the United States. New Orleans was poor, black, segregated, unequal, violent—and exposed.

New Orleans sits below sea level, and five years before Katrina made landfall, an article about the flood dangers facing the city was published in *Time* magazine. It included a computer-generated map showing how deep the waters would rise if a category 5 hurricane came barreling out of the Gulf of Mexico and headed straight toward the city. The analysis proved accurate. Katrina was no surprise.

Scientists knew not only *wha*t would happen if a Katrina-like hurricane struck. They knew why it would happen. First, the levee system along the Mississippi River eliminated the city's first line of defense against storm surge. Without levees along the Mississippi, silt from the river's floodwaters would stabilize land along the riverside and stop or at least slow down the sinking of coastal wetlands into the Gulf of Mexico. With the levees, silt is diverted into the Gulf, so the wetlands, which protect New Orleans from storm surge, are disappearing at an alarming rate. Second, levees along Lake Pontchartrain, to the north of the city, were last reinforced with higher walls in 1965, when they were built to withstand a category 3 storm. It was only a matter of time before a more severe storm would cause water to break through. Third, some climate scientists believe that, in recent years, hurricanes had become more severe, partly because global warming due to the excessive burning of fossil fuels has put more moisture into the atmosphere. Thus, hurricane Katrina was in part a social disaster caused by deep racial inequality, poor planning, neglect, and careless disregard for the human impact on nature.

A hundred thousand people failed to evacuate New Orleans. They were predominantly poor, black, elderly, and disabled. Most of them didn't own cars or have access to other means of transportation. Many of them had little or no money; all they owned was in their homes. They were trapped for sociological reasons as the waters began to rise and people began scrambling to their attics, the Louisiana Superdome, and the New Orleans Convention Center, where survivors remained for days without food, water, or sanitation. Poor planning by inefficient government bureaucracies slowed the relief and recovery effort. About 2,300 people died in hurricane Katrina.

Most of the predominantly white, well-off districts of New Orleans are on high ground. They escaped the worst of the flooding. Most of the predominantly African American, poor districts are on low ground. There, flooding was most severe. Four years after Katrina, many of the poor districts were substantially depopulated or deserted. The new New Orleans is thus likely to be smaller, richer, and whiter, partly due to environmental racism.

Environmental Risk and the Less Developed Countries

What is true for disadvantaged classes and racial groups in the United States also holds for the world's less developed countries. The underprivileged face more environmental dangers than the privileged (Kennedy, 1993: 95–121). In North America, western Europe, and Japan, population growth is low and falling. Industry and government are eliminating some of the worst excesses of industrialization. In contrast, world population will grow to about 7 billion by 2012, and nearly all of that growth will be in the less developed countries. Moreover, Mexico, Brazil, China, India, and many other countries are industrializing rapidly. This is putting tremendous strain on their natural resources. Rising demand for water, electricity, fossil fuels, and consumer products is creating more polluted rivers, dead lakes, and industrial waste sites. At a quickening pace, rain forests, grazing land, cropland, and wetlands are giving way to factories, roads, airports, and housing complexes. Smog-blanketed megacities continue to sprawl.

Given the picture just sketched, it should come as no surprise that on average, people in less developed countries are more concerned about the environment than people in rich countries (Brechin and Kempton, 1994). However, the developing countries cannot afford much in the way of pollution control, so antipollution regulations are lax by North American, western European, and Japanese standards. This is an incentive for some multinational corporations to site some of their most environmentally unfriendly operations in the less developed countries (Clapp, 1998). It is also the reason the industrialization of the less developed countries is proving so punishing to the environment.

For the time being, however, the rich countries do most of the world's environmental damage. That is because their inhabitants earn and consume more than the inhabitants of less developed countries. How much more? In the second half of the twentieth century, the richest one-fifth of humanity doubled its per capita consumption of energy, meat, timber, steel, and copper and quadrupled its car ownership. In that same period, the per capita consumption of the poorest one-fifth hardly changed. The United States has only 4.5 percent of the world's population, but it uses about 25 percent of the Earth's resources. It also produces more than 20 percent of global emissions of carbon dioxide, the pollutant responsible for about one-half of global warming (Ehrlich et al., 1997). Thus, the inhabitants of the developed countries cause a disproportionately large share of the world's environmental problems, enjoy a disproportionate share of the benefits of technology, and live with fewer environmental risks than do people in the less developed countries.

What Is to Be Done?

The Market and High-Tech Solutions

Some people believe the environmental crisis will resolve itself. More precisely, they think we already have two weapons that will work together to end the crisis: the market and high technology. The case of oil illustrates how these weapons can presumably combine forces. If oil reserves drop or producers withhold oil from the market for political reasons, the price of oil goes up. This makes it worthwhile for oil exploration companies to develop new technologies to discover and recover more oil. When they bring more oil to market, prices fall back to where they were. Generalizing these experiences and projecting them into the future, optimists believe that we will deal similarly with global warming, industrial pollution, and other forms of environmental degradation. In their view, human inventiveness and the profit motive will combine to create the new technologies we need to survive and prosper in the 21st century.

Some evidence supports this optimistic scenario. For example, following the oil shocks of 1973 (when prices tripled) and 1978–79 (when prices tripled again), new discoveries were made and new efficiencies were implemented, so oil reserves grew and prices fell. Moreover, in recent years, we have adopted new technologies to combat some of the worst excesses of environmental degradation. For example, we have replaced brain-damaging leaded gas with unleaded gas. We have developed environmentally friendly refrigerants and stopped the production of ozone-destroying CFCs. In a model of international cooperation, rich countries have even subsidized the cost of replacing CFCs in the developing countries. Efficient windmills and solar panels are now common. More factories are equipped with high-tech pollution control devices, preventing dangerous chemicals from seeping into the air and water. We have introduced cost-effective ways to recycle metal, plastic, paper, and glass. New methods are being developed for eliminating carbon dioxide emissions from the burning of fossil fuels. We can now buy hybrid cars, and electric cars will soon be on the market.

Although market forces are helping to bring environmentally friendly technologies online, four factors suggest that they cannot solve environmental problems on their own:

1. *Imperfect price signals.* The price of many commodities does not reflect their actual cost to society. Gasoline costs less than $2 a gallon at the time of this writing, but the social cost, including the cost of repairing the environmental damage caused by burning the gas, may be three or four times that. Due to this and other price distortions, the market often fails to send signals that might result in the speedy adoption of technological and policy fixes.

2. *The slow pace of change.* So far, our efforts to deal with the environmental consequences of rapid technological change are just not good enough. For example, global warming continues to accelerate, partly because automobile use is increasing quickly worldwide. The world's renewable resources continue to decline (▶Figure 16.10).

3. *The importance of political pressure.* Political pressure exerted by environmental activists, community groups, and public opinion is often necessary to motivate corporate and government action on environmental issues. For instance, organizations like Greenpeace have successfully challenged the practices of logging companies, whalers, the nuclear industry, and other groups engaged in environmentally dangerous practices. Without the efforts of such organizations, it is doubtful that corporations and governments would define many environmental issues as social problems.

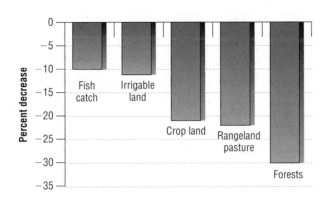

▶FIGURE 16.10
Renewable Resources, World, Percent Change, 1990–2010

Source: Postel (1994: 11)

4. *The resistance of powerful interest groups.* The oil and automobile industries in the United States benefit from things staying the way they are and have acted as a brake on change.

The United States imports about half the petroleum it uses. About a third of its imports come from the Middle East, especially Saudi Arabia, Iraq, and Kuwait. American allies in Western Europe depend somewhat more heavily on Middle Eastern oil, whereas Japan buys more than three-quarters of its oil from the region. We pay a heavy price economically, environmentally, and politically for this dependence. We even went to war with Iraq in 1991 and 2003, partly (some would say mainly) to protect our oil interests in the region.

Meanwhile, the United States is the world's second biggest producer of automobiles. Cars use much of our petroleum and are the single biggest source of carbon emissions. As has often been said, Americans have a love affair with the automobile, and we consider it our right to enjoy among the lowest gas prices in the world. The oil and automobile industries employ millions of Americans, and their owners have exerted enormous influence on the White House. For example, the Bush and Cheney families earned their personal wealth in the oil industry, and they have many friends and business associates in it.

Given the extent and depth of these interests in the status quo, proposals to adopt cleaner and less expensive alternatives to gas-burning cars have until recently met with little response from government or industry. For instance, the movement to improve fuel efficiency gained force after the 1973 oil crisis, but it petered out when the government allowed sport utility vehicles (SUVs) to be classified as small trucks and thereby avoid stringent fuel-economy regulation.

To help resolve the environmental crisis, the Obama presidency has promised to break with the past and overcome the resistance of powerful interest groups in the oil and automobile industries. We conclude our discussion by outlining what the new environmental policy might involve.

The Cooperative Alternative

The alternative to the market and high-tech approach involves increased cooperation among citizens, governments, and corporations aimed at the following goals (Livernash and Rodenburg, 1998):

● Reducing wasteful consumption;

● Increasing environmentally related research and development;

● Investing more in energy-saving technologies;

● Cleaning up the environment more effectively and quickly;

● Giving more aid to the developing countries for environmentally friendly industrialization;

● Placing caps on carbon emissions; and

● Introducing new taxes or at least eliminating tax cuts to the wealthy such as those that were implemented during the Bush era.

Cooperation on these issues would require renewed commitment to voluntary efforts and willingness to pass new laws and create new enforcement bodies.

Is the solution realistic? Not in the short term. It would be political suicide for anyone in the rich countries to propose a quick implementation of the measures just listed. For example, not too many American drivers would be happy paying $8 a gallon for gas tomorrow. For the solution to be politically acceptable, the broad public in North America, Western Europe, and Japan must be aware of the gravity of the environmental problem and be willing to make substantial sacrifices to get the job done.

Data from the General Social Survey and other polls suggest that nearly all Americans are aware of environmental problems. The great majority of people believe that the government and individuals can and should do more to solve them. However, fewer than half of Americans are willing to pay much higher prices to protect the environment, and only about a third are willing to pay much higher taxes or cut back on their driving (National Opinion Research Center, 2008b). In 2005, researchers at Yale and Columbia Universities calculated an "environmental sustainability index" for each of the world's countries and found that the United States ranked only 47th—behind Russia (33rd) and the Congo (39th)—in its effort to protect the environment (Yale Center, 2005). A "climate protection index" calculated by German researchers in 2009 placed the United States in 58th place out of 60 industrialized countries (Figure ▶16.11).

Sociologist Sheldon Ungar shows in his analysis of the global warming issue that only when a social scare occurs are more people prepared to make bigger sacrifices to deal with the perceived problem. That is, people have to be able to connect real-life events, such as long droughts, catastrophic storms, scorching summers, and mild winters, with what they hear in the mass media about the environmental crisis before taking the problem more seriously and making the necessary commitment to help save the planet (Ungar, 1992, 1995, 1998, 1999). It follows that more and bigger environmental catastrophes may have

▶FIGURE 16.11
Climate Protection Performance of Industrialized Countries, 2009

Source: Germanwatch (2009).

Top Ten Performers	Bottom Ten Performers
1. Sweden	51. Greece
2. Germany	52. Malaysia
3. France	53. Cyprus
4. India	54. Russia
5. Brazil	55. Australia
6. UK	56. Kazakhstan
7. Denmark	57. Luxembourg
8. Norway	58. United States
9. Hungary	59. Canada
10. Iceland	60. Saudi Arabia

to occur before more people are willing to take remedial action. The good news is that there is still time to change our culture of environmental degradation.

 ## The Points of the Compass

For many thousands of years, humans have done well on this planet. That is because we have created cultural practices, including technologies, that allowed us to adapt to and thrive in our environment. Nonetheless, there have been some failures along the way. Many tribes and civilizations are extinct. And our success to date as a species is no warrant for the future. If we persist in using technologies that create an inhospitable environment, Nature will deal with us in the same way it always deals with species that cannot adapt.

Broadly speaking, we have two survival strategies to cope with the challenges that lie ahead: competition and cooperation. Charles Darwin wrote famously about competition in *The Origin of Species* (1859). He observed that members of each species struggle against each other and against other species in their struggle to survive. Most of the quickest, the strongest, the best camouflaged, and the smartest live long enough to bear offspring. Most of the rest are killed off. Thus, the traits passed on to offspring are those most valuable for survival. Ruthless competition, it turns out, is a key survival strategy of all species, including humans.

In *The Descent of Man,* Darwin mentioned our second important survival strategy: cooperation. In some species mutual assistance is common. The species members that flourish are those that best learn to help each other (Darwin, 1871:163). The Russian geographer and naturalist Petr Kropotkin (1908 [1902]) elaborated this idea. After spending five years studying animal life in Siberia, he concluded that "mutual aid" is at least as important a survival strategy as competition. Competition takes place when members of the same species compete for limited resources, said Kropotkin. Cooperation occurs when species members struggle against adverse environmental circumstances. According to Kropotkin, survival in the face of environmental threat is best assured if species members help each other. Kropotkin also showed that the most advanced species in any group—ants among insects, mammals among vertebrates, humans among mammals—are the most cooperative. Many evolutionary biologists now accept Kropotkin's ideas (Gould 1988; Nowak, May, and Sigmund 1995:81).

As we have seen, a strictly competitive approach to dealing with the environmental crisis—relying on the market alone to solve our problems—now seems inadequate. Instead, it appears we require more cooperation and self-sacrifice. This involves substantially reducing consumption, paying higher taxes for environmental cleanup and energy-efficient industrial processes, subsidizing the developing countries to industrialize in an environmentally friendly way, and so forth. Previously, we outlined some grave consequences of relying too little on a cooperative survival strategy at this historical juncture. But which strategy you emphasize in your own life is, of course, your choice.

Similarly, throughout this book—when we discussed families, gender inequality, crime, race, population, and many other topics—we raised social issues lying at the intersection of history, social structure, and biography. We arrayed these issues on our sociological compass, set out alternative courses of action, and outlined their consequences. We thus followed our disciplinary mandate: helping people make informed choices based on sound sociological knowledge (Wilensky, 1997). In the context of the present chapter, however, we can make an even bolder claim for the discipline. Conceived at its broadest, sociology promises to help in the rational and equitable evolution of humankind.

Calvin and Hobbes

by Bill Watterson

CHAPTER SUMMARY

1. What is the Malthusian theory of population growth? Does it apply today?

Robert Malthus argued that while food supplies increase slowly, populations grow quickly. Because of these presumed natural laws, only war, pestilence, and famine can keep human population growth in check. Several developments have cast doubt on Malthus's theory. Food production has increased rapidly. The limits to population size are higher than Malthus expected. Some populations are large yet prosperous. Some countries provide generous social welfare and still maintain low population growth rates. The use of contraception is widespread.

2. What is demographic transition theory?

Demographic transition theory holds that the main factors underlying population dynamics are industrialization and the growth of modern cultural values. In the preindustrial era, both crude birthrates and crude deathrates were high, and population growth was therefore slow. In the first stages of industrialization, crude deathrates fell, so population growth was rapid. As industrialization progressed and people's values about having children changed, the crude birthrate fell, resulting in slow growth again. Finally, in the postindustrial era, the crude deathrate has risen above the crude birthrate in many societies. As a result, their populations shrink unless in-migration augments their numbers.

3. What factors aside from the level of industrialization affect population growth?

The level of social inequality between women and men and between classes affects population dynamics, with lower levels of social inequality typically resulting in lower crude birth rates and therefore lower population growth rates.

4. Is urbanization a function of industrialization?

Much urbanization is associated with the growth of factories. However, religious, political, and commercial need gave rise to cities in the preindustrial era. Moreover, the fastest-growing cities in the world today are in semi-industrialized countries.

5. What did members of the Chicago school contribute to our understanding of the growth of cities?

The members of the Chicago school described and explained the spatial and social dimensions of the industrial city. They developed a theory of human ecology that explained urban growth as the outcome of differentiation, competition, and ecological succession. They described the spatial arrangement of the industrial city as a series of expanding concentric circles. The main business/entertainment/shopping area stood in the center, with the class position of residents increasing as one moved from inner to outer rings.

6. What are the main weaknesses of the Chicago school's analysis of cities?

Subsequent research has shown that the city is not as anomic as the Chicago sociologists made it appear. Moreover, the concentric zone pattern applies best to the American industrial city in the first quarter of the 20th century. The new urban sociology criticized the Chicago school for making city growth seem like an almost natural process, playing down the power conflicts and profit motives that prompted the evolution of cities.

7. What are corporate and postmodern cities?

The corporate city that emerged after World War II was a vehicle for capital accumulation that stimulated the growth of the suburbs and resulted in the decline of inner cities. The postmodern city that took shape in the last decades of the 20th century is characterized by the increased globalization of culture, fragmentation of lifestyles, and privatization of space.

8. **What are some of the other major changes that have taken place in city life in recent decades?**

   Cities have become suburbanized and exurbanized as they sprawl into the surrounding countryside.

9. **What are the major forms of environmental degradation and who is most exposed to the risks associated with them?**

   The major forms of environmental degradation include global warming, industrial pollution, and the destruction of biodiversity. The people most exposed to the risks associated with the various forms of environmental degradation include members of racial minorities, lower classes, and less developed societies.

10. **How is social constructionism applied to the study of environmental problems?**

    Social constructionism emphasizes that social problems do not emerge spontaneously. Instead, they are contested phenomena whose prominence depends on the ability of supporters and detractors to make the public aware of them.

11. **Are market and high-tech solutions capable of dealing with the problem of environmental degradation?**

    Market and high-tech solutions can help solve many environmental problems. However, four issues suggest that they are insufficient by themselves. First, price signals do not always mirror market conditions. Second, political pressure is often needed to motivate governments and corporations to take action on environmental issues. Third, the pace of change is too slow. Fourth, some interest groups oppose change.

12. **What needs to be done to solve the problem of environmental degradation?**

    Increased cooperation among citizens, governments, and corporations is required to solve the environmental crisis. This strategy involves renewed commitment to voluntary efforts, new laws and enforcement bodies to ensure compliance, increased investment in energy-saving research and development by industry and government, more environmentally directed foreign aid, and new taxes to help pay for some if it. Many Americans are unwilling to undergo the personal sacrifices and changes in lifestyle required to deal with the problem of environmental degradation, and some interest groups with a deep stake in things as they are resist change. However, repeated environmental catastrophes could change the context of U.S. politics in a way that would make the cooperative strategy more popular in this country.

Questions to Consider

1. Do you think rapid global population growth is cause for alarm? If not, why not? If so, what aspects of global population growth are especially worrisome? What should be done about them?

2. Do you think of the city mainly as a place of innovation and tolerance or mainly as a site of crime, prejudice, and anomie? Where does your image of the city come from? Your own experience? the mass media? your sociological reading?

3. What are the main environmental problems in your community? How are they connected to global environmental issues?

4. Take an inventory of your environmentally friendly and environmentally dangerous habits. In what ways can you act in a more environmentally friendly way?

Web Resources

CENGAGENOW™

Maximize your study time by using CengageNOW's diagnostic study plan to help you review this chapter. The Study Plan will

- help you identify areas on which you should concentrate;

- provide interactive exercises to help you master the chapter concepts; and

- provide a post-test to confirm you are ready to move on to the next chapter.

The Companion Website for *Sociology: Your Compass for a New World, The Brief Edition*, Enhanced Second Edition

www.cengage.com/sociology/brym

Supplement your review of this chapter by going to the companion website to take one of the tutorial quizzes, use flash cards to master key terms, and check out the many other study aids you'll find there. You'll also find special features such as GSS Data and Census 2000 information that will put data and resources at your fingertips to help you with that special project or help you do some research on your own.

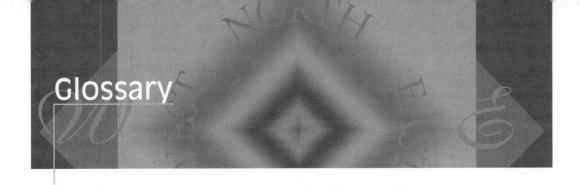

Glossary

A

Ablism: Prejudice and discrimination against disabled people.

Absolute deprivation: A condition of extreme poverty.

Abstraction: The human capacity to create general ideas or ways of thinking that are not linked to particular instances.

Achieved status: A voluntary status.

Achievement-based stratification system: A stratification system in which the allocation of rank depends on a person's accomplishments.

Acid rain: Precipitation whose acidity destroys forests and the ecosystems of lakes. It is formed by sulfur dioxide and other gases emitted by coal-burning power plants, pulp and paper mills, and motor-vehicle exhaust.

Affirmative action: A policy that gives preference to women or minority-group members if equally qualified people are available for a position, thus compensating for past discrimination.

Age cohort: A category of people born in the same range of years.

Age stratification: Social inequality among age cohorts.

Ageism: Prejudice and discrimination against people based on their age.

Altruistic suicide: Durkheim's term for suicide that occurs in high-solidarity settings, where norms tightly govern behavior. *Altruism* means devotion to the interests of others. Altruistic suicide is suicide in the group interest.

Analysis of existing documents and official statistics: A nonreactive research method that involves the analysis of diaries, newspapers, published historical works, and statistics produced by government agencies, all of which are created by people other than the researcher for purposes other than sociological research.

Anomic suicide: Durkheim's term for a type of suicide that occurs in low-solidarity settings, where norms governing behavior are vaguely defined. *Anomie* (from which the adjective is derived) means "without order."

Anticipatory socialization: Involves beginning to take on the norms and behaviors of a role to which one aspires but does not yet occupy.

Apartheid: A caste system based on race that existed in South Africa from 1948 until 1992. It consigned the large black majority to menial jobs, prevented marriage between blacks and whites, and erected separate public facilities for members of the two races. Asians and people of "mixed race" enjoyed privileges between these two extremes.

Ascribed status: An involuntary status.

Ascription-based stratification system: A stratification system in which the allocation of rank depends on the characteristics a person is born with.

Assimilation: The process by which a minority group blends into the majority population and eventually disappears as a distinct group.

Association: Exists between two variables if the value of one variable changes with the value of the other.

Authoritarian leadership: A leadership style that demands strict compliance from subordinates. Authoritarian leaders are most effective in a crisis such as a war or in the emergency room of a hospital.

Authoritarian: States that sharply restrict citizen control of government.

Authority: Legitimate, institutionalized power.

Autocracy: Form of government in which absolute power resides in a single person or party.

B

Biodiversity: The enormous variety of plant and animal species inhabiting the Earth.

Bisexuals: People who prefer sexual partners of both sexes.

Bourgeoisie: According to Marx, owners of the means of production, including factories, tools, and land. They do not do any physical labor. Their income derives from profits.

Breakdown theory: Holds that social movements emerge when traditional norms, expectations, and patterns of social organization are disrupted.

Bureaucracy: A large, impersonal organization composed of many clearly defined positions arranged in a hierarchy. A bureaucracy has a permanent, salaried staff of qualified experts and written goals, rules, and procedures. Staff members always try to find ways of running the bureaucracy more efficiently.

Bureaucratic inertia: The tendency of large, rigid bureaucracies to continue their policies even when their clients' needs change.

Bureaucratic ritualism: A situation that involves bureaucrats becoming so preoccupied with rules and regulations that they make it difficult for the organization to fulfill its goals.

C

Capitalism: The dominant economic system in the world today. Capitalist economies are characterized by private ownership of property and competition in the pursuit of profit.

Caste system: An almost pure ascription-based stratification system in which occupation and marriage partners are assigned on the basis of caste membership.

Charismatic authority: Authority based on belief in the claims of extraordinary individuals to be inspired by a god or some higher principle.

Chicago school: Group of researchers in the first decades of the 20th century who founded urban sociology in the United States. Its members distinguished themselves by their vivid and detailed descriptions and analyses of urban life and their development of the theory of human ecology.

Church: A bureaucratic religious organization that has accommodated itself to mainstream society and culture.

Civil religion: A set of quasi-religious beliefs and practices that bind a population together and justify its way of life.

Civil society: The private sphere of social life.

Class: In Marx's sense of the term, class is determined by one's relationship to the means of production, or the *source* of income (e.g., ownership of factories vs. wage labor). In Weber's usage, class is determined by one's "market situation."

Class conflict: The struggle between classes to resist and overcome the opposition of other classes.

Class consciousness: Awareness of being a member of a class.

Closed-ended question: In a survey, a type of question that provides the respondent with a list of permitted answers. Each answer is given a numerical code so that the data can later be easily input into a computer for statistical analysis.

Collective action: Occurs when people act in unison to bring about or resist social, political, and economic change.

Collective conscience: The common sentiments and values that people share as a result of living together.

Colonialism: The political control of developing societies by more powerful, developed societies.

Communism: A political and economic system characterized by public ownership of property and government planning of the economy.

Comparable worth: The equal dollar value of different jobs. It is established in gender-neutral terms by comparing jobs in terms of the education and experience needed to do them and the stress, responsibility, and working conditions associated with them.

Competition: A mode of interaction in which power is unequally distributed but the degree of inequality is less than in systems of domination. Envy is an important emotion in competitive interactions. In human-ecology theory, the struggle by different groups for optimal locations in which to reside and set up their businesses.

Conflict crimes: Illegal acts that many people consider harmful to society and that other people think are not very harmful. Such crimes are punishable by the state.

Conflict theories of deviance and crime: A category of theories which hold that deviance and crime arise out of the conflict between the powerful and the powerless.

Conflict theories of social interaction: Theories which emphasize that when people interact, their statuses are often arranged in a hierarchy. Those on top enjoy more power than those on the bottom. The degree of inequality strongly affects the character of social interaction between the interacting parties.

Conflict theory: Generally focuses on large, macro-level structures, such as the relations between or among classes. It shows how major patterns of inequality in society produce social stability in some circumstances and social change in others. It stresses how members of privileged groups try to maintain their advantages, while subordinate groups struggle to increase theirs. It typically leads to the suggestion that eliminating privilege will lower the level of conflict and increase the sum total of human welfare.

Conglomerates: Large corporations that operate in several industries at the same time.

Consensus crimes: Illegal acts that nearly all people agree are bad and harm society greatly. The state inflicts severe punishment for consensus crimes.

Constraint theories: Theories that identify the social factors that impose deviance and crime (or conventional behavior) on people.

Consumerism: The tendency to define oneself in terms of the goods one purchases.

Contagion: The process by which extreme passions supposedly spread rapidly through a crowd like a contagious disease.

Control group: The group in an experiment that is not exposed to the independent variable.

Control theory: This theory holds that the rewards of deviance and crime are ample. Therefore, nearly everyone would engage in deviance and crime if they could get away with it, and the degree to which people are prevented from violating norms and laws accounts for variations in the level of deviance and crime.

Cooperation: A mode of social interaction in which power is more or less equally distributed between people of different status. The dominant emotion in cooperative interaction is trust. Also, more generally, the human capacity to create a complex social life.

Core capitalist countries: Capitalist countries that are rich and are the major sources of capital and technology in the world: the United States, Japan, and Germany.

Corporate city: The growing post–World War II perception and organization of the North American city as a vehicle for capital accumulation.

Corporations: Legal entities that can enter into contracts and own property. They are taxed at a lower rate than individuals, and their owners typically are not liable for the corporation's debt or any harm it may cause the public.

Countercultures: Subversive subcultures. They oppose dominant values and seek to replace them.

Crime: Deviance that is against the law.

Crossnational variations in internal stratification: Differences between countries in their stratification systems.

Crude birthrate: The annual number of live births per 1,000 women in a population.

Crude deathrate: The annual number of deaths per 1,000 people in a population.

Cults: Small groups of people deeply committed to a religious vision that rejects mainstream culture and society.

Cultural capital: Widely shared, high-status cultural signals (attitudes, preferences, formal knowledge, behaviors, goals, and credentials) used for social and cultural exclusion.

Cultural lag: The tendency of symbolic culture to change more slowly than material culture.

Cultural relativism: The belief that all cultures have equal value.

Culture: The sum of practices, languages, symbols, beliefs, values, ideologies, and material objects that people create to deal with real-life problems. Cultures enable people to adapt to and thrive in their environments.

D

Dehumanization: Occurs when bureaucracies treat clients as standard cases and personnel as cogs in a giant machine. This treatment frustrates clients and lowers worker morale.

Democracy: A political system in which citizens exercise a high degree of control over the state. They do this by choosing representatives in regular, competitive elections and enjoying freedoms and constitutional protections that make political participation and competition meaningful.

Democratic leadership: A leadership style that offers more guidance than the *laissez-faire* variety but less control than the authoritarian type. Democratic leaders try to include all group members in the decision-making process, taking the best ideas from the group and molding them into a strategy with which all can identify. Outside of crisis situations, democratic leadership is usually the most effective leadership style.

Democratic Revolution: Began about 1750, during which the citizens of the United States, France, and other countries broadened their participation in government. This revolution suggested that people organize society and that human intervention can therefore resolve social problems.

Democratic socialism: A political system in which democratically elected governments own certain basic industries entirely or in part and intervene vigorously in the market to redistribute income.

Demographers: Social-scientific analysts of human population.

Demographic transition theory: Explains how changes in fertility and mortality have affected population growth from preindustrial to postindustrial times.

Denominations: The various streams of belief and practice that some churches allow to coexist under their overarching authority.

Dependency theory: Explains economic underdevelopment as the consequence of exploitative relations between rich and poor countries.

Dependent variable: The presumed effect in a cause-and-effect relationship.

Deskilling: The process by which work tasks are broken into simple routines requiring little training to perform. Deskilling is usually accompanied by the use of machinery to replace labor wherever possible and increased management control over workers.

Detached observation: A type of field research that involves classifying and counting the behavior of interest according to a predetermined scheme.

Deviance: Occurs when someone departs from a norm and evokes a reaction from others.

Differential association theory: Holds that people learn to value deviant or nondeviant lifestyles depending on whether their social environment leads them to associate more with deviants or nondeviants.

Differentiation: In human-ecology theory, the process by which urban populations and their activities become more complex and heterogeneous over time.

Disability: The inability of people to perform within the range of what is widely regarded as normal human activity.

Discrimination: Unfair treatment of people due to their group membership.

Division of labor: Specialization of work tasks. The more specialized the work tasks in a society, the greater the division of labor.

Divorce rate: The number of divorces that occur in a year for every 1,000 people in the population.

Domination: A mode of interaction in which nearly all power is concentrated in the hands of people with similar status. Fear is the dominant emotion in systems of interaction based on domination.

Dramaturgical analysis: An approach that views social interaction as a sort of play in which people present themselves so that they appear in the best possible light.

Dyad: A social relationship between two nodes, or social units (people, firms, organizations, countries).

Dysfunctions: Effects of social structures that create social instability.

E

Ecclesia: State-supported churches.

Ecological succession: In human-ecology theory, the process by which a distinct urban group moves from one area to another and a second group comes in to replace the group that has moved out.

Ecological theory: A theory of ethnic succession arguing that ethnic groups pass through five stages in their struggle for territory: invasion, resistance, competition, accommodation/cooperation, and assimilation.

Economy: The institution that organizes the production, distribution, and exchange of goods and services.

Edge cities: Exurban clusters of malls, offices, and entertainment complexes that arise at the convergence point of major highways.

Educational achievement: Refers to how much students actually learn.

Educational attainment: Refers to the number of years of school students complete.

Ego: According to Freud, a psychological mechanism that balances the conflicting needs of the pleasure-seeking id and the restraining superego.

Egoistic suicide: Durkheim's term for a type of suicide that occurs in low-solidarity settings. It results from a lack of integration of the individual into society because of weak social ties to others.

Elite theory: Holds that small groups occupying the command posts of America's most influential institutions make the important decisions that profoundly affect all members of society. Moreover, they do so without much regard for elections or public opinion.

Elites: Small groups that occupy the command posts of a society's most influential institutions.

Emigration: Or out-migration; the outflow of people from one country and their settlement in one or more other countries.

Emotion labor: Emotion management that many people do as part of their job and for which they are paid.

Emotion management: Involves people obeying "feeling rules" and responding appropriately to the situations in which they find themselves.

Environmental racism: The tendency to heap environmental dangers on the disadvantaged, especially on disadvantaged racial minorities.

Essentialism: A school of thought that sees gender differences as a reflection of biological differences between women and men.

Ethnic enclave: A spatial concentration of ethnic group members who establish businesses that serve and employ mainly members of the ethnic group and reinvest profits in the businesses and organizations of the ethnic community.

Ethnic group: Composed of people whose perceived cultural markers are deemed socially significant. Ethnic groups differ from one another in terms of language, religion, customs, values, ancestors, and the like.

Ethnocentrism: The tendency to judge other cultures exclusively by the standards of one's own.

Ethnomethodology: The study of how people make sense of what others do and say by adhering to preexisting norms.

Euthanasia: Involves a doctor prescribing or administering medication or treatment that is intended to end a terminally ill patient's life.

Exchange theory: Holds that social interaction involves trade in valued resources.

Experiment: A carefully controlled artificial situation that allows researchers to isolate hypothesized causes and measure their effects precisely.

Experimental group: The group in an experiment that is exposed to the independent variable.

Expulsion: The forcible removal of a population from a territory claimed by another population.

Extended family: Expands the nuclear family "vertically" by adding another generation—one or more of the spouses' parents—to the household.

Exurbs: Rural residential areas within commuting distance of a city.

F

Female–male earnings ratio: Women's earnings expressed as a percentage of men's earnings.

Feminist theory: Claims that patriarchy is at least as important as class inequality in determining a person's opportunities in life. It holds that male domination and female subordination are determined not by biological necessity but by structures of power and social convention. It examines the operation of patriarchy in both micro- and macro-level settings and contends that existing patterns of gender inequality can and should be changed for the benefit of all members of society.

Field research: Research based on the observation of people in their natural settings.

Folkways: A relatively unimportant norm that many people prefer to uphold. The violation of a folkway evokes mild punishment.

Formal organizations: Secondary groups designed to achieve specific and explicit objectives.

Formal punishment: Punishment that takes place when the judicial system penalizes someone for breaking a law.

Frame alignment: The process by which individual interests, beliefs, and values are made congruent and complementary with the activities, goals, and ideology of a social movement.

Free market: An economic arrangement in which prices are determined only by supply and demand.

Functional theory of stratification: Argues that (1) some jobs are more important than others; (2) people have to make sacrifices to train for important jobs; and (3) inequality is required to motivate people to undergo these sacrifices.

Functionalist theory: Stresses that human behavior is governed by relatively stable social structures. It underlines how social structures maintain or undermine social stability. It emphasizes that social structures are based mainly on shared values or preferences, and it suggests that reestablishing equilibrium can best solve most social problems.

Fundamentalists: Religious people who interpret their scriptures literally, seek to establish a direct, personal relationship with the higher being(s) they worship, and are relatively intolerant of nonfundamentalists.

G

Gated communities: Expensive, upper middle-class residential developments patrolled by security guards and walled off from the outside world.

Gender: One's sense of being male or female and playing masculine and feminine roles in ways defined as appropriate by one's culture and society.

Gender discrimination: A practice that involves rewarding men and women differently for the same work.

Gender identity: One's identification with, or sense of belonging to, a particular sex—biologically, psychologically, and socially.

Gender ideology: A set of ideas about what constitutes appropriate masculine and feminine roles and behavior.

Gender roles: The set of behaviors associated with widely shared expectations about how males and females are supposed to act.

Generalized other: According to Mead, a person's image of cultural standards and how they apply to him or her.

Genocide: The intentional extermination of an entire population defined as a race or a people.

Gentrification: The process of middle-class people moving into rundown areas of the inner city and restoring them.

Gerontocracy: A society ruled by elderly people.

Gini index: A measure of income inequality. Its value ranges from 0 (which means that every household earns exactly the same amount of money) to 1 (which means that all income is earned by a single household).

Glass ceiling: A social barrier that makes it difficult for women to rise to the top level of management.

Global commodity chain: A worldwide network of labor and production processes whose end result is a finished commodity.

Global inequality: Differences in the economic ranking of countries.

Global structures: Patterns of social relations that lie outside and above the national level. They include international organizations, patterns of worldwide travel and communication, and the economic relations between and among countries.

Global warming: The gradual worldwide increase in average surface temperature.

Globalization: The process by which formerly separate economies, states, and cultures are being tied together and people are becoming increasingly aware of their growing interdependence.

Glocalization: The simultaneous homogenization of some aspects of life and the strengthening of some local differences under the impact of globalization.

Greenhouse effect: The accumulation of carbon dioxide in the atmosphere that allows more solar radiation to enter the atmosphere and less solar radiation to escape.

Groupthink: Group pressure to conform despite individual misgivings.

H

Hate crimes: Criminal acts motivated by a person's race, religion, or ethnicity.

Health care system: Composed of a nation's clinics, hospitals, and other facilities for ensuring health and treating illness.

Heterosexuality: The preference to have members of the opposite sex as sexual partners.

Hidden curriculum: Instruction in what will be expected of students as conventionally good citizens once they leave school.

High culture: Culture consumed mainly by upper classes.

Holistic medicine: Emphasizes disease prevention. Holistic practitioners treat disease by taking into account the relationship between mind and body and between the individual and his or her social and physical environment.

Homophobia: Fear of homosexuals.

Homosexuals: People who prefer sexual partners of the same sex. People usually call homosexual men *gay* and homosexual women *lesbians.*

Hostile environment sexual harassment: Involves sexual jokes, comments, and touching that interfere with work or create an unfriendly work setting.

Human ecology: A theoretical approach to urban sociology that borrows ideas from biology and ecology to highlight the links between the physical and social dimensions of cities and identify the dynamics and patterns of urban growth.

I

I: According to Mead, the subjective and impulsive aspect of the self that is present from birth.

Id: According to Freud, the part of the self that demands immediate gratification.

Immigration: Or in-migration; the inflow of people into one country from one or more other countries and their settlement in the destination country.

Impaired: A description of people considered deficient in physical or mental capacity.

Imperialism: The economic domination of one country by another.

Independent variable: The presumed cause in a cause-and-effect relationship.

Industrial Revolution: The rapid economic transformation that began in Britain in the 1780s. It involved the large-scale application of science and technology to industrial processes, the creation of factories, and the formation of a working class. It created a host of new and serious social problems that attracted the attention of many social thinkers.

Infant mortality: The number of deaths before the age of 1 year for every 1,000 live births in a population in 1 year.

Informal punishment: Involves a mild sanction that is imposed during face-to-face interaction, not by the judicial system.

In-group: Composed of people who belong to a group.

Initiation rite: A ritual that signifies the transition of the individual from one group to another and ensures his or her loyalty to the new group.

Institutional racism: Bias that is inherent in social institutions and is often not noticed by members of the majority group.

Intergenerational mobility: Social mobility that occurs between generations.

Interlocking directorates: Structures formed by one or more individuals sitting on the board of directors of two or more noncompeting companies.

Internal colonialism: Involves one race or ethnic group subjugating another in the same country. It prevents assimilation by segregating the subordinate group in terms of jobs, housing, and social contacts.

Intersexed: People born with ambiguous genitals due to a hormone imbalance in their mother's womb or some other cause.

Intragenerational mobility: Social mobility that occurs within a single generation.

L

Labeling theory: Holds that deviance results not so much from the actions of the deviant as from the response of others, who label the rule breaker a deviant.

Labor market segmentation: The division of the market for labor into distinct settings. In these settings, work is found in different ways and workers have different characteristics. There is only a slim chance of moving from one setting to another.

Laissez-faire **leadership:** A leadership style that allows subordinates to work things out largely on their own, with almost no direction from above. It is the least effective type of leadership.

Language: A system of symbols strung together to communicate thought.

Latent functions: Invisible and unintended effects of social structures.

Law: A norm stipulated and enforced by government bodies.

Legal-rational authority: A type of authority typical of modern societies. It derives from respect for the law. Laws specify how one can achieve office. People generally believe these laws are rational. If someone achieves office by following these laws, people respect his or her authority.

Life expectancy: The average number of years a person can expect to live.

Lobbies: Organizations formed by special-interest groups to advise and influence politicians.

Looking-glass self: Cooley's description of the way our feelings about who we are depend largely on how we see ourselves evaluated by others.

M

Macrostructures: Overarching patterns of social relations that lie outside and above one's circle of intimates and acquaintances. Macrostructures include classes and power systems such as patriarchy.

Malthusian trap: A cycle of population growth followed by an outbreak of war, pestilence, or famine that keeps population growth in check.

Manifest functions: Visible and intended effects of social structures.

Markets: Social relations that regulate the exchange of goods and services. In a market, the prices of goods and services are established by how plentiful they are (supply) and how much they are wanted (demand).

Marriage: A socially approved, presumably long-term, sexual and economic union between a man and a woman. It involves reciprocal rights and obligations between spouses and between parents and their children.

Marriage rate: The number of marriages that occur in a year for every 1,000 people in the population.

Mass culture: (See *popular culture*).

Mass media: Means of mass communication that in a democracy are supposed to help keep the public informed about the quality of government.

Master status: The status that is most influential in shaping one's life at a given time and hence one's overriding public identity.

Material culture: Culture composed of the tools and objects that enable people to get tasks accomplished.

Maximum average human life span: The average age of death for a population under ideal conditions. It is currently about 85 years.

McDonaldization: A form of rationalization. Specifically, it refers to the spread of the principles of fast-food restaurants, such as efficiency, predictability, and calculability, to all spheres of life.

Me: According to Mead, the objective component of the self that emerges as people communicate symbolically and learn to take the role of the other.

Media imperialism: The domination of a mass medium by a single national culture and the undermining of other national cultures.

Medicalization of deviance: The process by which medical definitions of deviant behavior are becoming more prevalent.

Meritocracy: A stratification system in which equality of opportunity allows people to rise or fall to a position that matches their talent and effort.

Metropolitan areas: Downtown city cores and their surrounding suburbs.

Microstructures: Patterns of social relations formed during face-to-face interaction. Families, friendship circles, and work associations are all examples of microstructures.

Minority group: A group of people who are socially disadvantaged although they may be in the numerical majority.

Modernization theory: Holds that economic underdevelopment results from poor countries lacking Western attributes, including Western values, business practices, levels of investment capital, and stable governments.

Moral panic: Occurs when many people fervently believe that some form of deviance or crime poses a profound threat to society's well-being.

More: A core norm that most people believe must be upheld. The violation of a more evokes moderately harsh punishment.

Motivational theories: Theories that identify the social factors that drive people to commit deviant and criminal acts.

Multiculturalism: The view that the curricula of America's public schools and colleges should reflect the country's ethnic and racial diversity and recognize the equality of all cultures.

N

Neoliberal globalization: A policy that promotes private control of industry, minimal government interference in the running of the economy, the removal of taxes, tariffs, and restrictive regulations that discourage the international buying and selling of goods and services, and the encouragement of foreign investment.

New urban sociology: Emerged in the 1970s and stresses that city growth is a process rooted in power relations and the urge to profit.

Nonmaterial culture: Culture composed of symbols, norms, and other nontangible elements of culture.

Norms: Generally accepted ways of doing things.

Nuclear family: Consists of a cohabiting man and woman who maintain a socially approved sexual relationship and have at least one child.

O

Oligarchy: Means "rule by the few." Bureaucracies have a supposed tendency for power to become increasingly concentrated in the hands of a few people at the top of the organizational pyramid.

Open-ended question: In a survey, a type of question that allows respondents to answer in their own words.

Organizational environment: A host of economic, political, cultural, and other factors that lie outside an organization and affect the way it works.

Out-group: Composed of people who are excluded from the in-group.

Ozone layer: Lies 5 to 25 miles above the Earth's surface. It is depleted by CFCs. The depletion of the ozone layer allows more ultraviolet light to enter the Earth's atmosphere, increasing the rate of skin cancer.

P

Participant observation: A type of field research that involves carefully observing people's face-to-face interactions and participating in their lives over a long period, thus achieving a deep and sympathetic understanding of what motivates them to act in the way they do.

Parties: In Weber's usage, organizations that seek to impose their will on others.

Patriarchy: The traditional system of economic and political inequality between women and men.

Peer group: A group composed of people who are about the same age and of similar status. The peer group acts as an agent of socialization.

Peripheral capitalist countries: Countries that are former colonies; they are poor and are major sources of raw materials and cheap labor.

Placebo effect: The positive influence on healing of strong belief in the effectiveness of a cure.

Pluralism: The retention of racial and ethnic culture combined with equal access to basic social resources.

Pluralist theory: Holds that power is widely dispersed, as a result of which, no group enjoys disproportionate influence, and decisions are usually reached through negotiation and compromise.

Political opportunities: Chances for collective action and social-movement growth that emerge during election campaigns, when influential allies offer insurgents support, when ruling political alignments become unstable, and when elite groups become divided and conflict with one another.

Political parties: Organizations that compete for control of government in regular elections. In the process, they give voice to policy alternatives and rally adult citizens to vote.

Political revolution: Overthrow of political institutions by an opposition movement and replacement by new institutions.

Polygamy: Expands the nuclear family "horizontally" by adding one or more spouses (usually women) to the household.

Popular culture (or **mass culture**): Culture consumed by all classes.

Population: The entire group about which a researcher wishes to generalize.

Postindustrial Revolution: The technology-driven shift from manufacturing to service industries and the consequences of that shift for virtually all human activities.

Postmodern city: A new urban form that is more privatized, socially and culturally fragmented, and globalized than the corporate city.

Postmodernism: A style of thought characterized by an eclectic mixing of cultural elements and the erosion of authority and of consensus around some core values.

Poverty rate: The percentage of people living below the poverty threshold, which is three times the minimum food budget established by the U.S. Department of Agriculture.

Power: The probability that one actor in a social relationship will be in a position to carry out his or her own will despite resistance.

Power resource theory: Holds that change in the distribution of power between major classes partly accounts for the successes and failures of different political parties in the long term.

Prejudice: An attitude that judges a person on his or her group's real or imagined characteristics.

Primary groups: Groups in which norms, roles, and statuses are agreed upon but are not put in writing. Social interaction leads to strong emotional ties. It extends over a long period and involves a wide range of activities. It results in group members knowing one another well.

Primary labor market: A labor market that is composed disproportionately of highly skilled or well-educated white males. They are employed in large corporations that enjoy high levels of capital investment. In the primary labor market, employment is secure, earnings are high, and fringe benefits are generous.

Primary socialization: The process of acquiring the basic skills needed to function in society during childhood. Primary socialization usually takes place in a family.

Probability sample: Sample in which units have a known and nonzero chance of being selected.

Production: The human capacity to make and use tools that improve our ability to take what we want from nature.

Productivity: The amount of goods or services produced for every hour worked.

Profane: The secular, everyday world.

Professionalization: The process by which people gain control and authority over their occupation and clients.

Proletariat: According to Marx, the working class. Members of the proletariat perform physical labor but do not own means of production. They are thus in a position to earn wages.

Protestant ethic: The 16th- and 17th-century Protestant belief that religious doubts could be reduced and a state of grace assured if people worked diligently and lived ascetically. According to Weber, the Protestant ethic had the unintended effect of increasing savings and investment and thus stimulating capitalist growth.

Public health system: Composed of government-run programs that ensure access to clean drinking water, basic sewage and sanitation services, and inoculation against infectious diseases.

Public opinion: The values and attitudes of the adult population as a whole. It is expressed mainly in polls and letters to lawmakers and gives politicians a reading of citizen preferences.

Public policy: Involves the creation of laws and regulations by organizations and governments.

Q

Quid pro quo sexual harassment: Takes place when sexual threats or bribery are made a condition of employment decisions.

R

Race: A social construct used to distinguish people in terms of one or more physical markers, usually with profound effects on their lives.

Racism: The belief that a visible characteristic of a group, such as skin color, indicates group inferiority and justifies discrimination.

Randomization: In an experiment, involves assigning individuals to experimental and control groups by chance processes.

Rational choice theory: Focuses on the way interacting people weigh the benefits and costs of interaction. According to rational choice theory, interacting people always try to maximize benefits and minimize costs.

Rationalization: The application of the most efficient means to achieve given goals and the unintended, negative consequences of doing so.

Reactivity: The tendency of people who are observed by a researcher to react to the presence of the researcher by concealing certain things or acting artificially to impress the researcher.

Reference group: A group composed of people against whom an individual evaluates his or her situation or conduct.

Regionalization: The division of the world into different and often competing economic, political, and cultural areas.

Regulated market: An economic arrangement that limits the capacity of supply and demand to determine prices.

Rehabilitation: Curing disabilities to the extent possible through medical and technological intervention; trying to improve the lives of those with disabilities by means of care, training, and education; and integrating them into mainstream society.

Relative deprivation: An intolerable gap between the social rewards people expect to receive and the social rewards they actually receive.

Reliability: The degree to which a measurement procedure yields consistent results.

Religiosity: Refers to how important religion is to people.

Replacement level: The number of children that each woman must have on average for population size to remain stable. Ignoring any inflow of population from other countries and any outflow to other countries, the replacement level is 2.1.

Research: The process of systematically observing reality to assess the validity of a theory.

Resocialization: Occurs when powerful socializing agents deliberately cause rapid change in one's values, roles, and self-conception, sometimes against one's will.

Resource mobilization: The process by which social movements crystallize due to increasing organizational, material, and other resources of movement members.

Respondents: People who answer survey questions.

Revised secularization thesis: Holds that worldly institutions break off from the institution of religion over time. As a result, religion governs an ever smaller part of most people's lives and becomes largely a matter of personal choice.

Rights revolution: The process by which socially excluded groups have struggled to win equal rights under the law and in practice since the 1960s.

Rites of passage: Cultural ceremonies that mark the transition from one stage of life to another (e.g., from childhood to adulthood) or from life to death (e.g., funerals).

Rituals: Public practices designed to connect people to the sacred.

Role: The behavior (or set of behaviors) expected of a person occupying a particular position in society.

Role conflict: Occurs when two or more statuses held at the same time place contradictory role demands on a person.

Role distancing: Involves giving the impression that we are just going through the motions and that we lack serious commitment to a role.

Role set: A cluster of roles attached to a single status.

Role strain: Occurs when incompatible role demands are placed on a person in a single status.

Routinization of charisma: Weber's term for the transformation of the unique gift of divine enlightenment into a permanent feature of everyday life. It involves turning religious inspiration into a stable social institution with defined roles (interpreters of the divine message, teachers, dues-paying laypeople, and so forth).

Rumors: Claims about the world that are not supported by authenticated information. They are a form of communication that takes place when people try to construct a meaningful interpretation of an ambiguous situation. They are often short-lived, although they may recur.

S

Sacred: The religious, transcendent world.

Sample: Part of the population of research interest that is selected for analysis.

Sampling frame: A list of all the people (or other social units, such as organizations) in the population of interest to a researcher.

Sanctions: Actions indicating disappoval of deviance.

Sapir-Whorf thesis: Holds that we experience certain things in our environment and form concepts about those things. We then develop language to express our concepts. Finally, language itself influences how we see the world.

Scapegoat: A disadvantaged person or category of people whom others blame for their own problems.

Scientific management: A system of improving productivity developed in the first decade of the 20th century by Frederick W. Taylor. After analyzing the movements of workers as they did their jobs, Taylor trained them to eliminate unnecessary actions and greatly improve their efficiency.

Scientific Revolution: Began in Europe about 1550. It encouraged the view that sound conclusions about the workings of society must be based on solid evidence, not just speculation.

Secondary groups: Groups that are larger and more impersonal than primary groups. Compared with primary groups, social interaction in secondary groups creates weaker emotional ties. It extends over a shorter period, and it involves a narrow range of activities. It results in most group members having at most a passing acquaintance with one another.

Secondary labor market: A labor market that contains a disproportionately large number of women and members of racial minorities, particularly African and Hispanic Americans. Employees in the secondary labor market tend to be unskilled and lack higher education. They work in small firms with low levels of capital investment. Employment is insecure, earnings are low, and fringe benefits are meager.

Secondary socialization: Socialization outside the family after childhood.

Sects: Religious groups that usually form by breaking away from churches due to disagreement about church doctrine. Sects are less integrated into society and less bureaucratized than churches. They are often led by charismatic leaders, who tend to be relatively intolerant of religious opinions other than their own.

Secularization thesis: Holds that religious institutions, actions, and consciousness are on the decline worldwide.

Segregation: Involves the spatial and institutional separation of racial or ethnic groups.

Self: Consists of one's ideas and attitudes about who one is.

Self-fulfilling prophecy: An expectation that helps bring about the result that it predicts.

Self-report surveys: In such surveys, respondents are asked to report their involvement in criminal activities, either as perpetrators or as victims.

Self-socialization: Involves choosing socialization influences from the wide variety of mass media offerings.

Semiperipheral capitalist countries: Countries, comprising former colonies, that are making considerable headway in their attempts to industrialize, such as South Korea, Taiwan, and Israel.

Sex: An aspect of one's biological makeup that depends on whether one is born with distinct male or female genitals and a genetic program that releases either male or female hormones to stimulate the development of one's reproductive system.

Sex ratio: The ratio of women to men in a geographical area.

Sick role: According to Talcott Parsons, involves (1) the nondeliberate suspension of routine responsibilities, (2) wanting to be well, (3) seeking competent help, and (4) cooperating with health care practitioners at all times.

Significant others: A category that is composed of people who play important roles in the early socialization experiences of children.

Slavery: The ownership and control of people.

Social category: A category that is composed of people who share similar status but do not identify with one another.

Social constructionism: A school of thought which argues that apparently natural or innate features of life are often sustained by *social* processes that vary historically and culturally. For example, gender differences are seen by social constructionists as a reflection of the different social positions occupied by women and men and the social institutions and processes that support those differences.

Social control: In the study of social movements, social control refers to the containment of collective action by co-optation, concessions, and coercion.

Social deviations: Noncriminal departures from norms that are nonetheless subject to official control. Some members of the public regard them as somewhat harmful, whereas other members of the public do not.

Social diversion: A minor act of deviance that is generally perceived as relatively harmless and that evokes, at most, a mild societal reaction such as amusement or disdain.

Social group: A group that is composed of one or more networks of people who identify with one another and adhere to defined norms, roles, and statuses.

Social interaction: Involves people communicating face-to-face or via computer, acting and reacting in relation to other people. It is structured around norms, roles, and statuses.

Social movements: Collective attempts to change all or part of the social order by stepping outside the rules of normal politics and rioting, petitioning, striking, demonstrating, and establishing lobbies, unions, and political parties.

Social network: A bounded set of individuals who are linked by the exchange of material or emotional resources. The patterns of exchange determine the boundaries of the network. Members exchange resources more frequently with each other than with nonmembers. They also think of themselves as network members. Social networks may be formal (defined in writing), but they are more often informal (defined only in practice).

Social solidarity: (1) The degree to which group members share beliefs and values and (2) the intensity and frequency of their interaction.

Social stratification: Refers to the way society is organized in layers or strata.

Social structures: Stable patterns of social relations.

Socialization: The process by which people learn their culture. They do so by entering and disengaging from a succession of roles and becoming aware of themselves as they interact with others.

Society: People who interact, usually in a defined territory, and share a culture.

Socioeconomic index (SEI) of occupational status: An index developed by Blau and Duncan that combines, for each occupation, average earnings and years of education of men employed full time in the occupation.

Socioeconomic status (SES): Combines income, education, and occupational prestige data in a single index of one's position in the socioeconomic hierarchy.

Sociological imagination: The quality of mind that enables one to see the connection between personal troubles and social structures.

Sociology: The systematic study of human behavior in social context.

Solidarity theory: Holds that social movements are social organizations that emerge when potential members can mobilize resources, take advantage of new political opportunities, and avoid high levels of social control by authorities.

Split labor markets: A situation in which low-wage workers of one race and high-wage workers of another race compete for the same jobs. High-wage workers are likely to resent the presence of low-wage competitors, and conflict is bound to result. Consequently, racist attitudes develop or get reinforced.

State: The institutions responsible for formulating and carrying out a country's laws and public policies.

State-centered theory: Holds that the state itself can structure political life to some degree independently of the way in which power is distributed between classes and other groups at a given time.

Status: A recognized social position that an individual can occupy.

Status cues: Visual indicators of a person's social position.

Status groups: Groups that differ from one another in terms of the prestige or social honor they enjoy and in terms of their lifestyle.

Status set: The entire ensemble of statuses occupied by an individual.

Stereotype threat: The impact of negative stereotypes on the school performance of disadvantaged groups.

Stereotypes: Rigid views of how members of various groups act, regardless of whether individual group members really behave that way.

Stigma: A marker that distinguishes some people from others and allows them to be negatively evaluated and treated.

Strain: Breakdown in traditional norms that precede collective action.

Strain theory: A theory which holds that people may turn to deviance when they experience strain. Strain results when a culture teaches people the value of material success and society fails to provide enough legitimate opportunities for everyone to succeed.

Street crimes: Crimes that include arson, burglary, assault, and other illegal acts disproportionately committed by people from lower classes.

Structural mobility: Social mobility that results from change in the distribution of occupations.

Subcultural theory: This theory argues that gangs are a collective adaptation to social conditions. Distinct norms and values that reject the legitimate world crystallize in gangs.

Subculture: A set of distinctive values, norms, and practices within a larger culture.

Suburbanism: A way of life outside city centers that is organized mainly around the needs of children and involves higher levels of conformity and sociability than life in the central city.

Superego: According to Freud, the part of the self that acts as a repository of cultural standards.

Survey: Asks people questions about their knowledge, attitudes, or behavior, either in a face-to-face interview, telephone interview, or paper-and-pencil format.

Symbol: Ideas that carry a particular meaning, including the components of language, mathematical notations, and signs.

Symbolic ethnicity: A nostalgic allegiance to the culture of the immigrant generation, or that of the old country, that is not usually incorporated into everyday behavior.

Symbolic interactionist theory: Focuses on interpersonal communication in micro-level social settings. It emphasizes that an adequate explanation of social behavior requires understanding the subjective meanings people attach to their social circumstances. It stresses that people help create their social circumstances and do not merely react to them. By underscoring the subjective meanings people create in small social settings, it validates unpopular and nonofficial viewpoints. This increases our understanding and tolerance of people who may be different from us.

T

Taboos: The strongest and most central norms. When someone violates a taboo, it causes revulsion in the community, and punishment is severe.

Techniques of neutralization: The rationalizations that deviants and criminals use to justify their activities. Techniques of neutralization make deviance and crime seem normal, at least to the deviants and criminals themselves.

Thomas theorem: States that "situations we define as real become real in their consequences."

Total fertility rate: The average number of children that would be born to a woman over her lifetime if she had the same average number of children as women in each age cohort in a given year.

Total institutions: Settings where people are isolated from the larger society and under the strict control and constant supervision of a specialized staff.

Totems: Objects that symbolize the sacred.

Tracking: The procedure of sorting students into high-ability, middle-ability, and low-ability classes based on the results of IQ and other tests.

Traditional authority: The norm in tribal and feudal societies, involving rulers inheriting authority through family or clan ties. The right of a family or clan to monopolize leadership is widely believed to be derived from a god's will.

Traditional nuclear family: A nuclear family in which the husband works outside the home for money and the wife works in the home without pay.

Transgendered: People who break society's gender norms by defying the rigid distinction between male and female. They may be heterosexual or homosexual.

Transnational corporations: Large businesses that rely increasingly on foreign labor and foreign production; skills and advances in design, technology, and management; world markets; and massive advertising campaigns. They are increasingly autonomous from national governments.

Transsexuals: People who believe they were born with the "wrong" body. They identify with, and want to live fully as, members of the "opposite" sex, and to do so they often change their appearance or resort to medical intervention. They may be heterosexual or homosexual.

Triad: A social relationship among three nodes, or social units (people, firms, organizations, countries).

U

Unconscious: According to Freud, the part of the self that contains repressed memories that we are not normally aware of.

Union density: Union members as a percent of nonfarm workers.

Unions: Organizations of workers that seek to defend and promote their members' interests.

Urban sprawl: The spread of cities into ever-larger expanses of the surrounding countryside.

Urbanism: A way of life that, according to Louis Wirth, involves increased tolerance but also emotional withdrawal and specialized, impersonal, and self-interested interaction.

V

Validity: The degree to which a measure actually measures what it is intended to measure.

Values: Ideas about what is right and wrong, good and bad, beautiful and ugly.

Vertical social mobility: Movement up or down the stratification system.

Victimless crimes: Crimes that involve violations of the law in which no victim steps forward and is identified.

Virtual community: An association of people, scattered across the country, continent, or planet, who communicate via computer and modem about a subject of common interest.

W

White-collar crime: An illegal act committed by a respectable, high-status person in the course of work.

References

Abelmann, Nancy, and John Lie. 1995. *Blue Dreams: Korean Americans and the Los Angeles Riots.* Cambridge, MA: Harvard University Press.

Abraham, Laurie Kaye. 1993. *Mama Might Be Better Off Dead: The Failure of Health Care in Urban America.* Chicago: University of Chicago Press.

Abramsky, Sasha. 1999. "When They Get Out." *The Atlantic Monthly* June. On the World Wide Web at http://www.theatlantic.com/issues/99jun/9906prisoners.htm (29 April 2000).

Achilles, Rhona. 1993. "Desperately Seeking Babies: New Technologies of Hope and Despair." Pp. 214–229 in Bonnie J. Fox, ed. *Family Patterns, Gender Relations.* Toronto: Oxford University Press.

Adams, Henry E., Lester W. Wright, Jr., and Bethany A. Lohr. 1998. "Is Homophobia Associated with Homosexual Arousal?" *Journal of Abnormal Psychology* 105: 440–445.

Adherents.com. 2001. "Religion Statistics: Predominant Religions." On the World Wide Web at http://www.adherents.com/adh_predonm.html (30 November 2001).

Adler, Patricia A., and Peter Adler. 1998. *Peer Power: Preadolescent Culture and Identity.* New Brunswick, NJ: Rutgers University Press.

Agenda Inc. "American Bandstand 2005." On the World Wide Web at http://www.agendainc.com/brandstand05.pdf (26 March 2005).

Ahmad, Imad-ad-Dean. 2000. "Female Genital Mutilation: An Islamic Perspective." On the World Wide Web at http://www.minaret.org/fgm-pamphlet.htm (20 January 2003).

Akin, David. 2002 "Kevin Warwick is a Borg." *Globe and Mail* June 1: F7.

Albelda, Randy, and Nancy Folbre. 1996. *The War on the Poor: A Defense Manual.* New York: New Press.

Albrow, Martin. 1997. *The Global Age: State and Society Beyond Modernity.* Stanford, CA: Stanford University Press.

Aldrich, Howard E. 1979. *Organizations and Environments.* Englewood Cliffs, NJ: Prentice-Hall.

Alford, Robert R., and Roger Friedland. 1985. *Powers of Theory: Capitalism, the State, and Democracy.* Cambridge: Cambridge University Press.

Althaus, Scott. L. 2005. "How Exceptional Was Turnout in 2004?" *Political Communication Report* 15, 1. On the World Wide Web at http://www.ou.edu/policom/1501_2005_winter/commentary.htm (21 August 2005).

Amato, Paul R., and Bruce Keith. 1991. "Parental Divorce and the Well-Being of Children: A Meta-Analysis." *Psychological Bulletin* 110: 26–46.

American Association of Retired People. 2001. *A Profile of Older Americans 2001.* On the World Wide Web at http://research.aarp.org/general/profile_2001.pdf (23 April 2003).

American Association of Suicidology. 2008. "U.S.A. Suicide: 2005 Official Final Data." On the World Wide Web at http://www.suicidology.org/assocations/1045/files/2005datapgs.pdf (7 August 2008).

American Chiropractic Association. 1999. "Two More Surveys Show Demand for Alternative Care is Rising." On the World Wide Web at http://www.amerchiro.org/research/new_research.html (2 May 2000).

American Psychological Association. "Answers to Your Questions About Sexual Orientation and Homosexuality." 1998. On the World Wide Web at http://www.apa.org/pubinfo/orient.html (14 June 2000).

American Society of Plastic Surgeons. 2008. "National Clearinghouse of Plastic Surgery Statistics." On the World Wide Web at http://www.plasticsurgery.org/media/statistics/index.cfm (6 March 2009).

American Sociological Association. 1999. *Code of Ethics and Policies and Procedures of the ASA Committee on Professional Ethics.* Washington DC: Author.

Anderson, Ben. 1999. "GOP Combats Census Sampling with Money, Logistics." *Conservative News Service.* On the World Wide Web at http://www.conservativenews.net/InDepth/archive/199903/IND19990316b.html (6 May 2000).

Anderson, Benedict O. 1991. *Imagined Communities: Reflections on the Origin and Spread of Nationalism.* London: Verso.

Anderson, Craig, and Brad J. Bushman. 2002. "The Effects of Media Violence on Society." *Science* 295, 5564: 2377–2379.

Anderson, Elijah. 1990. *Streetwise: Race, Class, and Change in an Urban Community.* Chicago: University of Chicago Press.

Anderson, Gerald F., Uwe E. Reinhardt, Peter S. Hussey, and Varduhi Petrosyan. 2003. "It's the Prices, Stupid: Why the United States Is So Different from Other Countries." *Health Affairs* 22, 3: 89–105.

Anderson, Michael. 2003. "Reading Violence in Boys' Writing." *Language Arts* 80, 3: 223–231.

Anderson, Robert N. 2002. "Deaths: Leading Causes for 2000." *National Vital Statistics Reports* 50, 16. On the World Wide Web at http://www.cdc.gov/nchs/data/nvsr/nvsr50/nvsr50_16.pdf (13 June 2003).

Angier, Natalie. 2000. "Do Races Differ? Not Really, DNA Shows." *The New York Times on the Web* 22 August. On the World Wide Web at http://www.nytimes.com/library/national/science/082200sci-genetics-race.html (24 August 2000).

Angus Reid. 2007. "Death Penalty Backed in Four Countries." On the World Wide Web at http://www.angus-reid.com/polls/view/death_penalty_backed_in_four_countries/ (9 August 2008).

Annie E. Casey Foundation. 1998. *Child Care You Can Count On: Model Programs and Policies.* Baltimore. On the World Wide Web at http://www.kidscount.org/publications/child/afford.htm (30 April 2000).

Anti-Defamation League. 1999. "School Vouchers: The Wrong Choice for Public Education." On the World Wide Web at http://www.adl.org/frames/front_vouchers.html (10 August 2000).

Ariès, Phillipe. 1962 [1960]. *Centuries of Childhood: A Social History of Family Life,* Robert Baldick, trans. New York: Knopf.

_____. 1982. *The Hour of Our Death.* New York: Knopf.

Arnett, Jeffrey Jensen. 1995. "Adolescents' Uses of Media for Self-Socialization." *Journal of Youth and Adolescence* 24: 519–533.

Asch, Solomon. 1955. "Opinion and Social Pressure." *Scientific American* July: 31–35.

Associated Press. 2002. "More People on Welfare after Years of Decline." *New York Times* December 31. On the World Wide Web at http://www.nytimes.com (31 December 2002).

Averett, Susan, and Sanders Korenman. 1996. "The Economic Reality of *The Beauty Myth.*" *Journal of Human Resources* 31: 304–330.

Avery, Christopher, Andrew Fairbanks, and Richard Zeckhauser. 2003. *The Early Admission Game: Joining the Elite.* Cambridge, MA: Harvard University Press.

Baca Zinn, M., and D. Stanley Eitzen. 1993 [1988]. *Diversity in American Families,* 3rd ed. New York: HarperCollins.

Bairoch, Paul. 1988 [1985]. *Cities and Economic Development: From the Dawn of History to the Present.* Christopher Braider, trans. Chicago: University of Chicago Press.

Bales, Kevin. 1999. *Disposable People: New Slavery in the Global Economy.* Berkeley: University of California Press.

_____. 2002. "The Social Psychology of Modern Slavery." *Scientific American* 286, 4: 80–88.

Baltzell, E. Digby. 1964. *The Protestant Establishment: Aristocracy and Caste in America.* New York: Vintage.

Banner, Lois W. 1992. *In Full Flower: Aging Women, Power, and Sexuality.* New York: Knopf.

Baran, Paul A. 1957. *The Political Economy of Growth.* New York: Monthly Review Press.

Barber, Benjamin. 1992. "Jihad vs. McWorld," *The Atlantic Monthly* March. On the World Wide Web at http://www.theatlantic.com/politics/foreign/barberf.htm (28 April 2000).

_____. 1996. *Jihad vs. McWorld: How Globalism and Tribalism are Reshaping the World.* New York: Ballantine Books.

Bardes, Barbara A., and Robert W. Oldendick. 2003. *Public Opinion: Measuring the American Mind.* Belmont, CA: Wadsworth.

Barlett, Donald L., and James B. Steele. 2002. "Playing the Political Slots." *Time* December 23: 38–47.

Barnard, Chester I. 1938. *The Functions of the Executive.* Cambridge, MA: Harvard University Press.

Barnet, Richard J., and John Cavanagh. 1994. *Global Dreams: Imperial Corporations and the New World Order.* New York: Simon & Schuster.

Barnett, Cynthia. n.d. "The Measurement of White-Collar Crime Using Uniform Crime Reporting (UCR) Data." U.S. Department of Justice, Federal Bureau of Investigation, Criminal Justice Information Services (CJIS) Division. On the World Wide Web at http://www.fbi.gov/ucr/whitecollarforweb.pdf (21 February 2003).

Bar-On, Dan. 1999. *The Indescribable and the Undiscussable: Reconstructing Human Discourse After Trauma.* Ithaca, NY: Cornell University Press.

Barry, Patricia. 2002a. "Ads, Promotions Drive up Drug Costs." *AARP.* On the World Wide Web at http://www.aarp.org/bulletin/departments/2002/medicare/0310_medicare_1.html (17 June 2003).

_____. 2002b. "Drug Industry Spends Huge Sums Guarding Prices." *AARP.* On the World Wide Web at http://www.aarp.org/bulletin/departments/2002/medicare/0510_medicare_1.html (17 June 2003).

_____. 2002c. "Drug Profits vs. Research." *AARP.* On the World Wide Web at http://www.aarp.org/bulletin/departments/2002/medicare/0605_medicare_1.html (17 June 2003).

Bartfeld, Judi. 2000. "Child Support and the Postdivorce Economic Well-Being of Mothers, Fathers, and Children." *Demography* 37: 203–213.

Barth, Fredrik, ed. 1969. *Ethnic Groups and Boundaries: The Social Organization of Cultural Difference.* Boston: Little, Brown.

Baudrillard, Jean. 1988 [1986]. *America.* Chris Turner, trans. London: Verso.

Bauman, Zygmunt. 1991 [1989]. *Modernity and the Holocaust.* Ithaca, NY: Cornell University Press.

Bayer, Ada-Helen, and Leon Harper. 2000. *Fixing to Stay: A National Survey of Housing and Home Modification Issues.* Washington, DC: AARP. On the World Wide Web at http://research.aarp.org/il/home_mod.pdf (13 August 2000).

Bean, Frank D., and Marta Tienda. 1987. *The Hispanic Population of the United States.* New York: Russell Sage Foundation.

Beauvoir, Simone de. 1972 [1970]. *The Coming of Age,* Patrick O'Brian, trans. New York: G.P. Putnam's Sons.

Becker, Elizabeth. 2003. "U.S. Ready to End Tariffs on Textiles in Hemisphere." *New York Times* February 11. On the World Wide Web at http://www.nytimes.com (13 February 2003).

Becker, Ernest. 1973. *The Denial of Death.* New York: Free Press.

Becker, Gaylene. 1980. *Growing Old in Silence.* Berkeley: University of California Press.

Becker, Howard. 1963. *Outsiders: Studies in the Sociology of Deviance.* New York: Free Press of Glencoe.

Beil, Laura. 2007. "For Struggling Black College, Hopes of a Revival." *New York Times* December 5. On the World Wide Web at http://www.nytimes.com/2007/12/05/education/05wiley.html?scp=1&sq=wiley%20college&st=cse (19 August 2008).

Bell, Daniel. 1973. *The Coming of Post-Industrial Society: A Venture in Social Forecasting.* New York: Basic Books.

Bell, Wendell, and Robert V. Robinson. 1980. "Cognitive Maps of Class and Racial Inequalities in England and the United States." *American Journal of Sociology* 86: 320–349.

Bellah, Robert A. 1975. *The Broken Covenant: American Civil Religion in a Time of Trial.* New York: Seabury Press.

Belluck, Pam. 2002. "New Wave of the Homeless Floods Cities' Shelters." *New York Times* December 18. On the World Wide Web at http://www.nytimes.com (18 December 2002).

Benford, Robert D. 1997. "An Insider's Critique of the Social Movement Framing Perspective." *Sociological Inquiry* 67: 409–439.

Benson, John M. 1999. "End-of-Life Issues." *Public Opinion Quarterly* 63: 263–277.

Berger, Peter L., and Thomas Luckmann. 1966. *The Social Construction of Reality: A Treatise in the Sociology of Knowledge.* Garden City, NY: Doubleday.

Berk, Richard A. 1974. *Collective Behavior.* Dubuque, IA: Wm. C. Brown.

Berk, Sarah Fenstermaker. 1985. *The Gender Factory: The Apportionment of Work in American Households.* New York: Plenum.

Berliner, Wendy. 2004. "Where Have All the Young Men Gone?" *Manchester Guardian* 18 May: 8.

Besserer, Sandra. 1998. "Criminal Victimization: An International Perspective." *Juristat* 18, 6.

Bianchi, Suzanne M., and Lynne M. Casper. 2000. "American Families." *Population Bulletin* 55, 4. On the World Wide Web at http://www.ameristat.org/Template.cfm?Section=Population_Bulletin1&template=/ContentManagement/ContentDisplay.cfm&ContentID=5885 (9 June 2003).

_____ and Daphne Spain. 1996. "Women, Work, and Family in America." *Population Bulletin* 51, 3: 2–48.

Biegler, Rebecca S. 1999. "Psychological Interventions Designed to Counter Sexism in Children: Empirical Limitations and Theoretical Foundations." Pp. 129–152 in W. B. Swann, Jr., J. H. Langlois and L. A. Gilbert, eds. *Sexism and Stereotypes in Modern Society: The Gender Science of Janet Taylor Spence.* Washington, DC: American Psychological Association.

Bierstedt, Robert. 1974. "An Analysis of Social Power." Pp. 220–41 in *Power and Progress: Essays in Sociological Theory.* New York: McGraw-Hill.

Birdsall, Nancy. 2005. "Rising Inequality in the New Global Economy." *Wider Angle* 2: 1–3.

Black, Donald. 1989. *Sociological Justice.* New York: Oxford University Press.

Blau, Peter M. 1963 [1955]. *The Dynamics of Bureaucracy: A Study of Interpersonal Relationships in Two Government Agencies,* rev. ed. Chicago: University of Chicago Press.

_____. 1964. *Exchange and Power in Social Life.* New York: Wiley.

_____ and Otis Dudley Duncan. 1967. *The American Occupational Structure.* New York: Wiley.

Blazer, Dan G., Ronald C. Kessler, Katherine A. McGonagle, and Marvin S. Swartz. 1994. "The Prevalence and Distribution of Major Depression in a National Community Sample: The National Comorbidity Survey." *American Journal of Psychiatry* 151: 979–86.

Blauner, Robert. 1972. *Racial Oppression in America.* New York: Harper & Row.

Block, Fred. 1979. "The Ruling Class Does Not Rule." Pp. 128–140 in R. Quinney, ed. *Capitalist Society.* Homewood, IL: Dorsey Press.

Bluestone, Barry, and Bennett Harrison. 1982. *The Deindustrialization of America.* New York: Basic Books.

Blum, Deborah. 1997. *Sex on the Brain: The Biological Differences Between Men and Women.* New York: Penguin.

Blumer, Herbert. 1969. *Symbolic Interactionism: Perspective and Method.* Englewood Cliffs, NJ: Prentice-Hall.

Bonacich, Edna. 1972. "A Theory of Ethnic Antagonism: The Split Labor Market." *American Sociological Review* 37: 547–559.

_____. 1973. "A Theory of Middleman Minorities." *American Sociological Review* 38: 583–594.

Bornholt, Laurel. 2001. "Self-Concepts, Usefulness, and Behavioral Intentions in the Social Context of Schooling." *Educational Psychology* 21: 67–78.

Bornschier, Volker, and Christopher Chase-Dunn. 1985. *Transnational Corporations and Underdevelopment.* New York: Praeger.

Boston Women's Health Book Collective, ed. 1998. *Our Bodies, Our Selves for the New Century: A Book by and for Women.* New York: Simon & Schuster.

Boswell, A. Ayres, and Joan Z. Spade. 1996. "Fraternities and Collegiate Rape Culture: Why Are Some Fraternities More Dangerous Places for Women." *Gender and Society* 10: 133–147.

Bourdieu, Pierre. 1977 [1972]. *Outline of a Theory of Practice,* Richard Nice, trans. Cambridge: Cambridge University Press.

_____. 1998. *Acts of Resistance: Against the Tyranny of the Market,* Richard Nice, trans. New York: New Press.

Bourdieu, Pierre, and Jean-Claude Passeron. 1990 [1977]. *Reproduction in Education, Society and Culture,* 2nd ed., Richard Nice, trans. London: Sage.

Bowen, William G., and Derek Bok. 1998. *The Shape of the River: Long-Term Consequences of Considering Race in College and University Admissions.* Princeton, NJ: Princeton University Press.

Bowles, Samuel, and Herbert Gintis. 1976. *Schooling in Capitalist America: Educational Reform and the Contradictions of Economic Life.* New York: Basic Books.

Boyd, Monica. 1997. "Feminizing Paid Work." *Current Sociology* 45: 49–73.

Bradbury, Bruce, and Markus Jäntti. 2001. "Child Poverty across Twenty-five Countries." Pp. 62–91 in Bruce Bradbury, Stephen P. Jenkins, and John Micklewright, eds. *The Dynamics of Child Poverty in Industrialised Countries.* Cambridge: Cambridge University Press.

Bracey, Gerald W. 1998. "Are U.S. Students Behind?" On the World Wide Web at http://www.prospect.org/archives/37/37bracfs.htlm (1 May 2000).

Brains, Craig Leonard. 1999. "When Registration Barriers Fall, Who Votes?" *Public Choice* 35: 161–176.

Braithwaite, John. 1989. *Crime, Shame and Reintegration.* New York: Cambridge University Press.

Braverman, Harry. 1974. *Labor and Monopoly Capital: The Degradation of Work in the Twentieth Century.* New York: Monthly Review Press.

Brazzini, D. G., W. D. McIntosh, S. M. Smith, S. Cook and C. Harris. 1997. "The Aging Woman in Popular Film: Underrepresented, Unattractive, Unfriendly, and Unintelligent." *Sex Roles* 36: 531–543.

Bray, Dennis, and Hans von Storch. 2005. "Survey of Climate Scientists: 1996, 2003." On the World Wide Web at http://w3g.gkss.de/G/Mitarbeiter/bray.html/BrayGKSSsite/BrayGKSS/surveyframe.html (21 December 2005).

Breault, K. D. 1986. "Suicide in America: A Test of Durkheim's Theory of Religious and Family Integration, 1933–1980." *American Journal of Sociology* 92: 628–656.

Brechin, Steven R., and Willett Kempton. 1994. "Global Environmentalism: A Challenge to the Postmaterialism Thesis." *Social Science Quarterly* 75: 245–269.

Brennan, Teresa. 2003. *Globalization and Its Terrors: Daily Life in the West.* London: Routledge.

Brinkhoff, Thomas. 2007. "The Principal Agglomerations of the World." On the World Wide Web at http://www.citypopulation.de/World.html (21 August 2008).

Brint, Stephen. 1984. "New Class and Cumulative Trend Explanations of the Liberal Political Attitudes of Professionals." *American Journal of Sociology* 90: 30–71.

"British Magazines Agree to Ban Ultra-thin Models." 2000. *National Post* 23 June: A2.

Brooks, Clem, and Jeff Manza. 1997. "Social Cleavages and Political Alignments: U.S. Presidential Elections, 1960 to 1992." *American Sociological Review* 62: 937–946.

Brouwer, Steve. 1998. *Sharing the Pie: A Citizen's Guide to Wealth and Power in America.* New York: Holt.

Brower, David. 1975. *Training the Nihilists: Education and Radicalism in Tsarist Russia.* Ithaca, NY: Cornell University Press.

Brown, Dee A. 1970. *Bury My Heart at Wounded Knee: An Indian History of the American West.* New York: Henry Holt.

Brown, Lyn Mikel, and Carol Gilligan. 1992. *Meeting at the Crossroads: Women's Psychology and Girls' Development.* Cambridge, MA: Harvard University Press.

Brown, Peter. 1996. *The Rise of Western Christendom: Triumph and Diversity, A.D. 200–1000.* Oxford: Blackwell.

Browne, Kevin D., and Catherine Hamilton-Giachritsis. 2005. "The Influence of Violent Media on Children and Adolescents: A Public-Health Approach." *The Lancet* 365, 9460: 702–710.

Browning, Christopher R. 1992. *Ordinary Men: Reserve Police Battalion 101 and the Final Solution in Poland.* New York: HarperCollins.

Bruce, Steve. 1988. *The Rise and Fall of the New Christian Right: Conservative Protestant Politics in America 1978–1988.* Oxford: Clarendon Press.

_____. 1990. *Pray TV: Televangelism in America.* London: Routledge.

Brumberg, Joan Jacobs. 1997. *The Body Project: An Intimate History of American Girls.* New York: Random House.

Brym, Robert J. 1979. "Political Conservatism in Atlantic Canada." Pp. 59–79 in Robert J. Brym and R. James Sacouman, eds. *Underdevelopment and Social Movements in Atlantic Canada.* Toronto: New Hogtown Press.

_____. 1980. *Intellectuals and Politics.* London: George Allen & Unwin.

_____. 2002. "Canadian Sociology: An Introduction to the Upper Thirteen." *American Sociologist* 33: 5–11.

_____. 2007. "Six lessons of suicide bombers." *Contexts* 6, 4: 40–45.

_____. 2009a. "Affluence, strikes, and power in Canada, 1973-2005." Pp. 61–75 in Edward Grabb and Neil Guppy, eds. *Social Inequality in Canada: Patterns, Problems, Policies,* 5th ed. Scarborough, ON: Prentice-Hall Canada.

_____. 2009b. *Sociology as a Life or Death Issue.* Belmont, CA: Wadsworth Cengage Learning.

_____ and Bader Araj. 2006. "Suicide bombing as strategy and interaction: The case of the second *intifada*," *Social Forces* 84: 165–82.

_____ and Evel Economakis. 1994. "Peasant or proletarian? Blacklisted Pskov Workers in St. Petersburg, 1913." *Slavic Review* 53: 120–139.

_____ with Bonnie J. Fox. 1989. *From Culture to Power: The Sociology of English Canada.* Toronto: Oxford University Press.

_____, Michael Gillespie, and A. Ron Gillis. 1985. "Anomie, Opportunity, and the Density of Ethnic Ties: Another View of Jewish Outmarriage in Canada." *Canadian Review of Sociology and Anthropology* 22: 102–112.

_____, Michael Gillespie, and Rhonda L. Lenton. 1989. "Class Power, Class Mobilization, and Class Voting: The Canadian Case." *Canadian Journal of Sociology* 14: 25–44.

_____ and Rhonda Lenton. 2001. *Love Online: A Report on Digital Dating in Canada.* Toronto: MSN. CA. On the World Wide Web at http://www.nelson .com/nelson/harcourt/sociology/newsociety3e/socplus .htm (30 December 2003).

Bryson, Ken, and Lynne M. Casper. 1998. *Household and Family Characteristics: March 1997.* Washington, DC: U.S. Department of Commerce, Economics and Statistics Administration. On the World Wide Web at http://www.census.gov/prod/3/98pubs/p20-509.pdf (1 May 2000).

Brzezinski, Zbigniew. 1993. *Out of Control: Global Turmoil on the Eve of the Twenty-first Century.* New York: Scribner.

_____. 2002. "Confronting Anti-American Grievances." *New York Times* 1 September. On the World Wide Web at http://www.nytimes.com (1 September 2002).

Bullard, Robert D. 1994 [1990]. *Dumping in Dixie: Race, Class and Environmental Quality,* 2nd ed. Boulder, CO: Westview Press.

Bumiller, Elisabeth. 2002. "Bush Calls Ruling About Vouchers 'Historic'." 2002. *New York Times* July 2. On the World Wide Web at http://www.nytimes.com (July 2).

_____. 2003. "Evangelicals Sway White House on Human Rights Issue Abroad." *New York Times* October 26. On the World Wide Web at http://www.nytimes.com (26 October 2003).

Burawoy, Michael. 1979. *Manufacturing Consent: Changes in the Labor Process under Monopoly Capitalism.* Chicago: University of Chicago Press.

Bureau of Justice Statistics. 2002. *Sourcebook of Criminal Justice Statistics, 2001.* On the World Wide Web at http://www.albany.edu/sourcebook/1995 (15 February 2003).

Burleigh, Michael. 2000. *The Third Reich: A New History.* New York: Hill & Wang.

Burns, Tom, and G. M. Stalker. 1961. *The Management of Innovation.* London: Tavistock.

Bush, George W. 2001. "Address to a Joint Session of Congress and the American People." On the World Wide Web at http://www.whitehouse.gov/news/ releases/2001/09/20010920-8.html (22 December 2002).

"The Business of Touch." 2006. On the World Wide Web at http://www.businessoftouch.com/index2.html (7 April 2006).

Buss, D. M. 1998. "The Psychology of Human Mate Selection: Exploring the Complexity of the Strategic Repertoire." Pp. 405–29 in C. Crawford and D. L. Krebs, eds. *Handbook of Evolutionary Psychology: Ideas, Issues, and Applications.* Mahwah, NJ: Erlbaum.

Butterfield, Fox. 2001. "Killings Increase in Many Big Cities." *New York Times on the Web.* On the World Wide Web at http://www.nytimes.com/2001/12/21/ national/21CRIM.html?todaysheadlines (21 December 2001).

Camarillo, Albert. 1979. *Chicanos in a Changing Society: From Mexican Pueblos to American Barrios in Santa Barbara and Southern California, 1848–1930.* Cambridge, MA: Harvard University Press.

Campbell, Donald, and Julian Stanley. 1963. *Experimental and Quasi-Experimental Designs for Research.* Chicago: Rand McNally.

Campbell, Frances A., and Craig T. Ramey. 1994. "Effects of Early Intervention on Intellectual and Academic Achievement: A Follow-up Study of Children from Low income Families." *Child Development* 65: 684–698.

_____, _____, E. P. Pungello, S. Miller-Johnson, and J. Sparling. 2002. "Early Childhood Education: Young Adult Outcomes from the Abecedarian Project." *Applied Developmental Science.*

Campbell, Jane, and Mike Oliver. 1996. *Disability Politics: Understanding Our Past, Changing Our Future.* London: Routledge.

Campion, Edward W. 1993. "Why Unconventional Medicine?" *New England Journal of Medicine* 328: 282.

Cancio, A. Silvia, T. David Evans, and David J. Maume, Jr. 1996. "Reconsidering the Declining Significance of Race: Racial Differences in Early Career Wages." *American Sociological Review* 61: 541–556.

Canedy, Dana. 2002. "Florida Court Bans Use of Vouchers." *New York Times* August 6. On the World Wide Web at http://www.nytimes.com (6 August 2002).

Cardoso, Fernando Henrique, and Enzo Faletto. 1979. *Dependency and Development in Latin America,* Marjory Mattingly Urquidi, trans. Berkeley: University of California Press.

Carpenter, Dave. 2003. "McDonald's High-Tech With Kitchen, Kiosks." KioskCom. On the World Wide Web at http://www.kioskcom.com/articles_detail.php?ident 1856 (23 October 2003).

Carter, Stephen L. 1991. *Reflections of an Affirmative Action Baby.* New York: Basic Books.

Case, Anne C., I-Fen Lin, and Sara S. McLanahan. 2003. "Explaining Trends in Child Support: Economic, Demographic, and Policy Effects." *Demography* 40: 171–189.

Casper, Lynne M., Sara S. McLanahan, and Irwin Garfinkel. 1994. "The Gender-Poverty Gap: What Can We Learn From Other Countries?" *American Sociological Review* 59: 594–605.

Cassidy, John. 1999. "Schools Are Her Business." *New Yorker* 18–25 October: 144–160.

Cavalli-Sforza, L. Luca, Paolo Menozzi, and Alberto Piazza. 1994. *The History and Geography of Human Genes.* Princeton, NJ: Princeton University Press.

CBC. 2007. "Casualties in the Iraq war." On the World Wide Web at http://www.cbc.ca/news/background/iraq/casualties.html (13 January 2008).

Centers for Disease Control and Prevention. 1995a. *Monthly Vital Statistics Report* 43, 9(S): 22 March.

_____. 1995b. *Monthly Vital Statistics Report* 43, 12(S): 14 July.

_____. 1998. *Monthly Vital Statistics Report* 46, 12: 28 July.

_____. 1999a. *National Vital Statistics Reports* 47, 25: 5 October. On the World Wide Web at http://www.cdc.gov/nchs/data/nvs47_25.pdf (27 April 2000).

_____. 1999b. *National Vital Statistics Reports* 47, 25: 5 October. On the World Wide Web at http://www.cdc.gov/nchs/data/nvs47_25.pdf (27 April 2000).

_____. 2000. "Cumulative Age of Initiation of Cigarette Smoking—United States, 1991." On the World Wide Web at http://www.cdc.gov/tobacco/init.htm (1 May 2000).

_____. 2001. *National Vital Statistics Reports* 49, 6. On the World Wide Web at http://www.cdc.gov/nchs/data/nvsr/nvsr49/nvsr49_06.pdf (8 June 2003).

_____. 2002a. "Work Table 12. Death Rates for 358 Selected Causes, by 10-Year Age Groups, Race, and Sex: United States, 1999–2000." On the World Wide Web at http://www.cdc.gov/nchs/data/dvs/v500100.WTABLE12.pdf (25 January 2003).

_____. 2003. *National Vital Statistics Reports* 51, 6. On the World Wide Web at http://www.cdc.gov/nchs/data/nvsr/nvsr51/nvsr51_06.pdf (8 June 2003).

_____. 2005. *National Vital Statistics Reports* 53, 16. On the World Wide Web at http://www.cdc.gov/nchs/data/nvsr/nvsr53/nvsr53_16.pdf (7 March 2005).

_____. 2007a. "Births: Final Data for 2005." *National Vital Statistics Reports* 56, 6: August. On the World Wide Web at http://www.cdc.gov/nchs/data/nvsr/nvsr56/nvsr56_06.pdf (18 August 2008).

_____. 2007b. "Births, Marriages, Divorces, and Deaths: Provisional Data for 2006." *National Vital Statistics Reports* 55, 20: August. On the World Wide Web at http://www.cdc.gov/nchs/data/nvsr/nvsr55/nvsr55_20.pdf (18 August 2008).

_____. 2008. "Births, Marriages, Divorces, and Deaths: Provisional Data for 2007." *National Vital Statistics Reports* 56, 21: August. On the World Wide Web at http://www.cdc.gov/nchs/data/nvsr/nvsr56/nvsr56_21.htm (18 August 2008).

Central Intelligence Agency. 2002. *The World Factbook 2002.* On the World Wide Web at http://www.cia.gov/cia/publications/factbook (6 February 2003).

_____. 2005. *The World Factbook.* On the World Wide Web at http://www.cia.gov/cia/publications/factbook (March 2006).

Centre for Economic Policy Research. 2002. *Making Sense of Globalization: A Guide to the Economic Issues.* London.

Chambliss, William J. 1989. "State-Organized Crime." *Criminology* 27: 183–208.

Chagnon, Napoleon. 1992. *Yanomamö: The Last Days of Eden.* New York: Harcourt, Brace Yovanovich.

Chang, Ha-Joon. 2002. *Kicking Away the Ladder: Development Strategy in Historical Perspective.* London: Anthem Press.

Charlton, James I. 1998. *Nothing About Us Without Us: Disability Oppression and Empowerment.* Berkeley: University of California Press.

Chauncey, George. 2005. *Why Marriage? The History Shaping Today's Debate over Gay Equality.* New York: Basic Books.

Chaves, Mark. 1994. "Secularization as Declining Religious Authority." *Social Forces* 72: 749–774.

Cherlin, Andrew J. 1992 [1981]. *Marriage, Divorce, Remarriage,* rev. ed. Cambridge, MA: Harvard University Press.

_____, Frank F. Furstenberg, Jr., P. Lindsay Chase-Lansdale, Kathleen E. Kiernan, Philip K. Robins, Donna Ruane Morrison, and Julien O. Teitler. 1991. "Longitudinal Studies of Effects of Divorce on Children in Great Britain and the United States." *Science* 252: 1386–1389.

Chesnais, Jean-Claude. 1992 [1986]. *The Demographic Transition: Stages, Patterns, and Economic Implications.* Elizabeth Kreager and Philip Kreager, trans. Oxford: Clarendon Press.

Cicourel, Aaron V. 1968. *The Social Organization of Juvenile Justice.* New York: Wiley.

Clapp, Jennifer. 1998. "Foreign Direct Investment in Hazardous Industries in Developing Countries: Rethinking the Debate." *Environmental Politics* 7, 4: 92–113.

Clarke-Stewart, K. Alison, Christian P. Gruber, and Linda May Fitzgerald. 1994. *Children at Home and in Day Care.* Hillsdale, NJ: Lawrence Erlbaum.

Clawson, Dan. 1980. *Bureaucracy and the Labor Process: The Transformation of U.S. Industry, 1860–1920.* New York: Monthly Review Press.

_____ and Mary Ann Clawson. 1999. "What Has Happened to the US Labor Movement? Union Decline and Renewal." *Annual Review of Sociology* 25: 95–119.

_____, Alan Neustadtl, and Denise Scott. 1992. *Money Talks: Corporate PACS and Political Influence.* New York: Basic Books.

Clemetson, Lynette. 2003. "More Americans in Poverty in 2002, Census Study Says." *New York Times.* On the World Wide Web at http://www.nytimes.com (27 September 2003).

Clinton, William J. 1998. "Statement on Signing the Child Support Performance and Incentive Act of 1998." *Weekly Compilation of Presidential Documents* 34, 29: 1396.

Cloward, Richard A., and Lloyd E. Ohlin. 1960. *Delinquency and Opportunity: A Theory of Delinquent Gangs.* New York: Free Press.

CNN.COM. 1998. "Prosecutor: Attackers Planned to Rob Gay Student." On the World Wide Web at http://www .htt.com/cnn.com/US/9811/19/shepard.01/index.html (1 November 1999).

CNNPolitics.com. 2008. "U.S. chooses 'change,' redraws electoral divide." On the World Wide Web at http:// www.cnn.com/2008/POLITICS/11/05/election.president/ index.html?iref=newssearch (5 November 2008).

Coale, Ansley J. 1974. "The History of Human Population." *Scientific American* 23, 3: 41–51.

_____ and Susan C. Watkins, eds. 1986. *The Decline of Fertility in Europe.* Princeton, NJ: Princeton University Press.

Coghlan, Benjamin, Richard J. Brennan, Pascal Ngoy, David Dofara, Brad Otto, Mark Clements, and Tony Stewart. 2006. "Mortality in the Democratic Republic of Congo: A Nationwide Survey." *The Lancet* 367: 44–51.

Cohen, Albert. 1955. *Delinquent Boys: The Subculture of a Gang.* New York: Free Press.

Cohen, Arthur M., and Florence B. Brawer. 2003 [1981]. *The American Community College*, 4th ed. San Francisco: Jossey-Bass.

Cohen, Stanley. 1972. *Folk Devils and Moral Panics: The Creation of the Mods and Rockers.* London: MacGibbon & Kee.

Colapinto, John. 1997. "The True Story of John/Joan." *Rolling Stone* 11 December: 54–73, 92–97.

_____. 2001. *As Nature Made Him: The Boy Who was Raised as a Girl.* New York: Harper Collins.

Cole, Michael. 1995. *Cultural Psychology.* Cambridge, MA: Harvard University Press.

Coleman, James S. 1961. *The Adolescent Society.* New York: Free Press.

_____. 1990. *Foundations of Social Theory.* Cambridge, MA: Harvard University Press.

_____ et al. 1966. *Equality of Educational Opportunity.* Washington, DC: U.S. Department of Health, Education, and Welfare, Office of Education.

College Entrance Examination Board. 2005. "SAT Scores Hold Steady for College-Bound Seniors." On the World Wide Web at http://www.collegeboard.com/prod _downloads/about/news_info/cbsenior/yr2004/ CBS2004Report.pdf (26 July 2006).

Collins, Randall. 1982. *Sociological Insight: An Introduction to Nonobvious Sociology.* New York: Oxford University Press.

_____ and Scott Coltrane. 1991 [1985]. *Sociology of Marriage and the Family: Gender, Love, and Property*, 3rd ed. Chicago: Nelson-Hall.

Commins, Patricia. 1997. "Foreign Sales Prop Up McDonald's." *Globe and Mail* 26 August: B8.

"Comparable Worth." 1990. *Issues in Ethics* 3, 2. On the World Wide Web at http://www.scu.edu/SCU/Centers/ Ethics/publications/iie/v3n2/comparable.shtml (30 April 2000).

Comte, Auguste. 1975. *Auguste Comte: The Foundation of Sociology*, Kenneth Thompson, ed. New York: Wiley.

Condry, J., and S. Condry. 1976. "Sex Differences: The Eye of the Beholder." *Child Development* 47: 812–819.

Conley, Dalton. 1999. *Being Black, Living in the Red: Race, Wealth, and Social Policy in America.* Berkeley: University of California Press.

Conrad, Peter, and Joseph W. Schneider. 1992 [1980]. *Deviance and Medicalization: From Badness to Sickness*, expanded ed. Philadelphia: Temple University Press.

Converse, Jean M., and Stanley Presser. 1986. *Survey Questions: Handcrafting the Standardized Questionnaire.* Newbury Park, CA: Sage.

Conwell, Chic. 1937. *The Professional Thief: By a Professional Thief*, annotated and interpreted by Edwin H. Sutherland. Chicago: University of Chicago Press.

Cooley, Charles Horton. 1902. *Human Nature and the Social Order.* New York: Scribner's.

Coontz, Stephanie. 1992. *The Way We Never Were: American Families and the Nostalgia Trip.* New York: Basic Books.

Cornell, Stephen. 1988. *The Return of the Native: American Indian Political Resurgence.* New York: Oxford University Press.

Coser, Rose Laub. 1960. "Laughter among Colleagues: A Study of the Functions of Humor among the Staff of a Mental Hospital." *Psychiatry* 23: 81–95.

Cramton, Peter, and Joseph Tracy. 1998. "The Use of Replacement Workers in Union Contract Negotiations: The U.S. Experience, 1980–1989." *Journal of Labor Economics* 16: 667–701.

Creedon, Jeremiah. 1998. "God With a Million Faces." *Utne Reader* July–August: 42–48.

Creighton, Sarah and Catherine Mihto. 2001. "Managing Intersex." *British Medical Journal*, 323(7324), December 1264–1265.

Critser, Greg. 2003. *Fat Land: How Americans Became the Fattest People in the World.* Boston: Houghton Mifflin.

Crothers, Charles. 1979. "On the Myth of Rural Tranquility: Comment on Webb and Collette." *American Journal of Sociology* 84: 429–437.

Crozier, Michel. 1964 [1963]. *The Bureaucratic Phenomenon.* Chicago: University of Chicago Press.

Crystal, David. 2003 [1997]. *English as a Global Language*, 2nd ed. Cambridge: Cambridge University Press.

Curtis, James, John Loy and Wally Karnilowicz. 1986. "A Comparison of Suicide-Dip Effects of Major Sport Events and Civil Holidays." *Sociology of Sport Journal* 3: 1–14.

Dahl, Robert A. 1961. *Who Governs?* New Haven, CT: Yale University Press.

Darder, Antonia, and Rodolfo D. Torres, eds. 1998. *The Latino Studies Reader: Culture, Economy and Society.* Malden, MA: Blackwell.

Darwin, Charles. 1859. *On the Origin of Species by Means of Natural Selection.* London: John Murray.

_____. 1871. *The Descent of Man.* London: John Murray.

Davidoff, Judith. 1999. "The Fatherhood Industry: Welfare Reformers Set Their Sights on Wayward Dads." *The Progressive.* November: 28–31.

Davies, Christine. 1998. *Jokes and Their Relation to Society.* Berlin: Mouton de Gruyter.

Davies, James C. 1969. "Toward a Theory of Revolution." Pp. 85–108 in Barry McLaughlin, ed. *Studies in Social Movements: A Social Psychological Perspective.* New York: Free Press.

Davies, Mark, and Denise B. Kandel. 1981. "Parental and Peer Influences on Adolescents' Educational Plans: Some Further Evidence." *American Journal of Sociology* 87: 363–387.

Davis, Kingsley, and Wilbert E. Moore. 1945. "Some Principles of Stratification." *American Sociological Review* 10: 242–249.

Davis, Lennard J. 1995. *Enforcing Normalcy: Disability, Deafness, and the Body.* London: Verso.

Davis, Mike. 1990. *City of Quartz: Excavating the Future in Los Angeles.* New York: Verso.

Day, Jennifer Cheeseman, and Eric Newburger. 2002. "The Big Payoff: Educational Attainment and Synthetic Estimates of Work-Life Earnings." On the World Wide Web at http://www.census.gov/prod/2002pubs/p23-210 .pdf (27 April 2003).

DeFine, Michael Sullivan. 1997. "A History of Governmentally Coerced Sterilization: The Plight of the Native American Woman." On the World Wide Web at http://www.geocities.com/CapitolHill/9118/mike2 .html (24 April 2003).

DeFrancis, Marc. 2002. "U.S. Elder Care Is in a Fragile State." *Population Today* 30, 1: 1–3.

de la Garza, Rodolpho O., Luis DiSipio, F. Chris Garcia, John Garcia, and Angelo Falcon. 1992. *Latino Voices: Mexican, Puerto Rican, and Cuban Perspectives on American Politics.* Boulder, CO: Westview.

De Long, J. Bradford. 1998. *Global Trends: 1980–2015 and Beyond.* Ottawa: Industry Canada.

Denzin, Norman K. 1992. *Symbolic Interactionism and Cultural Studies: The Politics of Interpretation.* Oxford: Blackwell.

Department of Geography, Slippery Rock University. 1997. "World's Largest Cities, 1900." On the World Wide Web at http://www.sru.edu/depts/artsci/ges/discover/ d-6-8.htm (2 May 2000).

_____. 2003. "World's Largest Urban Agglomerations, 2015." On the World Wide Web at http://www1.sru .edu/gge/faculty/hughes/100/100-6/d-6-9b.htm (August 2).

Department of Justice, Canada. 1995. "A Review of Firearm Statistics and Regulations in Selected Countries." On the World Wide Web at http://www.cfc-ccaf.gc.ca/ research/publications/reports/1990%2D95/reports/ siter_rpt_en.html (29 April 2000).

Derber, Charles. 1979. *The Pursuit of Attention: Power and Individualism in Everyday Life.* New York: Oxford University Press.

DeSoya, Indra, and John Oneal. 1999. "Boon or Bane? Reassessing the Productivity of Foreign Direct Investment with New Data." *American Sociological Review* 64: 766–782.

de Villiers, Marq. 1999. *Water.* Toronto: Stoddart Publishing.

de Waal, Alexander. 1989. *Famine That Kills: Darfur, Sudan, 1984–1985.* Oxford: Clarendon Press.

DiCarlo, Lisa. 2000. "32 Debut on the List." *Forbes.com.* On the World Wide Web at http://www.forbes.com/tool/ toolbox/rich400 (22 September 2000).

Dietz, Tracy L. 1998. "An Examination of Violence and Gender Role Portrayals in Video Games: Implications for Gender Socialization and Aggressive Behavior." *Sex Roles* 38: 425–442.

"Digital Dilemmas." 2003. *The Economist* 25 January: 3–26. On the World Wide Web at http://www.economist.com/ displayStory.cfm?Story_id 1534303 (29 May 2003).

Dillon, Sam. 2005. "Students Ace State Tests, but Earn D's from U.S." *New York Times* 26 November. On the World Wide Web at www.nytimes.com (26 November 2005).

DiMaggio, Paul. 1982. "Cultural Capital and School Success: The Impact of Status Culture Participation on the Grades of U.S. High School Students." *American Sociological Review* 47: 189–201.

_____ and Walter W. Powell. 1983. "The Iron Cage Revisited: Institutional Isomorphism and Collective Rationality in Organizational Fields." *American Sociological Review* 48: 147–160.

Dines, Gail, and Jean McMahon Humez. 1995. *Gender, Race, and Class in Media: A Text-Reader.* Thousand Oaks, CA: Sage.

Donahue III, John J., and Steven D. Levitt. 2001. "The Impact of Legalized Abortion on Crime." *Quarterly Journal of Economics* 116: 379–420.

Dolnick, Edward. 1993. "Deafness as culture." *The Atlantic Monthly* 272, 3: 37–48.

Dore, Ronald. 1983. "Goodwill and the Spirit of Market Capitalism." *British Journal of Sociology* 34: 459–482.

Douglas, Emily N. and Murray A. Straus. 2006. "Assault and injury of dating partners by university students in 19 nations and its relations to corporal punishment experienced as a child." *Journal of Criminology* 3: 293–318.

Doyle, Aaron, Brian Elliott, and David Tindall. 1997 [1992]. "Framing the Forests: Corporations, the B.C. Forest Alliance, and the Media." Pp. 240–68 in William Carroll, ed., *Organizing Dissent: Contemporary Social Movements in Theory and Practice,* 2nd ed. Toronto: Garamond Press.

Du Bois, W. E. B. 1967 [1899]. *The Philadelphia Negro: A Social Study.* New York: Schocken.

Dudley, Kathryn Marie. 1994. *The End of the Line: Lost Jobs, New Lives in Postindustrial America.* Chicago: University of Chicago Press.

Duffy, Elizabeth A., and Idana Goldberg. 1997. *Crafting a Class: Admissions and Financial Aid, 1955–1994.* Princeton, NJ: Princeton University Press.

Durham, William H. 1979. *Scarcity and Survival in Central America: Ecological Origins of the Soccer War.* Stanford, CA: Stanford University Press.

Durkheim, Émile. 1951 [1897]. *Suicide: A Study in Sociology,* G. Simpson, ed., J. Spaulding and G. Simpson, trans. New York: Free Press.

_____. 1956. *Education and Sociology,* Sherwood D. Fox, trans. New York: Free Press.

_____. 1961 [1925]. *Moral Education: A Study in the Theory and Application of the Sociology of Education,* Everett K. Wilson and Herman Schnurer, trans. New York: Free Press.

_____. 1964 [1895]. *The Division of Labor in Society.* New York: Free Press.

_____. 1973 [1899–1900]. "Two Laws of Penal Evolution." *Economy and Society* 2: 285–308.

_____. 1976 [1915]. *The Elementary Forms of the Religious Life,* Joseph Ward Swain, trans. New York: Free Press.

Dutton, Judy. 2000. "Detect His Lies Every Time." *Cosmopolitan* April: 126.

Eagley, Alice H., and Wendy Wood. 1999. "The Origins of Sex Differences in Human Behavior: Evolved Dispositions Versus Social Roles." *American Psychologist* 54: 408–423.

Eccles, J. S., J. E. Jacobs, and R. D. Harold. 1990. "Gender Role Stereotypes, Expectancy Effects and Parents' Socialization of Gender Differences." *Journal of Social Issues* 46: 183–201.

Economakis, Evel, and Robert J. Brym. 1995. "Marriage and Militance in a Working Class District of St. Petersburg, 1896–1913." *Journal of Family History* 20: 23–43.

Edelman, Peter. 2002. "The True Purpose of Welfare Reform." *New York Times* May 29. On the World Wide Web at http://www.nytimes.com (29 May 2002).

Edmundson, Mark. 2003. "How Teachers Can Stop Cheaters." *New York Times.* On the World Wide Web at www.nytimes.com (9 September 2003).

Ehrenreich, Barbara. 2001. *Nickel and Dimed: On (Not) Getting by in America.* New York: Henry Holt.

Ehrlich, Paul R. 1968. *The Population Bomb.* New York: Ballantine.

_____ and Anne H. Ehrlich. 1990. *The Population Explosion.* New York: Simon & Schuster.

Eisenberg, David M., Ronald C. Kessler, Cindy Foster, Frances E. Norlock, David R. Calkins, and Thomas L. Delbanco. 1993. "Unconventional Medicine in the United States—Prevalence, Costs, and Patterns of Use." *New England Journal of Medicine* 328: 246.

Ekman, Paul. 1978. *Facial Action Coding System.* New York: Consulting Psychologists Press.

Elias, Norbert. 1985 [1982]. *The Loneliness of the Dying,* Edmund Jephcott, trans. Oxford: Blackwell.

_____. 1994 [1939]. *The Civilizing Process,* Edmund Jephcott, trans. Oxford: Blackwell.

Elliott, H. L. 1995. "Living Vicariously Through Barbie." On the World Wide Web at http://ziris.syr.edu/path/public_html/barbie/main.html (19 November 1998).

Emanuel, Kerry. 2005. "Increasing Destructiveness of Tropical Cyclones over the Past 30 Years." *Nature* 436, 4: 686–88.

Engels, Frederick. 1970 [1884]. *The Origins of the Family, Private Property and the State,* Eleanor Burke Leacock, ed., Alec West, trans. New York: International Publishers.

England, Paula. 1992a. *Comparable Worth: Theories and Evidence.* Hawthorne, NY: Aldine de Gruyter.

_____. 1992b. "From Status Attainment to Segregation and Devaluation." *Contemporary Sociology* 21: 643–647.

Entine, John. 2000. *Taboo: Why Black Athletes Dominate Sports and Why We Are Afraid to Talk About It.* New York: Public Affairs.

Epstein, Helen. 1998. "Life and Death on the Social Ladder." *New York Review of Books* 45, 12: 16 July: 26–30.

Epstein, Steven. 1996. *Impure Science: AIDS, Activism, and the Politics of Knowledge.* Berkeley: University of California Press.

Erikson, Robert, and John H. Goldthorpe. 1992. *The Constant Flux: A Study of Class Mobility in Industrial Societies.* Oxford: Clarendon Press.

Esping-Andersen, Gøsta. 1990. *The Three Worlds of Welfare Capitalism.* Princeton, NJ: Princeton University Press.

Estrich, Susan. 1987. *Real Rape.* Cambridge, MA: Harvard University Press.

"Ethnic Groups in the World." 2001. *Scientific American.* On the World Wide Web at http://www.sciam.com/1998/0998issue/0998numbers.html (4 December 2001).

Evans, Peter B., Dietrich Rueschemeyer, and Theda Skocpol. 1985. *Bringing the State Back In.* Cambridge: Cambridge University Press.

Evans, Robert G. 1999. "Social Inequalities in Health." *Horizons* (Policy Research Secretariat, Government of Canada) 2, 3: 6–7.

"Excerpts from Justices' Opinions on Michigan Affirmative Action Cases." 2003. *New York Times* June 24. On the World Wide Web at http://www.nytimes.com (24 June 2003).

Executive Office of the President of the United States. 2000. "A Citizen's Guide to the Federal Budget." On the World Wide Web at http://usgovinfo.about.com/newsissues/usgovinfo/gi/dynamic/offsite.htm?site=http://w3.access.gpo.gov/usbudget (8 June 2000).

Fagot, Beverly I., Caire S. Rodgers, and Mary D. Leinbach. 2000. "Theories of Gender Socialization." Pp. 65–89 in Thomas Eckes, ed. *The Developmental Social Psychology of Gender.* Mahwah, NJ: Lawrence Erlbaum Associates.

Fall Colors 2001–02: Prime Time Diversity Report. 2002. Oakland and Los Angeles: Children Now. On the World Wide Web at http://www.childrennow.org/media/fc2002/fc-2002-report.pdf (29 May 2002).

Farley, Christopher John. 1998. "Rock Star." *Time* July 20. On the World Wide Web at http://www.time.com/time/sampler/article/0,8599,166239,00.html (9 April 2003).

Fass, Paula S. 1989. *Outside In: Minorities and the Transformation of American Education.* New York: Oxford University Press.

Fava, Sylvia Fleis. 1956. "Suburbanism as a Way of Life." *American Sociological Review* 21: 34–37.

Feagin, Joe R., and Melvin P. Sikes. 1994. *Living with Racism: The Black Middle-Class Experience.* Boston: Beacon Press.

Featherman, David L., and Robert M. Hauser. 1976. "Sexual Inequalities and Socioeconomic Achievement in the U.S., 1962–1973." *American Sociological Review* 41: 462–483.

_____, and _____. 1978. *Opportunity and Change.* New York: Academic Press.

_____, F. Lancaster Jones, and Robert M. Hauser. 1975. "Assumptions of Mobility Research in the United States: The Case of Occupational Status." *Social Science Research* 4: 329–360.

Felson, Richard B. 1996. "Mass Media Effects on Violent Behavior." *Annual Review of Sociology* 22: 103–128.

Feminist.com. "The Wage Gap." 1999. On the World Wide Web at http://www.feminist.com/wgot.htm (30 April 2000).

Fernandez-Dols, Jose-Miguel, Flor Sanchez, Pilar Carrera, and Maria-Angeles Ruiz-Belda. 1997. "Are Spontaneous Expressions and Emotions Linked? An Experimental Test of Coherence." *Journal of Nonverbal Behavior* 21: 163–177.

Figart, Deborah M., and June Lapidus. 1996. "The Impact of Comparable Worth on Earnings Inequality." *Work and Occupations* 23: 297–318.

Fine, Gary Alan, and Patricia A. Turner. 2001. *Whispers on the Color Line: Rumor and Race in America.* Berkeley: University of California Press.

Finke, Roger, Avery Guest, and Rodney Stark. 1996. "Mobilizing Religious Markets: Religious Pluralism in the Empire State, 1865." *American Sociological Review* 61: 203–218.

_____, and Rodney Starke. 1992. *The Churching of America, 1776–1990: Winners and Losers in Our Religious Economy.* New Brunswick, NJ: Rutgers University Press.

Finsterbusch, Kurt. 2001. *Clashing Views on Controversial Social Issues.* Guilfod, CT: Dushkin.

Firebaugh, Glenn, and Frank D. Beck. 1994. "Does Economic Growth Benefit the Masses? Growth, Dependence and Welfare in the Third World." *American Journal of Sociology* 59: 631–653.

Fischer, Claude S. 1981. "The Public and Private Worlds of City Life." *American Sociological Review* 46: 306–316.

_____. 1984 [1976]. *The Urban Experience,* 2nd ed. New York: Harcourt Brace Jovanovich.

_____, Michael Hout, Martín Sánchez Jankowski, Samuel R. Lucas, Ann Swidler, and Kim Voss. 1996. *Inequality by Design: Cracking the Bell Curve Myth.* Princeton, NJ: Princeton University Press.

Fitzgerald, Frances. 1979. *America Revised: History Schoolbooks in the Twentieth Century.* Boston: Little, Brown.

Flexner, Eleanor. 1975. *Century of Struggle: The Woman's Rights Movement in the United States,* rev. ed. Cambridge, MA: Harvard University Press.

Flood, Gavin D. 1996. *An Introduction to Hinduism.* Cambridge: Cambridge University Press.

Flowers, Paul and Katie Buston. 2001. "'I Was Terrified of Being Different:' Exploring Gay Men's Accounts of Growing-Up in a Heterosexist Society." *Journal of Adolescence.* Special Issue: Gay, Lesbian, and Bisexual Youth. 24: 51–65.

Fong, Eric W., and William T. Markham. 2002. "Anti-Chinese Politics in California in the 1870s: An Intercounty Analysis." *Sociological Perspectives* 45: 183–210.

"Forbes 500 Annual Directory." 2000. On the World Wide Web at http://www.forbes.com/tool/toolbox/forbes500s/asp/rankindex.asp (30 April 2000).

Forbes.com. 2006. "Fortune Global 500." On the World Wide Web at http://money.cnn.com/magazines/fortune/global500/2006/performers/companies/biggest_employers/index.html (21 August 2008).

_____. 2007. "The 400 Richest Americans." On the World Wide Web at http://www.forbes.com/lists/2007/54/richlist07_The-400-Richest-Americans_Rank_print.html (11 August 2008).

Foucault, Michel. 1990 [1978]. *The History of Sexuality: An Introduction,* Vol. 1. Robert Hurley, trans. New York: Vintage.

Franco, Zeno and Philip Zimbardo. 2006–2007. "The Banality of Heroism." *Greater Good* 3, 2: 33–34. On the World Wide Web at http://greatergood.berkeley.edu/greatergood/archive/2006fallwinter/francozimbardo.html (3 January 2008).

Frank Porter Graham Child Development Center. 1999. "Early Learning, Later Success: The Abecedarian Study." On the World Wide Web at http://www.fpg.unc.edu/~abc/abcedarianWeb/index.htm (10 August 2000).

Frank, Robert H. 1988. *Passions Within Reason: The Strategic Role of the Emotions.* New York: W.W. Norton.

Frank, Thomas. 1997. *The Conquest of Cool.* Chicago: University of Chicago Press.

_____ and Matt Weiland, eds. 1997. *Commodify Your Dissent: Salvos from the Baffler.* New York: W.W. Norton.

Franke, Richard W., and Barbara H. Chasin. 1992. *Kerala: Development Through Radical Reform.* San Francisco: Institute for Food and Development Policy.

Frankel, Glenn. 1996. "U.S. Aided Cigarette Firms in Conquests Across Asia." *Washington Post* November 17: A01. On the World Wide Web at http://www.washingtonpost.com/wp-srv/national/longterm/tobacco/stories/asia.htm (8 February 2003).

Franklin, Karen. 1998. "Psychosocial Motivations of Hate Crime Perpetrators." Paper presented at the annual meetings of the American Psychological Association (San Francisco: 16 August).

Freedman, Jonathan L. 2002. *Media Violence and Its Effect on Aggression: Assessing the Scientific Evidence.* Toronto: University of Toronto Press.

Freedom House. 2004. *Freedom in the World,* 2004. On the World Wide Web at http://www.freedomhouse.org/research/survey2004.htm (2 May 2004).

_____. 2008. "Tables and Charts." On the World Wide Web at http://www.freedomhouse.org/template.cfm?page=25&year=2008 (21 August 2008).

Freidson, Eliot. 1986. *Professional Powers: A Study of the Institutionalization of Formal Knowledge.* Chicago: University of Chicago Press.

Freire, Paolo. 1972. *The Pedagogy of the Oppressed.* New York: Herder and Herder.

Freud, Sigmund. 1962 [1930]. *Civilization and Its Discontents.* James Strachey, trans. New York: W.W. Norton.

_____. 1973 [1915–17]. *Introductory Lectures on Psychoanalysis.* James Strachey, trans., James Strachey and Angela Richards, eds. Harmondsworth, UK: Penguin.

Friedenberg, Edgar Z. 1959. *The Vanishing Adolescent.* Boston: Beacon Press.

Fröbel, Folker, Jürgen Heinrichs, and Otto Kreyre. 1980. *The New International Division of Labour: Structural Unemployment in Industrialised Countries and Industrialisation in Developing Countries.* Pete Burgess, trans. Cambridge: Cambridge University Press.

Froissart, Jean. 1968 [c. 1365]. *Chronicles,* selected and translated by Geoffrey Brereton. Harmondsworth, UK: Penguin.

"Funeral Help." 2008. On the World Wide Web at http://www.funeralhelp.com/index2.php?option=com_content&do_pdf=1&id=62 (24 March 2009).

Furstenberg, Frank F., Jr., and Andrew Cherlin. 1991. *Divided Families: What Happens to Children When Parents Part.* Cambridge, MA: Harvard University Press.

_____, Sheela Kennedy, Vonnie C. Mcloyd, Rubén G. Rumbaut, and Richard A. Settersten, Jr. 2004. "Growing up is harder to do." *Contexts* 3, 3. On the World Wide Web at http://www.contextsmagazine.org/content_sample_v3-3.php (26 March 2007).

Gado, Mark. 2003. "A Cry in the Night: The Kitty Genovese Murder." *Court TV's Crime Library.* On the World Wide Web at http://www.crimelibrary.com/serial_killers/predators/kitty_genovese/1.html (23 July 2003).

Galewitz, Phil. 2000. "Firm Settles Fraud Case: Hospital Chain Columbia/HCA to pay $745 Million." *ABCNEWS.com* May 18. On the World Wide Web at http://abcnews.go.com/sections/business/DailyNews/columbiahca_990518.html (12 June 2003).

Galper, Joseph. 1998. "Schooling for Society." *American Demographics* 20, 3: 33–34.

Gambetta, Diego, ed. 1988. *Trust: Making and Breaking Cooperative Relations.* Oxford: Blackwell.

Gamson, William A. 1975. *The Strategy of Social Protest.* Homewood, IL: Dorsey Press.

_____, Bruce Fireman, and Steven Rytina. 1982. *Encounters with Unjust Authority.* Homewood, IL: Dorsey Press.

Gans, Herbert. 1962. *The Urban Villagers: Group and Class in the Life of Italian-Americans.* New York: Free Press.

_____. 1979, "Symbolic Ethnicity: The Future of Ethnic Groups and Cultures in America." Pp. 193–220 in Herbert Gans et al., eds. *On the Making of Americans: Essays in Honor of David Reisman.* Philadelphia: University of Pennsylvania Press.

_____. 1995. *The War Against Poverty: The Underclass and Antipoverty Policy.* New York: Basic Books.

Ganz, Marshall. 1996. "Motor Voter or Motivated Voter?" *The American Prospect* 28. On the World Wide Web at http://www.prospect.org/archives/28/28ganz.html (21 November 2000).

Gap.com. "Gap." 1999. On the World Wide Web at http://www.gap.com/onlinestore/gap/advertising/khakitv.asp (28 April 2000).

"Garciaparra Explains His Superstitions." 2000. On the World Wide Web at http://www.geocities.com/Colosseum/Track/4242/nomar3.wav (28 April 2000).

Garfinkel, Harold. 1967. *Studies in Ethnomethodology.* Englewood Cliffs, NJ: Prentice-Hall.

Garkawe, Sam. 1995. "The Impact of the Doctrine of Cultural Relativism on the Australian Legal System." *E Law* 2, 1. On the World Wide Web at http://www.murdoch.edu.au/elaw/issues/v2n1/garkawe.txt (10 May 2000).

Garland, David. 1990. *Punishment and Modern Society: A Study in Social Theory.* Chicago: University of Chicago Press.

Garner, David M. 1997. "The 1997 Body Image Survey Results." *Psychology Today* 30, 1: 30–44.

Garrau, Joel. 1991. *Edge City: Life on the New Frontier.* New York: Doubleday.

Garson, Barbara. 2001. *Money Makes the World Go Around.* New York: Viking.

Gaubatz, Kathlyn Taylor. 1995. *Crime in the Public Mind.* Ann Arbor: University of Michigan Press.

Gauvain, Mary, Beverly I. Fagot, Craige Leve, and Kate Kavanagh. 2002. "Instruction by Mothers and Fathers During Problem Solving with Their Young Children." *Journal of Family Psychology* 6: 81–90.

Gearon, Christopher J. 2002. "States Forming Alliances to Deal with Drugmakers." *AARP.* On the World Wide Web at http://www.aarp.org/bulletin/departments/2002/medicare/0410_medicare_1.html (17 June 2003).

Gelbspan, Ross. 1999. "Trading Away Our Chances to End Global Warming." *Boston Globe,* May 16: E2.

Gelles, Richard J. 1997 [1985]. *Intimate Violence in Families,* 3rd ed. Thousand Oaks, CA: Sage.

Gellner, Ernest. 1988. *Plough, Sword and Book: The Structure of Human History.* Chicago: University of Chicago Press.

Gerbner, George. 1998. "Casting the American Scene: A Look at the Characters on Prime Time and Daytime Television from 1994–1997." *The 1998 Screen Actors Guild Report.* On the World Wide Web at http://www.media-awareness.ca/eng/issues/minrep/resource/reports/gerbner.htm (5 August 2000).

Germanwatch. 2009. "Climate Change Performance Index 2009." On the World Wide Web at http://www.germanwatch.org/ccpi (27 January 2009).

Gerschenkron, Alexander. 1962. *Economic Backwardness in Historical Perspective: A Book of Essays.* Cambridge, MA: Harvard University Press.

Giddens, Anthony. 1987. *Sociology: A Brief but Critical Introduction,* 2nd ed. New York: Harcourt Brace Jovanovich.

_____. 1990. *The Consequences of Modernity.* Stanford, CA: Stanford University Press.

Gillis, John R. 1981. *Youth and History: Tradition and Change in European Age Relations, 1770–Present,* expanded student ed. New York: Academic Press.

Gilpin, Robert. 2001. *Global Political Economy: Understanding the International Economic Order.* Princeton, NJ: Princeton University Press.

Gladwell, Malcolm. 2002. "The Politics of Politesse." *New Yorker* December 23–30: 57–58.

Glaser, Barney, and Anselm Straus. 1967. *The Discovery of Grounded Theory.* Chicago: Aldine.

Glazer, Nathan. 1997. *We Are All Multiculturalists Now.* Cambridge, MA: Harvard University Press.

Gleick, James. 2000 [1999]. *Faster: The Acceleration of Just About Everything.* New York: Vintage.

Global Reach, 2003. "Global Internet Statistics (by Language)." On the World Wide Web at http://www.glreach.com/globstats/index.php3 (25 March 2004).

_____. 2004. "Global Internet Statistics (by Language)." On the World Wide Web at http://www.glreach.com/globstats/index.php3 (11 February 2004).

Glock, Charles Y. 1962. "On the Study of Religious Commitment." *Religious Education* 62, 4: 98–110.

"Gnutella." 2000. On the World Wide Web at http://gnutella.wego.com (7 August 2000).

Goddard Institute for Space Studies. 2008. "Global Temperature Anomalies in .01 C, base period: 1951-1980." On the World Wide Web at http://data.giss.nasa.gov/gistemp/tabledata/GLB.Ts.txt (12 January 2008).

Goffman, Erving. 1959 [1956]. *The Presentation of Self in Everyday Life.* Garden City, NY: Anchor.

_____. 1961. *Asylums: Essays on the Social Situation of Mental Patients and Other Inmates.* Garden City, NY: Anchor Books.

_____. 1963a. *Behavior in Public Places: Notes on the Social Organization of Gatherings.* New York: Free Press.

_____. 1963b. *Stigma: Notes on the Management of Spoiled Identity.* Englewood Cliffs, NJ: Prentice-Hall.

_____. 1974. *Frame Analysis.* Cambridge, MA: Harvard University Press.

Goldthorpe, John H. in collaboration with Catriona Llewellyn and Clive Payne. 1987 [1980]. *Social Mobility and Class Structure in Modern Britain,* 2nd ed. Oxford: Clarendon Press.

Goll, David. 2002. "True Priority of Office Ethics Clouded by Scandals." *East Bay Business Times* August 19. On the World Wide Web at http://eastbay.bizjournals.com/eastbay/stories/2002/08/19/smallb3.html (13 January 2003).

Gombrich, Richard Francis. 1996. *How Buddhism Began: The Conditioned Genesis of the Early Teachings.* London: Athlone.

Goode, Erich, and Nachman Ben-Yehuda. 1994. *Moral Panics: The Social Construction of Deviance.* Cambridge, MA: Blackwell.

Gordon, David M. 1996. *Fat and Mean: The Corporate Squeeze of Working Americans and the Myth of Managerial "Downsizing."* New York: Free Press.

Gordon, Sarah. 1984. *Hitler, Germans, and the Jewish Question.* Princeton, NJ: Princeton University Press.

Gorman, Christine. 1998. *"Playing the HMO Game."* Time 152, 2: 13 July. On the World Wide Web at http://www.time.com/time/magazine/1998/dom/980713/cover1.html (2 May 2000).

Gormley, Jr., William T. 1995. *Everybody's Children: Child Care as a Public Problem.* Washington, DC: Brookings Institution.

Gottdiener, Mark, and Ray Hutchison. 2000 [1994]. *The New Urban Sociology,* 2nd ed. Boston: McGraw-Hill.

Gottfredson, Michael, and Travis Hirschi. 1990. *A General Theory of Crime.* Stanford, CA: Stanford University Press.

Gottwald, Norman K. 1979. *The Tribes of Yahweh: A Sociology of the Religion of Liberated Israel, 1250–1050 B.C.E.* Maryknoll, NY: Orbis.

Goubert, Jean-Pierre. 1989 [1986]. *The Conquest of Water,* Andrew Wilson, trans. Princeton, NJ: Princeton University Press.

Gould, Stephen J. 1988. "Kropotkin Was No Crackpot." *Natural History* 97, 7: 12–18.

_____. 1996 [1981]. *The Mismeasure of Man,* rev. ed. New York: W.W. Norton.

Government of Canada. 2002. "Study Released on Firearms in Canada." On the World Wide Web at http://www.cfc-ccaf.gc.ca/media/news_releases/2002/survey-08202002_e.asp (29 December 2005).

Graff, Harvey J. 1995. *Conflicting Paths: Growing Up in America.* Cambridge, MA: Harvard University Press.

Granovetter, Mark. 1973. "The Strength of Weak Ties." *American Sociological Review* 78: 1360–1380.

_____. 1995 [1974]. *Getting a Job: A Study of Contacts and Careers.* Cambridge, MA: Harvard University Press.

_____. 1984. "Small is Bountiful." *American Sociological Review* 49: 323–334.

Gratz and Hamacher v. Bollinger et al. 1997. Supreme Court of the United States. On the World Wide Web at http://www.moraldefense.com/Campaigns/Equality/gratz_v_bollinger_SupCt_brief.pdf (30 December 2003).

Greeley, Andrew. 1989. *Religious Change in America.* Cambridge, MA: Harvard University Press.

Green, Donald, Eric Schickler, and Bradley Palmquist. 2002. *Partisan Hearts and Minds.* New Haven, CT: Yale University Press.

Greenpeace. 2000. "Greenpeace Contacts Worldwide." 2000. On the World Wide Web at http://adam.greenpeace.org/information.shtml (2 May 2000).

Greenstein, Theodore N. 1996. "Husbands' Participation in Domestic Labor: Interactive Effects of Wives' and Husbands' Gender Ideologies." *Journal of Marriage and the Family* 58: 585–595.

Grescoe, P. 1996. *The Merchants of Venus: Inside Harlequin and the Empire of Romance.* Vancouver: Raincoast.

Groce, Nora Ellen. 1985. *Everyone Here Spoke Sign Language: Hereditary Deafness on Martha's Vineyard.* Cambridge, MA: Harvard University Press.

Grusky, David B., and Robert M. Hauser. 1984. "Comparative Social Mobility Revisited: Models of Convergence and Divergence in 16 Countries." *American Sociological Review* 49: 19–38.

Grutter v. Bollinger et al., 1997. Supreme Court of the United States. On the World Wide Web at http://www.moraldefense.com/Campaigns/Equality/grutter_v_bollinger_SupCt_brief.pdf (30 December 2003).

Guillén, Mauro F. 2001. "Is Globalization Civilizing, Destructive or Feeble? A Critique of Five Key Debates in the Social Science Literature." *Annual Review of Sociology* 27. On the World Wide Web at http://knowledge.wharton.upenn.edu/PDFs/938.pdf (6 February 2003).

Gunderson, Edna, Bill Keveney, and Ann Oldenburg. 2002. "'The Osbournes' Find a Home in America's Living Rooms." *USA Today* April 19: 1A, 2A.

Gurr, Ted Robert. 1970. *Why Men Rebel.* Princeton, NJ: Princeton University Press.

Gutiérrez, David G. 1995. *Walls and Mirrors: Mexican Americans, Mexican Immigrants, and the Politics of Ethnicity.* Berkeley: University of California Press.

Haas, Jack, and William Shaffir. 1987. *Becoming Doctors: The Adoption of a Cloak of Competence.* Greenwich, CT: JAI Press.

Haas, Jennifer. 1998. "The Cost of Being a Woman." *New England Journal of Medicine* 338: 1694–1695.

Hacker, Andrew. 1992. *Two Nations: Black and White, Separate, Hostile, Unequal.* New York: Ballantine Books.

Hacker, Jacob S. 1997. *The Road to Nowhere: The Genesis of President Clinton's Plan for Health Security.* Princeton, NJ: Princeton University Press.

Hacsi, Timothy A. 2002. *Children as Pawns: The Politics of Educational Reform.* Cambridge, MA: Harvard University Press.

Hagan, John. 1989. *Structuralist Criminology.* New Brunswick, NJ: Rutgers University Press.

_____. 1994. *Crime and Disrepute.* Thousand Oaks, CA: Pine Forge Press.

_____, John Simpson, and A. R. Gillis. 1987. "Class in the Household: A Power-Control Theory of Gender and Delinquency." *American Journal of Sociology* 92: 788–816.

Haines, Herbert H. 1996. *Against Capital Punishment: The Anti-Death Penalty Movement in America, 1972–1994.*

Hall, Edward. 1959. *The Silent Language.* New York: Doubleday.

_____. 1966. *The Hidden Dimension.* New York: Doubleday.

Hamachek, D. 1995. "Self-concept and School Achievement: Interaction Dynamics and a Tool for Assessing the Self-concept Component." *Journal of Counseling and Development* 73: 419–425.

Hamilton, Roberta. 1996. *Gendering the Vertical Mosaic: Feminist Perspectives on Canadian Society.* Toronto: Copp-Clark.

Hamlin, Cynthia Lins, and Robert J. Brym. 2006. "The Return of the Native: A Cultural and Social-Psychological Critique of Durkheim's *Suicide* Based on the Guarani-Kaiowá of Southwestern Brazil." *Sociological Theory* 24: 42–57.

Hammer, Michael. 1999. "Is Work Bad for You?" *The Atlantic Monthly* August: 87–93.

Hampton, Janie, ed. 1998. *Internally Displaced People: A Global Survey.* London: Earthscan.

Hancock, Graham. 1989. *Lords of Poverty: The Power, Prestige, and Corruption of the International Aid Business.* New York: Atlantic Monthly Press.

Handy, Bruce. 2002. "Glamour with Altitude." *Vanity Fair* October: 214–228.

Haney, Craig, W. Curtis Banks, and Philip G. Zimbardo. 1973. "Interpersonal Dynamics in a Simulated Prison." *International Journal of Criminology and Penology* 1: 69–97.

Hanke, Robert. 1998. "'Yo Quiero Mi MTV!' Making Music Television for Latin America." Pp. 219–45 in Thomas Swiss, Andrew Herman, and John M. Sloop, eds. *Mapping the Beat: Popular Music and Contemporary Theory.* Oxford: Blackwell.

Hannigan, John. 1995a. "The Postmodern City: A New Urbanization?" *Current Sociology* 43, 1: 151–217.

_____. 1995b. *Environmental Sociology: A Social Constructionist Perspective.* London: Routledge.

_____. 1998a. *Fantasy City: Pleasure and Profit in the Postmodern Metropolis.* New York: Routledge.

_____. 1998b [1995]. "Urbanization." Pp. 337–59 in Robert J. Brym, ed. *New Society: Sociology for the 21st Century,* 2nd ed. Toronto: Harcourt Brace Canada.

Hannon, Roseann, David S. Hall, Todd Kuntz, Van Laar, and Jennifer Williams. 1995. "Dating Characteristics Leading to Unwanted vs. Wanted Sexual Behavior." *Sex Roles* 33: 767–783.

Hao, Xiaoming. 1994. "Television Viewing Among American Adults in the 1990s." *Journal of Broadcasting and Electronic Media* 38: 353–360.

Harden, Blaine. 2001. "Two-Parent Families Rise After Changes in Welfare." *The New York Times Online.* On the World Wide Web at http://www.nytimes.com/2001/08/12/national/12FAMI.html?todaysheadlines &pagewanted print (12 August 2001).

Harding, David J., Cybelle Fox, and Jal D. Mehta. 2002. "Studying Rare Events through Qualitative Case Studies: Lessons from a Study of Rampage School Shootings." *Sociological Methods and Research* 31, 2: 174–217.

Harris, Chauncy D. 1997. "The Nature of Cities and Urban Geography in the Last Half Century." *Urban Geography* 18: 15–35.

_____ and Edward L. Ullman. 1945. "The Nature of Cities." *Annals of the American Academy of Political and Social Science* 242: 7–17.

Harris, Kathleen Mullan. 1997. *Teen Mothers and the Revolving Welfare Door.* Philadelphia: Temple University Press.

Harris, Marvin. 1974. *Cows, Pigs, Wars and Witches: The Riddles of Culture.* New York, Random House.

Harrison, Bennett. 1994. *Lean and Mean: The Changing Landscape of Corporate Power in the Age of Flexibility.* New York: Basic Books.

Harvey, Andrew S., Katherine Marshall, and Judith A. Frederick. 1991. *Where Does the Time Go?* Ottawa: Statistics Canada.

Harvey, Elizabeth. 1999. "Short-term and Long-term Effects of Early Parental Employment on Children of the National Longitudinal Survey of Youth." *Developmental Psychology* 35: 445–449.

Hastings, Arthur C., James Fadiman, and James C. Gordon, eds. 1980. *Health for the Whole Person: The Complete Guide to Holistic Medicine.* Boulder, CO: Westview Press.

Haub, Carl. 2000. "How Many People Have Ever Lived on Earth?" On the World Wide Web at http://www.discover.com/ask/main57.html (5 June 2003).

Hauser, Robert M., John Robert Warren, Min-Hsiung Huang, and Wendy Y. Carter. 2000. "Occupational Status, Education, and Social Mobility in the Meritocracy." Pp. 179–229 in Kenneth Arrow, Samuel Bowles, and Steven Durlauf, eds. *Meritocracy and Economic Inequality.* Princeton, NJ: Princeton University Press.

Hawley, Amos. 1950. *Human Ecology: A Theory of Community Structure.* New York: Ronald Press.

Haythornwaite, Caroline, and Barry Wellman. 2002. "The Internet in Everyday Life: An Introduction." Pp. 3–41 in *The Internet in Everyday Life.* Oxford: Blackwell.

"Health Care Systems: An International Comparison." 2001. Ottawa: Strategic Policy and Research, Intergovernmental Affairs. On the World Wide Web at http://www.pnrec.org/2001papers/DaigneaultLajoie.pdf (13 June 2003).

Hechter, Michael. 1974. *Internal Colonialism: The Celtic Fringe in British National Development, 1536–1966.* Berkeley: University of California Press.

_____. 1987. *Principles of Group Solidarity.* Berkeley: University of California Press.

Helsing, Knud J., Moyses Szklo, and George W. Comstock. 1981. "Factors Associated with Mortality After Widowhood." *American Journal of Public Health* 71: 802–809.

Herdt, Gilbert. 2001. "Social Change, Sexual Diversity, and Tolerance for Bisexuality in the United States." Pp. 267–283 in Anthony R. D'Augelli and Charlotte J. Patterson, eds. *Lesbian, Gay, and Bisexual Identities and Youth: Psychological Perspectives.* New York: Oxford University Press.

Herlihy, David. 1998. *The Black Death and the Transformation of the West.* Cambridge, MA: Harvard University Press.

Herman, Edward S., and Gerry O'Sullivan. 1989. *The "Terrorism" Industry: The Experts and Institutions That Shape Our View of Terror.* New York: Pantheon.

Herrnstein, Richard J., and Charles Murray. 1994. *The Bell Curve: Intelligence and Class Structure in American Life.* New York: Free Press.

Hersch, Patricia. 1998. *A Tribe Apart: A Journey into the Heart of American Adolescence.* New York: Ballantine Books.

Hertzman, Clyde, 2000. "The Case for Early Childhood Development Strategy." *Isuma: Canadian Journal of Policy Research* 1, 2: 11–18.

Hesse-Biber, Sharlene. 1996. *Am I Thin Enough Yet? The Cult of Thinness and the Commercialization of Identity.* New York: Oxford University Press.

_____ and Gregg Lee Carter. 2000. *Working Women in America: Split Dreams.* New York: Oxford University Press.

Hewitt, Joseph J., Jonathan Wilkenfeld, and Ted Robert Gurr. 2008. "Peace and Conflict 2008: Executive Summary." On the World Wide Web at http://www.cidcm.umd.edu/pc/executive_summary/pc_es_20070613.pdf (21 August 2008).

Hirschi, Travis. 1969. *Causes of Delinquency.* Berkeley: University of California Press.

Hirschman, Albert O. 1970. *Exit, Voice, and Loyalty: Responses to Decline in Firms, Organizations, and States.* Cambridge, MA: Harvard University Press.

Hobbes, Thomas. 1968 [1651]). *Leviathan.* Middlesex, UK: Penguin.

Hoberman, John. 1997. *Darwin's Athletes: How Sport Has Damaged Black America and Preserved the Myth of Race.* Boston: Houghton Mifflin.

Hochberg, Fred P. 2002. "American Capitalism's Other Side." *New York Times* July 25. On the World Wide Web at http://www.nytimes.com (25 July 2002).

Hochschild, Arlie Russell. 1973. *The Unexpected Community: Portrait of an Old Age Subculture.* Berkeley: University of California Press.

_____. 1979. "Emotion Work, Feeling Rules, and Social Structure." *American Journal of Sociology* 85: 551–575.

_____. 1983. *The Managed Heart: Commercialization of Human Feeling.* Berkeley: University of California Press.

_____ with Anne Machung. 1989. *The Second Shift: Working Parents and the Revolution at Home.* New York: Viking.

Hodgson, Marshall G. S. 1974. *The Venture of Islam: Conscience and History in a World Civilization,* 3 vols. Chicago: University of Chicago Press.

Hodson, Randy, and Teresa Sullivan. 1995 [1990]. *The Social Organization of Work,* 2nd ed. Belmont, CA: Wadsworth.

Homans, George Caspar. 1950. *The Human Group.* New York: Harcourt, Brace.

_____. 1961. *Social Behavior: Its Elementary Forms.* New York: Harcourt, Brace and World.

hooks, bell. 1984. *Feminist Theory: From Margin to Center.* Boston: South End Press.

Hopkins, Terence K., and Immanuel Wallerstein. 1986. "Commodity Chains in the World Economy Prior to 1800." *Review* 10: 157–170.

Horan, Patrick M. 1978. "Is Status Attainment Research Atheoretical?" *American Sociological Review* 43: 534–541.

Houpt, Simon. 2004. "Pass the popcorn, save the world." *Globe and Mail 29* May: R1, R13.

Houseknecht, Sharon K., and Jaya Sastry. 1996. "Family 'Decline' and Child Well-Being: A Comparative Assessment." *Journal of Marriage and the Family* 58: 726–739.

Hout, Michael. 1988. "More Universalism, Less Structural Mobility: The American Occupational Structure in the 1980s." *American Journal of Sociology* 93: 1358–1400.

_____ and William R. Morgan. 1975. "Race and Sex Variations in the Causes of the Expected Attainments of High School Seniors." *American Journal of Sociology* 81: 364–394.

_____, Adrian E. Raftery, and Eleanor O. Bell. 1993. "Making the Grade: Educational Stratification in the United States, 1925–1989." Pp. 25–49 in *Persistent Inequality: Changing Inequality in 13 Countries,* Yossi Shavit and Hans-Peter Blossfeld, eds. Boulder, CO: Westview.

Hoyt, Homer. 1939. *The Structure and Growth of Residential Neighborhoods in American Cities.* Washington, DC: Federal Housing Authority.

Huesmann, L. Rowell, et al. 2003. "Longitudinal Relations between Children's Exposure to TV Violence and their Aggressive and Violent Behavior in Young Adulthood: 1977–1992." *Developmental Psychology* 39, 2: 201–221.

Hughes, Fergus P. 1995 [1991]. *Children, Play and Development,* 2nd ed. Boston: Allyn and Bacon.

Human Rights Campaign. 1999. "The Hate Crime Prevention Act of 1999." On the World Wide web at http://www.hrc.org/issues/leg/hcpa/index.html (30 April 2000).

Human Rights Watch. 1995. *The Human Rights Watch Global Report on Women's Human Rights.* New York: Human Rights Watch.

Hunter, James Davison. 1991. *Culture Wars: The Struggle to Define America.* New York: Basic Books.

Hunter, Shireen T. 1998. *The Future of Islam and the West: Clash of Civilizations or Peaceful Coexistence?* Westport, CT: Praeger.

"Hunting bin Laden." 1999. On the World Wide Web at http://www.pbs.org/wgbh/pages/frontline/shows/binladen (13 September 2001).

Huntington, Samuel P. 1996. *The Clash of Civilizations and the Remaking of World Order.* New York: Simon and Schuster.

Ignatieff, Michael. 2000. *The Rights Revolution.* Toronto: Anansi.

Ignatiev, Noel. 1995. *How the Irish Became White.* New York: Routledge.

Illich, Ivan. 1976. *Limits to Medicine: Medical Nemesis: The Expropriation of Health.* New York: Penguin.

Infocom. 2003. "Bureaucracy." On the World Wide Web at http://infocom.elsewhere.org/gallery/bureaucracy/bureaucracy.html (14 March 2003).

Infoplease.com. 2001. "The Death Penalty Worldwide." On the World Wide Web at http://www.infoplease.com/ipa/A0777460.html (5 December 2002).

_____. 2003. "Federal Minimum Wage Rates, 1955–2002." On the World Wide Web at http://www.infoplease.com/ipa/A0774473.html (21 May 2003).

_____. 2005a. "Average SAT I Scores by Race and Ethnicity." On the World Wide Web at http://www.infoplease.com/ipa/A0883611.html (3 March 2006).

_____. 2005b. "The Death Penalty Worldwide." On the World Wide Web at http://www.infoplease.com/ipa/A0777460.html (11 March 2005).

_____. 2005c. "Federal Minimum Wage Rates, 1955–2005. On the World Wide Web at http://www.infoplease.com/ipa/A0774473.html (4 March 2006).

_____. 2005d. "Infant Mortality and Life Expectancy for Selected Countries, 2005." On the World Wide Web at http://www.infoplease.com/ipa/A0004393.html (4 March 2006).

_____. 2005e. "Families by Type, Race, and Hispanic Origin, 2002." On the World Wide Web at http://www.infoplease.com/ipa/a0880691.html (8 March 2005).

_____. 2009. "Federal Minimum Wage Rates, 1955–2009." On the World Wide Web at http://www.infoplease.com/ipa/A0774473.html (3 March 2009).

Inkeles, Alex, and David H. Smith. 1976. *Becoming Modern: Individual Change in Six Developing Countries.* Cambridge, MA: Harvard University Press.

Intergovernmental Panel on Climate Change. 2007. On the World Wide Web at http://www.ipcc.ch/ (2 May 2007).

"Internet Growth." 2000. On the World Wide Web at http://citywideguide.com/InternetGrowth.html (29 April 2000).

Internet Movie Database. 2003. On the World Wide Web at http://us.imdb.com (13 March 2003).

Internet Systems Consortium. 2007. "ISC Internet Domain Survey." On the World Wide Web at http://www.isc.org/index.pl (19 December 2007).

"Internet Usage Statistics." 2008. On the World Wide Web at http://www.internetworldstats.com/stats.htm (8 August 2008).

"Internet Usage Statistics—The Big Picture." 2005. On the World Wide Web at http://www.internetworldstats.com/stats.htm (25 February 2005).

Internet World Statistics. 2008. "Internet World Users by Language." On the World Wide Web at http://www.internetworldstats.com/stats7.htm (7 August 2008).

Inter-University Consortium for Political and Social Research. 1992. "Description-Study No. 9593." On the World Wide Web at http://www.icpsr.umich.edu:8080/ICPSR-STUDY/09593.xml (9 March 2003).

"Iraq Body Count." 2008. On the World Wide Web at http://www.iraqbodycount.org/ (12 January 2008).

"Iraq Coalition Casualty Count." 2008. On the World Wide Web at http://icasualties.org/oif/ (12 January 2008).

Isajiw, W. Wsevolod. 1978. "Olga in Wonderland: Ethnicity in a Technological Society." Pp. 29–39 in Leo Driedger, ed. *The Canadian Ethnic Mosaic: A Quest for Identity.* Toronto: McClelland & Stewart.

Jackman, Mary R., and Robert W. Jackman. 1983. *Class Awareness in the United States.* Berkeley: University of California Press.

Jackson, Carolyn and Ian David Smith. 2000. "Poles Apart? An Exploration of Single-Sex and Mixed-Sex Educational Environments in Australia and England." *Educational Studies* 26: 409–22.

James, William. 1976 [1902]. *The Varieties of Religious Experience: A Study in Human Nature.* New York: Collier Books.

Janis, Irving. 1972. *Victims of Groupthink.* Boston: Houghton Mifflin.

Jargowsky, Paul A. 2003. *Stunning Progress, Hidden Problems: The Dramatic Decline of Concentrated Poverty in the 1990s.* Washington, DC: Center on Urban and Metropolitan Policy, The Brookings Institution. On the World Wide Web at http://www.brookings.edu/dybdocroot/es/urban/publications/jargowskypoverty.pdf (5 August 2003).

Jencks, Christopher, Marshall Smith, Henry Acland, Mary Jo Bane, David Cohen, Herbert Gintis, Barbara Heyns, and Stephan Michelson. 1972. *Inequality: A Reassessment of the Effect of Family and Schooling in America.* New York: Basic Books.

Jensen, Margaret Ann. 1984. *Love's Sweet Return. The Harlequin Story.* Toronto: Women's Press.

"Jim Crow Laws: Texas." 2008. On the World Wide Web at http://www.jimcrowhistory.org/scripts/jimcrow/insidesouth.cgi?state=Texas (19 August 2008).

Johansen, Bruce E. 1998. "Sterilization of Native American Women." On the World Wide Web at http://www.ratical.org/ratville/sterilize.html (24 April 2003).

Johnson, Chalmers. 2000. *Blowback: The Costs and Consequences of American Empire.* New York: Metropolitan Books.

Johnson, Jeffrey G., et al. 2002. "Television Viewing and Aggressive Behavior During Adolescence and Adulthood." *Science* 295, 5564: 2468–2471.

Johnson, Michael P., and Kathleeen J. Ferraro. 2000. "Research on Domestic Violence in the 1990s: Making Distinctions." *Journal of Marriage and the Family* 62: 948–63.

Johnson, Neil F., and Sushil Jajodia. 1998. "Exploring Steganography: Seeing the Unseen." *IEEE Computer* February. On the World Wide Web at http://www.jjtc.com/pub/r2026a.htm (13 September 2001).

Jones, Brian J., Bernard J. Gallagher III, and Joseph A. McFalls, Jr. 1995. *Sociology: Micro, Macro, and Mega Structures.* Fort Worth, TX: Harcourt Brace College Publishers.

Jones, Christopher. 1999. "Chiapas' Well-Connected Rebels." *Wired News* 1 February. On the World Wide Web at http://www.wired.com/news/print/0,1294,17633,00.html (30 July 2000).

Jones, Jacqueline. 1986. *Labor of Love, Love of Sorrow: Black Women, Work and Slavery from Slavery to the Present.* New York: Random House.

Jones, Laura. 1997. "Global Warming Is All the Rage These Days . . . Which Enrages Many Doubting Scientists." *The Fraser Institute.* On the World Wide Web at http://oldfraser.lexi.net/media/media_releases/1997/19971201a.html (5 May 2002).

Jones, Patrice M. 2003. "Drug Lords Do What Officials Don't—Control Brazil's Slums." *Chicago Tribune* 2 February. On the World Wide Web at http://www.il-rs.com.br/ilingles/informative/marco_2003/informative_drugs.htm (5 August 2003).

Joyce, Terrence, and Lloyd Keigwin. 2004. "Abrupt Climate Change: Are We on the Brink of a New Little Ice Age?" Ocean and Climate Change Institute, Woods Hole Oceanographic Institution. On the World Wide Web at http://www.whoi.edu/institutes/occi/currenttopics/abruptclimate_joyce_keigwin.html (29 May 2004).

Jubilee Debt Campaign. 2005. "The Problem: Facts and Figures." On the World Wide Web at www.jubileedebtcampaign.org.uk/?lid=247 (21 July 2006).

Juergensmeyer, Mark. 2000. *Terror in the Mind of God: The Global Rise of Religious Violence.* Berkeley: University of California Press.

Kaiser, Scott. 2008. "Kerry Outperformed Obama among LGBT Voters: Why?" On the World Wide Web at http://www.bilerico.com/2008/11/kerry_outperformed_obama_among_lgbt_vote.php (27 January 2009).

Kalmijn, Matthijs. 1998. "Intermarriage and Homogamy: Causes, Patterns, Trends." *Annual Review of Sociology* 24: 395–421.

Kanter, Rosabeth Moss. 1977. *Men and Women of the Corporation.* New York: Basic Books.

_____. 1989. *When Giants Learn to Dance: Mastering the Challenges of Strategy, Management, and Careers in the 1990s.* New York: Simon & Schuster.

Kantor, Jodi. 2009. "A Portrait of Change: Nation's Many Faces in Extended First Family" New York Times. 21 January. On the World Wide Web at http://www.nytimes.com/2009/01/21/us/politics/21family.html?_r=1&scp=1&sq=kantor&st=cse (21 January 2009).

Karabel, Jerome. 1986. "Community Colleges and Social Stratification in the 1980s." In L. S. Zwerling, ed. *The Community College and its Critics.* San Francisco: Jossey-Bass.

Karl, Thomas R., and Kevin E. Trenberth. 1999. "The Human Impact on Climate." *Scientific American* 281, 6: September: 100–05.

Katznelson, Ira. 2005. *When Affirmative Action Was White: An Untold History of Racial Inequality in Twentieth-Century America.* New York: W.W. Norton.

Kaufman, Bruce E. 1982. "The Determinants of Strikes in the United States, 1900–1977." *Industrial and Labor Relations Review* 35: 473–490.

Keister, Lisa A. 2000. *Wealth in America: Trends in Wealth Inequality.* Cambridge: Cambridge University Press.

_____ and Stephanie Moller. 2000. "Wealth Inequality in the United States." *Annual Review of Sociology* 26: 63–81.

Keller, Larry. 2000. "Dual Earners: Double Trouble." On the World Wide Web at http://www.cnn.com/2000/CAREER/trends/11/13/dual.earners (13 November 2000).

Kelley, Jack. 2001. "Terror Groups Hide Behind Web Encryption." *USA Today* (June 19). On the World Wide Web at http://www.usatoday.com/life/cyber/tech/2001-02-05-binladen.htm (13 September 2001).

Kennedy, Paul. 1993. *Preparing for the Twenty-First Century.* New York: HarperCollins.

Kerig, Patricia K., Philip A. Cowan, and Carolyn Pape Cowan. 1993. "Marital Quality and Gender Differences in Parent-Child Interaction." *Developmental Psychology* 29: 931–939.

Kimmerling, Baruch, ed. 2001. *The Invention and Decline of Israeliness: State, Society, and the Military.* Berkeley: University of California Press.

_____. 2003. *Politicide: Ariel Sharon's War against the Palestinians.* London: Verso.

Kingston, Paul W. 2001. "The Unfulfilled Promise of Cultural Capital Theory." *Sociology of Education* Supplement: 88–91.

Kinsey, Alfred C., Wardell B. Pomeroy, and Clyde E. Martin. 1948. *Sexual Behavior in the Human Male.* Philadelphia: W. B. Saunders.

Kinsley, Michael. 2003. "How Affirmative Action Helped George W." On the World Wide Web at http://www.cnn.com/2003/ALLPOLITICS/01/20/timep.affirm.action.tm (1 February 2003).

Kleege, Georgina. 1999. *Sight Unseen.* New Haven, CT: Yale University Press.

Klein, Naomi. 2000. *No Logo: Taking Aim at the Brand Bullies.* New York: HarperCollins.

Kling, Kristen C., Janet Shibley Hyde, Carolin J. Showers, and Brenda N. Buswell. 1999. "Gender Differences in Self-Esteem: A Meta-Analysis." *Psychological Bulletin* 125, 4: 470–500.

Klockars, Carl B. 1974. *The Professional Fence.* New York: Free Press.

Kluegel, James R., and Eliot R. Smith. 1986. *Beliefs about Inequality: Americans' Views of What Is and What Ought to Be.* New York: Aldine de Gruyter.

Kluger, Richard. 1996. *Ashes to Ashes: America's Hundred-Year Cigarette War, the Public Health, and the Unabashed Triumph of Philip Morris.* New York: Knopf.

Koepke, Leslie, Jan Hare, and Patricia B. Moran. 1992. "Relationship Quality in a Sample of Lesbian Couples with Children and Child-Free Lesbian Couples." *Family Relations* 41: 224–229.

Kohlberg, Lawrence. 1981. *The Psychology of Moral Development: The Nature and Validity of Moral Stages.* New York: Harper & Row.

Kolko, Gabriel. 2002. *Another Century of War?* New York: New Press.

Koring, Paul. 2004. "The Iraq War: One Year Later." *Globe and Mail* 6 March: A1, A19.

Kornblum, William. 1997 [1988]. *Sociology in a Changing World,* 4th ed. Fort Worth, TX: Harcourt Brace College Publishers.

Korpi, Walter. 1983. *The Democratic Class Struggle.* London: Routledge & Kegan Paul.

_____, and Joakim Palme. 2003. "New Politics and Class Politics in the Context of Austerity and Globalization: Welfare State Regress in 18 Countries, 1975–95." *American Political Science Review* 97: 425–446.

Kosmin, Barry A. 1991. *Research Report of the National Survey of Religious Identification.* New York: CUNY Graduate Center.

Koss, Mary P., Christine A. Gidycz, and Nadine Wisniewski. 1987. "The Scope of Rape: Incidence and Prevalence of Sexual Aggression and Victimization in a National Sample of Higher Education Students." *Journal of Consulting and Clinical Psychology* 55: 162–170.

Kozol, Jonathan. 1991. *Savage Inequalities: Children in America's Schools.* New York: Crown.

Kropotkin, Petr. 1908 [1902]. *Mutual Aid: A Factor of Evolution,* revised ed. London: W. Heinemann.

Kübler-Ross, Elisabeth. 1969. *On Death and Dying.* New York: Macmillan.

Kurdek, Lawrence A. 1996. "The Deterioration of Relationship Quality for Gay and Lesbian Cohabiting Couples: A Five-Year Prospective Longitudinal Study." *Personal Relationships* 3: 417-42.

Kurzweil, Ray. 1999. *The Age of Spiritual Machines: When Computers Exceed Human Intelligence.* New York: Viking Penguin.

Kuttner, Robert. 1998a. "In This For-Profit Age, Preventive Medicine Means Avoiding Audits." *Boston Globe* 22 March: E7.

_____. 1998b. "Toward Universal Coverage." *The Washington Post* 14 July: A15.

LaFeber, Walter. 1993. *Inevitable Revolutions: The United States in Central America,* 2nd ed. New York: W.W. Norton.

_____. 1999. *Michael Jordan and the New Global Capitalism.* New York: W.W. Norton.

LaFree, Gary D. 1980. "The Effect of Sexual Stratification by Race on Official Reactions to Rape." *American Sociological Review* 45: 842–854.

Lahmeyer, Jan. 2003. "Brazil: Historical Demographical Data of the Whole Country." On the World Wide Web at http://www.library.uu.nl/wesp/populstat/Americas/brazilc.htm (5 August 2003).

Lamanna, Mary Ann, and Agnes Riedmann. 2003. *Marriages and Families: Making Choices in a Diverse Society,* 8th ed. Belmont, CA: Wadsworth.

Lamont, Michele and Annette Lareau. 1988. "Cultural Capital: Allusions, Gaps, and Glissandos in Recent Theoretical Developments." *Sociological Theory* 6: 153–168.

Lane, Harlan. 1992. *The Mask of Benevolence: Disabling the Deaf Community.* New York: Alfred A. Knopf.

Lantz, Herman, Martin Schultz, and Mary O'Hara. 1977. "The Changing American Family from the Preindustrial to the Industrial Period: A Final Report." *American Sociological Review* 42: 406–421.

Lapidus, Gail Warshofsky. 1978. *Women in Soviet Society: Equality, Development, and Social Change.* Berkeley: University of California Press.

Lapidus, Ira M. 2002 [1998]. *A History of Islamic Societies,* 2nd ed. Cambridge: Cambridge University Press.

Laslett, Peter. 1991 [1989]. *A Fresh Map of Life: The Emergence of the Third Age.* Cambridge, MA: Harvard University Press.

Lasswell, Harold. 1936. *Politics: Who Gets What, When and How.* New York: McGraw-Hill.

Laumann, Edward O., John H. Gagnon, Robert T. Michael, and Stuart Michaels. 1994. *The Social Organization of Sexuality: Sexual Practices in the United States.* Chicago: University of Chicago Press.

Lazare, Daniel. 1999. "Your Constitution Is Killing You: A Reconsideration of the Right to Bear Arms." *Harper's* 299, 1793, October: 57–65.

Le Bon, Gustave. 1969 [1895]. *The Crowd: A Study of the Popular Mind.* New York: Ballantine Books.

Lefkowitz, Bernard. 1997a. "Boys Town: Did Glen Ridge Raise Its Sons to Be Rapists?" *Salon* August 13. On the World Wide Web at http://www.salon.com/aug97/mothers/

_____. 1997b. *Our Guys: The Glen Ridge Rape and the Secret Life of the Perfect Suburb.* Berkeley: University of California Press.

Lehoczky, Etelka. 2003. "Stewardess Chic." *Chicago Tribune Online Edition.* April 2. On the World Wide Web at http://www.chicagotribune.com/shopping/chi-0304020338apr02,0,3507596.story?coll chi-shopping-hed (6 April 2003).

Lenski, Gerhard. 1966. *Power and Privilege: A Theory of Social Stratification.* New York: McGraw-Hill.

_____, Patrick Nolan, and Jean Lenski. 1995. *Human Societies: An Introduction to Macrosociology,* 7th ed. New York: McGraw-Hill.

Lenton, Rhonda L. 1989. "Homicide in Canada and the U.S.A." *Canadian Journal of Sociology* 14: 163–178.

Levine, R. A., and D. T. Campbell. 1972. *Ethnocentrism: Theories of Conflict, Ethnic Attitudes, and Group Behavior.* New York: Wiley.

Levine, Robert, Suguru Sato, Tsukasa Hashimoto, and Jyoti Verma. 1995. "Love and Marriage in Eleven Countries." *Journal of Cross-Cultural Psychology* 26: 554–71.

Levy, Frank. 1998. *The New Dollars and Dreams: American Incomes and Economic Change.* New York: Russell Sage Foundation.

Lewis, Bernard. 2002. *What Went Wrong? Western Impact and Middle Eastern Response.* New York: Oxford University Press.

Lewontin, Richard C. 1991. *Biology as Ideology: The Doctrine of DNA.* New York: HarperCollins.

Lie, John. 1992. "The Concept of Mode of Exchange." *American Sociological Review* 57: 508–523.

_____. 1998. *Han Unbound: The Political Economy of South Korea.* Stanford, CA: Stanford University Press.

_____. 2001. *Multiethnic Japan.* Cambridge, MA: Harvard University Press.

_____. 2004. *Modern Peoplehood.* Cambridge, MA: Harvard University Press.

Lieberson, Stanley. 1980. *A Piece of the Pie: Blacks and White Immigrants Since 1880.* Berkeley: University of California Press.

_____.1991. "A New Ethnic Group in the United States." Pp. 444–57 in Norman R. Yetman, ed. *Majority and Minority: The Dynamics of Race and Ethnicity in American Life,* 5th ed. Boston: Allyn & Bacon.

Liebow, Elliot. 1993. *Tell Them Who I Am: The Lives of Homeless Women.* New York: Free Press.

Light, Ivan. 1991. "Immigrant and Ethnic Enterprise in North America." Pp. 307–18 in Norman R. Yetman, ed. *Majority and Minority: The Dynamics of Race and Ethnicity in American Life,* 5th ed. Boston: Allyn & Bacon.

Lightfoot-Klein, Hanny, Cheryl Chase, Tim Hammond and Ronald Goldman. 2000. "Genital Surgery on Children below the Age of Consent." Pp. 440-479 in Lenore T. Szuchman and Frank Muscarella, eds. *Psychological Perspectives on Human Sexuality.* New York: John Wiley & Sons.

Lijphart, Arend. 1997. "Unequal Participation: Democracy's Unresolved Dilemma." *American Political Science Review* 91: 1–14.

Lindner, Rolf. 1996 [1990]. *The Reportage of Urban Culture: Robert Park and the Chicago School.* Adrian Morris, trans. Cambridge: Cambridge University Press.

Lino, Mark. 2005. *Expenditures on Children by Families, 2004.* Alexandria, VA: U.S. Department of Agriculture, Center for Nutrition Policy and Promotion. On the World Wide Web at http://www.cnpp.usda.gov/Crc/crc2004.pdf (9 March 2006).

Linton, Ralph. 1936. *The Study of Man.* New York: Appleton-Century-Croft.

Lips, Hilary M. 1999. *A New Psychology of Women: Gender, Culture and Ethnicity.* Mountain View, CA: Mayfield Publishing Company.

Lipset, Seymour Martin. 1971 [1951]. *Agrarian Socialism: The Cooperative Commonwealth Federation in Saskatchewan,* rev. ed. Berkeley: University of California Press.

_____ and Reinhard Bendix. 1963. *Social Mobility in Industrial Society.* Berkeley: University of California Press.

_____ and Stein Rokkan. 1967. "Cleavage Structures, Party Systems, and Voter Alignments: An Introduction." Pp. 1–64 in Seymour Martin Lipset and Stein Rokkan, eds. *Party Systems and Voter Alignments: Cross-National Perspectives.* New York: Free Press.

_____, Martin A. Trow, and James S. Coleman. 1956. *Union Democracy: The Internal Politics of the International Typographical Union.* Glencoe, IL: Free Press.

Liptak, Adam. 2003. "Death Row Numbers Decline as Challenges to System Rise." *New York Times* January 11. On the World Wide Web at http://www.nytimes.com (11 January 2003).

_____. 2005. "Court Takes Another Step in Reshaping Capital Punishment." *New York Times,* March 2. On the World Wide Web at www.nytimes.com (2 March 2005).

Lisak, David. 1992. "Sexual Aggression, Masculinity, and Fathers." *Signs* 16: 238–262.

Livernash, Robert, and Eric Rodenburg. 1998. "Population Change, Resources, and the Environment." *Population Bulletin* 53, 1. On the World Wide Web at http://www.prb.org/pubs/population_bulletin/bu53-1.htm (25 August 2000).

Livi-Bacci, Massimo. 1992. *A Concise History of World Population.* Cambridge, MA: Blackwell.

Lock, Margaret. 2002. *Twice Dead: Organ Transplants and the Reinvention of Death.* Berkeley: University of California Press.

Lofland, John, and Lyn H. Lofland. 1995 [1971]. *Analyzing Social Settings: A Guide to Qualitative Observation and Analysis,* 3rd ed. Belmont, CA: Wadsworth.

Lofland, L. H. 1985. "The Social Shaping of Emotion: Grief in Historical Perspective." *Symbolic Interaction* 8: 171–190.

Logan, John R., and Harvey L. Molotch. 1987. *Urban Fortunes: The Political Economy of Place.* Berkeley: University of California Press.

Lopez, Donald S. 2001. *The Story of Buddhism: A Concise Guide to Its History and Teachings.* San Francisco: Harper.

Lowe, Graham. 2000. *The Quality of Work: A People-Centred Agenda.* Toronto: Oxford University Press.

Lucas, Samuel Roundfield. 1999. *Tracking Inequality: Stratification and Mobility in American High Schools.* New York: Teachers College Press.

Lurie, Alison. 1981. *The Language of Clothes.* New York: Random House.

Luxembourg Income Study. 1999a. "LIS Inequality Indices." On the World Wide Web at http://lissy.ceps.lu/ineq.htm (29 April 2000).

_____. 1999b. "LIS Low Income Measures." On the World Wide Web at http://lissy.ceps.lu/lim.htm (29 April 2000).

Lynch, Michael, and David Bogen. 1997. "Sociology's Asociological 'Core': An Examination of Textbook Sociology in Light of the Sociology of Scientific Knowledge." *American Sociological Review* 62: 481–493.

MacCarthy, Fiona. 1999. "Skin Deep." *New York Review of Books* 46, 15: 19–21.

MacDonald, K., and R. D. Parke. 1986. "Parent-Child Physical Play: The Effects of Sex and Age on Children and Parents." *Sex Roles* 15: 367–378.

Macionis, John J. 1997 [1987]. *Sociology,* 6th ed. Upper Saddle River, NJ: Prentice-Hall.

MacKinnon, Catharine A. 1979. *Sexual Harassment of Working Women.* New Haven, CT: Yale University Press.

Macklin, Eleanor D. 1980. "Nontraditional Family Forms: A Decade of Research." *Journal of Marriage and the Family* 42: 905–922.

Maguire, Kathleen, and Ann L. Pastore, eds. 1998. *Sourcebook of Criminal Justice Statistics 1997.* On the World Wide Web at http://www.albany.edu/sourcebook/1995/pdf/t256.pdf (29 April 2000).

Mahony, Rhona. 1995. *Kidding Ourselves: Breadwinning, Babies, and Bargaining Power.* New York: Basic Books.

Maines, David. 1982. "In Search of Mesostructure: Studies in the Negotiated Order." *Urban Life* 11: 267–79.

Malthus, Thomas Robert. 1966 [1798]. *An Essay on the Principle of Population.* J. R. Bodnar, ed. London: Macmillan.

Manga, Pran, Douglas E. Angus, and William R. Swan. 1993. "Effective Management of Low Back Pain: It's Time to Accept the Evidence." *Journal of the Canadian Chiropractic Association* 37: 221–229.

Mankiw, N. Gregory. 2003. "China's Trade and U.S. Manufacturing Jobs." Testimony before the House Committee on Ways and Means. Washington, DC. October 30. On the World Wide Web at http://www.whitehouse.gov/cea/mankiw_testimony_house_ways_and_means_oct_30.pdf (1 April 2005).

Mann, Susan A., Michael D. Grimes, Alice Abel Kemp, and Pamela J. Jenkins. 1997. "Paradigm Shifts in Family Sociology? Evidence From Three Decades of Family Textbooks." *Journal of Family Issues* 18: 315–349.

Manza, Jeff, Michael Hout, and Clem Brooks. 1995. "Class Voting in Capitalist Democracies Since World War II: Dealignment, Realignment, or Trendless Fluctuation?" *Annual Review of Sociology* 21: 137–162.

Marger, Martin M. 2003. *Race and Ethnic Relations: American and Global Perspectives,* 6th ed. Belmont, CA: Wadsworth.

Marklein, Mary Beth. 2002. "Students Say College Studies Take a Back Seat to Longer Work Hours." *USA Today* April 17: 8D.

Marmor, Theodore R. 1994. *Understanding Health Care Reform.* New Haven, CT: Yale University Press.

Marshall, Monty G., and Ted Robert Gurr. 2003. *Peace and Conflict 2003.* College Park: CIDCM, University of Maryland. On the World Wide Web at http://www.cidcm.umd.edu/inscr/PC03print.pdf (3 June 2003).

Marshall, S. L. A. 1947. *Men Against Fire: The Problem of Battle Command in Future War.* New York: Morrow.

Marshall, T. H. 1965. "Citizenship and Social Class." Pp. 71–134 in T. H. Marshall, ed. *Class, Citizenship, and Social Development: Essays by T. H. Marshall.* Garden City, NY: Anchor.

Martineau, Harriet. 1985. *Harriet Martineau on Women,* Gayle Graham Yates, ed. New Brunswick, NJ: Rutgers University Press.

Marx, Karl. 1904 [1859]. *A Contribution to the Critique of Political Economy,* N. Stone, trans. Chicago: Charles H. Kerr.

_____. 1970 [1843]. *Critique of Hegel's "Philosophy of Right,"* Annette Jolin and Joseph O'Malley, trans. Cambridge: Cambridge University Press.

_____ and Friedrich Engels. 1972 [1848]. "Manifesto of the Communist Party." Pp. 331–62 in R. Tucker, ed. *The Marx-Engels Reader.* New York: W.W. Norton.

Massey, Douglas S., and Nancy A. Denton. 1993. *American Apartheid: Segregation and the Making of the Underclass.* Cambridge, MA: Harvard University Press.

_____, Camille Z. Charles, Garvey F. Lundy, and Mary J. Fischer. 2003. *The Source of the River: The Social Origins of Freshman at America's Selective Colleges and Universities.* Princeton, NJ: Princeton University Press.

Massing, Michael. 1999. "The End of Welfare?" *New York Review of Books* 46, 15: 22–26.

_____ et al. 1999. "Beyond Legalization: New Ideas for Ending the War on Drugs." *The Nation* 20 September: 11–48.

Matalon, Jean-Marc. 1997. "Jeanne Calment, World's Oldest Person, Dead at 122." *The Shawnee News-Star* 5 August. On the World Wide Web at http://www.news-star.com/stories/080597/life1.html (2 May 2000).

Mathis, William J. 2003. "No Child Left Behind: Costs and Benefits." *Phi Delta Kappan* May. On the World Wide Web at http://www.pdkintl.org/kappan/k0305mat.htm (29 March 2005).

Matsueda, Ross L. 1988. "The Current State of Differential Association Theory." *Crime and Delinquency* 34: 277–306.

_____. 1992. "Reflected Appraisals, Parental Labeling, and Delinquency: Specifying a Symbolic Interactionist Theory." *American Journal of Sociology* 97: 1577–1611.

Mauer, Marc. 1994. "Americans Behind Bars: The International Use of Incarceration, 1992–1993." On the World Wide Web at http://www.druglibrary.org/schaffer/Other/sp/abb.htm (29 April 2000).

McAdam, Doug. 1982. *Political Process and the Development of Black Insurgency, 1930–1970.* Chicago: University of Chicago Press.

_____, John D. McCarthy, and Mayer N. Zald. 1996. "Introduction: Opportunities, Mobilizing Structures, and Framing Processes—Toward a Synthetic, Comparative Perspective on Social Movements." Pp. 1–20 in Doug McAdam, John D. McCarthy, and Mayer N. Zald, eds. *Comparative Perspectives on Social Movements: Political Opportunities, Mobilizing Structures, and Cultural Framing.* New York: Cambridge University Press.

McClendon, McKee J. 1976. "The Occupational Status Attainment Processes of Males and Females." *American Sociological Review* 41: 52–64.

McConaghy, Nathaniel. 1999. "Unresolved Issues in Scientific Sexology." *Archives of Sexual Behavior* 28, 4: 285–318.

McCrum, Robert, William Cran, and Robert MacNeil. 1992. *The Story of English,* new and rev. ed. London: Faber and Faber.

McCullagh, Declan. 2000a. "Bin Laden: Steganography Master?" *Wired* February 7. On the World Wide Web at http://www.wired.com/news/print/0.1294.41658.00.html (13 September 2001).

_____. 2000b. "Regulating Privacy: At What Cost?" *Wired* September 19. On the World Wide Web at http://www.wired.com/news/print/0.1294.38878.00.html (13 September 2001).

McDonald, Michael P. 2008a. "This may be the election of the century." On the World Wide Web at http://www.politico.com/news/stories/0908/13798.html (5 November 2008).

_____. 2008b. "Voter Turnout." On the World Wide Web at http://elections.gmu.edu/voter_turnout.htm (5 November 2008).

McGovern, James R. 1982. *Anatomy of a Lynching: The Killing of Claude Neal.* Baton Rouge: Louisiana State University Press.

McGinn, Anne Platt. 1998. "Promoting Sustainable Fisheries." In Lester R. Brown, Christopher Flavin, Hilary French, et al., eds., *State of the World 1998,* pp. 59–78. New York: W.W. Norton.

McLuhan, Marshall. 1964. *Understanding Media: The Extensions of Man.* New York: McGraw-Hill.

McMahon, Walter W. 1999. *Education and Development: Measuring the Social Benefits.* Oxford: Oxford University Press.

McManners, John, ed. 1990. *Oxford Illustrated History of Christianity.* Oxford: Oxford University Press.

McNeill, William H. 1976. *Plagues and Peoples.* Garden City, NY: Anchor Press.

_____. 1990. *Population and Politics since 1750.* Charlottesville, WV: University Press of Virginia.

McPhail, Clark. 1991. *The Myth of the Madding Crowd.* New York: Aldine de Gruyter.

_____. 1994. "The Dark Side of Purpose: Individual and Collective Violence in Riots." *The Sociological Quarterly* 35: 1–32.

_____ and Ronald T. Wohlstein. 1983. "Individual and Collective Behaviors Within Gatherings, Demonstrations, and Riots." *Annual Review of Sociology* 9: 579–600.

Mead, G. H. 1934. *Mind, Self and Society.* Chicago: University of Chicago Press.

Meek, Ronald L., ed. 1971. *Marx and Engels on the Population Bomb: Selections from the Writings of Marx and Engels Dealing with the Theories of Thomas Robert Malthus.* Dorothea L. Meek and Ronald L. Meek, trans. Berkeley, CA: Ramparts Press.

Meier, Deborah. 2002. *In Schools We Trust.* Boston: Beacon Press.

Meier, Diane E., Carol-Ann Emmons, Sylvan Wallenstein, Timothy Quill, R. Sean Morrison, and Christine K. Cassell. 1998, "A National Survey of Physician Assisted Suicide and Euthanasia in the United States." *New England Journal of Medicine* 338: 1193–1201.

Melton, J. Gordon. 1996 [1978]. *Encyclopedia of American Religions,* 5th ed. Detroit: Gale.

Melucci, Alberto. 1980. "The New Social Movements: A Theoretical Approach." *Social Science Information* 19: 199–226.

_____. 1995. "The New Social Movements Revisited: Reflections on a Sociological Misunderstanding." Pp. 107–19 in Louis Maheu, ed. *Social Classes and Social Movements: The Future of Collective Action.* London: Sage.

Merton, Robert K. 1938. "Social Structure and Anomie." *American Sociological Review* 3: 672–682.

_____. 1968 [1949]. *Social Theory and Social Structure.* New York: Free Press.

Messner, Michael. 1995 [1989]. "Boyhood, Organized Sports, and the Construction of Masculinities." Pp. 102–14 in Michael S. Kimmel and Michael A. Messner *Men's Lives,* 3rd ed. Boston: Allyn & Bacon.

Metropolitan Museum of Art. 2000. "Mrs. Charles Dana Gibson (1873–1956)" On the World Wide Web at http://costumeinstitute.org/gibson.htm (13 June 2000).

Meyer, John W., Francisco O. Ramirez, and Yasemin Nuhoglu Soysal. 1992. "World Expansion of Mass Education, 1870–1980." *Sociology of Education* 65: 128–49.

_____, and W. Richard Scott. 1983. *Organizational Environments: Ritual and Rationality.* Beverly Hills, CA: Sage.

Michael, Robert T., John H. Gagnon, Edward O. Laumann, and Gina Kolata. 1994. *Sex in America: A Definitive Survey.* Boston: Little, Brown.

Michels, Robert. 1949 [1911]. *Political Parties: A Sociological Study of the Oligarchical Tendencies of Modern Democracy,* E. and C. Paul, trans. New York: Free Press.

Milem, Jeffrey F. 1998. "Attitude Change in College Students: Examining the Effect of College Peer Groups and Faculty Normative Groups." *The Journal of Higher Education* 69: 117–140.

Miles, Robert. 1989. *Racism.* London: Routledge.

Milgram, Stanley. 1974. *Obedience to Authority: An Experimental View.* New York: Harper.

Miller, Jerome G. 1996. *Search and Destroy: African-American Males in the Criminal Justice System.* New York: Cambridge University Press.

Mills, C. Wright. 1956. *The Power Elite.* New York: Oxford University Press.

_____. 1959. *The Sociological Imagination.* New York: Oxford University Press.

Ministério de Ciência e Tecnologia Brasil. 2002. "Brazil Urban Population." On the World Wide Web at http://www.mct.gov.br/clima/ingles/comunic_old/res7_1_1.htm (5 August 2003).

Minkel, J. R. 2002. "A Way with Words." *Scientific American* 25 March. On the World Wide Web at http://www.mit.edu/~lera/sciam (21 January 2003).

Mintz, Alexander. 1946. "A Re-Examination of Correlations Between Lynchings and Economic Indices." *Journal of Abnormal and Social Psychology* 41: 154–160.

Mintz, Beth. 1989. "United States of America." Pp. 207–36 in Tom Bottomore and Robert J. Brym, eds. *The Capitalist Class: An International Study.* New York: New York University Press.

_____ and Michael Schwartz. 1985. *The Power Structure of American Business.* Chicago: University of Chicago Press.

Mishel, Lawrence, Jared Bernstein, and John Schmitt. 1999. *The State of Working America, 1998–99.* Ithaca, NY: Cornell University Press.

Mitford, Jessica. 1998 [1963]. *The American Way of Death Revisited.* New York: Vintage.

Mittelman, James H. 2000. *The Globalization Syndrome: Transformation and Resistance.* Princeton, NJ: Princeton University Press.

Mittelstaedt, Martin. 2001. "When a Car's Tailpipe Is More Lethal than a Car Crash." *Globe and Mail,* September 29: F9.

Mizruchi, Mark S. 1982. *The American Corporate Network, 1904–1974.* Beverly Hills, CA: Sage.

_____. 1992. *The Structure of Corporate Political Action: Interfirm Relations and Their Consequences.* Cambridge, MA: Harvard University Press.

Money, John and Anke Ehrhardt. 1972. *Man and Woman, Boy and Girl.* Boston: Little Brown.

Mooney, Linda, Caroline Schact, David Knox and Adie Nelson. 2003. *Understanding Social Problems,* 2nd ed. Toronto: Nelson.

Morris, Aldon D. 1984. *The Origins of the Civil Rights Movement: Black Communities Organizing for Change.* New York: Free Press.

Morris, Charles R. 1996. *The AARP: America's Most Powerful Lobby and the Clash of Generations.* New York: Times Books.

Morris, Norval, and David J. Rothman, eds. 1995. *The Oxford History of the Prison: The Practice of Punishment in Western Society.* New York: Oxford University Press.

Mortimer, Jeylan T., and Roberta G. Simmons. 1978. "Adult Socialization." *Annual Review of Sociology* 4: 421–454.

MSNBC. 2008. "United States—President." On the World Wide Web at http://www.msnbc.msn.com/id/26843704 (5 November 2008).

Mumford, Lewis. 1961. *The City in History: Its Origins, Its Transformations, and Its Prospects.* New York: Harcourt, Brace, & World.

Murdoch, Guy. 1995. "Child Care Centers." *Consumers' Research Magazine* 78, 10: 2.

Murdock, George Peter. 1937. "Comparative Data on the Division of Labor by Sex." *Social Forces* 15: 551–553.

_____. 1949. *Social Structure.* New York: Macmillan.

Mustard, Cameron A., Patricia Kaufert, Anita Kozyrskyj, and Teresa Mayer. 1998. "Sex Differences in the Use of Health Care Services." *New England Journal of Medicine* 338: 1678–1683.

Myerhoff, Barbara. 1978. *Number Our Days.* New York: Dutton.

Myers, Ransom A., and Boris Worm. 2003. "Rapid Worldwide Depletion of Predatory Fish Communities." *Nature* 423: 280–283.

Myles, John. 1988. "The Expanding Middle: Some Canadian Evidence on the Deskilling Debate." *Canadian Review of Sociology and Anthropology* 25: 335–364.

Nagel, Joane. 1996. *American Indian Ethnic Renewal: Red Power and the Resurgence of Identity and Culture.* New York: Oxford University Press.

Nash, Gary, Charlotte Crabtree, and Ross Dunn. 1997. *History on Trial: Culture Wars and the Teaching of the Past.* New York: Knopf.

National Basketball Association. 2000. "New York Knicks History." On the World Wide at http://nba.com/knicks/00400499.html#2 (29 May 2000).

National Center for Education Statistics. 2004. *The Condition of Education, 2004.* Washington, DC: Institute of Education Sciences, U.S. Department of Education. On the World Wide Web at http://nces.ed.gov/programs/coe (12 June 2004).

_____. 2008. "The Condition of Education 2008." On the World Wide Web at http://nces.ed.gov/programs/coe/2008/pdf/25_2008.pdf (20 August 2008).

National Center for Health Statistics. 2008. "Deaths, Percent of Total Deaths, and Death Rates for the 15 Leading Causes of Death: United States and Each State, 1999-2005." On the World Wide Web at http://www.cdc.gov/nchs/datawh/statab/unpubd/mortabs/lcwk9_10.htm (22 August 2008).

National Center for Injury Prevention and Control. 2000. "Suicide in the United States." On the World Wide Web at http://www.cdc.gov/ncipc/factsheets/suifacts.htm (27 April 2000).

National Commission on Excellence in Education. 1983. *A Nation at Risk.* Washington D.C.

National Counterterrorism Center. 2007. "Annex of Statistical Information." On the World Wide Web at http://www.state.gov/documents/organization/83396.pdf (12 January 2008).

National Gay and Lesbian Task Force. 2004. "Specific Anti-Same-Sex Marriage Laws in the U.S. January 2004." On the World Wide Web at http://www.ngltf.org/downloads/marriagemap0400.gif (6 March 2004).

_____. 2005. "Anti-Gay Marriage Measures in the U.S. as of February 2005." On the World Wide Web at http://www.thetaskforce.org/downloads/marriagemap.pdf (8 March 2005).

National Office of Vital Statistics. 1947. "Deaths and Death Rates for Leading Causes of Death: Death Registration States, 1900–1940." Special tabulation prepared for the authors.

National Opinion Research Center. 2006. *General Social Survey, 1972–2004.* Chicago: University of Chicago. Machine readable file.

_____. 2008a. "General Social Survey." On the World Wide Web at http://www.norc.org/GSS+Website/Data+Analysis/ (8 August 2008).

_____. 2008b. *General Social Survey, 1972–2006.* Chicago: University of Chicago.

National Organization for Men Against Sexism. 2000. On the World Wide Web at http://nomas.idea-net.com (15 June 2000).

National Rifle Association. 2005. "Guns, Gun Ownership, & RTC at All-Time Highs, Less 'Gun Control,' and Violent Crime at 30-Year Low." On the World Wide Web at http://www.nraila.org/Issues/FactSheets/Read.aspx?ID=126 (29 December 2005).

Neugarten, Bernice. 1974. "Age Groups in American Society and the Rise of the Young Old." *Annals of the American Academy of Political and Social Science* 415: 187–198.

Nevitte, Neil. 1996. *The Decline of Deference.* Peterborough, Canada: Broadview Press.

Newcomb, Theodore M. 1943. *Personality and Social Change: Attitude Formation in a Student Community.* New York: Holt, Rinehart & Winston.

Newman, Katherine S. 1988. *Falling From Grace: The Experience of Downward Mobility in the American Middle Class.* New York: Free Press.

_____. 1999. *No Shame in My Game: The Working Poor in the Inner City.* New York: Knopf and the Russell Sage Foundation.

Newport, Frank. 2000. "Support for Death Penalty Drops to Lowest Level in 19 Years, Although Still High at 66%." The Gallup Organization. On the World Wide Web at http://www.gallup.com/poll/releases/pr000224.asp (8 August 2000).

New York City Department of Consumer Affairs. 2001. "The High Cost of Dying." On the World Wide Web at http://home.nyc.gov/html/dca/html/dcafuneralreport.html (27 April 2003).

Nie, Norman H., Sidney Verba, and John R. Petrocik. 1979 [1976]. *The Changing American Voter,* rev. ed. Cambridge, MA: Harvard University Press.

Nielson Media Research. 2008. "Top TV Ratings." On the World Wide Web at http://www.nielsenmedia.com/nc/portal/site/Public/menuitem.43afce2fac27e890311ba0a347a062a0/?vgnextoid=9e4df9669fa14010VgnVCM100000880a260aRCRD (9 August 2008).

Nisbett, Richard E., Kaiping Peng, Incheol Choi, and Ara Norenzayan. 2001. "Culture and Systems of Thought: Holistic Versus Analytic Cognition." *Psychological Review* 108: 291–310.

Nolen, Stephanie. 1999. "Gender: The Third Way." *Globe and Mail* September 25: D1, D4.

Norton, Kevin I., Timothy S. Olds, Scott Olive and Stephen Dank. 1996. "Ken and Barbie at Life Size." *Sex Roles* 34: 287–94.

Nowak, Martin A., Robert M. May, and Karl Sigmund. 1995. "The Arithmetics of Mutual Help." *Scientific American* 272, 6: 76–81.

Nowell, Amy, and Larry V. Hedges. 1998. "Trends in Gender Differences in Academic Achievement from 1960 to 1994: An Analysis of Differences in Mean, Variance, and Extreme Scores." *Sex Roles* 39: 21–43.

Nuland, Sherwin B. 1993. *How We Die: Reflections on Life's Final Chapter.* New York: Vintage.

Oates, Joyce Carol. 1999. "The Mystery of JonBenét Ramsey." *New York Review of Books* 24 June: 31–37.

Oberschall, Anthony. 1973. *Social Conflict and Social Movements.* Englewood Cliffs, NJ: Prentice-Hall.

O'Connor, Julia S., and Robert J. Brym. 1988. "Public Welfare Expenditure in OECD Countries: Towards a Reconciliation of Inconsistent Findings." *British Journal of Sociology* 39: 47–68.

_____and Gregg M. Olsen, eds. 1998. *Power Resources Theory and the Welfare State: A Critical Approach.* Toronto: University of Toronto Press.

Ogbu, John U. 2003. *Black American Students in an Affluent Suburb: A Study of Academic Disengagement.* Mahwah, NJ: L. Erlbaum Associates.

Ogburn, William F. 1966 [1922]. *Social Change with Respect to Culture and Original Nature.* New York: Dell.

O'Hare, William P. 1996. "A New Look at Poverty in America." *Population Bulletin* 51, 2: 2–46.

Oliver, Melvin L., and Thomas M. Shapiro. 1995. *Black Wealth/White Wealth: A New Perspective on Racial Inequality.* New York: Routledge.

Oliver, Mike. 1996. *Understanding Disability: From Theory to Practice.* Basingstoke, UK: Macmillan.

Olsen, Gregg. 2002. *The Politics of the Welfare State: Canada, Sweden, and the United States.* Toronto: Oxford University Press.

_____ and Robert J. Brym. 1996. "Between American Exceptionalism and Swedish Social Democracy: Public and Private Pensions in Canada." Pp. 261–79 in Michael Shalev, ed. *The Privatization of Social Policy? Occupational Welfare and the Welfare State in America, Scandinavia and Japan.* London: Macmillan.

Olshansky, S. Jay, Bruce A. Carnes, and Aline Desesquelles. 2001. "Prospects for Human Longevity." *Science* 291, 5508: 1491–1492.

Omi, Michael, and Howard Winant. 1986. *Racial Formation in the United States.* New York: Routledge.

Oregon Department of Human Services. 2003. *Fifth Annual Report on Oregon's Death with Dignity Act.* Portland, OR. On the World Wide Web at http://www.dhs.state.or.us/publichealth/chs/pas/ar-index.cfm (25 April 2003).

Oreskes, Naomi. 2004. "The Scientific Consensus on Climate Change." *Science* 306: 1686.

Orfield, Gary, and Susan E. Eaton. 1996. *Dismantling Desegregation: The Quiet Reversal of Brown v. Board of Education.* New York: Free Press.

Organization of African Unity. 2000. *Rwanda: The Preventable Genocide.* On the World Wide Web at http://www.visiontv.ca/RememberRwanda/Report.pdf (15 January 2005).

Ornstein, Michael. 1998. "Survey Research." *Current Sociology* 46, 4: 1–87.

Ossowski, Stanislaw. 1963. *Class Structure in the Social Consciousness,* S. Patterson, trans. London: Routledge & Kegan Paul.

Oziewicz, Estanislao. 2006. "Poll Finds Support Soft for Iraq War." *Globe and Mail* 1 March: A 11.

Pammett, Jon H. 1997. "Getting Ahead Around the World." Pp. 67–86 in Alan Frizzell and Jon H. Pammett, eds. *Social Inequality in Canada.* Ottawa: Carleton University Press.

Pape, Robert A. 2003 "The Strategic Logic of Suicide Terrorism." *American Political Science Review* 97: 343–361.

_____. 2005. *Dying to Win: The Strategic Logic of Suicide Terrorism.* New York: Random House.

Parillo, Vincent N., John Stimson, and Ardyth Stimson. 1999. *Contemporary Social Problems,* 4th ed. Boston: Allyn & Bacon.

Park, Robert Ezra. 1914. "Racial Assimilation in Secondary Groups." *Publications of the American Sociological Society* 8: 66–72.

_____. 1950. *Race and Culture.* New York: Free Press.

_____, Ernest W. Burgess, and Roderick D. McKenzie. 1967 [1925]. *The City.* Chicago: University of Chicago Press.

Parsons, Talcott. 1942. "Age and Sex in the Social Structure of the United States." *American Sociological Review* 7: 604–616.

_____. 1951. *The Social System.* New York: Free Press.

_____. 1955. "The American Family: Its Relation to Personality and to the Social Structure." Pp. 3–33 in Talcott Parsons and Robert F. Bales, eds. *Family, Socialization and Interaction Process.* New York: Free Press.

Patent Medicine Prices Review Board. 2002. *Annual Report.* Ottawa. On the World Wide Web at http://www.pmprb-cepmb.gc.ca/CMFiles/ar-2002e21IRA-6162003-196.pdf (17 June 2003).

Patterson, Orlando. 1982. *Slavery and Social Death.* Cambridge, MA: Harvard University Press.

Peacock, Mary. 2000. "The Cult of Thinness." On the World Wide Web at http://www.womenswire.com/image/toothin.html (13 June 2000).

Pear, Robert. 2003. "House Endorses Stricter Work Rules for Poor." *New York Times* February 14. On the World Wide Web at http://www.nytimes.com (14 February 2003).

Peritz, Ingrid. 2006. "Spreading the (English) word." *Globe and Mail* 11 February 2006: A1, A7.

Peters, John F. 1994. "Gender Socialization of Adolescents in the Home: Research and Discussion." *Adolescence* 29: 913–934.

Pettersson, Jan. 2003. "Democracy, Regime Stability, and Growth." *Scandinavian Working Papers in Economics.* On the World Wide Web at http://swopec.hhs.se/sunrpe/abs/sunrpe2002_0016.htm (13 February 2003).

Pew Forum on Religion and Public Life. 2008. "U.S. Religious Landscape Survey." On the World Wide Web at http://religions.pewforum.org/ (19 August 2008).

Pew Research Center for the People and the Press. 2002. "Among Wealthy Nations U.S. Stands Alone in its Embrace of Religion." On the World Wide Web at http://people-press.org/reports/display.php3?ReportID 167 (3 May 2003).

Phillips, Kevin. 1990. *The Politics of Rich and Poor: Wealth and the American Electorate in the Reagan Aftermath.* New York: Random House.

Piaget, Jean, and Bärbel Inhelder. 1969. *The Psychology of the Child,* Helen Weaver, trans. New York: Basic Books.

PISA (The Programme for International Student Assessment). 2007. "Executive Summary." On the World Wide Web at http://www.pisa.oecd.org/dataoecd/15/13/39725224.pdf (20 August 2008).

Piven, Frances Fox, and Richard A. Cloward. 1977. *Poor People's Movements: Why They Succeed, How They Fail.* New York: Vintage.

_____ and _____.1989 [1988]. *Why Americans Don't Vote.* New York: Pantheon.

_____and _____.1993 [1971]. *Regulating the Poor: The Functions of Public Welfare,* updated ed. New York: Vintage.

A Place Called Chiapas. 1998. Vancouver: Canada Wild Productions. (Movie).

Podolny, Joel M., and Karen L. Page. 1998. "Network Forms of Organization." *Annual Review of Sociology* 24: 57–76.

Polanyi, Karl. 1957 [1944]. *The Great Transformation: The Political and Economic Origins of Our Time.* Boston: Beacon Press.

PollingReport.com. 2005. "Crime." On the World Wide Web at http://www.pollingreport.com/crime.htm (11 March 2005).

Polsby, Nelson W. 1959. "Three Problems in the Analysis of Community Power." *American Sociological Review* 24: 796–803.

Pool, Robert. 1997. *Beyond Engineering: How Society Shapes Technology.* New York: Oxford University Press.

Popenoe, David. 1988. *Disturbing the Nest: Family Change and Decline in Modern Societies.* New York: Aldine de Gruyter.

_____. 1991. "Family Decline in the Swedish Welfare State." *Public Interest* 102: 65–78.

_____. 1992. "Family Decline: A Rejoinder." *Public Interest* 109: 116–118.

_____. 1993. "American Family Decline, 1960–1990: A Review and Appraisal." *Journal of Marriage and the Family* 55: 527–555.

_____. 1996. *Life Without Father: Compelling New Evidence that Fatherhood and Marriage are Indispensable for the Good of Children and Society.* New York: Martin Kessler Books.

Population Reference Bureau. 2002. "World Population Data Sheet 2002." On the World Wide Web at http://www.prb.org/pdf/WorldPopulationDS02_Eng.pdf (13 June 2003).

_____. 2004. "Transitions in World Population." *Population Bulletin* 59, 1. On the World Wide Web at http://www.prb.org/Template.cfm?Section=PRB&template=/ContentManagement/ContentDisplay.cfm&ContentID=12488 (17 March 2006).

_____. 2008. "Word Population Data Sheet 2008." On the World Wide Web at http://www.prb.org/pdf08/08WPDS_Eng.pdf (21 August 2008).

Portes, Alejandro, and Robert D. Manning. 1991. "The Immigrant Enclave: Theory and Empirical Examples." Pp. 319–32 in Norman R. Yetman, ed. *Majority and Minority: The Dynamics of Race and Ethnicity in American Life,* 5th ed. Boston: Allyn & Bacon.

_____and Cynthia G. Truelove. 1991."Making Sense of Diversity: Recent Research on Hispanic Minorities in the United States." Pp. 402–19 in Norman R. Yetman, ed. *Majority and Minority: The Dynamics of Race and Ethnicity in American Life,* 5th ed. Boston: Allyn & Bacon.

Postel, Sandra. 1994. "Carrying Capacity: Earth's Bottom Line." Pp. 3–21 in Linda Starke, ed. *State of the World 1994.* New York: W.W. Norton.

Postman, Neil. 1982. *The Disappearance of Childhood.* New York: Delacorte.

Pred, Allan R. 1973. *Urban Growth and the Circulation of Information.* Cambridge, MA: Harvard University Press.

Prejean, Sister Helen. 2005. "Death in Texas." *New York Review of Books,* 52, 1: 13 January. On the World Wide Web at http://www.nybooks.com/articles/17670 (12 March 2005).

Priestly, Mark. 2001. "Introduction: The Global Context of Disability." Pp. 3–25 in *Disability and the Life Course: Global Perspectives,* Mark Priestly, ed. Cambridge: Cambridge University Press.

Proctor, Robert N. 1988. *Racial Hygiene: Medicine under the Nazis.* Cambridge, MA: Harvard University Press.

Provine, Robert R. 2000. *Laughter: A Scientific Investigation.* New York: Penguin.

Public Broadcasting System. 1997. "Double Talk?" On the World Wide Web at http://www.pbs.org/newshour/bb/education/july-dec97/bilingual_9-21.html (11 August 2000).

Public Citizen. 2004. "U.S. Workers' Jobs, Wages and Economic Security." On the World Wide Web at http://www.citizen.org/documents/NAFTA_10_jobs.pdf (31 March 2005).

Quadagno, Jill. 1994. *The Color of Welfare: How Racism Undermined the War on Poverty.* New York: Oxford University Press.

Quaschning, Volker. 2003. "Development of Global Carbon Dioxide Emissions and Concentration in Atmosphere." On the World Wide Web at http://www.volker-quaschning.de/datserv/CO2/index_e.html (2 March 2005).

Raag, Tarja, and Christine L. Rackliff. 1998. "Preschoolers' Awareness of Social Expectations of Gender: Relationships to Toy Choices." *Sex Roles* 38: 685–700.

Ramirez, Roberto R., and G. Patricia de la Cruz. 2003. "The Hispanic Population in the United States: March 2002." Washington, DC: U.S. Census Bureau. On the World Wide Web at http://www.census.gov/prod/2002pubs/c2kbr01-16.pdf (24 June 2003).

Rank, Mark Robert. 1994. *Living on the Edge: The Politics of Welfare in America.* New York: Columbia University Press.

Rapp, R., and E. Ross. 1986. "The 1920s: Feminism, Consumerism and Political Backlash in the U.S." Pp. 52–62 in J. Friedlander, B. Cook, A. Kessler-Harris, and C. Smith-Rosenberg, eds. *Women in Culture and Politics.* Bloomington: Indiana University Press.

Reich, Robert B. 1991. *The Work of Nations: Preparing Ourselves for 21st-Century Capitalism.* New York: Knopf.

Reimann, Renate. 1997. "Does Biology Matter?: Lesbian Couples Transition to Parenthood and Their Division of Labor." *Qualitative Sociology* 20: 153–85.

Reinarman, Craig, and Harry G. Levine, eds. 1999. *Crack in America: Demon Drugs and Social Justice.* Berkeley: University of California Press.

ReligiousTolerance.org. 2000. "Homosexual (Same-Sex) Marriages." On the World Wide Web at http://www.religioustolerance.org/hom_marr.htm (20 August).

Remennick, Larissa I. 1998. "The Cancer Problem in the Context of Modernity: Sociology, Demography, Politics." *Current Sociology* 46, 1: 1–150.

Rennison, Callie. 2002. "Criminal Victimization 2001: 2000–2001 Changes with Trends 1993–2001." U.S. Department of Justice. Office of Justice Programs. Bureau of Justice Statistics. On the World Wide Web at http://www.ojp.usdoj.gov/bjs/abstract/cv01.htm (16 February 2003).

Reskin, Barbara, and Irene Padavic. 2002 [1994]. *Women and Men at Work,* 2nd ed. Thousand Oaks, CA: Pine Forge.

Ridgeway, Cecilia L. 1983. *The Dynamics of Small Groups.* New York: St. Martin's Press.

Riedmann, Agnes. 1993. *Science That Colonizes: A Critique of Fertility Studies in Africa.* Philadelphia: Temple University Press.

Rier, David A. 2000. "The Missing Voice of the Critically Ill: A Medical Sociologist's First-Person Account." *Sociology of Health and Illness* 22: 68–93.

Rifkin, Jeremy. 1995. *The End of Work: The Decline of the Global Labor Force and the Dawn of the Post Market Era.* New York: G. P. Putnam's Sons.

Riley, Nancy. 1997. "Gender, Power, and Population Change." *Population Bulletin* 52, 1. On the World Wide Web at http://www.prb.org/pubs/population_bulletin/bu52-1.htm (25 August 2000).

Ritzer, George. 1996a. *The McDonaldization of Society,* rev. ed. Thousand Oaks, CA: Pine Forge Press.

Roberts, Sam. 2008. "In a Generation, Minorities May Be the U.S. Majority." *New York Times* 14 August. On the World Wide Web at www.nytimes.com (14 August 2008).

Robertson, Ian. 1987 [1977]. *Sociology,* 3rd ed. New York: Worth.

Robinson, John P., and Suzanne Bianchi. 1997. "The Children's Hours." *American Demographics* December: 20–24.

Robinson, Richard H., and Willard L. Johnson. 1997 [1982]. *The Buddhist Religion: A Historical Introduction,* 4th ed. Belmont, CA: Wadsworth.

Robinson, Robert V., and Wendell Bell. 1978. "Equality, Success, and Social Justice in England and the United States." *American Sociological Review* 43: 125–143.

Roche, Maurice. 1995. "Rethinking Citizenship and Social Movements: Themes in Contemporary Sociology and Neoconservative Ideology." Pp. 186–219 in Louis Maheu, ed. *Social Classes and Social Movements: The Future of Collective Action.* London: Sage.

Rodinson, Maxime. 1996. *Muhammad,* 2nd ed. Anne Carter, trans. London: Penguin.

Roediger, David R. 1991. *The Wages of Whiteness: Race and the Making of the American Working Class.* London: Verso.

Roethlisberger, Fritz J., and William J. Dickson. 1939. *Management and the Worker.* Cambridge, MA: Harvard University Press.

Rogers, Jackie Krasas, and Kevin D. Henson. 1997. "'Hey, Why Don't You Wear a Shorter Skirt?' Structural Vulnerability and the Organization of Sexual Harassment in Temporary Clerical Employment." *Gender and Society* 11: 215–237.

Rollins, Boyd C., and Kenneth L. Cannon. 1974. "Marital Satisfaction over the Family Life Cycle." *Journal of Marriage and the Family* 36: 271–284.

Ron, James. 2007. Personal communication. Norman Paterson School of International Affairs, Carleton University, Ottawa. December 20.

Rones, Philip L., Randy E. Ilg, and Jennifer M. Gardner. 1997. "Trends in Hours of Work Since the Mid-1970s." *Monthly Labor Review* April. On the World Wide Web at http://www.bls.gov/opub/mlr/1997/04/art1full.pdf (26 January 2003).

Rootes, Chris. 1995. "A New Class? The Higher Educated and the New Politics." Pp. 220–35 in Louis Maheu, ed. *Social Classes and Social Movements: The Future of Collective Action.* London: Sage.

Roscoe, Lori A., L. J. Dragovic, and Donna Cohen. 2000. "Dr. Jack Kevorkian and Cases of Euthanasia in Oakland County, Michigan, 1990–1998." On the World Wide Web at http://www.nejm.org/content/2000/0343/0023/1735.asp (12 July 2000).

Rose, Michael S. 2001. "The Facts Behind the Massacre." *Catholic World News* 17 October. On the World Wide Web at http:///www.cwnews.com/news/viewstory.cfm?recnum=20654 (15 January 2005).

Rosenbluth, Susan C. 1997. "Is Sexual Orientation a Matter of Choice?" *Psychology of Women Quarterly* 21: 595–610.

Rosenfeld, Michael. 2008. "Increasing Percentage of Marriages in the US That Are Interracial." On the World Wide Web at http://www.stanford.edu/~mrosenfe/Rosenfeld_pct_interracial.pdf (7 August 2008).

Rosenthal, Robert, and Lenore Jacobson. 1968. *Pygmalion in the Classroom: Teacher Expectation and Pupils' Intellectual Development.* New York: Holt, Rinehart, & Winston.

Roslin, Alex. 2000. "Black & Blue." *Saturday Night* 23 September: 44–49.

Rostow, W. W. 1960. *The Stages of Economic Growth: A Non-Communist Manifesto.* New York: Cambridge University Press.

Roth, Cecil. 1961. *A History of the Jews.* New York: Schocken.

Rothman, Barbara Katz. 1982. *In Labor: Women and Power in the Birthplace.* New York: W.W. Norton.

_____. 1989. *Recreating Motherhood: Ideology and Technology in a Patriarchal Society.* New York: W.W. Norton.

Rothman, David J. 1991. *Strangers at the Bedside: A History of How Law and Bioethics Transformed Medical Decision Making.* New York: Basic Books.

_____. 1998. "The International Organ Traffic." *New York Review of Books* 45, 5: 14–17.

Rothman, Stanley, and Amy E. Black. 1998. "Who Rules Now? American Elites in the 1990s." *Society* 35, 6: 17–20.

Rubin, J. Z., F. J. Provenzano, and Z. Lurra. 1974. "The Eye of the Beholder." *American Journal of Orthopsychiatry* 44: 512–519.

Ruggles, Steven. 1997. "The Effects of AFDC on American Family Structure, 1940–1990." *Journal of Family History* 22: 307–325.

Russett, Cynthia Eagle. 1966. *The Concept of Equilibrium in American Social Thought.* New Haven, CT: Yale University Press.

Ryan, Kathryn M., and Jeanne Kanjorski. 1998. "The Enjoyment of Sexist Humor, Rape Attitudes, and Relationship Aggression in College Students." *Sex Roles* 38: 743–756.

Rytina, Steve. 1992. "Scaling the Intergenerational Continuity of Occupation: Is Occupational Inheritance Ascriptive After All?" *American Journal of Sociology* 97: 1658–1688.

Sampson, Robert. 1997. "The Embeddedness of Child and Adolescent Development: A Community-Level Perspective on Urban Violence." Pp. 31–77 in Joan McCord, ed. *Violence and Childhood in the Inner City.* Cambridge: Cambridge University Press.

_____ and William J. Wilson. 1995. "Toward a Theory of Race, Crime and Urban Inequality." Pp. 37–54 in John Hagan and Ruth D. Peterson, eds., *Crime and Inequality.* Stanford, CA: Stanford University Press.

Samuelson, Paul A. 2004. "Where Ricardo and Mill Rebut and Confirm Arguments of Mainstream Economists Supporting Globalization." *Journal of Economic Perspectives* 18: 135–46.

Samuelsson, Kurt. 1961 [1957]. *Religion and Economic Action,* E. French, trans. Stockholm: Scandinavian University Books.

Sanday, Peggy Reeves. 1990. *Fraternity Gang Rape: Sex, Brotherhood, and Privilege on Campus.* New York: New York University Press.

Sandqvist, Karin, and Bengt-Erik Andersson. 1992. "Thriving Families in the Swedish Welfare State." *Public Interest* 109: 114–116.

Sanmartin, Claudia, Edward Ng, Debra Blackwell, Jane Gentleman, Michael Martinez, and Catherine Simile. 2004. *Joint Canada/United States Survey of Health.* Ottawa: Statistics Canada. On the World Wide Web at http://www.statcan.ca/english/freepub/82M0022XIE/2003001/pdf/82M0022XIE2003001.pdf (14 March 2005).

Sartre, Jean-Paul. 1965 [1948]. *Anti-Semite and Jew,* George J. Becker, trans. New York: Schocken.

Sassen, Saskia. 1991. *The Global City: New York, London, Tokyo.* Princeton, NJ: Princeton University Press.

Saunders, Doug. 2003. "U.S. FDA Blocks Mail-Order Drugs." *Globe and Mail* November 8: A23.

Savelsberg, Joachim, with contributions by Peter Brühl. 1994. *Constructing White-Collar Crime: Rationalities, Communication, Power.* Philadelphia: University of Pennsylvania Press.

Saxton, Lloyd. 1990. *The Individual, Marriage, and the Family,* 9th ed. Belmont, CA: Wadsworth.

Schemo, Diana Jean. 2002. "Neediest Schools Receive Less Money, Report Finds." *New York Times* August 9. On the World Wide Web at http://www.nytimes.com (9 August 2002).

Schiff, Michel, and Richard Lewontin. 1986. *Education and Class: The Irrelevance of IQ Genetic Studies.* Oxford: Clarendon Press.

Schippers, Mimi. 2002. *Rockin' Out of the Box: Gender Maneuvering in Alternative Hard Rock.* New Brunswick, NJ: Rutgers University Press.

Schlesinger, Arthur. 1991. *The Disuniting of America: Reflections on a Multicultural Society.* New York: W.W. Norton.

Schlosser, Eric. 1998. "The Prison-Industrial Complex." *The Atlantic Monthly* December. On the World Wide Web at http://www.theatlantic.com/issues/98dec/prisons.htm (29 April 2000).

Schneider, Barbara, and David Stevenson. 1999. *The Ambitious Generation: America's Teenagers: Motivated But Directionless.* New Haven, CT: Yale University Press.

Schoen, Cathy, Michelle M. Doty, Sara R. Collins, and Alyssa L. Holmgren. 2005. "Insured But Not Protected: How Many Adults Are Underinsured?" *Health Affairs Web Supplement* W5. 289, 1. On the World Wide Web at http://content.healthaffairs.org/cgi/reprint/hlthaff.w5.289v1 (2 July 2005).

Schor, Juliet B. 1992. *The Overworked American: The Unexpected Decline of Leisure.* New York: Basic Books.

_____. 1999. *The Overspent American: Why We Want What We Don't Need.* New York: Harper.

Schrag, Peter. 2004. "Bush's Education Fraud." *The American Prospect,* February 1. On the World Wide Web at http://www.prospect.org/web/page.ww?section=root&name=ViewPrint&articleId=6998 (29 March 2005).

Schuettler, Darren. 2002. "Earth Summit Bogs Down in Bitter Trade Debate." *Yahoo! Canada News* 28 August. On the World Wide Web at http://ca.news.yahoo.com/020828/5/olia.html (12 February 2002).

Schumer, Charles, and Paul Craig Roberts. 2004. "Exporting Jobs Is Not Free Trade." *International Herald Tribune,* January 7. On the World Wide Web at http://www.iht.com/articles/123898.html (31 March 2005).

Schwartz, Stephen. 2003. *The Two Faces of Islam: The House of Sa'ud from Tradition to Terror.* New York: Doubleday.

Schweingruber, David, and Clark McPhail. 1999. "A Method for Systematically Observing and Recording Collective Action." *Sociological Methods and Research* 27: 451–498.

Scott, Janny. 1998. "Manners and Civil Society." *Journal* 2, 3. On the World Wide Web at http://www.civnet.org/journal/issue7/ftjscott.htm (12 April 2003).

Scott, Peter Dale, and Jonathan Marshall. 1991. *Cocaine Politics: Drugs, Armies, and the CIA in Central America.* Berkeley: University of California Press.

Scott, Shirley Lynn. 2003. "The Death of James Bulger." *Court TV's Crime Library.* On the World Wide Web at http://www.crimelibrary.com/notorious_murders/young/bulger/1.html?sect 10 (23 July 2003).

Scott, Wilbur J. 1990. "PTSD in *DSM-III*: A Case in the Politics of Diagnosis and Disease." *Social Problems,* 37: 294–310.

Scully, Diana. 1990. *Understanding Sexual Violence: A Study of Convicted Rapists.* Boston: Unwin Hyman.

"Search Engines of All Countries in All Languages as of August 27, 2002." 2002. *WebMasterAid.com.* On the World Wide Web at http://webmasteraid.com/cgi-bin/d.cgi (25 May 2003).

Seccombe, Wally. 1992. *A Millennium of Family Change: Feudalism to Capitalism in Northwestern Europe.* London: Verso.

Seeman, Neil. 2000. "Capital Questions." *The National Post* 6 August: B1, B6.

Sen, Amartya. 1990. "More than 100 Million Women are Missing." *New York Review of Books* 20 December: 61–66.

_____. 1994. "Population: Delusion and Reality." *New York Review of Books* 41, 15: 62–71.

_____. 2001. "Many Faces of Gender Inequality." *The Frontline* 9 November. On the World Wide Web at http://www.ksg.harvard.edu/gei/Text/Sen-Pubs/Sen_many_faces_of_gender_inequality.pdf (5 August 2003).

The Sentencing Project. 1997. "Americans Behind Bars: U.S. and International Use of Incarceration, 1995." On the World Wide Web at http://www.sentencingproject.org/pubs/tsppubs/9030data.html (29 April 2000).

_____. 2001. "U.S. Surpasses Russia as World Leader in Rate of Incarceration." On the World Wide Web at http://www.sentencingproject.org/brief/usvsrus.pdf (27 June 2001).

Sewell, William H. 1958. "Infant Training and the Personality of the Child." *American Journal of Sociology* 64: 150–159.

_____, and Robert Hauser. 1993. "A Review of the Wisconsin Longitudinal Study of Social and Psychological Factors in Aspirations and Achievements 1963–1992." *CDE Working Paper No. 92–01.* Center for Demography and Ecology, University of Wisconsin-Madison. On the World Wide Web at http://www.ssc.wisc.edu/cde/cdewp/92-01.pdf (15 May 2003).

Shakur, Sanyika (a.k.a. Monster Kody Scott). 1993. *Monster: The Autobiography of an L.A. Gang Member.* New York: Penguin.

Shapiro, Andrew L. 1992. *We're Number One.* New York: Vintage.

Shapiro, Joseph P. 1993. *No Pity: People with Disabilities Forging a New Civil Rights Movement.* New York: Times Books.

Shattuck, Roger. 1980. *The Forbidden Experiment: The Story of the Wild Boy of Aveyron.* New York: Farrar, Straus, & Giroux.

Shaw, Martin. 2000. *Theory of the Global State: Globality as Unfinished Revolution.* Cambridge: Cambridge University Press.

Shea, Sarah E., Kevin Gordon, Ann Hawkins, Janet Kawchuk, and Donna Smith. 2000. "Pathology in the Hundred Acre Wood: A Neurodevelopmental Perspective on A. A. Milne." *Canadian Medical Association Journal,* 163(12): 1557–59. On the World Wide Web at http://www.cma.ca/cmaj/vol-163/issue-12/1557.htm (12 December 2000).

Shekelle, Paul G. 1998. "What Role for Chiropractic in Health Care?" *New England Journal of Medicine* 339: 1074–1075.

Shelton, Beth Anne, and Daphne John. 1996. "The Division of Household Labor." *Annual Review of Sociology* 22: 299–322.

Sherif, M., L. J. Harvey, B. J. White, W. R. Hood, and C. W. Sherif. 1988 [1961]. *The Robber's Cave Experiment: Intergroup Conflict and Cooperation.* Middletown, CT: Wesleyan University Press.

Sherkat, Darren E. 1998. "Counterculture or Continuity? Competing Influences on Baby Boomers' Religious Orientations and Participation." *Social Forces* 76: 1087–1115.

_____ and Christopher G. Ellison. 1999. "Recent Developments and Current Controversies in the Sociology of Religion." *Annual Review of Sociology* 25: 363–394.

Sherrill, Robert. 1997. "A Year in Corporate Crime." *The Nation* 7 April: 11–20.

Shibutani, Tamotsu. 1966. *Improvised News: A Sociological Study of Rumor.* Indianapolis, IN: Bobbs-Merrill.

Shipler, David K. 1997. *A Country of Strangers: Blacks and Whites in America.* New York: Knopf.

Short, James F., Jr., and Fred L. Strodtbeck. 1965. *Group Process and Gang Delinquency.* Chicago: University of Chicago Press.

Shorter, Edward. 1997. *A History of Psychiatry: From the Era of the Asylum to the Age of Prozac.* New York: Wiley.

Siegel, Jacob. 1996. "Aging into the 21st Century." Administration on Aging. On the World Wide Web at http://www.aoa.dhhs.gov/aoa/stats/aging21/default.htm (2 May 2000).

Silberman, Steve. 2000. "Talking to Strangers." *Wired* 8, 5: 225–233, 288–296. On the World Wide Web at http://www.wired.com/wired/archive/8.05/translation.html (23 May 2000).

Silverstein, Louise B., and Carl F. Auerbach. 1999. "Reconstructing the Essential Father." *American Psychologist* 54: 397–407.

Simmel, Georg. 1950. *The Sociology of Georg Simmel,* Kurt H. Wolff, trans and ed. New York: Free Press.

Simon, Jonathan. 1993. *Poor Discipline: Parole and the Social Control of the Underclass, 1890–1990.* Chicago: University of Chicago Press.

Simons, Ronald L., Chyi-In Wu, Christine Johnson, and Rand D. Conger. 1995. "A Test of Various Perspectives on the Intergenerational Transmission of Domestic Violence." *Criminology* 33: 141–60.

Skocpol, Theda. 1996. *Boomerang: Clinton's Health Security Effort and the Turn Against Government in U.S. Politics.* New York: W.W. Norton.

Skolnick, Arlene. 1991. *Embattled Paradise: The American Family in an Age of Uncertainty.* New York: Basic Books.

Skolnick, Jerome K. 1997. "Tough Guys." *The American Prospect* 30: 86–91. On the World Wide Web at http://www.prospect.org/archives/30/fs30jsko.html (29 April 2000).

Smeeding, Timothy M. 2004. "Public Policy and Economic Inequality: The United States in Comparative Perspective." *Working Paper No. 367.* Syracuse, NY: Maxwell School of Citizenship and Public Affairs, Syracuse University. On the World Wide Web at http://www.lisproject.org/publications/liswps/367.pdf (30 January 2005).

Smelser, Neil. 1963. *Theory of Collective Behavior.* New York: Free Press.

Smith, Christian. 1996. *Disruptive Religion: The Force of Faith in Social-Movement Activism.* London: Routledge.

_____. 2000. *Christian America? What Evangelicals Really Want.* Berkeley: University of California Press.

Smith, Jackie. 1998. "Global Civil Society? Transnational Social Movement Organizations and Social Capital." *American Behavioral Scientist* 42: 93–107.

Smock, Pamela J. 2000. "Cohabitation in the United States: An Appraisal of Research Themes, Findings, and Implications." *Annual Review of Sociology* 26: 1–20.

"A Snapshot of Annual High-Risk College Drinking Consequences." 2007. On the World Wide Web at http://www.collegedrinkingprevention.gov/StatsSummaries/snapshot.aspx (8 August 2008).

Snow, David A., E. Burke Rochford, Jr., Steven K. Worden, and Robert D. Benford. 1986. "Frame Alignment Processes, Micromobilization, and Movement Participation." *American Sociological Review* 51: 464–481.

Sofsky, Wolfgang. 1997 [1993]. *The Order of Terror: The Concentration Camp,* William Templer, trans. Princeton, NJ: Princeton University Press.

Sorenson, Elaine. 1994. *Comparable Worth: Is It a Worthy Policy?* Princeton, NJ: Princeton University Press.

Soule, Sarah A. 1992. "Populism and Black Lynching in Georgia, 1890–1900." *Social Forces* 71: 431–449.

Southern Poverty Law Center. 2000. "Intelligence Report." On the World Wide Web at http://www.splcenter.org/intelligenceproject/ip-index.html (29 April 2000).

_____. 2003. "Active U.S. Hate Groups in 2003." On the World Wide Web at http://www.splcenter.org/intel/map/hate.jsp (12 May 2004).

Spade, Joan Z. 2001. "Gender and Education in the United States." Pp. 270–8. In Jeanne H. Ballantine and Joan Z. Spade, eds. *Schools and Society: A Sociological Approach to Education.* Belmont, CA: Wadsworth.

Spilerman, Seymour. 2000. "Wealth and Stratification Processes." *Annual Review of Sociology* 26: 497–524.

Spitz, René A. 1945. "Hospitalism: An Inquiry into the Genesis of Psychiatric Conditions in Early Childhood." Pp. 53–74 in *The Psychoanalytic Study of the Child,* Vol. 1. New York: International Universities Press.

_____. 1962. "Autoerotism Re-examined: The Role of Early Sexual Behavior Patterns in Personality Formation." Pp. 283–315 in *The Psychoanalytic Study of the Child,* Vol. 17. New York: International Universities Press.

Spitzer, Steven. 1980. "Toward a Marxian Theory of Deviance." Pp. 175–91 in Delos H. Kelly, ed. *Criminal Behavior: Readings in Criminology.* New York: St. Martin's Press.

Srinivas, M. N. 1952. *Religion and Society among the Coorgs of South India.* Oxford: Oxford University Press.

Stack, Stephen, and J. Ross Eshleman. 1998. "Marital Status and Happiness: A 17-Nation Study." *Journal of Marriage and the Family* 60: 527–536.

Staples, Brent. 2004. "Why Some Politicians Need Their Prisons to Stay Full." *New York Times,* December 27. On the World Wide Web at www.nytimes.com (27 December 2005).

Starbuck, Gene H. 2002. *Families in Context.* Belmont, CA: Wadsworth.

Stark, Rodney. 1985. *Sociology.* Belmont, CA: Wadsworth.

_____, and William Sims Bainbridge. 1979. "Of Churches, Sects, and Cults: Preliminary Concepts for a Theory of Religious Movements." *Journal for the Scientific Study of Religion* 18: 117–131.

Starr, Paul. 1982. *The Social Transformation of American Medicine.* New York: Basic Books.

_____. 1994 [1992]. *The Logic of Health Care Reform: Why and How the President's Plan Will Work,* rev. ed. New York: Penguin.

Stearns, Carol Zisowitz, and Peter N. Stearns. 1985. "Emotionology: Clarifying the History of Emotions and Emotional Standards." *American Historical Review* 90: 813–836.

Steele, Claude M. 1992. "Race and the Schooling of Black Americans." *The Atlantic Monthly* April. On the World Wide Web at http://www.theatlantic.com/unbound/flashbks/blacked/steele.htm (2 May 2000).

_____. 1997. "A Threat in the Air: How Stereotypes Shape the Intellectual Identities and Performance of Women and African-Americans." *American Psychologist* 52: 613–29.

Steinberg, Jacques. 2002. "Cleveland Case Poses New Test for Vouchers." *New York Times* February 10. On the World Wide Web at http://www.nytimes.com (10 February 2002).

_____. 2003. "Of Sheepskins and Greenbacks." *New York Times* February 13: A20.

Steinberg, Stephen. 1989 [1981]. *The Ethnic Myth: Race, Ethnicity, and Class in America,* updated ed. Boston: Beacon Press.

Stenger, Richard. 2003. "NASA Chief Blasted over Shuttle Memos." On the World Wide Web at http://www.cnn.com/2003/TECH/space/02/27/sprj.colu.memo/index.htm (6 March 2003).

Sternberg, Robert J. 1998 [1995]. *In Search of the Human Mind,* 2nd ed. Fort Worth, TX: Harcourt Brace.

Stewart, Abigail, Anne P. Copeland, Nia Lane Chester, Janet E. Malley, and Nicole B. Barenbaum. 1997. *Separating Together: How Divorce Transforms Families.* New York: The Guilford Press.

Stiglitz, Joseph E. 2002. *Globalization and Its Discontents.* New York: W.W. Norton.

Stiker, Henri-Jacques. 1999 [1982]. *A History of Disability,* William Sayers, trans. Ann Arbor: University of Michigan Press.

Stipp, David. 2003. "The Pentagon's Weather Nightmare." *Fortune* 26 January. On the World Wide Web at http://paxhumana.info/article.php3?id_article 400 (29 May 2004).

Stolzenberg, Ross. M. 1990. "Ethnicity, Geography, and Occupational Achievement of Hispanic Men in the United States." *American Sociological Review* 55: 143–154.

Stone, Lawrence. 1977. *The Family, Sex and Marriage in England, 1500–1800.* New York: Harper & Row.

Stouffer, Samuel A., et al. 1949. *The American Soldier,* 4 vols. Princeton, NJ: Princeton University Press.

Straus, Murray A. 1994. "State-to-State Differences in Social Inequality and Social Bonds in Relation to Assaults on Wives in the United States." *Journal of Comparative Family Studies* 25: 7–24.

Strauss, Anselm L. 1993. *Continual Permutations of Action.* New York: Aldine de Gruyter.

Stretesky, Paul, and Michael J. Hogan. 1998. "Environmental Justice: An Analysis of Superfund Sites in Florida." *Social Problems* 45: 268–87.

Sullivan, Mercer L. 2002. "Exploring Layers: Extended Case Method as a Tool for Multilevel Analysis of School Violence." *Sociological Methods and Research* 31, 2: 255–285.

Sumner, William Graham. 1940 [1907]. *Folkways.* Boston: Ginn.

Superbowl.com. 2004. "Super Bowl Information." On the World Wide Web at http://www.superbowl.com/features/general_info (7 March 2004).

"A Survey of Human Rights Law." 1998. *The Economist.* December 5.

Sutherland, Edwin H. 1939. *Principles of Criminology.* Philadelphia: Lippincott.

_____. 1949. *White Collar Crime.* New York: Dryden.

Suttles, Gerald D. 1968. *The Social Order of the Slum: Ethnicity and Territory in the Inner City.* Chicago: University of Chicago Press.

Sweezy, Kate, and Jill Tiefenthaler. 1996. "Do State-Level Variables Affect Divorce Rates?" *Review of Social Economy* 54: 47–65.

Swiss Re. 2003. "Natural Catastrophes and Reinsurance." On the World Wide Web at http://www.swissre.com (28 July 2003).

_____. 2004. "Sigma: Natural Catastrophes and Man-Made Disasters in 2003." On the World Wide Web at http://www.swissre.com (2 March 2005).

_____. 2005. "Sigma: Natural Catastrophes and Man-Made Disasters in 2004." On the World Wide Web at http:// www.swissre.com (2 March 2005).

_____. 2007. "Natural catastrophes and man-made disasters in 2006." On the World Wide Web at http://www.swissre.com/INTERNET/pwswpspr.nsf/fmBookMarkFrameSet?ReadForm&BM=http://www.swissre.com/INTERNET/pwswpspr.nsf/vwAllByIDKeyLu/SBAR-59FDAE (30 April 2007).

Sykes, Gresham, and David Matza. 1957. "Techniques of Neutralization: A Theory of Delinquency." *American Sociological Review* 22: 664–670.

Sylwester, Kevin. 2002. "Democracy and Changes in Income Inequality." *International Journal of Business and Economics* 1: 167–178.

Szasz, Andrew, and Michael Meuser. 1997. "Environmental Inequalities: Literature Review and Proposals for New Directions in Research and Theory." *Current Sociology* 45, 3: 99–120.

Szreter, Simon. 1996. *Fertility, Class and Gender in Britain, 1860–1940.* Cambridge: Cambridge University Press.

Tajfel, Henri. 1981. *Human Groups and Social Categories: Studies in Social Psychology.* Cambridge: Cambridge University Press.

Takaki, Ronald. 1989. *Strangers from a Different Shore: A History of Asian Americans.* New York: Penguin.

Tal, Benjamin. 2004. "Assessing US Job Quality." *CIBC World Markets: Economics and Strategy,* June 21. On the World Wide Web at http://research.cibcwm.com/economic_public/download/eqi-us-062004.pdf (1 April 2005).

Tannen, Deborah. 1990. *You Just Don't Understand Me: Women and Men in Conversation.* New York: William Morrow.

_____. 1994a. *Talking from 9 to 5: How Women's and Men's Conversational Styles Affect Who Gets Heard, Who Gets Credit, and What Gets Done at Work.* New York: William Morrow.

_____. 1994b. *Gender and Discourse.* New York: Oxford University Press.

Tarrow, Sidney. 1994. *Power in Movement: Social Movements, Collective Action and Politics.* Cambridge: Cambridge University Press.

Tasker, Fiona L., and Susan Golombok. 1997. *Growing Up in a Lesbian Family: Effects on Child Development.* New York: The Guilford Press.

Tec, Nechama. 1986. *When Light Pierced the Darkness: Christian Rescue of Jews in Nazi-Occupied Poland.* New York: Oxford University Press.

Terry, Jennifer, and Jacqueline Urla, eds. 1995. *Deviant Bodies: Critical Perspectives on Difference in Science and Popular Culture.* Bloomington: Indiana University Press.

"The United States of the World," *The Globe and Mail,* March 8, 2003, p. F1.

Thernstrom, Stephan, and Abigail Thernstrom. 1997. *America in Black and White: One Nation, Indivisible.* New York: Simon & Schuster.

Thoits, Peggy A. 1989. "The Sociology of Emotions." *Annual Review of Sociology* 15: 317–342.

Thomas, Keith. 1971. *Religion and the Decline of Magic.* London: Weidenfeld and Nicholson.

Thomas, William Isaac. 1966 [1931]. "The Relation of Research to the Social Process." Pp. 289–305 in Morris Janowitz, ed. *W. I. Thomas on Social Organization and Social Personality.* Chicago: University of Chicago Press.

Thompson, Charis. 2005. *Making Parents: The Ontological Choreography of Reproductive Technologies.* Cambridge, MA: MIT Press.

Thompson, E. P. 1967. "Time, Work Discipline, and Industrial Capitalism." *Past and Present* 38: 59–67.

Thorne, Barrie. 1993. *Gender Play: Girls and Boys in School.* New Brunswick, NJ: Rutgers University Press.

Tienda, Marta, and Ding-Tzann Lii. 1987. "Minority Concentration and Earnings Inequality: Blacks, Hispanics, and Asians Compared." *American Journal of Sociology* 93: 141–165.

Tilly, Charles. 1979a. "Collective Violence in European Perspective." Pp. 83–118 in H. Graham and T. Gurr, eds. *Violence in America: Historical and Comparative Perspective,* 2nd ed. Beverly Hills, CA: Sage.

_____. 1979b. "Repertoires of Contention in America and Britain, 1750–1830." Pp. 126–55 in Mayer N. Zald and John D. McCarthy, eds. *The Dynamics of Social Movements: Resource Mobilization, Social Control, and Tactics.* Cambridge, MA: Winthrop Publishers.

_____. 2002. "Violence, Terror, and Politics as Usual." *Boston Review* 27: 3. On the World Wide Web at http://www.bostonreview.net/BR27.3/tilly.html (1 May 2004).

_____, Louise Tilly, and Richard Tilly. 1975. *The Rebellious Century, 1830–1930.* Cambridge, MA: Harvard University Press.

Toffler, Alvin. 1990. *Powershift: Knowledge, Wealth, and Violence at the Edge of the 21st Century.* New York: Bantam.

Tolnay, Stewart E., and E. M. Beck. 1995. *A Festival of Violence: An Analysis of Southern Lynchings, 1882–1930.* Urbana: University of Illinois Press.

Tönnies, Ferdinand. 1988 [1887]. *Community and Society (Gemeinschaft und Gesselschaft).* New Brunswick, NJ: Transaction.

Tonry, Michael. 1995. *Malign Neglect: Race, Crime, and Punishment in America.* New York: Oxford University Press.

Toor, Rachel. 2001. *Admissions Confidential: An Insider's Account of the Elite College Selection Process.* New York: St. Martin's Press.

"Top 20 Network Primetime Series by Households: Season-To-Date 09/23/02–02/09/03." 2003. On the World Wide Web at http://tv.zap2it.com/news/ratings/season/030209season.html (15 February 2003).

Tornquist, Cynthia. 1998. "Students Head Back to Decaying Classrooms." *Cnn.com* 30 August. On the World Wide Web at http://www.cnn.co.uk/US/9808/30/hazardous.schools (11 August 2000).

Travers, Jeffrey, and Stanley Milgram. 1969. "An Experimental Study of the Small World Problem." *Sociometry* 32: 425–443.

Troeltsch, Ernst. 1931 [1923]. *The Social Teaching of the Christian Churches,* Olive Wyon, trans. 2 vols. London: George Allen and Unwin.

Troy, Leo. 1986. "The Rise and Fall of American Trade Unions: The Labor Movement from FDR to RR." Pp. 75–109 in Seymour Martin Lipset, ed. *Unions in Transition: Entering the Second Century.* San Francisco: ICS Press.

Tschannen, Olivier. 1991. "The Secularization Paradigm: A Systematization." *Journal for the Scientific Study of Religion* 30: 395–415.

Tsutsui, William M. 1998. *Manufacturing Ideology: Scientific Management in Twentieth-Century Japan.* Princeton, NJ: Princeton University Press.

Tuljapurkar, Shripad, Nan Li, and Carl Boe. 2000. "A Universal Pattern of Mortality Decline in the G7 Countries." *Nature* 405: 789–792.

Tumin, Melvin. 1953. "Some Principles of Stratification: A Critical Analysis." *American Sociological Review* 18: 387–394.

Turkle, Sherry. 1995. *Life on the Screen: Identity in the Age of the Internet.* New York: Simon & Schuster.

Turner, Bryan S. 1986. *Citizenship and Capitalism: The Debate over Reformism.* London: Allen & Unwin.

Turner, Ralph H., and Lewis M. Killian. 1987 [1957] *Collective Behavior,* 3rd ed. Englewood Cliffs, NJ: Prentice-Hall.

Tyree, Andrea, Moshe Semyonov, and Robert W. Hodge. 1979. "Gaps and Glissandos: Inequality, Economic Development, and Social Mobility in 24 Countries." *American Sociological Review* 44: 410–424.

UNESCO (United Nations Educational, Scientific and Cultural Organization). 1999. "The Globalization of Tourism." On the World Wide Web at http://unesdoc.unesco.org/images/0011/001165/116578e.pdf#116585 (27 February 2006).

UNESCO. 2002. "Education Goals Remain Elusive in More Than 70 Countries." On the World Wide Web at http://portal.unesco.org/uis/ev.php?URL_ID 5175&URL_DO DO _TOPIC&URL_SECTION 201&reload 1044561680 (6 February 2003).

Ungar, Sheldon. 1992. "The Rise and (Relative) Decline of Global Warming as a Social Problem." *Sociological Quarterly* 33: 483–501.

_____. 1995. "Social Scares and Global Warming: Beyond the Rio Convention." *Society and Natural Resources* 8: 443–56.

_____. 1998. "Bringing the Issue Back In: Comparing the Marketability of the Ozone Hole and Global Warming." *Social Problems* 45: 510–27.

_____. 1999. "Is Strange Weather in the Air? A Study of U.S. National Network News Coverage of Extreme Weather Events." *Climatic Change* 41: 133–50.

Union of International Associations Inc. "International Organizations by Year and Type (Table 2)." 2001. *Yearbook of International Organizations.* On the World Wide Web at http://www.uia.org/uiastats/ytb299 .htm (6 February 2003).

Union of International Associations. 2007. "Number of international organizations in this edition by type (2005/2006)." On the World Wide Web at http://www .uia.be/en/stats (19 December 2007).

United Airlines. 2003. "Flight Attendant History." On the World Wide Web at http://www.ual.com/page/ article/0,1360,3191,00.html (6 April 2003).

United Nations. 1997. "Percentage of Population Living in Urban Areas in 1996 and 2030." On the World Wide Web at http://www.undp.org/popin/wdtrends/ura/ uracht1.htm (2 May 2000).

_____. 1998a. *Human Development Report 1998.* New York: Oxford University Press.

_____. 1998b. "Universal Declaration of Human Rights." On the World Wide Web at http://www.un.org/ Overview/rights.html (25 January 2003).

_____. 2000. "Table 1. Total Population by Sex and Sex Ratio, by Country, 2000 (medium-variant)." On the World Wide Web at http://www.un.org/esa/population/ publications/wpp2000/annex-tables.pdf (5 August 2003).

_____. 2002. *Human Development Report 2002.* New York: Oxford University Press. On the World Wide Web at http://hdr.undp.org/reports/global/2002/en (16 April 2003).

_____. 2003a. *Human Development Report 2003.* On the World Wide Web at http://www.undp.org/hdr2003/ indicator/pdf/hdr03_table_23.pdf (22 January 2004).

_____. 2003b. "Statistical Databases." On the World Wide Web at http://millenniumindicators.un.org/unsd/ mi/mi_series_results.asp?rowID 563 (15 June 2003).

_____. 2005. "Millennium Indicators Database." On the World Wide Web at http://unstats.un.org/unsd/mi/ mi_series_results.asp?rowID=563 (4 March 2006).

_____. 2007a. "Gender empowerment measure." On the World Wide Web at http://hdrstats.undp.org/ indicators/279.html (18 August 2008).

_____. 2007b. *Human Development Report 2007/2008.* New York. On the World Wide Web at http://hdr .undp.org/en/media/hdr_20072008_en_complete.pdf (19 December 2007).

_____. 2008. *Human Development Report 2007/2008.* On the World Wide Web at http://hdr.undp.org/en/ media/HDR_20072008_EN_Complete.pdf (11 August 2008).

United Nations Conference on Trade and Development. 2007. *World Investment Report 2007.* Geneva. On the World Wide Web at http://www.unctad.org/en/docs/ wir2007p1_en.pdf (19 December 2007).

United Nations World Tourism Organization. 2007a. "International Tourist Arrivals." On the World Wide Web at http://unwto.org/facts/eng/pdf/historical/ITA_ 1950_2005.pdf (19 December 2007).

_____. 2007b. *Tourism Highlights 2007 Edition.* Madrid. On the World Wide Web at http://unwto.org/ facts/eng/pdf/highlights/highlights_07_eng_hr.pdf (19 December 2007).

University of Virginia. 2003. "The Oracle of Bacon at Virginia." On the World Wide Web at: http://www .cs.virginia.edu/oracle (13 March 2003).

Unschuld, Paul. 1985. *Medicine in China.* Berkeley: University of California Press.

U.S. Administration on Aging. 1999. "Older Population by Age: 1900 to 2050." On the World Wide Web at http:// www.aoa.dhhs.gov/aoa/stats/AgePop2050.html (2 May 2000).

U.S. Census Bureau. 1993. "We the American . . . Foreign Born." On the World Wide Web at http://www.census .gov/apsd/wepeople/we-7.pdf (29 April 2000).

_____. 1997. "Country of Origin and Year of Entry into the US of the Foreign Born, by Citizenship Status: March 1997." On the World Wide Web at http://www .bls.census.gov/cps/pub/1997/for_born.htm (29 April 2000).

_____. 1998. *Statistical Abstract of the United States: 1998.* On the World Wide Web at http://www .census.gov/prod/www/statistical-abstract-us.html (29 April 2000).

_____. 1999a. "Households, by Type: 1940 to Present." On the World Wide Web at http://www.census.gov/ population/socdemo/hh-fam/htabHH-1.txt (1 May 2000).

_____. 1999b. *Statistical Abstract of the United States: 1999.* On the World Wide Web at http://www.census .gov/prod/99pubs/99statab/sec04.pdf (15 January 2001).

_____. 1999c. "Region and Country or Area of Birth of the Foreign-Born Population, With Geographic Detail Shown in Decennial Census Publications of 1930 or Earlier: 1850 to 1930 and 1960 to 1999." On the World Wide Web at http://www.census.gov/ population/www/ documentation/twps0029/tab04.html (29 April 2000).

_____. 2000a. "Countries Ranked by Population: 2000." On the World Wide Web at http://www.census .gov/cgi-bin/ipc/idbrank.pl (29 April 2000).

_____. 2000b "Percentage of Industry Statistics Accounted for by Largest Companies: 1992." On the World Wide Web at http://www.census.gov:80/mcd/ mancen/download/mc92cr.sum (30 April 2000).

_____. 2001a. "Census 2000 Shows Resident Population of 281,421,906; Apportionment Counts Delivered to President." On the World Wide Web at http://www.census.gov/Press-Release/www/2000/ cb00cn64.html(12 August 2001).

_____. 2001b. *Mapping Census 2000: The Geography of U.S. Diversity.* On the World Wide Web at http://www .census.gov/population/cen2000/atlas/censr01-1.pdf (12 August 2003).

_____. 2001c. "Profile of the Foreign-Born Population in the United States: 2000." *Current Population Reports.* On the World Wide Web at http://www.census.gov/ prod/2002pubs/p23-206.pdf (19 June 2003).

_____. 2001d. *Statistical Abstract of the United States 2001.* On the World Wide Web at http://www.census.gov/prod/2002pubs/01stat-ab01.html (12 August 2004), p. 48.

_____. 2002a. "Historical Income Tables—Households." On the World Wide Web at http://www.census.gov/hhes/income/histinc/ho2.html (9 March 2003).

_____. 2002b. "Selected Characteristics of Households, by Total Money Income in 2000." On the World Wide Web at http://ferret.bls.census.gov/macro/032002/hhinc/new01_001.htm (8 March 2003).

_____. 2002c. *Statistical Abstract of the United States 2002.* On the World Wide Web at http://www.census.gov/prod/www/statistical-abstract-02.html (19 June 2003).

_____. 2002d. "Table FINC-02. Age of Reference Person, by Total Money Income in 2001, Type of Family, Race and Hispanic Origin of Reference Person." On the World Wide Web at http://ferret.bls.census.gov/macro/032002/faminc/new02_000.htm (19 June 2003).

_____. 2002e. "Table 1.1: Population by Sex, Age, and Citizenship Status: March 2002 (Numbers in Thousands)." On the World Wide Web at http://www.census.gov/population/socdemo/foreign/ppl-162/tab01-01.txt (19 June 2003).

_____. 2002f. "Table 1. United States—Race and Hispanic Origin: 1790 to 1990." On the World Wide Web at http://www.census.gov/population/documentation/twps0056/tab01.pdf (20 June 2003).

_____. 2003a. "DP-1. Profile of General Demographic Characteristics: 2000." On the World Wide Web at http://factfinder.census.gov/servlet/QTTable?ds_name=DEC_2000_SF1_U&geo_id 01000US&qr_name DEC_2000_SF1_U_DP1 (15 February 2003).

_____. 2003b. "2000 Population Distribution in the United States." On the World Wide Web at http://www.census.gov/geo/www/mapGallery/images/2k_night.jpg (3 August 2003).

_____. 2003c. "Population Estimates for Cities and Towns." On the World Wide Web at http://eire.census.gov/popest/data/cities/tables/SUB-EST2002-01.php (2 August 2003).

_____. 2004. "Historical Poverty Tables—People." On the World Wide Web at http://www.census.gov/hhes/poverty/histpov/perindex.html (30 January 2005).

_____. 2005a. "American Community Survey: General Demographic Characteristics 2004." On the World Wide Web at http://factfinder.census.gov/servlet/ADPTable?_bm=y&-geo_id=01000US&-ds_name=ACS_2004_EST_G00_&-_lang=en&-_caller=geoselect&-format= (3 March 2006).

_____. 2005b. "Countries Ranked by Population: 2006." On the World Wide Web at http://www.census.gov/cgi-bin/ipc/idbrank.pl (11 March 2005).

_____. 2006. "Statistical Abstract of the United States." On the World Wide Web at http://www.census.gov/statab/www (4 March 2006)

_____. 2007a. "Census Bureau Announces Most Populous Cities." On the World Wide Web at http://www.census.gov/Press-Release/www/releases/archives/population/010315.html (21 August 2008).

_____. 2007b. "Income, Poverty, and Health Insurance Coverage in the United States: 2006." *Current Population Reports.* On the World Wide Web at http://www.census.gov/prod/2007pubs/p60-233.pdf (11 August 2008).

_____. 2007c. "The American Community—Asians: 2004." On the World Wide Web at http://www.census.gov/prod/2007pubs/acs-05.pdf (17 August 2008).

_____. 2008a. "America's Families and Living Arrangements: 2007." On the World Wide Web at http://www.census.gov/population/www/socdemo/hh-fam/cps2007.html (18 August 2008).

_____. 2008b. "Historical Income Tables—Households." On the World Wide Web at http://www.census.gov/hhes/www/income/histinc/h02ar.html (11 August 2008).

_____. 2008c. "Historical Poverty Tables—People." On the World Wide Web at http://www.census.gov/hhes/www/poverty/histpov/hstpov19.html (11 August 2008).

_____. 2008d. "International Database (IDB)." On the World Wide Web at http://www.census.gov/ipc/www/idb/pyramids.html (21 August 2008).

_____. 2008e. "Table 672. Money Income of Families—Number and Distribution by Race and Hispanic Origin: 2005." On the World Wide Web at http://www.census.gov/compendia/statab/cats/income_expenditures_poverty_wealth/family_income.html (17 August 2008).

_____. 2008f. "Total Midyear Population for the World: 1950-2050." On the World Wide Web at http://www.census.gov/ipc/www/idb/worldpop.html (21 August 2008).

_____. 2008g. "Who's Minding the Kids: Child Care Arrangements: Spring 2005." On the World Wide Web at http://www.census.gov/population/www/socdemo/childcare.html (19 March 2009).

U.S. Code. 1998. "Title 18—Crimes and Criminal Procedure. Part I. Crimes. Chapter 7, Assault." On the World Wide Web at http://www.fgm.org/USCode.html (20 January 2003).

U.S. Department of Commerce. 1997. *News.* September 29. On the World Wide Web at http://www.census.gov/Press-Release/cb97-162.html (15 June 2003).

_____. 2001. *News* "Nation's Household Income Stable in 2000, Poverty Rate Virtually Equals Record Low, Census Bureau Reports." September 25. On the World Wide Web at http://www.census.gov/Press-Release/www/2001/cb01-158.html (9 March 2003).

_____. 2002a. *A Nation Online: How Americans are Expanding Their Use of the Internet.* Washington DC. On the World Wide Web at http://www.ntia.doc.gov/ntiahome/dn (5 June 2003).

_____. 2002b. "Poverty Rate Rises, Household Income Declines, Census Bureau Reports." September 24. On the World Wide Web at http://www.census.gov/Press-Release/www/2002/cb02-124.html (9 March 2003).

U.S. Department of Commerce, National Oceanic and Atmospheric Administration. 2008. "Trends in Atmospheric Carbon Dioxide—Mauna Loa." On the World Wide Web at http://www.esrl.noaa.gov/gmd/ccgg/trends/ (12 January 2008).

U.S. Department of Health and Human Services. 2002. "Child Health USA 2002." On the World Wide Web at http://www.mchb.hrsa.gov/chusa02/main_pages/page_12.htm (25 April 2003).

_____. 2003. "The 2003 HHS Poverty Guidelines." On the World Wide Web at http://aspe.hhs.gov/poverty/03poverty.htm (23 February 2004).

_____. 2004. "Youth Risk Behavior Surveillance—United States, 2003." *Morbidity and Mortality Weekly Report* 53, May 21. On the World Wide Web at http://www.cdc.gov/mmwr/PDF/SS/SS5302.pdf (24 February 2005).

U.S. Department of Justice. 2007. "Intimate Partner Violence in the United States." On the World Wide Web at http://www.ojp.usdoj.gov/bjs/intimate/ipv.htm (18 August 2008).

_____. 2008. "Gangs." On the World Wide Web at http://www.cops.usdoj.gov/Default.asp?Item=1593 (9 August 2008).

U.S. Department of Labor, Bureau of Labor Statistics. 1999a. *Report on the American Workforce.* Washington D.C. On the World Wide Web at http://www.bls.gov/opub/rtaw/pdf/rtaw1999.pdf (26 January 2003).

_____. 1999b. "Table 5. Civilian Labor Force by Sex, Age, Race, and Hispanic Origin, 1978, 1988, 1998, and projected 2008." On the World Wide Web at http://stats.bls.gov/emplt985.htm (30 April 2000).

_____. 1999c. "Value of the Federal Minimum Wage." On the World Wide Web at http://www.dol.gov/dol/esa/public/minwage/chart2.htm (30 April 2000).

_____. 2000a. "Union Members Summary." On the World Wide Web at http://stats.bls.gov/news.release/union2.nws.htm (30 April 2000).

_____. 2000b. "Union Membership Data from the National Directory Series." On the World Wide Web at ftp://146.142.4.23/pub/special.requests/collbarg/unmem.txt (1 August 2000).

_____. 2000c. "Work Stoppages Involving 1,000 Workers or More, 1947–2000." On the World Wide Web at http://stats.bls.gov/news.release/wkstp.t01.htm (28 April 2000).

_____. 2002a. "Employed persons by detailed occupation, sex, race, and Hispanic origin." On the World Wide Web at http://www.bls.gov/cps/cpsaat11.pdf (16 April 2003).

_____. 2002b. "Median usual weekly earnings of full-time wage and salary workers by detailed occupation and sex." On the World Wide Web at ftp://ftp.bls.gov/pub/special.requests/lf/aat39.txt (16 April 2003).

_____. 2003a. "Labor force data files." On the World Wide Web at http://www.bls.gov/emp/emplab1.htm (16 April 2003).

_____. 2003b. "Leading Occupations of Employed Women, 2001 Annual Averages." On the World Wide Web at http://www.dol.gov/wb/wb_pubs/20lead2001.htm (17 April 2003).

_____. 2003c. "Comparative Civilian Labor Force Statistics, Ten Countries, 1959–2002." Bureau of Labor Statistics, Office of Productivity and Technology. On the World Wide Web at ftp://ftp.bls.gov/pub/special.requests/foreignlabor/flslforc.txt (21 May 2003).

_____. 2004a. "Where Can I Find the Unemployment Rate for Previous Years?" On the World Wide Web at http://www.bls.gov/cps/prev_yrs.htm (3 March 2005).

_____. 2004b. "November 2003 National Occupational Employment and Wage Estimates: All Occupations." On the World Wide Web at http://www.bls.gov/oes/2003/november/oes_00al.htm (26 March 2006).

_____. 2004c. "Median weekly earnings of full-time wage and salary workers by detailed occupation and sex." On the World Wide Web at ftp://ftp.bls.gov/pub/special.requests/lf/aat39.txt (23 February 2005).

_____. 2004d. "National Compensation Survey: Occupational Wages in the United States, July 2003 Supplementary Tables." Washington, D.C.: Bureau of Labor Statistics. On the World Wide Web at http://www.bls.gov/ncs/ocs/sp/ncbl0636.pdf (30 January 2005).

_____. 2005a. "Comparative Civilian Labor Force Statistics, 10 Countries, 1960-2004." On the World Wide Web at http://www.bls.gov/fls/flslforc.pdf (4 March 2006).

_____. 2007a. "Table 18. Median usual weekly earnings of full-time wage and salary workers by detailed occupation and sex, 2006 annual averages." On the World Wide Web at http://www.bls.gov/cps/wlf-table18-2007.pdf (17 August 2008).

_____. 2007b. "Tomorrow's Jobs." On the World Wide Web at http://www.bls.gov/oco/oco2003.htm (22 March 2009).

_____. 2008a. "Unemployment Rate." On the World Wide Web at http://data.bls.gov/PDQ/servlet/SurveyOutputServlet?data_tool=latest_numbers&series_id=LNS14000000 (21 August 2008).

_____. 2008b. "Work Stoppages." On the World Wide Web at http://www.bls.gov/wsp/ (21 August 2008).

_____. 2009. "Consumer Price Index—All Urban Consumers." On the World Wide Web at http://data.bls.gov/PDQ/servlet/SurveyOutputServlet?data_tool=latest_numbers&series_id=CUSR0000SA0&output_view=pct_1mth (27 March 2009).

U.S. Department of State. 1997. *1996 Patterns of Global Terrorism Report.* On the World Wide Web at http://www.state.gov/www/global/terrorism/1996Report/1996index.html#table (3 June 2003).

_____. 2003. *Patterns of International Terrorism 2002.* On the World Wide Web at http://www.state.gov/s/ct/rls/pgtrpt/2002/pdf (3 June 2003).

_____. 2004. *Patterns of Global Terrorism 2003.* Washington, D.C. On the World Wide Web at http://www.state.gov/documents/organization31912.pdf (1 May 2004).

U.S. Environmental Protection Agency, Office of Air Quality Planning and Standards. 2000. *National Air Pollutant Emission Trends, 1900–1998.* On the World Wide Web at http://www.epa.gov/ttn/chief/trends98/emtrnd.html (3 August 2000).

U.S. Federal Bureau of Investigation. 1999. *Uniform Crime Reports for the United States 1998.* On the World Wide Web at http://www.fbi.gov/ucr/98cius.htm (25 May 2000).

_____. 2001. *Hate Crime Statistics 2001.* Washington, D.C. On the World Wide Web at http://www.fbi.gov/ucr/01hate.pdf (23 June 2003).

_____. 2002a. *Crime in the United States, 2001.* On the World Wide Web at http://www.fbi.gov/ucr/cius_01/01crime.pdf (15 February 2003).

_____. 2002b. "Hate Crime Fact Sheet." On the World Wide Web at http://www2.fbi.gov/pressrel/pressrel02/2001hc.htm (7 August 2003).

_____. 2003. *Crime in the United States, 2002.* On the World Wide Web at http://www.fbi.gov/ucr/cius_02/html/web/index.html (16 February 2004).

_____. 2007a. "2006 Hate Crime Statistics." On the World Wide Web at http://www.fbi.gov/ucr/hc2006/incidents.html (17 August 2008).

_____. 2007b. *Crime in the United States 2006.* On the World Wide Web at http://www.fbi.gov/ucr/cius2006/offenses/index.html (9 August 2008).

"The U.S. Inflation Rate—1948–2007." On the World Wide Web at http://www.miseryindex.us/irbyyear.asp (21 August 2008).

U.S. Information Agency. 1998–1999. *The People Have Spoken: Global Views of Democracy,* 2 vols. Washington, DC: Office of Research and Media Reaction.

Useem, Bert. 1998. "Breakdown Theories of Collective Action." *Annual Review of Sociology* 24: 215–238.

_____, and Jack A. Goldstone. 2002. "Forging Social Order and Its Breakdown: Riot and Reform in U.S. Prisons." *American Sociological Review* 67: 499–525.

Valelly, Richard. 1999. "Voting Rights in Jeopardy." *The American Prospect* 46: 43–49 On the World Wide Web at http://www.prospect.org/archives/46/46valelly.html (14 January 2001).

Valocchi, Steve. 1996. "The Emergence of the Integrationist Ideology in the Civil Rights Movement." *Social Problems* 43: 116–130.

Van de Kaa, Dirk. 1987. "Europe's Second Demographic Transition." *Population Bulletin* 42, 1: 1–58.

van Kesteren, John, Pat Mayhew, and Paul Nieuwbeerta. 2001. "Criminal Victimisation in Seventeen Industrialised Countries: Key Findings from the 2000 International Crime Victims Survey." On the World Wide Web at http://www.minjust.nl:8080/b_organ/wodc/reports/ob187i.htm (11 March 2005).

Vanneman, Reeve, and Lynn Weber Cannon. 1987. *The American Perception of Class.* Philadelphia: Temple University Press.

Veblen, Thorstein. 1899. *The Theory of the Leisure Class.* On the World Wide Web at http://socserv2.socsci.mcmaster.ca/~econ/ugcm/3ll3/veblen/leisure/index.html (29 April 2000).

Verba, Sidney, Kay Lehman Schlozman, and Henry E. Brady. 1997. "The Big Tilt: Participatory Inequality in America." *The American Prospect* 32: 74–80.

Vincent, David. 2000. *The Rise of Mass Literacy: Reading and Writing in Modern Europe.* Cambridge: Polity Press.

Vygotsky, Lev S. 1987. *The Collected Works of L. S. Vygotsky,* Vol. 1, N. Minick, trans. New York: Plenum.

Wagner, Tony. 2002. *Making the Grade: Reinventing America's Schools.* New York: RoutledgeFalmer.

Wald, Matthew L., and John Schwartz. 2003. "Alerts Were Lacking, NASA Shuttle Manager Says." *New York Times* July 23. On the World Wide Web at http://www.nytimes.com (23 July 2003).

Waldfogel, Jane. 1997. "The Effect of Children on Women's Wages." *American Sociological Review* 62: 209–217.

Wallace, James, and Jim Erickson. 1992. *Hard Drive: Bill Gates and the Making of the Microsoft Empire.* New York: Wiley.

Wallerstein, Immanuel. 1974–1989. *The Modern World-System,* 3 vols. New York: Academic Press.

Wallerstein, Judith S., and Sandra Blakeslee. 1989. *Second Chances: Men, Women, and Children a Decade After Divorce.* New York: Ticknor & Fields.

_____, Julia Lewis, and Sandra Blakeslee. 2000. *The Unexpected Legacy of Divorce: A 25 Year Landmark Study.* New York: Hyperion.

Wasserman, Stanley, and Katherine Faust. 1994. *Social Network Analysis: Methods and Applications.* Cambridge: Cambridge University Press.

Waters, Mary C. 1990. *Ethnic Options: Choosing Identities in America.* Berkeley: University of California Press.

Watson, James L., ed. 1997. *Golden Arches East: McDonald's in East Asia.* Stanford, CA: Stanford University Press.

Watts, Duncan J. 2003. *Six Degrees: The Science of a Connected Age.* New York: W.W. Norton.

Webb, Eugene J., Donald T. Campbell, Richard D. Schwartz, and Lee Sechrest. 1966. *Unobtrusive Measures: Nonreactive Research in the Social Sciences.* Chicago: Rand McNally.

Webb, Stephen D., and John Collette. 1977. "Rural–Urban Differences in the Use of Stress-Alleviating Drugs." *American Journal of Sociology* 83: 700–707.

_____. 1979. "Reply to Comment on Rural–Urban Differences in the Use of Stress-Alleviating Drugs." *American Journal of Sociology* 84: 1446–1452.

Weber, Max. 1946. *From Max Weber: Essays in Sociology,* Hans Gerth and C. Wright Mills, ed. and trans. New York: Oxford University Press.

_____. 1947. *The Theory of Social and Economic Organization,* T. Parsons, ed., A. M. Henderson and T. Parsons, trans. New York: Free Press.

_____. 1958 [1904–5]. *The Protestant Ethic and the Spirit of Capitalism.* New York: Charles Scribner's Sons.

_____. 1978 [1968]. *Economy and Society,* Guenther Roth and Claus Wittich, eds. Berkeley: University of California Press.

Weeks, Jeffrey. 1986. *Sexuality.* London: Routledge.

Weinstein, Rhona S. 2002. *Reaching Higher: The Power of Expectations in Schooling.* Cambridge, MA: Harvard University Press.

Weisbrot, Mark, and Dean Baker. 2002. "The Relative Impact of Trade Liberalization on Developing Countries." Center for Economic and Policy Research, 11 June. Washington, DC. On the World Wide Web at http://www.cepr.net/relative_impact_of_trade_liberal.htm (10 February 2003).

Welch, Michael. 1997. "Violence Against Women by Professional Football Players: A Gender Analysis of Hypermasculinity, Positional Status, Narcissism, and Entitlement." *Journal of Sport and Social Issues* 21: 392–411.

Wellman, Barry. 1979. "The Community Question: The Intimate Networks of East Yorkers." *American Journal of Sociology* 84: 201–231.

_____ and Stephen Berkowitz, eds. 1997 [1988]. *Social Structures: A Network Approach,* updated ed. Greenwich, CT: JAI Press.

_____, Peter J. Carrington, and Alan Hall. 1997 [1988]. "Networks as Personal Communities." Pp. 130–184 in Barry Wellman and S. D. Berkowitz, eds., *Social Structures: A Network Approach,* updated ed., Greenwich, CT: JAI Press.

Wells, H. G. 1927. "The Country of the Blind." Pp. 123–146 in *Selected Short Stories.* Harmondsworth, UK: Penguin. On the World Wide Web at http://www.fantasticfiction.co.uk/etexts/y3800.htm (24 April 2003).

Welsh, Sandy. 1999. "Gender and Sexual Harassment." *Annual Review of Sociology* 25: 169–190.

West, Candace, and Don Zimmerman. 1987. "Doing Gender." *Gender and Society* 1: 125–151.

Wheeler, Stanton. 1961. "Socialization in Correctional Communities." *American Sociological Review* 26: 697–712.

Whitman, David. 2000. "When East Beats West Old Money Bests New." *Business Week* 8 May: 28.

Whorf, Benjamin Lee. 1956. *Language, Thought, and Reality,* John B. Carroll, ed. Cambridge, MA: MIT Press.

Whyte, William Foote. 1981 [1943]. *Street Corner Society: The Social Structure of an Italian Slum,* 3rd revised and expanded ed. Chicago: University of Chicago Press.

Wiegand, Steve, and Steve Gibson. 1999. "The Business of Death." On the World Wide Web at http://www.sacbee.com/static/archive/news/projects/cost_of_dying (16 February 2003).

Wilder, D. A. 1990. "Some Determinants of the Persuasive Power of Ingroups and Outgroups: Organization of Information and Attribution of Independence." *Journal of Personality and Social Psychology* 59: 1202–13.

Wilensky, Harold L. 1967. *Organizational Intelligence: Knowledge and Policy in Government and Industry.* New York: Basic Books.

_____. 1997. "Social Science and the Public Agenda: Reflections on the Relation of Knowledge to Policy in the United States and Abroad." *Journal of Health Politics, Policy and Law* 22: 1241–65.

Wiley College. 2007. "Mission Statement." On the World Wide Web at http://www.wileyc.edu/wly_content/departments/administrative/mission.php (19 August 2008).

Wilgoren, Jodi. 2003. "Governor Assails System's Errors as He Empties Illinois Death Row." *New York Times* 12 January. On the World Wide Web at http://www.nytimes.com (12 January 2003).

Wilkinson, Richard G. 1996. *Unhealthy Societies: The Afflictions of Inequality.* London: Routledge.

Willardt, Kenneth. 2000. "The Gaze He'll Go Gaga For." *Cosmopolitan* April: 232–237.

Williams, Daniel T. 1970. "The Lynching Records at Tuskegee Institute." *Eight Negro Bibliographies.* New York: Kraus Reprint Co.

Williams, David R., and Chiquita Collins. 1995. "U.S. Socioeconomic and Racial Differences in Health: Patterns and Explanations." *Annual Review of Sociology* 21: 349–386.

Williams, Jr., Robin M. 1951. *American Society: A Sociological Interpretation.* New York: Knopf.

Willis, Paul. 1984 [1977]. *Learning to Labour: How Working-Class Kids Get Working-Class Jobs.* New York: Columbia University Press.

Wilson, William Julius. 1980 [1978]. *The Declining Significance of Race: Blacks and Changing American Institutions,* 2nd ed. Chicago: University of Chicago Press.

_____. 1987. *The Truly Disadvantaged: The Inner City, the Underclass, and Public Policy.* Chicago: University of Chicago Press.

_____. 1996. *When Work Disappears: The World of the New Urban Poor.* New York: Knopf.

Winch, Donald. 1987. *Malthus.* Oxford: Oxford University Press.

Wirth, Louis. 1938. "Urbanism as a Way of Life." *American Journal of Sociology* 44: 1–24.

Wolf, Diane Lauren. 1992. *Factory Daughters: Gender, Household Dynamics, and Rural Industrialization in Java.* Berkeley and Los Angeles: University of California Press.

Wolf, Naomi. 1997. *Promiscuities: The Secret Struggle for Womanhood.* New York: Vintage.

Wood, Julia. 1999 [1996]. *Everyday Encounters: An Introduction to Interpersonal Communication,* 2nd ed. Belmont, CA: Wadsworth.

Woodbury, Anthony. 2003. "Endangered Languages." *Linguistic Society of America.* On the World Wide Web at http://www.lsadc.org/web2/endangeredlgs.htm (19 July 2003).

Wordsworth, Araminta. 2000. "Family Planning Officials Drown Baby in Rice Paddy." *National Post* 25 August: A10.

"Work-related Stress: A Condition Felt 'Round the World'." 1995. *HR Focus* 72, 4: 17.

World Bank. 1999. "GNP Per Capita 1997, Atlas Method and PPP." On the World Wide Web at http://www.worldbank.org/data/databytopic/GNPPC97.pdf (10 July 1999).

_____. 2008. "Monitoring the MDGs: Selected Indicators." On the World Wide Web at http://siteresources.worldbank.org/INTGLOMONREP2008/Resources/4737994-1207342962709/251-268_GMR08_mdg_web.pdf (27 January 2009).

World Health Organization. 2001. "Female Genital Mutilation." On the World Wide Web at http://www.who.int/frh-whd/FGM (20 January 2003).

_____. 2002. *World Health Report 2002.* On the World Wide Web at http://www.who.int/whr/2002/en (13 June 2003).

_____. 2003. "Countries." On the World Wide Web at http://www.who.int/countries/en (4 March 2006).

_____. 2005. "Global Atlas of the Health Workforce." On the World Wide Web at http://www.who.int/globalatlas/default.asp (4 March 2006).

_____. 2007. "Aids Epidemic Update 2007." On the World Wide Web at http://data.unaids.org/pub/EPISlides/2007/2007_epiupdate_en.pdf (22 August 2008).

World Values Survey. 2004. Machine readable data set.

Worth, Robert. 1995. "A Model Prison." *The Atlantic Monthly* November. On the World Wide Web at http://www.theatlantic.com/issues/95nov/prisons/prisons.htm (28 May 2000).

Wright, Erik Olin. 1985. *Classes.* London: Verso.

_____. 1997. *Class Counts: Comparative Studies in Class Analysis.* Cambridge: Cambridge University Press.

X, Malcolm. 1965. *The Autobiography of Malcolm X.* New York: Grove.

Yale Center for Law and Policy and Center for International Earth Science Information Network, Columbia University. 2005. *2005 Environmental Sustainability Index.* On the World Wide Web at http://www.yale.edu/esi (2 March 2005).

Yamane, David. 1997. "Secularization on Trial: In Defense of a Neosecularization Paradigm." *Journal for the Scientific Study of Religion* 36: 109–122.

Yancey, William L., Eugene P. Ericksen, and George H. Leon. 1976. "Emergent Ethnicity: A Review and Reformulation." *American Sociological Review* 41: 391–403.

York, Geoffrey. 2006. "Asian Trade Bloc Would Rival NAFTA, EU." *Globe and Mail* 24 August: B1, B8.

Zald, Meyer N., and John D. McCarthy. 1979. *The Dynamics of Social Movements.* Cambridge, MA: Winthrop.

Zangwill, Israel. 1909. *The Melting Pot: Drama in Four Acts.* New York: Macmillan.

Zaslavsky, Victor, and Robert J. Brym. 1978. "The Functions of Elections in the USSR." *Soviet Studies* 30: 62–71.

Zelikow, Philip and John Brennan. 2005 "Remarks on Release of 'Country Reports on Terrorism' for 2004." U.S. Department of State. On the World Wide Web at http://www.state.gov/s/ct/rls/rm/45279.htm (12 January 2008).

Zijderveld, Anton C. 1983. "The Sociology of Humour and Laughter." *Current Sociology* 31, 3: 1–103.

Zimbardo, Philip G. 1972. "Pathology of Imprisonment." *Society* 9, 6: 4–8.

Zimmermann, Francis. 1987 [1982]. *The Jungle and the Aroma of Meats: An Ecological Theme in Hindu Medicine,* Janet Lloyd, trans. Berkeley: University of California Press.

Zimring, Franklin E., and Gordon Hawkins. 1995. *Incapacitation: Penal Confinement and the Restraint of Crime.* New York: Oxford University Press.

Zogby International. 2001. "Arab American Institute Polls Results: Arab Americans are strong advocates of war against terrorism; Overwhelmingly endorse President Bush's actions; Significant numbers have experienced discrimination since Sept. 11." On the World Wide Web at http://www.zogby.com/news/ReadNews.dbm?ID 487 (21 December 2002).

Zola, Irving Kenneth. 1982. *Missing Pieces: A Chronicle of Living with a Disability.* Philadelphia: Temple University Press.

Zuboff, Shoshana. 1988. *In the Age of the Smart Machine: The Future of Work and Power.* New York: Basic Books.

Zukin, Sharon. 1980. "A Decade of the New Urban Sociology." *Theory and Society* 9: 539–574.

Zurcher, Louis A., and David A. Snow. 1981. "Collective Behavior and Social Movements." Pp. 447–82 in Morris Rosenberg and Ralph Turner, eds. *Social Psychology: Sociological Perspectives.* New York: Basic Books.

Zussman, Robert. 1992. *Intensive Care: Medical Ethics and the Medical Profession.* Chicago: University of Chicago Press.

_____. 1997. "Sociological Perspectives on Medical Ethics and Decision-Making." *Annual Review of Sociology* 23: 171–189.

Zwick, Rebecca. 2002. *Fair Game? The Use of Standardized Academic Tests in Higher Education.* New York: RoutledgeFalmer.

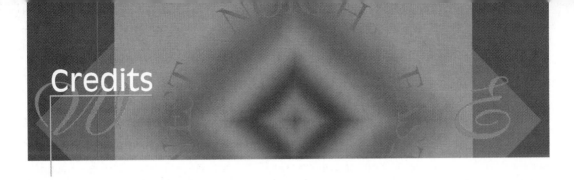

Credits

This page constitutes an extension of the copyright page. We have made every effort to trace the ownership of all copyrighted material and to secure permission from copyright holders. In the event of any question arising as to the use of any material, we will be pleased to make the necessary corrections in future printings. Thanks are due to the following authors, publishers, and agents for permission to use the material indicated.

Chapter 1

xxxiv: Zigy Kaluzny/Getty Images **3:** Courtesy of A. C. Fine Art, Nova Scotia. Photographer: James Chambers **6:** Brown Brothers, Sterling PA **7:** 20TH CENTURY FOX/DREAMWORKS/THE KOBAL COLLECTION **8:** Peter Willi/SuperStock **9:** Bettmann/CORBIS **10:** Courtesy of Columbia University **11:** The Art Archive/Corbis **12, top:** Brown Brothers, Sterling PA **12, bottom:** Bettmann/CORBIS **13:** The Granger Collection, New York **14:** Hulton-Deutsch Collection/CORBIS **17:** Courtesy of Carol Wainio, London, Ontario, Canada **20:** David Turnley/CORBIS **22:** Jeff Greenberg/PhotoEdit

Chapter 2

32: Kevin Frayer/CP PHOTO **34:** Andrew Woolley **35:** Mark Richards/PhotoEdit **39:** Photo By Ilpo Musto/Rex USA, Courtesy Everett Collection **41:** World Religions Photo Library/Alamy **42:** © 1992 Joel Gordon **45:** Courtesy of Kellogg's **49:** Owen Franken/CORBIS **51:** Photo by Peter Macdiarmid/Getty Images Europe **53:** HAL ROACH/PATHE EXCHANGE/THE KOBAL COLLECTION **56:** Jim Ruymen/REUTERS/CORBIS **57:** Kurt Krieger/Corbis

Chapter 3

60: Jim West/The Image Works **62:** Nina Leen/Time Life Pictures/Getty Images **64:** Bettmann/CORBIS **66:** Courtesy of Carol Gilligan. Photo by Jerry Bauer **68:** © New Line/courtesy Everett Collection **75:** Mills and Boon **76:** Jonathan Blair/CORBIS **77:** Myrleen F. Cate/PhotoEdit **82:** Spencer Grant/PhotoEdit

Chapter 4

86: Henry Diltz/CORBIS **89:** Bettmann/CORBIS **90:** Everett Collection **92:** Sipkin Corey/Corbis Sygma **95:** Christie's Images/SuperStock **98, left:** PAUL BUCK/AFP/Getty Images **98, right:** Ewing Galloway/Index Stock Imagery/Photolibrary **100:** RON BATZDORFF/CASTLE ROCK/FORTIS/THE KOBAL COLLECTION **103:** Robert J. Brym **104:** Appeared in *Leatherneck,* March, 1945/Pantheon Books/Random House, Inc.

Chapter 5

110: Andersen Ross/Brand X/Corbis **112:** Everett Collection **113:** Time Inc./Time Life Pictures/Getty Images **117:** Reuters/CORBIS **118:** Everett Collection **122:** Brian Leng/CORBIS **125:** Hulton-Deutsch Collection/CORBIS **127:** Infocom, 2000/Activision **128:** Ryan Remiorz/CP PHOTO **131:** Rob Lewine/Corbis

Chapter 6

138: image100/Corbis **140:** Bettmann/CORBIS **141:** Lloyd Manufacturing Co./National Library of Medicine, Washington, DC **142:** Weegee(Arthur Fellig)/International Center of Photography/Getty Images **143:** New York Public Library **148:** The Everett Collection **154:** Everett Collection **159:** Ted Streshinsky/CORBIS **160:** New York Public Library **165:** LUMEN FILMS/LAMA PRODS/THE KOBAL COLLECTION **166:** The Everett Collection

Chapter 7

170: Bruce Ayres/Stone/Getty Images **172:** The Granger Collection, New York **174, left and right:** Reuters/CORBIS **176:** TOUCHSTONE/THE KOBAL COLLECTION/IOVINO, PETER **182:** Art Resource, NY **185, left:** © 1995 Alex Webb/Magnum Photos, Inc. **185, right:** Richard T. Nowitz/CORBIS **193:** [LC-USF34-009058-C]/Dorthea Lange/Library of Congress Prints and Photographs Division Washington, DC 20540

Chapter 8

200: Michael S. Yamashita/Corbis **202, left:** Chuck Savage/CORBIS **202, right:** Ariel Skelley/CORBIS **204, left:** Brian A. Vikander/CORBIS **204, right:** Roy McMahon/CORBIS **206:** Sandy Felsenthal/CORBIS **208:** John Van Hasselt/CORBIS SYGMA **214:** Francis Malasig/epa/Corbis **218:** From Eric Hobsbawm's *The Age of Empire* (Vintage Books), copyright © 1987 by E. J. Hobsbawm. **222:** Panorama Images/The Image Works **226:** WARNER BROS/THE KOBAL COLLECTION

Chapter 9

230: Michael Ainsworth/Dallas Morning News/Corbis **232:** From *The Mismeasurement of Man* by Stephen Jay Gould (Norton)/W.W. Norton & Co. **233:** Kevork Djansezian/AP Photo **234:** Obama For America/Handout/Reuters/Corbis **235:** Copyright 1941 Time, Inc./Timepix/Getty Images **237:** Morton Beebe/CORBIS **243:** LIONS GATE/THE KOBAL COLLECTION **245, both:** Saskatchewan Archives Board, R-A8223 **248:** Museum of History and Industry, Seattle **249:** David Turnley/CORBIS **254:** Lewis W. Hine/Getty Images

Chapter 10

260: Rolf Bruderer/CORBIS **264:** Carol Beckwith & Angela Fisher/HAGA/The Image Works **267, top:** Pascal Le Segretain/CORBIS SYGMA **267, bottom:** Brian Snyder/Reuters/CORBIS **269:** David Young-Wolff/PhotoEdit **271, left and right:** Courtesy of the White Rock Beverage Company **275:** Hollandse Hoogte/Corbis Sygma **277:** FOCUS FEATURES/THE KOBAL COLLECTION **279:** Janette Beckman/Corbis **281:** Rachel Epstein/PhotoEdit **286:** SuperStock, Inc. **287:** Joseph Sohm/Visions of America/Corbis

Chapter 11

292: David Ellis/Digital Vision/Getty Images **295:** FOX 2000/20TH CENTURY FOX/THE KOBAL COLLECTION **299:** The Everett Collection **302:** The Everett Collection **305:** Andrew Benjei, *Pink Couch,* 1993. Fiberglass, 24 x 15 x 19 inches. Photo: Ron Giddings, Reproduced with permission of the artist. **307:** Scott Barrow, Inc./SuperStock **310:** Jacques M. Chenet/CORBIS **311:** Michael Newman/ PhotoEdit **314:** Serge J.F. Levy/AP Photo **317:** Laura Dwight/CORBIS **321:** Jonathan Blair/ CORBIS

Chapter 12

326: Charles O'Rear/CORBIS **329:** Michael Newman/PhotoEdit **333:** Bettmann/CORBIS **335:** A. Ramey/PhotoEdit **336:** Everett Collection, Inc. **346:** Ted Horowitz/CORBIS **347:** Diane Bondareff/AP Photo **357:** Paul Conklin/Photo Edit

Chapter 13

360: Chet Gordon/The Image Works **362:** John Duricka/AP Photo **365, top:** The Art Archive/ Corbis, Center Prisma/SuperStock **365, middle:** Prisma/SuperStock **365, bottom:** CORBIS **367:** © Zeitgeist Films/courtesy Everett Collection **368, top:** Rick Friedman/Corbis **368, bottom:** AP Photo/Morry Gash **369:** Mark Richards/PhotoEdit **376:** Patrick Robert/Corbis **388:** The Granger Collection, New York **390:** Beth A. Keiser/AP Photo

Chapter 14

394: Karen Kasmauski/Science Faction/ Corbis **396:** Museo del Prado, Madrid, Spain/SuperStock **398:** Ian Cook/Time Life Pictures/Getty Images **400, left:** Mark Richards/ PhotoEdit **400, right:** Mike Hutchings/Reuters/ Corbis **410:** Lisa M. McGeady/CORBIS **413:** Lightscapes Photography, Inc./CORBIS **415:** © Lions Gate/Courtesy Everett Collection **420:** Ron Dahlquist/Stone/Getty Images **422:** John Hillary/Reuters/Corbis

Chapter 15

426: Mark Peterson/Corbis **430:** National Association for the Advancement of Colored People, 1934 **433:** Achmad Ibrahim/AP Photo **439:** Neville Elder/CORBIS **440:** AP Photo **442:** Joseph Sohm/Visions of America/Corbis **445:** Henry Diltz/CORBIS **447:** 20TH CENTURY FOX/THE KOBAL COLLECTION **449:** Bibliotheque Nationale, Paris/SuperStock **450:** Sean White/Copyright 2007 Canadian Press Images **451:** Daniel Aguilar/REUTERS/CORBIS

Chapter 16

454: Paul A. Souders/CORBIS **456:** Don Klein/ SuperStock **457:** Carl & Ann Purcell/CORBIS **460:** Scala/Art Resource, NY **465:** Christopher Morris/Black Star Publishing **467:** The Granger Collection, New York **470:** Alan Schein Photography/Corbis **472:** Universal/courtesy Everett Collection **480:** Dave Martin/AP Photo **486:** Copyright 1990 Watterson. Reprinted with permission of Universal Press Syndicate. All rights reserved.

Name Index

Subject Index